*"I like that the key terms are given at the beginning of the chapter. It
what is important while reading. I also like that the key definitions are put in the
margins. It makes it easier for reviewing and studying."*

—Joe Hoff, student at University of Wisconsin–LaCrosse

Prepare for Class

Improve Your Grade

ACE the Test

Do you find the marginal callouts useful?

#	Answer		Number of Responses	Percentage
1	Strongly agree		166	38.16%
2	Agree		207	47.59%
3	Somewhat agree		55	12.64%
4	Disagree		7	1.61%
	TOTAL:		**435**	**100.00%**

Mean : 1.777 Mean Percentile : 80.57% Standard Deviation : 0.723

*"It's nice that the book specifically tells you the resources you can
use and where you can find them."*

—Kristin Chimento, student at Miami University

Do you find the concept checks useful?

#	Answer		Number of Responses	Percentage
1	Strongly agree		117	27.08%
2	Agree		205	47.45%
3	Somewhat agree		86	19.91%
4	Disagree		24	5.56%
	TOTAL:		**432**	**100.00%**

Mean : 2.039 Mean Percentile : 74.02% Standard Deviation : 0.831

CONCEPT CHECK
What factors affect
a person's choice of
careers? What values
do you have that
might affect your
career choice?

I like the quizzes and that the [text] is short and to the point."
—Fernando Monzon, student at Miami Dade College

Do you find the test prepper useful?

#	Answer		Number of Responses	Percentage
1	Strongly agree		163	38.08%
2	Agree		194	45.33%
3	Somewhat agree		65	15.19%
4	Disagree		6	1.40%
	TOTAL:		**428**	**100.00%**

Mean : 1.799 Mean Percentile : 80.02% Standard Deviation : 0.741

Data in barcharts from student survey at San Francisco State University.

Foundations
of Business

THIS BOOK IS DEDICATED

TO NANCY, ALLEN, AND MICHAEL PRIDE

TO MY MOTHER, BARBARA Y. HUGHES, AND MY WIFE, PEGGY, AND IN MEMORY OF PAT THOMAS

TO MY FATHER, RAM KAPOOR, AND IN MEMORY OF MY MOTHER, SHEELA; MY WIFE, THERESA;
AND MY CHILDREN, KAREN, KATHRYN, AND DAVE

STUDENT ACHIEVEMENT SERIES

Foundations of Business

William M. Pride
Texas A & M University

Robert J. Hughes
Dallas County Community Colleges

Jack R. Kapoor
College of DuPage

SOUTH-WESTERN
CENGAGE Learning™

Australia • Brazil • Japan • Korea • Mexico • Singapore • Spain • United Kingdom • United States

SOUTH-WESTERN
CENGAGE Learning

Student Achievement Series: Foundations of Business
William M. Pride, Robert J. Hughes, and Jack R. Kapoor

Vice President, Executive Publisher:
  George Hoffman

Executive Editor, Business and Economics:
  Lise Johnson

Sponsoring Editor: Mike Schenk

Marketing Manager: Nicole Mollica

Discipline Product Manager: Damaris Curran

Senior Development Editor: Julia Perez

Senior Project Editor: Nancy Blodget

Senior Media Producer: Nancy Hiney

Content Manager: Rachel Wimberly

Art and Design Manager: Jill Haber

Cover Design Director: Tony Saizon

Senior Photo Editor: Jennifer Meyer Dare

Senior Composition Buyer: Chuck Dutton

Editorial Assistant: Matt DiGangi

New Title Project Manager: James Lonergan

Marketing Assistant: Lauren Foye

Editorial Assistant: Jill Clark

Cover Photo: © Jim Scherer Photography

For product information and technology assistance, contact us at
Cengage Learning Customer & Sales Support, 1-800-354-9706

For permission to use material from this text or product,
submit all requests online at **www.cengage.com/permissions**
Further permissions questions can be emailed to
permissionrequest@cengage.com

Library of Congress Control Number: 2007940800

ISBN-13: 978-0-618-95193-2

ISBN-10: 0-618-95193-8

South-Western
5191 Natorp Boulevard
Mason, OH 45040
USA

Cengage Learning is a leading provider of customized learning solutions with office locations around the globe, including Singapore, the United Kingdom, Australia, Mexico, Brazil, and Japan. Locate your local office at **international.cengage.com/region**

Cengage Learning products are represented in Canada by Nelson Education, Ltd.

To learn more about South-Western, visit **www.cengage.com/southwestern**

Purchase any of our products at your local college store or at our preferred online store **www.ichapters.com**

Printed in the United States of America
3 4 5 6 7 11 10 09

Brief Contents

Contents

CHAPTER 6

Small Business, Entrepreneurship, and Franchises 178

Part 3   Management and Organization

CHAPTER 7

Understanding the Management Process 210

CHAPTER 8

Creating a Flexible Organization 236

CHAPTER 11

Motivating and Satisfying Employees and Teams 330

Part 5   Marketing

CHAPTER 12

Building Customer Relationships Through Effective Marketing 364

CHAPTER 13

Creating and Pricing Products that Satisfy Customers 392

CHAPTER 16

Mastering Financial Management ... 508

Preface

A Team Approach: Built by Professors and Students, For Professors and Students

Over the past four years Cengage Learning has conducted research and focus groups with a diverse cross-section of professors and students from across the country to create the first textbook that truly reflects what professors and students want and need in an educational product. Everything we have learned has been applied to create and build a brand new educational experience and product model, from the ground up, for our two very important customer bases. *Student Achievement Series: Foundations of Business* is based on extensive professor and student feedback and is specifically designed to meet the teaching needs of today's instructors as well as the learning, study, and assessment goals of today's students. Professors and students have been involved with every key decision regarding this new product development model and learning system—from content structure, to design, to packaging, to the title of the textbook, and even to marketing and messaging. Professors have also played an integral role as content advisers through their reviews, creative ideas, and contributions to this new textbook.

It has long been a Cengage Learning tradition and honor to partner closely with professors to gain valuable insights and recommendations during the development process. Partnering equally as closely with students through the entire product development and product launch process has proved to also be extremely gratifying and productive.

What Students Told Us

Working closely with students has been both rewarding and enlightening. Their honest and candid feedback and their practical and creative ideas have helped us to develop an educational learning model like no other on the market today.

Students have told us many things. While price is important to them, they are just as interested in having a textbook that reflects the way they actually learn and study. As with other consumer purchases and decisions they make, they want a textbook that is of true value to them. *Student Achievement Series: Foundations of Business* accomplishes both of their primary goals: it provides them with a price-conscious textbook, and it presents the concepts in a way that pleases them.

Today's students are busy individuals. They go to school, they work, some have families, they have a wide variety of interests, and they are involved in many activities. They take their education very seriously. Their main goal is to master the materials so they can perform well in class, get a good grade, graduate, land a good job, and be successful.

Different students learn in different ways; some learn best by reading, some are more visually oriented, and some learn best by doing through practice and assessment. While students learn in different ways, almost all students told us the same things regarding what they want their textbook to "look like."

The ideal textbook for students:

- Gets to the point quickly
- Is easy to understand and read
- Has fewer and/or shorter chapters
- Has pedagogical materials designed to reinforce key concepts
- Has a strong supporting website for quizzing, testing and assessment of materials
- Is cost conscious
- Provides students with real value for their dollar

Students want smaller chunks of information rather than the long sections and paragraphs found in traditional textbooks. This format provides them with immediate reinforcement and allows them to assess the concepts they have just studied. They like to read materials in more bulleted formats that are easier to digest than long sections and paragraphs. They almost always pay special attention to key terms and any materials that are boldfaced or highlighted in the text. In general, they spend little time reading or looking at materials that they view as superficial, such as many of the photographs (although they want some photos for visual enhancement) and long, drawn out boxed materials. However, they do want a textbook that is visually interesting, holds their interest, and is designed in an open, friendly, and accessible format. They want integrated study and assessment materials that help them reinforce, master, and test their knowledge of key concepts. They also want integrated Web and technology components that focus on quizzing and provide them with an interactive place to go to for help and assessment. They don't want websites that simply repeat the textual information in the book or that provide superficial information that is not primary to the key concepts in the text.

While students learn and study in a variety of different ways, a number of students told us that they often attend class first to hear their professor lecture and to take notes. Then they go back to read the chapter after (not always before) class. They use their textbook in this fashion to not only get the information they need but to also reinforce what they have learned in class. Students told us that they study primarily by using index or flashcards that highlight key concepts and terms, by reading lecture notes, and by using the supporting book website for quizzing and testing of key concepts. They also told us that they are far more likely to purchase and use a textbook if their professor actively uses the textbook in class and tells them that they need it.

Taking What Professors and Students Told Us to Create: *Student Achievement Series: Foundations of Business*

Student Achievement Series: Foundations of Business provides exactly what students want and need pedagogically in an educational product. While other textbooks on the market include some of these features, *Student Achievement Series* is the first textbook to fully incorporate all of these cornerstones, as well as to introduce innovative new learning methods and study processes that completely meet the wishes of today's students. It does this by:

- Being concise and to the point
- Presenting more content in bulleted or more succinct formats
- Highlighting and boldfacing key concepts and information
- Organizing content in more bite-size and chunked-up formats
- Providing a system for immediate reinforcement and assessment of materials throughout the chapter
- Creating a design that is open, user friendly, and interesting for today's students
- Eliminating or reducing traditional chapter components that students view as superficial
- Creating a product that is easier for students to read and study
- Providing students with a price-conscious product
- Providing students with a product they feel is valuable
- Developing a supporting and integrated Web component that focuses on quizzing and assessment of key concepts
- Developing a supporting and integrated web component that focuses on quizzing and assessment of key concepts
- Developing a total instructional package that helps students learn and professors teach. See inside back covers for more information on package components

When we asked students to compare a chapter from this new learning model to chapters from traditional competing textbooks, students overwhelmingly rated this new product model as far superior. In one focus group, ten students were asked to rank each "blind" chapter on a scale from 1 to 5, with 5 being the highest mark. *Student Achievement Series: Foundations of Business* received six 5's, while three competing books collectively received two 5's. Students told us that *Student Achievement Series: Foundations of Business* is "a very valuable text," is "easier to read and easier to study from," is "more modern," and is "more of what [they] want in a text."

Professors and Students: We Couldn't Have Done It Without You

We are very grateful to all the students across the country who participated in one form or another in helping us to create and build the first educational product pedagogically designed specifically for them and their learning and educational goals. Working with these students was an honor, as well as a lot of fun, for all of us at Cengage Learning. We sincerely appreciate their honesty, candor, creativeness, and interest in helping us to develop a better learning experience. We also appreciate their willingness to meet with us for lengthy periods of time and to allow us to videotape them and use some of their excellent quotes. We wish them much success as they complete their college education, begin their careers, and go about their daily lives.

STUDENT PARTICIPANTS

Katie Aiken, *Miami University*

O'Neil Barrett, *Borough of Manhattan Community College*

Joe Barron, *Providence College*

Laura Beal, *Miami University*

Ryan Bis, *Boston University*

Gerius Brantley, *Florida Atlantic University*

Angie Brewster, *Boston College*

Cyleigh Brez, *Miami University*

Veronica Calvo, *Keiser College*

Kristin Chimento, *Miami University*

Catie Connolly, *Anna Marie College*

Angelique Cooper, *DePaul University*

Adam Delaney-Winn, *Tufts University*

Stephanie DiSerio, *Miami University*

Rita Diz, *Lehman College*

Maggie Dolehide, *Miami University*

Matthew Dripps, *Miami University*

Gabriel Duran, *Florida International University*

Giovanni Espinoza, *Hunter College*

Tanya Fahrenbach, *Benedictine University*

Christina Fischer, *University of Illinois at Chicago*

Danielle Gagnon, *Boston University*

Paulina Glater, *DePaul University*

Donna Gonzalex, *Florida International University*

Barry Greenbaum, *Cooper Union*

Rachel Hall, *Miami University*

Emma Harris, *Miami University*

Erika Hill, *University of Florida*

Joe Hoff, *University of Wisconsin–LaCrosse*

Matt Janko, *University of Massachusetts–Amherst*

Travis Keltner, *Boston College*

Matthew Konigsberg, *Baruch University*

Fritz Kuhnlenz, *Boston University*

Lindsey Lambalot, *Northeastern University*

Cheng Lee, *University of Wisconsin–LaCrosse*

Steven Lippi, *Boston College*

Henry Lopez, *Florida International University*

Jessie Lynch, *Miami University*

Sarah Marith, *Boston University*

Nichelina Mavros, *Fordham University*

Marika Michalos, *City College of New York*

Evan Miller, *Parsons School of Design*

Fernando Monzon, *Miami Dade College*

Matt Nitka, *University of Wisconsin–LaCrosse*

Rehan Noormohammad, *Northeastern Illinois University*

Caitlin Offinger, *Amherst College*

Durrell Queen, *University of New York*

Adrienne Rayski, *Baruch University*

Kevin Ringel, *Northwestern University*

Alison Savery, *Tufts University*

Laura Schaffner, *Miami University*

Jordan Simkovi, *Northwestern University*

Karissa Teekah, *Lehman College*

Patrick Thermitus, *Bentley College*

Gregory Toft, *Baruch University*

Rebecca Tolles, *Miami University*

Sam Trzyzewski, *Boston University*

Vanessa Uribe, *Florida International University*

Kristin Vayda, *Miami University*

Michael Werner, *Baruch University*

Robert White, *DePaul University*

Helen Wong, *Hunter College*

Aliyah Yusuf, *Lehman College*

525 Students in MKTG 431: Principles of Marketing, San Francisco State University

We are equally grateful to all the professors across the country who participated in the development and creation of this new textbook through content reviews, advisory boards, and/or focus group work regarding the new pedagogical learning system. As always, professors provided us with invaluable information, ideas, and suggestions that consistently helped to strengthen our final product. We owe them great thanks and wish them much success in and out of their classrooms.

PROFESSOR PARTICIPANTS AND REVIEWERS

Jackie Anderson, *Davenport*

Lydia Anderson, *Fresno City College*

Richard Bartlett, *Columbus State Community College*

Kay Bloisingame-Boike, *Middle Tennessee State University*

Paula E. Brown, *Northern Illinois University*

Bruce Fisher, *Elmhurst College*

Mark Fox, *Indiana University South Bend*

Linda Hefferin, *Elgin Community College*

Paula Hladik, *Waubonsie Community College*

Mark Levine, *California Sate Chico*

Fred Mayerson, *Kingsborough Community College*

Lisa McConnel, *Oklahoma State University*

Steven Nichols, *Metro Community College Omaha*

Lori Oriatti, *College of Lake County*

Suzanne Peterson, *Arizona State University*

Patricia Setlik, *William Harper College Palatine*

Gerald Silver, *Purdue University–Calumet*

Nancy Thannert, *Robert Morris College*

Ron Thomas, *Oakton Community College*

Kenneth Thompson, *DePaul University*

Timothy Weaver, *Moorpark College*

Benjamin Weeks, *St. Xavier University*

ACKNOWLEDGMENTS

As we began the process of creating this text, we asked many individuals for ideas and suggestions that would help professors teach better and help students learn more efficiently. We have incorporated those ideas and suggestions into this edition of *Foundations of Business*. We are especially proud to say that we have included extensive student feedback in our text and instructional package. We can only say *thank you* for your suggestions, ideas, and support. Without you—both instructors and students—we would have no reason to write *Foundations of Business*.

For the generous gift of their time and for their thoughtful and useful comments and suggestions, we are indebted to:

- Samira Hussein (Johnson County Community College) for helping us make decisions about content coverage in each chapter.
- Brahm Canzer (John Abbot College) for his continued advice on technology and e-business content.
- Carmen Powers (Monroe Community College and Kaplan University) and her husband Jack for their contributions to the instructional package. In addition we'd like to thank the other contributors to the instructional package: Pat Menard, Deniz Hackner, Milton Pressley, Mari Florence, Jill Whaley, Chuck Bowles, and Adilia James.

Many talented professionals at Cengage Learning have contributed to the development of *Foundations of Business*. We are especially grateful to George Hoffman for his vision and dedication to this project, Mike Schenk, our sponsoring editor whose help, guidance, and friendship are invaluable, Julia Perez, our developmental editor, for her patience, support, and encouragement, Nicole Mollica, our marketing manager, for her market savvy and enthusiasm, and Nancy Blodget, for her detail oriented approach. We are especially grateful for the dedication and professionalism of Mary Stone and Sally Gregg at Xplana Learning, Inc. Their expertise helped to change this book from a dream into a reality.

We especially thank our families for their love, care, and patience. Without them, life would be meaningless.

Special Note to Students and Professors—Our Customers

Since a text always should be evaluated by the students and instructors who use it, we would welcome and sincerely appreciate your comments and suggestions. Please feel free to contact us by using one of the following e-mail addresses:

Bill Pride: w-pride@tamu.edu

Bob Hughes: bhughes@dcccd.edu

Jack Kapoor: kapoorj@cdnet.cod.edu

Foundations of Business

CHAPTER 1

Exploring the World of Business and Economics

Your Guide to Success in Business

Why this chapter matters
Studying business will help you to choose a career, become a successful employee, perhaps start your own business, and become a better-informed consumer and investor.

LEARNING OBJECTIVES

1. Examine the reasons why you would want a career in the world of business.

2. Define *business* and identify potential risks and rewards.

3. Define *economics* and describe the two types of economic systems: capitalism and command economy.

4. Examine the importance of productivity in the study of economics and how it relates to the measures of economic performance.

5. Examine the different economic cycles and their management through fiscal and monetary policies.

6. Analyze the economic forces of supply and demand and how they affect the four different types of business competition.

7. Summarize the historical factors that have affected the current business environment and the challenges American businesses will encounter in the future.

PepsiCo + Gatorade = Healthy Profits

From Gatorade to Flat Earth crisps, PepsiCo has a bold plan to make healthier profits by making healthier beverages and foods. For over a hundred years, PepsiCo, based in Purchase, New York, has adapted well to the changing consumer market. Its four divisions, PepsiCo Beverages, PepsiCo International, Frito-Lay, and Quaker Foods, employ 168,000 people worldwide and sell foods and beverages in nearly 200 countries. With increased consumer awareness of healthy eating habits, PepsiCo is filling its global pantry with healthier products to move way beyond its current $35 billion in annual sales.

Gatorade, the best-selling sports drink in the United States, plays a big role in Pepsi's big-profit plans. Since it acquired Gatorade in 2001 with the purchase of Quaker Foods, PepsiCo has made the bottle with a lightning bolt a familiar sight at all kinds of sports events, from basketball games to car racing. Gatorade's sales continue to thrive—particularly among consumers with a taste for noncarbonated soft drinks—despite competition from global rivals such as Coca-Cola's Powerade and GlaxoSmithKline's Lucozade.

PepsiCo has expanded further into healthier products by purchasing Naked Juice fortified drinks, Izze sparkling juices, Stacy's Pita Chips, Mother's Natural Cereals, and Tropicana juices. The company also has taken an entrepreneurial, customer-oriented route to placing newer products in health food stores. For example, knowing that health food customers like to discover unique, non-mass-marketed items, the company got its Sun Snack line and Fuelosophy smoothies onto the shelves of Whole Foods Markets with little fanfare.

Although some of PepsiCo's products are high in caffeine, sugar, or fat, the company is increasingly responsive to the changing social attitudes of health-conscious consumers. It has reduced the fat and sugar content of snacks and beverages sold in schools and will spend more on advertising healthier snack foods for children under 12 years of age. Partnering with Ocean Spray, the Massachusetts juice company, has enabled PepsiCo to keep expanding its line of healthy beverages. Ocean Spray uses PepsiCo's marketing clout to obtain more shelf space and better placement in grocery stores. What's next on PepsiCo's shopping list for business success?[1]

DID YOU KNOW?

PepsiCo's Gatorade is thriving despite competition from global rivals such as Coca-Cola's Powerade and GlaxoSmithKline's Lucozade.

KEY TERMS

free enterprise (4)
cultural (or workplace) diversity (7)
business (10)
profit (12)
stakeholders (13)
economics (14)
economy (14)
microeconomics (14)
macroeconomics (14)
factors of production (15)
entrepreneur (15)

capitalism (15)
invisible hand (15)
market economy (16)
mixed economy (16)
consumer products (16)
command economy (17)
productivity (19)
gross domestic product (GDP) (20)
inflation (20)
deflation (20)
business cycle (22)

recession (22)
depression (22)
monetary policies (22)
fiscal policy (22)
federal deficit (23)
national debt (23)
competition (24)
supply (24)
demand (24)
market price (25)
perfect (or pure) competition (25)

monopolistic competition (26)
product differentiation (26)
oligopoly (26)
monopoly (26)
natural monopoly (26)
standard of living (27)
barter (28)
domestic system (28)
factory system (28)
specialization (28)
e-business (30)

ACE the Test
Crossword Puzzle
Flashcards

Wow! What a challenging world we live in. Just for a moment, think about the changes that both individuals and businesses have experienced since the beginning of the twenty-first century. The economy took a nosedive and now shows signs of recovery. We have experienced the tragic events of September 11 and are now involved in a war on terrorism. There has been an escalation of tensions in the Middle East and other parts of the world. The stock market lost approximately a third of its value and then began to rebound to reach new record highs. There have been hurricanes that affected not only the people who live in the coastal areas of the country but also businesses and consumers around the globe. The cost of energy has risen. There were a large number of business failures—especially in high-technology industries. And yet, make no mistake about it, our economic system will survive. In fact, our economy continues to adapt and change to meet the challenges of an ever-changing world.

Think for a moment about PepsiCo, the corporation profiled in the opening case for this chapter. The firm's drinks and snack foods don't magically appear on store shelves. In fact, there is a whole lot more to producing Pepsi's products than most consumers can imagine. And once the firm's products are produced, they must be distributed and marketed to consumers in order to generate sales in a very competitive business world. While PepsiCo has four major divisions that generate more than $35 billion in sales each year, the company continues to examine the way it does business and the way it treats both its customers and its employees.[2] As a result of constantly working to improve the way it does business, PepsiCo is an excellent example of what American business should be doing.

free enterprise the system of business in which individuals are free to decide what to produce, how to produce it, and at what price to sell it

Our economic system provides an amazing amount of freedom that allows businesses that range in size from the small corner grocer to General Electric, AT&T, and Toyota to adapt to changing business environments. This system of business, in which individuals decide *what to produce, how to produce it, and at what price to sell it*, is called **free enterprise**. **EXAMPLE** Our free-enterprise system ensures, for example, that Dell Computer can buy parts from Intel and software from Microsoft and manufacture its own computers. Our system gives Dell's owners and stockholders the right to make a profit from the company's success. It gives Dell's management the right to compete with Hewlett-Packard and IBM. And it gives computer buyers the right to choose.

In this chapter

* We look briefly at what business is and how it got that way.

* We define *business*, noting how business organizations satisfy needs and earn profits.

* We examine how capitalism, socialism, and communism answer four basic economic questions.

* Then our focus shifts to how the nations of the world measure economic performance and the four types of competitive situations.

* Finally, we look at the events that helped shape today's business system, the current business environment, and the challenges that businesses face.

Your Future in the Changing World of Business

Learning Objective

Examine the reasons why you would want a career in the world of business.

The key word in this heading is *changing*. When faced with both economic problems and increasing competition not only from firms in the United States but also from firms located in other parts of the world, employees and managers now began to ask the question: What do we do now? Although this is a fair question, it is difficult to answer. Certainly, for a college student taking business courses or a beginning employee just starting a career, the question is even more difficult to answer. And yet there are still opportunities out there for people who are willing to work hard, continue to learn, and possess the ability to adapt to change. Let's begin our discussion in this section with three basic questions.

* What do you want?
* Why do you want it?
* Did you write it down?

During a segment on the *Oprah* television show, Joe Dudley, one of the world's most successful black business owners, gave the preceding advice to anyone who wants to succeed in business. And his advice is an excellent way to begin our discussion of what free enterprise is all about. What is so amazing about Dudley's success is that he started a manufacturing business in his own kitchen, with his wife and children serving as the new firm's only employees. He went on to develop his own line of hair-care products and to open a chain of beauty schools and beauty supply stores. Today Mr. Dudley has built a multimillion-dollar empire and is president of Dudley Products, Inc—one of the most successful minority-owned companies in the nation. Not only a successful business owner, Dudley is also a winner of the Horatio Alger Award—an award given to outstanding individuals who have succeeded in the face of adversity.[3] According to Mr. Dudley, "Success is a journey, not just a destination."[4]

Whether you want to obtain part-time employment to pay college and living expenses, begin your career as a full-time employee, or start a business, you must *bring something to the table* that makes you different from the next person. Employers and our capitalistic economic system are more demanding than ever before. Ask yourself:

1. What can I do that will make employers want to pay me a salary?
2. What skills do I have that employers need?

With these two questions in mind, we begin the next section with another basic question: Why study business?

Prepare for Class
Career Snapshot

SPOTLIGHT

Who makes the most money!

The amount of education you have can make a difference. Dollar amounts represent median yearly income for each group.

$88,216

$50,600

$35,026

$27,526

| High school graduate | Some college, no degree | Bachelor's degree | Professional degree |

Source: *2006–2007 Statistical Abstract of the United States.*

CONCEPT CHECK

What factors affect a person's choice of careers? What values do you have that might affect your career choice?

Why Study Business?

The potential benefits of higher education and a career in business are enormous. To begin with, there are economic benefits. Over their lifetimes, college graduates, on average, earn much more than high school graduates. And while lifetime earnings are substantially higher for college graduates, so are annual income amounts.

The nice feature of education and knowledge is that once you have them, no one can take them away. They are yours to use for a lifetime. In this section we explore what you may expect to get out of this business course and text. You will find at least four quite compelling reasons for studying business:

* For help in choosing a career
* To be a successful employee
* To start your own business
* To become a better-informed consumer and investor

For Help in Choosing a Career What do you want to do with the rest of your life? Someplace, sometime, someone probably has asked you this same question. And like many people, you may find it a difficult question to answer. This business course will introduce you to a wide array of employment opportunities. In private enterprise, these range from small, local businesses owned by one individual to large companies such as American Express and Marriott International that employ thousands of employees. There are also employment opportunities with federal, state, county, and local governments and with not-for-profit organizations such as the Red Cross and Save the Children. For help in deciding what career might be right for you, go to the student website **college.cengage.com/pic/prideSASfound** and read *Careers in Business*. In addition to career information on the text website, a number of additional websites provide information about career development. For more information, visit the following sites:

* Career Builder at **www.careerbuilder.com**
* Career One Stop at **www.careeronestop.org**
* Monster at **monster.com**
* Yahoo! Hot Jobs at **http://hotjobs.yahoo.com**

One thing to remember as you think about what your ideal career might be is that a person's choice of a career ultimately is just a reflection of what he or she values and holds most important. What will give one individual personal satisfaction may not satisfy another. For example, one person may dream of a career as a corporate executive and becoming a millionaire before the age of thirty, whereas another may choose a career that has more modest monetary rewards but that provides the opportunity to help others. What you choose to do with your life will be based on what you feel is most important. And the *you* is a very important part of that decision.

To Be a Successful Employee Deciding on the type of career you want is only a first step. To get a job in your chosen field and to be successful at it, you will have to develop a plan, or road map, that ensures that you have the skills and knowledge the job requires. You will be expected to have both the technical skills needed to accomplish a specific task and the ability to work well with many types of people in a culturally diverse work force. Cultural (or workplace) diversity refers to the differences among people in a work force owing to race, ethnicity, and gender. These skills, together with a working knowledge of the American business system and an appreciation for a culturally diverse workplace, can give you an inside edge when you are interviewing with a prospective employer.

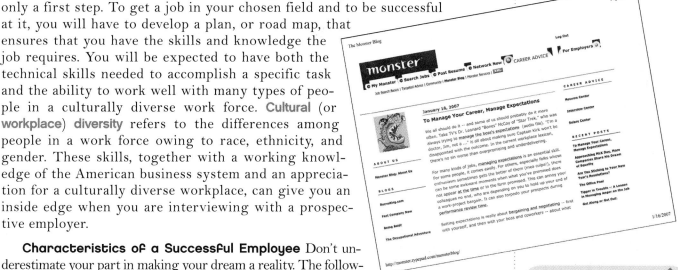

Characteristics of a Successful Employee Don't underestimate your part in making your dream a reality. The following skills are going to set you apart from others:

* Hard work, dedication, perseverance, and time-management skills.

* Communication skills. Today, most employers are looking for employees who can compose a business letter and get it into mailable form. They also want employees who can talk with customers and use e-mail to communicate with people within and outside the organization.

* On-the-job skills that you may have developed in cooperative work/school programs, during summer vacations, or in part-time jobs during the school year.

To Start Your Own Business Some people prefer to work for themselves, and they open their own businesses. To be successful, business owners must possess many of the same skills that successful employees have. And they must be willing to work hard and put in long hours.

It also helps if your small business can provide a product or service that customers want. **EXAMPLE** Mark Cuban started a small Internet company called Broadcast.com that provided hundreds of live and on-demand audio and video programs ranging from rap music to sporting events to business events over the Internet. When Cuban sold Broadcast.com to Yahoo! Inc., he became a billionaire. Today he is an expert on how the Internet will affect society in the future and believes that there is a real need for all companies, not just technology companies, to provide something that their customers want. If they don't do that, their company could very well fail.[5]

Unfortunately, many small-business firms fail; 70 percent of them fail within the first five years. Typical reasons for business failures include *poor management, undercapitalization* (not enough money), *poor business location, poor customer service,* and *lack of a proper business plan.* The material in Chapter 6 and selected topics and examples throughout this text will help you to decide whether you want to open your own business.

cultural (or workplace) diversity differences among people in a work force owing to race, ethnicity, and gender

To Become a Better-Informed Consumer and Investor The world of business surrounds us. You cannot buy a home, a new Grand Prix from the local Pontiac dealer, a Black & Decker sander at an ACE Hardware store, a pair of jeans at the Gap, or a hot dog from a street vendor without entering a business transaction. Because you no doubt will engage in business transactions almost every day of your life, one very good reason for studying business is to become a more fully informed consumer. Many people also rely on a basic understanding of business to help them to invest for the future. According to Julie Stav, Hispanic stockbroker-turned-author/radio-personality, "Take $25, add to it drive plus determination and then watch it multiply into an empire."[6] The author of *Get Your Share*, a *New York Times* best-seller, believes that it is important to learn the basics about the economy and business, stocks, mutual funds, and other alternatives before investing your money. And while this is an obvious conclusion, just dreaming of being rich doesn't make it happen. In fact, like many facets of life, it takes planning and determination to establish the type of investment program that will help you to accomplish your financial goals.

Special Note to Students

It is important to begin reading this text with one thing in mind: *This business course does not have to be difficult.* In fact, *learning about business and how you can be involved as an employee, business owner, consumer, or investor can be fun!*

We have done everything possible to eliminate the problems that students encounter in a typical class. All the features in each chapter have been evaluated and recommended by instructors with years of teaching experience. In addition, business students were asked to critique each chapter component. Based on this feedback, the text includes the following features:

* *Your Guide to Success in Business* is placed at the beginning of each chapter and provides learning objectives, key terms, and helpful suggestions for mastering chapter content.

* *An Opening Inside Business Case* highlights how successful companies do business on a day-to-day basis.

* *Margin notes* are used throughout the text to reinforce both learning objectives and key terms.

* *Boxed features* highlight career information, starting a business, ethical behavior, global issues, and the impact of technology on business today.

* *Spotlight features* highlight interesting facts about business and society and often provide a real-world example of an important concept within a chapter.

* *End-of-chapter materials* provide questions about the opening case, a chapter summary, and a video case. The last section of every chapter is entitled Building Skills for Career Success and includes exercises devoted to exploring the Internet, building team skills, and researching different careers.

* *End-of-part case* provides a continuing video case about the Finagle A Bagel Company that operates a chain of retail outlets in the northeastern section of the United States.

In addition to the text, a number of student supplements will help you to explore the world of business. We are especially proud of the website that accompanies this

1. *Prepare before you go to class.*	Early preparation is the key to success in many of life's activities. Certainly, early preparation can help you to participate in class, ask questions, and improve your performance on exams.	**TABLE 1.1** **Seven Ways to Use This Text and Its Resources**
2. *Read the chapter.*	Although it may seem like an obvious suggestion, many students never take the time to really read the material. Find a quiet space where there are no distractions, and invest enough time to become a "content expert."	
3. *Underline or highlight important concepts.*	Make this text yours. Don't be afraid to write on the pages of your text. It is much easier to review material if you have identified important concepts.	
4. *Take notes.*	While reading, take the time to jot down important points and summarize concepts in your own words. Also, take notes in class.	
5. *Apply the concepts.*	Learning is always easier if you can apply the content to your real-life situation. Think about how you could use the material either now or in the future.	
6. *Practice critical thinking.*	Test the material in the text. Do the concepts make sense? To build critical-thinking skills, answer concept checks within each chapter. Also, many of the exercises in the Building Skills for Career Success require critical thinking.	
7. *Prepare for exams.*	Allow enough time to review the material before exams. Check out the summary and Test Prepper questions. Then use the resources on the text website.	

edition. There, you will find online study aids, including interactive study tools, practice tests, audio reviews for each chapter, flashcards, and other resources. If you want to take a look at the Internet support materials available for this edition of *Foundations of Business,*

1. Make an Internet connection and go to **college.cengage.com/pic/prideSASfound**
2. Choose one of the topics and click.

As authors, we want you to be successful. We know that your time is valuable and that textbooks are expensive. In order to help you get off to a good start, a number of suggestions for developing effective study skills and using this text are provided in Table 1.1. Why not take a look at these suggestions and use them to help you succeed in this course and earn a higher grade. Remember what Joe Dudley said, "Success is a journey, not a destination."

Since a text always should be evaluated by the students and instructors who use it, we would welcome and sincerely appreciate your comments and suggestions. Please feel free to contact us by using one of the following e-mail addresses:

Bill Pride: w-pride@tamu.edu

Bob Hughes: bhughes@dcccd.edu

Jack Kapoor: kapoorj@cdnet.cod.edu

TEST PREPPER 1.1

True or False?

F 1. The majority of small business firms are successful within the first five years.

T 2. One thing to remember as you think about what your ideal career might be is that your personal choice mirrors your most highly held values.

Multiple Choice

D 3. What quality would *not* make you appealing to the business world?

  a. You bring something unique to the workplace.
  b. You are willing to work hard.
  c. You are able to adapt to rapidly changing environments.
  d. A business degree leads to higher income.
  e. You have very few technical skills but score high on conceptual skills.

B 4. Which one is a compelling reason to study business?

  a. A study of business will guarantee success.
  b. Learn the skills necessary to start your own business.
  c. Virtually all business owners are successful.
  d. Studying business will make you rich quick.
  e. Business studies will make you popular with the right people.

C 5. Cultural diversity in the workplace involves such things as

  a. race, religion, and gender.
  b. age, religion, and ethnicity.
  c. race, ethnicity, and gender.
  d. religion, age, and personality.
  e. dress, language, and religion.

ACE the Test
ACE & ACE+
Practice Test 1.1

Business: A Definition

Learning Objective 2

Define *business* and identify potential risks and rewards.

business the organized effort of individuals to produce and sell, for a profit, the goods and services that satisfy society's needs

Business is the organized effort of individuals to produce and sell, for a profit, the goods and services that satisfy society's needs. The general term *business* refers to all such efforts within a society (as in "American business") or within an industry (as in "the steel business"). However, a *business* is a particular organization, such as Kraft Foods, Inc., or Cracker Barrel Old Country Stores. To be successful, a business must perform three activities:

1. It must be *organized.*
2. It must *satisfy needs.*
3. It must *earn a profit.*

The Organized Effort of Individuals

For a business to be organized, it must combine four kinds of resources: material, human, financial, and informational. *Material* resources include the raw materials used in manufacturing processes, as well as buildings and machinery. **EXAMPLE** Sara Lee Corporation needs flour, sugar, butter, eggs, and other raw materials to produce the food products it sells worldwide. In addition, this Illinois-based company needs human, financial, and informational resources. *Human* resources are the people who furnish their labor to the business in return for wages. The *financial* resources are the money required to pay employees, purchase materials, and generally keep the business operating. And *information* is the resource that tells the managers of the business how effectively the other resources are being combined and used (see Figure 1.1).

Today, businesses usually are organized as one of three specific types. *Manufacturing businesses* process various materials into tangible goods, such as delivery trucks or towels. **EXAMPLE** Intel produces computer chips that, in turn, are sold to companies that manufacture computers. *Service businesses* produce services, such as haircuts, legal advice, or tax preparation. And some firms called *marketing intermediaries* buy products from manufacturers and then re-sell them. Sony Corporation is a manufacturer that produces computers and televisions, among other things. These products may be sold to a marketing intermediary such as Best Buy or Circuit City, which then resells the manufactured goods to consumers.

Advertising that works.

To increase sales and profits, marketing intermediaries like Best Buy often advertise. In fact, Best Buy changes its newspaper and Web-based advertising every Sunday in order to showcase weekly specials for all kinds of products that include electronics, computers, appliances, and the latest video and music products.

Satisfying Needs

The ultimate objective of every firm must be to satisfy the needs of its customers. People generally do not buy goods and services simply to own them; they buy products and services to satisfy particular needs. Some of us may feel that the need for transportation is best satisfied by an air-conditioned BMW with stereo compact-disc player, automatic transmission, power seats and windows, and remote-control side mirrors. Others may believe that a Ford Focus with a stick shift will do just fine. Both products are available to those who want them, along with a wide variety of other products that satisfy the need for transportation.

When firms lose sight of their customers' needs, they are likely to find the going rough. However, when businesses understand their customers' needs and work to satisfy those needs, they are usually successful. **EXAMPLE** Back in 1962, Sam Walton opened his first discount store in Rogers, Arkansas. Although the original store was quite different from the Wal-Mart Superstores you see today, the basic ideas of providing customer service and offering goods that satisfied needs at low prices are part of the reason why this firm has grown to become the largest retailer in the world. Today, Wal-Mart provides its products

CONCEPT CHECK

Describe the four resources that must be combined to organize and operate a business.

FIGURE 1.1

Combining Resources

A business must combine all four resources effectively to be successful.

and services to more than 176 million customers each week and has more than 3,800 retail stores in the United States and over 2,600 retail stores in fifteen different countries.[7]

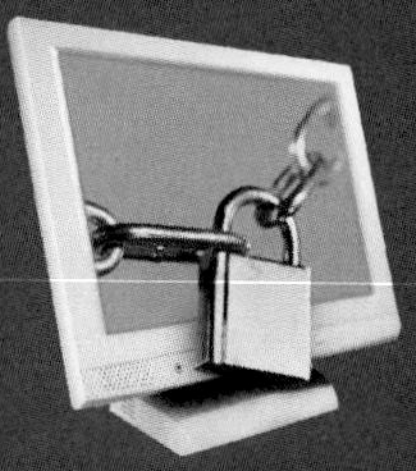

Business Profit

A business receives money (sales revenue) from its customers in exchange for goods or services. It also must pay out money to cover the expenses involved in doing business. If the firm's sales revenues are greater than its expenses, it has earned a profit. More specifically, as shown in Figure 1.2, **profit** is what remains after all business expenses have been deducted from sales revenue. A negative profit, which results when a firm's expenses are greater than its sales revenue, is called a *loss.* A business cannot continue to operate at a loss for an indefinite period of time. Management and employees must find some way to increase sales revenues and/or reduce expenses in order to return to profitability. In some cases, the pursuit of profits is so important that some corporate executives, including those from such corporations as Enron, WorldCom, and Adelphia Communications, have fudged their profit

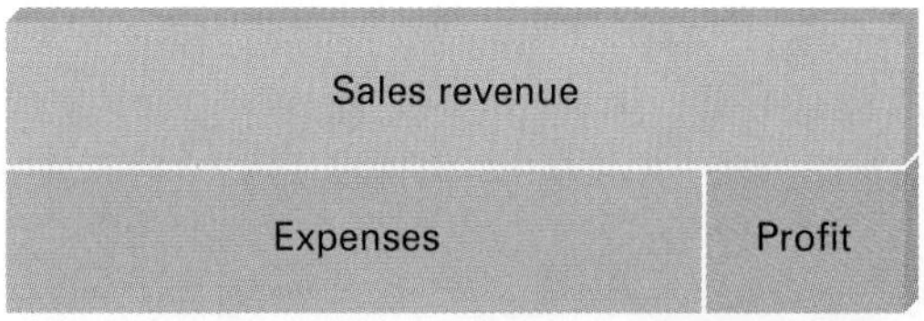

profit what remains after all business expenses have been deducted from sales revenue

FIGURE 1.2

The Relationship Between Sales Revenue and Profit

Profit is what remains after all business expenses have been deducted from sales revenue.

Sales revenue	
Expenses	Profit

figures to avoid disappointing shareholders, directors, Wall Street analysts, lenders, and other stakeholders. The term **stakeholders** is used to describe
all the different people or groups of people who are
affected by the policies, decisions, and activities of an
organization.

The profit earned by a business becomes the property of its owners. Thus, in one sense, profit is the reward business owners receive for producing goods and
services that consumers want. Profit is also the payment that business owners receive for assuming the
considerable risks of ownership. One of these is the risk
of not being paid. Everyone else—employees, suppliers,
and lenders—must be paid before the
owners. A second risk that owners
undertake is the risk of losing whatever they have invested into the business. A business that cannot earn a
profit is very likely to fail, in which
case the owners lose whatever money,
effort, and time they have invested.

To satisfy society's needs and make a profit, a business must operate within the
parameters of a nation's economic system. In the next section we define economics
and describe two different types of economic systems.

No Need for Gas!

Toronto-based Feel Good Cars has created the "ultimate" luxury neighborhood electric vehicle. At a cost of around $14,000, the company plans
to meet the needs of customers while earning a profit by providing a fully electric vehicle that seats two and, offers zero emission, and no noise.

stakeholders all the
different people or
groups of people who are
affected by the policies,
decisions, and activities
of an organization

TEST PREPPER 1.2

True or False?

F 1. For a business to be successful, certain
characteristics such as organization, satisfying
needs, and earning a profit are nice but not
required.

T 2. Profit is the payment that business owners
receive for assuming considerable risks.

Multiple Choice

D 3. Business, as an organization of individuals, has
certain goals and objectives common to all such
enterprises. What are they?

   a. To make as much money as possible regardless
   of the consequences
   b. To produce and sell goods and services at a
   profit that harms the consumer
   c. To produce and sell goods and services that benefit society with no regard to a profit motive
   d. To produce and sell goods and services for a
   profit that satisfies the needs of the society

   e. To produce, assemble, distribute, and sell goods
   or services that society has no interest in
   consuming

C 4. Business can be broadly categorized into the
following:

   a. service, distribution, and investment.
   b. marketing, advertising, and lobbying.
   c. manufacturing, service, and marketing
   d. distribution, retail, and shipping.
   e. service, advertising, and manufacturing.

A 5. Profit is positive when

   a. the firm's sales revenues are greater than its
   expenses.
   b. the firm's expenses equal its sales revenues.
   c. the cost of making the product exceeds the
   selling price.
   d. the firm's revenues are mostly higher than its
   sales but not always.
   e. when the economy is positive.

ACE the Test
ACE & ACE+
Practice Test 1.2

economics the study of how wealth is created and distributed

economy the way in which people deal with the creation and distribution of wealth

microeconomics the study of the decisions made by individuals and businesses

macroeconomics the study of the national economy and the global economy

Meet Sharon Cote.

Back in 2000, Ms Cote became an entrepreneur when she decided to risk her time, effort, and money and open a small business. Today her company, SBH Services is successful (and profitable) because it provides construction contracting and trucking services to commercial and residential customers in Anchorage Alaska.

Types of Economic Systems

Learning Objective ③

Define *economics* and describe the two types of economic systems: capitalism and command economy.

Economics is the study of how wealth is created and distributed. By *wealth*, we mean "anything of value," including the products produced and sold by business. *How wealth is distributed* simply means "who gets what." Experts often use economics to explain the choices we make and how those choices change as we cope with the demands of everyday life. **EXAMPLE** You want to take a weekend trip to some exotic vacation spot, and you also want to begin an investment program. Because of your financial resources, though, you cannot do both. You must decide what is more important. Individuals, along with business firms, governments, and to some extent society, must deal with scarcity when making important decisions. In this case, *scarcity* means "lack of resources"—money, time, natural resources, etc.—that are needed to satisfy a want or need. The decisions that individuals, business firms, government, and society make and the way in which people deal with the creation and distribution of wealth determine the kind of economic system, or **economy**, that a nation has.

Today, experts often study economics from two different perspectives: microeconomics and macroeconomics. **Microeconomics** is the study of the decisions made by individuals and businesses. Microeconomics, for example, examines how the prices of homes affect the number of homes built and sold. On the other hand, **macroeconomics** is the study of the national economy and the global economy. Macroeconomics examines the economic effect of taxes, government spending, interest rates, and similar factors on a nation and society.

Over the years, the economic systems of the world have differed in essentially two ways: (1) the ownership of the factors of production and (2) how they answer four basic economic questions that direct a nation's economic activity. **Factors of production** are the resources used to produce goods and services. There are four such factors:

* *Land and natural resources*—elements in their natural state that can be used in the production process to make appliances, automobiles, and other products. Typical examples include crude oil, forests, minerals, land, water, and even air.

* *Labor*—the time and effort that we use to produce goods and services. It includes human resources such as managers and employees.

* *Capital*—the facilities, equipment, machines, *and* money used in the operation of organizations. While most people think of capital as just money, it also can be the manufacturing equipment on a Ford automobile assembly line or a computer used in the corporate offices of ACE Hardware.

* *Entrepreneurship*—the resources that organize land, labor, and capital. It is the willingness to take risks and the knowledge and ability to use the other factors of production efficiently. An **entrepreneur** is a person who risks his or her time, effort, and money to start and operate a business.

A nation's economic system significantly affects all the economic activities of its citizens and organizations. This far-reaching impact becomes more apparent when we consider that a country's economic system determines how the factors of production are used to meet the needs of society. Today, two different economic systems exist: *capitalism* and *command* economies. The way each system answers the four basic economic questions below determines a nation's economy.

1. What goods and services—and how much of each—will be produced?
2. How will these goods and services be produced?
3. For whom will these goods and services be produced?
4. Who owns and who controls the major factors of production?

Capitalism

Capitalism is an economic system in which individuals own and operate the majority of businesses that provide goods and services. Capitalism stems from the theories of the eighteenth-century Scottish economist Adam Smith. In his book *Wealth of Nations*, published in 1776, Smith argued that a society's interests are best served when the individuals within that society are allowed to pursue their own self-interest. In other words, people will work hard only if they can earn more pay or profits in the case of a business owner. According to Smith, when an individual is acting to improve his or her own fortunes, he or she indirectly promotes the good of his or her community and the people of that community. Smith went on to call this concept the "invisible hand." The **invisible hand** is a term created by Adam Smith to describe how an individual's own personal gain benefits others and a nation's economy. **EXAMPLE** The only way a small-business owner who produces shoes can increase personal wealth is to sell shoes to customers. To become even more prosperous, the small-business owner must hire workers to produce even more shoes. According to the invisible hand, people in the small-business owner's community not only would have shoes, but some workers also would have jobs working for the shoemaker. Thus the success of people in the community and, to some extent, the nation's economy is tied indirectly to the success of the small-business owner.

factors of production the resources used to produce goods and services

entrepreneur a person who risks time, effort, and money to start and operate a business

Improve Your Grade
Hangman

capitalism an economic system in which individuals own and operate the majority of businesses that provide goods and services

invisible hand a term created by Adam Smith to describe how an individual's own personal gain benefits others and a nation's economy

Laissez-faire capitalism

| Right to create wealth |
| Right to own private property and resources |
| Right to economic freedom and freedom to compete |
| Right to limited government intervention |

FIGURE 1.3

Basic Assumptions for Adam Smith's Laissez-Faire Capitalism

---

market economy an economic system in which businesses and individuals decide what to produce and buy, and the market determines quantities sold and prices

---

CONCEPT CHECK

What are the four basic economic questions? How are they answered in a capitalist economy?

---

mixed economy an economy that exhibits elements of both capitalism and socialism

---

consumer products goods and services purchased by individuals for personal consumption

Adam Smith's capitalism is based on four fundamental issues illustrated in Figure 1.3.

1. Smith argued that the creation of wealth is properly the concern of private individuals, not government.

2. Private individuals must own the resources used to create wealth. Smith argued that the owners of resources should be free to determine how those resources are used and also should be free to enjoy the income, profits, and other benefits derived from the ownership of those resources.

3. Smith contended that economic freedom ensures the existence of competitive markets that allow both sellers and buyers to enter and exit as they choose. This freedom to enter or leave a market at will has given rise to the term *market economy*. A **market economy** (sometimes referred to as a *free-market economy*) is an economic system in which businesses and individuals decide what to produce and buy, and the market determines quantities sold and prices.

4. In Smith's view, the role of government should be limited to providing defense against foreign enemies, ensuring internal order, and furnishing public works and education. With regard to the economy, government should act only as rule maker and umpire. The French term *laissez faire* describes Smith's capitalistic system and implies that there should be no government interference in the economy. Loosely translated, this term means "let them do" (as they see fit).

Capitalism in the United States

Our economic system is rooted in the laissez-faire capitalism of Adam Smith. However, our real-world economy is not as laissez faire as Smith would have liked because government participates as more than umpire and rule maker. Our economy is, in fact, a **mixed economy**, one that exhibits elements of both capitalism and socialism.

In a mixed economy, the four basic economic questions discussed at the beginning of this section (what, how, for whom, and who) are answered through the interaction of households, businesses, and governments. The interactions among these three groups are shown in Figure 1.4.

Households Households, made up of individuals, are the consumers of goods and services, as well as owners of some of the factors of production. As *resource owners*, the members of households provide businesses with labor, capital, and other resources. In return, businesses pay wages, rent, and dividends and interest, which households receive as income.

As *consumers*, household members use their income to purchase the goods and services produced by business. Today, approximately 70 percent of our nation's total production consists of **consumer products**—goods and services purchased by individuals for personal consumption. (The remaining third is purchased by businesses and governments.[8]) This means that consumers, as a group, are the biggest customers of American business.

Businesses Like households, businesses are engaged in two different exchanges:

* First, they exchange money for natural resources, labor, and capital and use those resources to produce goods and services.

* Then they exchange their goods and services for sales revenue. This sales revenue, in turn, is exchanged for additional resources, which are used to produce and sell more goods and services. Thus the circular flow of Figure 1.4 is continuous.

Along the way, of course, business owners would like to *remove* something from the circular flow in the form of profits. And households try to *retain* some income as savings. But are profits and savings really removed from the flow? Usually not! When the economy is running smoothly, households are willing to invest their savings in businesses. They can do so *directly* by buying stocks in businesses, by purchasing shares in mutual funds that purchase stocks in businesses, or by lending money to businesses. They also can invest *indirectly* by placing their savings in bank accounts. Banks and other financial institutions then invest these savings as part of their normal business operations.

When business profits are distributed to business owners, these profits become household income. (Business owners are, after all, members of households.) And, as we saw, household income is retained in the circular flow as either *consumer spending* or *invested savings*. Thus business profits, too, are retained in the business system, and the circular flow is complete. How, then, does government fit in?

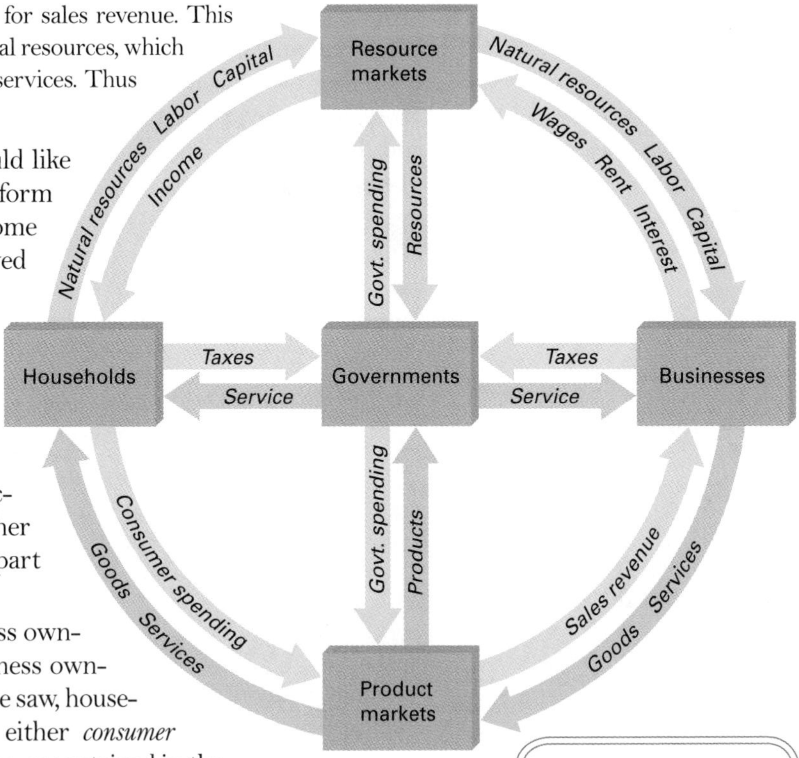

Governments The framers of our Constitution desired as little government interference with business as possible. At the same time, the Preamble to the Constitution sets forth the responsibility of government to protect and promote the public welfare. Local, state, and federal governments discharge this responsibility through regulation and the provision of services. The numerous government services are important but either (1) would not be produced by private business firms or (2) would be produced only for those who could afford them. Typical services include national defense, police and fire protection, education, and construction of roads and highways. To pay for all these services, governments collect a variety of taxes from households (such as personal income taxes and sales taxes) and from businesses (corporate income taxes). Figure 1.4 shows the exchange of taxes for government services. It also shows government spending of tax dollars for resources and products required to provide those services.

Actually, with government included, our circular flow looks more like a combination of several flows. In reality, it is. The important point is that together the various flows make up a single unit—a complete economic system that effectively provides answers to the basic economic questions. Simply put, the system works.

Command Economies

Before we discuss how to measure a nation's economic performance, we look quickly at another economic system called a *command economy*. A **command economy** is an economic system in which the government decides what goods and services will be

FIGURE 1.4

The Circular Flow in Our Mixed Economy
Our economic system is guided by the interaction of buyers and sellers, with the role of government being taken into account.

CONCEPT CHECK
Why is the American economy called a mixed economy?

command economy an economic system in which the government decides what goods and services will be produced, how they will be produced, for whom available goods and services will be produced, and who owns and controls the major factors of production

produced, how they will be produced, for whom available goods and services will be produced, and who owns and controls the major factors of production. The answers to all four basic economic questions are determined, at least to some degree, through centralized government planning. Today, two types of economic systems—*socialism* and *communism*—serve as examples of command economies.

Socialism In a *socialist* economy, the key industries are owned and controlled by the government. Such industries usually include transportation, utilities, communications, banking, and industries producing important materials such as steel. Land, buildings, and raw materials also may be the property of the state in a socialist economy. Depending on the country, private ownership of smaller businesses is permitted to varying degrees. People usually may choose their own occupations, but many work in state-owned industries.

* *What to produce and how to produce it* are determined in accordance with national goals, which are based on projected needs and the availability of resources.

* The distribution of goods and services—*who gets what*—is also controlled by the state to the extent that it controls taxes, rents, and wages. Among the professed aims of socialist countries are the equitable distribution of income, the elimination of poverty, and the distribution of social services (such as medical care) to all who need them.

* *Disadvantages* of socialism include increased taxation and loss of incentive and motivation for both individuals and business owners.

Today, many of the nations that traditionally have been labeled as socialist nations, including France, the Netherlands, Sweden, and India, are transitioning to a free-market economy. And currently, many countries that once were thought of as communist countries are now often referred to as socialist countries. Examples of former communist countries often referred to as socialist (or even capitalist) include most of the nations that were formerly part of the Union of Soviet Socialist Republics (USSR), China, and Vietnam. Other, more authoritarian countries actually may have socialist economies; however, we tend to think of them as communist because of their almost total lack of freedom.

Communism If Adam Smith was the father of capitalism, Karl Marx was the father of communism. In his writings during the mid-nineteenth century, Marx advocated a classless society whose citizens together owned all economic resources. All workers then would contribute to this *communist* society according to their ability and would receive benefits according to their need.

Since the breakup of the Soviet Union and economic reforms in China and most of the Eastern European Countries, the best remaining examples of communism are North Korea and Cuba. Today these so-called communist economies seem to practice a strictly controlled kind of socialism. Typical conditions in a communist economy include:

* The government owns almost all economic resources. The basic economic questions are answered through centralized state planning, which sets prices and wages as well.

* Emphasis is placed on the production of goods the government needs rather than on products that consumers might want, so there are frequent shortages of consumer goods.

* Workers have little choice of jobs, but special skills or talents seem to be rewarded with special privileges.

* Various groups of professionals (bureaucrats, university professors, and athletes, for example) fare much better than, say, factory workers.

TEST PREPPER 1.3

True or False?

<u>T</u>   1. Socialism and communism are examples of command economies.

<u>F</u>   2. Macroeconomics is the study of the decisions made by individuals and businesses.

Multiple Choice

<u>D</u>   3. Economics is the study of
   a. anything of value.
   b. how the government impacts the economy.
   c. the allocation of a firm's resources to the highest use.
   d. how wealth is created and distributed.
   e. money as central among resources.

<u>C</u>   4. From an economist's view, which of the following describes the factors of production.
   a. Land, education, natural resources, and capital labor

   b. Labor, workforce training, and natural resources
   c. Land and natural resources, labor, capital, and entrepreneurship
   d. Entrepreneurship, education, capital, and workers
   e. Capitalism, communism, socialism, and democracy

<u>E</u>   5. Karl Marx, the father of communism, advocated which of the following fundamental principles?
   a. The invisible hand.
   b. Wealth creation is the responsibility of individuals.
   c. Private individuals must own the resources to create wealth.
   d. Competition should be dictated by buyers and sellers in a free market.
   e. None of the above.

ACE the Test
ACE & ACE+
Practice Test 1.3

Measuring Economic Performance

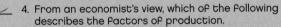

Learning Objective 4

Examine the importance of productivity in the study of economics and how it relates to the measures of economic performance.

Today it is hard to turn on the radio, watch the news on television, or read the newspaper without hearing or seeing something about the economy. Consider for just a moment the following questions:

* Are U.S. workers as *productive* as workers in other countries?

* Is the *gross domestic product* for the United States increasing or decreasing?

* Why is the *unemployment rate* important?

The information needed to answer these questions, along with the answers to other similar questions, is easily obtainable from many sources. More important, the answers to these and other questions can be used to gauge the economic health of a nation.

The Importance of Productivity in the Global Marketplace

One way to measure a nation's economic performance is to assess its productivity. **Productivity** is the average level of output per worker per hour. An increase in productivity results in economic growth because a larger number of goods and services are

productivity the average level of output per worker per hour

Can you tell where this car was manufactured?

In an effort to improve productivity, lower costs, and increase world-wide market share, General Motors has joined forces with Shanghai Automotive Industry Corporation to produce cars in China. At the time of publication, General Motors is the only U.S. carmaker with four factories in China.

gross domestic product (GDP) the total dollar value of all goods and services produced by all people within the boundaries of a country during a one-year period

inflation a general *rise* in the level of prices

deflation a general *decrease* in the level of prices

produced by a given labor force. When measuring the health of the nation's economy, economists often refer to the *productivity rate*—a measure that tracks the increase and decrease in the average level of output per worker. Productivity growth in the United States has increased dramatically over the last several years. And yet, before you think that all the nation's economic problems are over, consider the following questions:

Question: How does productivity growth affect the economy?

Answer: Because of productivity growth, it now takes just 90 workers to produce what 100 workers produced in 2001.[9] As a result, employers have reduced costs, earned more profits, and/or sold their products for less. Finally, productivity growth helps American business to compete more effectively with other nations in a competitive world.

Question: How does a nation improve productivity?

Answer: Reducing costs and enabling employees to work more efficiently are at the core of all attempts to improve productivity. Methods that can be used to increase productivity are discussed in detail in Chapter 9.

Question: Is productivity growth always good.

Answer: While economists always point to increased efficiency and the ability to produce goods and services for lower costs as a positive factor, at least two factors must be considered when answering this question.

* *Higher productivity.* First, fewer workers producing more goods and services is good for employers. As mentioned earlier, increased productivity enables business owners to reduce costs, make more profit, and/or sell their products for less.

* *Higher unemployment.* Increased productivity can lead to higher unemployment rates. And unemployed workers often find that employers are not hiring as many new employees because existing employees are more productive.

Employers throughout the world are also concerned about productivity. **EXAMPLE** Today, China, the "sleeping dragon," as Napoleon called it, is awake and is shaking the world. Increased productivity has enabled the Chinese to manufacture products that range from trinkets to sophisticated electronic and computer products. And China is just one country. There are many other countries that understand the economic benefits of increased productivity.

Important Economic Indicators That Measure a Nation's Economy

In addition to productivity, a measure called *gross domestic product* can be used to measure the economic well-being of a nation. **Gross domestic product (GDP)** is the total dollar value of all goods and services produced by all people within the boundaries of a country during a one-year period. **EXAMPLE** The value of automobiles produced by employees in an American-owned General Motors plant and the value of automobiles produced by employees in a Japanese-owned Toyota plant *in the United States* are both included in the GDP for the United States. The U.S. GDP was $12,456 billion in 2005—the last year that complete results are available.[10]

Question: Why is it important to know the GDP of a country?

Answer:

* The GDP figure facilitates comparisons between the United States and other countries because it is the standard used in international guidelines for economic accounting.

* It is also possible to compare the GDP for one nation over several different time periods.

* Finally, this comparison allows observers to determine the extent to which a nation is experiencing economic growth.

To make accurate comparisons of the GDP for different years, we must adjust the dollar amounts for inflation. **Inflation** is a general *rise* in the level of prices. (The opposite of inflation is deflation.) **Deflation** is a general *decrease* in the level of prices. By using inflation-adjusted figures, we are able to measure the *real* GDP for a nation. In effect, it is now possible to compare the products and services produced by a nation in constant dollars—dollars that will purchase the same amount of goods and services. Figure 1.5 depicts the GDP of the United States in current dollars and the real GDP in inflation-adjusted dollars. Note that between 1990 and 2005, America's *real* GDP grew from $7,113 billion to $11,049 billion.[11]

In addition to GDP and *real* GDP, other economic measures exist that can be used to evaluate a nation's economy. Some additional terms that are often reported in news reports on the radio, television, or the Internet are described in Table 1.2. Like the

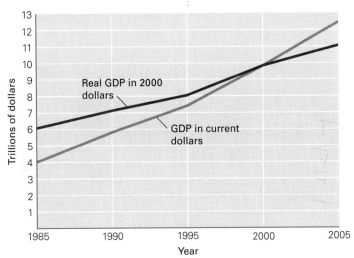

FIGURE 1.5

GDP in Current Dollars and in Inflation-Adjusted Dollars

The changes in GDP and *real* GDP for the United States from one year to another year can be used to measure economic growth.

Source: U.S. Bureau of Economic Analysis website at **www.bea.gov**; accessed September 10, 2006.

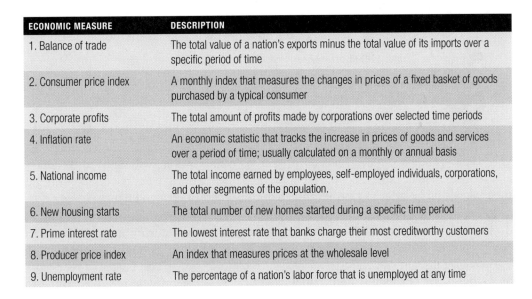

ECONOMIC MEASURE	DESCRIPTION
1. Balance of trade	The total value of a nation's exports minus the total value of its imports over a specific period of time
2. Consumer price index	A monthly index that measures the changes in prices of a fixed basket of goods purchased by a typical consumer
3. Corporate profits	The total amount of profits made by corporations over selected time periods
4. Inflation rate	An economic statistic that tracks the increase in prices of goods and services over a period of time; usually calculated on a monthly or annual basis
5. National income	The total income earned by employees, self-employed individuals, corporations, and other segments of the population.
6. New housing starts	The total number of new homes started during a specific time period
7. Prime interest rate	The lowest interest rate that banks charge their most creditworthy customers
8. Producer price index	An index that measures prices at the wholesale level
9. Unemployment rate	The percentage of a nation's labor force that is unemployed at any time

TABLE 1.2

Common Measures Used to Evaluate a Nation's Economic Health

CONCEPT CHECK

Is gross domestic product a reliable indicator of a nation's economic health? What might be a better indicator?

measures for GDP, these measures can be used to compare one economic statistic over different periods of time and to measure economic growth.

ACE the Test
ACE & ACE+
Practice Test 1.4

TEST PREPPER 1.4

True or False?

___T___ 1. Productivity is the average level of output per worker per hour.

___F___ 2. Deflation is a general rise in the level of prices.

___F___ 3. The balance of trade measures prices at the wholesale level.

___T___ 4. The consumer price index (CPI) is a monthly index that measures the changes in prices of a fixed basket of goods purchased by a typical consumer.

Multiple Choice

___A___ 5. It is important to know the gross domestic product (GDP) because the GDP figure

    a. facilitates comparisons between the United States and other countries.

    b. can measure the amount of employment in a nation.

    c. stays the same from year to year for most countries.

    d. usually decreases when the economy is strong.

CONCEPT CHECK

What are the four steps in a typical business cycle? How are monetary and fiscal policy related to the business cycle?

business cycle the recurrence of periods of growth and recession in a nation's economic activity

recession two or more consecutive three-month periods of decline in a country's GDP

depression a severe recession that lasts longer than a recession

monetary policies Federal Reserve decisions that determine the size of the supply of money in the nation and the level of interest rates

fiscal policy government influence on the amount of savings and expenditures; accomplished by altering the tax structure and by changing the levels of government spending

The Business Cycle

Learning Objective 5

Examine the different economic cycles and their management through fiscal and monetary policies.

All industrialized nations of the world seek economic growth, full employment, and price stability. However, a nation's economy fluctuates rather than grows at a steady pace every year. In fact, if you were to graph the economic growth rate for a country such as the United States, it would resemble a roller coaster ride with peaks (high points) and troughs (low points). These fluctuations generally are referred to as the **business cycle**, that is, the recurrence of periods of growth and recession in a nation's economic activity. Generally, the business cycle consists of four states:

* *Peak* (sometimes called *prosperity*)
* *Recession*
* *Trough*
* *Recovery* (sometimes called *expansion*)

During the *peak period*, unemployment is low, and total income is relatively high. As long as the economic outlook remains prosperous, consumers are willing to buy products and services. In fact, businesses often expand and offer new products and services during the peak period in order to take advantage of consumers' increased buying power.

Economists define a **recession** as two or more consecutive three-month periods of decline in a country's GDP. Because unemployment rises during a recession, total buying power declines. As buying power decreases, consumers tend to become more value conscious and reluctant to purchase frivolous items. In response to a recession, many businesses focus on the products and services that provide the most value to their customers. Economists define a **depression** as a severe recession that lasts longer than a recession. A depression is characterized by extremely high unemployment rates, low wages, reduced purchasing power, lack of confidence in the economy, and a general decrease in business activity.

Economists refer to the third phase of the business cycle as the *trough*. The trough of a recession or depression is the turning point when a nation's output and employment bottom out and reach their lowest levels. To offset the effects of recession and depression, the federal government uses both monetary and fiscal policies. **Monetary policies** are the Federal Reserve's decisions that determine the size of the supply of money in the nation and the level of interest rates. Through **fiscal policy**, the government can influence the amount of savings and expenditures by altering the tax structure and changing the levels of government spending.

Although the federal government collects approximately $2 trillion in annual revenues, the government often spends more than it receives, resulting in a **federal deficit**. For example, the government had a federal deficit for each year between 2002 and 2004. The total of all federal deficits is called the **national debt**. Today, the U.S. national debt is about $8 trillion, or approximately $27,000 for every man, woman, and child in the United States.[12]

Some experts believe that effective use of monetary and fiscal policies can speed up recovery and reduce the amount of time the economy is in recession. *Recovery* (or *expansion*) is movement of the economy from depression or recession to prosperity. High unemployment rates decline, income increases, and both the ability and the willingness of consumers to buy rise.

Distressing information!

Douglas Durst, the owner of this building in New York City, believes you should know the dollar amount of the U.S. national debt and also your family's share of the national debt. For more information about the national debt, go to http://www.treasurydirect.gov.

federal deficit a shortfall created when the federal government spends more in a fiscal year than it receives

national debt the total of all federal deficits

TEST PREPPER 1.5

True or False?

___T___ 1. The total of all federal deficits is called the *national debt*.

___T___ 2. Some experts believe that effective use of monetary and fiscal policies can speed up recovery and reduce the amount of time the economy is in recession.

___T___ 3. Through monetary policy, the Federal Reserve determines the size of the supply of money in the nation and the level of interest rates.

Multiple Choice

___C___ 4. The business cycle consists of various stages of expansion and contraction. In the peak of the business cycle, what are the defining characteristics?

a. Increased employment, consumers buy less, increased buying power, and total income high
b. Decreased buying power, high unemployment, consumers buy more, and total income stagnant
c. Increased employment, increased buying power, total higher income, and consumers buy more
d. Decreased employment, consumers buy less, decreased buying power, and total income lower
e. The peak of the business cycle defines recession.

___B___ 5. Recession means that the GDP has declined for

a. three or more consecutive months.
b. six or more consecutive months.
c. nine or more consecutive months.
d. six or more nonconsecutive months.
e. twelve or more nonconsecutive months.

ACE the Test
ACE & ACE+
Practice Test 1.5

Types of Competition

Learning Objective 6

Analyze the economic forces of supply and demand and how they affect the four different types of business competition.

Our capitalist system ensures that individuals and businesses make the decisions about what to produce, how to produce it, and what price to charge for the product. **EXAMPLE** Mattel, Inc., for example, can introduce new versions of its famous Barbie doll, license the Barbie name, change the doll's price and method of distribution, and attempt to produce and market Barbie in other countries or over the Internet at **www.mattel.com.** Our system also allows customers the right to choose between Mattel's products and those produced by competitors.

Competition like that between Mattel and other toy manufacturers is a necessary and extremely important by-product of capitalism. Business **competition** is essentially a rivalry among businesses for sales to potential customers. In a capitalistic economy, competition also ensures that a firm will survive only if it serves its customers well by providing products and services that meet needs. In a competitive economic environment, the price of each product is determined by the actions of *all buyers and all sellers together* through the forces of supply and demand.

The Basics of Supply and Demand

The **supply** of a particular product is the quantity of the product that *producers* are willing to sell at each of various prices. Producers are rational people, so we would expect them to offer more of a product for sale at higher prices and to offer less of the product at lower prices, as illustrated by the supply curve in Figure 1.6.

The **demand** for a particular product is the quantity that *buyers* are willing to purchase at each of various prices. Buyers, too, are usually rational, so we would expect them—as a group—to buy more of a product when its price is low and to buy less of the product when its price is high, as depicted by the demand curve in Figure 1.6.

The Equilibrium, or Market, Price

There is always one certain price at which the demanded quantity of a product is exactly equal to the

competition rivalry among businesses for sales to potential customers

supply the quantity of a product that *producers* are willing to sell at each of various prices

demand the quantity of a product that *buyers* are willing to purchase at each of various prices

FIGURE 1.6

Supply Curve and Demand Curve

The intersection of a supply curve and a demand curve is called the *equilibrium,* or *market, price.* This intersection indicates a single price and quantity at which suppliers will sell products and buyers will purchase them.

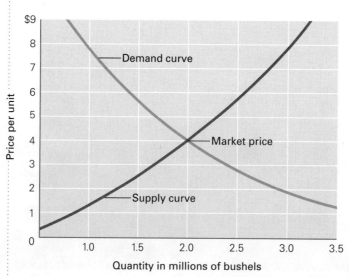

quantity of that product produced. Suppose that producers are willing to *supply* two million bushels of wheat at a price of $4 per bushel and that buyers are willing to *purchase* two million bushels at a price of $4 per bushel. In other words, supply and demand are in balance, or *in equilibrium*, at the price of $4. Economists call this price the *market price*. The **market price** of any product is the price at which the quantity demanded is exactly equal to the quantity supplied. If suppliers produce two million bushels, then no one who is willing to pay $4 per bushel will have to go without wheat, and no producer who is willing to sell at $4 per bushel will be stuck with unsold wheat.

In theory and in the real world, market prices are affected by anything that affects supply and demand. The *demand* for wheat, for example, might change if researchers suddenly discovered that it offered a previously unknown health benefit. Then buyers would demand more wheat at every price. Or the *supply* of wheat might change if new technology permitted the production of greater quantities of wheat from the same amount of acreage. Other changes that can affect competitive prices are shifts in buyer tastes, the development of new products, fluctuations in income owing to inflation or recession, or even changes in the weather that affect the production of wheat.

Types or Degrees of Competition

Economists recognize four different degrees of competition ranging from ideal, complete competition to no competition at all. These are perfect competition, monopolistic competition, oligopoly, and monopoly. For a quick overview of the different types of competition, including numbers of firms and examples for each type, look at Table 1.3.

TYPE OF COMPETITION	NUMBER OF BUSINESS FIRMS OR SUPPLIERS	REAL-WORLD EXAMPLES
1. Perfect	Many	Corn, wheat, peanuts
2. Monopolistic	Many	Clothing, shoes
3. Oligopoly	Few	Automobiles, cereals
4. Monopoly	One	Software protected by copyright, local public utilities

Perfect Competition Perfect (or pure) competition is the market situation in which there are many buyers and sellers of a product, and no single buyer or seller is powerful enough to affect the price of that product.

Characteristics of Perfect Competition

* We are discussing the market for a single product, say, bushels of wheat.
* All sellers offer essentially the same product for sale.
* All buyers and sellers know everything there is to know about the market (including, in our example, the prices that all sellers are asking for their wheat).
* The overall market is not affected by the actions of any one buyer or seller.

When perfect competition exists, every seller should ask the same price that every other seller is asking. Why? Because if one seller wanted 50 cents more per bushel of

market price the price at which the quantity demanded is exactly equal to the quantity supplied

TABLE 1.3

Four Different Types of Competition

The number of firms determines the degree of competition within an industry.

perfect (or pure) competition the market situation in which there are many buyers and sellers of a product, and no single buyer or seller is powerful enough to affect the price of that product

wheat than all the others, that seller would not be able to sell a single bushel. Buyers could—and would—do better by purchasing wheat from the competition. On the other hand, a firm willing to sell below the going price would sell all its wheat quickly. But that seller would lose sales revenue (and profit) because buyers actually are willing to pay more. Perfect competition is quite rare in today's world. Many real markets, however, are examples of monopolistic competition.

Monopolistic Competition Monopolistic competition is a market situation in which there are many buyers along with a relatively large number of sellers.

Characteristics of Monopolistic Competition

* The various products available in a monopolistically competitive market are very similar in nature, and they are intended to satisfy the same need.

* Each seller attempts to make its product different from the others by providing unique product features, an attention-getting brand name, unique packaging, or services such as free delivery or a "lifetime" warranty.

* Product differentiation is the process of developing and promoting differences between one's products and all similar products. **EXAMPLE** A furniture manufacturer such as Thomasville sees what looks like a mob of competitors, all trying to chip away at its market. By differentiating each of its products from all similar products produced by competitors, Thomasville obtains some limited control over the market price of its product.

Oligopoly An oligopoly is a market (or industry) in which there are few sellers. Generally, these sellers are quite large, and sizable investments are required to enter into their market. **EXAMPLE** Oligopolies include the automobile, car rental, cereal, and farm implement industries.

Characteristics of an Oligopoly

* There are few sellers in an oligopoly.

* The market actions of each seller can have a strong effect on competitors' sales and prices. **EXAMPLE** If General Motors reduces its automobile prices, Ford, Chrysler, Toyota, and Nissan usually do the same to retain their market shares.

* Product differentiation becomes the major competitive weapon; this is very evident in the advertising of the major auto manufacturers. **EXAMPLE** When Toyota began offering hybrid automobiles, General Motors and Ford also introduced competitive hybrid models.

Monopoly A monopoly is a market (or industry) with only one seller.

Characteristics of a Monopoly

* In a monopoly, there is no close substitute for the product or service.

* Because only one firm is the supplier of a product, it appears that it has complete control over price. However, no firm with a monopoly can set its price at some astronomical figure; the firm soon would find that it had no customers or sales revenue either. The firm in a monopoly position must consider the demand for its product and set the price at the most profitable level.

* Examples of monopolies in the United States include many public utilities. Each utility firm operates in a natural monopoly, an industry that requires a huge investment in

monopolistic competition a market situation in which there are many buyers along with a relatively large number of sellers who differentiate their products from the products of competitors

product differentiation the process of developing and promoting differences between one's products and all similar products

oligopoly a market (or industry) in which there are few sellers

monopoly a market (or industry) with only one seller

natural monopoly an industry that requires a huge investment in capital and within which any duplication of facilities would be wasteful capital and within which any duplication of facilities would be wasteful. Natural monopolies are permitted to exist because the public interest is best served by their existence, but they operate under the scrutiny of various state and federal agencies. While many utilities are still classified as natural monopolies, there is increased demand for competition in many industries.

* A legal monopoly—sometimes referred to as a *limited monopoly*—is created when the federal government issues a copyright, patent, or trademark. Each of these exists for a specific period of time and can be used to protect the owners of written materials, ideas, or product brands from unauthorized use by competitors that have not shared in the time, effort, and expense required for their development. **EXAMPLE** Because Microsoft owns the copyright on its popular Windows software, it enjoys a limited-monopoly position. Except for natural monopolies and monopolies created by copyrights, patents, and trademarks, federal antitrust laws prohibit both monopolies and attempts to form monopolies.

> **CONCEPT CHECK**
>
> Discuss this statement, "Business competition encourages efficiency of production and leads to improved product quality."

TEST PREPPER 1.6

True or False?

_T_ 1. In a capitalistic economy, competition ensures that a firm will survive only if it serves its customers well by providing products and services that meet needs.

_F_ 2. A market in which there are few sellers and many buyers is a monopoly.

_T_ 3. There is always one certain price at which the demanded quantity of a product is exactly equal to the quantity of that product produced, and this is called the *market price*.

Multiple Choice

_D_ 4. An electric utility company is an example of

    a. perfect competition.
    b. oligopoly.
    c. limited monopoly.
    d. natural monopoly.
    e. monopolistic competition.

_B_ 5. When there are few sellers, the actions of each seller can have a strong effect on competitors' sales and prices, and product differentiation becomes the major competitive weapon, this is a type of

    a. monopoly.
    b. oligopoly.
    c. pure competition.
    d. monopolistic competition.
    e. None of the above.

ACE the Test
ACE & ACE+
Practice Test 1.6

American Business Today

Learning Objective 7

Summarize the historical factors that have affected the current business environment and the challenges American businesses will encounter in the future.

While our economic system is far from perfect, it provides Americans with a high standard of living compared with people in other countries throughout the world. **Standard of living** is a loose, subjective measure of how well off an individual or a society is mainly in terms of want satisfaction through goods and services.

> **standard of living** a loose, subjective measure of how well off an individual or a society is mainly in terms of want satisfaction through goods and services

To understand the current business environment and the challenges ahead, it helps to understand how business developed.

Early Business Development

Our American business system has its roots in the knowledge, skills, and values that the earliest settlers brought to this country. Refer to Figure 1.7 for an overall view of our nation's history, the development of our business system, and some major inventions that influenced the nation and our business system.

The first settlers in the New World were concerned mainly with providing themselves with basic necessities—food, clothing, and shelter. Almost all families lived on farms, and the entire family worked at the business of surviving. They used their surplus for trading, mainly by barter, among themselves and with the English trading ships that called at the colonies. **Barter** is a system of exchange in which goods or services are traded directly for other goods and/or services without using money. As this trade increased, small-scale business enterprises began to appear. Some settlers were able to use their skills and their excess time to work under the domestic system of production. The **domestic system** was a method of manufacturing in which an entrepreneur distributed raw materials to various homes, where families would process them into finished goods. The merchant entrepreneur then offered the goods for sale.

Then, in 1789, a young English apprentice mechanic named Samuel Slater decided to sail to America. At this time, British law forbade the export of machinery, technology, and skilled workers. To get around the law, Slater painstakingly memorized the plans for Richard Arkwright's water-powered spinning machine, which had revolutionized the British textile industry, and left England disguised as a farmer. A year later he set up a textile factory in Pawtucket, Rhode Island, to spin raw cotton into thread. Slater's ingenuity resulted in America's first use of the **factory system** of manufacturing, in which all the materials, machinery, and workers required to manufacture a product are assembled in one place. The Industrial Revolution in America was born. A manufacturing technique called *specialization* was used to improve productivity. **Specialization** is the separation of a manufacturing process into distinct tasks and the assignment of the different tasks to different individuals.

The years from 1820 to 1900 were the golden age of invention and innovation in machinery. At the same time, new means of transportation greatly expanded the domestic markets for American products. Many business historians view the period from 1870 to 1900 as the second Industrial Revolution. Certainly, many characteristics of our modern business system took form during this time period.

The Twentieth Century

Industrial growth and prosperity continued well into the twentieth century. Henry Ford's moving automotive assembly line, which brought the work to the worker, refined the concept of specialization and helped to spur on the mass production of

barter a system of exchange in which goods or services are traded directly for other goods and/or services without using money

domestic system a method of manufacturing in which an entrepreneur distributes raw materials to various homes, where families process them into finished goods to be offered for sale by the merchant entrepreneur

factory system a system of manufacturing in which all the materials, machinery, and workers required to manufacture a product are assembled in one place

specialization the separation of a manufacturing process into distinct tasks and the assignment of the different tasks to different individuals

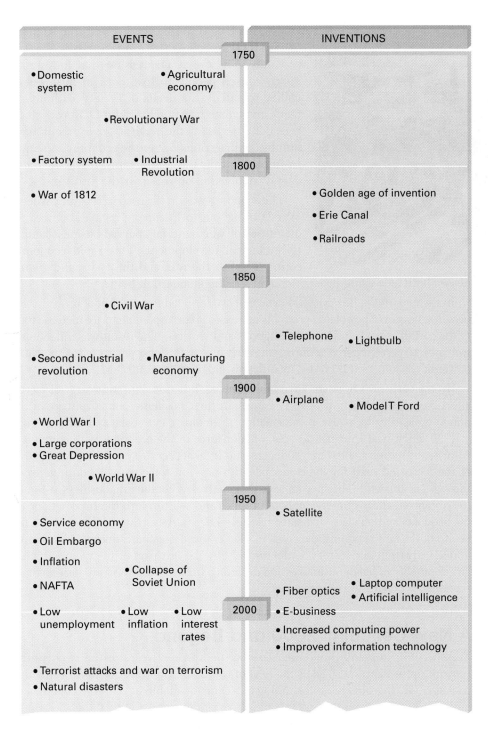

FIGURE 1.7

Time Line of American Business

Throughout the history of the United States, invention and innovation have led naturally to change and a more industrialized economy.

consumer goods. Fundamental changes occurred in business ownership and management as well. No longer were the largest businesses owned by one individual; instead, ownership was in the hands of thousands of corporate shareholders who were willing to invest in—but not to operate—a business.

Both men and women worked on Henry Ford's Early Assembly Line.

Because of the factory system and specialization, the amount of consumer goods produced in the United States increased dramatically during the early 1900s. While this Ford outdoor assembly line is crude by today's standards, it was a state-of-the-art manufacturing facility during the early economic development of the United States.

e-Business the organized effort of individuals to produce and sell through the Internet, for a profit, the products and services that satisfy society's needs

The Roaring Twenties ended with the sudden crash of the stock market in 1929 and the near collapse of the economy. The Great Depression that followed in the 1930s caused people to lose faith in business and its ability to satisfy the needs of society without government involvement. After Franklin D. Roosevelt became president in 1933, the federal government devised a number of programs to get the economy moving again. In implementing these programs, the government got deeply involved in business for the first time.

The economy was on the road to recovery when World War II broke out in Europe in 1939. The need for vast quantities of war material spurred business activity and technological development. This rapid economic pace continued after the war, and the 1950s and 1960s witnessed both increasing production and a rising standard of living.

In the mid-1970s, however, a shortage of crude oil led to a new set of problems for business. As the cost of petroleum products increased, a corresponding price increase took place in the cost of energy and the cost of goods and services. The result was inflation at a rate well over 10 percent per year during the early 1980s. Business profits fell as the purchasing power of consumers was eroded by inflation and high interest rates.

By the early 1990s, unemployment numbers, inflation, and interest—all factors that affect business—were now at record lows. In turn, business took advantage of this economic prosperity to invest in information technology, cut costs, and increase flexibility and efficiency. The Internet became a major force in the economy, with computer hardware manufacturers, software producers, and Internet service providers taking advantage of the increased need for information. e-Business—a topic we will continue to explore throughout this text—became an accepted method of conducting business. **e-Business** is the organized effort of individuals to produce and sell through the Internet, for a profit, the products and services that satisfy society's needs. As further evidence of the financial health of the new economy, the stock market enjoyed the longest period of sustained economic growth in our history. Unfortunately, by the last part of the twentieth century, a larger number of business failures and declining stock values were initial signs that larger economic problems were on the way.

A New Century: 2000 and Beyond

According to many economic experts, the first few years of the twenty-first century might be characterized as the best of times and the worst of times rolled into one package. On the plus side, technology became available at an affordable price. Both individuals and businesses now could access information with the click of a button. They also could buy and sell merchandise online.

In addition to information technology, the growth of service businesses and increasing opportunities for global trade also changed the way American firms do business in the twenty-first century. Because they employ over 80 percent of the American work force, service businesses are a very important component of our economy.[13] As a result, service businesses must find ways to improve productivity and cut costs while at the same time providing jobs for an even larger portion of the work force.

On the negative side, it is hard to watch television, surf the web, listen to the radio, or read the newspaper without hearing some news about the economy. Even though many of the economic indicators described in Table 1.2 on page 21 remain strong or show signs of improvement, there is still a certain amount of pessimism surrounding the economy.

The Current Business Environment

Before reading on, answer the following question:

In today's competitive business world, which of the following environments affects business?

a. *The competitive environment*   d. *The economic environment*
b. *The global environment*   e. All the above
c. *The technological environment*

The correct answer is e. All the environments listed affect business today. For example, businesses operate in a *competitive environment.* As noted earlier in this chapter, competition is a basic component of capitalism. Every day, business owners must figure out what makes their businesses successful and how their businesses are different from the competition. Often the answer is contained in the basic definition of business. Just for a moment, review the definition on page 10.

Note the phrase *satisfy society's needs.* Those three words say a lot about how well a successful firm competes with competitors. If you meet customer needs, then you have a better chance at success.

Related to the competitive environment is the *global environment.* Not only do American businesses have to compete with other American businesses, but they also must compete with businesses from all over the globe. According to global experts, China is the fastest-growing economy in the world. And China is not alone. Other countries around the world also compete with U.S. firms. According to Richard Haass, president of the Council on Foreign Relations, "There will be winners and losers from globalization. We win every time we go shopping because prices are lower. Choice is greater because of globalization. But there are losers. There are people who will lose their jobs either to foreign competition or [to] technological innovation."[14]

In addition to competition and globalization, the use of technology has changed the way we do business. In fact, the *technological environment* for U.S. businesses has never been more challenging. Changes in manufacturing equipment, communication with customers, and distribution of products are all examples of how technology has changed everyday business practices. And the technology will continue to change. New technology will require businesses to spend additional money to keep abreast of an ever-changing technology environment.

In addition to the competitive, global, and technological environments, the *economic environment* always must be considered when making business decisions. While many people believe that business has unlimited resources, the truth is that managers and business owners realize that there is never enough money to fund all the activities a business might want to fund. This fact is especially important when the nation's economy takes a nosedive or an individual firm's sales revenue and profits are declining.

When you look back at the original question we asked at the beginning of this section, clearly, each different type of environment affects the way a business does *business*. As a result, there are always opportunities for improvement and challenges that must be considered.

The Challenges Ahead

There it is—the American business system in brief. When it works well, it provides jobs for those who are willing to work, a standard of living that few countries can match, and many opportunities for personal advancement. However, like every other system devised by humans, it is not perfect. Our business system may give us prosperity, but it also gave us the Great Depression of the 1930s and the economic problems of the 1970s, the late 1980s, and the first part of the twenty-first century.

Obviously, the system can be improved. Certainly there are plenty of people who are willing to tell us exactly what *they* think the American economy needs. But these people provide us only with conflicting opinions. Who is right and who is wrong? Even the experts cannot agree.

The experts do agree, however, that several key issues will challenge our economic system (and our nation) over the next decade. Some of the questions to be resolved include

* How can we encourage Iraq and Afghanistan to establish a democratic and free society and resolve possible conflict with North Korea, Iran, and other countries throughout the world?

* How can we create a more stable economy and create new jobs?

Your Career

What Does It Take to Get to the Top?

Building a successful career in the changing world of business requires more than ambition, determination, and hard work. You'll need to develop these skills to get to the top:

* Become fluent in the financial language of business.
* Be adaptable and open to new ideas.
* Practice making informed decisions.
* Hone your people skills to motivate others.
* Set high goals and standards.

Patricia Woertz became the first woman CEO of the food-processing giant Archer Daniels Midland by employing savvy financial strategies, working well with employees at all levels, and staying focused on her career goals. She knows how to listen, learn from colleagues, and create an atmosphere of trust, capabilities she needs as she builds on the company's strengths to keep sales and profits growing.

Gary Pruitt, CEO of McClatchy, the second-largest U.S. newspaper chain, uses analytical thinking and clear goals to guide such difficult decisions as which newspapers to keep and which to sell. "This is an era where CEOs have to be hands on, deeply engaged, and knowledgeable about operations," Pruitt states.

What can you do right now to start preparing for your successful career?

Sources: Based on information from Geoffrey Colvin, "What It Takes to Be Great," *Fortune*, October 30, 2006, pp. 88–96; Carol Hymowitz, "Leaders Must Produce *Bold New Blueprints in Era of Architect CEO*," *Wall Street Journal*, April 17, 2006, p. B1; Carol Hymowitz, "After a 14-Year Run, A Technology CEO Shares Some Advice," *Wall Street Journal*, March 20, 2006, p. B1; Jon Birger, "The Outsider," *Fortune*, October 16, 2006, pp. 167–176.

* As a nation, how can we develop a disaster crisis management program that will help people in times of peril?

* How can we meet the challenges of managing culturally diverse work forces to address the needs of a culturally diverse marketplace?

* How can we make American manufacturers more productive and more competitive with foreign producers who have lower labor costs?

* How can we preserve the benefits of competition and small businesses in our American economic system?

* How can we encourage economic growth and at the same time continue to conserve natural resources, protect our environment, and meet the needs of society?

* How can we best market American-made products in foreign nations?

* How can we meet the needs of two-income families, single parents, older Americans, and the less fortunate?

The answers to these questions are anything but simple. In the past, Americans always have been able to solve their economic problems through ingenuity and creativity. Now, as we continue the journey through the twenty-first century, we need that same ingenuity and creativity not only to solve our current problems but also to compete in the global marketplace.

According to economic experts, if we as a nation can become more competitive, we may solve many of our current domestic problems. As an added bonus, increased competitiveness also will enable us to meet the economic challenges posed by other industrialized nations of the world. The way we solve these problems will affect our own future, our children's future, and that of our nation. Within the American economic and political system, the answers are ours to provide.

The American business system is not perfect by any means, but it does work reasonably well. We discuss some of its problems in Chapter 2 as we examine the topics of social responsibility and business ethics.

> **CONCEPT CHECK**
> What do you consider the most important challenges that will face people in the United States in the years ahead?

TEST PREPPER 1.7

True or False?

 1. In the early 1990s, unemployment numbers, inflation, and interest—all factors that affect business—were at record lows.

2. The organized effort of individuals to produce and sell through the Internet, for a profit, the products and services that satisfy society's needs is referred to as *e-business*.

Multiple Choice

 3. Segmenting the production process into distinct processes is

   a. the barter system.
   b. specialization.
   c. the domestic system.
   d. the factory system.
   e. e-business.

4. A system of exchange in which goods or services are traded directly for other goods and/or services without using money is

   a. the barter system.
   b. specialization.
   c. the domestic system.
   d. the factory system.
   e. e-business.

5. Samuel Slater used which of the following concepts to introduce America to a new form of manufacturing?

   a. Barter system
   b. Foreign trade
   c. Domestic system
   d. Factory system
   e. e-Business

ACE the Test
ACE & ACE+
Practice Test 1.7

Prepare for Class
CL News Feeds
CL News Now

→ **RETURN TO INSIDE BUSINESS**

By any measure, business is bubbling at PepsiCo. With $6 billion in annual sales, Gatorade is a shining star among Pepsi's seventeen mega-brands, and it plays a major role in the company's international success. Gatorade was developed originally as a sports drink for college football players. However, its thirst-quenching benefits have won fans in many sports and among health-conscious consumers of all ages.

In recent years, PepsiCo has broadened its customer base by adding a variety of new flavors and formulations, such as Gatorade A.M. and Gatorade Endurance Formula. As a result, demand for Gatorade has been so strong that the company is expanding production capacity. Looking ahead, PepsiCo is counting on Gatorade's widespread appeal to add fizz to its profitability in markets around the world.

Questions

1. What factors have led to PepsiCo's business success for more than 100 years?
2. What steps should PepsiCo take to maintain stakeholder satisfaction while competing in the global marketplace?

LEARNING OBJECTIVES REVIEW

1 Examine the reasons why you would want a career in the world of business.

- There are many opportunities out there for people who are willing to work hard, continue to learn, and possess the ability to adapt to change.
- Employers and our capitalistic economic system are more demanding than ever before.
- As you begin this course, ask yourself: What can I do that will make employers want to pay me a salary? What skills do I have that employers need?
- To get a job in your chosen field and to be successful at it, you will have to develop a plan, or road map, that ensures that you have the necessary skills and the knowledge the job requires to become a better employee.

2 Define *business* and identify potential risks and rewards.

- *Business* is the organized effort of individuals to produce and sell, for a profit, the products and services that satisfy society's needs.
- Four kinds of resources—material, human, financial, and informational—must be combined to start and operate a business.

- The three general types of businesses are manufacturers, service businesses, and marketing intermediaries.
- Profit is what remains after all business expenses are deducted from sales revenue. It is the payment that owners receive for assuming the risks of business—primarily the risks of not receiving payment and of losing whatever has been invested in the firm.

3 Define *economics* and describe the two types of economic systems: capitalism and command economy.

- *Economics* is the study of how wealth is created and distributed.
- Capitalism (on which our economic system is based) is an economic system in which individuals own and operate the majority of businesses that provide goods and services.
- The U.S. economic system today is a mixed economy.
- In a command economy, government, rather than individuals, owns the major factors of production and provides the answers to the three other economic questions.

- Socialist and communist economies are—at least in theory—command economies. In the real world, however, communists seem to practice a strictly controlled kind of socialism.

4 **Examine the importance of productivity in the study of economics and how it relates to the measures of economic performance.**

- One way to evaluate the performance of an economic system is to assess changes in productivity, which is the average level of output per worker per hour.

- Gross domestic product (GDP) also can be used to measure a nation's economic well-being and is the total dollar value of all goods and services produced by all people within the boundaries of a country during a one-year period.

- The GDP figure facilitates comparisons between the United States and other countries because it is the standard used in international guidelines for economic accounting.

- It is also possible to adjust GDP for inflation and thus to measure *real* GDP.

- In addition to GDP, other economic indicators include a nation's balance of trade, consumer price index (CPI), corporate profits, inflation rate, national income, new housing starts, prime interest rate, producer price index (PPI), productivity rate, and unemployment rate.

5 **Examine the different economic cycles and their management through fiscal and monetary policies.**

- A nation's economy fluctuates rather than grows at a steady pace every year. These fluctuations generally are referred to as the *business cycle*.

- Generally, the business cycle consists of four states: the peak (sometimes referred to as *prosperity*), recession, the trough, and recovery.

- Some experts believe that effective use of monetary policy (the Federal Reserve's decisions that determine the size of the supply of money and the level of interest rates) and fiscal policies (the government's influence on the amount of savings and expenditures) can speed up recovery and reduce the amount of time the economy is in recession.

6 **Analyze the economic forces of supply and demand and how they affect the four different types of business competition.**

- Competition is essentially a rivalry among businesses for sales to potential customers.

- In a capitalist economy, competition works to ensure the efficient and effective operation of business.

- Competition also ensures that a firm will survive only if it serves its customers well.

- *Supply* of a particular product is the quantity of the product that *producers* are willing to sell at each of various prices.

- *Demand* is the quantity of a product that *buyers* are willing to purchase at each of various prices.

- The *equilibrium*, or *market*, *price* is the one price at which the demanded quantity of a product is exactly equal to the quantity of that product supplied.

- Economists recognize four degrees of competition, ranging from most to least competitive.

- The four degrees are perfect competition, monopolistic competition, oligopoly, and monopoly.

7 **Summarize the historical factors that have affected the current business environment and the challenges American businesses will encounter in the future.**

- *Standard of living* is a loose subjective measure of how well off an individual or a society is mainly in terms of want satisfaction through goods and services.

- Increased use of the Internet and e-business and the increasing importance of services and global trade is changing the way that firms do business.

- The way a business operates is affected by the competitive environment, global environment, technological environment, and economic environment.

- The United States can solve many of its current domestic problems by becoming more competitive.

- Increased competitiveness will enable us to meet the economic challenges posed by other industrialized nations of the world.

Improve Your Grade
Learning Objectives Review
Audio Chapter Review & Quiz

VIDEO CASE

Stonyfield Farm's "Yogurt on a Mission"

Stonyfield Farm's "Yogurt on a Mission" is changing the culture of at least one multinational corporation. Stonyfield Farm, founded in New Hampshire in 1983, began with three Jersey cows. Today it owns the third largest-selling yogurt brand in America. The company's extensive line of organic foods includes refrigerated yogurts, ice cream, frozen yogurt, soft-serve yogurt, cultured soy snacks, and drinkable yogurts. All its products meet rigorous guidelines for organic certification because the ingredients are produced without synthetic fertilizers or pesticides, antibiotics, and hormones. Although organic foods were not as popular when Stonyfield was established, they currently account for a whopping $9 billion in yearly sales.

Stonyfield is pursuing a five-part mission to (1) support family farmers, (2) be profitable, (3) offer quality products, (4) protect the environment, and (5) be a great place for employees to work. All Stonyfield's decisions and actions reflect this ambitious mission. Managers are dedicated to using only the highest-quality ingredients to make all-natural food products that are both healthy and tasty. They use product packaging to educate customers about environmental causes such as global warming and recycling. They also are firmly committed to the family farms that supply organic milk for Stonyfield's products, paying a higher price so that the farmers can survive even when competing yogurt makers cut the amount they pay for milk. And they ensure that workplace conditions allow employees the opportunity to develop their skills and advance into new positions.

Following company policy to "reduce, reuse, recycle," Stonyfield's personnel always look for the most environmentally friendly ways to operate. For example, the company currently recycles 60 percent of its yogurt plant's waste. However, CEO Gary Hirshberg wants to increase that recycling level to 80 percent or higher. Even milk that does not meet the company's strict quality standards is not wasted—it goes to local farmers, who feed it to their pigs. The company also collects used yogurt cups and turns them over to a company that recycles the plastic into handles for razors and toothbrushes.

Stonyfield's continuing success proves that caring for the environment can be profitable. Using less energy or water actually lowers operating costs. Similarly, reducing or recycling waste lowers waste-removal costs. Just as important, communicating with customers about environmental issues creates a closer connection and builds sales by reinforcing brand loyalty. In fact, Stonyfield's sales have been growing rapidly, and it donates 10 percent of its profits to environmental causes every year.

Hirshberg is also using his entrepreneurial talents to move into the lucrative fast-food market with O'Natural's restaurants. The chain serves healthy fast food in a comfortable, family-friendly setting—with environmental education as a side dish. "We call it 'fast food with a mission,'" the CEO states.

Now Stonyfield is entering a new phase of its business life. In 2001, France's Groupe Danone—maker of Dannon, the world's best-selling yogurt—acquired a 40 percent holding in Stonyfield. In 2004, Groupe Danone increased that stake to 80 percent. If Stonyfield's president leaves the company, Groupe Danone will keep donating 10 percent of Stonyfield's profits to environmental causes for at least a decade afterward.

Groupe Danone's chairman sees Stonyfield as a model for doing business in the future. "We are driven by social values similar to Gary's," he notes. "We have to think not only in terms of economics, but also in terms of social responsibility." This fits with Hirshberg's long-term view of socially responsible businesses and healthier customers: "If you make the right choices, then future generations will have a healthier planet and healthier, more enjoyable lives."[15] For more information about this company, go to www.stonyfield.com.

Questions

1. As a business, what needs does Stonyfield satisfy for its customers?
2. Does the yogurt market reflect monopolistic competition or an oligopoly? Support your answer by discussing how Stonyfield's diverse line of organic foods helps the company to compete.
3. Why would a firm like Stonyfield embrace environmental causes *and* the concept of increasing sales and profits?

BUILDING SKILLS FOR CAREER SUCCESS

1. Exploring the Internet

To familiarize you with the wealth of information available through the Internet and its usefulness to business students, this exercise focuses on information services available from a few popular search engines used to explore the web. Each of the remaining chapters in this text also contains an Internet exercise that is in some way associated with the topics covered in the chapter. After completing these exercises, not only will you be familiar with a variety of sources of business information, but you also will be better prepared to locate information you might need in the future.

To use one of these search engines, enter its *Internet address* in your web browser. The addresses of some popular search engines are

www.google.com, www.msn.com, www.yahoo.com.

Visit the text website for updates to this exercise.

Assignment

1. Examine the ways in which two search engines present categories of information on their opening screens. Which search engine was better to use in your opinion? Why?

2. Think of a business topic that you would like to know more about, for example, careers, gross domestic product, etc. Using your preferred search engine, explore a few articles on your topic. Briefly summarize your findings.

2. Building Team Skills

Over the past few years, employees have been expected to function as productive team members instead of working alone. People often believe that they can work effectively in teams, but many people find working with a group of people to be a challenge. Being an effective team member requires skills that encourage other members to participate in the team endeavor.

College classes that function as teams are more interesting and more fun to attend, and students generally learn more about the topics in the course.

Prepare for Class
Exploring the Internet

Assignment

1. Find a partner, preferably someone you do not know and ask in two to three minutes the following questions:
   a. What is your name, and where do you work?
   b. What interesting or unusual thing have you done in your life? (Do not talk about work or college; rather, focus on such things as hobbies, travel, family, and sports.)
   c. Why are you taking this course, and what do you expect to learn? (Satisfying a degree requirement is not an acceptable answer.)

2. Introduce your partner to the class. Use one to two minutes, depending on the size of the class.

3. Researching Different Careers

In this chapter, *entrepreneurship* is defined as the willingness to take risks and the knowledge and ability to use the other factors of production efficiently. An *entrepreneur* is a person who risks his or her time, effort, and money to start and operate a business. Often people believe that these terms apply only to small business operations, but recently, employees with entrepreneurial attitudes have advanced more rapidly in large companies.

Assignment

1. Go to the local library or use the Internet to research how large firms, especially corporations, are rewarding employees who have entrepreneurial skills.

2. Find answers to the following questions and write a two-page report that summarizes your findings.
   a. Why is an entrepreneurial attitude important in corporations today?
   b. What makes an entrepreneurial employee different from other employees?
   c. How are these employees being rewarded, and are the rewards worth the effort?

CHAPTER 2

Being Ethical and Socially Responsible

Your Guide to Success in Business

Why this chapter matters

Business ethics and social responsibility issues have become extremely relevant in today's business world. Business schools teach business ethics to prepare managers to be more responsible. Corporations are developing ethics and social responsibility programs to help meet these needs in the work place.

LEARNING OBJECTIVES

1. Understand what is meant by *business ethics*.

2. Identify the types of ethical concerns that arise in the business world.

3. Discuss the factors that affect the level of ethical behavior in organizations.

4. Explain how ethical decision making can be encouraged.

5. Describe the historical progression of how our current views on social responsibility of business have evolved.

6. Explain the two views on the social responsibility of business and understand the arguments for and against increased social responsibility.

7. Discuss the factors that led to the consumer movement and list some of its results.

8. Analyze how present employment practices are being used to counteract past abuses.

9. Describe how the different forces behind social consciousness are dealing with major types of pollution, their causes, and their cures.

10. Identify the steps a business must take to implement a program of social responsibility.

3M Takes Innovative Steps with a Smaller Environmental Footprint

"Hire good people and let them do their job in their own way. And tolerate mistakes" is 3M's corporate philosophy. From Scotch tape to Post-It Notes, industrial adhesives to energy-efficient window coatings, 3M has been launching innovative products for more than 125 years. Based in St. Paul, Minnesota, 3M employs 69,000 people with worldwide sales of over $21 billion. How does this diversified multinational firm remain a leader in innovation and environmental responsibility?

"If you are going to be an innovative company, organic growth and new products have to be what drives the company," explains Larry Wendling, vice president of 3M's corporate research labs. To encourage innovation,

- 3M devotes over 6 percent of its budget to new product development.
- 3M's senior managers provide employees with a broad base of technological support and encourage communication and networking.
- 3M monitors market reaction to determine whether its research and development funds have been well spent.
- 3M rewards employees for outstanding work.

Satisfying customers' needs with innovative products of superior quality and acting with honesty and integrity are key to 3M's corporate values. Employees spend considerable time with consumers and business customers to better understand and meet their needs. As just one example, its engineers developed the 3M Ergonomic Optical Mouse to provide wrist and finger comfort for computer users at home and at work.

Yet 3M is also able to balance its drive for innovation with a strong sense of environmental responsibility. The U.S. Environmental Protection Agency (EPA) has included 3M in its National Environmental Performance Track Program and honored 3M with numerous awards because of the company's achievements in reducing pollution and conserving both water and energy. Just recently, 3M received the EPA's Energy Star Sustained Excellence Award for reducing energy usage even further. "From potato chips to Post-it Notes, our Energy Star award winners are proving that saving energy dollars just makes sense," states the EPA's Stephen Johnson.[1]

> **DID YOU KNOW?**
>
> For more than 125 years, 3M has been balancing its drive for innovation with a strong sense of environmental responsibility and ethics.

KEY TERMS

ethics (41)
business ethics (41)
Sarbanes-Oxley Act of 2002 (46)
code of ethics (46)
whistle-blowing (47)

social responsibility (49)
caveat emptor (54)
economic model of social responsibility (56)
socioeconomic model of social responsibility (56)

consumerism (58)
minority (62)
affirmative action program (63)
Equal Employment Opportunity Commission (EEOC) (63)

hard-core unemployed (64)
National Alliance of Business (NAB) (64)
pollution (65)
social audit (70)

ACE the Test
Crossword Puzzle
Flashcards

Obviously, organizations like 3M want to be recognized as responsible corporate citizens. Most managers today, like those at 3M, are finding ways to balance a growing agenda of socially responsible activities with the drive to generate profits. This also happens to be a good way for a company to demonstrate its values and to attract like-minded employees, customers, and stockholders. In a highly competitive business environment, an increasing number of companies are, like 3M, seeking to set themselves apart by developing a reputation for ethical and socially responsible behavior.

We begin this chapter by

* Defining *business ethics* and examining ethical issues.
* Looking at the standards of behavior in organizations and how ethical behavior can be encouraged.
* Examining the topic of social responsibility. We compare and contrast two present-day models of social responsibility and present arguments for and against increasing the social responsibility of business.
* Examining the major elements of the consumer movement.
* Discussing how social responsibility in business has affected employment practices and environmental concerns.
* Considering the commitment, planning, and funding that go into a firm's program of social responsibility.

—EXAMINING ETHICS—
Is It Spying?

How far can a company go to protect its sensitive information and still be a prudent employer? In particular, employers are concerned about the amount of time their employees spend on the Internet and the possibility that company secrets will be shared with outsiders.

In a recent survey, the American Management Association found that, of the responding companies,

* 76 percent monitor employee visits to websites,
* 36 percent track e-mail content, and
* 55 percent retain and review all e-mail.

Many companies monitor their employees' phone calls, e-mail, Internet usage, and computer activities using software such as Websense. Even the magnetic cards needed to open doors in the workplace can track employees' movements within company buildings. As more monitoring devices and software are developed, it is important for employers to follow best management practices and provide employees with a written policy to explain monitoring procedures.

Sources: Based on information from Amy Joyce, "Every Move You Make," *The Washington Post*, October 1, 2006, p. F1; Phred Dvorak and Vauhini Vara, "At Many Companies, Hunt for Leakers Expands Arsenal of Monitoring Tactics," *Wall Street Journal*, September 11, 2006, p. B1; Michael Orey, "Corporate Snoops," *BusinessWeek*, October 9, 2006, pp. 47–49.

Business Ethics Defined

Learning Objective

Understand what is meant by business ethics.

Ethics is the study of right and wrong and of the morality of the choices individuals make. An ethical decision or action is one that is "right" according to some standard of behavior. **Business ethics** is the application of moral standards to business situations. Recent court cases involving unethical behavior have helped to make business ethics a matter of public concern. **EXAMPLE** Copley Pharmaceutical, Inc., pled guilty to federal criminal charges (and paid a $10.65 million fine) for falsifying drug manufacturers' reports to the Food and Drug Administration. In another much-publicized case, lawsuits against tobacco companies have led to $246 billion in settlements, although there has been only one class-action lawsuit filed on behalf of all smokers. That case, *Engle v. R. J. Reynolds*, could cost tobacco companies an estimated $500 billion.

ethics the study of right and wrong and of the morality of the choices individuals make

business ethics the application of moral standards to business situations

Ethical Issues

Learning Objective

Identify the types of ethical concerns that arise in the business world.

Ethical issues often arise out of a business's relationship with investors, customers, employees, creditors, or competitors. Each of these groups has specific concerns and usually exerts pressure on the organization's managers. For example,

* *Investors* want management to make sensible financial decisions that will boost sales, profits, and returns on their investments.
* *Customers* expect a firm's products to be safe, reliable, and reasonably priced.
* *Employees* demand to be treated fairly in hiring, promotion, and compensation decisions.
* *Creditors* require accounts to be paid on time and the accounting information furnished by the firm to be accurate.
* *Competitors* expect the firm's competitive practices to be fair and honest.

EXAMPLE Consider TAP Pharmaceutical Products, Inc., whose sales representatives offered every urologist in the United States a big-screen TV, computers, fax machines, and golf vacations if the doctors prescribed TAP's new prostate cancer drug Lupron. Moreover, the sales representatives sold Lupron at cut-rate prices or gratis while defrauding Medicare. Recently, the federal government won an $875 million judgment against TAP.[2]

In late 2006, Hewlett-Packard Co.'s chairman, Patricia Dunn, and general counsel, Ann Baskins, resigned amid allegations that the company used intrusive tactics in observing the personal lives of journalists and company's directors, thus tarnishing Hewlett-Packard's reputation for integrity. According to Congressman John Dingell of

Michigan, "We have before us witnesses from Hewlett-Packard to discuss a plumbers' operation that would make [former president] Richard Nixon blush were he still alive."

Business people face ethical issues every day, and some of these issues can be difficult to assess. Although some types of issues arise infrequently, others occur regularly. Let's take a closer look at several ethical issues.

Fairness and Honesty

Fairness and honesty in business are two important ethical concerns. Besides obeying all laws and regulations, business people are expected to refrain from knowingly deceiving, misrepresenting, or intimidating others. The consequences of failing to do so can be expensive. **EXAMPLE** Recently, Keith E. Anderson and Wayne Anderson, the leaders of an international tax shelter scheme known as Anderson's Ark and Associates, were sentenced to as many as twenty years in prison. The Andersons, among their associates, were ordered to pay over $200 million in fines and restitution.[3] In yet another 2005 case, the accounting firm PriceWaterhouseCoopers LLP agreed to pay the U.S. government $42 million to resolve allegations that it made false claims in connection with travel reimbursements it collected for several federal agencies.[4]

Organizational Relationships

A business person may be tempted to place his or her personal welfare above the welfare of others or the welfare of the organization. For example, in late 2002, former CEO of Tyco International, Ltd., Leo Dennis Kozlowski was indicted for misappropriating $43 million in corporate funds to make philanthropic contributions in his own name, including $5 million to Seton Hall University, which named its new business-school building Kozlowski Hall. Furthermore, according to Tyco, the former CEO took $61.7 million in interest-free relocation loans without the board's permission. He allegedly used the money to finance many personal luxuries, including a $15 million yacht and a $3.9 million Renoir painting, and to throw a $2 million party for his wife's birthday.[5] Relationships with customers and coworkers often create ethical problems. Unethical behavior in these areas includes taking credit for others' ideas or work, not meeting one's commitments in a mutual agreement, and pressuring others to behave unethically.

Conflict of Interest

Conflict of interest results when a business person takes advantage of a situation for his or her own personal interest rather than for the employer's interest. Such conflict may occur when payments and gifts make their way into business deals. A wise rule to remember is that anything given to a person that might unfairly influence that person's business decision is a bribe, and all bribes are unethical.

EXAMPLE At Procter & Gamble Company (P&G), all employees are obligated to act at all times solely in the best interests of the company. A conflict of interest arises when an employee has a personal relationship or financial or other interest that could interfere with this obligation or when an employee uses his or her position with the company for personal gain. P&G requires employees to disclose all potential conflicts of interest and to take prompt actions to eliminate a conflict when the company asks them to do so. Receiving gifts, entertainment, or other gratuities from people with whom P&G does business generally is not acceptable because doing so could imply an obligation on the part of the company and potentially pose a conflict of interest.

Communications

Business communications, especially advertising, can present ethical questions. False and misleading advertising is illegal and unethical, and it can infuriate customers. Sponsors of advertisements aimed at children must be especially careful to avoid misleading messages. Advertisers of health-related products also must take precautions to guard against deception when using such descriptive terms as *low fat, fat free,* and *light*. In fact, the Federal Trade Commission has issued guidelines on the use of these labels.

ACE the Test
ACE & ACE+
Practice Test 2.1, 2.2

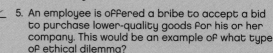

TEST PREPPER 2.1 2.2

True or False?

_I_ 1. Fairness and honesty are two important ethical concerns.

_F_ 2. Ethics and business ethics have nothing in common and are completely separate applications.

Multiple Choice

_B_ 3. Fairness and honesty are ethical components that
   a. may be optional.
   b. customers, investors, employees, creditors, and competitors always have a right to expect.
   c. should be applied only when advantageous to the business owner.
   d. can conflict with good business practices.
   e. have no basis in moral standards.

 4. Placing personal interest above the welfare of others is an illustration of
   a. fairness.
   b. conflict of interest.
   c. an organizational relationship.
   d. communication.
   e. honesty.

_C_ 5. An employee is offered a bribe to accept a bid to purchase lower-quality goods for his or her company. This would be an example of what type of ethical dilemma?
   a. Communication
   b. Organizational relationship
   c. Conflict of interest
   d. Fairness and honesty
   e. Communication and organizational relationship

Factors Affecting Ethical Behavior

Learning Objective ❸

Discuss the factors that affect the level of ethical behavior in organizations.

Is it possible for an individual with strong moral values to make ethically questionable decisions in a business setting? What factors affect a person's inclination to make either ethical or unethical decisions in a business organization? Although the answers to these questions are not entirely clear, three general sets of factors do appear to influence the standards of behavior in an organization. As shown in Figure 2.1, the sets consist of *individual factors, social factors,* and *opportunity*.

LEVEL OF ETHICAL BEHAVIOR

| Individual factors | Social factors | Opportunity |

FIGURE 2.1

Factors That Affect the Level of Ethical Behavior in an Organization

Source: Based on O. C. Ferrell and Larry Gresham, "A Contingency Framework for Understanding Ethical Decision Making in Marketing," *Journal of Marketing*, Summer 1985, p. 89.

CONCEPT CHECK

Why might an individual with high ethical standards act less ethically in businessn than in his or her personal life?

Individual Factors Affecting Ethics

Several individual factors influence the level of ethical behavior in an organization.

* *Individual knowledge of an issue.* How much an individual knowsabout an issue is one factor: A decision maker with a greater amount of knowledge regarding a situation may take steps to avoid ethical problems, whereas a less-informed person may take action unknowingly that leads to an ethical quagmire.

* *Personal values.* An individual's moral values and central, value-related attitudes also clearly influence his or her business behavior. Most people join organizations to accomplish personal goals.

* *Personal goals.* The types of personal goals an individual aspires to and the manner in which these goals are pursued have a significant impact on that individual's behavior in an organization. The actions of specific individuals in scandal-plagued companies such as Adelphia, Arthur Anderson, Enron, Halliburton, Qwest, and WorldCom often raise questions about individuals' personal character and integrity.

Social Factors Affecting Ethics

* *Cultural norms.* A person's behavior in the workplace, to some degree, is determined by cultural norms, and these social factors vary from one culture to another. For example, in some countries it is acceptable and ethical for customs agents to receive gratuities for performing ordinary, legal tasks that are a part of their jobs, whereas in other countries these practices would be viewed as unethical and perhaps illegal.

* *Coworkers.* The actions and decisions of coworkers constitute another social factor believed to shape a person's sense of business ethics. For example, if your coworkers make long-distance telephone calls on company time and at company expense, you might view that behavior as acceptable and ethical because everyone does it.

* *Significant others.* The moral values and attitudes of "significant others"—spouses, friends, and relatives, for instance—also can affect an employee's perception of what is ethical and unethical behavior in the workplace.

* *Use of the Internet.* Even the Internet presents new challenges for firms whose employees enjoy easy access to sites through convenient high-speed connections at work. An employee's behavior online can be viewed as offensive to coworkers and possibly lead to lawsuits against the firm if employees engage in unethical behavior on controversial websites not related to their job. As a result, research by Websense and the Center for Internet Studies reveals that nearly two out of three companies nationwide have disciplined employees and that nearly one out of three have fired employees for Internet misuse in the workplace.[6] Interestingly, one recent survey of employees found that most workers assume that their use of technology at work will be monitored. A large majority of employees approved of most monitoring methods such as monitoring faxes and e-mail, tracking web use, and even recording telephone calls.

"Opportunity" as a Factor Affecting Ethics

* *Presence of opportunity. Opportunity* refers to the amount of freedom an organization gives an employee to behave unethically if he or she makes that choice. In some organizations, certain company policies and procedures reduce the opportunity to be unethical. For example, at some fast-food restaurants, one employee takes your order and receives your payment, and another fills the order. This procedure reduces the opportunity to be unethical because the person handling the money is not dispensing the product, and the person giving out the product is not handling the money.

* *Ethical codes.* The existence of an ethical code and the importance management places on this code are other determinants of opportunity (codes of ethics are discussed in more detail in the next section).

* *Enforcement.* The degree of enforcement of company policies, procedures, and ethical codes is a major force affecting opportunity. When violations are dealt with consistently and firmly, the opportunity to be unethical is reduced.

Now that we have considered some of the factors believed to influence the level of ethical behavior in the workplace, let's explore what can be done to encourage ethical behavior and to discourage unethical behavior.

SPOTLIGHT

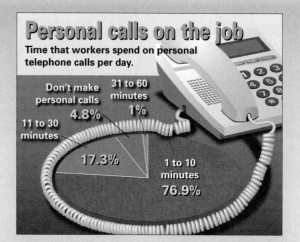

Personal calls on the job
Time that workers spend on personal telephone calls per day.

Don't make personal calls **4.8%**
31 to 60 minutes **1%**
11 to 30 minutes **17.3%**
1 to 10 minutes **76.9%**

Source: At-A-Glance survey of 1,385 office workers. Margin of error +2.7 percentage points. O.C. Ferrel, John Fraedrich and Linda Ferrell, *Business Ethics*, 6th ed. Copyright © 2008 by Houghton Mifflin Company. Reprinted with Permission of Houghton Mifflin.

TEST PREPPER 2.3

True or False?

I 1. In general, there are three factors that affect standards of behavior in an organization.

I 2. The actions of individuals in scandal-plagued companies can have a significant impact on the behavior of others in those companies.

I 3. The degree to which a company enforces ethical standards is a major force affecting opportunity.

Multiple Choice

C 4. A social factor that can affect ethics is
  a. individual knowledge of an issue.
  b. personal goals.
  c. cultural norms.
  d. the presence of opportunity.
  e. ethical codes.

B 5. The existence of an ethical code and the importance management places on this code are an application of which of the following?
  a. Enforcement
  b. Opportunity
  c. Internet usage
  d. Coworkers
  e. Significant others

ACE the Test
ACE & ACE+
Practice Test 2.3

Encouraging Ethical Behavior

Learning Objective 4

Explain how ethical decision making can be encouraged.

Most authorities agree that there is room for improvement in business ethics. A more problematic question is: Can business be made more ethical in the real world? The majority opinion on this issue suggests that *government, trade associations, and individual firms* indeed can establish acceptable levels of ethical behavior.

Government's Role in Encouraging Ethics

The government can encourage ethical behavior by legislating more stringent regulations. For example, the landmark **Sarbanes-Oxley Act of 2002** provides sweeping new legal protection for employees who report corporate misconduct. At the signing ceremony, President George W. Bush stated, "The act adopts tough new provisions to deter and punish corporate and accounting fraud and corruption, ensure justice for wrongdoers, and protect the interests of workers and shareholders." Among other things, the law deals with corporate responsibility, conflicts of interest, and corporate accountability. However, rules require enforcement, and the unethical business person frequently seems to "slip something by" without getting caught. Increased regulation may help, but it surely cannot solve the entire ethics problem.

Trade Associations' Role in Encouraging Ethics

Trade associations can and often do provide ethical guidelines for their members. These organizations, which operate within particular industries, are in an excellent position to exert pressure on members who stoop to questionable business practices. For example, recently, a pharmaceutical trade group adopted a new set of guidelines to halt the extravagant dinners and other gifts sales representatives often give to physicians. However, enforcement and authority vary from association to association. And because trade associations exist for the benefit of their members, harsh measures may be self-defeating.

Individual Companies' Role in Encouraging Ethics

Codes of ethics that companies provide to their employees are perhaps the most effective way to encourage ethical behavior. A **code of ethics** is a written guide to acceptable and ethical behavior as defined by an organization; it outlines uniform policies, standards, and punishments for violations. Because employees know what is expected of them and what will happen if they violate the rules, a code of ethics goes a long way toward encouraging ethical behavior. However, codes cannot possibly cover every situation. Companies also must create an environment in which employees recognize the importance of complying with the written code. Managers must provide direction by fostering communication, actively model and encourage ethical decision making, and train employees to make ethical decisions.

Sarbanes-Oxley Act of 2002 provides sweeping new legal protection for employees who report corporate misconduct

code of ethics a guide to acceptable and ethical behavior as defined by the organization

ACE the Test
Hangman

CONCEPT CHECK

How would an organizational code of ethics help to ensure ethical business behavior?

During the 1980s, an increasing number of organizations created and implemented ethics codes. In a recent survey of *Fortune* 1000 firms, 93 percent of the companies that responded reported having a formal code of ethics. Some companies are now even taking steps to strengthen their codes. **EXAMPLE** To strengthen its account-ability, S. C. Johnson & Son, makers of Pledge, Drano, Windex, and many other household products, is a firm that recognizes that it must behave in ways the public perceives as ethical; its code includes expectations for employees and its commitment to consumers, the community, and society in general. As shown in Figure 2.2, included in the ethics code of electronics giant Texas Instruments (TI) are issues relating to policies and procedures; laws and regulations; relationships with customers, suppliers, and competitors; conflicts of interest; handling of proprietary information; and code enforcement.

Assigning an ethics officer who coordinates ethical conduct gives employees someone to consult if they are not sure of the right thing to do. An ethics officer meets with employees and top management to provide ethical advice; establishes and maintains an anonymous, confidential service to answer questions about ethical issues; and takes action on ethics code violations.

Sometimes even employees who want to act ethically may find it difficult to do so. Unethical practices can become ingrained in an organization. Employees with high personal ethics then may take a controversial step called *whistle-blowing*. **Whistle-blowing** is informing the press or government officials about unethical practices within one's organization.

The year 2002 was labeled as the "Year of the Whistleblower." Consider Joe Speaker, a 40-year-old acting chief financial officer (CFO) at Rite Aid Corp. in 1999. He discovered that inventories at Rite Aid had been overvalued and that millions in expenses had not been reported properly. Further digging into Rite Aid's books revealed that $541 million in earnings over the previous two years were really $1.6 billion in losses. Mr. Speaker was a main government witness when former Rite Aid Corp. Chairman and CEO Martin L. Grass went on trial. Mr. Speaker is among dozens of corporate managers who have blown the whistle. Enron's Sherron S. Watkins and WorldCom's Cynthia Cooper are now well-known whistle-blowers and *Time* magazine's persons of the year 2002. According to Linda Chatman Thomsen, deputy director for enforcement at the Securities and Exchange Commission, "Whistle-blowers give us an insider's perspective and have advanced our investigation immeasurably." Stephen Meagher, a former federal prosecutor who represents whistle-blowers, calls Watkins and Cooper national champions and says, "The business of whistle-blowing is booming."[7]

Whistle-blowing could have averted disaster and prevented needless deaths in the *Challenger* space shuttle disaster, for example. How could employees have known about life-threatening problems and let them pass? Whistle-blowing, on the other hand, can have serious repercussions for employees: Those who "blow whistles" sometimes lose their jobs. However, the Sarbanes-Oxley Act of 2002 protects whistle-blowers who report corporate misconduct. Any executive who retaliates against a whistle-blower can be held criminally liable and imprisoned for up to ten years.

Retaliations do occur, however. For example, in 2005, the U.S. Court of Appeals for the 8th Circuit unanimously upheld the right of Jane Turner, a twenty-five-year veteran

whistle-blowing
informing the press or government officials about unethical practices within one's organization

The Year of the Whistle Blowers.

Meet Cynthia Cooper of WorldCom, Colleen Rowley of the FBI, and Sherron Watkins of Enron who couldn't take it any more. These employees with high personal ethics blew the whistle on unethical practices in their organizations. For their bold stands, which had profound effects, they were featured on the cover of *Time* magazine as *Time*'s Persons of the Year.

FIGURE 2.2

Defining Acceptable Behavior: Texas Instruments' Code of Ethics

Texas Instruments encourages ethical behavior through an extensive training program and a written code of ethics and shared values.

Source: Courtesy of Texas Instruments, www.ti.com/corp/docs/ company/citizen/ethics/ brochure/integrity .shtml; accessed September 24, 2006.

TEXAS INSTRUMENTS CODE OF ETHICS

"Integrity is the foundation on which TI is built. There is no other characteristic more essential to a TIer's makeup. It has to be present at all levels. Integrity is expected of managers and individuals when they make commitments. They are expected to stand by their commitments to the best of their ability.

One of TI's greatest strengths is its values and ethics. We had some early leaders who set those values as the standard for how they lived their lives. And it is important that TI grew that way. It's something that we don't want to lose. At the same time, we must move more rapidly. But we don't want to confuse that with the fact that we're ethical and we're moral. We're very responsible, and we live up to what we say."

Tom Engibous, President and CEO
Texas Instruments, 1997

We Respect and Value People By:

Treating others as we want to be treated.

- Exercising the basic virtues of respect, dignity, kindness, courtesy and manners in all work relationships.
- Recognizing and avoiding behaviors that others may find offensive, including the manner in which we speak and relate to one another and the materials we bring into the workplace, both printed and electronically.
- Respecting the right and obligation of every TIer to resolve concerns relating to ethics questions in the course of our duties without retribution and retaliation.
- Giving all TIers the same opportunity to have their questions, issues and situations fairly considered while understanding that being treated fairly does not always mean that we will all be treated the same.
- Trusting one another to use sound judgment in our use of TI business and information systems.
- Understanding that even though TI has the obligation to monitor its business information systems activity, we will respect privacy by prohibiting random searches of individual TIers' communications.
- Recognizing that conduct socially and professionally acceptable in one culture and country may be viewed differently in another.

We Are Honest By:

Representing ourselves and our intentions truthfully.

- Offering full disclosure and withdrawing ourselves from discussions and decisions when our business judgment appears to be in conflict with a personal interest.
- Respecting the rights and property of others, including their intellectual property. Accepting confidential or trade secret information only after we clearly understand our obligations as defined in a nondisclosure agreement.
- Competing fairly without collusion or collaboration with competitors to divide markets, set prices, restrict production, allocate customers or otherwise restrain competition.
- Assuring that no payments or favors are offered to influence others to do something wrong.
- Keeping records that are accurate and include all payments and receipts.
- Exercising good judgment in the exchange of business courtesies, meals and entertainment by avoiding activities that could create even the appearance that our decisions could be compromised.
- Refusing to speculate in TI stock through frequent buying and selling or through other forms of speculative trading.

1. *Listen and learn.*	Recognize the problem or decision-making opportunity that confronts your company, team, or unit. Don't argue, criticize, or defend yourself—keep listening and reviewing until you are sure that you understand others.
2. *Identify the ethical issues.*	Examine how coworkers and consumers are affected by the situation or decision at hand. Examine how you feel about the situation, and attempt to understand the viewpoint of those involved in the decision or in the consequences of the decision.
3. *Create and analyze options.*	Try to put aside strong feelings such as anger or a desire for power and prestige and come up with as many alternatives as possible before developing an analysis. Ask everyone involved for ideas about which options offer the best long-term results for you and the company. Then decide which option will increase your self-respect even if, in the long run, things don't work out the way you hope?
4. *Identify the best option from your point of view.*	Consider it and test it against some established criteria, such as respect, understanding, caring, fairness, honesty, and openness.
5. *Explain your decision and resolve any differences that arise.*	This may require neutral arbitration from a trusted manager or taking "time out" to reconsider, consult, or exchange written proposals before a decision is reached.

TABLE 2.1

Guidelines for Making Ethical Decisions

Source: Tom Rusk with D. Patrick Miller, "Doing the Right Thing," *Sky* (Delta Airlines), August 1993, pp. 18–22.

FBI agent, to obtain monetary damages and a jury trial against the FBI. The court held that Ms. Turner presented sufficient facts to justify a trial by jury based on the FBI's retaliatory transfer of Ms. Turner from her investigatory position in Minot, North Dakota, to a demeaning desk job in Minneapolis. Kris Kolesnik, executive director of the National Whistle Blower Center, said, "Jane Turner is an American hero. She refused to be silent when her co-agents committed misconduct in a child rape case. She refused to be silent when her co-agents stole property from Ground Zero. She paid the price and lost her job. The 8th Circuit Court did the right thing and insured that justice will take place in her case."[8]

When firms set up anonymous hotlines to handle ethically questionable situations, employees actually may be more likely to engage in whistle-blowing. When firms instead create an environment that educates employees and nurtures ethical behavior, fewer ethical problems arise, and ultimately, the need for whistle-blowing is greatly reduced.

It is difficult for an organization to develop ethics codes, policies, and procedures to deal with all relationships and every situation. When no company policy or procedures exist or apply, a quick test to determine if a behavior is ethical is to see if others—coworkers, customers, and suppliers—approve of it. Ethical decisions always will withstand scrutiny. Openness and communication about choices often will build trust and strengthen business relationships. Table 2.1 provides some general guidelines for making ethical decisions.

Social Responsibility

Social responsibility is the recognition that business activities have an impact on society and the consideration of that impact in business decision making. **EXAMPLE** In the first few days after hurricane Katrina hit New Orleans, Wal-Mart delivered $20 million in cash (including $4 million to employees displaced by the storm), 100 truckloads of free merchandise, and food for 100,000 meals. The company also promised a job elsewhere for every one of its workers affected by the catastrophe. Obviously, social responsibility costs money. It is perhaps not so obvious—except in isolated cases—that

social responsibility the recognition that business activities have an impact on society and the consideration of that impact in business decision making

Responding to the Needs of Communities.

Bechtel's commitment is to deliver quality and value to its customers. But its commitment also extends to improving the standard of living and quality of life of the communities where the company does business. Here, a Bechtel employee, James Beard, receives a thankful handshake from Hurricane Katrina's victim, John F. Smith.

social responsibility is also good business. Customers eventually find out which firms are acting responsibly and which are not. And just as easily as they cast their dollar votes for a product made by a company that is socially responsible, they can vote against the firm that is not.

Consider the following examples of organizations that are attempting to be socially responsible:

* Social responsibility can take many forms—including flying lessons. Through Young Eagles, underwritten by S. C. Johnson, Phillips Petroleum, Lockheed Martin, Jaguar, and other corporations, 22,000 volunteer pilots have taken a half million youngsters on free flights designed to teach flying basics and inspire excitement about flying careers. Young Eagles is just one of the growing number of education projects undertaken by businesses building solid records as good corporate citizens.

* Dell employees contributed more than $2 million to the Asian tsunami relief effort. Globally, Dell employees are dedicating thousands of hours and donating millions of dollars every year to organizations such as the International Red Cross, Habitat for Humanity, United Way, Second Harvest, and Earth Share. In 2005,

    * Dell awarded Healthy Community Grants to nineteen organizations that provide children's basic needs such as food, shelter, safety and health care.

    * Dell recognized seventy-five individuals and sixteen employee teams for their outstanding volunteer work in 2004 and donated $100,000 on behalf of the employees to organizations in Brazil, Canada, China, India, Ireland, Japan, Malaysia, Panama, Portugal, Slovakia, Spain, the United Kingdom, and the United States.

    * Dell employees pledged more than $3 million to assist organizations around the world.

    * Dell employees collected food and necessities for donation to Katrina and Rita victims while also donating more than $1.5 million to the American Red Cross. In addition, Dell contributed almost $3 million in technology and support to aid emergency response operations for hurricane victims.[9]

* Social responsibility is the recognition that business activities have an impact on society and the consideration of that impact in business decision making. Recently, IBM contributed $150 million in technology, talent, technical services, and cash to social and educational institutions worldwide. In the wake of natural disasters, IBM's Crisis Response Team works with local governments to deploy appropriate technologies, services, and solutions to help affected communities. In the last ten years, this team has contributed to relief operations in the wake of more than seventy major disasters, including the earthquake in Gujarat, India, in 2001, the attacks of September 11, 2001, in the United States, the tsunami that struck Southeast Asia, and most recently, the 2005 earthquakes in Pakistan and India. Within hours of that tragedy, IBM was working in India, Indonesia, Sri Lanka, and Thailand to establish secure wireless systems, operate relief sites, and deploy applications to track displaced and missing

persons. IBM's commitment of $3 million in services and equipment for relief efforts was supplemented by $1.2 million in donations by IBM employees. So far IBM has committed more than $6.4 million to the victims of the Asian tsunami and hurricane Katrina. Recently, IBM was featured as one of the top ten improvers and within the top twenty-five on AccountAbility's Accountability Rating Report, which measures the extent to which companies put responsible practices at the heart of their businesses.[10]

Did you know that, on average, each family moving into a Habitat for Humanity house invests 423 hours to building not only their own home, but homes for other Habitat families? That adds up to a total of 38,916 hours for the 92 families moving into this year's Jimmy Carter Work Project (JCWP) 2003 homes. To help with this endeavor Whirlpool and Lowe's, the Premier Sponsors of the JCWP 2003, will send hundreds of employees to the JCWP 2005 week, dedicating a total of 6,200 volunteer hours.

* General Electric Company (GE) has a long history of supporting the communities where its employees work and live through GE's unique combination of resources, equipment, and employees' and retirees' hearts and souls. In 2005, GE employees and retirees contributed more than one million hours of service to local community projects. Today, there are 200 GE Volunteer Councils located in thirty-six countries around the world. Each is responsible for mobilizing volunteers to address the serious social issues facing their communities, including mentoring students, protecting the environment, community development, and applying their professional expertise to help school systems and nonprofit organizations. No wonder GE was honored to receive broad recognition for its citizenship initiatives. GE received the Catalyst Award for excellence in developing and promoting women and the Executive Leadership Council Award for excellence in its work with African-American employees. In addition, GE was added to the Dow Jones Sustainability Index, joining a highly selective group of companies representing the top 10 percent in sixty industry groups across thirty-four countries chosen for their environmental, social, and economic programs.[11]

* At Merck & Co., Inc., the Patient Assistance Program makes the company's medicines available to low-income Americans and their families at no cost. When patients don't have health insurance or a prescription drug plan and are unable to afford the Merck medicines their doctors prescribe, they can work with their physicians to contact the Merck Patient Assistance Program. In 2005, Merck's philanthropic contributions totaled just over $1 billion, consisting of cash contributions ($60 million), product donations through the U.S. Patient Assistance Program ($542 million), and product donations through the Merck Medical Outreach Program ($437 million). Merck reacted quickly in response to the tsunami tragedy that struck Asia and the eastern coast of Africa. The company contributed a total of more than $10 million, including $3 million to the American Red Cross, the U.S. Fund for UNICEF, and several local agencies. Its donation also includes more than $7.4 million in medicines.[12]

A Good Investment.

Whirlpool Corporation demonstrates its commitment to community and society through its partnership with Habitat for Humanity. Whirlpool Corporation is the largest Cornerstone Partner of Habitat for Humanity. The company led the effort to build 100,000 homes between 2001 and 2005.

Help Change the World.

No other technological breakthrough has demonstrated the power of individuals more than grid computing. By donating your unused computer time, you can begin to change the world for better.

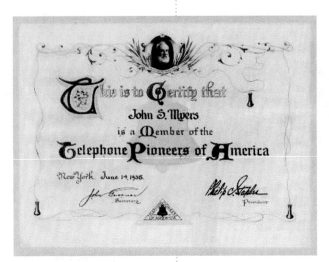

* 3M is a company of dedicated employees who also strive to be good citizens. 3M Community Giving is about the collective effort of 3M, the 3M Foundation, and 3M employees and retirees in giving cash, products, and time to meet ongoing and emergency community needs. In 2005, more than 1,530 retirees participated in more than seventy volunteer activities.[13]

* AT&T has built a tradition of supporting education, health and human services, the environment, public policy, and the arts in the communities it serves since Alexander Graham Bell founded the company over a century ago. Since 1996, AT&T and the AT&T Foundation have distributed more than $439 million to enhance quality of life and to strengthen communities. In 2005, AT&T contributed more than $101 million through corporate, employee, and foundation giving programs to enhance education, community vitality, and technology access.[14]

* In 2006, the ExxonMobil Foundation announced a grant for $250,000 to the Intrepid Fallen Heroes Fund. Since 2000, the fund has provided financial assistance

ENTREPRENEURIAL CHALLENGE

Local First and the Triple Bottom Line

Michigan entrepreneur Guy Bazzani didn't know he would one day be part of a nationwide business network when he started promoting socially responsible, ecofriendly business practices. Using environmentally safe building materials to restore old buildings in Grand Rapids, his green business practices took off. Then he founded Local First, a local business network allied with the nonprofit Business Alliance for Local Living Economies (BALLE).

The Local First movement encourages consumers and businesses to buy from environmentally responsible local businesses where possible. The idea is to create more local jobs, build the local tax base, and keep money in the community. "The small businesses are the heart of this

community," observes economist Michael Shuman. "Dollars spent locally tend to stay in the community."

Local First is one of fifty similar business networks in the United States and Canada that help small businesses achieve the "triple bottom line" of profitability, social responsibility, and environmental sustainability by promoting 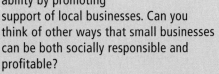 support of local businesses. Can you think of other ways that small businesses can be both socially responsible and profitable?

Sources: Based on information from Glenn Rifkin, "Making a Profit and a Difference," *New York Times*, October 5, 2006, p. C5; Kristina Riggle, "Economist Sees Small Businesses Holding Their Own," *Grand Rapids Press*, November 14, 2006; www.MLive.com.

to the families of those who lost their lives in the service of their country in Iraq and Afghanistan. The fund also supports The Center for the Intrepid, a world-class physical rehabilitation center at Brooke Army Medical Center at Fort Sam Houston in San Antonio, Texas. The center will offer the best-available cutting-edge technology and techniques for military personnel who have been catastrophically disabled in operations in Iraq and Afghanistan, as well as for veterans who suffered injuries in previous conflicts. The fund has raised approximately 80 percent of its goal of $35 million for a 60,000-square-foot facility, including components such as family living accommodations, a prosthetics workshop, and various simulators where patients can readjust to daily activities using their new limbs. More than 12,000 ExxonMobil employees, retirees, and their families volunteered 826,000 hours to more than 5,800 charitable organizations in twenty-two countries during 2005 through company-sponsored volunteer programs. Employees and retirees also donated $35 million of their own money to charity and relief organizations through company-sponsored programs. ExxonMobil Corporation and its affiliates donated $9 million to the charitable organizations where employees and retirees volunteered.[15]

ACE the Test
ACE & ACE+
Practice Test 2.4

TEST PREPPER 2.4

True or False?

_T_   1. Government regulation can encourage ethics with legislation.

_T_   2. An established code of ethics can help to promote ethical behavior.

_F_   3. Voluntary codes of conduct will always be followed.

Multiple Choice

_D_   4. Which of the following items would not be an instrument to promote ethical behavior?

    a. Anonymous hotlines
    b. Ethics officer
    c. Code of ethics
    d. Management indifference
    e. Trade organizations

_C_   5. Whistle-blowing is best used when

    a. the organization has a long track record of ethical behavior.
    b. a disgruntled employee wants to damage a company.
    c. the corporate culture has ingrained ethical lapses.
    d. attention is desired by the whistle-blower.
    e. personal grievances are to be addressed.

The Evolution of Social Responsibility in Business

Learning Objective 5

Describe the historical progression of how our current views on social responsibility of business have evolved.

Business is far from perfect in many respects, but its record of social responsibility today is much better than in past decades. In fact, present demands for social responsibility have their roots in outraged reactions to the abusive business practices of the early 1900s.

Historical Evolution of Business Social Responsibility

* During the first quarter of the twentieth century, businesses were free to operate pretty much as they chose. Government protection of workers and consumers was minimal. As a result, people either accepted what business had to offer or they did without.

* Working conditions often were deplorable by today's standards. The average work week in most industries exceeded sixty hours, no minimum-wage law existed, and employee benefits were almost nonexistent. Work areas were crowded and unsafe, and industrial accidents were the rule rather than the exception. To improve working conditions, employees organized and joined labor unions. During the early 1900s, however, businesses—with the help of government—were able to use court orders, brute force, and even the few existing antitrust laws to defeat union attempts to improve working conditions.

caveat emptor a Latin phrase meaning "let the buyer beware"

* During this period, consumers generally were subject to the doctrine of **caveat emptor,** a Latin phrase meaning "let the buyer beware." In other words, "what you see is what you get," and if it is not what you expected, too bad. Although victims of unscrupulous business practices could take legal action, going to court was very expensive, and consumers rarely won their cases. Moreover, no consumer groups or government agencies existed to publicize consumer grievances or to hold sellers accountable for their actions.

* Prior to the 1930s, most people believed that competition and the action of the marketplace would, in time, correct abuses. Government therefore became involved in day-to-day business activities only in cases of obvious abuse of the free-market system. Six of the more important business-related federal laws passed between 1887 and 1914 are described in Table 2.2. As you can see, these laws were aimed more at encouraging competition than at correcting abuses, although two of them did deal with the purity of food and drug products.

The collapse of the stock market on October 29, 1929, triggered the Great Depression and years of dire economic problems for the United States. Factory production fell by almost half, and up to 25 percent of the nation's work force was unemployed.

* Franklin D. Roosevelt was inaugurated as president in 1933, and he instituted programs to restore the economy and improve social conditions. Laws were passed to correct what many viewed as the monopolistic abuses of big business, and various

TABLE 2.2

Early Government Regulations That Affected American Business

GOVERNMENT REGULATION	MAJOR PROVISIONS
Interstate Commerce Act (1887)	First federal act to regulate business practices; provided regulation of railroads and shipping rates
Sherman Antitrust Act (1890)	Prevented monopolies or mergers where competition was endangered
Pure Food and Drug Act (1906)	Established limited supervision of interstate sale of food and drugs
Meat Inspection Act (1906)	Provided for limited supervision of interstate sale of meat and meat products
Federal Trade Commission Act (1914)	Created the Federal Trade Commission to investigate illegal trade practices
Clayton Antitrust Act (1914)	Eliminated many forms of price discrimination that gave large businesses a competitive advantage over smaller firms

social services were provided for individuals. These massive federal programs became the foundation for increased government involvement in the dealings between business and society.

* As government involvement has increased, so has everyone's awareness of the social responsibility of business. Today's business owners are concerned about the return on their investment, but at the same time most of them demand ethical behavior from employees. In addition, employees demand better working conditions, and consumers want safe, reliable products. Various advocacy groups echo these concerns and also call for careful consideration of our earth's delicate ecological balance. Managers therefore must operate in a complex business environment—one in which they are just as responsible for their managerial actions as for their actions as individual citizens.

> **CONCEPT CHECK**
>
> How and why did the American business environment change after the Great Depression?

TEST PREPPER 2.5

True or False?

___I___ 1. Government intervention has made business more socially responsible.

___F___ 2. The phrase *caveat emptor* no longer applies today.

Multiple Choice

___C___ 3. The Sherman Antitrust Act has provisions that regulate

 a. railroad and shipping rates.
 b. supervision of interstate sale of drugs and food.
 c. illegal trade practices.
 d. meat sales and products.
 e. monopolies and mergers that endanger competition.

___B___ 4. The Great Depression

 a. caused the stock market crash of October 29, 1929.
 b. increased unemployment to 25 percent.
 c. caused insignificant factory production changes.
 d. was not caused by a lack of government regulation.
 e. lasted only six months.

___B___ 5. Today, most authorities agree that

 a. there is no room for improvement in business ethics.
 b. there is room for improvement in business ethics.
 c. the government cannot encourage ethical behavior.
 d. the Sarbanes-Oxley Act discourages businesses to be ethical.
 e. codes of ethics are not an effective way to encourage ethical behavior.

ACE the Test
ACE & ACE+
Practice Test 2.5

Two Views of Social Responsibility

Learning Objective 6

Explain the two views on the social responsibility of business and understand the arguments for and against increased social responsibility.

Government regulation and public awareness are *external* forces that have increased the social responsibility of business. But business decisions are made *within* the firm—and there, social responsibility begins with the attitude of management. Two contrasting philosophies, or models, define the range of management attitudes toward social responsibility.

economic model of social responsibility the view that society will benefit most when business is left alone to produce and market profitable products that society needs

The Economic Model

According to the traditional concept of business, a firm exists to produce quality goods and services, earn a reasonable profit, and provide jobs. In line with this concept, the economic model of social responsibility holds that society will benefit most when business is left alone to produce and market profitable products that society needs. The economic model has its origins in the eighteenth century, when businesses were owned primarily by entrepreneurs or owner-managers. Competition was vigorous among small firms, and short-run profits and survival were the primary concerns.

To the manager who adopts this traditional attitude, social responsibility is someone else's job. After all, stockholders invest in a corporation to earn a return on their investment, not because the firm is socially responsible, and the firm is legally obligated to act in the economic interest of its stockholders. Moreover, profitable firms pay federal, state, and local taxes that are used to meet the needs of society. Thus managers who concentrate on profit believe that they fulfill their social responsibility indirectly through the taxes paid by their firms. As a result, social responsibility becomes the problem of government, various environmental groups, charitable foundations, and similar organizations.

socioeconomic model of social responsibility the concept that business should emphasize not only profits but also the impact of its decisions on society

The Socioeconomic Model

In contrast, some managers believe that they have a responsibility not only to stockholders but also to customers, employees, suppliers, and the general public. This broader view is referred to as the socioeconomic model of social responsibility, which places emphasis not only on profits but also on the impact of business decisions on society.

Recently, increasing numbers of managers and firms have adopted the socioeconomic model, and they have done so for at least three reasons:

1. Business is dominated by the corporate form of ownership, and the corporation is a creation of society. If a corporation does not perform as a good citizen, society can and will demand changes.
2. Many firms have begun to take pride in their social responsibility records, among them Starbucks Coffee, Hewlett-Packard, Colgate-Palmolive, and Coca-Cola. Each of these companies is a winner of a Corporate Conscience Award in the areas of environmental concern, responsiveness to employees, equal opportunity, and community involvement. And of course, many other corporations are much more socially responsible today than they were ten years ago.
3. Many business people believe that it is in their best interest to take the initiative in this area. The alternative may be legal action brought against the firm by some special-interest group; in such a situation, the firm may lose control of its activities.

CONCEPT CHECK
Overall, would it be more profitable for a business to follow the economic model or the socioeconomic model of social responsibility?

The Pros and Cons of Social Responsibility

Business owners, managers, customers, and government officials have debated the pros and cons of the economic and socioeconomic models for years. Each side seems to have four major arguments to reinforce its viewpoint.

Arguments for Increased Social Responsibility Proponents of the socioeconomic model maintain that a business must do more than simply seek profits. To support their position, they offer the following arguments:

1. Because business is a part of our society, it cannot ignore social issues.
2. Business has the technical, financial, and managerial resources needed to tackle today's complex social issues.
3. By helping resolve social issues, business can create a more stable environment for long-term profitability.
4. Socially responsible decision making by firms can prevent increased government intervention, which would force businesses to do what they fail to do voluntarily.

These arguments are based on the assumption that a business has a responsibility not only to its stockholders but also to its customers, employees, suppliers, and the general public.

Arguments Against Increased Social Responsibility Opponents of the socioeconomic model argue that business should do what it does best: earn a profit by manufacturing and marketing products that people want. Those who support this position argue as follows:

1. Business managers are responsible primarily to stockholders, so management must be concerned with providing a return on owners' investments.
2. Corporate time, money, and talent should be used to maximize profits, not to solve society's problems.
3. Social problems affect society in general, so individual businesses should not be expected to solve these problems.
4. Social issues are the responsibility of government officials who are elected for that purpose and who are accountable to the voters for their decisions.

These arguments obviously are based on the assumption that the primary objective of business is to earn profits and that government and social institutions should deal with social problems.

Table 2.3 compares the economic and socioeconomic viewpoints in terms of business emphasis. Today, few firms are either purely economic or purely socioeconomic in outlook; most have chosen some middle ground between the two extremes. However, our society generally seems to want—and even to expect—some degree of social responsibility from business. Thus, within this middle ground, businesses

CONCEPT CHECK

What are the arguments for and against increasing the social responsibility of business?

TABLE 2.3

A Comparison of the Economic and Socioeconomic Models of Social Responsibility as Implemented in Business

Source: Adapted from Keith Davis, William C. Frederick, and Robert L. Blomstron, *Business and Society: Concepts and Policy Issues* (New York: McGraw-Hill, 1980), p. 9. Used by permission of McGraw-Hill Book Company.

ECONOMIC MODEL PRIMARY EMPHASIS		SOCIOECONOMIC MODEL PRIMARY EMPHASIS
1. Production		1. Quality of life
2. Exploitation of natural resources		2. Conservation of natural resources
3. Internal, market-based decisions		3. Market-based decisions, with some community controls
4. Economic return (profit)	Middle ground	4. Balance of economic return and social return
5. Firm's or manager's interest		5. Firm's and community's interests
6. Minor role for government		6. Active government

are leaning toward the socioeconomic view. In the next several sections we look at some results of this movement in four specific areas: consumerism, employment practices, concern for the environment, and implementation of social responsibility programs.

TEST PREPPER 2.6

True or False?

F 1. The two views of social responsibility are *economic* and *ethical* models of social responsibility.

T 2. One argument against social responsibility is that managers are responsible primarily to their stockholders.

T 3. Today, most firms have chosen a middle ground of social responsibility.

A 4. An increasing number of managers have adopted the socioeconomic model because

    a. that is the right thing to do.
    b. many firms are taking pride in their superior products.
    c. many firms are interested in making the most money possible.

    d. many firms are increasingly concentrating on domestic growth.
    e. most of the firms are moving toward global ethics.

C 5. One argument for social responsibility is

    a. that it is good for firms to be social.
    b. that it is always good to be following the ethics of the day.
    c. that being socially responsible prevents government intervention in the firm's affairs.
    d. that being socially responsible is good because it does not cost extra.
    e. that since other firms engage in it, it is best to emulate others.

ACE the Test
ACE & ACE+
Practice Test 2.6

Consumerism

Learning Objective 7

Discuss the factors that led to the consumer movement and list some of its results.

consumerism all activities undertaken to protect the rights of consumers

Consumerism consists of all activities undertaken to protect the rights of consumers. The fundamental issues pursued by the consumer movement fall into three categories: *environmental protection, product performance and safety,* and *information disclosure.* Although consumerism has been with us to some extent since the early nineteenth century, the consumer movement became stronger in the 1960s. It was then that President John F. Kennedy declared that the consumer was entitled to a new "bill of rights."

The Six Basic Rights of Consumers

President Kennedy's consumer bill of rights asserted that consumers have a right to safety, to be informed, to choose, and to be heard. Two additional rights added since 1975 are the right to consumer education and the right to courteous service.

The Right to Safety The consumers' right to safety means that the products they purchase must be safe for their intended use, must include thorough and explicit directions for proper use, and must be tested by the manufacturer to ensure product quality and reliability. There are several reasons why American business firms must be concerned about product safety.

* *Corrective actions can be expensive.* Federal agencies such as the Food and Drug Administration and the Consumer Product Safety Commission have the power to force businesses that make or sell defective products to take corrective actions. Such actions include offering refunds, recalling defective products, issuing public warnings, and reimbursing consumers—all of which can be expensive.

* *Increasing number of lawsuits.* Business firms also should be aware that consumers and the government have been winning an increasing number of product liability lawsuits against sellers of defective products. Moreover, the amount of the awards in these suits has been increasing steadily. Fearing the outcome of numerous lawsuits filed around the nation, tobacco giants Philip Morris and R. J. Reynolds, which for decades had denied that cigarettes cause illness, began negotiating in 1997 with state attorneys general, plaintiffs' lawyers, and antismoking activists.

* *Consumer demand.* Yet another major reason for improving product safety is consumers' demand for safe products. People simply will stop buying a product they believe is unsafe or unreliable.

The Right to Be Informed The right to be informed means that consumers must have access to complete information about a product before they buy it. Detailed information about ingredients and nutrition must be provided on food containers, information about fabrics and laundering methods must be attached to clothing, and lenders must disclose the true cost of borrowing the money they make available to customers who purchase merchandise on credit. In addition, manufacturers must inform consumers about the potential dangers of using their products. Manufacturers that fail to provide such information can be held responsible for personal injuries suffered because of their products. For example, Maytag provides customers with a lengthy booklet that describes how they should use an automatic clothes washer. Sometimes such warnings seem excessive, but they are necessary if user injuries (and resulting lawsuits) are to be avoided.

The Right to Choose The right to choose means that consumers must have a choice of products, offered by different manufacturers and sellers, to satisfy a particular need. The government has done its part by encouraging competition through antitrust legislation. The greater the competition, the greater is the choice available to consumers. Competition and the resulting freedom of choice provide additional benefits for customers by reducing prices. For example, when personal computers were introduced, they cost over $5,000. Thanks to intense competition and technological advancements, personal computers today can be purchased for less than $500.

The Right to Be Heard This fourth right means that someone will listen and take appropriate action when customers complain. Actually, management began to listen to consumers after World War II, when competition between businesses that manufactured and sold consumer goods increased. One way that firms got a competitive edge was to listen to consumers and provide the products they said they wanted and needed. Today, businesses are listening even more attentively, and many larger firms have consumer relations departments that can be contacted easily via toll-free phone numbers. Other groups listen, too. Most large cities and some states have consumer affairs offices to act on citizens' complaints.

Additional Consumer Rights In 1975, President Gerald Ford added to the consumer bill of rights the right to consumer education, which entitles people to be fully informed about their rights as consumers. In 1994, President Bill Clinton added a sixth right, the right to service, which entitles consumers to convenience, courtesy, and responsiveness from manufacturers and sellers of consumer products.

Major Consumerism Forces

The major forces in consumerism are *individual consumer advocates and organizations, consumer education programs,* and *federal laws protecting the consumer.* Consumer advocates, such as Ralph Nader, take it on themselves to protect the rights of consumers. They band together into consumer organizations, either independently or under government sponsorship. **EXAMPLE** Some organizations, such as the National Consumers' League and the Consumer Federation of America, operate nationally, whereas others are active at state and local levels. They inform and organize other consumers, raise issues, help businesses to develop consumer-oriented programs, and pressure lawmakers to enact consumer protection laws. Some consumer advocates and organizations encourage consumers to boycott products and businesses to which they have objections. Today, the consumer movement has adopted corporate-style marketing and addresses a broad range of issues. Current campaigns include efforts (1) to curtail the use of animals for testing purposes, (2) to reduce liquor and cigarette billboard advertising in low-income, inner-city neighborhoods, and (3) to encourage recycling.

Educating consumers to make wiser purchasing decisions is perhaps one of the most far-reaching aspects of consumerism. Increasingly, consumer education is becoming a part of high school and college curricula and adult-education programs. These programs cover many topics—for instance, what major factors should be considered when buying specific products, such as insurance, real estate, automobiles, appliances and furniture, clothes, and food; the provisions of certain consumer-protection laws; and the sources of information that can help individuals become knowledgeable consumers.

Major advances in consumerism have come through federal legislation. Some laws enacted in the last forty-eight years to protect your rights as a consumer are listed and described in Table 2.4. Most business people now realize that they ignore consumer issues only at their own peril. Managers know that improper handling of consumer complaints can result in lost sales, bad publicity, and lawsuits.

LEGISLATION	MAJOR PROVISIONS
Federal Hazardous Substances Labeling Act (1960)	Required warning labels on household chemicals if they are highly toxic
Kefauver-Harris Drug Amendments (1962)	Established testing practices for drugs and required manufacturers to label drugs with generic names in addition to trade names
Cigarette Labeling Act (1965)	Required manufacturers to place standard warning labels on all cigarette packages and advertising
Fair Packaging and Labeling Act (1966)	Called for all products sold across state lines to be labeled with net weight, ingredients, and manufacturer's name and address
Motor Vehicle Safety Act (1966)	Established standards for safer cars
Wholesome Meat Act (1967)	Required states to inspect meat (but not poultry) sold within the state
Flammable Fabrics Act (1967)	Extended flammability standards for clothing to include children's sleepwear in sizes 0 to 6X
Truth in Lending Act (1968)	Required lenders and credit merchants to disclose the full cost of finance charges in both dollars and annual percentage rates
Child Protection and Toy Act (1969)	Banned toys with mechanical or electrical defects from interstate commerce
Credit Card Liability Act (1970)	Limited credit-card holder's liability to $50 per card and stopped credit-card companies from issuing unsolicited cards
Fair Credit Reporting Act (1971)	Required credit bureaus to provide credit reports to consumers regarding their own credit files; also provided for correction of incorrect information
Consumer Product Safety Commission Act (1972)	Established the Consumer Product Safety Commission
Trade Regulation Rule (1972)	Established a "cooling off" period of 72 hours for door-to-door sales
Fair Credit Billing Act (1974)	Amended the Truth in Lending Act to enable consumers to challenge billing errors
Equal Credit Opportunity Act (1974)	Provided equal credit opportunities for males and females and for married and single individuals
Magnuson-Moss Warranty-Federal Trade Commission Act (1975)	Provided for minimum disclosure standards for written consumer product warranties for products that cost more than $15
Amendments to the Equal Credit Opportunity Act (1976, 1994)	Prevented discrimination based on race, creed, color, religion, age, and income when granting credit
Fair Debt Collection Practices Act (1977)	Outlawed abusive collection practices by third parties
Drug Price Competition and Patent Restoration Act (1984)	Established an abbreviated procedure for registering certain generic drugs
Orphan Drug Act (1985)	Amended the original 1983 Orphan Drug Act and extended tax incentives to encourage the development of drugs for rare diseases
Nutrition Labeling and Education Act (1990)	Required the Food and Drug Administration to review current food labeling and packaging focusing on nutrition label content, label format, ingredient labeling, food descriptors and standards, and health messages
Telephone Consumer Protection Act (1991)	Prohibited the use of automated dialing and prerecorded-voice calling equipment to make calls or deliver messages
Consumer Credit Reporting Reform Act (1997)	Placed more responsibility for accurate credit data on credit issuers; required creditors to verify that disputed data are accurate and to notify a consumer before reinstating the data
Children's Online Privacy Protection Act (2000)	Placed parents in control over what information is collected online from their children under age 13; required commercial website operators to maintain the confidentiality, security, and integrity of the personal information collected from children

TABLE 2.4

Major Federal Legislation Protecting Consumers Since 1960

TEST PREPPER 2.7

True or False?

 1. John F. Kennedy believed that the consumer was entitled to a bill of rights.

2. One of the major forces in consumerism is the federal laws protecting the consumers.

Multiple Choice

 3. There are several reasons why firms must be concerned about product safety. Which one of the following is not one of the reasons?

   a. Corrective actions can be expensive.
   b. There can be an increasing number of lawsuits.
   c. There can be a foreign reaction to inferior products.

   d. Consumers demand safe products.
   e. Government has the power to force corrective actions.

_e_ 4. Which is *not* one of the rights listed in the consumer bill of rights.

   a. Right to be heard
   b. Right to choose
   c. Right to be informed
   d. Right to safety
   e. Right to make money

 5. One of the biggest consumer advocates has been

   a. Oprah Winfrey.
   b. Ralph Nader.
   c. Jay Leno.
   d. George Bush.
   e. Mother Teresa.

ACE the Test
ACE & ACE+
Practice Test 2.7

Employment Practices

Learning Objective 8

Analyze how present employment practices are being used to counteract past abuses.

minority a racial, religious, political, national, or other group that is regarded as different from the larger group of which it is a part and that is often singled out for unfavorable treatment

We have seen that managers who subscribe to the socioeconomic view of business's social responsibility, together with significant government legislation enacted to protect the buying public, have broadened the rights of consumers. The last four decades have seen similar progress in affirming the rights of employees to equal treatment in the workplace. Everyone should have the opportunity to land a job for which he or she is qualified and to be rewarded on the basis of ability and performance. This is an important issue for society, and it also makes good business sense. Yet, over the years, this opportunity has been denied to members of various minority groups. A **minority** is a racial, religious, political, national, or other group that is regarded as different from the larger group of which it is a part and that is often singled out for unfavorable treatment.

The federal government responded to the outcry of minority groups during the 1960s and 1970s by passing a number of laws forbidding discrimination in the workplace. (These laws are discussed in Chapter 10 in the context of human resources management.) Now, forty-four years after passage of the first of these (the Civil Rights Act of 1964), abuses still exist. **EXAMPLE** An example is the disparity in income levels for whites, blacks, Hispanics, and Asians, as illustrated in Figure 2.3. Lower incomes and higher unemployment rates also characterize Native Americans, handicapped persons, and women. Responsible managers have instituted a number of programs to counteract the results of discrimination.

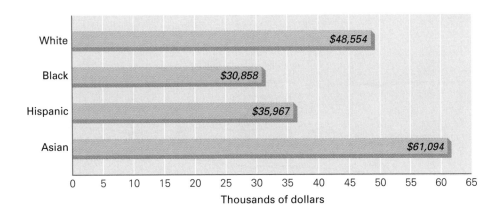

FIGURE 2.3

Comparative Income Levels

This chart shows the median household incomes of white, black, Hispanic, and Asian workers in 2005. (Hispanic persons may be of any race.)

Source: U.S. Census Bureau, *Current Population Survey*, 1968–2006 Annual Demographic Supplements, **www .census.gov/hhes/www/ img/incpov03/Fig07.jpg;** accessed September 30, 2006.

Affirmative Action Programs

An **affirmative action program** is a plan designed to increase the number of minority employees at all levels within an organization. Employers with federal contracts of more than $50,000 per year must have written affirmative action plans. The objective of such programs is to ensure that minorities are represented within the organization in approximately the same proportion as in the surrounding community. If 25 percent of the electricians in a geographic area in which a company is located are African-American, then approximately 25 percent of the electricians it employs also should be African-American. Affirmative action plans encompass all areas of human resources management: recruiting, hiring, training, promotion, and pay.

affirmative action program a plan designed to increase the number of minority employees at all levels within an organization

Equal Employment Opportunity Commission (EEOC) a government agency with power to investigate complaints of employment discrimination and power to sue firms that practice it

Unfortunately, affirmative action programs have been plagued by two problems. The first involves quotas. In the beginning, many firms pledged to recruit and hire a certain number of minority members by a specific date. To achieve this goal, they were forced to consider only minority applicants for job openings; if they hired nonminority workers, they would be defeating their own purpose. However, the courts have ruled that such quotas are unconstitutional, even though their purpose is commendable. They are, in fact, a form of discrimination called *reverse discrimination.*

The second problem is that although most such programs have been reasonably successful, not all business people are in favor of affirmative action programs. Managers not committed to these programs can "play the game" and still discriminate against workers. To help solve this problem, Congress created (and later strengthened) the **Equal Employment Opportunity Commission (EEOC)**, a government agency with the power to investigate complaints of employment discrimination and sue firms that practice it.

Protecting the Rights of Workers.

Do female employees receive fewer promotions than their male counterparts? The Equal Employment Opportunity Commission is a government agency with the power to investigate complaints of employment discrimination and sue firms that practice it.

Relative Earnings of Male and Female Workers

The ratio of women's to men's annual full-time earnings was 77 percent in 2005, a new all-time high, up from 74 percent first reached in 1996.

Source: U.S. Census Bureau, *Current Population Survey,* 1960–2006 Annual Demographic Supplements, **www.census.gov/;** accessed September 30, 2006.

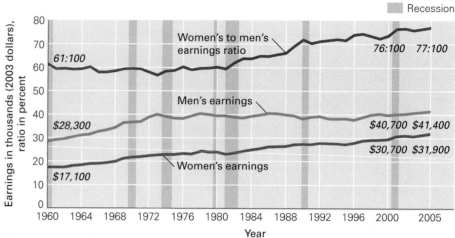

Note: Income rounded to nearest $100.

CONCEPT CHECK

There are more women than men in the United States. Why, then, are women considered a minority with regard to employment?

hard-core unemployed workers with little education or vocational training and a long history of unemployment

National Alliance of Business (NAB) a joint business-government program to train the hard-core unemployed

CONCEPT CHECK

Why should business take on the task of training the hard-core unemployed?

The threat of legal action has persuaded some corporations to amend their hiring and promotional policies, but the discrepancy between men's and women's salaries still exists, as illustrated in Figure 2.4. For more than forty years, women have consistently earned only about 70 cents for each dollar earned by men.

Training Programs for the Hard-Core Unemployed

For some firms, social responsibility extends far beyond placing a help-wanted ad in the local newspaper. These firms have assumed the task of helping the **hard-core unemployed**, workers with little education or vocational training and a long history of unemployment. **EXAMPLE** A few years ago, General Mills helped establish Siyeza, a frozen soul-food processing plant in North Minneapolis. Through the years, Siyeza has provided stable, high-quality full-time jobs for a permanent core of eighty unemployed or underemployed minority inner-city residents. In addition, groups of up to a hundred temporary employees are called in when needed. Recently, Siyeza had a regular payroll of almost $1.9 million and is an example of the persistent commitment necessary to make positive changes in the community.

In the past, such workers often were turned down routinely by personnel managers, even for the most menial jobs. Obviously, such workers require training; just as obviously, this training can be expensive and time-consuming. To share the costs, business and community leaders have joined together in a number of cooperative programs. One particularly successful partnership is the **National Alliance of Business (NAB)**, a joint business-government program to train the hard-core unemployed. The alliance's 5,000 members include companies of all sizes and industries, their CEOs and senior executives, as well as educators and community leaders. NAB, founded in 1968 by President Lyndon Johnson and Henry Ford II, is a major national business organization focusing on education and work force issues.

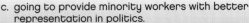

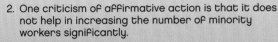**TEST PREPPER** 2.8

True or False?

 1. *Minority* is defined solely on the basis of religion.

 2. One criticism of affirmative action is that it does not help in increasing the number of minority workers significantly.

 3. Workers with little education and no vocational training are called **truly unemployed** *workers*.

Multiple Choice

___A___ 4. An affirmative action plan is

    a. designed to increase the number of minority workers at all levels within an organization.
    b. designed to give more pay to minority workers.

    c. going to provide minority workers with better representation in politics.
    d. designed to place minority workers in better supervisory positions.
    e. designed to encourage a better relationship between white males and minority females.

___B___ 5. A joint business-government program to employ the hard-core unemployed is called the

    a. National Government Alliance.
    b. National Alliance of Business.
    c. National Unemployed Alliance.
    d. National Alliance of Government and Business.
    e. National Unemployment Insurance.

ACE the Test
ACE & ACE+
Practice Test 2.8

Concern for the Environment

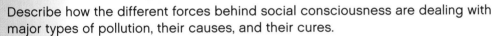

Learning Objective 9

Describe how the different forces behind social consciousness are dealing with major types of pollution, their causes, and their cures.

The social consciousness of responsible business managers, the encouragement of a concerned government, and an increasing concern on the part of the public have led to a major effort to reduce environmental pollution, conserve natural resources, and reverse some of the worst effects of past negligence in this area. **Pollution** is the contamination of water, air, or land through the actions of people in an industrialized society. For several decades, environmentalists have been warning us about the dangers of industrial pollution. Unfortunately, business and government leaders either ignored the problem or were not concerned about it until pollution became a threat to life and health in America. Today, Americans expect business and government leaders to take swift action to clean up our environment—and to keep it clean.

pollution the contamination of water, air, or land through the actions of people in an industrialized society

Effects of Environmental Legislation

As in other areas of concern to our society, legislation and regulations play a crucial role in pollution control. The laws outlined in Table 2.5 reflect the scope of current environmental legislation: laws to promote clean air, clean water, and even quiet work and living environments. Of major importance was the creation of the Environmental Protection Agency (EPA), the federal agency charged with enforcing laws designed to protect the environment.

When they are aware of a pollution problem, many firms respond to it rather than wait to be cited by the EPA. Other owners and managers, however, take the position

TABLE 2.5

Summary of Major Environmental Laws

LEGISLATION	MAJOR PROVISIONS
National Environmental Policy Act (1970)	Established the Environmental Protection Agency (EPA) to enforce federal laws that involve the environment
Clean Air Amendment (1970)	Provided stringent automotive, aircraft, and factory emission standards
Water Quality Improvement Act (1970)	Strengthened existing water pollution regulations and provided for large monetary fines against violators
Resource Recovery Act (1970)	Enlarged the solid-waste disposal program and provided for enforcement by the EPA
Water Pollution Control Act Amendment (1972)	Established standards for cleaning navigable streams and lakes and eliminating all harmful waste disposal by 1985
Noise Control Act (1972)	Established standards for major sources of noise and required the EPA to advise the Federal Aviation Administration on standards for airplanes
Clean Air Act Amendment (1977)	Established new deadlines for cleaning up polluted areas; also required review of existing air-quality standards
Resource Conservation and Recovery Act (1984)	Amended the original 1976 act and required federal regulation of potentially dangerous solid-waste disposal
Clean Air Act Amendment (1987)	Established a national air-quality standard for ozone
Oil Pollution Act (1990)	Expanded the nation's oil-spill prevention and response activities; also established the Oil Spill Liability Trust Fund
Clean Air Act Amendments (1990)	Required that motor vehicles be equipped with onboard systems to control about 90 percent of refueling vapors

that environmental standards are too strict. (Loosely translated, this means that compliance with present standards is too expensive.) Consequently, it often has been necessary for the EPA to take legal action to force firms to install antipollution equipment and to clean up waste storage areas.

Experience has shown that the combination of environmental legislation, voluntary compliance, and EPA action can succeed in cleaning up the environment and keeping it clean. However, much still remains to be done.

Water Pollution The Clean Water Act has been credited with greatly improving the condition of the waters in the United States. This success comes largely from the control of pollutant discharges from industrial and wastewater treatment plants. Although the quality of our nation's rivers, lakes, and streams has improved significantly in recent years, many of these surface waters remain severely polluted. Currently, one of the most serious water-quality problems results from the high level of toxic pollutants found in these waters.

Air Pollution Aviation emissions are a potentially significant and growing percentage of greenhouse gases that contribute to global warming. Aircraft emissions are significant for several reasons:

1. Jet aircraft are the main source of human emissions deposited directly into the upper atmosphere, where they may have a greater warming effect than if they were released at the earth's surface.

2. Carbon dioxide—the primary aircraft emission—is the main focus of international concern.

3. Carbon dioxide emissions, combined with other gases and particles emitted by jet aircraft, could have two to four times as great an effect on the atmosphere as carbon dioxide alone.

4. The Intergovernmental Panel recently concluded that the rise in aviation emissions owing to the growing demand for air travel would not be fully offset by reductions in emissions achieved solely through technological improvements.

How effective is air pollution control? The EPA estimates that the Clean Air Act and its amendments eventually will result in the removal of fifty-six billion pounds of pollution from the air each year, thus measurably reducing lung disease, cancer, and other serious health problems caused by air pollution. Other authorities note that we have already seen improvement in air quality. A number of cities have cleaner air today than they did thirty years ago. Even in southern California, bad air-quality days have dropped to less than forty days a year, about 60 percent lower than just a decade ago.

Land Pollution Air and water quality may be improving, but land pollution is still a serious problem in many areas. The fundamental issues are

1. How to restore damaged or contaminated land at a reasonable cost
2. How to protect unpolluted land from future damage

The land pollution problem has been worsening over the past few years because modern technology has continued to produce increasing amounts of chemical and radioactive waste.

To help pay the enormous costs of cleaning up land polluted with chemicals and toxic wastes, Congress created a $1.6 billion Superfund in 1980. Originally, money was to flow into the Superfund from a tax paid by 800 oil and chemical companies that produce toxic waste. The EPA was to use the money in the Superfund to finance the cleanup of hazardous waste sites across the nation.

U.S. agricultural activities also can impair the nation's water, air, and soil; disrupt habitat for endangered species; and constrain groundwater resources. For example, sediment produced during routine agricultural activities may run off the land and reach surface waters, including rivers and lakes. Sediment can destroy or degrade aquatic habitat and can further impair water quality by transporting into area waters the pesticides applied to cropland and the nutrients found in fertilizers and animal waste. The Environmental Quality Incentive Program (EQIP), managed by the U.S. Department of Agriculture, provides about $1 billion annually in financial and technical assistance to agricultural producers who agree to install conservation practices on their land.[16]

CONCEPT CHECK
To what extent should the blame for vehicular air pollution be shared by manufacturers, consumers, and government?

BIZ TECH

Reduce, Reuse, Recycle Your e-Waste

Electronic waste—*e-waste*—is a growing problem as technology advances and personal computers become obsolete at a rapid rate.

Tons of Trash

Since the personal computer (PC) was invented in 1985, more than sixty million have been sent to landfills as Americans trade up to newer, faster models. The National Safety Council estimates that by 2009, 136,000 PCs will be thrown away every day. Because some of the metals in PCs can leach into soil and water, pollution is a real concern.

Recycling Options

The major computer manufacturers all offer recycling programs. For a modest fee, Hewlett-Packard, Dell, and other companies will send you a shipping label and arrange to pick up your old PC. Or nonprofits such as the National Cristina Foundation and Per Scholas may take your PC if it's not too outdated.

Find Out More

For more information on e-waste and PC recycling, check Earth 911 (**www.earth911.org**), the Rethink Initiative (**rethink.ebay.com**), or the Computer Takeback Campaign (**www.computertakeback.com**).

TIP No. 417
Get recycled.
Buying recycled products, like this jacket, reduces waste and pollution.
TO LEARN MORE
www.reduce.org

What Does Reducing Waste Mean?

When you avoid making garbage in the first place, you don't have to worry about disposing of waste or recycling it later. Changing your habits is the key—think about ways you can reduce your waste when you shop, work and play. Americans throw away enough office paper each year to build a 12-foot high wall stretching from New York to San Francisco—that's 10,000 or so sheets per person!

Noise Pollution Excessive noise caused by traffic, aircraft, and machinery can do physical harm to human beings. Research has shown that people who are exposed to loud noises for long periods of time can suffer permanent hearing loss. The Noise Control Act of 1972 established noise emission standards for aircraft and airports, railroads, and interstate motor carriers. The act also provided funding for noise research at state and local levels.

Noise levels can be reduced by two methods. The source of noise pollution can be isolated as much as possible. (Thus many metropolitan airports are located outside the cities.) And engineers can modify machinery and equipment to reduce noise levels. If it is impossible to reduce industrial noise to acceptable levels, workers should be required to wear earplugs to guard against permanent hearing damage.

Who Should Pay for a Clean Environment?

Governments and businesses are spending billions of dollars annually to reduce pollution—over $35 billion to control air pollution, $25 billion to control water pollution, and $12 billion to treat hazardous wastes. To make matters worse, much of the money required to purify the environment is supposed to come from already depressed industries, such as the chemical industry. And a few firms have discovered that it is cheaper to pay a fine than to install expensive equipment for pollution control.

Who, then, will pay for the environmental cleanup? Many business leaders offer one answer—tax money should be used to clean up the environment and to keep it clean. They reason that business is not the only source of pollution, so business should not be forced to absorb the entire cost of the cleanup. Environmentalists disagree. They believe that the cost of proper treatment and disposal of industrial wastes is an expense of doing business. In either case, consumers probably will pay a large part of the cost—either as taxes or in the form of higher prices for goods and services.

ACE the Test
ACE & ACE+
Practice Test 2.9

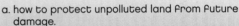
TEST PREPPER 2.9

True or False?

F 1. Pollution is mainly contamination of air.

F 2. Currently, there are no programs to recycle your old computers.

Multiple Choice

C 3. The act that is concerned with improving the condition of the waters in the United States is the
   a. Clean Waters of the United States.
   b. Clean Air and Water Act.
   c. Clean Water Act.
   d. Clean U.S. Water Act.
   e. Clean American Water Act.

A 4. One of the issues of land pollution is
   a. how to protect unpolluted land from future damage.
   b. how to protect land from waterlogging.
   c. how to prevent forest fires.
   d. how to use land efficiently.
   e. how to designate certain lands only for contamination.

A 5. The Noise Control Act of 1972 was *not* meant for the emission standards of
   a. private cars.
   b. railways.
   c. airports.
   d. interstate motor carriers.
   e. aircraft.

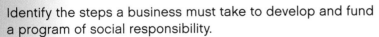
Implementing a Program of Social Responsibility

Learning Objective 10

Identify the steps a business must take to develop and fund a program of social responsibility.

A firm's decision to be socially responsible is a step in the right direction—but only the first step. The firm then must develop and implement a program to reach this goal. The program will be affected by the firm's size, financial resources, past record in the area of social responsibility, and competition. Above all, however, the program must have the firm's total commitment or it will fail.

Developing a Program of Social Responsibility

An effective program for social responsibility takes time, money, and organization. In most cases, developing and implementing such a program will require four steps:

1. Commitment of top executives
2. Planning
3. Appointing a director
4. Preparing a social audit

Commitment of Top Executives Without the support of top executives, any program will soon falter and become ineffective. **EXAMPLE** The Boeing Company's Ethics and Business Conduct Committee is responsible for the ethics program. The committee is appointed by the Boeing board of directors, and its members include the company chairman and CEO, the president and chief operating officer, the presidents of the operating groups, and senior vice presidents. As evidence of their commitment to social responsibility, top managers should develop a policy statement that outlines key areas of concern. This statement sets a tone of positive support and later will serve as a guide for other employees as they become involved in the program.

Planning Next, a committee of managers should be appointed to plan the program. Whatever form their plan takes, it should deal with each of the issues described in the top managers' policy statement. If necessary, outside consultants can be hired to help develop the plan.

Appointment of a Director After the social responsibility plan is established, a top-level executive should be appointed to implement the organization's plan. This individual should be charged with recommending specific policies and helping individual departments to understand and live up to the social responsibilities the firm has assumed. Depending on the size of the firm, the director may require a staff to handle the program on a day-to-day basis. For example, at the Boeing Company, the director of ethics and business conduct administers the ethics and business conduct program.

The Social Audit At specified intervals, the program director should prepare a social audit for the firm. A social audit is a comprehensive report of what an organization has done and is doing with regard to social issues that affect it. This document provides the information the firm needs to evaluate and revise its social responsibility program. Typical subject areas include human resources, community involvement, the quality and safety of products, business practices, and efforts to reduce pollution and improve the environment. The information included in a social audit should be as accurate and as quantitative as possible, and the audit should reveal both positive and negative aspects of the program.

Funding the Program

We have noted that social responsibility costs money. Thus, just like any other corporate undertaking, a program to improve social responsibility must be funded. Funding can come from three sources:

1. *Consumers.* Management can pass the cost on to consumers in the form of higher prices.

social audit a comprehensive report of what an organization has done and is doing with regard to social issues that affect it

2. *Corporation.* The corporation may be forced to absorb the cost of the program if, for example, the competitive situation does not permit a price increase. In this case, the cost is treated as a business expense, and profit is reduced.

3. *Federal government.* The federal government may pay for all or part of the cost through tax reductions or other incentives.

TEST PREPPER 2.10

True or False?

I   1. An effective program for social responsibility takes time, money and influence.

T   2. A social audit is a comprehensive report of what an organization has done and is doing regarding social issues that affect it.

Multiple Choice

D   3. Without the support of the _____, any program of social responsibility in an organization will soon fail.

   a. customer
   b. front-line managers
   c. shareholders of the firm
   d. top executives
   e. staff of the firm

C   4. Funding a program to improve social responsibility can come from several sources. Which of the following is one of the sources?

   a. Foreign donors
   b. Shareholders
   c. Consumers
   d. Civic organizations
   e. Churches

ACE the Test
ACE & ACE+
Practice Test 2.10

Prepare for Class
CL News Feeds
CL News Now

→ RETURN TO INSIDE BUSINESS

3M meets a variety of customer needs through diverse businesses covering five broad product areas: consumer and office, display and graphics, electro and communications, health care, industrial and transportation, and safety, security, and protection services. Over the years, customers worldwide have gained admiration for 3M's innovation and its strong commitment to ethical behavior and social responsibility.

Will CEO George Buckley's renewed focus on higher efficiency hurt the innovative spirit of the company? Buckley believes that 3M's future depends on making this type of difficult decision: "Courage is necessary for a person to get off the dime and make the right decision, a courageous decision, in order to make a company grow and improve." He also will have to maintain that critical balance between healthy profits and environmental responsibility that has been an integral part of 3M's history for many decades.

Questions

1. Why would 3M want to be a leader in environmental responsibility?
2. In what other ways could a multinational corporation like 3M show its commitment to ethics and social responsibility?

LEARNING OBJECTIVES REVIEW

1 Understand what is meant by *business ethics.*

- Ethics is the study of right and wrong and of the morality of choices.
- Business ethics is the application of moral standards to business situations.

2 Identify the types of ethical concerns that arise in the business world.

- Ethical issues arise often in business situations out of relationships with investors, customers, employees, creditors, or competitors.
- Business people should make every effort to be fair, to consider the welfare of customers and others within the firm, to avoid conflicts of interest, and to communicate honestly.

3 Discuss the factors that affect the level of ethical behavior in organizations.

- Individual, social, and opportunity factors all affect the level of ethical behavior in an organization.
- Individual factors include knowledge level, moral values and attitudes, and personal goals. Social factors include cultural norms and the actions and values of coworkers and significant others. Opportunity factors refer to the amount of leeway in an organization for employees to behave unethically.

4 Explain how ethical decision making can be encouraged.

- Governments, trade associations, and individual firms all can establish guidelines for defining ethical behavior.
  - Governments can pass stricter regulations.
  - Trade associations provide ethical guidelines for their members.
  - Companies provide codes of ethics—and create an atmosphere in which ethical behavior is encouraged.
- An ethical employee working in an unethical environment may resort to whistle-blowing to bring a questionable practice to light.

5 Describe the historical progression of how our current views on social responsibility of business have evolved.

- Before the 1930s, workers, consumers, and government had very little influence on business activities; as a result, business leaders gave little thought to social responsibility.
- All this changed with the Great Depression. Government regulations, employee demands, and consumer awareness combined to create a demand that businesses act in socially responsible ways.

6 Explain the two views on the social responsibility of business and understand the arguments for and against increased social responsibility.

- The basic premise of the economic model of social responsibility is that society benefits most when business is left alone to produce profitable goods and services.
- According to the socioeconomic model, business has as much responsibility to society as it has to its owners.

7 Discuss the factors that led to the consumer movement and list some of its results.

- Consumerism consists of all activities undertaken to protect the rights of consumers.
- The consumer movement generally has demanded—and received—attention from business in the areas of product safety, product information, product choices through competition, and the resolution of complaints about products and business practices.
- Consumer rights became more powerful in the 1960s when President John F. Kennedy initiated the consumer "bill of rights."
- The six basic rights of consumers include the right to
  - safety
  - be informed
  - choose
  - be heard
  - consumer education and courteous service

Improve Your Grade
Learning Objectives Review
Audio Chapter Review & Quiz

8 Analyze how present employment practices are being used to counteract past abuses.

- Legislation and public demand have prompted some businesses to correct past abuses in employment practices—mainly with regard to minority groups.
- Two types of programs that have been used successfully with regard to minority groups are Affirmative Action and training of the hard-core unemployed

9 Describe how the different forces behind social consciousness are dealing with major types of pollution, their causes, and their cures.

- Industry has contributed to the noise pollution and the pollution of our land and water through the dumping of wastes and to air pollution through vehicle and smokestack emissions.

- This contamination can be cleaned up and controlled, but the big question is: Who will pay?
- Present cleanup efforts are funded partly by government tax revenues, partly by business, and in the long run by consumers.

10 Identify the steps a business must take to implement a program of social responsibility.

- A program to implement social responsibility in a business begins with total commitment by top management.
- The program should be planned carefully, and a capable director should be appointed to implement it.
- Social audits should be prepared periodically as a means of evaluating and revising the program.
- Programs may be funded through price increases, reduction of profit, or federal incentives.

New Belgium Brews Up Earth-Friendly Operations

New Belgium, America's first wind-powered brewery, aims to make both a better beer and a better society. Founded by husband-and-wife entrepreneurs Jeff Lebesch and Kim Jordan, the company offers European-style beers under intriguing brand names such as Fat Tire and Sunshine Wheat. Lebesch hatched the idea for brewing his own beers after sipping local beers while touring Belgium on bicycle. Returning home with a special yeast strain, Lebesch experimented in his basement and came up with a beer he dubbed Fat Tire Amber Ale in honor of his bicycle trip.

By 1991, he and his wife were bottling and delivering five Belgian-style beers to liquor stores and other retailers in and around their hometown of Fort Collins, Colorado. Within a few years, sales had grown so rapidly that New Belgium needed much more space. Two moves later, the company was operating out of an 80,000-square-foot state-of-the-art brewery designed with the environment in mind.

For example, sun tubes bring daylight to areas that lack windows, which reduces the brewery's energy requirements. As another energy-saving example, the brewery's kettles have steam condensers to capture and reuse hot water again and again. The biggest energy-conservation measure is a cooling device that reduces the need for air conditioning in warm weather.

Soon after opening the new brewery, the entire staff voted to convert it to wind power, which is kinder to the environment because it doesn't pollute or require scarce fossil fuels. In addition to saving energy and natural resources, New Belgium is actually transforming the methane from its waste stream into energy through the process of cogeneration. It also has found ways to cut carbon dioxide emissions and reuse brewing by-products as cattle feed. Soon it will expand with a new facility, built from earth-friendly materials, that can produce 700 bottles of beer per minute. And to ensure that every aspect of New Belgium's operations is as "green" as possible, it employs a sustainability coordinator.

Going further, New Belgium donates $1 to charitable causes for every barrel of beer it sells. Over the years, the company has contributed more than $2 million to nonprofit organizations in the states where it does business. Moreover, it donates the proceeds of its annual Tour de Fat biking event to nonprofit bicycling organizations.

Still, customers are most concerned with the taste of New Belgium's beers, which have won numerous awards and attracted a large, loyal customer base. Many people become customers after hearing about the beer from long-time fans, and as its popularity grows, the word spreads even further. New Belgium's advertising emphasizes its ecofriendly values and shows customers that the company is made up of "real people making real beer."

Clearly, sales and profits are vital ingredients in New Belgium's long-term recipe, but they are not the only important elements. Jordan stresses that the company is not just about making beer—it's about creating what she calls "magic." Reflecting on her continued involvement in New Belgium, she says: "How do you support a community of people? How do you show up in the larger community? How do you strive to be a business role model? That's the part that keeps me really engaged here."

Jordan points to the sustainability impact of new beers featuring organic malts and hops, noting that as the company buys organic ingredients in higher volume, more growers will be encouraged to use organic agricultural methods. In fact, New Belgium has integrated social responsibility into its operations so effectively that it received an award from *Business Ethics* magazine. Success has definitely changed New Belgium—giving it additional resources to make great beer, protect the environment, and urge everyone to "follow your folly."[17]

Questions

1. What do you think Kim Jordan means when she talks about how New Belgium Brewing strives to be a "business role model," not just a beer maker?
2. Given New Belgium Brewing's emphasis on social responsibility, what would you suggest the company look at when preparing a social audit?
3. Should businesses charge more for products that are produced using more costly but environmentally friendly methods such as wind power? Should consumers pay more for products that are *not* produced using environmentally friendly methods because of the potential for costly environmental damage? Explain your answers.

BUILDING SKILLS FOR CAREER SUCCESS

1. Exploring the Internet

Socially responsible business behavior can be as simple as donating unneeded older computers to schools, mentoring interested learners in good business practices, or supplying public speakers to talk about career opportunities. Students, as part of the public at large, perceive a great deal of information about a company, its employees, and its owners by the positive social actions taken and perhaps even more by actions not taken. Microsoft donates millions of dollars of computers and software to educational institutions every year. Some people consider this level of corporate giving to be insufficient given the scale of the wealth of the corporation. Others believe that firms have no obligation to give back any more than they wish and that recipients should be grateful. Visit the text website for updates to this exercise.

Assignment

1. Select any firm involved in high technology and the Internet such as Microsoft or IBM. Examine its website and report its corporate position on social responsibility and giving as the company has stated it. What activities are the company involved in? What programs does the company support, and how does it support them?

2. Search the Internet for commentary on business social responsibility, form your own opinions, and then evaluate the social effort demonstrated by the firm you have selected. What more could the firm have done?

2. Building Team Skills

A firm's code of ethics outlines the kinds of behaviors expected within the organization and serves as a guideline for encouraging ethical behavior in the workplace. It reflects the rights of the firm's workers, shareholders, and consumers.

Assignment

1. Working in a team of four, find a code of ethics for a business firm. Start the search by asking firms in your community for a copy of

their code, by visiting the library, or by searching and downloading information from the Internet.

2. Analyze the code of ethics you have chosen, and answer the following questions:

   a. What does the company's code of ethics say about the rights of its workers, shareholders, consumers, and suppliers? How does the code reflect the company's attitude toward competitors?

   b. How does this code of ethics resemble the information discussed in this chapter? How does it differ?

   c. As an employee of this company, how would you personally interpret the code of ethics? How might the code influence your behavior within the workplace? Give several examples.

3. Researching Different Careers

Business ethics has been at the heart of many discussions over the years and continues to trouble employees and shareholders. Stories about dishonesty and wrongful behavior in the workplace appear on a regular basis in newspapers and on the national news.

Assignment

Prepare a written report on the following:

1. Why can it be so difficult for people to do what is right?

2. What is your personal code of ethics? Prepare a code outlining what you believe is morally right. The document should include guidelines for your personal behavior.

3. How will your code of ethics affect your decisions about

   a. the types of questions you should ask in a job interview?

   b. selecting a company in which to work?

   Prepare for Class
   Exploring the Internet

CHAPTER 3

Exploring Global Business

Your Guide to Success in Business

Why this chapter matters

Free trade—are you for or against it? Most economists support free-trade policies, but public support can be lukewarm, and certain groups are adamantly opposed, alleging that "trade harms large segments of U.S. workers," "degrades the environment," and "exploits poor countries."

LEARNING OBJECTIVES

1 Explain the economic basis for international business.

2 Discuss the different types of international trade restrictions nations engage in and the arguments for and against such restrictions.

3 Outline the extent of international trade and identify the organizations working to foster it.

4 Define the methods by which a firm can organize for and enter into international markets.

5 Describe the various sources of export assistance and identify the institutions that help firms and nations finance international business.

Procter & Gamble

What do Pampers and Pringles have in common? Both are "billion-dollar brands" in the $68 billion global empire built by Cincinnati-based Procter & Gamble. P&G, which makes personal-care products, household cleaners, razors, and batteries, has twenty-two billion-dollar brands and expects sixteen more to join that exclusive club within a few years. The company employs 138,000 people worldwide and rings up 53 percent of its annual sales outside North America. To do business on such a large scale, P&G casts an international net for products and managers while staying in touch with local needs.

Have You Heard of the Tough Mr. Clean?

Take a look at the globe-trotting adventures of Mr. Clean, the brand represented by a brawny bald guy who has appeared on the label of P&G's household cleaners for many decades. Just a few years ago, a P&G employee browsing in a market in Osaka, Japan, noticed an unusual stain-removing sponge. He bought one and sent it to P&G researchers in Cincinnati, who quickly recognized its cleaning advantages. Within months, P&G had purchased the technology from its owners—a German chemical company—and was working with the German scientists on an improved sponge. That sponge, renamed the Mr. Clean Magic Eraser, has emerged as one of P&G's fastest-selling household products.

Developing exceptional managers is as important to P&G's global success as developing exceptional products. Because most of the workforce is based outside the United States, P&G recruits from all over the world, training managers to absorb and adapt the best business practices of different regions. Most of the company's top executives, including the CEO, have managed overseas divisions during their careers.

Despite P&G's global reach, it never loses sight of what local customers like and lack. P&G managers have tagged along with Venezuelan shoppers and visited Vietnamese mothers at home, for example, to see how P&G products are used and get ideas for new products. Moreover, P&G profits by manufacturing products close to the markets where they will be sold. Those containers of Head & Shoulders shampoo in Shanghai supermarkets may have American cachet, but they're actually produced in China.[1]

> **DID YOU KNOW?**
>
> Procter & Gamble has twenty-two billion-dollar brands and rings up 53 percent of its $68 billion in annual sales outside the United States.

KEY TERMS

international business (78)
absolute advantage (79)
comparative advantage (79)
exporting (80)
importing (80)
balance of trade (80)
trade deficit (80)
balance of payments (80)

import duty (tariff) (83)
dumping (83)
nontariff barrier (84)
import quota (84)
embargo (84)
foreign-exchange control (84)
currency devaluation (85)
General Agreement on Tariffs and Trade (GATT) (89)

World Trade Organization (WTO) (90)
economic community (90)
licensing (93)
letter of credit (94)
bill of lading (94)
draft (94)
strategic alliance (96)
trading company (96)

countertrade (97)
multinational enterprise (97)
Export-Import Bank of the United States (100)
multilateral development bank (MDB) (100)
International Monetary Fund (IMF) (101)

ACE the Test
Crossword Puzzle
Flashcards

Procter & Gamble is just one of a growing number of U.S. companies, large and small, that are doing business with firms in other countries. Some companies, such as Coca-Cola, sell to firms in other countries; others, such as Pier 1 Imports, buy goods around the world to import into the United States. Whether they buy or sell products across national borders, these companies are all contributing to the volume of international trade that is fueling the global economy.

Theoretically, international trade is every bit as logical and worthwhile as interstate trade between, say, California and Washington. Yet nations tend to restrict the import of certain goods for a variety of reasons. For example, in the early 2000s, the United States restricted the import of Mexican fresh tomatoes because they were undercutting price levels of domestic fresh tomatoes.

Despite such restrictions, international trade has increased almost steadily since World War II. Many of the industrialized nations have signed trade agreements intended to eliminate problems in international business and to help less-developed nations participate in world trade. Individual firms around the world have seized the opportunity to compete in foreign markets by exporting products and increasing foreign production, as well as by other means.

In his national best-seller, *The World Is Flat*, Thomas L. Friedman states, "The flattening of the world has presented us with new opportunities, new challenges, new partners but, also, alas, new dangers, particularly as Americans it is imperative that we be the best global citizens that we can be—because in a flat world, if you don't visit a bad neighborhood, it might visit you." In this chapter we

* Discuss modern specialization, whereby each country trades the surplus goods and services it produces most efficiently for products in short supply.

* Examine the restrictions nations place on products and services from other countries and present some of the possible advantages and disadvantages of these restrictions.

* Analyze the extent of international trade and identify the organizations working to foster it.

* Describe several methods of entering international markets and the various sources of export assistance available from the federal government.

* Identify some of the institutions that provide the complex financing necessary for modern international trade.

The Basis for International Business

Learning Objective ❶

Explain the economic basis for international business.

international business
all business activities that
involve exchanges across
national boundaries

International business encompasses all business activities that involve exchanges across national boundaries. Thus a firm is engaged in international business when it buys some portion of its input from or sells some portion of its output to an organization located in a foreign country. (A small retail store may sell goods produced in some other country. However, because it purchases those goods from American distributors, it is not engaged in international trade.)

absolute advantage
the ability to produce a specific product more efficiently than any other nation

Absolute and Comparative Advantage

Some countries are better equipped than others to produce particular goods or services. The reason may be a country's natural resources, its labor supply, or even customs or a historical accident. Such a country would be best off if it could *specialize* in the production of such products because it can produce them most efficiently. The country could use what it needed of these products and then trade the surplus for products it could not produce efficiently on its own.

Saudi Arabia thus has specialized in the production of crude oil and petroleum products; South Africa, in diamonds; and Australia, in wool. Each of these countries is said to have an absolute advantage with regard to a particular product. An **absolute advantage** is the ability to produce a specific product more efficiently than any other nation.

One country may have an absolute advantage with regard to several products, whereas another country may have no absolute advantage at all. Yet it is still worthwhile for these two countries to specialize and trade with each other. **EXAMPLE** Imagine that you are the president of a successful manufacturing firm and that you can accurately type ninety words per minute. Your assistant can type eighty words per minute but would run the business poorly. Thus you have an absolute advantage over your assistant in both typing and managing. However, you cannot afford to type your own letters because your time is better spent in managing the business. That is, you have a **comparative advantage** in managing. A comparative advantage is the ability to produce a specific product more efficiently than any other product.

Boeing flies high around the world.

Since the beginning of the jet era, Japan has been the largest single-country international market for Boeing commercial airplanes. In the past decade, more than 80 percent of the airplanes ordered by Japanese customers have been Boeing products. During the next 20 years, Japan is expected to be one of the largest non-U.S. purchasers of commercial airplanes. Boeing expects to sell 1,176 airplanes valued at approximately $147 billion during this period. Japan Airlines was the first airline company to take delivery of a Boeing 747 more than 30 years ago.

comparative advantage
the ability to produce a specific product more efficiently than any other product

Your assistant, on the other hand, has a comparative advantage in typing because he or she can do that better than managing the business. Thus you spend your time managing, and you leave the typing to your assistant. Overall, the business is run as efficiently as possible because you are each working in accordance with your own comparative advantage.

The same is true for nations. Goods and services are produced more efficiently when each country specializes in the products for which it has a comparative advantage. Moreover, by definition, every country has a comparative advantage in *some* product. The United States has many comparative advantages—in research and development, high-technology industries, and identifying new markets, for instance.

CONCEPT CHECK

What is the difference between an absolute and a comparative advantage in international trade? How are both types of advantages related to the concept of specialization?

exporting selling and shipping raw materials or products to other nations

importing purchasing raw materials or products in other nations and bringing them into one's own country

balance of trade the total value of a nation's exports *minus* the total value of its imports over some period of time

trade deficit a negative balance of trade

balance of payments the total flow of money into a country *minus* the total flow of money out of that country over some period of time

Exporting and Importing

Suppose that the United States specializes in producing corn. It then will produce a surplus of corn, but perhaps it will have a shortage of wine. France, on the other hand, specializes in producing wine but experiences a shortage of corn. To satisfy both needs—for corn and for wine—the two countries should trade with each other. The United States should export corn and import wine. France should export wine and import corn.

Exporting is selling and shipping raw materials or products to other nations. The Boeing Company, for example, exports its airplanes to a number of countries for use by their airlines.

Importing is purchasing raw materials or products in other nations and bringing them into one's own country. Thus buyers for Macy's department stores may purchase rugs in India or raincoats in England and have them shipped back to the United States for resale.

Importing and exporting are the principal activities of international trade. They give rise to an important concept called the *balance of trade*. A nation's **balance of trade** is the total value of its exports *minus* the total value of its imports over some period of time. If a country imports more than it exports, its balance of trade is negative and is said to be *unfavorable*. (A negative balance of trade is unfavorable because the country must export money to pay for its excess imports.) In 2006, the United States imported $1,860 billion worth of merchandise and exported $1,024 billion worth. It thus had a trade deficit of $836 billion. A **trade deficit** is a negative balance of trade (see Figure 3.1). However, the United States has consistently enjoyed a large and rapidly growing surplus in services. For example, in 2006, the United States imported $342.4 billion worth and exported $413.1 billion worth of services, thus creating a favorable balance of $70.7 billion.[2]

Question: Are trade deficits bad?

Answer: In testimony before the Senate Finance Committee, Daniel T. Griswold, associate director of the Center for Trade Policy at the Cato Institute, remarked, "The trade deficit is not a sign of economic distress, but of rising domestic demand and investment. Imposing new trade barriers will only make Americans worse off while leaving the trade deficit virtually unchanged."

On the other hand, when a country exports more than it imports, it is said to have a *favorable* balance of trade. This has consistently been the case for Japan over the last two decades or so.

A nation's **balance of payments** is the total flow of money into a country *minus* the total flow of money out of that country over some period of time. Balance of payments therefore is a much broader concept than balance of trade. It includes imports and exports, of course. But it also includes investments, money spent by foreign tourists,

SP⊙TLIGHT

The growing deficit
After a small surplus in 1991, the U.S. balance of payments has consistently run large deficits since 1992.

Deficit in billions of dollars

Year	Deficit
1996	-125
1998	-214
2000	-416
2002	-475
2004	-668
2005	-805

Source: U.S. Department of Commerce, Bureau of Economic Analysis, *News Release*, **www.bea.doc.gov/bea/Articles/2005/07July/0705_ita%**; accessed March 14, 2006.

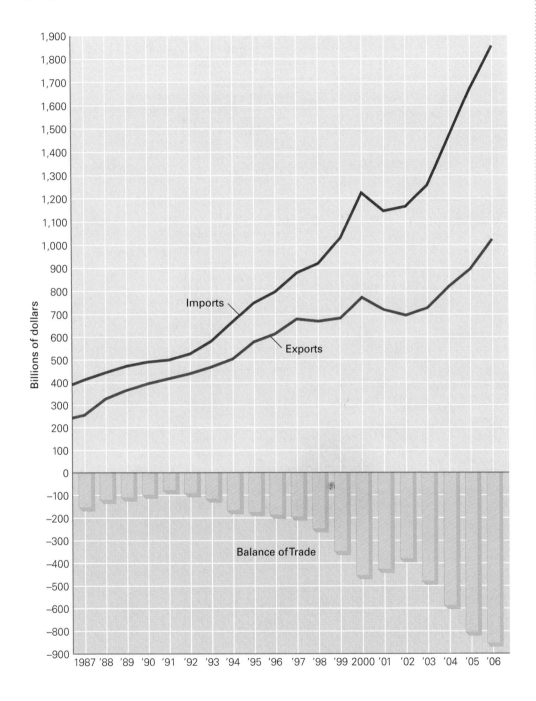

FIGURE 3.1

International Trade in Goods

If a country imports more goods than it exports, the balance of trade is negative, as it was in the United States from 1987 to 2006.

Source: U.S. Department of Commerce, International Trade Administration, U.S. Census Bureau, **www.census.gov/foreign -trade/Press-Release/ current-press-release/ exh1.pdf**; accessed May 18, 2007.

payments by foreign governments, aid to foreign governments, and all other receipts and payments.

A continual deficit in a nation's balance of payments (a negative balance) can cause other nations to lose confidence in that nation's economy. A continual surplus may indicate that the country encourages exports but limits imports by imposing trade restrictions.

CONCEPT CHECK

What is a favorable balance of trade? In what way is it "favorable"?

TEST PREPPER 3.1

True or False?

1. A buyer for Macy's department store buys $10,000 worth of rugs from India that are sold for $45,000 in a New York outlet. This is an example of exporting to other countries from the United States.

Multiple Choice

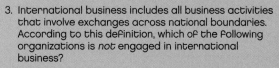

2. Procter & Gamble (P&G) drives its success by being aware of local needs. Which of the following is a good example of responsiveness to local preferences?

   a. Duplicating marketing strategies for products that are successful in the United States in countries all over the world
   b. Hiring managerial staff from all over the world while restricting senior management to recruitment and training within the United States
   c. Going house to house in Vietnam to sell products that have been successful in the United States
   d Interacting with consumers in different parts of the world to see how P&G products are used
   e. Taking advantage of tax-free export-processing zones by producing in third world countries

3. International business includes all business activities that involve exchanges across national boundaries. According to this definition, which of the following organizations is *not* engaged in international business?

   a. Mattel, a U.S.-based brand that manufactures toys in China for sale exclusively in the United States

   b. A Toyota retailer in the United States selling Japanese-manufactured cars
   c. A local grocery store that sells tomatoes imported from Mexico
   d. A computer manufacturer that manufactures and assembles all its parts in the United States for laptops that are sold in the United States and the United Kingdom
   e. An American telecommunications company that outsources some of its help-line services to call centers in Bangalore, India

4. Which of the following is the best definition of *comparative advantage*?

   a. The ability to produce a product more efficiently than anyone else
   b. The ability to produce a product more efficiently than any other product
   c. The ability of the United States to engage in research and development more effectively than any other nation
   d. The efficiency that results from each country specializing in producing a particular type of good or service
   e. The ability to produce all goods and services more effectively than anyone else

5. Suppose that in 2007 the United States imports $2,660 billion worth of merchandise and exports $1,964 billion worth. Which of the following situations will this lead to?

   a. A trade deficit of $836 billion
   b. A trade surplus of $696 billion
   c. A trade surplus of $1,128 billion
   d. A trade deficit of $696 billion
   e. A trade surplus of $800 billion

ACE the Test
ACE & ACE+
Practice Test 3.1

Restrictions to International Business

> **Learning Objective** 2
>
> Discuss the different types of international trade restrictions nations engage in and the arguments for and against such restrictions.

Specialization and international trade can result in the efficient production of want-satisfying goods and services on a worldwide basis. As we have noted, international business generally is increasing. Yet the nations of the world continue to erect barriers to free trade. They do so for reasons ranging from *internal political* and *economic pressures* to simple *mistrust of other nations*. We examine first the types of restrictions that are applied and then the arguments for and against trade restrictions.

Types of Trade Restrictions

Nations generally are eager to export their products. They want to provide markets for their industries and to develop a favorable balance of trade. Hence most trade restrictions are applied to imports from other nations.

Tariffs Perhaps the most commonly applied trade restriction is the customs (or import) duty. An **import duty** (also called a **tariff**) is a tax levied on a particular foreign product entering a country. **EXAMPLE** The United States imposes a 2.2 percent import duty on fresh Chilean tomatoes, 8.7 percent if tomatoes are dried and pack-

aged, and nearly 12 percent if tomatoes are made into ketchup or salsa. The two types of tariffs are *revenue tariffs* and *protective tariffs*; both have the effect of raising the price of the product in the importing nations, but for different reasons. *Revenue tariffs* are imposed solely to generate income for the government. For example, the United States imposes a duty on Scotch whiskey solely for revenue purposes. *Protective tariffs*, on the other hand, are imposed to protect a domestic industry from competition by keeping the price of competing imports level with or higher than the price of similar domestic products. Because fewer units of the product will be sold at the increased price, fewer units will be imported. The French and Japanese agricultural sectors would both shrink drastically if their nations abolished the protective tariffs that keep the price of imported farm products high. Today, U.S. tariffs are the lowest in history, with average tariff rates on all imports of under 3 percent.

Some countries rationalize their protectionist policies as a way of offsetting an international trade practice called *dumping*. **Dumping** is the exportation of large quantities of a product at a price lower than that of the same product in the home market. Thus dumping drives down the price of the domestic item. **EXAMPLE** Recently, the Pencil Makers Association, which represents eight U.S. pencil manufacturers, charged that low-priced pencils from Thailand and the People's Republic of China were being sold in the United States at less than fair-value prices. Unable to compete with these inexpensive imports, several domestic manufacturers had to shut down. To protect themselves, domestic manufacturers can obtain an antidumping duty through the government to offset the advantage of the foreign product. Recently, for example, the U.S. Department of Commerce imposed preliminary antidumping duties of up to 30 percent on a variety of steel products imported from Europe, Japan, and Russia; 29 percent on Canadian soft lumber; and up to 60 percent on orange juice from Brazil.

import duty (tariff) a tax levied on a particular foreign product entering a country

dumping exportation of large quantities of a product at a price lower than that of the same product in the home market

China Upsets U.S. Apple Cart.

China's 1.3 billion consumers, with a growing middle class, can afford high quality U.S. apples, but a 30 percent tariff imposed by the Chinese government limits the imports of Washington apples to China. Here, the U.S. Agriculture Secretary Dan Glickman inspects a display of Washington apples in Beijing, China.

nontariff barrier a nontax measure imposed by a government to favor domestic over foreign suppliers

import quota a limit on the amount of a particular good that may be imported into a country during a given period of time

embargo a complete halt to trading with a particular nation or in a particular product

foreign-exchange control a restriction on the amount of a particular foreign currency that can be purchased or sold

Nontariff Barriers A **nontariff barrier** is a nontax measure imposed by a government to favor domestic over foreign suppliers. Nontariff barriers create obstacles to the marketing of foreign goods in a country and increase costs for exporters. The following are a few examples of government-imposed nontariff barriers:

* An **import quota** is a limit on the amount of a particular good that may be imported into a country during a given period of time. The limit may be set in terms of either quantity (so many pounds of beef) or value (so many dollars' worth of shoes). Quotas also may be set on individual products imported from specific countries. Once an import quota has been reached, imports are halted until the specified time has elapsed.

* An **embargo** is a complete halt to trading with a particular nation or in a particular product. The embargo is used most often as a political weapon. At present, the United States has import embargoes against Cuba and North Korea—both as a result of extremely poor political relations.

* A **foreign-exchange control** is a restriction on the amount of a particular foreign currency that can be purchased or sold. By limiting the amount of foreign currency importers can obtain, a government limits the amount of goods importers can purchase with that currency. This has the effect of limiting imports from the country whose foreign exchange is being controlled.

* A nation can increase or decrease the value of its money relative to the currency of other nations. **Currency devaluation** is the reduction of the value of a nation's currency relative to the currencies of other countries.

  Devaluation increases the cost of foreign goods while it decreases the cost of domestic goods to foreign firms. For example, suppose that the British pound is worth $2. Then an American-made $2,000 computer can be purchased for £1,000. However, if the United Kingdom devalues the pound so that it is worth only $1, that same computer will cost £2,000. The increased cost, in pounds, will reduce the import of American computers—and all foreign goods—into England.

  On the other hand, before devaluation, a £500 set of English bone china would cost an American $1,000. After the devaluation, the set of china would cost only $500. The decreased cost would make the china—and all English goods—much more attractive to U.S. purchasers.

* *Bureaucratic red tape* is more subtle than the other forms of nontariff barriers. Yet it can be the most frustrating trade barrier of all. A couple of examples include unnecessarily restrictive application of standards and complex requirements related to product testing, labeling, and certification.

Another type of nontariff barrier is related to cultural attitudes. Cultural barriers can impede acceptance of products in foreign countries. **EXAMPLE** Mexican cars have not been viewed by the world as being quality products. Volkswagen, for example, may not want to advertise that some of its models sold in the United States are made in Mexico.

Reasons for Trade Restrictions

Various reasons are advanced for trade restrictions either on the import of specific products or on trade with particular countries. We have noted that political considerations usually are involved in trade embargoes. Other frequently cited reasons for restricting trade include the following:

* *To equalize a nation's balance of payments.* This may be considered necessary to restore confidence in the country's monetary system and in its ability to repay its debts.

* *To protect new or weak industries.* A new, or *infant*, industry may not be strong enough to withstand foreign competition. Temporary trade restrictions may be used to give it a chance to grow and become self-sufficient. The problem is that once an industry is protected from foreign competition, it may refuse to grow, and "temporary" trade restrictions will become permanent.

* *To protect national security.* Restrictions in this category generally apply to technological products that must be kept out of the hands of potential enemies. For example, strategic and defense-related goods cannot be exported to unfriendly nations.

* *To protect the health of citizens.* Products may be embargoed because they are dangerous or unhealthy (e.g., farm products contaminated with insecticides).

* *To retaliate for another nation's trade restrictions.* A country whose exports are taxed by another country may respond by imposing tariffs on imports from that country.

* *To protect domestic jobs.* By restricting imports, a nation can protect jobs in domestic industries. However, protecting these jobs can be expensive. For example, protecting 9,000 jobs in the U.S. carbon-steel industry costs $6.8 billion, or $750,000 per job.

Reasons Against Trade Restrictions

Trade restrictions have immediate and long-term economic consequences—both within the restricting nation and in world trade patterns. These include

* *Higher prices for consumers.* Higher prices may result from the imposition of tariffs or the elimination of foreign competition, as described earlier. For example, imposing quota restrictions and import protections adds $25 billion annually to U.S. consumers' apparel costs by directly increasing costs for imported apparel.

* *Restriction of consumers' choices.* Again, this is a direct result of the elimination of some foreign products from the marketplace and of the artificially high prices that importers must charge for products that still are imported.

* *Misallocation of international resources.* The protection of weak industries results in the inefficient use of limited resources. The economies of both the restricting nation and other nations eventually suffer because of this waste.

* *Loss of jobs.* The restriction of imports by one nation must lead to cutbacks—and the loss of jobs—in the export-oriented industries of other nations. Furthermore, trade protection has a significant effect on the composition of employment. U.S. trade restrictions—whether on textiles, apparel, steel, or automobiles—benefit only a few industries while harming many others. The gains in employment accrue to the protected industries and their primary suppliers, and the losses are spread across all other industries. A few states gain employment, but many other states lose employment.

currency devaluation the reduction of the value of a nation's currency relative to the currencies of other countries

CONCEPT CHECK
What are the general effects of import restrictions on trade?

CONCEPT CHECK
What are the reasons given for and against imposing trade restrictions?

TEST PREPPER **3.2**

True or False?

 1. A tax levied on a particular foreign product entering a country in order to protect an industry within that country is known as a *protective tariff.*

 2. Restrictions on the amount of foreign currency importers can obtain is a good example of a nontariff barrier.

Multiple Choice

3. Based on your understanding of trade restrictions, which of the following is *not* a reason why a country might want to restrict its trade with other countries?

   a. To encourage competition for local manufactures
   b. To encourage the growth of infant industries
   c. To protect national security
   d. To protect domestic jobs
   e. To retaliate for another nation's trade restrictions

4. Which of the following is a good example of a nontariff barrier?

   a. Import duty on luxury cars from Germany in order to raise government revenue
   b. Antidumping regulation on wheat to protect farmers in the United States
   c. A limit on the amount of Japanese cars that may be imported into the country during one year
   d. Subsidies for local manufacturers in order to compete with imports
   e. Restrictions on the total output of local manufacturers for export purposes

 5. Perhaps the most commonly applied trade restriction is

   a. an import quota.
   b. an embargo.
   c. a foreign exchange control.
   d. cultural barriers.
   e. the customs (or import) duty.

ACE the Test
ACE & ACE+
Practice Test 3.2

The Extent of International Business

Learning Objective ③

Outline the extent of international trade and identify the organizations working to foster it.

Restrictions or not, international business is growing. Although the worldwide recessions of 1991 and 2001–2002 slowed the rate of growth, globalization is a reality of our time. Since the early 1980s, total trade in goods accounted for 36 percent of world gross domestic product (GDP); 26 years later, that ratio increased to 50 percent.[3] In the United States, international trade now accounts for over one-fourth of GDP. As trade barriers decrease, new competitors enter the global marketplace, creating more choices for consumers and new opportunities for job seekers. International business will grow along with the expansion of commercial use of the Internet.

The World Economic Outlook for Trade

While the U.S. economy had been growing steadily until 2000 and recorded the longest peacetime expansion in the nation's history, the worldwide recession has slowed the rate of growth. The International Monetary Fund (IMF), an international bank with 185 member nations, estimated that the U.S. economy grew by slightly less than 4.2 percent in 2004 and, despite hurricanes Katrina and Rita, by 3.5 percent in 2005 and 3.3 percent in 2006. However, global growth in 2004 was the highest in three decades when world output increased by over 5 percent.[4] International experts expected global economic growth of 4.3 percent in 2005 and 2006 despite the high oil prices and two hurricanes in the United States. At this rate of growth, world production of goods and services will double by the year 2020.

Canada and Western Europe
Our leading export-import partner, Canada, is projected to show the fastest economic growth from 2.9 percent in 2005 to 3.2 percent predicted in 2006. The inflation rate in Canada is about half the U.S. rate, and our exports to Canada are booming. However, economies in western Europe have been growing slowly. Recent growth in Austria, Belgium, the Netherlands, and Portugal has been slow at less than 1 percent in 2005, whereas growth in Greece, Ireland, and Spain has been somewhat stronger.

Prepare for Class
Career Snapshot

Mexico and South America Our second-largest export-import partner, Mexico, suffered its sharpest recession ever in 1995, but its growth rate has rebounded in the 2000s to about 4 percent in 2005. In general, the growth in the Latin American economies is beginning to slow down to 4.1 percent in 2005 versus 5.6 percent in 2004. The economies of Argentina, Uruguay, Paraguay, Brazil, Venezuela, Ecuador, Peru, and a few other countries in that region have been sluggish owing to political, economic, and financial market problems.

Japan Japan's economy is regaining momentum with the IMF estimated growth at 2 percent for 2005 and 2006. Stronger consumer demand and business investment make Japan less reliant on exports for growth.

Asia The economic recovery in Asia increased significantly in recent years with economic growth at 7.8 percent in 2005 and 7.2 percent in 2006. For example, in China and India, the GDP increased 9.0 and 7.0 percent, respectively. Even in the hardest-hit economies in the region, Singapore and Taiwan Province of China, the recovery continues.

China's emergence as a global economic power has been among the most dramatic economic developments of recent decades. From 1980 to 2004, China's economy averaged a real GDP annual growth rate of 9.5 percent and became the world's sixth-largest economy, China had become the third-largest trading nation in dollar terms, behind the United States and Germany and just ahead of Japan.[5]

Central and Eastern Europe and Russia After World War II, trade between the United States and the communist nations of central and Eastern Europe was minimal. The United States maintained high tariff barriers on imports

ENTREPRENEURIAL CHALLENGE

The Fair Trade Marketplace Expands

Until very recently, small entrepreneurs in developing countries had no way to participate in the global economy. Now fair-trade groups such as World of Good and Ten Thousand Villages are helping basket weavers in Swaziland, cocoa growers in Ghana, and artists in Cambodia sell their wares thousands of miles from home. Fair trade aims to encourage eco-friendly, sustainable small businesses and get entrepreneurs a fair price for their goods.

Here's a quick look at these groups:

- World of Good, based in California, has fair-trade kiosks in 1,100 U.S. stores, including branches of Whole Foods Market and hundreds of college bookstores. To date, it has distributed 500,000 fair-trade items made by entrepreneurs in thirty-one countries.
- Ten Thousand Villages, operated by a division of the Mennonite Church, is a nonprofit organization that rings up $23 million in annual sales through 100 stores and a website. Its buyers negotiate a fair price with craftspeople, pay half the price in advance, and pay the rest after the items sell.

Sources: Based on information from Evelyn Iritani, "Creating a Market for Fair Trade," *Los Angeles Times*, August 5, 2006, p. C1; Rob Walker, "Values Chain," *New York Times Magazine*, March 19, 2006, p. 20.

from most of these countries and also restricted its exports. However, since the disintegration of the Soviet Union and the collapse of communism, trade between the United States and central and Eastern Europe has expanded substantially.

U.S. exports to central and Eastern Europe and Russia will increase, as will U.S. investment in these countries, as demand for capital goods and technology opens new markets for U.S. products. There already has been a substantial expansion in trade between the United States and the Czech Republic, the Republic of Slovakia, Hungary, and Poland.

Exports and the U.S. Economy Globalization represents a huge opportunity for all countries—rich or poor. The fifteen-fold increase in trade volume over the past fifty years has been one of the most important factors in the rise of living standards around the world. During this time, exports have become increasingly important to the U.S. economy. Exports as a percentage of U.S. GDP have increased steadily since 1985, except in the 2001 recession. And our exports to developing and newly industrialized countries are on the rise. Table 3.1 shows the value of U.S. merchandise exports to and imports from each of the nation's ten major trading partners. Note that Canada and Mexico are our best partners for our exports; Canada and China, for imports. Figure 3.2 shows the U.S. goods export and import shares in 2006. Major U.S. exports and imports are manufactured goods, agricultural products, and mineral fuels.

CONCEPT CHECK

Which nations are the principal trading partners of the United States? What are the major U.S. imports and exports?

RANK	TRADING PARTNER	EXPORTS ($ BILLIONS)
1	Canada	230.6
2	Mexico	134.2
3	Japan	59.6
4	China	55.2
5	United Kingdom	45.4
6	Germany	41.3
7	Korea, South	32.5
8	Netherlands	31.1
9	Singapore	24.7
10	France	24.2

RANK	TRADING PARTNER	IMPORTS ($ BILLIONS)
1	Canada	303.4
2	China	287.8
3	Mexico	198.3
4	Japan	148.1
5	Germany	89.1
6	United Kingdom	53.4
7	Korea, South	45.8
8	Taiwan	38.2
9	Venezuela	37.2
10	France	37.1

TABLE 3.1

Value of U.S. Merchandise Exports and Imports, 2006

Source: www.census.gov/foreign-trade/statistics/highlights/top/top0612.html; accessed May 18, 2007. Used by permission.

General Agreement on Tariffs and Trade (GATT) an international organization of 132 nations dedicated to reducing or eliminating tariffs and other barriers to world trade

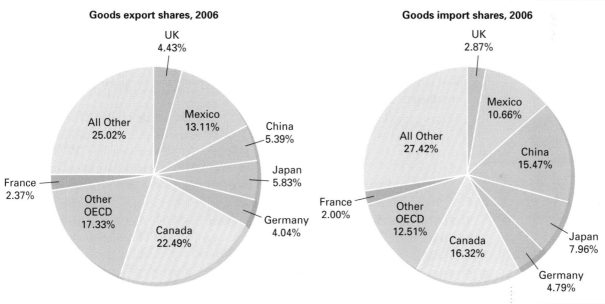

FIGURE 3.2

U.S. Goods Export and Import Shares in 2006

About 37 percent of U.S. exports and 27 percent of U.S. imports in 2006 were from Canada and Mexico.

Source: Federal Reserve Bank of St. Louis, *National Economic Trends*, May 2007, p. 18.

International Trade Agreements

The General Agreement on Tariffs and Trade and the World Trade Organization

At the end of World War II, the United States and twenty-two other nations organized the body that came to be known as *GATT*. The **General Agreement on Tariffs and Trade (GATT)** was an international organization of 132 nations dedicated to reducing or eliminating tariffs and other barriers to world trade. These 132 nations accounted for 90 percent of the world's merchandise trade. GATT, headquartered in Geneva, Switzerland, provided a forum for tariff negotiations and a means for settling international trade disputes and problems. *Most-favored-nation status* (MFN) was the famous principle of GATT. It meant that each GATT member nation was to be treated equally by all contracting nations. MFN therefore ensured that any tariff reductions or other trade concessions were extended automatically to all GATT members. From 1947 to 2001, the body sponsored nine rounds of negotiations to reduce trade restrictions. Three of the most fruitful were the Kennedy Round, the Tokyo Round, and the Uruguay Round.

The Kennedy Round (1964–1967) In 1962, the U.S. Congress passed the Trade Expansion Act. This law gave President John F. Kennedy the authority to negotiate reciprocal trade agreements that could reduce U.S. tariffs by as much as 50 percent. These negotiations were aimed at reducing tariffs and other barriers to trade in both industrial and agricultural products. The participants succeeded in reducing tariffs on these products by an average of more than 35 percent.

The Tokyo Round (1973–1979) In 1973, representatives of approximately one hundred nations gathered in Tokyo for another round of GATT negotiations. The participants negotiated tariff cuts of 30 to 35 percent, which were to be implemented over an eight-year period.

The Uruguay Round (1986–1993) In 1986, the Uruguay Round was launched to extend trade liberalization and widen the GATT treaty to include textiles, agricultural products, business services, and intellectual-property rights. The agreement included provisions to lower tariffs by greater than one-third, to reform trade in agricultural goods, to write new rules of trade for intellectual property and services, and to strengthen the dispute-settlement process.

The Uruguay Round also created the **World Trade Organization (WTO)** on January 1, 1991. The WTO was established by GATT to oversee the provisions of the Uruguay Round and to resolve any resulting trade disputes. Membership in the WTO obliges 151 member nations to observe GATT rules. The WTO has judicial powers to mediate among members disputing the new rules. It incorporates trade in goods, services, and ideas and exerts more binding authority than GATT.

The Doha Round (2001) In 2001, in Doha, Qatar, the WTO members agreed to further reduce trade barriers through multilateral trade negotiations. This new round of negotiations focuses on industrial tariffs and nontariff barriers, agriculture, services, and easing trade rules. Some experts suggest that U.S. exporters of industrial and agricultural goods and services should have improved access to overseas markets, whereas others disagree.

International Economic Organizations Working to Foster Trade

The primary objective of the WTO is to remove barriers to trade on a worldwide basis. On a smaller scale, an **economic community** is an organization of nations formed to promote the free movement of resources and products among its members and to create common economic policies. A number of economic communities now exist.

* The *European Union* (EU), also known as the *European Economic Community* and the *Common Market*, was formed in 1957 by six countries—France, the Federal Republic of Germany, Italy, Belgium, the Netherlands, and Luxembourg. Its objective was freely conducted commerce among these nations and others that might later join. As shown in Figure 3.3, many more nations have joined the EU since then.

World Trade Organization (WTO) powerful successor to GATT that incorporates trade in goods, services, and ideas

CONCEPT CHECK The United States restricts imports but, at the same time, supports the WTO and international banks whose objective is to enhance world trade. As a member of Congress, how would you justify this contradiction to your constituents?

economic community an organization of nations formed to promote the free movement of resources and products among its members and to create common economic policies

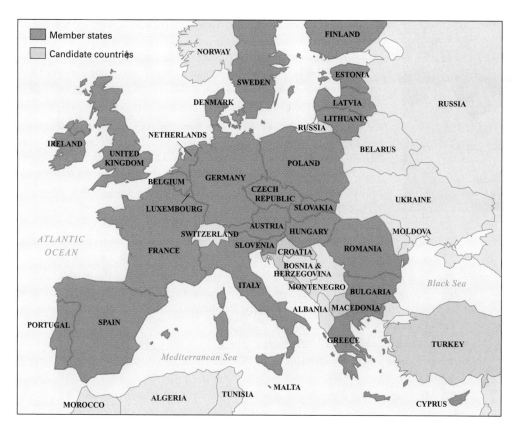

Member states
Candidate countries

FINLAND
NORWAY
SWEDEN
ESTONIA
DENMARK
LATVIA
RUSSIA
LITHUANIA
RUSSIA
IRELAND
NETHERLANDS
BELARUS
UNITED
KINGDOM
POLAND
BELGIUM
GERMANY
CZECH
REPUBLIC
UKRAINE
LUXEMBOURG
SLOVAKIA
AUSTRIA
HUNGARY
MOLDOVA
ATLANTIC
OCEAN
SWITZERLAND
SLOVENIA
FRANCE
CROATIA
ROMANIA
BOSNIA &
HERZEGOVINA
Black Sea
ITALY
MONTENEGRO
BULGARIA
ALBANIA
MACEDONIA
PORTUGAL
SPAIN
GREECE
TURKEY
Mediterranean Sea
MALTA
MOROCCO
ALGERIA
TUNISIA
CYPRUS

FIGURE 3.3

The Evolving European Union

The European Union is now an economic force, with a collective economy larger than that of the United States or Japan.

Source: **http://europa.eu/ abc/european_countries/ index_en.htm**; accessed on June 2, 2007.

On January 1, 2007, the twenty-five nations of the EU became the EU27 as Bulgaria and Romania became new members. The EU is now an economic force with a collective economy larger than that of the United States or Japan.

In celebrating the EU's fiftieth anniversary in 2007, the president of the European Commission, Jose Manuel Durao Baroso, declared, "Let us first recognize fifty years of achievement. Peace, liberty, and prosperity, beyond the dreams of even the most optimistic founding fathers of Europe. In 1957, fifteen of our twenty-seven members were either under dictatorship or were not allowed to exist as independent countries. Now we are all prospering democracies. The EU of today is around fifty times more prosperous and with three times the population of the EU of 1957."

Since January 2002, twelve member nations of the EU are participating in the new common currency, the euro. The euro is the single currency of the European Monetary Union nations. But three EU members, Denmark, the United Kingdom, and Sweden, still keep their own currencies.

* The *European Economic Area* (EEA) became effective in January 1994. This pact consists of Iceland, Norway, and the fifteen member nations of the EU. The EEA allows for the free movement of goods throughout all seventeen countries.

* The *North American Free Trade Agreement* (NAFTA) joined the United States with its first- and second-largest trading partners, Canada and Mexico. Implementation of NAFTA on January 1, 1994, created a market of over 439 million people. This market consists of Canada (population 33 million), the United States (300 million), and Mexico (106 million).

From Tolars to Euros.

Slovenia got the green light to change Slovenian tolars to euros on January 1, 2007. A recent European Commission meeting gave Slovenia the chance to be the first Eastern European country with a euro currency. The Slovenians still pay with tolars but receive the return change in euro, causing calculation difficulties to the cashiers and customers.

ACE the Test
ACE & ACE+
Practice Test 3.3

Since 1994, trade among the three countries has increased more than 200 percent. Mexico's exports have increased threefold, with nearly 90 percent coming to the United States.

NAFTA will gradually eliminate all tariffs on goods produced and traded among Canada, Mexico, and the United States to provide for a totally free-trade area by 2009.

* The *Central America Free Trade Agreement* (CAFTA) was created in 2003 by the United States and four Central American countries—El Salvador, Guatemala, Honduras, and Nicaragua. CAFTA immediately eliminates tariffs on nearly 80 percent of U.S. exports and is expected to generate billions of dollars in increased sales of U.S. goods and farm exports.[6]

* The *Association of Southeast Asian Nations* (ASEAN), with headquarters in Jakarta, Indonesia, was established in 1967 to promote political, economic, and social cooperation among its seven member countries: Indonesia, Malaysia, Philippines, Singapore, Thailand, Brunei, and Vietnam.

* The *Pacific Rim*, referring to countries and economies bordering the Pacific Ocean, is an informal, flexible term generally regarded as a reference to East Asia, Canada, and the United States. At a minimum, the Pacific Rim includes Canada, Japan, China, Taiwan, and the United States.

* The *Commonwealth of Independent States* (CIS) was established in December 1991 by the newly independent states (NIS) as an association of eleven republics of the former Soviet Union.

* The *Organization of Petroleum Exporting Countries* (OPEC) was founded in 1960 in response to reductions in the prices that oil companies were willing to pay for crude oil. The organization was conceived as a collective-bargaining unit to provide oil-producing nations with some control over oil prices.

* The *Organization for Economic Cooperation and Development* (OECD) is a group of thirty industrialized market-economy countries of North America, Europe, the Far East, and the South Pacific. OECD, headquartered in Paris, was established in 1961 to promote economic development and international trade.

TEST PREPPER 3.3

True or False?

_T_ 1. The commercial use of the Internet will be instrumental in expanding opportunities for international trade between businesses.

_F_ 2. Japan's decreased dependency on exports for growth is due to greater emphasis on savings and not on consumption.

_T_ 3. The Organization of Petroleum Exporting Countries (OPEC) was conceived as a collective-bargaining unit to provide oil-producing nations with control over oil prices.

Multiple Choice

_C_ 4. Which of the following is the name of the international organization dedicated to reducing or eliminating tariffs and other barriers to world trade?

 a. The Doha round of negotiations
 b. The Kennedy round of negotiations
 c. The World Trade Organization (WTO)
 d. The North American Free Trade Agreement (NAFTA)
 e. International Monetary Fund (IMF)

_D_ 5. Which of the following organizations is the United States not a participating member of?

 a. NAFTA
 b. WTO
 c. OECD
 d. CIS
 e. UN

Methods of Entering International Business

ACE the Test
Hangman

Learning Objective ❹
Define the methods by which a firm can organize for and enter into international markets.

A firm that has decided to enter international markets can do so in several ways. We will discuss several different methods. These different approaches require varying degrees of involvement in international business. Typically, a firm begins its international operations at the simplest level. Then, depending on its goals, it may progress to higher levels of involvement.

Licensing

Licensing is a contractual agreement in which one firm permits another to produce and market its product and use its brand name in return for a royalty or other compensation. **EXAMPLE** Yoplait yogurt is a French yogurt licensed for production in the United States. The Yoplait brand maintains an appealing French image, and in return, the U.S. producer pays the French firm a percentage of its income from sales of the product.

licensing a contractual agreement in which one firm permits another to produce and market its product and use its brand name in return for a royalty or other compensation

Advantages of Licensing

* Licensing is especially advantageous for small manufacturers wanting to launch a well-known domestic brand internationally. For example, all Spalding sporting products are licensed worldwide. The licensor, the Questor Corporation, owns the Spalding name but produces no goods itself.

* Licensing provides a simple method for expanding into a foreign market with virtually no investment.

Disadvantages of Licensing

* If the licensee does not maintain the licensor's product standards, the product's image may be damaged.

* A licensing arrangement may not provide the original producer with any foreign marketing experience.

CONCEPT CHECK
The methods of engaging in international business may be categorized as either direct or indirect. How would you classify each of the methods described in this chapter? Why?

Exporting

A firm also may manufacture its products in its home country and export them for sale in foreign markets. As with licensing, exporting can be a relatively low-risk method of entering foreign markets. Unlike licensing, however, it is not a simple method; it opens up several levels of involvement to the exporting firm.

At the most basic level, the exporting firm may sell its products outright to an *export-import merchant*, which is essentially a merchant wholesaler. The merchant assumes all the risks of product ownership, distribution, and sale. It may even purchase the goods in the producer's home country and assume responsibility for exporting the goods.

letter of credit issued by a bank on request of an importer stating that the bank will pay an amount of money to a stated beneficiary

bill of lading document issued by a transport carrier to an exporter to prove that merchandise has been shipped

draft issued by the exporter's bank, ordering the importer's bank to pay for the merchandise, thus guaranteeing payment once accepted by the importer's bank

An important and practical issue for domestic firms dealing with foreign customers is securing payment. This is a two-sided issue that reflects the mutual concern rightly felt by both parties to the trade deal: The exporter would like to be paid before shipping the merchandise, whereas the importer obviously would prefer to know that it has received the shipment before releasing any funds. The solution for this mutual mistrust is for both parties to use a mutually trusted go-between who can ensure that the payment is held until the merchandise is in fact delivered according to the terms of the trade contract. The go-between representatives employed by the importer and exporter are still, as they were in the past, the local domestic banks involved in international business.

Here is a simplified version of how it works. After signing contracts detailing the merchandise sold and terms for its delivery, an importer will ask its local bank to issue a **letter of credit** for the amount of money needed to pay for the merchandise. The letter of credit is issued "in favor of the exporter," meaning that the funds are tied specifically to the trade contract involved. The importer's bank forwards the letter of credit to the exporter's bank, which also normally deals in international transactions.

The exporter's bank then notifies the exporter that a letter of credit has been received in its name, and the exporter can go ahead with the shipment. The carrier transporting the merchandise provides the exporter with evidence of the shipment in a document called a **bill of lading**. The exporter signs over title to the merchandise (now in transit) to its bank by delivering signed copies of the bill of lading and the letter of credit.

In exchange, the exporter issues a **draft** from the bank that orders the importer's bank to pay for the merchandise. The draft, bill of lading, and letter of credit are sent from the exporter's bank to the importer's bank. Acceptance by the importer's bank leads to return of the draft and its sale by the exporter to its bank, meaning that the exporter receives cash and the bank assumes the risk of collecting the funds from the foreign bank. The importer is obliged to pay its bank on delivery of the merchandise, and the deal is complete.

In most cases, the letter of credit is part of a lending arrangement between the importer and its bank, and of course, both banks earn fees for issuing of letters of credit and drafts and for handling the import-export services for their clients. Furthermore, the process incorporates the fact that both importer and exporter will have different local currencies and might even negotiate their trade in a third currency. The banks look after all the necessary exchanges. For example, the vast majority of international business is negotiated in U.S. dollars, even though the trade may be between countries other than the United States. Thus, although the importer may end up paying for the merchandise in its local currency and the exporter may receive payment in another local currency, the banks involved will exchange all necessary foreign funds in order to allow the deal to take place.

The exporting firm instead may ship its products to an *export-import agent*, which for a commission or fee arranges the sale of the products to foreign intermediaries. The agent is an independent firm—like other agents—that sells and may perform other marketing functions for the exporter. The exporter, however, retains title to the products during shipment and until they are sold.

An exporting firm also may establish its own *sales offices*, or *branches*, in foreign countries. These installations are international extensions of the firm's distribution system. They represent a deeper involvement in international business than the other exporting techniques we have discussed—and thus they carry a greater risk. The exporting firm maintains control over sales, and it gains both experience in and knowledge of foreign markets. Eventually, the firm also may develop its own sales force to operate in conjunction with foreign sales offices.

Joint Ventures

A *joint venture* is a partnership formed to achieve a specific goal or to operate for a specific period of time. A joint venture with an established firm in a foreign country provides immediate market knowledge and access, reduced risk, and control over product attributes. However, joint-venture agreements established across national borders can become extremely complex. As a result, joint-venture agreements generally require a very high level of commitment from all the parties involved.

A joint venture may be used to produce and market an existing product in a foreign nation or to develop an entirely new product. Recently, for example, Archer Daniels Midland Company (ADM), one of the world's leading food processors, entered into a joint venture with Gruma SA, Mexico's largest corn flour and tortilla company. Besides a 22 percent stake in Gruma, ADM also received stakes in other joint ventures operated by Gruma.

Totally Owned Facilities

At a still deeper level of involvement in international business, a firm may develop *totally owned facilities*, that is, its own production and marketing facilities in one or more foreign nations. This *direct investment* provides complete control over operations, but it carries a greater risk than the joint venture. The firm is really establishing a subsidiary in a foreign country. Most firms do so only after they have acquired some knowledge of the host country's markets.

Direct investment may take either of two forms:

* *Form A.* In this type of direct investment, the firm builds or purchases manufacturing and other facilities in the foreign country. It uses these facilities to produce its own established products and to market them in that country and perhaps in neighboring countries. Firms such as General Motors, Union Carbide, and Colgate-Palmolive are multinational companies with worldwide manufacturing facilities. Colgate-Palmolive factories are becoming *Eurofactories*, supplying neighboring countries as well as their own local markets.

* *Form B.* This is the purchase of an existing firm in a foreign country under an arrangement that allows it to operate independently of the parent company. When Sony Corporation (a Japanese firm) decided to enter the motion-picture business in the United States, it chose to purchase Columbia Pictures Entertainment, Inc., rather than start a new motion-picture studio from scratch.

Venturing into joint ventures.

Tata BlueScope Steel Limited, a 50-50 joint venture between BlueScope Steel and India's Tata Steel, opens its manufacturing facility near Chennai in southern India. Here, Chetan Tolia, managing director of Tata BlueScope Steel, poses with Kathryn Fagg, chairperson of Tata BlueScope Steel at their manufacturing unit near Chennai.

—EXAMINING ETHICS—
Who Should Police Overseas Factories?

Gap, Apple Computer, Nike, and Hewlett-Packard are among the many companies that keep costs down by limiting direct investment in totally owned factories. Instead, these firms buy some parts and finished products from suppliers in China, Jordan, and other countries. But when an overseas supplier is criticized for abuses such as excessive overtime, child labor, or unsafe working conditions, who should police the factory? Different companies handle this situation in different ways.

- *Company monitoring.* Gap has ninety-two inspectors on staff to check suppliers' factories. It has dropped some suppliers because of abuses and publicly reports on factory conditions every year.
- *Outside monitoring.* Responding to a report of problems in the Chinese factory where iPods are made, Apple investigated and forced the supplier to eliminate excessive overtime. Now it has a nonprofit group monitoring the factory.
- *Industry code.* Nike and other apparel firms created the Fair Labor Association to set labor standards and check that suppliers are complying. The computer industry follows the Electronic Industry Code of Conduct, but individual companies such as Hewlett-Packard must enforce the code.

Sources: Based on information from John Markoff, "Apple Finds No Forced Labor at iPod Factory in South China," *New York Times*, August 18, 2006, p. C3; Peter Burrows, "Stalking High-Tech Sweatshops," *BusinessWeek*, June 19, 2006, pp. 62–63; "Gap Lists Plants Abusing Workers," *Los Angeles Times*, July 14, 2005, p. C2.

Strategic Alliances

strategic alliance a partnership formed to create competitive advantage on a worldwide basis

A **strategic alliance**, the newest form of international business structure, is a partnership formed to create competitive advantage on a worldwide basis. Strategic alliances are very similar to joint ventures. The number of strategic alliances is growing at an estimated rate of about 20 percent per year. In fact, in the automobile and computer industries, strategic alliances are becoming the predominant means of competing. International competition is so fierce and the costs of competing on a global basis are so high that few firms have all the resources needed to do it alone. Thus individual firms that lack the internal resources essential for international success may seek to collaborate with other companies.

An example of such an alliance is the New United Motor Manufacturing, Inc. (NUMMI), formed by Toyota and General Motors to make automobiles for both firms. This enterprise united the quality engineering of Japanese cars with the marketing expertise and market access of General Motors.[7]

Trading Companies

trading company provides a link between buyers and sellers in different countries

A **trading company** provides a link between buyers and sellers in different countries. A trading company, as its name implies, is not involved in manufacturing or owning assets related to manufacturing. It buys products in one country at the lowest price consistent with quality and sells to buyers in another country. An important function of trading companies is taking title to products and performing all the activities necessary to move the products from the domestic country to a foreign country. For example, large grain-trading companies operating out of home offices both in the United States and overseas control a major portion of the world's trade in basic food commodities. These trading companies sell homogeneous agricultural commodities that can be stored and moved rapidly in response to market conditions. The best-known U.S. trading company is Sears World Trade, which specializes in consumer goods, light industrial items, and processed foods.[8]

Countertrade

In the early 1990s, many developing nations had major restrictions on converting domestic currency into foreign currency. Exporters therefore had to resort to barter agreements with importers. Countertrade is essentially an international barter transaction in which goods and services are exchanged for different goods and services. Examples include Saudi Arabia's purchase of ten 747 jets from Boeing with payment in crude oil, Philip Morris's sale of cigarettes to Russia in return for chemicals used to make fertilizers, and Iraq's barter of crude oil for warships from Italy.

Multinational Firms

A multinational enterprise is a firm that operates on a worldwide scale without ties to any specific nation or region. The multinational firm represents the highest level of involvement in international business. It is equally "at home" in most countries of the world. In fact, as far as the operations of the multinational enterprise are concerned, national boundaries exist only on maps. It is, however, organized under the laws of its home country.

Table 3.2 shows the ten largest foreign and U.S. public multinational companies; the ranking is based on a composite score reflecting each company's best three out of four rankings for sales, profits, assets, and market value. Table 3.3 describes steps in entering international markets.

1,000 首歌在你口袋里。 **iPod + iTunes**

China's iPod sweatshops.

This iPod assembly plant in Longhua, China, employs 200,000 workers who live in dormitories that house 100 workers.

countertrade an international barter transaction

multinational enterprise a firm that operates on a worldwide scale without ties to any specific nation or region

2006 RANK	COMPANY	BUSINESS	COUNTRY	REVENUE ($ MILLIONS)
1	Exxon Mobil	Energy	United States	339,938
2	Wal-Mart Stores	General Merchandiser	United States	315,654
3	Royal Dutch/Shell Group	Energy	Netherlands/United Kingdom	306,731
4	BP	Energy	United Kingdom	267,600
5	General Motors	Automobiles	United States	192,604
6	Chevron	Energy	United States	189,481
7	DaimlerChrysler	Automobiles	Germany	186,106
8	Toyota Motor	Automobiles	Japan	185,805
9	Ford Motor	Automobiles	United States	177,210
10	Conoco Phillips	Energy	United States	166,683

TABLE 3.2

The Ten Largest Foreign and U.S. Multinational Corporations

Source: "Global 500", http://money.cnn.com/magazines/fortune/global500/2006/full_list; accessed May 19, 2007. The Ten Largest Foreign and U.S. Multinational Corporations from FORTUNE, July 23, 2007. Copyright © 2007 Time Inc. All rights reserved. Reprinted by permission.

TABLE 3.3

Steps in Entering International Markets

Source: U.S. Department of Commerce, International Trade Administration, Washington, D.C

STEP	ACTIVITY	MARKETING TASKS
1	Identify exportable products	Identify key selling features Identify needs that they satisfy Identify the selling constraints that are imposed
2	Identify key foreign markets for the products	Determine who the customers are Pinpoint what and when they will buy Do market research Establish priority, or "target," countries
3	Analyze how to sell in each priority market (methods will be affected by product characteristics and unique features of country/market)	Locate available government and private-sector resources Determine service and backup sales requirements
4	Set export prices and payment terms, methods, and techniques	Establish methods of export pricing Establish sales terms, quotations, invoices, and conditions of sale Determine methods of international payments, secured and unsecured
5	Estimate resource requirements and returns	Estimate financial requirements Estimate human resources requirements (full- or part-time export department or operation?) Estimate plant production capacity Determine necessary product adaptations
6	Establish overseas distribution network	Determine distribution agreement and other key marketing decisions (price, repair policies, returns, territory, performance, and termination) Know your customer (use U.S. Department of Commerce international marketing services)
7	Determine shipping, traffic, and documentation procedures and requirements	Determine methods of shipment (air or ocean freight, truck, rail) Finalize containerization Obtain validated export license Follow export-administration documentation procedures
8	Promote, sell, and be paid	Use international media, communications, advertising, trade shows, and exhibitions Determine the need for overseas travel (when, where, and how often?) Initiate customer follow-up procedures
9	Continuously analyze current marketing, economic, and political situations	Recognize changing factors influencing marketing strategies Constantly reevaluate

TEST PREPPER 3.4

True or False?

___ 1. The solution to mutual mistrust on the part of both importer and exporter is to use a letter of credit from a bank that will ensure that the payment will be made to the beneficiary.

___ 2. A bill of lading is a document issued by the exporter's bank ordering the importer's bank to pay for the merchandise.

___ 3. A trading company enables an international barter transaction in which goods and services are exchanged for different goods and services.

Multiple Choice

___ 4. Licensing is a contractual agreement in which one firm permits another to produce and market its product and use its brand name in return for a royalty or other compensation. Based on this definition, which of the following is not an advantage of licensing?

    a. It allows small manufacturers the ability to launch a well-known domestic brand internationally.

    b. It provides small manufacturers with a way to increase sales worldwide without committing capital.

    c. It provides a simple method for expanding into a foreign market with virtually no investment.

    d. It provides the original producer with extensive foreign marketing experience.

    e. It allows firms to earn revenue by sharing a percentage of the manufacturer's income from sales of the product.

___ 5. Different approaches to international trade require varying degrees of involvement in international business. Which of the following describes the greatest degree of involvement in international business?

    a. Totally owned facilities
    b. Licensing
    c. Company monitoring
    d. Strategic alliance
    e. Joint ventures

ACE the Test
ACE & ACE+
Practice Test 3.4

Sources of Export Assistance

Learning Objective 5

Describe the various sources of export assistance, and identify the institutions that help firms and nations finance international business.

In September 1993, President Bill Clinton announced the *National Export Strategy* (NES) to revitalize U.S. exports. Under the NES, the *Trade Promotion Coordinating Committee* (TPCC) assists U.S. firms in developing export-promotion programs. The export services and programs of the nineteen TPCC agencies can help American firms to compete in foreign markets and create new jobs in the United States. Table 3.4 provides an overview of selected export-assistance programs.

These and other sources of export information enhance the business opportunities of U.S. firms seeking to enter expanding foreign markets. Another vital entry factor is financing.

CONCEPT CHECK

How can a firm obtain the expertise needed to produce and market its products in, for example, the EU?

Financing International Business

International trade compounds the concerns of financial managers. Currency exchange rates, tariffs and foreign-exchange controls, and the tax structures of host nations all affect international operations and the flow of cash. In addition,

TABLE 3.4

U.S. Government Export Assistance Programs

AGENCY	SERVICES PROVIDED
1. U.S. Export Assistance Centers, www.sba.gov/oit/export/useac.html	Provide assistance in export marketing and trade finance.
2. International Trade Administration, www.ita.doc.gov/	Offers assistance and information to exporters through its domestic and overseas commercial officers
3. U.S. and Foreign Commercial Services, www.export.gov/	Helps U.S. firms compete more effectively in the global marketplace and provides information on foreign markets.
4. Advocacy Center, www.ita.doc.gov/advocacy	Facilitates advocacy to assist U.S. firms competing for major projects and procurements worldwide.
5. Trade Information Center, www.ita.doc.gov/td/tic/	Provides U.S. companies information on federal programs and activities that support U.S. exports.
6. STATUSA/Internet, www.stat-usa.gov/	Offers a comprehensive collection of business, economic, and trade information on the web.
7. Small Business Administration, www.sba.gov/oit/	Publishes many helpful guides to assist small and medium-sized companies.
8. National Trade Data Bank, www.stat-usa.gov/tradtest.nsf	Provides international economic and export promotion information supplied by over twenty U.S. agencies.

financial managers must be concerned both with the financing of their international operations and with the means available to their customers to finance purchases.

Fortunately, along with business in general, a number of large banks have become international in scope. Many have established branches in major cities around the world. Thus, like firms in other industries, they are able to provide their services where and when they are needed. In addition, financial assistance is available from U.S. government and international sources.

Several of today's international financial organizations were founded many years ago to facilitate free trade and the exchange of currencies among nations. Some, such as the Inter-American Development Bank, are supported internationally and focus on developing countries. Others, such as the Export-Import Bank, are operated by one country but provide international financing.

The Export-Import Bank of the United States   The Export-Import Bank of the United States, created in 1934, is an independent agency of the U.S. government whose function it is to assist in financing the exports of American firms. *Eximbank*, as it is commonly called, extends and guarantees credit to overseas buyers of American goods and services and guarantees short-term financing for exports. It also cooperates with commercial banks in helping American exporters to offer credit to their overseas customers.

Multilateral Development Banks   A multilateral development bank (MDB) is an internationally supported bank that provides loans to developing countries to help them grow. The most familiar is the World Bank, which operates worldwide. Four other MDBs operate primarily in Central and South America, Asia, Africa, and Eastern and Central Europe. All five are supported by the industrialized nations, including the United States.

Export-Import Bank of the United States an independent agency of the U.S. government whose function it is to assist in financing the exports of American firms

multilateral development bank (MDB) an internationally supported bank that provides loans to developing countries to help them grow

The *Inter-American Development Bank* (IDB), the oldest and largest regional bank, was created in 1959 by ten Latin American countries and the United States. The bank, which is headquartered in Washington, D.C., makes loans and provides technical advice and assistance to countries.

With sixty-six member nations, the *Asian Development Bank* (ADB), created in 1966 and headquartered in the Philippines, promotes economic and social progress in Asian and Pacific regions. The U.S. government is the second-largest contributor to the ADB's capital, after Japan.

The *African Development Bank* (AFDB), also known as *Banque Africaines de Developpment*, was established in 1964 with headquarters in Abidjan, Ivory Coast. Its members include fifty-three African and twenty-four non-African countries from the Americas, Europe, and Asia. The AFDB's goal is to foster the economic and social development of its African members. The bank pursues this goal through loans, research, technical assistance, and the development of trade programs.

Established in 1991 to encourage reconstruction and development in the Eastern and Central European countries, the London-based *European Bank for Reconstruction and Development* (EBRD) is owned by sixty countries and two intergovernmental institutions. Its loans are geared toward developing market-oriented economies and promoting private enterprise.

The International Monetary Fund The International Monetary Fund (IMF) is an international bank with 184 member nations that makes short-term loans to developing countries experiencing balance-of-payment deficits. This financing is contributed by member nations, and it must be repaid with interest. Loans are provided primarily to fund international trade.

International Monetary Fund (IMF) an international bank with 184 member nations that makes short-term loans to developing countries experiencing balance-of-payment deficits

CONCEPT CHECK

In what ways do Eximbank, multilateral development banks, and the IMF enhance international trade?

ACE the Test
ACE & ACE+
Practice Test 3.5

TEST PREPPER 3.5

True or False?

_F_ 1. The International Trade Administration facilitates advocacy to assist U.S. firms competing for major projects and procurements worldwide.

_T_ 2. The National Trade Data Bank provides international economic and export promotion information supplied by over twenty U.S. agencies.

_F_ 3. The London-based European Bank for Reconstruction and Development (EBRD) is an example of a bank that is operated by one country but provides international financing.

Multiple Choice

_E_ 4. The export services and programs of the nineteen TPCC agencies can help American firms to compete in foreign markets and create new jobs in the United States. Which agency publishes helpful guides to assist small and medium-sized companies?

  a. U.S. and Foreign Commercial Service
  b. Advocacy Center
  c. Trade Information Center
  d. STATUSA/Internet
  e. Small Business Administration

_A_ 5. Which of the following is the stated objective of the U.S. and Foreign Commercial Services?

  a. Helping U.S. firms compete more effectively in the global marketplace and providing information on foreign markets
  b. Facilitating advocacy to assist U.S. firms competing for major projects and procurements worldwide
  c. Providing U.S. companies with information on federal programs and activities that support U.S. exports
  d. Providing assistance in export marketing and trade finance
  e. Offering assistance and information to exporters through its domestic and overseas commercial officers

_C_ 6. Which important utility provides firms with a comprehensive collection of business, economic, and trade information on the web?

   a. Advocacy Center
   b. Trade Information Center
   c. STATUSA/Internet
   d. Small Business Administration
   e. National Trade Data Bank

_C_ 7. According to your understanding of the financial requirements of international business, which of the following is not an example of the role the Eximbank plays in international financing?

   a. It guarantees short-term financing for exports.
   b. It cooperates with commercial banks to offer credit to their overseas customers.

   c. It is operated by the United States to provide financing exclusively for U.S. firms.
   d. It is an independent agency of the U.S. government whose function it is to assist in financing the exports of American firms.
   d. It extends and guarantees credit to overseas buyers of American goods.

_D_ 8. The World Bank, the Inter-American Development Bank, and the Asian Development Bank are all examples of which kind of international financial institution?

   a. Multinational firms
   b. Trading companies
   c. Company monitoring institutions
   d. Multilateral development banks
   e. Unilateral development agencies

Prepare for Class
CL News Feeds
CL News Now

→ **RETURN TO INSIDE BUSINESS**

Procter & Gamble waited seventy-eight years to build its first factory outside the United States, yet today it's a multinational giant with totally owned facilities in eighty countries. CEO A. G. Lafley has accelerated P&G's international expansion by reminding employees that "the consumer is boss."

In particular, Lafley is boosting direct investment in China, where P&G's sales have risen from $93 million to $3 billion over the past fifteen years. Meanwhile, deep-pocketed global rivals such as Unilever are building plant after plant in China even as locally owned firms are fighting to hold onto their customers. Faced with intense competition in developing countries throughout Asia and Latin America as well as slowing economic growth in some regions, how can P&G maintain its worldwide sales and profit momentum?

Questions

1. Most of the products P&G sells in China are manufactured locally in its totally owned facilities. What are the implications for the U.S. balance of payments with China?
2. To fuel growth without the expense of direct investment, should P&G license its billion-dollar brands in countries where they are not currently available? Support your answer.

LEARNING OBJECTIVES REVIEW

1 Explain the economic basis for international business.

- International business encompasses all business activities that involve exchanges across national boundaries.

- International trade is based on specialization, whereby each country produces the goods and services that it can produce more efficiently than any other goods and services.

- A nation is said to have a comparative advantage relative to those goods. International trade develops when each nation trades its surplus products for those in short supply.

- A nation's balance of trade is the difference between the value of its exports and the value of its imports. Its balance of payments is the difference between the flow of money into and out of the nation.

2 Discuss the different types of international trade restrictions nations engage in and the arguments for and against such restrictions.

- Despite the benefits of world trade, nations tend to use tariffs and nontariff barriers (import quotas, embargoes, and other restrictions) to limit trade.

- These restrictions typically are justified as being needed to protect a nation's economy, industries, citizens, or security.

- They can result in the loss of jobs, higher prices, fewer choices in the marketplace, and the misallocation of resources.

3 Outline the extent of international trade and identify the organizations working to foster it.

- World trade is generally increasing. Trade between the United States and other nations is increasing in dollar value but decreasing in terms of our share of the world market.

- The General Agreement on Tariffs and Trade (GATT) was formed to dismantle trade barriers and provide an environment in which international business can grow.

- Today, the World Trade Organization (WTO) and various economic communities carry on that mission.

Improve Your Grade
Learning Objective Review
Audio Chapter Review & Quiz

4 Define the methods by which a firm can organize for and enter into international markets.

- It may *license* a foreign firm to produce and market its products.

- It may *export* its products and sell them through *foreign intermediaries* or its own sales organization abroad.

- It may sell its *exports* outright to an *export-import merchant*.

- It may enter into a *joint venture* with a foreign firm.

- It may *establish its own foreign subsidiaries*.

- Or it may develop into a *multinational enterprise*.

- Generally, each of these methods represents an increasingly deeper level of involvement in international business, with licensing being the simplest and the development of a multinational corporation the most involved.

5 Describe the various sources of export assistance. Identify the institutions that help firms and nations finance international business.

- Many government and international agencies provide export assistance to U.S. and foreign firms. The export services and programs of the nineteen agencies of the U.S. Trade Promotion Coordinating Committee (TPCC) can help U.S. firms to compete in foreign markets and create new jobs in the United States.

- Sources of export assistance include
  - U.S. Export Assistance Centers
  - The International Trade Administration
  - U.S. and Foreign Commercial Services
  - Advocacy Center
  - National Trade Data Bank
  - Other government and international agencies

- The financing of international trade is more complex than that of domestic trade.

- Institutions such as the Eximbank and the International Monetary Fund have been established to provide financing and ultimately to increase world trade for American and international firms.

VIDEO CASE

IDG Profits Globally from Local Differences

For more than four decades, International Data Group (IDG) has prospered by allowing each of its publishing, online, research, and conference businesses to find their own keys to success, nation by nation. A business idea that works spectacularly well in one country may fail miserably in another. This is why IDG's careful focus on meeting local needs—in the local language—makes all the difference in fulfilling the company's mission of spreading the computer revolution around the world.

All of IDG's businesses deal with information about technology. Its newspapers and magazines, such as *PCWorld* and *ComputerWorld,* keep business people up-to-date on technology developments. The company maintains 400 technology news websites and manages hundreds of technology conferences and exhibitions every year, such as the popular MacWorld Expo. In addition, its International Data Corporation unit specializes in researching and analyzing worldwide technology trends for business clients.

IDG's combined annual revenue from operations in eighty-five countries soon will reach $3 billion. The company is looking ahead to even higher revenue as different units expand to meet growing demand for timely technology information in Southeast Asia, China, and other areas. In each country, local interests and language preferences shape the goods and services offered by IDG's local businesses. Moreover, the company sometimes teams up with local government agencies to develop and launch new offerings. For example, it has partnered with the Ministry of Science and Technology to produce information technology conferences in Vietnam.

Unlike multinational corporations that embrace the "one size fits all" strategy, the IDG businesses in each country are expected to be entrepreneurs, investigating what their customers want and need. Top executives have given local managers the authority to make decisions based on local trends and changes. As one example, the unit in South Korea decided to introduce online services before offering magazine subscriptions because it found that most local business people rely on high-speed Internet and web-enabled cell phones to access information. IDG is not only looking at the outcome in South Korea, but it is also considering how this approach might work in other areas. Thus, in the future, IDG might decide to deliver technology news solely through wireless media in some countries rather than relying on more traditional print media.

In China, IDG is already one of the top international publishers because of its joint ventures with local companies, which publish *ComputerWorld China* and other magazines in Chinese. IDG's success here has led other U.S. publishers to seek its help in launching Chinese editions of popular U.S. consumer magazines such as *Cosmopolitan*. Having gained in-depth market knowledge and forged close ties with local businesses, IDG began investing in Chinese high-tech companies in the early 1990s. Over the years, some of these firms went bankrupt, whereas others began selling stock or became acquisition targets—vastly increasing the value of IDG's investment stake.

CEO Patrick Kenealy says that his job is to let the best ideas of IDG's businesses rise to the surface and then "help everyone share best practices." However, he and his management team recognize the potential for misinterpretation when employees from different cultures try to communicate. Because IDG's local employees speak so many languages, presentations for multinational internal audiences are made in English. Even when employees are using the same language—English—employees from the United States, United Kingdom, and Australia may not glean the same meaning from a presentation or report. This is why Gigi Wang, senior vice president of strategy, stresses that "it's not what you say that's important; it's what the listener hears."[9]

Questions

1. What are some of the advantages and disadvantages of IDG's intense focus on meeting local needs and using the local language in every country?
2. Why do you think IDG partners with government agencies rather than private firms in some countries?
3. Considering that IDG's main product is information, which trade restrictions might affect its profitability?

BUILDING SKILLS FOR CAREER SUCCESS

1. Exploring the Internet

A popular question debated among firms actively involved on the Internet is whether or not there exists a truly global Internet-based customer, irrespective of any individual culture, linguistic, or nationality issues. Does this Internet-based universal customer see the Internet and products sold there in pretty much the same way? If so, then one model might fit all customers. For example, although Yahoo.com translates its web pages so that they are understood around the world, the pages look pretty much the same regardless of which international site you use. Is this good strategy, or should the sites reflect local customers differently? Visit the text website for updates to this exercise.

Assignment

1. Examine a website such as Yahoo's (**www.yahoo.com**) and its various international versions that operate in other languages around the world. Compare their similarities and differences as best you can, even if you do not understand the individual languages.

2. After making your comparison, do you now agree that there are indeed universal Internet products and customers? Explain your decision.

2. Building Team Skills

The North American Free Trade Agreement among the United States, Mexico, and Canada went into effect on January 1, 1994. It has made a difference in trade among the countries and has affected the lives of many people.

Assignment

1. Working in teams and using the resources of your library, investigate NAFTA. Answer the following questions:
   a. What are NAFTA's objectives?
   b. What are its benefits?
   c. What impact has NAFTA had on trade, jobs, and travel?
   d. Some Americans were opposed to the implementation of NAFTA. What were their objections? Have any of these objections been justified?
   e. Has NAFTA influenced your life? How?

2. Summarize your answers in a written report. Your team also should be prepared to give a class presentation.

3. Researching Different Careers

Today, firms around the world need employees with special skills. In some countries such employees are not always available, and firms then must search abroad for qualified applicants. One way they can do this is through global work force databases. As business and trade operations continue to grow globally, you may one day find yourself working in a foreign country, perhaps for an American company doing business there or for a foreign company. In what foreign country would you like to work? What problems might you face?

Assignment

1. Choose a country in which you might like to work.

2. Research the country. The National Trade Data Bank (NTDB) is a good place to start. Find answers to the following questions:
   a. What language is spoken in this country? Are you proficient in it? What would you need to do if you are not proficient?
   b. What are the economic, social, and legal systems like in this nation?
   c. What is its history?
   d. What are its culture and social traditions like? How might they affect your work or your living arrangements?

3. Describe what you have found out about this country in a written report. Include an assessment of whether you would want to work there and the problems you might face if you did.

Prepare for Class
Exploring the Internet

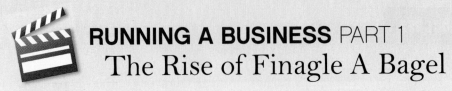

RUNNING A BUSINESS PART 1
The Rise of Finagle A Bagel

Would bagels sell in Hong Kong? Laura Beth Trust and Alan Litchman planned to find out. Trust was in Hong Kong working in the garment manufacturing industry, and Litchman was in real estate, but they were eager to start their own business. They were particularly interested in running a business where they would have direct customer contact and be able to get firsthand feedback about their products and services. And no matter what kind of business they started, it would be a family undertaking: The two entrepreneurs had recently decided to get married.

Looking around Hong Kong, Litchman and Trust noticed numerous Western-style food chains such as McDonald's, Pizza Hut, KFC, and Starbucks, but no bagel places. Yet they believed that Hong Kong's sophisticated, multicultural population would welcome authentic New York–style bagels. Although both the entrepreneurs had MBA degrees from the Sloan School of Management, neither had any restaurant experience or knew how to make a bagel. Still, because they sensed a profitable opportunity and possessed solid business skills, Trust and Litchman decided to move ahead. The two incorporated a company, found a partner, and then returned to the United States to investigate the bagel business. As part of their research, they approached two knowledgeable experts for advice.

One of the bagel experts was Larry Smith, who in 1982 had cofounded a tiny cheesecake store in Boston's historic Quincy Market. When business was slow, the store began selling bagels topped with leftover cream cheese. By the late 1980s, this sideline was doing so well that Smith and his partners changed their focus from cheesecakes to bagels and changed the store's name from Julian's Cheesecakes to Finagle A Bagel. They relocated the store from a cramped 63-square-foot storefront into a more spacious 922-square-foot space in the same busy market complex. Soon so many customers were lining up for bagels that the owners began opening more Finagle A Bagel stores around downtown Boston.

New Ownership, New Growth

By the time Trust and Litchman met Smith, he was operating six successful bagel stores, was ringing up $10 million in annual sales, and was looking for a source of capital to open more stores. Therefore, instead of helping the entrepreneurs launch a business in Hong Kong, Smith suggested they stay and become involved in Finagle A Bagel. Because Litchman and Trust had roots in the Boston area, the opportunity to join a local bagel business was appealing both personally and professionally. Late in 1998, they bought a majority stake in Finagle A Bagel from Smith. The three owners agreed on how to divide management responsibilities and collaborated on plans for more aggressive expansion. Within a few years, Trust and Litchman completed a deal to buy the rest of the business and became the sole owners and copresidents.

The business has grown every year since the conversion to bagels. Today, Finagle A Bagel operates twenty (soon to be twenty-one) stores in downtown Boston and the surrounding suburbs. When Finagle A Bagel outgrew its original production facilities, it moved the corporate headquarters and production center to Newton, Massachusetts. This is where tens of thousands of bagels are prepared every day, along with enough cream cheese and cookies to supply a much larger network of stores. The headquarters also houses a Bagel Museum with bagel memorabilia and more.

Branding the Bagel

Over time, the owners have introduced a wide range of bagels, sandwiches, salads, and soups linked to the core bagel product. Bagels are baked fresh every day, and the stores receive daily deliveries of fresh salad fixings and other ingredients. Employees make each menu item to order while the customer watches. Some of the most popular offerings include a breakfast bagel pizza, salads with bagel-chip croutons, and BLT (bacon-lettuce-tomato) bagel sandwiches.

In addition, Finagle A Bagel wholesales its bagels to thousands of universities, hospitals, and corporate cafeterias. It also sells several varieties of bagels under the Finagle A Bagel brand to the Shaw's Market grocery chain. Shaw's has been expanding in New England through mergers and acquisitions, opening new opportunities for its bagel supplier. "As they grow, we grow with them," comments Litchman. "More importantly, it gets our name into markets where we're not. And we can track the sales and see how we're doing." If a particular Shaw's supermarket registers unusually strong bagel sales, the copresidents will consider opening a store in or near that community.

The Bagel Economy

Although Finagle A Bagel competes with other bagel chains in and around Boston, its competition goes well beyond restaurants in that category. "You compete with a person selling a cup of coffee, you compete with a grocery store selling a salad," Litchman notes. "People only have so many 'dining dollars' and you need to convince them to spend those dining dollars in your store." Finagle A Bagel's competitive advantages are high-

quality, fresh products; courteous and competent employees; and clean, attractive, and inviting restaurants.

During a recent economic recession, Boston's tourist traffic slumped temporarily, and corporate customers cut back on catering orders from Finagle A Bagel. After the company's sales revenues remained flat for about a year, they began inching up as the economy improved. Now the business sells more than $20 million worth of bagels, soups, sandwiches, and salads every year.

Social Responsibility Through Bagels

Social responsibility is an integral part of Finagle A Bagel's operations. Rather than simply throw away unsold bagels at the end of the day, the owners donate the bagels to schools, shelters, and other non-profit organizations. When local nonprofit groups hold fund-raising events, the copresidents contribute bagels to feed the volunteers. Over the years, Finagle A Bagel has provided bagels to bicyclists raising money for St. Jude Children's Research Hospital, to swimmers raising money for breast cancer research, and to people building community playgrounds. Also, the copresidents are strongly committed to being fair to their customers by offering good value and a good

experience. "Something that we need to remember and instill in our people all the time," Trust emphasizes, "is that customers are coming in and your responsibility is to give them the best that you can give them."

Even with 320-plus employees, the copresidents find that owning a business is a nonstop proposition. "Our typical day never ends," says Trust. They are constantly visiting stores, dealing with suppliers, reviewing financial results, and planning for the future. Despite all these responsibilities, this husband-and-wife entrepreneurial team enjoys applying their educational background and business experience to build a company that satisfies thousands of customers every day.

Questions

1. How has the business cycle affected Finagle A Bagel?

2. What is Finagle A Bagel doing to differentiate itself from competitors that want a share of customers' dining dollars?

3. Why would Finagle A Bagel donate bagels to local charities rather than give them away to customers or employees?

4. If you wanted to open a bagel restaurant in Hong Kong, would you license the Finagle A Bagel brand? Why or why not?

CHAPTER 4

Understanding Information and e-Business

Your Guide to Success in Business

Why this chapter matters
Question: How important is information for a successful business?
Answer: It would be extremely difficult to manage even a small business without information.

LEARNING OBJECTIVES

1 Examine how information can reduce risk when making a decision.

2 Discuss management's information requirements.

3 Outline the five functions of an information system.

4 Describe how the Internet helps in decision making, communications, sales, and recruiting and training.

5 Analyze how computers and technology change the way information is acquired, organized, and used.

6 Explain the meaning of e-business.

7 Describe the fundamental models of e-business.

8 Explore the factors that will affect the future of e-business.

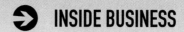

Carol's Daughter Expands Electronically and Mall by Mall

Carol's Daughter has quite a story to tell about building a small business into an international enterprise. Founder Lisa Price, whose mother was named Carol, began her business by mixing fragrances and skin lotions in her New York City kitchen. In 1999, after years of selling her beauty products at events such as the International African Arts Festival, Price opened her first Carol's Daughter store in Brooklyn, New York.

The Brooklyn store is thriving under the management of Price's son, Aerol Hutson. These days, however, Carol's Daughter has grown into much more than a family business. With celebrity backing, the company is building its name through a snazzy online presence (**www.carolsdaughter .com**), seasonal catalogs, a sophisticated flagship store in Harlem, two mall stores, and distribution through the Sephora cosmetics chain.

Now, as a multimillion-dollar company, Carol's Daughter continues to expand by selling personal-care products for men, women, and children through its colorful, user-friendly website. Customers can search the site for specific products, click to browse through the product lines, and sign up to receive e-mail newsletters and promotions. For a small fee, they also can join "Members of the Family" and receive discounts on every electronic order as well as invitations to special store events.

Behind the scenes of this busy e-business, the managers of Carol's Daughter rely on powerful technology to monitor sales, update customer records, communicate with suppliers, track tax payments, and other daily tasks. For her part, founder Lisa Price is deeply involved in developing new products, packaging, and promotion. "We used to shoot the catalog in my kitchen; now we can use the best photographers," she says. "It's a dream come true."[1]

> **DID YOU KNOW?**
>
> Carol's Daughter received a $10 million investment from celebrities such as Will Smith, Jada Pinkett Smith, Steve Stoute, Jay-Z, and Thalia.

KEY TERMS

data (111)
information (112)
database (112)
knowledge management (KM) (113)
management information system (MIS) (113)
information technology (IT) officer (113)
data processing (118)

statistic (119)
decision-support system (DSS) (122)
executive information system (EIS) (122)
expert system (122)
groupware (122)
collaborative learning system (123)
information society (125)
Internet (125)

World Wide Web (the web) (126)
Internet service providers (ISPs) (126)
broadband technology (126)
intranet (126)
computer network (126)
wide-area network (WAN) (126)
local-area network (LAN) (127)
e-business (electronic business) (128)

outsourcing (130)
revenue stream (131)
business model (133)
business-to-business (B2B) model (133)
business-to-consumer (B2C) model (134)

ACE the Test
Crossword Puzzle
Flashcards

These ambitious expansion plans took shape after an investment group, headed by record executive and marketing expert Steve Stoute, put $10 million into Carol's Daughter. The investors include actor Will Smith, his wife Jada Pinkett Smith, singer Thalia, rapper Jay-Z, and other celebrities. Stoute explains, "Our job (as investors) is to nurture this business's growth—to take it from a crawl to a walk."[2] Now, the business is expanding faster than Lisa Price (the entrepreneur behind the business) and the investors could imagine. While there are many reasons for the firm's success, Price's original vision, the investment capital, *and* technology and information have enabled the firm to open both a chain of retail stores and create an online presence that is generating sales revenues and profits.

While some believe that we may be reaching an information saturation point, managers at Carol's Daughter know how important information is. To improve the decision-making process, the information used by both individuals and business firms must be relevant or useful to meet a specific need. Using relevant information results in better decisions.

Relevant information → better intelligence and knowledge → better decisions

For businesses, better intelligence and knowledge that lead to better decisions are especially important because they can provide a *competitive edge* over competitors and improve a firm's *profit*s. We begin this chapter by describing why employees need information.

The first three major sections in this chapter answer the following questions:

* How can information reduce risk when making a decision?
* What is a management information system?
* How do employees use an information system?

Next, we discuss how computers, the Internet, and software—all topics covered in this chapter—are used to obtain the information needed to make decisions on a daily basis. In the last part of this chapter we take a close look at how firms conduct business on the Internet and what growth opportunities may be available to both new and existing firms.

ACE the Test
Hangman

How Can Information Reduce Risk When Making a Decision?

Learning Objective ①

Examine how information can reduce risk when making a decision.

As we noted in Chapter 1, information is one of the four major resources (along with material, human, and financial resources) managers must have to operate a business. While a successful business uses all four resources efficiently, it is information that helps managers reduce risk when making a decision.

Information and Risk

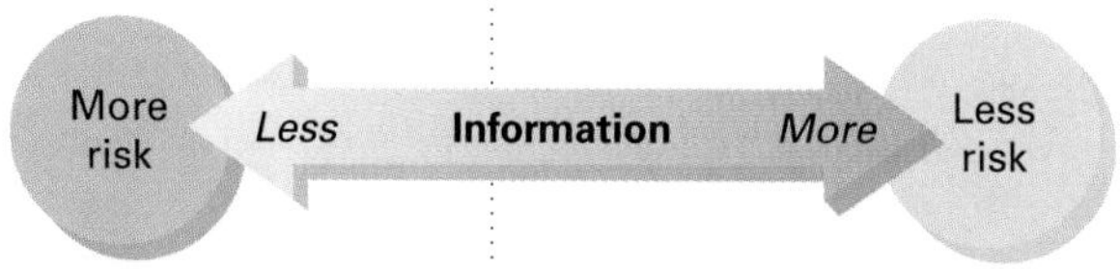

Theoretically, with accurate and complete information, there is no risk whatsoever. On the other hand, a decision made without any information is a gamble. These two extreme situations are rare in business. For the most part, business decision makers see themselves located someplace between either extreme. As illustrated in Figure 4.1, when the amount of available information is high, there is less risk; when the amount of available information is low, there is more risk.

EXAMPLE Suppose that a marketing manager for Procter & Gamble (P&G) responsible for the promotion of a well-known shampoo such as Pantene Pro-V has called a meeting of her department team to consider the selection of a new magazine advertisement. The company's advertising agency has submitted two new advertisements in sealed envelopes. Neither the manager nor any of her team has seen them before. Only one selection will be made for the new advertising campaign. Which advertisement should be chosen?

Without any further information, the team might as well make the decision by flipping a coin. If, however, team members were allowed to open the envelopes and examine the advertisements, they would have more information. If, in addition to allowing them to examine the advertisements, the marketing manager circulated a report containing the reactions of a group of target consumers to each of the two advertisements, the team would have even more information with which to work. Thus information, when understood properly, produces knowledge and empowers managers and employees to make better decisions.

FIGURE 4.1

The Relationship Between Information and Risk

When the amount of available information is high, managers tend to make better decisions.

Information Rules

Marketing research continues to show that discounts influence almost all car buyers. Simply put, if dealers lower their prices, they will sell more cars. This relationship between buyer behavior and price can be thought of as an *information rule* that usually will guide the marketing manager correctly. An information rule emerges when research confirms the same results each time that it studies the same or a similar set of circumstances. Because of the volume of information they receive each day and their need to make decisions on a daily basis, business people try to accumulate information rules to shorten the time they spend analyzing choices.

Information rules are the "great simplifiers" for all decision makers. Business research is continuously looking for new rules that can be put to good use and looking to discredit old ones that are no longer valid. This ongoing process is necessary because business conditions rarely stay the same for very long.

The Difference Between Data and Information

Many people use the terms *data* and *information* interchangeably, but the two differ in important ways. Data are numerical or verbal descriptions that usually result from some sort of measurement. (The word *data* is plural; the singular form is *datum*.) **EXAMPLE** Your current wage level, the amount of last year's after-tax profit for Motorola, and the current retail prices of Honda automobiles are all data.

data numerical or verbal descriptions that usually result from some sort of measurement

Check this out if you're interested in buying a new Ford.

Often carmakers like Ford offer cash bonuses and special purchase programs for specific groups of customers—in this case college students. The fact that marketing activities like these increase sales is an information rule that helps Ford executives make marketing decisions.

information data presented in a form that is useful for a specific purpose

database a single collection of data stored in one place that can be used by people throughout an organization to make decisions

CONCEPT CHECK

What is the difference between data and information? Give one example of accounting data and one example of accounting information.

Most people think of data as being numerical only, but they can be nonnumerical as well. A description of an individual as a "tall, athletic person with short, dark hair" certainly would qualify as data.

Information is data presented in a form that is useful for a specific purpose. **EXAMPLE** Suppose that a human resources manager wants to compare the wages paid to male and female employees over a period of five years. The manager might begin with a stack of computer printouts listing every person employed by the firm, along with each employee's current and past wages. The manager would be hard pressed to make any sense of all the names and numbers. Such printouts consist of data rather than information.

Now suppose that the manager uses a computer to graph the average wages paid to men and to women in each of the five years. The result is information because the manager can use it for the purpose at hand—to compare wages paid to men with those paid to women over the five-year period. When summarized in the graph, the wage data from the printouts become information. For a manager, information presented in a practical, useful form such as a graph simplifies the decision-making process.

The average company maintains a great deal of data that can be transformed into information. Typical data include records pertaining to personnel, inventory, sales, and accounting. Often each type of data is stored in individual departments within an organization. However, the data can be used more effectively when they are organized into a database. A **database** is a single collection of data stored in one place that can be used by people throughout an organization to make decisions. Today, most companies have several different types of databases. While databases are important, the way the data and information are used is even more important—and more valuable to the firm. As a result, management information experts now use the term **knowledge management (KM)** to describe a firm's procedures for generating, using, and sharing the data and information contained in the firm's databases. Typically, data, information, databases, and knowledge management all become important parts of a firm's management information system.

What Is a Management Information System?

A **management information system (MIS)** is a system that provides managers and employees with the information they need to perform their jobs as effectively as possible (see Figure 4.2).

The purpose of an MIS (sometimes referred to as an *information technology system* or simply *IT system*) is to distribute timely and useful information from both internal and external sources to the managers and employees who need it. Today, most medium-sized to large business firms have an information technology (IT) officer. An **information technology (IT) officer** is a manager at the executive level who is responsible for ensuring that a firm has the equipment necessary to provide the information the firm's employees and managers need to make effective decisions.

Today's typical MIS is built around a computerized system of record-keeping and communications software so that it can provide information based on a wide variety of data. After all, the goal is to provide needed information to all managers and employees.

knowledge management (KM) a firm's procedures for generating, using, and sharing the data and information contained in the firm's databases

management information system (MIS) a system that provides managers and employees with the information they need to perform their jobs as effectively as possible

information technology (IT) officer a manager at the executive level who is responsible for ensuring that a firm has the equipment necessary to provide the information the firm's employees and managers need to make effective decisions

CONCEPT CHECH

Why are computers so well suited to management information systems (MISs)? What are some things computers cannot do in dealing with data and information?

MANAGEMENT INFORMATION SYSTEM

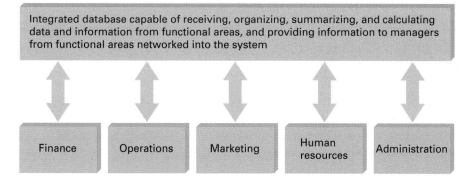

Integrated database capable of receiving, organizing, summarizing, and calculating data and information from functional areas, and providing information to managers from functional areas networked into the system

| Finance | Operations | Marketing | Human resources | Administration |

FIGURE 4.2

Management Information System (MIS)

After an MIS is installed, a user can get information directly from the MIS without having to go through other people in the organization.

Source: Ricky W. Griffin, MANAGEMENT, 9/e (Boston: Houghton Mifflin Company, 2008). Reprinted by permission.

TEST PREPPER 4.1

True or False?

_____ 1. When the amount of available information is high, there is more risk; when the amount of available information is low, there is less risk.

_____ 2. An information technology (IT) officer is a manager at the executive level who is responsible for ensuring that a firm has the equipment necessary to provide the information the firm's employees and managers need to make effective decisions.

Multiple Choice

_____ 3. Based on your understanding of data as opposed to information, which of the following describes data?

   a. Flight details for a vacation trip to Florida
   b. A report containing the reactions of a group of target consumers toward two new Pantene Pro-V conditioners
   c. Timings, dates, and reviews for the new _Pirates of the Caribbean_ movie playing at a local Cinemark theater
   d. Daily sales for online company Carol's Daughter in the last year
   e. An e-mail newsletter to customers advertising the latest fragrance by Carol's Daughter

_____ 4. Select the most appropriate option: _Knowledge management_ can be defined as a firm's procedures for

   a. generating, using, and sharing the data and information contained in the firm's databases.

   b. finding customers, suppliers, competitors, and even new products available in the marketplace by business firms.
   c. obtaining up-to-the-minute news and information regarding the stock exchange.
   d. being able to communicate with suppliers and track tax payments.
   e. using powerful technology to monitor sales for an online website.

_____ 5. Based on your understanding of MIS, which of the following is the best example of a management information system?

   a. A system that provides managers and employees with the information they need to perform their jobs as effectively as possible.
   b. A website where customers can order specific products, browse through the product lines, and sign up to receive e-mail newsletters and promotions
   c. A website where users can obtain up-to-the-minute news and flight information
   d. A tool that allows managers to find customers, suppliers, competitors, and even new products available in the marketplace
   e. Any database where a user can get information directly without having to go through other people in the organization

ACE the Test
ACE & ACE+
Practice Test 4.1

Managers' Information Requirements

Learning Objective ②

Discuss management's information requirements.

Managers typically follow a three-step plan when collecting and using information:

1. _Plan_ for the future.
2. _Implement_ the plans in the present.
3. _Evaluate_ results against what has been accomplished in the past.

The specific types of information they need depend on their area of management.

Today, many firms are organized into five areas of management: _finance, operations, marketing, human resources,_ and _administration_. Managers in each of these areas need specific information in order to make decisions.

* *Financial managers* obviously are most concerned with their firm's finances. They study its debts and receivables, cash flow, future capitalization needs, financial statements, and other accounting information. Of equal importance to financial managers is information about the present state of the economy, interest rates, and predictions of business conditions in the future.

* *Operations managers* are concerned with present and future sales levels, current inventory levels of work in process and finished goods, and the availability and cost of the resources required to produce products and services. They also must keep abreast of any innovative production technology that might be useful to the firm.

* *Marketing managers* need to have detailed information about their firm's products and the products offered by competitors. Such information includes pricing strategies, new promotional campaigns, and products that competitors are test marketing. Information concerning the firm's customers, current and projected market share, and new and pending product legislation is also important to marketing managers.

* *Human resources managers* must be aware of anything that pertains to the firm's employees. Key examples include current wage levels and benefits packages both within the firm and in firms that compete for valuable employees, current legislation and court decisions that affect employment practices, union activities, and the firm's plans for growth, expansion, or mergers.

* *Administrative managers* are responsible for the overall management of the organization. Thus they are concerned with the coordination of information—just as they are concerned with the coordination of material, human, and financial resources. First, administrators must ensure that all employees have access to the information they need to do their jobs. Administrative managers also must make sure that

    * All information is used in a consistent manner throughout the firm.
    * All managers and employees receive the training required to use the firm's MIS.
    * Money is available to update the firm's MIS when needed.

Size and Complexity of the System

An MIS must be tailored to the needs of the organization it serves. In some firms, a tendency to save on initial costs may result in a system that is too small or overly simple. Such a system generally ends up serving only one or two management levels or a single department. Managers in other departments "give up" on the system as soon as they find that it cannot process their data. Often they look elsewhere for information, process their own data, or simply do without.

Almost as bad is an MIS that is too large or too complex for the organization. Unused capacity and complexity do nothing but increase the cost of owning and operating the system. In

CONCEPT CHECK
How do the information requirements of managers differ by management area?

Building employee diversification at Home Depot.

Barbara Serret, a human resources manager at Home Depot knows the value of bilingual employees for Home Depot—the world's largest home improvement chain. Like many retailers, Home Depot is recruiting Hispanic employees who can provide information to Hispanic customers.

addition, a system that is difficult to use probably will not be used at all. Obviously, much is expected of an effective MIS system. Let's examine the functions an MIS system must perform to provide the information managers need.

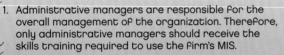

TEST PREPPER 4.2

True or False?

___F___ 1. Administrative managers are responsible for the overall management of the organization. Therefore, only administrative managers should receive the skills training required to use the firm's MIS.

___F___ 2. Once implemented, an organization's MIS is capable of running without extensive updates or investment in technology.

___T___ 3. A three-step plan typically followed by managers when collecting and using information involves planning, implementing and evaluating.

Multiple Choice

___b___ 4. Which of the following managers are required to keep abreast of innovative production technology that might be useful to the firm?
   a. Financial managers
   b. Operations managers
   c. Marketing managers
   d. Human resource managers
   e. Administrative managers

___C___ 5. Financial managers are most concerned with their firm's finances. Keeping this in mind, which of the following would be information relevant to their position in the firm?
   a. Inventory levels of work in process and finished goods
   b. Information concerning the firm's projected market share
   c. The firm's debts and receivables
   d. Information concerning the firm's customers
   e. Current wage levels and benefits packages

ACE the Test
ACE & ACE+
Practice Test 4.2

How Do Employees Use an Information System?

Learning Objective 3

Outline the five functions of an information system.

To provide information, an MIS must perform five specific functions:
1. It must collect data.
2. It must store the data.
3. It must update the data.
4. It must process the data into information.
5. It must present information to users (see Figure 4.3).

Collecting Data

A firm's employees, with the help of an MIS system, must gather the data needed to establish the firm's *data bank*. The data bank should include all past and current data that may be useful in managing the firm. Clearly, the data entered into the system must be *relevant* to the needs of the firm's managers. And perhaps most important, the data must be *accurate*. Irrelevant data are simply useless; inaccurate data can be disastrous. There are two data sources: *internal* and *external*.

Internal Sources of Data Typically, most of the data gathered for an MIS comes from internal sources. The most common internal sources of information are managers and employees, company records and reports, and minutes of meetings. **EXAMPLE** Past and present accounting data also can provide information about the firm's transactions with customers, creditors, and suppliers. Sales reports are a source of data on sales, pricing strategies, and the effectiveness of promotional campaigns. Human resources records are useful as a source of data on wage and benefits levels, hiring patterns, employee turnover, and other personnel variables.

Present and past production forecasts also should be included in the firm's data bank, along with data indicating how well these forecasts predicted actual events. And specific plans and management decisions—regarding capital expansion and new product development, for example—should be incorporated into the MIS system.

External Sources of Data External sources of data include customers, suppliers, bankers, trade and financial publications, industry conferences, online computer services, government sources, and firms that specialize in gathering data for organizations. **EXAMPLE** A marketing research company may acquire forecasts pertaining to product demand, consumer tastes, and other marketing variables. Suppliers are also an excellent source of information about the future availability and costs of raw materials and component parts. Bankers often can provide valuable economic insights and projections. And the information furnished by trade publications and industry conferences usually is concerned as much with future projections as with present conditions. Whether the source of the data is internal or external, always remember the following three cautions:

1. The cost of obtaining data from some external sources, such as marketing research firms, can be quite high.
2. Outdated or incomplete data usually yield inaccurate information.
3. Although computers generally do not make mistakes, the people who use them can make or cause errors. When data (or information) and your judgment disagree, always check the data.

Storing Data

An MIS must be capable of storing data until they are needed. Typically, the method chosen to store data depends on the size and needs of the organization. Small businesses may enter data and then store them directly on the hard drive inside an employee's computer. Generally, medium-sized to large businesses store data in a larger computer system and provide access to employees through a computer network. Today, networks take on many configurations and are designed by specialists who work with a firm's IT personnel to decide on what's best for the company.

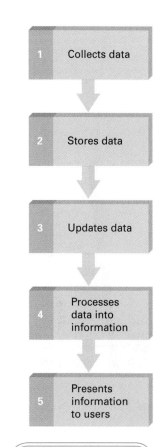

FIGURE 4.3

Five Management Information System Functions

Every MIS must be tailored to the organization it serves and must perform five functions.

1 Collects data

2 Stores data

3 Updates data

4 Processes data into information

5 Presents information to users

Updating Data

Today, an MIS must be able to update stored data regularly to ensure that the information presented to managers and employees is accurate, complete, and up-to-date. The frequency with which data are updated depends on how fast they change and how often they are used. When it is vital to have current data, updating may occur as soon as the new data are available. For example, Giant Food, a grocery-store chain operating in the eastern part of the United States, has cash registers that automatically transmit data on each item sold to a central computer. The computer adjusts the store's inventory records accordingly. In some systems the computer even may be programmed to reorder items whose inventories fall below some specified level. Data and information also may be updated according to a predetermined time schedule.

Processing Data

Some data are used in the form in which they are stored, whereas other data require processing to extract, highlight, or summarize the information they contain. **Data processing** is the transformation of data into a form that is useful for a specific purpose. For verbal data, this processing consists mainly of extracting the pertinent material from storage and combining it into a report. Most business data, however, are in the form of numbers—large groups of numbers, such as daily sales totals or production costs for a specific product. Such groups of numbers are

data processing the transformation of data into a form that is useful for a specific purpose

—EXAMINING ETHICS—
Screensavers That Save the World

If you have a computer connected to the Internet, you can help save the world. How? By downloading a screensaver that allows a nonprofit group to process a small amount of data from a giant research project during your computer's free time. With tens of thousands of PCs crunching data in spare moments, scientists see the results sooner. If you volunteer your PC, your personal files won't be touched, and your computer will be put to work only when it has spare processing power.

Here are a few sites that want to put your PC to work on large-scale projects:

- **grid.org** (to help find new cancer treatments)
- **folding.stanford.edu** (to help find a cure for Parkinson's or Alzheimer's)
- **setiathome.berkeley.edu** (to help search for extraterrestrial life)
- **boinc.berkeley.edu** (links to other projects such as those attempting to understand climate change)

Sources: Based on information from Courtney McCarty, "Save the World with Your Screensaver," *PC Magazine*, November 7, 2006, pp. 1561; Lee Gomes, "Wanted: Your PC's Spare Time," *Wall Street Journal*, June 19, 2006, p. R14.

difficult to handle and to comprehend, but their contents can be summarized through the use of statistics. A **statistic** is a measure that summarizes a particular characteristic of an entire group of numbers. Figure 4.4 is an example of statistics in use.

Presenting Information

An MIS must be capable of presenting information in a usable form. That is, the method of presentation—reports, tables, graphs, or charts, for example—must be appropriate for the information itself and for the uses to which it will be put.

Verbal information may be presented in list or paragraph form. Employees often are asked to prepare formal business reports. A typical business report includes (1) an introduction, (2) the body of the report, (3) the conclusions, and (4) the recommendations.

A *visual display* can also be used to present information and may be a diagram that represents several items of information in a manner that makes comparison easier. Figure 4.5 illustrates examples of visual displays generated by a computer. Typical visual displays include

Sky Cloud Manufacturing
Employee Salaries for April 2007

Employee	Monthly Salary
Thomas P. Ouimet	$ 3,500
Marina Ruiz	3,500
Ronald F. Washington	3,000
Sarah H. Abrams	3,000
Kathleen L. Norton	3,000
Martin C. Hess	2,800
Jane Chang	2,500
Margaret S. Fernandez	2,400
John F. O'Malley	2,000
Robert Miller	2,000
William G. Dorfmann	1,800
Total	$29,500

FIGURE 4.4

Statistics

Managers often examine statistics that describe trends in employee compensation.

statistic a measure that summarizes a particular characteristic of an entire group of numbers

The meaning behind the numbers.

Visual displays like these bar charts often are more interesting than if the same information were described in a written paragraph. Because it's easier to compare data when bar charts, pie charts, and graphs are used, the eye can quickly pick out the most important and least important information.

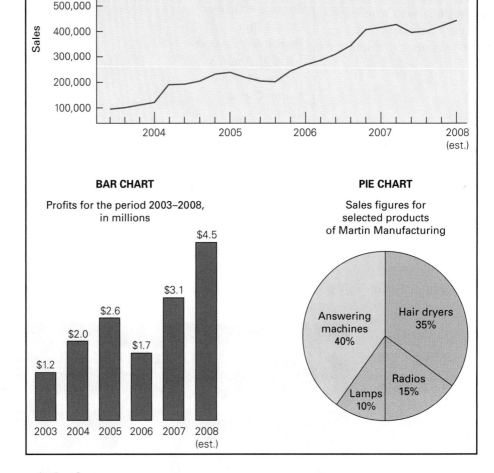

* *Graphs*
* *Bar charts*
* *Pie charts*

Tabular Displays A tabular display is used to present verbal or numerical information in columns and rows. It is most useful in presenting information about two or more related variables. A table, for example, can be used to illustrate the number of salespeople in each region of the country, sales for different types of products, and total sales for all products (see Table 4.1). And information that is to be manipulated—for example, to calculate loan payments—is usually displayed in tabular form.

Tabular displays generally have less impact than visual displays. However, displaying the information that could be contained in a multicolumn table such as Table 4.1 would require several bar or pie charts.

| All-Star Technology Projected Sales | | | |
SECTION OF THE COUNTRY	NUMBER OF SALESPEOPLE	CONSUMER PRODUCTS	INDUSTRIAL PRODUCTS
Eastern territory	15	$1,500,000	$ 3,500,000
Midwestern territory	20	$2,000,000	$ 5,000,000
Western territory	10	$1,000,000	$ 4,000,000
TOTAL	45	$4,500,000	$12,500,000

TABLE 4.1

Typical Three-Column Table Used in Business Presentations

Tables are most useful for displaying information about two or more variables.

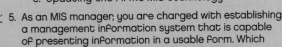

TEST PREPPER 4.3

True or False?

 1. Data processing is the transformation of data into a form that is useful for a specific purpose.

2. Visual displays are most useful for displaying detailed information about two or more variables, whereas tables can be used to make comparison easier.

Multiple Choice

3. Based on your understanding of *internal data*, which of the following is not an example of internal data?

   a. Last year's report on the effectiveness of a product's advertising campaign
   b. Sales reports for years 1999–2007
   c. Data from 2001 on pricing strategies for a product that is no longer manufactured by the company
   d. A 2005 production forecast that overestimated production by 2 percent for the year 2006–2007
   e. Information from the company's regular supplier of computer equipment regarding reduced costs for desktop computers

 4. "Present and past production forecasts should be included in the firm's data bank." Which of the following functions of MIS does this task describe?

   a. Data collection and update
   b. Data collection only
   c. Checking the data for relevance only
   d. Presenting information to users in the form of graphs and reports
   e. Updating the firm's MIS technology

5. As an MIS manager, you are charged with establishing a management information system that is capable of presenting information in a usable form. Which item below do you feel is not appropriate for presenting information in business report format?

   a. The introduction describes the problem and techniques used to gather data.
   b. The body of the report describes the facts.
   c. The conclusions describe the findings.
   d. The recommendations present suggestions for solving the problem.
   e. The database of research methods used by the author of the report.

ACE the Test
ACE & ACE+
Practice Test 4.3

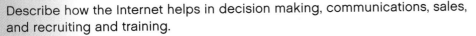

Improving Productivity with the Help of Computers and Technology

Learning Objective 4

Describe how the Internet helps in decision making, communications, sales, and recruiting and training.

In this section we examine several solutions to challenges created when a firm or its employees use computers and the Internet. In each case a solution is always evaluated in terms of its costs and compared with the benefits a firm receives, generally referred to as a *cost/benefit analysis*. Typical areas of concern for a business include decision making, communications, sales, recruiting and training employees, and business software applications.

Making Smart Decisions

How do managers and employees sort out relevant and useful information from the spam, junk mail, and useless data? Three different applications actually can help to improve and speed the decision-making process for people at different levels within an organization. First, a **decision-support system (DSS)** is a type of computer program that provides relevant data and information to help a firm's employees make decisions. It also can be used to determine the effect of changing different variables and answer "what if" type questions. **EXAMPLE** A manager at California-based KB Homes may use a DSS to determine prices for new homes built in an upscale, luxury subdivision. By entering the number of homes that will be built along with different costs associated with land, labor, materials, building permits, promotional costs, and all other costs, a DSS can help to determine a base price for each new home. It is also possible to increase or decrease the building costs and determine new home prices for each set of assumptions with a DSS.

Although similar to a DSS, an **executive information system (EIS)** is a computer-based system that facilitates and supports the decision-making needs of top managers and senior executives by providing easy access to both internal and external information. With an EIS, executives can obtain information by touching a computer screen, using a mouse, or using voice recognition and simply talking to the computer. Needed data and information can be displayed in graphs, charts, and spreadsheets.

An **expert system** is a type of computer program that uses artificial intelligence to imitate a human's ability to think. An expert system uses a set of rules that analyze information supplied by the user about a particular activity or problem. Based on the information supplied, the expert system then provides recommendations or suggests specific actions in order to help make decisions. **EXAMPLE** Expert systems have been used to schedule manufacturing tasks, diagnose illnesses, determine credit limits for credit-card customers, and develop electronic games.

Helping Employees Communicate

One of the first business applications of computer technology was e-mail. Once software was chosen and employees trained, communications could be carried out globally within and outside a firm at any time, twenty-four hours a day, seven days a week. Today, e-mail is also being used as a direct link between businesses and customers. **EXAMPLE** When investment bank Putnam Lovell Securities sent research reports to clients by e-mail instead of printing, packaging, and shipping the reports, the firm saved over $500,000 a year.[3]

Groupware is one of the latest types of software that facilitates the management of large projects among geographically dispersed employees, as well as such group activities as problem solving and brainstorming. **EXAMPLE** Suppose that the home office of a software development firm in a major city has been hired to prepare customized software for a client in another city. The project team leader uses groupware to establish guidelines for the project, check availability of employees around the world, give

decision-support system (DSS) a type of computer program that provides relevant data and information to help a firm's employees make decisions

executive information system (EIS) is a computer-based system that facilitates and supports the decision-making needs of top managers and senior executives by providing easy access to both internal and external information

expert system a type of computer program that uses artificial intelligence to imitate a human's ability to think

groupware one of the latest types of software that facilitates the management of large projects among geographically dispersed employees as well as such group activities as problem solving and brainstorming

individuals specific work assignments, and set up a schedule for work completion, testing, and final installation on the client's computer. The team leader is able to monitor work progress and may intervene if asked or if problems develop. When needed, people from various locations, possessing an array of knowledge and skills, can be called to the "workspace" created on the computer system for their contribution. When the work is finally completed, it can be forwarded to the client's computer and installed.

Besides being useful in project management, groupware provides an opportunity to establish a collaborative learning system to help solve a specific problem. A **collaborative learning system** is a work environment that allows problem-solving participation by all team members. By posting a question or problem on the groupware site, the team leader invites members, who may be located anywhere in the world, to submit messages that can help to move the group toward a solution.

collaborative learning system a work environment that allows problem-solving participation by all team members

Assisting the Firm's Sales Force

Internet-based software application programs sometimes referred to as *customer-relationship management* (CRM) programs focus on the special informational needs of sales personnel. For example, sales force automation programs support sales representatives with organized databases of information such as names of clients, status of pending orders, and sales leads and opportunities, as well as any related advice or recommendations from other company personnel. **EXAMPLE** When a sales representative for the pharmaceutical division of a company such as Johnson & Johnson is planning to visit doctors, health care providers, and hospitals in the Chicago area. A sales force automation software program can provide information about what the results were of the last contacts, who else in the pharmaceutical firm has interacted with the client, and previous purchases the client has made. As sales representatives complete their visits, information about what was learned should be entered into the sales force automation system as soon as possible so that everyone can use the latest information.

Recruiting and Training Employees

A common icon on most corporate websites is a link to "Careers" or "Employment Opportunities." Firms looking for people with specialized skills can post their employee needs on their websites and reach potential candidates from around the globe. This is an extremely important method of recruiting employees for positions where labor shortages are common and individuals with the *right* skills are in high demand.

Furthermore, software programs can help large firms such as General Electric, ExxonMobil, and Citigroup to establish a database of potential employees. This is an especially important function for a firm that receives thousands of unsolicited employment applications from people all over the world. The cost of organizing and processing this information is high, but software can reduce this expense when compared with a paper-based system.

Large and midsize companies also spend a great deal of money on educational and training programs for employees. By distributing information about the firm, the organization, products and services, new procedures, and general information to employees through the Internet for reading and study at convenient times and places, firms can reduce training costs dramatically. Furthermore, revision and distribution of changes to this type of information are much easier if the information is provided on the company's website.

Business Applications Software

Early software typically performed a single function. Today, however, *integrated software* combines many functions in a single package. Integrated packages allow for the easy *linking* of text, numerical data, graphs, photos, and even audiovisual clips. A business report prepared using the Microsoft Office package, for instance, can include all these components.

Integration offers at least two other benefits. Once data have been entered into an application in an integrated package, the data can be used in another integrated package without having to re-enter the data again. Also, once a user learns one application, it is much easier to learn another application in an integrated package. From a career standpoint, you should realize that firms will assume that you possess, or will possess after training, a high degree of working comfort with several of the software applications described in Table 4.2.

TABLE 4.2

Current Business Application Software Used to Improve Productivity

Word processing	Users can prepare and edit written documents and store them in the computer or on a memory device.
Desktop publishing	Users can combine text and graphics in reports, newsletters, and pamphlets in professional reports.
Accounting	Users can record routine financial transactions and prepare financial reports at the end of the accounting period.
Database management	Users can electronically store large amounts of data and transform the data into information.
Graphics	Users can display and print pictures, drawings, charts, and diagrams.
Spreadsheets	Users can organize numerical data into a grid of rows and columns.

ACE the Test
ACE & ACE+
Practice Test 4.4

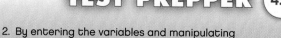 TEST PREPPER 4.4

Multiple Choice

1. A manager in a Kansas City–based firm posts a question on the project website. She then invites her liaisons in the United Kingdom and Canada to come up with innovative solutions to the problem. Within a week, five people have posted on the forum. This approach to problem solving using technology is a good example of which of the following?
   a. Executive information system (EIS)
   b. Desktop publishing
   c. Decision-support system (DSS)
   d. Expert system
   e. Collaborative learning system

2. By entering the variables and manipulating numbers, a program can help to project prices and therefore facilitate pricing strategies. It therefore can be used to determine the effect of changing different variables and answer "what if" type questions. Which of the following is this an example of?
   a. Executive information system (EIS)
   b. Groupware
   c. Decision-support system (DSS)
   d. Expert system
   e. Collaborative learning system

3. Suppose that your company is carrying out market research and wants to know the names of the people or retailers contacted and purchases made by clients. Which of the following is the program that would allow you to do this efficiently?

    a. Customer relationship management program
    b. Expert system
    c. Internet-based software application program
    d. Educational and training program
    e. Business applications software

4. Which of the following describes a process by which users can combine text and graphics in reports, newsletters, and pamphlets in professional reports?

    a. Accounting
    b. Database management
    c. Desktop publishing
    d. Graphics
    e. Spreadsheets

5. Which of the following describes a process by which users can organize numerical data into a grid of rows and columns?

    a. Word processing
    b. Desktop publishing
    c. Accounting
    d. Database management
    e. Spreadsheets

Using Computers and the Internet to Obtain Information

Learning Objective ⑤

Analyze how computers and technology change the way information is acquired, organized, and used.

We live in a rapidly changing **information society**— that is, a society in which large groups of employees generate or depend on information to perform their jobs. The need for more and better information will only continue to grow. Today, businesses are using the Internet to find and distribute information to global users. The Internet is also used for communicating between the firm's employees and its customers. Finally, businesses use the Internet to gather information about competitors' products, prices, and other business strategies. Clearly, the Internet is here to stay.

information society a society in which large groups of employees generate or depend on information to perform their jobs

Internet a worldwide network of computers linked through telecommunications

The Internet, the Intranet, and Networks

The **Internet** is a worldwide network of computers linked through telecommunications. Enabling users around the world to talk with each other electronically, the Internet provides access to a huge array of information sources. The Internet's most commonly used network

A picture is worth a 1000 words.

Because of wireless technology, Bob Hale, owner of American Onion, can use his laptop computer and the Internet to send pictures of his product—onions—right from a field in Hermiston, Oregon. Even as the most developed cities in the nation struggle with whether to offer free Wi-Fi access, one of the most rural counties in the nation has succeeded in creating the world's largest hot spot, a Wi-Fi cloud that stretches over the wide open landscape in Umatilla County, Oregon.

SPOTLIGHT

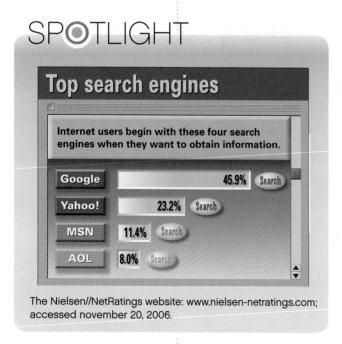

Top search engines

Internet users begin with these four search engines when they want to obtain information.

Google	45.9%	Search
Yahoo!	23.2%	Search
MSN	11.4%	Search
AOL	8.0%	Search

The Nielsen//NetRatings website: www.nielsen-netratings.com; accessed november 20, 2006.

World Wide Web (the web) the Internet's multimedia environment of audio, visual, and text data

Internet service providers (ISPs) provide customers with a connection to the Internet through various phone plugs and cables.

broadband technology a general term referring to higher-speed Internet connections that deliver data, voice, and video material

intranet a smaller version of the Internet for use within a firm

computer network a group of two or more computers linked together that allows users to share data and information

wide-area network (WAN) a network that connects computers over a large geographic area, such as a city, state, or even the world

for finding information is the World Wide Web. The **World Wide Web** (or more simply, **the web**) is the Internet's multimedia environment of audio, visual, and text data. To get on the Internet, you need a computer, a modem, and an Internet service provider (ISP), such as AT&T, America Online, or other companies that provide a connection to the web. **Internet service providers (ISPs)** provide customers with a connection to the Internet through various phone plugs and cables. Today, connections to the Internet include simple telephone lines or faster digital subscriber lines (DSLs) and cabled broadband that carry larger amounts of data at quicker transfer speeds. **Broadband technology** is a general term referring to higher-speed Internet connections that deliver data, voice, and video material.

In addition to business sites, the World Wide Web has a wide array of government and institutional sites that provide information to a firm's employees and the general public. There are also online sites available for most of the popular business periodicals.

An **intranet** is a smaller version of the Internet for use within a firm. Using a series of customized web pages, employees can quickly find information about their firm as well as connect to external sources. **EXAMPLE** An employee might use the intranet to access the firm's policy documents on customer warranties or even take a company-designed course on new products and how to introduce them to customers. Generally, intranet sites are protected, and users must supply both a user name and a password to gain access to a company's intranet site.

Both the Internet and intranets are examples of a computer network. A **computer network** is a group of two or more computers linked together that allows users to share data and information. To-day, two basic types of networks affect the way employees and the general public obtain data and information. A **wide-area network (WAN)** is a network that connects computers over a large geographic area, such as a city, state, or even the world. The world's largest WAN is the Internet.[4] In addition to the Internet, other WANs include private corporate networks (sometimes referred to as *virtual private networks*, or VPNs) and research networks. A **local-area network (LAN)** is a network that connects computers that are in close proximity to each other, such as an office building or a college campus. LANs allow users to share files, printers, games, or other applications.[5] Typically, LANs also will allow users to connect to the Internet.

Accessing the Internet

In order to access the Internet or an intranet, computers and software must be standardized. Establishing standards is vital to ensuring that a Hewlett-Packard computer in McPherson, Kansas, can "talk" with a Dell computer in San Francisco, California. It is just as important for software to be standardized if businesses and individuals are going to use computers to communicate and conduct business activities through the Internet.

The search for available information often begins with a specific website address or a search engine. Every website on the Internet is identified by its *Uniform Resource Locator* (URL), which acts as its address. To connect to a site, you enter its URL in your web browser. A web browser such as Microsoft Internet Explorer, Mozilla Firefox, or Netscape is software that helps users to navigate around the Internet and connect to different websites. The URLs of most corporate sites are similar to the organizations' real names. For instance, you can reach IBM by entering **http://www.ibm.com.** The first part of the entry, *http*, sets the software protocols for proper transfer of information between your computer and the one at the site to which you are connecting. *Http* stands for *HyperText Transfer Protocol* and frequently is omitted from a URL because your computer adds it automatically when you enter the rest of the address. *HyperText* refers to words or phrases highlighted or underlined on a web page; when you select these, they link you to other websites.

To find a particular website, you can take advantage of several free search programs available on the web, such as Google, Yahoo!, and AltaVista. To locate a search engine, enter its URL in your browser. Some URLs for popular search engines are **www.altavista.com, www.google.com, www.yahoo.com.**

The home page for many search engines provides a short list of primary topic divisions, such as *careers, finance, news, travel, health,* and *weather,* as well as a search window where you can enter the particular topic you are looking for.

Creating Web Pages

Today, employees and the general public connect to the Internet, enter a web address, or use a web search engine to access information. That information is presented on a website created and maintained by business firms; agencies of federal, state, or local governments; or educational or similar organizations. Because a website should provide accurate information, great care is required when creating a website. Generally, once a *template* or structure for the web page has been created, content such as text or images can be inserted or changed readily, allowing the site to remain current.

What the website says about a company is important and should be developed carefully to portray the "right" image. Therefore, it is understandable that a firm without the internal human resources to design and launch its website will turn to the talents of creative experts available through web consulting firms. Regardless of whether the website is developed by the firm's employees or outside consultants, the suggestions listed in Table 4.3 should be considered when creating materials for a firm's website.

Once a website is established, most companies prefer to manage their sites on their own computers. An alternative approach is to pay a hosting service that often will provide guaranteed user accessibility, e-business shopping software, site-updating services, and other specialized services.

local-area network (LAN) is a network that connects computers that are in close proximity to each other, such as an office building or a college campus

CONCEPT CHECK
Explain the difference between the Internet and an intranet. What is the difference between a wide-area network (WAN) and a local-area network (LAN)?

TABLE 4.3

Tips for Website Development

Whether you build your site from scratch, use a web design software program, or hire outside professionals, make sure that your website conveys not only the "right" image but also useful information about your company or organization.

1. Develop a theme.	A website is like a book and needs a theme to tie ideas together and tell an interesting story.
2. Determine how much information to include on your site.	Get a handle on the type and amount of information that will be contained on your site. Although it is tempting to include "everything," you must be selective.
3. Plan the layout of your site.	Think about how you want your site to look. Websites that combine color, art, and links to narrative material are the most useful.
4. Add graphics.	Obtain graphics that illustrate the types of data and information contained on your site. Choose colors and photos carefully to make sure that they add rather than detract from the site.
5. Outline the material for each page.	Generally, the opening, or home, page contains basic information with links to additional pages that provide more detailed information.
6. Develop plans to update the site.	It is important to develop a plan to update your site on a regular basis. Too often sites are "forgotten" and contain dated or inaccurate material.
7. Make sure that your site is easy to use.	Stand back and take a look at your site. Is your site confusing, or does it provide a road map to get from point A to point B? If you have trouble getting information, others will too.

TEST PREPPER 4.5

True or False?

 1. The intranet is a worldwide network of computers linked through telecommunications.

___ 2. Http stands for HyperText Transfer Protocol.

 3. When designing a company website, it is important to include every detail available so that there is a large amount of information contained on your site.

Multiple Choice

___ 4. Which of the following is the specific name for a network that connects computers that are in close proximity to each other, such as an office building or a college campus?

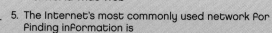
a. Wide-area network (WAN)
b. Internet service provider (ISP)
c. local-area network (LAN)
d. broadband network
e. World Wide Web

 5. The Internet's most commonly used network for finding information is

a. Google.
b. Yahoo.com.
c. URLs.
d. the World Wide Web.
e. broadband technology.

ACE the Test
ACE & ACE+
Practice Test 4.5

Defining e-Business

Learning Objective 6

Explain the meaning of e-business.

e-business (electronic business) the organized effort of individuals to produce and sell, for a profit, the products and services that satisfy society's needs *through the facilities available on the Internet*

Today, many business firms are using information technology to

1. Improve productivity
2. Communicate with both customers and employees

3. Recruit and train employees

4. Sell goods and services online

In Chapter 1 we defined *business* as the organized effort of individuals to produce and sell, for a profit, the products and services that satisfy society's needs. In a simple sense, then, **e-business**, or **electronic business**, can be defined as the organized effort of individuals to produce and sell, for a profit, the products and services that satisfy society's needs *through the facilities available on the Internet.* As you will see in the remainder of this chapter and throughout this book, e-business is transforming key business activities.

Organizing e-Business Resources

As noted in Chapter 1, to be organized, a business must combine *human, material, informational,* and *financial resources.* This is true of e-business, too (see Figure 4.6), but in this case, the resources may be more specialized than in a typical business.

Specialized Resources Needed for e-Business

Human Resources People who can design, create, and maintain websites are only a fraction of the specialized human resources required by e-businesses.

Material Resources These must include specialized computers, sophisticated equipment and software, and high-speed Internet connection lines.

Informational Resources Computer programs that track the number of customers to view a firm's website are generally among the specialized informational resources required.

Vietnam captures the attention of some of the largest players in the information technology industry.

Vietnam's young, educated, and affordable programmers are creating an international niche as a software outsourcing base for American, European, and Japanese high-tech firms.

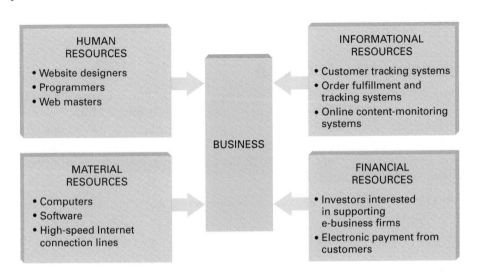

FIGURE 4.6

Combining e-Business Resources

While all businesses use four resources (human, material, informational, and financial), these resources typically are more specialized when used in an e-business.

Too Much Information

Planning a job search? Don't forget to polish your online presence as well as your résumé. Many employers check to see whether job applicants have posted photos, videos, or messages on public websites, blogs, or social networking sites. This is where too much information, sometimes referred to as *TMI*, can work against you. If an online search turns up revealing images, confessions of illegal or questionable activities, or other details that put you in an unprofessional light, that job interview or offer could very well evaporate.

To be safe, assume that some recruiter, at some point, will try to find you on Facebook.com, Blogger.com, MySpace.com, or a similar site. "It's becoming very much a common tool," says a group marketing manager at Microsoft. "For the first time ever, you suddenly have very public information about almost any candidate." In other words, TMI (especially the wrong kind of information) can sink your career even before it begins.

Sources: Based on information from Lindsey Gerdes, "Overexposed," *BusinessWeek*, November 13, 2006, p. 12; Amy Joyce, "So Much for 'Personal' Habits," *Washington Post*, October 15, 2006, p. F1; Alan Finder, "When a Risque Online Persona Undermines a Chance for a Job," *New York Times*, June 11, 2006, pp. A1+.

Financial Resources This is money required to start and maintain the firm and allow it to grow. Financial resources usually reflect greater participation by individual entrepreneurs and investors willing to invest in a high-tech firm instead of conventional financial sources such as banks.

In an effort to reduce the cost of specialized resources that are used in e-business, many firms have turned to outsourcing. **Outsourcing** is the process of finding outside vendors and suppliers that provide professional help, parts, or materials at a lower cost. **EXAMPLE** A firm that needs specialized software to complete a project may turn to an outside firm located in another part of the United States, India, or some Eastern European country.

outsourcing the process of finding outside vendors and suppliers that provide professional help, parts, or materials at a lower cost

Satisfying Needs Online

Think for a moment, why do people use the Internet? For most people, the Internet can be used to purchase products or services and as a source of information and interaction with other people. Today, more people use the Internet to satisfy these needs than ever before, and the number of people who use the Internet will continue to grow in the years to come. Because of the explosive growth of the Internet, let's start with two basic assumptions.

* The Internet has created some new customer needs that did not exist before creation of the Internet.
* e-Businesses can satisfy those needs, as well as more traditional ones.

CONCEPT CHECK

Is outsourcing good for an e-business firm? The firm's employees? Explain your answer.

EXAMPLE Restoration Hardware (**www.restorationhardware.com**) gives customers anywhere in the world access to the same virtual store of hardware and decorative items. And at eBay's global auction site, customers can, for a small fee, buy and sell almost anything. In each of these examples, customers can use the Internet to purchase a product or service.

General Uses of the Internet

In addition to purchasing products, the Internet can be used in the following ways that may benefit both individuals and business firms.

* Internet users also can access newspapers and magazines and radio and television programming at a time and place convenient to them.

* The Internet provides the opportunity for two-way interaction between the online program and the viewer. CNN.com and other news-content sites encourage dialogue among viewers in chat rooms and exchanges with the writers of articles posted to the site.

* Customers can respond to Internet programming by requesting more information about a product or posing specific questions, which may lead to purchasing a product or service.

* Finally, the Internet allows customers to choose the content they are offered. For example, individuals can custom design daily online newspapers and magazines with articles that are of interest to them. Knowing what is of interest to a customer allows an Internet firm to direct appropriate, *smart advertising* to a specific customer. **EXAMPLE** Someone wanting to read articles about the New York Yankees might be a potential customer for products and services related to baseball. For the advertiser, knowing that its advertisements are being directed to the most likely customers represents a better way to spend advertising dollars.

Creating e-Business Profit

Business firms can increase profits either by increasing sales revenue or by reducing expenses through a variety of e-business activities.

Increasing Sales Revenue Each source of sales revenue flowing into a firm is referred to as a **revenue stream**. One way to increase revenues is to sell merchandise on the Internet. Online merchants can reach a global customer base twenty-four hours a day, seven days a week because the opportunity to shop on the Internet is virtually unrestricted. And yet shifting revenues earned from customers inside a real store to revenues earned from those same customers online does not create any real new revenue for a firm. The goal is to find new customers and generate new sales so that total revenues are increased.

Intelligent informational systems also can help to generate sales revenue for Internet firms such as Amazon.com. Such systems store information about each

News you can use.

Today, more and more people are using the Internet and online newspapers, magazines, and radio and television programming to access news at a time and place convenient to them.

revenue stream a source of revenue flowing into a firm

CONCEPT CHECK
How do e-businesses generate revenue streams?

customer's purchases, along with a variety of other information about the buyer's preferences. Using this information, the system can assist the customer the next time he or she visits the website. For example, if the customer has bought a Clay Aiken or Kelly Clarkson CD in the past, the system might suggest CDs by similar artists who have appeared on the popular televised talent-search program *American Idol.*

While some customers in certain situations may not make a purchase online, the existence of the firm's website and the services and information it provides may lead to increased sales in the firm's physical stores. For example, Toyota.com can provide basic comparative information for shoppers so that they are better prepared for their visit to an automobile showroom.

In addition to selling products or services online, e-business revenue streams are created by advertising placed on web pages and by subscription fees charged for access to online services and content. **EXAMPLE** Hoover's Online (**www.hoovers.com**), a comprehensive source for company and industry information, makes some of its online content free for anyone who visits the site, but more detailed data are available only by paid subscription. In addition, it receives revenue from companies that are called *sponsors,* who advertise their products and services on Hoover's website.

Many Internet firms that distribute news, magazine and newspaper articles, and similar content generate revenue from commissions earned from sellers of products linked to the site. Online shopping malls, for example, now provide groups of related vendors of electronic equipment and computer hardware and software with a new method of selling their products and services. In many cases, the vendors share online sales revenues with the site owners.

Reducing Expenses Reducing expenses is the second major way in which e-business can help to increase profitability. Providing online access to information customers want can reduce the cost of dealing with customers. **EXAMPLE** Sprint Nextel (**www.sprint.com**) is just one company that maintains an extensive website where potential customers can learn more about cell phone products and services and current customers can access personal account information, send e-mail questions to customer service, and purchase additional products or services. With such extensive online services, Sprint Nextel does not have to maintain as many physical store locations as it would without these online services. We examine more examples of how e-business contributes to profitability throughout this chapter, especially as we focus on some of the business models for activity on the Internet.

TEST PREPPER 4.6

True or False?

 1. E-business is the organized effort of individuals to produce and sell, for a profit, the products and services that satisfy society's needs through the facilities available on the Internet.

 2. Outsourcing is a process by which a company takes advantage of outside vendors and suppliers providing professional help, parts, or materials at a lower cost.

 3. Smart advertising is the ability to know what is of interest to a customer and allows companies to target to a specific customer.

Multiple Choice

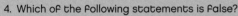 4. Which of the following statements is false?
   a. E-business guarantees that a firm will earn larger profits.
   b. E-business is transforming key business activities for many firms.

   c. E-business often requires specialized resources.
   d. E-business investors are often more involved in the business.
   e. E-business can reduce a firm's expenses.

5. Which of the following statements best describes a specific feature of *intelligent* informational systems that would lead to increased sales revenues online?
   a. They store general information about each customer.
   b. They enable companies to sell a wide variety of merchandise on the Internet.
   c. They can assist the customer the next time he or she visits the website by keeping track of preferences.
   d. They promote popular artist Clay Aiken over Kelly Clarkson.
   e. They enable companies to reach a global customer base interested in general merchandise.

Fundamental Models of e-Business

Learning Objective 7

Describe the fundamental models of e-business.

One way to get a better sense of how businesses are adapting to the opportunities available on the Internet is to identify e-business models. A **business model** represents a group of common characteristics and methods of doing business to generate sales revenues and reduce expenses. Each of the models discussed below represents a primary e-business model. Regardless of the type of business model, planning often depends on if the e-business is a new firm or an existing firm adding an online presence—see Figure 4.7.

Business-to-Business (B2B) Model

Many e-businesses can be distinguished from others simply by their customer focus. For instance, some firms use the Internet mainly to conduct business with other businesses. These firms generally are referred to as having a **business-to-business** (or **B2B**) **model**. Currently, the vast majority of e-business is B2B in nature.

When examining B2B business firms, two clear types emerge. In the first type, the focus is simply on facilitating sales transactions between businesses. For example, Dell manufactures computers to specifications that customers enter on the Dell website. The vast majority of Dell's online orders are from corporate clients who are well informed about the products they need and are looking for fairly priced, high-quality computer products that will be delivered quickly. Basically, by building only what is

business model represents a group of common characteristics and methods of doing business to generate sales revenues and reduce expenses

business-to-business (or **B2B**) **model** firms that conduct business with other businesses

FIGURE 4.7

Planning for a New Internet Business or Building an Online Presence for an Existing Business

The approach taken to creating an e-business plan will depend on whether you are establishing a new Internet business or adding an online component to an existing business.

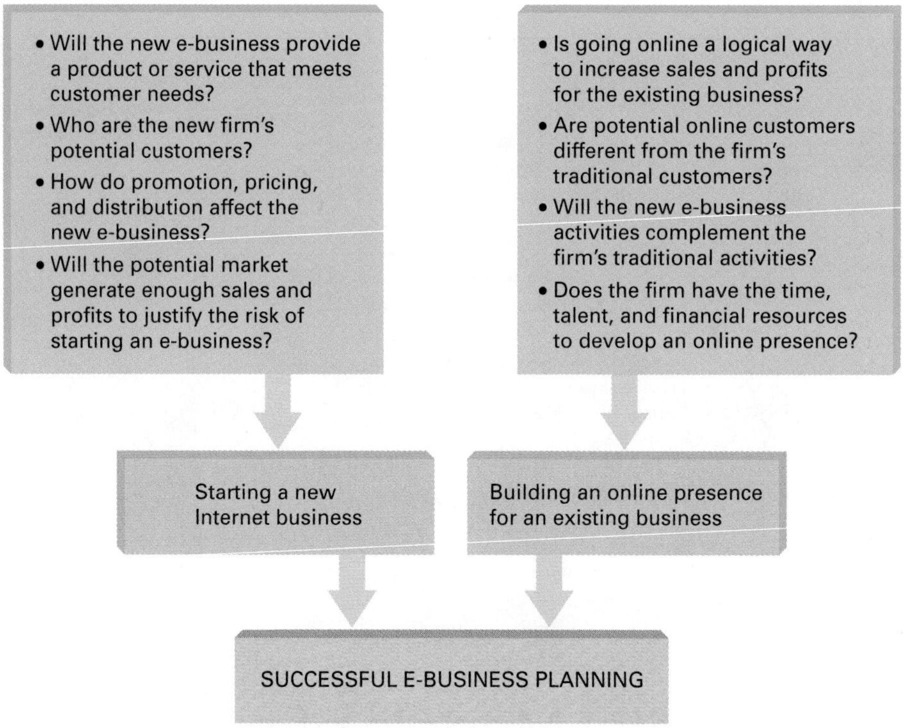

- Will the new e-business provide a product or service that meets customer needs?
- Who are the new firm's potential customers?
- How do promotion, pricing, and distribution affect the new e-business?
- Will the potential market generate enough sales and profits to justify the risk of starting an e-business?

- Is going online a logical way to increase sales and profits for the existing business?
- Are potential online customers different from the firm's traditional customers?
- Will the new e-business activities complement the firm's traditional activities?
- Does the firm have the time, talent, and financial resources to develop an online presence?

Starting a new Internet business

Building an online presence for an existing business

SUCCESSFUL E-BUSINESS PLANNING

ordered, Dell reduces storage and carrying costs and rarely is stuck with unsold inventory. By dealing directly with Dell, customers eliminate costs associated with wholesalers and retailers, thereby helping to reduce the price they pay for equipment.

A second, more complex type of B2B model involves a company and its suppliers. Today, suppliers use the Internet to bid on products and services they wish to sell to a customer and learn about the customer's rules and procedures that must be followed. For example, both General Motors and Ford have developed B2B models to link thousands of suppliers that sell the automobile makers parts worth billions of dollars each year. While the B2B sites are expensive to start and maintain, there are significant savings for General Motors and Ford. Given the potential savings, it is no wonder that many other manufacturers and their suppliers are beginning to use the same kind of B2B systems that are used by the automakers.

Business-to-Consumer (B2C) Model

In contrast to the B2B model, firms such as **Barnesandnoble.com** and **Landsend.com** clearly are focused on individual consumers and so are referred to as having a **business-to-consumer** (or **B2C**) **model**. In a B2C situation, understanding how consumers behave online is critical to a firm's success. Typically, a business firm that uses a B2C model must answer the following questions:

* Will consumers use websites merely to simplify and speed up comparison shopping?
* Will consumers purchase services and products online or end up buying at a traditional retail store?

business-to-consumer (or B2C) model firms that focus on conducting business with individual buyers

* What sorts of products and services are best suited for online consumer shopping?

* Which products and services are simply not good choices at this stage of online development?

In addition to providing round-the-clock global access to all kinds of products and services, B2C firms often attempt to build long-term relationships with their customers. Often firms will make a special effort to make sure that the customer is satisfied and that problems, if any, are solved quickly. While a "little special attention" may increase the cost of doing business for a B2C firm, the customer's repeated purchases will repay the investment many times over.

Today, B2B and B2C models are the most popular business models for e-business. And yet, there are other business models that perform specialized e-business activities to generate revenues. Most of the business models described in Table 4.4 are modified versions of the B2B and B2C models.

Advertising e-business model	Advertisements that are displayed on a firm's website in return for a fee. Examples include pop-up and banner advertisements on search engines and other popular Internet sites.
Brokerage e-business model	Online marketplaces where buyers and sellers are brought together to facilitate exchange of goods and services. Examples include eBay (**www.ebay.com**), which provides a site for buying and selling virtually anything.
Consumer-to-consumer model	Peer-to-peer software that allows individuals to share information over the Internet. Examples include Morpheus (**www.morpheus.com**), which allows users to exchange audio, document, photo, or video files.
Subscription and pay-per-view e-business models	Content that is available only to users who pay a fee to gain access to a website. Examples include investment information provided by Standard & Poor's (**www2.standardandpoors.com**) and business research provided by Forrester Research, Inc. (**www.forrester.com**).

TABLE 4.4

Other Business Models That Perform Specialized e-Business Activities

Although modified versions of B2B or B2C, these business models perform specialized e-business activities to generate revenues.

ACE the Test
ACE & ACE+
Practice Test 4.7

TEST PREPPER 4.7

True or False?

_T_ 1. Subscription and pay-per-view e-business models contain content that is available only to users who pay a fee to gain access to a website.

_F_ 2. A successful e-business would involve only those customers who are seeking the convenience of shopping online and not those who are using the website simply to view a retailer's merchandise and promotions before buying in a retail store.

Multiple Choice

_A_ 3. Interwood is a company that manufactures furniture and operates exclusively online. The majority of Interwood's online orders are from organizations such as schools and offices that are well informed about the furniture they need and are looking for fairly priced, high-quality items in bulk that will be delivered quickly. By manufacturing only what is ordered, Interwood reduces storage and carrying costs and rarely is stuck with unsold inventory. Which of the following business models is this a good example of?

   a. The business-to-business (B2B) model
   b. The business-to-consumer (B2C) model
   c. The consumer-to-consumer model
   d. The advertising e-business model
   e. The brokerage e-business model

 4. Amazon, the online book seller, uses a

   a. business-to-business (B2B) model.
   b. business-to-consumer (B2C) model.
   c. consumer-to-consumer model.
   d. pay-per-use model.
   e. brokerage e-business model.

5. Based on your understanding of Internet banking as an example of an e-business, why is it necessary to enable a strong customer-support system, especially during the initial phases of its introduction?
   a. It facilitates designing, installing, and testing of new technology.
   b. It tests the staff's ability to use it.
   c. It allows companies to train the staff to use it.
   d. It helps customers during the time it takes them to get used to the procedures required to bank online.
   e. Companies demand a rapid change to a new method of placing orders.

The Future of e-Business: Growth, Opportunities, and Challenges

Learning Objective 8

Explore the factors that will affect the future of e-business.

Prepare for Class
Career Snapshot

Since the beginning of commercial activity on the Internet, developments in e-business have been rapid and formidable with spectacular successes such as Google, eBay, and Yahoo!. However, the slowdown in e-business activity that began in 2000 caused a shakeout of excessive optimism in this new-business environment. By 2003, most firms involved in e-business used a more intelligent approach to development. Today, we can safely say that the long-term view held by the vast majority of analysts is that the Internet will continue to expand along with related technologies. For example, according to Forrester Research, Inc., the popularity and growth of consumer broadband access to the Internet have pushed marketers to allocate more money to advertising online in order to reach customers who are moving to the web and away from traditional media such as television and radio. As a result, Forrester predicts that by 2010, more than $26 billion, or about 8 percent of all advertising spending, will be online.[6]

Internet Growth Potential

To date, only a small percentage of the global population uses the Internet. Current estimates suggest that about one billion of the six billion people in the world use the web, and only about 60 percent of them are active users. Clearly, there is much more growth opportunity. Americans comprise 20 percent of all users—the largest group online.[7] Of the almost 300 million people making up the American population, 185 million use the Internet—140 million actively. And more than 40 percent of Americans enjoy fast broadband access at home, suggesting future development of more online activity requiring high-speed service such as downloading entertainment content and games.[8]

CONCEPT CHECK

How do internal and external forces change the way an e-business operates?

Even with any future economic downturn, the Internet will continue to offer great opportunities for growth. Firms that adapt existing business models to an online environment will continue to dominate development. Books, CDs, clothing, hotel accommodations, car rentals, and travel reservations are products and services well suited to online buying and selling. These products or services will continue to be sold in the traditional way, as well as in a more cost-effective and efficient fashion over the Internet.

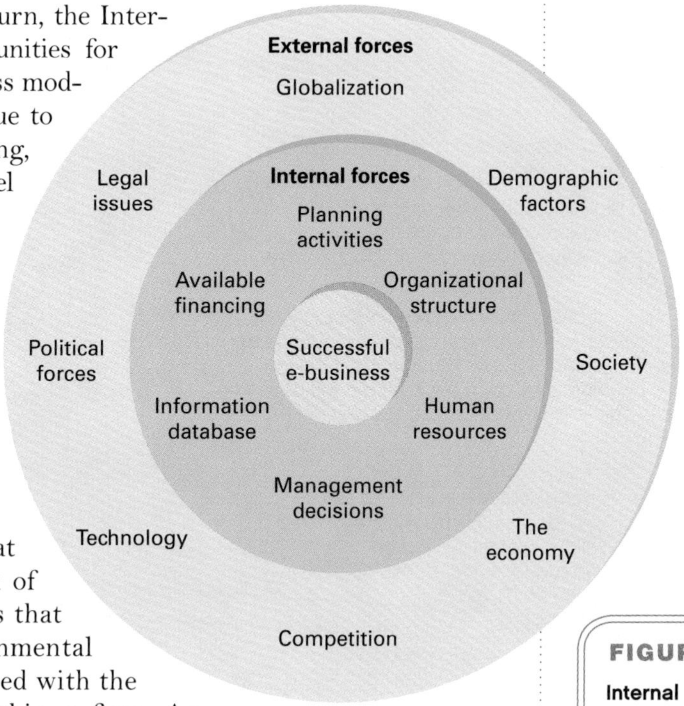

Environmental Forces Affecting e-Business

Although the environmental forces at work are complex, it is useful to think of them as either *internal* or *external* forces that affect an e-business. Internal environmental forces are those that are closely associated with the actions and decisions taking place within a firm. As shown in Figure 4.8, typical internal forces include a firm's planning activities, organization structure, human resources, management decisions, information database, and available financing. **EXAMPLE** A shortage of skilled employees needed for a specialized project can undermine a firm's ability to sell its services to clients. Unlike the external environmental forces affecting the firm, internal forces such as this one are more likely to be under the direct control of management. In this case, management can either hire the needed staff or choose to pass over a prospective project.

In contrast, external environmental forces are factors affecting e-business planning that originate from outside the organization. These forces are unlikely to be controllable by an e-business firm. Instead, managers and employees of an e-business firm generally will react to these forces, attempting to shield the organization from any undue negative effects and finding ways to take advantage of opportunities in the ever-changing e-business environment. **EXAMPLE** The primary external environmental forces affecting e-business planning include globalization, society, demographic, economic, competitive, technological, and political and legal forces.

This chapter has presented an overview of information on the fast-paced, emerging world of e-business. Throughout this book you will find more references to and examples of both information and e-business as they apply to the different aspects of business, such as management, marketing, and finance. In Chapters 5 and 6 we examine issues related to forms of business ownership and special considerations surrounding small business.

FIGURE 4.8

Internal and External Forces That Affect an e-Business

Today, managers and employees of an e-business must respond to internal forces within the organization and external forces outside the organization.

TEST PREPPER 4.8

True or False?

_T_ 1. To date, only a small percentage of the global population uses the Internet.

_F_ 2. Change in legislation regarding the way in which a candy manufacturer can advertise on children's websites is a good example of external forces that affect an e-business.

_F_ 3. Books, CDs, clothing, hotel accommodations, car rentals, and travel reservations are products and services well suited to online buying and selling. Experts predict that over time, these will cease to be sold in the traditional way, in stores.

Multiple Choice

_D_ 4. Internal environmental forces are those that are closely associated with the actions and decisions taking place within a firm. Based on this definition, which of the following is *not* an example of internal environmental forces?

   a. Variation in a firm's planning activities
   b. Overhaul of a company's organization structure
   c. Updating a company's information database
   d. Demand for a company's product owing to demographic change
   e. Cutbacks in financing available for the company

_B_ 5. Why is an accurate, up-to-date customer database so vital to the success of the e-business side of Carol's Daughter?

   a. It enables managers to track how customers respond to high-profile investors, such as Will Smith and Jada Pinkett Smith.
   b. The company consistently updates its strategy based on information from sources such as sales reports.
   c. It enables the marketing division to advertise the latest products.
   d. Customers are kept up-to-date through e-mail newsletters and promotions.
   e. It enables easy browsing for customers.

ACE the Test
ACE & ACE+
Practice Test 4.8

Prepare for Class
CL News Feeds
CL News Now

→ RETURN TO INSIDE BUSINESS

Although the beauty business is crowded and competitive, Carol's Daughter is making a splash with its unique products and its celebrity investors. Some of the high-profile investors, including Will Smith and Jada Pinkett Smith, have appeared in the company's advertising and on its website—which only adds to the company's glamour.

Based on information from sources such as sales reports, the company continually updates and improves its website and catalogs, dropping slower-selling products to make room for new items cooked up by founder Lisa Price. Steve Stoute, who put the investment group together, sees great long-term potential: "We're not stopping at skin care or hair care. We'll go into household goods like fabric and dishwashing liquids." In the future, says Stoute, Carol's Daughter will be "a billion-dollar opportunity."

Questions

1. Why is an accurate, up-to-date customer database so vital to the success of the e-business side of Carol's Daughter?
2. Now that Carol's Daughter has retail locations in New York and New Jersey, would you recommend using its website to recruit store employees? Explain your answer.

LEARNING OBJECTIVES REVIEW

1 Examine how information can reduce risk when making a decision.

- The more information a manager has, the less risk there is that a decision will be incorrect.

- Information produces knowledge and empowers managers and employees to make better decisions.

- Information rules shorten the time spent analyzing choices. Information rules emerge when business research confirms the same results each time it studies the same or a similar set of circumstances.

- Data are numerical or verbal descriptions that usually result from some sort of measurement.

- A database is a single collection of data stored in one place that can be used by people throughout an organization to make decisions.

- Knowledge management (KM) is a firm's procedures for generating, using, and sharing the data and information contained in the firm's databases.

- A management information system (MIS) is a means of providing managers with the information they need to perform their jobs as effectively as possible.

2 Discuss management's information requirements.

- An MIS distributes timely and useful information from both internal and external sources to the decision makers who need it.

- The specific types of information managers need depend on their area of management and level within the firm.

- The size and complexity of an MIS must be tailored to the information needs of the organization it serves.

3 Outline the five functions of an information system.

- The five functions performed by an MIS system are
  - Collecting data
  - Storing data
  - Updating data
  - Processing data into information
  - Presenting information to users

- Internal sources of data can be company records, reports, and minutes of meetings. External sources include customers, suppliers, bankers, trade and financial publications, industry conferences, online computer services, and information-gathering organizations.

- An MIS must be able to store data until they are needed and to update them regularly to ensure that the information presented to managers is accurate, complete, and timely.

- Large groups of numerical data usually are processed into summary numbers called *statistics.*

- Verbal information generally is presented in the form of a report.

- Numerical information most often is displayed in graphs, charts, or tables.

4 Describe how the Internet helps in decision making, communications, sales, and recruiting and training.

- Decision-support systems, executive information systems, and expert systems can help managers and employees to speed and improve the decision-making process.

- Groupware is software that facilitates the management of large projects among geographically dispersed employees as well as such group activities as problem solving and brainstorming.

- The Internet and a customer relationship management software program can provide a database of information that can be used to assist a sales representative.

- The Internet can be used to improve employee recruitment and training while lowering costs.

- Integrated software combines many functions in a single package and also allows for the easy linking of text, numerical data, graphs, photos, and even audiovisual clips. Once data have been entered into an application, the data can be used in another integrated package without having to be reentered into the system.

Improve Your Grade
Audio Chapter Review & Quiz

5 **Analyze how computers and technology change the way information is acquired, organized, and used.**

- The Internet is a worldwide network of computers linked through telecommunications. Firms also can use an intranet to distribute information within the firm.

- A computer network is a group of two or more computers linked together to allow users to share data and information.

- Two basic types of networks are local-area networks (LANs) and wide-area networks (WAN). These affect the way employees and the general public obtain data and information.

6 **Explain the meaning of e-business.**

- e-Business, or electronic business, can be defined as the organized effort of individuals to produce and sell, for a profit, the products and services that satisfy society's needs *through the facilities available on the Internet.*

- The human, material, information, and financial resources that any business requires are highly specialized for e-business.

- To reduce the cost of e-business resources, many firms have turned to outsourcing.

- Using e-business activities, it is possible to satisfy new customer needs created by the Internet as well as traditional ones in unique ways.

- Meeting customer needs is especially important when an e-business is trying to earn profits by increasing sales and reducing expenses.

- Each source of revenue flowing into a firm is referred to as a *revenue stream.*

7 **Describe the fundamental models of e-business.**

- e-Business models focus attention on the identity of a firm's customers.

- Firms that use the Internet mainly to conduct business with other businesses generally are referred to as having a business-to-business, or B2B, model.

- There are two types of B2B business firms:
  - The first type of B2B focuses on facilitating sales transactions between businesses.
  - A second, more complex type of the B2B model involves a company and its suppliers.

- In a B2C situation, understanding how consumers behave online is critical to the firm's success.

- Successful B2C firms often make a special effort to build long-term relationships with their customers.

8 **Explore the factors that will affect the future of e-business.**

- Since the advent of commercial activity on the Internet, developments in e-business have been rapid and formidable.

- The slowdown in e-business activity that began in 2000 caused a shakeout of excessive optimism in this new business environment. By 2003, most firms involved in e-business used a more intelligent approach to development.

- The long-term view held by the vast majority of analysts is that the Internet will continue to expand along with related technologies.

- Internal environmental forces are those that are closely associated with the actions and decisions taking place within a firm.

- External environmental forces are those affecting an e-business originating outside an organization.

VIDEO CASE

Travelocity Takes e-Business a Long Way

One of the original online travel agency sites, Travelocity, has been bookmarked by millions of people seeking low prices on airline tickets, hotel rooms, cruises, and rental cars. The site books $10 billion worth of travel annually to destinations near and far. Customers can search for flights on six major carriers, read descriptions before reserving at one of 20,000 participating hotels, compare car-rental prices, and click to browse and buy specially priced travel packages.

Travelocity began its e-business life as a site for finding the lowest airfares. However, its chief marketing officer notes that the company actually makes its money on hotel rooms and travel packages, not on airline tickets. This is why the site goes beyond emphasizing price to feature vacation packages and hotel choices more prominently—a change that has increased sales of these lucrative offerings dramatically.

Intense competition from Expedia and other online rivals has prompted Travelocity to find new ways of differentiating itself and keeping customers loyal. According to the CEO, the company is particularly interested in creating "an emotional connection with customers, one that builds more trust and bookings." Instead of focusing solely on low prices, Travelocity has invested $80 million in its "Roaming Gnome" ad campaign. The colorful garden gnome attracts attention and brings both personality and humor to the message that Travelocity stands for the whole travel experience, not just low prices.

In addition, the site has posted a "Customer Bill of Rights" guaranteeing customers that "everything about your booking will be right, or we'll work with our partners to make it right and right away." Although many e-businesses offer customer service by live chat, e-mail, and FAQ (frequently asked questions) pages, Travelocity encourages customers to call if something goes wrong with their travel arrangements so that company representatives can fix the problem. The CEO observes that customers whose problems are resolved satisfactorily have a 90 percent return rate,

compared with an 80 percent rate for customers who have a good experience.

Not long ago, Travelocity had the opportunity to put the spotlight on its guarantee when it posted a superlow airfare for flights to Fiji. The rock-bottom price was supposed to apply to companion tickets only, but because the fare was posted in error, travelers were unsure initially whether Travelocity really would issue the tickets. The company decided to honor the fare, despite the mistake, to prove its commitment to taking care of customers. This brought a lot of positive media coverage, further enhancing Travelocity's reputation.

The company recently redesigned its website so that customers can find exactly what they want and have more tools for planning all aspects of a trip. For example, customers can buy tickets to city tours, price travel insurance, buy gift certificates, check flight status, read about different destinations, and read what travelers have to say about the hotels.

Before making major changes to the site, Travelocity conducts usability testing to see how customers react to new features and to uncover problems customers might encounter when trying to buy. For example, the company learned that many people forgot their passwords and clicked away at the last minute because they needed the password to complete a purchase. To solve this problem, Travelocity removed the requirement and allowed customers to buy without inputting a password. Sales soared by 10 percent almost overnight, increasing revenue by millions of dollars.

Travelocity operates a number of other travel sites, including **lastminute.com, showtickets.com,** and **site59.com.** The company has been branching out into corporate travel services and specialized travel sites for international markets. It also provides travel services for the members of AARP and other organizations. Where in the world will Travelocity's Roaming Gnome turn up next?[9]

For more information about this company, go to **www .travelocity.com.**

Questions

1. Each year Travelocity helps millions of customers find low prices on airline tickets, hotel rooms, cruises, and rental cars by providing a website that is easy to use. What type of business model is Travelocity using? Support your answer.

2. Today, competition between Internet travel firms such as Travelocity, Expedia, and other online travel agencies has never been greater. What steps has Travelocity taken to retain its market share and increase revenues and profits?

3. Why would Travelocity publicize the availability of telephone customer service when higher call volume raises the company's costs?

4. AARP, an association for consumers over fifty years of age, has partnered with Travelocity to offer travel services to members through a site called "AARP Passport powered by Travelocity." From Travelocity's perspective, what are the pros and cons of having both the AARP and the Travelocity name on this travel site?

BUILDING SKILLS FOR CAREER SUCCESS

1. Exploring the Internet

Computer technology is a fast-paced, highly competitive industry in which product life cycles sometimes are measured in months or even weeks. To keep up with changes and trends in hardware and software, MIS managers routinely must scan computer publications and websites that discuss new products.

A major topic of interest among MIS managers is groupware, software that facilitates the management of large projects among geographically dispersed employees, as well as group activities such as problem solving and brainstorming.

Assignment

1. Use a search engine and enter the keyword "groupware" to locate companies that provide this type of software. Try the demonstration edition of the groupware if it is available.

2. Based on your research of this business application, why do you think groupware is growing in popularity?

3. Describe the structure of one of the groupware programs you examined as well as your impressions of its value to users.

2. Building Team Skills

An interesting approach taken by Yahoo.com and several other websites is to provide viewers with the tools needed to create a personal web page or community. Yahoo's GeoCities site (**http://geocities.yahoo.com**) provides simple instructions for creating a site and posting your own content, such as articles and photographs.

Assignment

1. Working in a group, examine some of the GeoCities communities and personal web pages. Discuss which sites you think work well and which do not. Explain your reasoning.

2. Develop an idea for your own website. Draw a sketch of how you would like the site to appear on the Internet. You may use ideas that look good on other personal pages.

3. Who is your target audience, and why do you think they will want to visit the site?

3. Researching Different Careers

Firms today expect employees to be proficient in using computers and computer software. Typical business applications include e-mail, word processing, spreadsheets, and graphics. By improving your skills in these areas, you can increase your chances not only of being employed but also of being promoted once you are employed.

Assignment

1. Assess your computer skills by placing a check in the appropriate column in the following table:

Skill level SOFTWARE	NONE	LOW	AVERAGE	HIGH
Word processing				
Desktop publishing				
Accounting				
Database management				
Graphics				
Spreadsheet				
Groupware				

2. Describe your self-assessment in a written report. Specify the software programs in which you need to become more proficient, and outline a plan for doing this.

Prepare for Class
Exploring the Internet

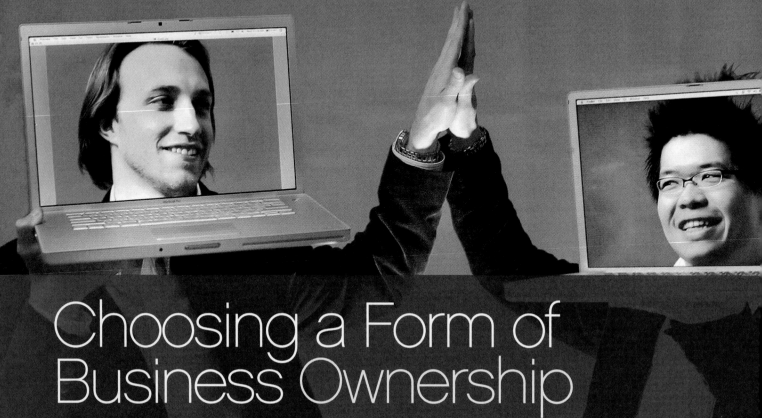

Choosing a Form of Business Ownership

Your Guide to Success in Business

Why this chapter matters
There's a good chance that during your lifetime you will work for a business or start a business. With this fact in mind, the material in this chapter can help you to understand how and why businesses are organized.

LEARNING OBJECTIVES

1. Describe a sole proprietorship and list its advantages and disadvantages.

2. Define and explain the different types of partnerships and the importance of partnership agreements.

3. Describe the advantages and disadvantages of partnerships.

4. Summarize how a corporation is formed.

5. Describe the advantages and disadvantages of a corporation.

6. Examine special types of corporations, including S-corporations, limited-liability companies, and not-for-profit corporations.

7. Discuss the purpose of a cooperative, joint venture, and syndicate.

8. Explain how growth from within and growth through mergers can enable a business to expand.

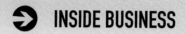

Johnson & Johnson: Brothers, Partners, Corporate Leaders

Band-Aid bandages and Johnson's Baby Powder might never have been invented without the partnership of three brothers. Today, after more than 120 years of spectacular growth, the Johnson & Johnson (J&J) partnership has evolved into a $50 billion corporation with 116,000 employees in fifty-seven countries. From contact lenses to coronary stents, surgical supplies to sugar substitutes, Johnson & Johnson now offers an extremely wide range of consumer and health care products.

However, antiseptic bandages and baby powder were not commercially available in 1886, when Robert Johnson joined the partnership his brothers Edward and James had founded a year earlier. The partners set up a factory in New Brunswick, New Jersey, and began manufacturing surgical dressings to sell to hospitals. They incorporated as Johnson & Johnson in 1887 and continued to develop innovative products for home and hospital use, including the well-known baby powder. The company went public in 1944, and it has paid dividends to stockholders every year since.

These days, J&J is admired as much for its credo as for its ground-breaking products. The credo details J&J's responsibilities to four groups, in this order: Customers come first, followed by employees and the community, and—finally—stockholders. When the credo was adopted in the 1940s, few corporations believed that a customer-oriented, socially responsible approach to business was the best way to serve their stockholders' interests. Yet decade after decade, following the credo has enabled J&J to prosper and polish its reputation, even during periods of crisis.

J&J has a long history of using acquisitions to fuel aggressive growth. In fact, some of the acquired companies went on to launch a number of J&J's biggest and best-known products, including Tylenol pain reliever and Splenda sweetener. Like the three founders, J&J's forward-thinking managers have, over the years, put special emphasis on product innovation. That emphasis has paid off: Today, one-third of the company's sales revenue comes from products that didn't exist five years ago. Looking ahead, what innovations and challenges will the future hold for J&J?[1]

> **DID YOU KNOW?**
>
> J&J, a partnership turned corporation, earns one-third of its $50 billion in annual sales from products that didn't exist five years ago.

K E Y   T E R M S

sole proprietorship (146)
unlimited liability (148)
partnership (150)
general partner (150)
limited partner (151)
master limited partnership (MLP) (151)
corporation (156)
stock (156)

stockholders (156)
closed corporation (156)
open corporation (157)
domestic corporation (158)
foreign corporation (158)
alien corporation (158)
corporate charter (158)
common stock (158)
preferred stock (158)

dividend (158)
proxy (158)
board of directors (159)
corporate officers (159)
limited liability (160)
S-corporation (164)
limited-liability company (LLC) (164)
not-for-profit corporation (165)

cooperative (166)
joint venture (167)
syndicate (168)
merger (169)
hostile takeover (169)
tender offer (169)
proxy fight (169)
leveraged buyout (LBO) (171)

ACE the Test
Crossword Puzzle
Flashcards

While most of us think of Johnson & Johnson (or simply J&J) as the corporation that manufacturers bandages, it is so much more. Consider three facts about this global giant. First, it is now a corporation. Although J&J started as a partnership, the corporate form of ownership was chosen because it offers a number of advantages when compared with other forms of ownership. We'll discuss each of the major forms of ownership in this chapter. Second, J&J is profitable. While some would-be business owners think that if they incorporate, their business will automatically be profitable, the fact is that there's more to earning a profit than the type of ownership you choose. In today's competitive business world, any corporation, sole proprietorship, *or* partnership must produce products and services that customers want. Finally, J&J is a good corporate citizen. The company is committed to giving back resources to the communities in which it operates. In today's competitive environment, it's common to hear of profitable companies. It is less common to hear of profitable companies that are held in high regard by their competitors. And yet, J&J has managed to do both—earn both profits and respect.

Many people dream of opening a business, and one of the first decisions they must make is *what form of ownership* to choose. In this chapter we

* Describe the three common forms of business ownership: sole proprietorships, partnerships, and corporations.

* Discuss how these types of businesses are formed and note the advantages and disadvantages of each.

* Consider several types of business ownership usually chosen for special purposes, including S-corporations, limited-liability companies, not-for-profit corporations, cooperatives, joint ventures, and syndicates.

* Conclude with a discussion of how businesses can grow through internal expansion or through mergers with other companies.

Sole Proprietorships

Learning Objective 1

Describe a sole proprietorship and list its advantages and disadvantages.

ACE the Test
Hangman

sole proprietorship a business that is owned (and usually operated) by one person

A **sole proprietorship** is a business that is owned (and usually operated) by one person. Although a few sole proprietorships are large and have many employees, most are small. Sole proprietorship is the simplest form of business ownership and the easiest to start. In most instances, the owner (the *sole* proprietor) simply decides that he or she is in business and begins operations. **EXAMPLE** Some of today's largest corporations, including Ford Motor Company, H.J. Heinz Company, and J.C. Penney Company, started out as tiny—and in many cases, struggling—sole proprietorships.

As you can see in Figure 5.1, there are more than 18.9 million sole proprietorships in the United States. They account for 72 percent of the country's business firms. Although the most popular form of ownership when compared with partnerships and corporations, they rank last in total sales revenues. As shown in Figure 5.2, sole proprietorships account for just over $1 trillion, or about 5 percent, of total sales.

Sole proprietorships are most common in retailing, service, and agriculture. Thus the clothing boutique, television repair shop down the street, and small, independent farmer are likely to be sole proprietorships. In addition to more traditional sole proprietorships, many entrepreneurs have started their own consulting services firms. Not only can they pick and choose which job assignments to accept, but they also have found that they can earn more money by not working exclusively for one firm as a salaried employee.

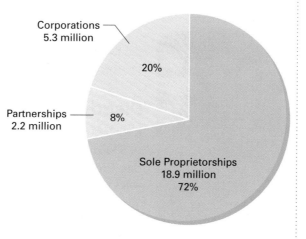

Corporations
5.3 million

20%

Partnerships
2.2 million

8%

Sole Proprietorships
18.9 million
72%

FIGURE 5.1

Relative Percentages of Sole Proprietorships, Partnerships, and Corporations in the United States

Sole proprietorships, the most widespread form of business ownership, are most common in retailing, the service industries, and agriculture.

Source: U.S. Bureau of the Census, *Statistical Abstract of the United States*, 125th ed., Washington, D.C.: U.S. Government Printing Office, 2006, p. 503, **www.census.gov.**

Advantages of Sole Proprietorships

Most of the advantages of sole proprietorships arise from the two main characteristics of this form of ownership: *simplicity* and *individual control*.

Ease of Start-up and Closure Sole proprietorship is the simplest and cheapest way to start a business. Often, start-up requires no contracts, agreements, or other legal documents. The legal requirements often are limited to registering the name of the business and obtaining any necessary licenses or permits.

If the enterprise does not succeed, the firm can be closed as easily as it was opened, after paying the creditors.

Pride of Ownership A successful sole proprietor is often very proud of her or his accomplishments—and rightfully so. In almost every case, the owner deserves a great deal of credit for assuming the risks and solving the day-to-day problems associated with operating a sole proprietorship. Unfortunately, the reverse is also true. When the business fails, it is often the sole proprietor who is to blame.

Retention of All Profits Because all profits become the personal earnings of the owner, the owner has a strong incentive to succeed. This direct financial reward attracts many entrepreneurs to the sole proprietorship form of business and, if the business succeeds, is a source of great satisfaction.

Flexibility of Being Your Own Boss A sole proprietor is completely free to make decisions about the firm's operations. Without asking or waiting for anyone's approval, a sole proprietor can switch from retailing to wholesaling, move a shop's location, open a new store, or close an old one.

No Special Taxes Profits earned by a sole proprietorship are taxed as the personal income of the owner. As a result, sole

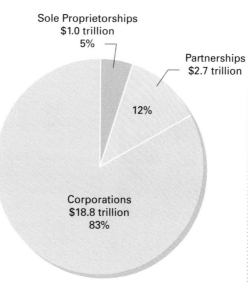

Sole Proprietorships
$1.0 trillion
5%

Partnerships
$2.7 trillion

12%

Corporations
$18.8 trillion
83%

FIGURE 5.2

Total Sales Receipts of American Businesses

Although corporations account for only about 20 percent of U.S. businesses, they bring in 83 percent of sales receipts.

Source: U.S. Bureau of the Census, *Statistical Abstract of the United States*, 125th ed., Washington, D.C.: U.S. Government Printing Office, 2006, p. 503, **www.census.gov.**

One Happy Business Owner!

John Avila's smile could be because his company—Avila Retail Development and Management—has successful retail stores in Albuquerque, Denver, and Phoenix. Avila started his company in New Mexico—a state that leads the nation in the percentage of Hispanic-owned businesses according to the U.S. Commerce Department.

unlimited liability a legal concept that holds a business owner personally responsible for all the debts of the business

SP☉TLIGHT

Profits for proprietors

As a reward for taking the risks of opening a business, proprietors receive profits. The amounts below are for all proprietors.

In billions of dollars

$ 728.4

$ 970.7

| 2000 | Today |

Source: The U.S. Department of Commerce and the Bureau of Economic Analysis. Website: **www.bea.gov**; accessed May 2, 2006.

proprietors must report certain financial information on their personal tax returns and make estimated quarterly tax payments to the federal government. Thus a sole proprietorship does not pay the special state and federal income taxes that corporations pay.

Disadvantages of Sole Proprietorships

The disadvantages of a sole proprietorship stem from the fact that these businesses are owned by one person. Some capable sole proprietors experience no problems. Individuals who start out with few management skills and little money are most at risk for failure.

Unlimited Liability Unlimited liability is a legal concept that holds a business owner personally responsible for all the debts of the business. There is no difference legally between the debts of the business and the debts of the proprietor. If the business fails, or if the business is involved in a lawsuit and loses, the owner's personal property—including savings and other assets—can be seized (and sold, if necessary) to pay creditors.

Unlimited liability is perhaps the major factor that tends to discourage would-be entrepreneurs with substantial personal wealth from using this form of business organization.

Lack of Continuity Legally, the sole proprietor *is* the business. If the owner retires, dies, or is declared legally incompetent, the business essentially ceases to exist. In many cases, however—especially when the business is a profitable enterprise—the owner's heirs take it over and either sell it or continue to operate it. An illness can be devastating if the sole proprietor's personal skills are what determine if the business is a success or a failure.

Lack of Money Banks, suppliers, and other lenders usually are unwilling to lend large sums of money to sole proprietorships. Only one person—the sole proprietor—can be held responsible for repaying such loans, and the assets of most sole proprietors usually are limited. Moreover, these assets may have been used already as the basis for personal borrowing (a home mortgage or car loan) or for short-term credit from suppliers. Lenders also worry about the lack of continuity of sole proprietorships: Who will repay a loan if the sole proprietor dies? Finally, many lenders are concerned about the large number of sole proprietorships that fail—a topic discussed in Chapter 6.

The limited ability to borrow money can prevent a sole proprietorship from growing. It is the main reason that many business owners, when in need of relatively large amounts of capital, change from a sole proprietorship to a partnership or corporate form of ownership.

Limited Management Skills The sole proprietor is often the sole manager—in addition to being the only salesperson, buyer, accountant, and on occasion, janitor. Even the most experienced business owner is unlikely to have expertise in all these areas. Consequently, unless he or she obtains the necessary expertise by hiring employees, assistants, or consultants, the business can suffer in the areas in which the owner is less knowledgeable. For the many sole proprietors who cannot hire the help they need, there just are not enough hours in the day to do everything that needs to be done.

Difficulty in Hiring Employees The sole proprietor may find it hard to attract and keep competent help. Potential employees may feel that there is no room for advancement in a firm whose owner assumes all managerial responsibilities. And when those who *are* hired are ready to take on added responsibility, they may find that the only way to do so is to quit the sole proprietorship and go to work for a larger firm or start their own businesses. The lure of higher salaries and increased benefits (especially hospitalization) also may cause existing employees to change jobs.

Beyond the Sole Proprietorship

Like many others, you may decide that the major disadvantage of a sole proprietorship is the limited amount that one person can do in a workday. One way to reduce the effect of this disadvantage (and retain many of the advantages) is to have more than one owner.

CONCEPT CHECK
If you were to start a business, which ownership form would you choose? What factors might affect your choice?

TEST PREPPER 5.1

True or False?

___F___ 1. In 1886, Robert Johnson joined Johnson & Johnson, the business his brothers Edward and James had founded a year earlier. This is an example of a sole proprietorship.

___T___ 2. *Lack of continuity* refers to a situation where if the owner of a company retires, dies, or is declared legally incompetent, the business essentially ceases to exist, and this is seen as a disadvantage of starting a sole proprietorship.

Multiple Choice

___a___ 3. During college, Elyssa Wood earned extra money by using her culinary skills to cater special parties. After graduation, she decided to turn her job into a full time business. She will *most likely* organize the business as a
   a. limited partnership.
   b. corporation.
   c. general partnership.
   d. sole proprietorship.
   c. cooperative.

___A___ 4. Simplicity and individual control are features of which one of the following types of organizations?
   a. Sole proprietorship
   b. Limited-Liability Company
   c. Not-for-profit corporation
   d. Multinational corporation
   e. Open Corporation

___E___ 5. Based on your understanding of sole proprietorships, which of the following is *not* an incentive for owners of a sole proprietorship over other types of business ownership?
   a. Ease of start-up and closure
   b. Pride of ownership
   c. Retention of all profits
   d. Flexibility of being your own boss
   e. Unlimited liability

ACE the Test
ACE & ACE+
Practice Test 5.1

Partalnerships

Learning Objective

Define and explain the different types of partnerships and
the importance of partnership agreements.

partnership a voluntary
association of two or
more persons to act as
co-owners of a business
for profit

The U.S. Uniform Partnership Act defines a **partnership** as a voluntary association
of two or more persons to act as co-owners of a business for profit. **EXAMPLE** In
1990, two young African-American entrepreneurs named Janet Smith and Gary
Smith started Ivy Planning Group—a company that provides strategic planning and
performance measurement for clients. Today, more than fifteen years later, the company has evolved into a multimillion-dollar company that has hired a diverse staff of
employees and provides cultural diversity training for *Fortune* 1000 firms and government agencies.[2]

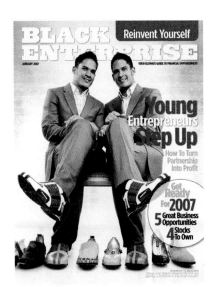

**Sometimes it takes
more than one
business owner!**

When an entrepreneur
doesn't have what it
takes to operate a
successful business,
many business owners
opt to form a partner-
ship. The ability to
attract a partner(s)
with the right combina-
tion of business skills,
knowledge, and man-
agement expertise can
increase the chances
of success and reduce
the risk of failure.

As shown in Figures 5.1 and 5.2, there are approximately 2.2 million partnerships in the United
States, and this type of ownership accounts for
about $2.7 trillion in sales receipts each year. Note,
however, that this form of ownership is much less
common than the sole proprietorship or the corporation. In fact, as Figure 5.1 shows, partnerships
represent only about 8 percent of all American
businesses. Although there is no legal maximum
on the number of partners a partnership may have,
most have only two. Large accounting, law, and
advertising partnerships, however, are likely to
have multiple partners. Regardless of the number
of people involved, a partnership often represents
a pooling of special managerial skills and talents;
at other times, it is the result of a sole proprietor's
taking on a partner for the purpose of obtaining
more capital.

Types of Partners

All partners are not necessarily equal. Some may be active in running the business,
whereas others may have a limited role.

general partner a person
who assumes full or
shared responsibility for
operating a business

General Partners A **general partner** is a person who assumes full or shared
responsibility for operating a business. General partners are active in day-to-day business operations, and each partner can enter into contracts on behalf of the other partners.
A general partner also assumes unlimited liability for all debts, including debts incurred
by any other general partner without his or her knowledge or consent. A *general partnership* is a business co-owned by two or more general partners who are liable for everything the business does. To avoid future liability, a general partner who withdraws from
the partnership must give notice to creditors, customers, and suppliers.

Limited Partners A **limited partner** is a person who contributes capital to a business but who has no management responsibility or liability for losses beyond his or her investment in the partnership. A *limited partnership* is a business co-owned by one or more general partners who manage the business and limited partners who invest money in it. Typically, the general partner or partners collect management fees and receive a percentage of profits. Limited partners receive a portion of profits and tax benefits.

Because of potential liability problems, special rules apply to limited partnerships. These rules are intended to protect customers and creditors who deal with limited partnerships. For example, prospective partners in a limited partnership must file a formal declaration, usually with the secretary of state or at their county courthouse, that describes the essential details of the partnership and the liability status of each partner involved in the business. At least one general partner must be responsible for the debts of the limited partnership. Also, some states prohibit the use of the limited partner's name in the partnership's name.

A special type of limited partnership is referred to as a *master limited partnership*. A **master limited partnership (MLP)** (sometimes referred to as a *publicly traded partnership*, or PTP) is a business partnership that is owned and managed like a corporation but often taxed like a partnership. This special ownership arrangement has a major advantage: Units of ownership in MLPs can be sold to investors to raise capital and often are traded on organized security exchanges. Because MLP units can be traded on an exchange, investors can sell their units of ownership at any time, hopefully for a profit. For more information on MLPs, visit the National Association of Publicly Traded Partnerships website at **www.naptp.org.**

The Internal Revenue Service has limited many of the tax advantages of MLPs. Also, people who invest in MLPs often must file additional complicated tax forms. While there are exceptions, most MLPs typically involve exploration for natural resources, oil or natural gas wells, or distribution companies for oil, natural gas, propane, or home heating oil.

The Partnership Agreement

Articles of partnership are an agreement listing and explaining the terms of the partnership. Although both oral and written partnership agreements are legal and can be enforced in the courts, a written agreement has an obvious advantage: It is not subject to lapses of memory.

Figure 5.3 shows a typical partnership agreement. The partnership agreement should state

* Who will make the final decisions
* What each partner's duties will be
* The investment each partner will make
* How much profit or loss each partner receives or is responsible for
* What happens if a partner wants to dissolve the partnership or dies

When entering into a partnership agreement, partners would be wise to let a neutral third party—a consultant, an accountant, a lawyer, or a mutual friend—assist with any disputes that might arise.

limited partner a person who contributes capital to a business but has no management responsibility or liability for losses beyond the amount he or she invested in the partnership

master limited partnership (MLP) a business partnership that is owned and managed like a corporation but often taxed like a partnership

CONCEPT CHECK

What is the difference between a general partner and a limited partner?

FIGURE 5.3

Articles of Partnership

Articles of partnership are a written or oral agreement that lists and explains the terms of a partnership.

Source: Adapted from Arnold Goldman and William Sigismond, *Business Law*, 5th edition. Boston: Houghton Mifflin, © 2007. Reprinted with permission.

PARTNERSHIP AGREEMENT

Names of partners — This agreement, made June 20, 2007, between Penelope Wolfburg of 783A South Street, Hazelton, Idaho, and Ingrid Swenson of RR 5, Box 96, Hazelton, Idaho.

Nature, name and address of business —
1. The above named persons have this day formed a partnership that shall operate under the name of W-S Jewelers, located at 85 Broad Street, Hazelton, Idaho 83335, and shall engage in jewelry sales and repairs.

Duration of partnership —
2. The duration of this agreement will be for a term of fifteen (15) years, beginning June 20, 2007, or for a shorter period if agreed upon in writing by both partners.

Contribution of capital —
3. The initial investment by each partner will be as follows: Penelope Wolfburg, assets and liabilities of Wolfburg's Jewelry Store, valued at a capital investment of $40,000; Ingrid Swenson, cash of $20,000. These investments are partnership property.

Duties of each partner —
4. Each partner will give her time, skill, and attention to the operation of this partnership and will engage in no other business enterprise unless permission is granted in writing by the other partner.

Salaries, withdrawals, and distribution of profits —
5. The salary for each partner will be as follows: Penelope Wolfburg, $40,000 per year; Ingrid Swenson, $30,000 per year. Neither partner may withdraw cash or other assets from the business without express permission in writing from the other partner. All profits and losses of the business will be shared as follows: Penelope Wolfburg, 60 percent; Ingrid Swenson, 40 percent.

Termination —
6. Upon the dissolution of the partnership due to termination of this agreement, or to written permission by each of the partners, or to the death or incapacitation of one or both partners, a new contract may be entered into by the partners or the sole continuing partner has the option to purchase the other partner's interest in the business at a price that shall not exceed the balance in the terminating partner's capital account. The payment shall be made in cash in equal quarterly installments from the date of termination.

7. At the conclusion of this contract, unless it is agreed by both partners to continue the operation of the business under a new contract, the assets of the partnership, after the liabilities are paid, will be divided in proportion to the balance in each partner's capital account on that date.

Signatures —
Penelope Wolfburg   *Ingrid Swenson*
_____   _____
Penelope Wolfburg   Ingrid Swenson

Date —
June 20, 2007   *June 20, 2007*
_____   _____
Date   Date

ACE the Test
ACE & ACE+
Practice Test 5.2

TEST PREPPER 5.2

True or False?

___ 1. A partnership is a voluntary association of two or more persons to act as co-owners of a business for profit.

___ 2. A major incentive to be a partner in a master limited partnership is that units of ownership can be traded on an exchange.

___ 3. Articles of partnership are an agreement listing and explaining the terms of the partnership. In order to be considered legal, a partnership agreement must be created by an attorney.

Multiple Choice

___ 4. Which of the following is the key difference between general and limited partners?

   a. Limited partners contribute capital to a business, whereas general partners do not.
   b. Limited partners can enter into contracts on behalf of the other partners, whereas general partners cannot.
   c. Limited partners receive a salary for investing in the business.
   d. Unlike general partners, limited partners who withdraw from the partnership must give notice to creditors.

e. A limited partner does not take liability for losses beyond the amount he or she invested in the partnership.

 5. Which of the following is *not* usually included in a partnership agreement?

    a. Who will make the final decisions
    b. What each partner's duties will be

c. The investment each partner will make
d. How many units of ownership each partner intends to sell
e. What happens if a partner wants to dissolve the partnership or dies

Advantages and Disadvantages of Partnerships

Learning Objective

Describe the advantages and disadvantages of partnerships.

Advantages of Partnerships

Partnerships have many advantages. The most important are described below.

Ease of Start-up Partnerships are relatively easy to form. As with a sole proprietorship, the legal requirements often are limited to registering the name of the business and obtaining any necessary licenses or permits. It may not even be necessary to prepare written articles of partnership, although doing so is generally a good idea.

Availability of Capital and Credit Because partners can pool their funds, a partnership usually has more capital available than a sole proprietorship does. This additional capital, coupled with the general partners' unlimited liability, can form the basis for a better credit rating. Banks and suppliers may be more willing to extend credit or grant larger loans to such a partnership than to a sole proprietor. This does not mean that partnerships can borrow all the money they need. Many partnerships have found it hard to get long-term financing simply because lenders worry about the possibility of management disagreements and lack of continuity.

Personal Interest General partners are very concerned with the operation of the firm—perhaps even more so than sole proprietors. After all, they are responsible for the actions of all other general partners, as well as for their own. The pride of ownership from solving the day-to-day problems of operating a business—with the help of another person(s)—is a strong motivating force and often makes all the people involved in the partnership work harder to become more successful.

Combined Business Skills and Knowledge Partners often have complementary skills. The weakness of one partner—in manufacturing, for example—may be offset by another partner's strength in that area. Moreover, the ability to discuss important decisions with another concerned individual often relieves some pressure and leads to more effective decision making.

Retention of Profits As in a sole proprietorship, all profits belong to the owners of the partnership. The partners share directly in the financial rewards and therefore are highly motivated to do their best to make the firm succeed. As noted, the partnership agreement should state how much profit or loss each partner receives or is responsible for.

No Special Taxes Although a partnership pays no income tax, the Internal Revenue Service requires partnerships to file an annual information return that states the names and addresses of all partners involved in the business. The return also must provide information about income and expenses and distributions made to each partner. Then each partner is required to report his or her share of profit (or loss) from the partnership business on his or her individual tax return and is taxed on his or her share of the profit—in the same way a sole proprietor is taxed.

Disadvantages of Partnerships

Although partnerships have many advantages when compared with sole proprietorships and corporations, they also have some disadvantages, which anyone thinking of forming a partnership should consider.

Unlimited Liability As we have noted, each *general* partner has unlimited liability for all debts of the business. Each partner is legally and personally responsible for the debts and actions of any other partner, even if that partner did not incur those debts or do anything wrong. General partners thus run the risk of having to use their personal assets to pay creditors. *Limited* partners, however, risk only their original investment.

Today, many states allow partners to form a *limited-liability partnership* (LLP), in which a partner may have limited-liability protection from legal action resulting from malpractice on the part of the other partners. Most states that allow LLPs restrict this type of ownership to certain types of professionals, such as accountants, architects, attorneys, and similar professionals. (Note the difference between a limited partnership and a limited-liability partnership. A limited partnership must have at least one general partner that has unlimited liability. On the other hand, all partners in a limited-liability partnership may have limited liability for the malpractice of the other partners.)

Management Disagreements What happens to a partnership if one of the partners brings a spouse or a relative into the business? What happens if a partner wants to withdraw more money from the business? Notice that each of the preceding situations—and for that matter, most of the other problems that can develop in a partnership—involves one partner doing something that disturbs the other partner(s). This human factor is especially important because business partners—with egos, ambitions, and money on the line—are especially susceptible to friction. When partners begin to disagree about decisions, policies, or ethics, distrust may build and get worse as time passes—often to the point where it is impossible to operate the business successfully.

Lack of Continuity Partnerships are terminated if any one of the general partners dies, withdraws, or is declared legally incompetent. However, the remaining partners can purchase that partner's ownership share. For example, the partnership agreement may permit surviving partners to continue the business after buying a deceased partner's interest from his or her estate. However, if the partnership loses an owner whose specific management or technical skills cannot be replaced, it is not likely to survive.

Frozen Investment It is easy to invest money in a partnership, but it is sometimes quite difficult to get it out. This is the case, for example, when remaining partners are unwilling to buy the share of the business that belongs to a partner who retires or wants to relocate to another city. To avoid such difficulties, the partnership agreement should include some procedure for buying out a partner.

In some cases, a partner must find someone outside the firm to buy his or her share. How easy or difficult it is to find an outsider depends on how successful the business is and how willing existing partners are to accept a new partner.

Beyond the Partnership

The main advantages of a partnership over a sole proprietorship are the added capital and management expertise of the partners. However, some of the basic disadvantages of the sole proprietorship also plague the general partnership. One disadvantage in particular—unlimited liability—can cause problems. A third form of business ownership, the corporation, overcomes this disadvantage.

TEST PREPPER 5.3

True or False?

___ 1. The difference between a limited partnership and a limited-liability partnership is that a limited-liability partnership must have at least one general partner that has unlimited liability.

___ 2. Partnerships are terminated if any one of the general partners dies, withdraws, or is declared legally incompetent. This is referred to as lack of continuity and is seen as a disadvantage of partnerships.

___ 3. In a partnership, each partner is required to report his or her share of profit (or loss) from the partnership business on his or her individual tax return and is taxed on his or her share of the profit.

Multiple Choice

___ 4. Which of the following features of a typical partnership helps to explain why partners

would have a better credit rating than sole proprietorships and therefore more access to capital?

   a. Ease of start-up and closure
   b. Combined business skills and knowledge
   c. Retention of all profits
   d. Unlimited liability of general partners
   e. No special taxes

___ 5. Which of the following situations can be avoided if the partnership agreement includes a procedure for buying out a partner?

   a. Unlimited liability
   b. Frozen investment
   c. Limited liability
   d. Management disagreements
   e. Lack of opportunity

ACE the Test
ACE & ACE+
Practice Test 5.3

Corporations

Learning Objective ❹

Summarize how a corporation is formed.

Back in 1837, William Procter and James Gamble—two sole proprietors—formed a partnership called Procter & Gamble and set out to compete with fourteen other soap and candle makers in Cincinnati, Ohio. Then, in 1890, Procter & Gamble incorporated to raise additional capital for expansion that eventually allowed the company to become a global giant. While not all sole proprietorships and partnerships become corporations, there are reasons why business owners choose the corporate form of ownership. Let's begin with a definition of a corporation. Perhaps the best definition of a corporation was given by Chief

TABLE 5.1

The Seven Largest U.S. Industrial Corporations, Ranked by Sales

Source: *Fortune 500.*
Copyright © 2006 Time, Inc., the Fortune website at **www .fortune.com;** accessed October 2, 2006.

	COMPANY	REVENUES ($ MILLIONS)	PROFITS ($ MILLIONS)
1	ExxonMobil, Irving, TX	339,938.0	36,130.0
2	Wal-Mart Stores, Bentonville, AR	315,654.0	11,231.0
3	General Motors, Detroit, MI	192,604.0	−10,600.0
4	Chevron, San Ramon, CA	189,481.0	14,099.0
5	Ford Motor, Dearborn, MI	177.210.0	2,024.0
6	ConocoPhillips, Houston, TX	166,683.0	13,529.0
7	General Electric, Fairfield, CT	157,153.0	16,353.0

corporation an artificial person created by law with most of the legal rights of a real person, including the rights to start and operate a business, to buy or sell property, to borrow money, to sue or be sued, and to enter into binding contracts

stock the shares of ownership of a corporation

stockholder a person who owns a corporation's stock

closed corporation a corporation whose stock is owned by relatively few people and is not sold to the general public

Justice John Marshall in a famous Supreme Court decision in 1819. A corporation, he said, "is an artificial being, invisible, intangible, and existing only in contemplation of the law." In other words, a **corporation** (sometimes referred to as a *regular* or *C-corporation*) is an artificial person created by law, with most of the legal rights of a real person. These include

* The right to start and operate a business
* The right to buy or sell property
* The right to borrow money
* The right to sue or be sued
* The right to enter into binding contracts

Unlike a real person, however, a corporation exists only on paper. There are 5.3 million corporations in the United States. They comprise only about 20 percent of all businesses, but they account for 83 percent of sales revenues (see Figures 5.1 and 5.2). Table 5.1 lists the seven largest U.S. industrial corporations, ranked according to sales.

Corporate Ownership

The shares of ownership of a corporation are called **stock**. The people who own a corporation's stock—and thus own part of the corporation—are called **stockholders** or sometimes *shareholders*. Once a corporation has been formed, it may sell its stock to individuals or other companies that want to invest in the corporation. It also may issue stock as a reward to key employees in return for certain services or as a return to investors (in place of cash payments).

A **closed corporation** is a corporation whose stock is owned by relatively few people and is not sold to the general public. **EXAMPLE** Mr. and Mrs. DeWitt Wallace owned virtually all the stock of Reader's Digest Association, making it one of the largest corporations of its kind. A person who wishes to sell the stock of a closed corporation generally arranges to sell it *privately* to another stockholder or a close acquaintance.

Although founded in 1922 as a closed corporation, the Reader's Digest Association became

A slice of pizza that led to corporate profits.

For Wolfgang Puck, the corporate form of ownership provided a number of advantages that allowed the famous chef/entrepreneur to create not only successful food items like all-natural pizzas, but also a successful business at the same time.

Wolfgang Puck

all natural spicy chicken pizza

an open corporation when it sold stock to investors for the first time in 1990. An **open corporation** is a corporation whose stock can be bought and sold by any individual. **EXAMPLE** Open corporations include General Motors, Microsoft, and Wal-Mart.

Steps Involved in Forming a Corporation

* Hire or consult an attorney.
* Decide where to incorporate.
* Submit articles of incorporation to the secretary of state to form a charter.
* Consider stockholders' rights and the importance of the organizational meeting.

GAP
gap.com

Forming a Corporation

Although you may think that incorporating a business guarantees success, it does not. There is no special magic about placing the word *Incorporated* or the abbreviation *Inc.* after the name of a business. Unfortunately, like sole proprietorships or partnerships, incorporated businesses can go broke. The decision to incorporate a business therefore should be made only after carefully considering whether the corporate form of ownership suits your needs better than the sole proprietorship or partnership forms.

If you decide that the corporate form is the best form of organization for you, most experts recommend that you begin the incorporation process by consulting a lawyer to be sure that all legal requirements are met. While it may be possible to incorporate a business without legal help, it is well to keep in mind the old saying, "A man who acts as his own attorney has a fool for a client." Table 5.2 lists some aspects of starting and running a business that may require legal help.

Where to Incorporate A business is allowed to incorporate in any state that it chooses. The decision on where to incorporate usually is based on two factors: (1) the cost of incorporating in one state compared with the cost in another state and (2) the advantages and disadvantages of each state's corporate laws and tax structure. Most small and medium-sized businesses are incorporated in the state where they do the most business. The founders of larger corporations or of those that will do business nationwide often compare the benefits that various states provide to corporations. Some states

1. Choosing either the sole proprietorship, partnership, or corporate form of ownership
2. Constructing a partnership agreement
3. Obtaining a corporate charter
4. Registering a corporation's stock
5. Obtaining a trademark, patent, or copyright
6. Filing for licenses or permits at the local, state, and federal levels
7. Purchasing an existing business or real estate
8. Creating valid contracts
9. Hiring employees and independent contractors
10. Extending credit and collecting debts

Why Did the Gap Incorporate?

While there are many reasons, incorporation allowed the Gap to sell stock and raise a lot of capital. Because stockholders enjoy limited liability, they were willing to invest in this company. In turn, the GAP used the stockholders' investments to grow the business and become a world leader in fashion retailing.

open corporation a corporation whose stock can be bought and sold by any individual

CONCEPT CHECK

Discuss the following statement: "Corporations are not really run by their owners."

TABLE 5.2

Ten Aspects of Business That May Require Legal Help

domestic corporation a corporation in the state in which it is incorporated

foreign corporation a corporation in any state in which it does business except the one in which it is incorporated

alien corporation a corporation chartered by a foreign government and conducting business in the United States

corporate charter a contract between a corporation and the state in which the state recognizes the formation of the artificial person that is the corporation

common stock stock owned by individuals or firms who may vote on corporate matters but whose claims on profit and assets are subordinate to the claims of others

preferred stock stock owned by individuals or firms who usually do not have voting rights but whose claims on dividends are paid before those of common-stock owners

dividend a distribution of earnings to the stockholders of a corporation

proxy a legal form listing issues to be decided at a stockholders' meeting and enabling stockholders to transfer their voting rights to some other individual or individuals

are more hospitable than others, and some offer fewer restrictions, lower taxes, and other benefits to attract new firms. **EXAMPLE** Delaware is often chosen by corporations that do business in more than one state because of its low organizational costs and its corporate tax structure.[3]

An incorporated business is called a **domestic corporation** in the state in which it is incorporated. In all other states where it does business, it is called a **foreign corporation**. **EXAMPLE** Sears Holdings Corporation, the parent company of Sears and Kmart, is incorporated in Delaware, where it is a domestic corporation. In the remaining forty-nine states, Sears is a foreign corporation. Sears must register in all states where it does business and also pay taxes and annual fees to each state. A corporation chartered by a foreign government and conducting business in the United States is an **alien corporation**. **EXAMPLE** Volkswagen AG, Sony Corporation, and the Royal Dutch/Shell Group are examples of alien corporations.

The Corporate Charter   Once a home state has been chosen, the incorporator(s) submits *articles of incorporation* to the secretary of state. When the articles of incorporation are approved, they become the firm's corporate charter. A **corporate charter** is a contract between a corporation and the state in which the state recognizes the formation of the artificial person that is the corporation. Usually the charter (and thus the articles of incorporation) includes the following information:

* The firm's name and address
* The incorporators' names and addresses
* The purpose of the corporation
* The maximum amount of stock and types of stock to be issued
* The rights and privileges of stockholders
* The length of time the corporation is to exist

To help you to decide if the corporate form of organization is the right choice, you may want to review the material available on the Yahoo! Small Business website (**http://smallbusiness.yahoo.com**). In addition, before making a decision to organize your business as a corporation, you may want to consider two additional areas: stockholders' rights and the importance of the organizational meeting.

Stockholders' Rights   There are two basic types of stock. Owners of **common stock** may vote on corporate matters. Generally, an owner of common stock has one vote for each share owned. However, any claims of common-stock owners on profit and assets of the corporation are subordinate to the claims of others. The owners of **preferred stock** usually have no voting rights, but their claims on dividends are paid before those of common-stock owners. While large corporations may issue both common and preferred stock, generally small corporations issue only common stock.

Perhaps the most important right of owners of both common and preferred stock is to share in the profit earned by the corporation through the payment of dividends. A **dividend** is a distribution of earnings to the stockholders of a corporation. Other rights include receiving information about the corporation, voting on changes to the corporate charter, and attending the corporation's annual stockholders' meeting, where they may exercise their right to vote.

Because common stockholders usually live all over the nation, very few actually may attend a corporation's annual meeting. Instead, they vote by proxy. A **proxy** is a legal form listing issues to be decided at a stockholders' meeting and enabling stockholders to transfer their voting rights to some other individual or individuals. The stockholder can register a vote and transfer voting rights simply by signing and returning the form. Today, most corporations also allow stockholders to exercise their right to vote by proxy by accessing the Internet or using a toll-free phone number.

Organizational Meeting As the last step in forming a corporation, the incorporators and original stockholders meet to adopt corporate by-laws and elect their first board of directors. (Later, directors will be elected or reelected at the corporation's annual meetings.) The board members are directly responsible to the stockholders for the way they operate the firm.

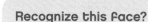

Recognize this face?

You may not recognize the face, but we bet you've used his firm's product. This is Eric Schmidt, the CEO of Google—Now—because of his success at Google—he has been asked to join the board of Apple Computer, adding another well-known name to the list of high-profile directors.

Corporate Structure

The organizational structure of most corporations is more complicated than that of a sole proprietorship or a partnership. This is especially true as the corporation begins to grow and expand. In a corporation, both the board of directors and the corporate officers are involved in management.

Board of Directors As an artificial person, a corporation can act only through its directors, who represent the corporation's stockholders. The **board of directors** is the top governing body of a corporation, and as we noted, directors are elected by the stockholders. Board members can be chosen from within the corporation or from outside it. *Note:* For a small corporation, only one director is required in most states, although you can choose to have more.

Directors who are elected from within the corporation are usually its top managers—the president and executive vice presidents, for example. Those elected from outside the corporation generally are experienced managers or entrepreneurs with proven leadership ability and/or specific talents the organization seems to need. In smaller corporations, majority stockholders usually serve as board members.

The major responsibilities of the board of directors are to set company goals and develop general plans (or strategies) for meeting those goals. The board also is responsible for the firm's overall operation.

Corporate Officers Corporate officers are appointed by the board of directors. The chairman of the board, president, executive vice presidents, corporate secretary, and treasurer are all corporate officers. They help the board to make plans, carry out strategies established by the board, hire employees, and manage day-to-day business activities. Periodically (usually each month), they report to the board of directors. And at the annual meeting, the directors report to the stockholders. In theory, then, the stockholders are able to control the activities of the entire corporation through its directors because they are the group that elects the board of directors (see Figure 5.4).

board of directors the top governing body of a corporation, the members of which are elected by the stockholders

corporate officers the chairman of the board, president, executive vice presidents, corporate secretary, treasurer, and any other top executive appointed by the board of directors

FIGURE 5.4

Hierarchy of Corporate Structure

Stockholders exercise a great deal of influence through their right to elect the board of directors.

Stockholders (owners) → *Elect* → Board of directors → *Appoints* → Officers → *Hire* → Employees

TEST PREPPER 5.4

True or False?

 1. A corporation chartered by a foreign government and conducting business in the United States is an alien corporation.

2. Owners of common stock may vote on corporate matters, but their claims on profit and assets are subordinate to the claims of others, whereas owners of preferred stock do not have voting rights, but their claims on dividends are paid before those of common-stock owners.

Multiple Choice

3. Based on your understanding of a corporation, which of the following is not a legal right of a corporation?

   a. The rights to start and operate a business
   b. The right to buy or sell property
   c. The right to borrow money
   d. Immunity from lawsuits
   e. The obligation to uphold binding contracts

 4. Once a corporation has been formed, it may sell its stock to individuals who want to invest in the corporation. These individuals are then known as

   a. shareholders.
   b. partners.
   c. limited partners.
   d. owners.
   e. clients.

5. A corporate charter is a contract between a corporation and the state in which the state recognizes the formation of the artificial person that is the corporation. Which of the following is not usually included in a corporate charter?

   a. The purpose of the corporation
   b. The maximum amount of stock and types of stock to be issued
   c. The rights and privileges of stockholders
   d. A statement of expected dividends for the first year
   e. The length of time the corporation is to exist

ACE the Test
ACE & ACE+
Practice Test 5.4

Advantages and Disadvantages of Corporations

> **Learning Objective 5**
> Describe the advantages and disadvantages of a corporation.

Prepare for Class
Career Snapshot

Back in October 2000, Manny Ruiz decided that it was time to start his own company. With the help of a team of media specialists, he founded Hispanic PR Wire. In a business where hype is the name of the game, Miami-based Hispanic PR Wire is the real thing and has established itself as the nation's leading news distribution service reaching U.S. Hispanic media and opinion leaders. Today, the business continues to build on its early success.[4] Mr. Ruiz chose to incorporate this business because it provided a number of advantages that other forms of business ownership did not offer. Typical advantages include limited liability, ease of raising capital, ease of transfer of ownership, perpetual life, and specialized management.

Advantages of Corporations

Limited Liability One of the most attractive features of corporate ownership is limited liability. With few exceptions, each owner's financial liability is limited to the amount of money he or she has paid for the corporation's stock. This feature arises from

limited liability a feature of corporate ownership that limits each owner's financial liability to the amount of money that he or she has paid for the corporation's stock

the fact that the corporation is itself a legal being, separate from its owners. If a corporation fails, creditors have a claim only on the corporation's assets, not on the owners' personal assets. Because it overcomes the problem of unlimited liability connected with sole proprietorships and general partnerships, limited liability is one of the chief reasons why entrepreneurs often choose the corporate form of organization.

Ease of Raising Capital The corporation is by far the most effective form of business ownership for raising capital. Like sole proprietorships and partnerships, corporations can borrow from lending institutions. However, they also can raise additional sums of money by selling stock. Individuals are more willing to invest in corporations than in other forms of business because of limited liability, and they can sell their stock easily—hopefully for a profit.

Ease of Transfer of Ownership Accessing a brokerage firm website or a telephone call to a stockbroker is all that is required to put stock up for sale. Willing buyers are available for most stocks at the current market price. Ownership is transferred when the sale is made, and few restrictions apply to the sale and purchase of stock issued by an open corporation.

Perpetual Life Since it is essentially a legal "person," a corporation exists independently of its owners and survives them. The withdrawal, death, or incompetence of a key executive or owner does not cause the corporation to be terminated. **EXAMPLE** Sears, Roebuck, which started as a partnership in 1887 and incorporated in 1893, is one of the nation's largest retailing corporations, even though its original owners, Richard Sears and Alvah Roebuck, have been dead for decades.

TABLE 5.3

Some Advantages and Disadvantages of a Sole Proprietorship, Partnership, and Corporation

	SOLE PROPRIETORSHIP	GENERAL PARTNERSHIP	REGULAR (C) CORPORATION
Protecting against liability for debts	Difficult	Difficult	Easy
Raising money	Difficult	Difficult	Easy
Ownership transfer	Difficult	Difficult	Easy
Preserving continuity	Difficult	Difficult	Easy
Government regulations	Few	Few	Many
Formation	Easy	Easy	Difficult
Income taxation	Once	Once	Twice

Specialized Management Typically, corporations are able to recruit more skilled, knowledgeable, and talented managers than proprietorships and partnerships. This is so because they pay bigger salaries, offer excellent fringe benefits, and are large enough to offer considerable opportunity for advancement. Within the corporate structure, administration, human resources, finance, marketing, and operations are placed in the charge of experts in these fields.

Disadvantages of Corporations

Like its advantages, many of a corporation's disadvantages stem from its legal definition as an artificial person or legal entity. The most serious disadvantages are described below. (See Table 5.3 for a comparison of some of the advantages and disadvantages of a sole proprietorship, general partnership, and corporation.)

Difficulty and Expense of Formation Forming a corporation can be a relatively complex and costly process. The use of an attorney usually is necessary to complete the legal forms and apply to the state for a charter. Charter fees, attorney's fees, registration costs associated with selling stock, and other organizational costs can amount to thousands of dollars for even a small or medium-sized corporation. The costs of incorporating, in terms of both time and money, discourage many owners of smaller businesses from forming corporations.

Government Regulation and Increased Paperwork A corporation must meet various government standards before it can sell its stock to the public. Then it must file many reports on its business operations and finances with local, state, and federal governments. In addition, the corporation must make periodic reports to its stockholders about various aspects of the business. To prepare all the necessary reports, even small corporations often need the help of an attorney, certified public accountant, and other professionals on a regular basis. In addition, a corporation's activities are restricted by law to those spelled out in its charter.

Conflict Within the Corporation Because a large corporation may employ thousands of employees, some conflict is inevitable. For example, the pressure to increase sales revenue, reduce expenses, and increase profits often leads to increased stress and tension for both managers and employees. This is especially true when a corporation operates in a competitive industry, attempts to develop and market new products, or must downsize the workforce to reduce employee salary expense.

Double Taxation Corporations must pay a tax on their profits. In addition, stockholders must pay a personal income tax on profits received as dividends. Corporate profits thus are taxed twice—once as corporate income and a second time as the personal income of stockholders. *Note:* Both the S-corporation and the limited-liability company discussed in the next section eliminate double taxation because they are taxed like a partnership and still provide the benefit of limited liability.

Lack of Secrecy Because open corporations are required to submit detailed reports to government agencies and to stockholders, they cannot keep their operations confidential. Competitors can study these corporate reports and then use the information to compete more effectively. In effect, every public corporation has to share some of its secrets with its competitors.

ACE the Test
ACE & ACE+
Practice Test 5.5

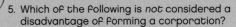
TEST PREPPER 5.5

True or False?

___ 1. Because corporations are able to pay bigger salaries and offer excellent fringe benefits to employees, they are able to stay functional long after the owner's death. This is referred to as the corporation having a perpetual life.

___ 2. Corporate profits are taxed twice—once as corporate income and a second time as the personal income of stockholders. This is considered one of the disadvantages of a corporation.

___ 3. Borrowing from lending institutions and selling stock are two ways in which corporations can raise capital.

Multiple Choice

___ 4. The corporation is itself a legal being, separate from its owners. If a corporation fails, creditors have a claim only on the corporation's assets,

not on the owners' personal assets. Which of the following terms defines this particular advantage of a corporation?

   a. Availability of capital
   b. Transfer of ownership
   c. Limited liability
   d. Perpetual life
   e. Specialized management

___ 5. Which of the following is *not* considered a disadvantage of forming a corporation?

   a. The expense
   b. Taxation of profits
   c. Conflict within the corporation
   d. The ability to transfer ownership by putting stock up for sale
   e. The obligation to submit detailed reports to government agencies and to stockholders

Special Types of Business Ownership

Learning Objective 6

Examine special types of corporations, including S-corporations, limited-liability companies, and not-for-profit corporations.

In addition to the sole proprietorship, partnership, and regular corporate form of organization, some entrepreneurs choose other forms of organization that meet their special needs. Additional organizational options include

* S-corporations
* Limited-liability companies
* Not-for-profit corporations

S-corporations

If a corporation meets certain requirements, its directors may apply to the Internal Revenue Service for status as an S-corporation. An **S-corporation** is a corporation that is taxed as though it were a partnership. In other words, the corporation's income is taxed only as the personal income of stockholders. Corporate profits or losses "pass through" the business and are reported on the owners' personal income tax returns.

Becoming an S-corporation can be an effective way to avoid double taxation while retaining the corporation's legal benefit of limited liability. To qualify for the special status of an S-corporation, a firm must meet the following criteria:[5]

1. No more than 100 stockholders are allowed.
2. Stockholders must be individuals, estates, or exempt organizations.
3. There can be only one class of outstanding stock.
4. The firm must be a domestic corporation eligible to file for S-corporation status.
5. There can be no nonresident-alien stockholders.
6. All stockholders must agree to the decision to form an S-corporation.

Limited-Liability Companies

In addition to the traditional forms of business ownership already covered, a new form of ownership called a *limited-liability company* has been approved in all fifty states—although each state's laws may differ. A **limited-liability company (LLC)** is a form of business ownership that combines the benefits of a corporation and a partnership while avoiding some of the restrictions and disadvantages of those forms of ownership. Chief advantages of an LLC are[6]

1. LLCs with at least two members are taxed like a partnership and thus avoid the double taxation imposed on most corporations. LLCs with just one member are taxed like a sole proprietorship.
2. Like a corporation, it provides limited-liability protection. An LLC thus extends the concept of personal-asset protection to small-business owners.
3. The LLC type of organization provides more management flexibility when compared with corporations. A corporation, for example, is required to have directors and corporate officers that follow guidelines established by the corporate charter. By comparison, an LLC generally is run by the owners or managers, who make all management decisions.

Although many experts believe that the LLC is nothing more than a variation of the S-corporation, there is a difference. An LLC is not restricted to 100 stockholders—a common drawback of the S-corporation. LLCs are also less restricted

S-corporation a corporation that is taxed as though it were a partnership

limited-liability company (LLC) a form of business ownership that provides limited-liability protection and is taxed like a partnership

CONCEPT CHECK
How do an S-corporation and a limited-liability company differ?

	REGULAR (C) CORPORATION	S-CORPORATION	LIMITED-LIABILITY COMPANY
Double taxation	Yes	No	No
Limited liability and personal-asset protection	Yes	Yes	Yes
Management flexibility	No	No	Yes
Restrictions on the number of owners/ stockholders	No	Yes	No
Internal Revenue Service tax regulations	Many	Many	Fewer

TABLE 5.4

Some Advantages and Disadvantages of a Regular Corporation, S-Corporation, and Limited-Liability Company

and have more flexibility than S-corporations in terms of who can become an owner. Although the owners of an LLC must file articles of organization with their state's secretary of state, they are not hampered by lots of Internal Revenue Service rules and government regulations that apply to corporations. As a result, experts are predicting that LLCs may become one of the most popular forms of business ownership available. For help in understanding the differences between a regular corporation, an S-corporation, and a limited-liability company, see Table 5.4.

Not-for-Profit Corporations

A **not-for-profit corporation** (sometimes referred to as *nonprofit*) is a corporation organized to provide a social, educational, religious, or other service rather than to earn a profit. Various charities, museums, private schools, and colleges are organized in this way, primarily to ensure limited liability. **EXAMPLE** Habitat for Humanity is a not-for-profit corporation and was formed to provide homes for qualified low-income people who could not afford housing. Even though this corporation may receive more money than it spends, any surplus funds are "reinvested" in building activities to provide low-cost housing. It is a not-for-profit corporation because its primary purpose is to provide a social service. Other examples include the Public Broadcasting System (PBS), the Girl Scouts of America, and the American Red Cross.

not-for-profit corporation a corporation organized to provide a social, educational, religious, or other service rather than to earn a profit

◀

SeaWorld and Busch Gardens Conservation Fund is all about service.

Each year the SeaWorld & Busch Gardens Conservation Fund, a private charitable foundation, works with purpose and passion on behalf of wildlife and habitats worldwide, encouraging sustainable solutions through research, animal rescue and rehabilitation, and conservation education. To pay the bills, this not-for-profit conservation fund accepts contributions from the Busch Entertainment Corporation, other businesses, and individuals. For more information, go to **www .swbg-conseravtionfund .org.**

TEST PREPPER 5.6

True or False?

 1. A firm may qualify for the special status of an S-corporation provided that its stockholders are individuals, estates, exempt organizations, and nonresident aliens.

 2. Limited-liability companies have been approved in all fifty states.

 3. Not-for-profit corporations are forbidden by federal law from making a profit.

Multiple Choice

 4. An S-corporation is a corporation that is taxed as though it were a partnership. Which of the following is not a criterion a firm must fulfill to become an S-corporation?

a. No more than 100 stockholders are allowed.
b. Stockholders must be individuals, estates, or exempt organizations.
c. There can be only one class of outstanding stock.
d. The firm must be a domestic corporation eligible to file for S-corporation status.
e. Stockholders must agree to the decision to form an S-corporation by a two-thirds majority.

C 5. Which of the following types of business ownership has the fewest government regulations?

a. Regular corporation
b. S-corporation
c. Limited-liability company
d. C-corporation
e. Merged corporation

ACE the Test
ACE & ACE+
Practice Test 5.6

Cooperatives, Joint Ventures, and Syndicates

> **Learning Objective 7**
> Discuss the purpose of a cooperative, joint venture, and syndicate.

CONCEPT CHECK

Why are cooperatives formed? Explain how they operate.

cooperative an association of individuals or firms whose purpose is to perform some business function for its members

Today, three additional types of business organizations—cooperatives, joint ventures, and syndicates—are used for special purposes. Each of these forms of organization is unique when compared with more traditional forms of business ownership.

Cooperatives

A **cooperative** is an association of individuals or firms whose purpose is to perform some business function for its members. The cooperative can perform its function more effectively than any member could by acting alone. **EXAMPLE** Cooperatives purchase goods in bulk and distribute them to members; thus the unit cost is lower than it would be if each member bought the goods in a much smaller quantity.

Although cooperatives are found in all segments of our economy, they are most prevalent in agriculture. **EXAMPLE** Farmers use cooperatives to purchase supplies, to buy services such as trucking and storage, and to process and market their products. Ocean Spray Cranberries, Inc., for example, is a cooperative of some 650 cranberry growers and more than 100 citrus growers spread throughout the country.

Joint Ventures

A **joint venture** is an agreement between two or more groups to form a business entity in order to achieve a specific goal or to operate for a specific period of time. Both the scope of the joint venture and the liabilities of the people or businesses involved usually are limited to one project. Once the goal is reached, the period of time elapses, or the project is completed, the joint venture is dissolved.

Corporations, as well as individuals, may enter into joint ventures. Major oil producers often have formed a number of joint ventures to share the extremely high cost of exploring for offshore petroleum deposits. **EXAMPLE** In the entertainment industry, Walt Disney formed a joint venture with Pixar Animation Studios to create movies. Finally, Japanese consumer electronics manufacturer Sony and Swedish telecom giant Ericsson

More Than a Pretty Face.

In this photo, models in Tokyo display new mobile phones—one result of the Sony Ericsson joint venture. Called the Renaissance Collection, the fashionable pink mobile face panel is available to fashion-conscious consumers for about 7,245 yen (US $60).

joint venture an agreement between two or more groups to form a business entity in order to achieve a specific goal or to operate for a specific period of time

BUSINESS AROUND THE WORLD

Caution Ahead for Automotive Joint Ventures?

Racing for higher revenues, car companies sometimes form joint ventures to enter or expand in overseas markets. However, joint ventures can have a dark side. Will carmakers put the brakes on joint ventures for fear that a partner might become a competitor?

- *In India.* India's Tata Motors and Italy's Fiat have a joint venture to build cars for India's fast-growing middle class. Both partners are pleased with this venture. Tata, India's second-largest car manufacturer, benefits from Fiat's technology and supplier network; Fiat gains from Tata's experience and customer knowledge.

- *In China.* General Motors (GM) and Volkswagen (VW) have separate joint ventures with the Shanghai Automotive Industry Corp. (SAIC) to produce cars in China. Yet SAIC recently created a new division, staffed by engineers who previously worked in the joint ventures, to make cars under a new brand. Publicly, VW and GM have said that they value their ventures with SAIC and understand its desire to develop cars independently. What will happen to these ventures as SAIC's division increases competitive tension in an already pressured industry?

Sources: Based on information from Paulo Soares de Oliveira, "SAIC Plans European Launch 2007," *Automotive News Europe*, August 21, 2006, p. 12; "Tata Motors, Ltd.: Truck Maker Joins with Fiat to Build, Sell Cars in India," *Wall Street Journal*, July 26, 2006, n.p.; Keith Bradsher and Micheline Mayner, "Chinese Partner of GM and VW to Offer Its Own Cars," *New York Times*, April 11, 2006, p. C6.

have formed a joint venture to manufacture and market mobile communications equipment. Now, after more than four years, the joint venture is profitable and projects even larger sales revenues and profits in the immediate future.[7]

Syndicates

syndicate a temporary association of individuals or firms organized to perform a specific task that requires a large amount of capital

A **syndicate** is a temporary association of individuals or firms organized to perform a specific task that requires a large amount of capital. The syndicate is formed because no one person or firm is willing to put up the entire amount required for the undertaking. Like a joint venture, a syndicate is dissolved as soon as its purpose has been accomplished.

Syndicates are used most commonly to underwrite large insurance policies, loans, and investments. Stock brokerage firms usually join together in the same way to market a new issue of stock. **EXAMPLE** Morgan Stanley, Credit Suisse First Boston, and other Wall Street firms formed a syndicate to sell shares of stock in Google. The initial public offering (IPO) was one of the largest in U.S. history—too large for Morgan Stanley and Credit Suisse First Boston to handle without help from other Wall Street firms. (*Initial public offering* is the term used to describe the first time a corporation sells stock to the general public.)

TEST PREPPER 5.7

True or False?

 1. When a corporation sells stock for the first time, it is called an IPO.

Multiple Choice

 2. Which of the following would be the term used to describe a company that, for example, purchases goods in bulk and distributes them to members, thus minimizing the cost for individual members?

   a. A not-for-profit corporation
   b. A cooperative
   c. A syndicate
   d. A joint venture
   e A limited-liability corporation

3. Japanese consumer electronics manufacturer Sony and Swedish telecom giant Ericsson have agreed to manufacture and market mobile communications equipment together for a ten-year period. Which of the following is the name given to such a collaborative effort?

   a. A not-for-profit venture
   b. A joint venture
   c. A cooperative
   d. A partnership
   e. An oligopoly

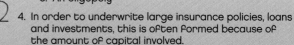 4. In order to underwrite large insurance policies, loans and investments, this is often formed because of the amount of capital involved.

   a. S-corporation
   b. Joint venture
   c. Cooperative
   d. Syndicate
   e C-corporation

5. Ocean Spray is a(n)

   a. cooperative.
   b. joint venture.
   c. agricultural partnership.
   d. syndicate
   e. merger.

ACE the Test
ACE & ACE+
Practice Test 5.7

Corporate Growth

Growth seems to be a basic characteristic of business. There are three main reasons why growth is important to a business. These are listed below.

1. A larger firm generally has greater sales revenue and thus greater profit.
2. In a growing economy, a business that does not grow actually is shrinking relative to the economy.
3. Business growth is a means by which some executives boost their power, prestige, and reputation.

Growth from Within

Most corporations grow by expanding their present operations. Some introduce and sell new but related products. Others expand the sale of present products to new geographic markets or to new groups of consumers in geographic markets already served. **EXAMPLE** Currently, Wal-Mart operates in fifteen countries and has over 6,500 stores worldwide.[8]

Growth from within, especially when carefully planned and controlled, can have relatively little adverse effect on a firm. For the most part, the firm continues to do what it has been doing, but on a larger scale. **EXAMPLE** For instance, Larry Ellison, founder and CEO of Oracle Corporation of Redwood City, California, built the firm's annual revenues up from a mere $282 million in 1988 to approximately $14.4 billion today.[9] Much of this growth has taken place since 1994 as Oracle capitalized on its global leadership in information management software.

Growth Through Mergers and Acquisitions

Another way a firm can grow is by purchasing another company. The purchase of one corporation by another is called a **merger**. An *acquisition* is essentially the same thing as a merger, but the term usually is used in reference to a large corporation's purchases of other corporations. Although most mergers and acquisitions are friendly, hostile takeovers also occur. A **hostile takeover** is a situation in which the management and board of directors of a firm targeted for acquisition disapprove of the merger.

When a merger or acquisition becomes hostile, a corporate raider—another company or a wealthy investor—may make a tender offer or start a proxy fight to gain control of the target company. A **tender offer** is an offer to purchase the stock of a firm targeted for acquisition at a price just high enough to tempt stockholders to sell their shares. Corporate raiders also may initiate a proxy fight. A **proxy fight** is a

merger the purchase of one corporation by another

hostile takeover a situation in which the management and board of directors of a firm targeted for acquisition disapprove of the merger

tender offer an offer to purchase the stock of a firm targeted for acquisition at a price just high enough to tempt stockholders to sell their shares

proxy fight a technique used to gather enough stockholder votes to control a targeted company

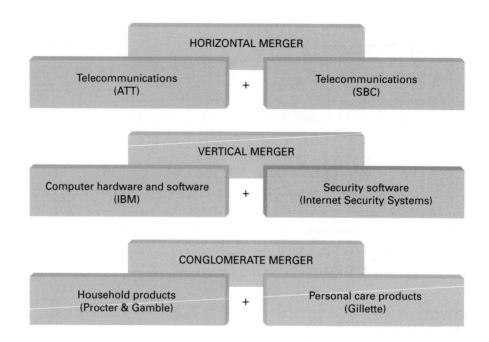

FIGURE 5.5

Three Types of Growth by Merger

Today mergers are classified as horizontal, vertical, or conglomerate.

CONCEPT CHECK

Are mergers and acquisitions good for the company, a firm's stockholders, or the economy? Explain your answer.

technique used to gather enough stockholder votes to control a targeted company. If the corporate raider is successful and takes over the targeted company, existing management usually is replaced. Faced with this probability, existing management may take specific actions sometimes referred to as "poison pills," "shark repellents," or "porcupine provisions" to maintain control of the firm and avoid the hostile takeover. Whether mergers are friendly or hostile, they are generally classified as *horizontal*, *vertical*, or *conglomerate* (see Figure 5.5).

Horizontal Mergers A *horizontal merger* is a merger between firms that make and sell similar products or services in similar markets. **EXAMPLE** The merger between SBC and AT&T is an example of a horizontal merger because both firms are in the telecommunications industry. This type of merger tends to reduce the number of firms in an industry—and thus may reduce competition. For this reason, each merger may be reviewed carefully by federal agencies before it is permitted.

Vertical Mergers A *vertical merger* is a merger between firms that operate at different but related levels in the production and marketing of a product. Generally, one of the merging firms is either a supplier or a customer of the other. **EXAMPLE** A vertical merger occurred when IBM acquired Internet Security Systems. At the time of the merger, Internet Security Systems was a leading provider of security software solutions to help customers protect networks, desktops, and servers from hackers and virus threats. At the same time, IBM needed this type of software to add to its own line of software products. Rather than develop its own software, IBM simply purchased the company.[10]

Conglomerate Mergers A *conglomerate merger* takes place between firms in completely different industries. **EXAMPLE** One of the largest conglomerate mergers in recent history occurred when Procter & Gamble merged with Gillette. While both companies were known for their consumer products, Procter & Gamble is the manufacturer and distributor for many household products, and Gillette is well known for personal-care products. According to Procter & Gamble, the addition of Gillette's products "will broaden the ways in which we can continue to provide the kinds of helpful solutions to assist our customers in taking care of their families, their homes—and themselves!"[11]

Current Merger Trends

Economists, financial analysts, corporate managers, and stockholders still hotly debate whether takeovers are good for the economy—or for individual companies—in the long run. One thing is clear, however: There are two sides to the takeover question.

Positive View of Takeovers Takeover advocates argue that for companies that have been taken over, the purchasers have been able to make the company more profitable and productive by installing a new top-management team and by forcing the company to concentrate on one main business.

Negative View of Takeovers Takeover opponents argue that takeovers do nothing to enhance corporate profitability or productivity. These critics argue that threats of takeovers have forced managers to devote valuable time to defending their companies from takeover, thus robbing time from new product development and other vital business activities. Finally, the opposition argues that the only people who benefit from takeovers are investment bankers, brokerage firms, and takeover "artists," who receive financial rewards by manipulating U.S. corporations rather than by producing tangible products or services.

Future Predictions Regarding Takeovers Most experts now predict that mergers and acquisitions during the first part of the twenty-first century will be the result of cash-rich companies looking to acquire businesses that will enhance their position in the marketplace. Analysts also anticipate more mergers that involve companies or investors from other countries. Regardless of the companies involved or where the companies are from, future mergers and acquisitions will be driven by solid business logic, the desire to compete in the international marketplace, and the explosion of information technology. Finally, experts predict more leveraged buyouts in the future. A **leveraged buyout (LBO)** is a purchase arrangement that allows a firm's managers and employees or a group of investors to purchase the company. (LBO activity is sometimes referred to as *taking a firm private.*)

Whether they are sole proprietorships, partnerships, corporations, or some other form of business ownership, most U.S. businesses are small. In the next chapter we focus on these small businesses. We examine, among other things, the meaning of the word *small* as it applies to business and the place of small business in the American economy.

CONCEPT CHECK
Describe the three types of mergers.

leveraged buyout (LBO) a purchase arrangement that allows a firm's managers and employees or a group of investors to purchase the company

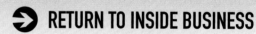

TEST PREPPER 5.8

True or False?

_____ 1. Growth from within, especially when carefully planned and controlled, can have relatively little adverse effect on a firm.

_____ 2. A proxy fight is a technique used to gather enough stockholder votes to control a targeted company and is used when a merger or acquisition becomes hostile.

_____ 3. Where one of the merging firms is either a supplier or a customer of the other, the merger is known as a conglomerate merger.

Multiple Choice

_____ 4. Which of the following is generally *not* a reason why corporations choose to grow?

a. To be able to generate greater sales revenue.
b. To earn larger corporate profits.
c. To be able to offer more employment to an expanding pool of highly skilled labor
d. To maintain the corporation's position in an industry when the economy is growing.
e. To bolster the CEO's sense of power and prestige

_____ 5. The purchase of one corporation by another is known as

a. a tender offer.
b. a competitive takeover.
c. a proxy fight.
d. a merger.
e. a corporate raider.

ACE the Test
ACE & ACE+
Practice Test 5.8

Prepare for Class
CL News Feeds
CL News Now

➡ RETURN TO INSIDE BUSINESS

Johnson & Johnson (J&J) consistently ranks among the ten most admired U.S. corporations. Its credo has won it admirers as well as customers, employees, suppliers, and investors. Although a good reputation helps to pave the way for profitability, it also raises expectations about what a major corporation can and should be doing about social responsibility. This is why, guided by its credo, J&J invests $600 million annually to enhance women's and children's health, aid disaster relief, improve access to care, advance health care knowledge, and support global public health.

Acquisitions have helped J&J steadily expand both sales and profits. The company recently bought Pfizer's consumer health care division for $16.6 billion. Now, Listerine and Rolaids are in the same corporate family as Band-Aid and Johnson's Baby Powder.

Questions

1. What are the advantages and disadvantages of J&J investing its shareholders' money in corporate citizenship projects with no immediate payback?
2. Would you like to work for a corporation like J&J? Why or why not?

LEARNING OBJECTIVES REVIEW

1 Describe a sole proprietorship and list its advantages and disadvantages.

- Advantages
  - All business profits become the property of the owner.
  - Sole proprietors have pride of ownership.
  - The sole proprietorship is the simplest form of business to enter, control, and leave.
  - It also pays no special taxes.
- Disadvantages
  - The owner is personally responsible for all business debts.
  - There is unlimited liability.
  - There are limits on one person's ability to borrow or to be an expert in all fields.
  - They account for only 5 percent of total revenues when compared with partnerships and corporations.

2 Define and explain the different types of partnerships and the importance of partnership agreements.

- Like sole proprietors, *general partners* are responsible for running the business and for all business debts.
- *Limited partners* receive a share of the profit in return for investing in the business. However, they are not responsible for business debts beyond the amount they have invested.
- *Master limited partnerships* (MLPs) sell units of ownership to raise capital.

3 Describe the advantages and disadvantages of partnerships.

- Advantages
  - Ease of start-up
  - Availability of capital and credit
  - Personal interest
  - Combined skills and knowledge
  - Retention of profits
- Disadvantages
  - Unlimited liability (in a general partnership)
  - Effects of management disagreements
  - Lack of continuity and frozen investment
  - Special requirements must be met if partners form either the limited partnership or the limited-liability partnership.

4 Summarize how a corporation is formed.

- A corporation is an artificial person created by law, with most of the legal rights of a real person, including the right to start and operate a business, to own property, to borrow money, to be sued or sue, and to enter into contracts.
- With the corporate form of ownership, stock can be sold to individuals to raise capital.
- Generally, corporations are classified as closed corporations (few stockholders) or open corporations (many stockholders).

5 Describe the advantages and disadvantages of a corporation.

- Advantages
  - Limited liability—stockholders are not liable for the corporation's debts beyond the amount they paid for its stock.
  - Ease of raising capital and of transfer of ownership, perpetual life, and specialized management.
- Disadvantages
  - Double taxation: All profits are taxed once as corporate income and again as personal income because stockholders must pay a personal income tax on the profits they receive as dividends.
  - Difficulty and expense of formation, government regulation, conflict within the corporation, and lack of secrecy.

6 Examine special types of corporations, including S-corporations, limited-liability companies, and not-for profit corporations.

- S-corporations are corporations that are taxed as though they were partnerships but that enjoy the benefit of limited liability.
- A limited-liability company (LLC) is a form of business ownership that provides limited liability for the investors and owners.
- When compared with a regular corporation or an S-corporation, an LLC is more flexible and has fewer government restrictions.
- Not-for-profit corporations are formed to provide social services rather than to earn profits.

Improve Your Grade
Audio Chapter Summary & Quiz

7 **Discuss the purpose of a cooperative, joint venture, and syndicate.**

- A cooperative is an association of individuals or firms whose purpose is to perform some business function for its members.

- A joint venture is formed when two or more groups form a business entity in order to achieve a specific goal or to operate for a specific period of time. Once the goal is reached, the joint venture is dissolved.

- A syndicate is a temporary association of individuals or firms organized to perform a specific task that requires large amounts of capital.

8 **Explain how growth from within and growth through mergers can enable a business to expand.**

- A corporation may grow by expanding its present operations or through a merger or acquisition. A hostile takeover is a situation in which the management and board of directors of a firm targeted for acquisition disapprove of the merger.

- Mergers generally are classified as horizontal, vertical, or conglomerate mergers.

- Experts predict that future mergers will be the result of cash-rich companies looking to acquire businesses that will enhance their position in the marketplace.

VIDEO CASE

Having Fun Is Serious Business at Jordan's Furniture

Jordan's Furniture is a unique retail chain. In fact, every one of its stores in New England is unique—and highly profitable. And that's what caught the eye of Warren Buffett, the head of conglomerate Berkshire Hathaway, who is famous for his astute investments. Buffet bought Jordan's Furniture in 1999 and has left the founding family in charge to continue the retailer's winning ways.

The company's history stretches back to 1918, when Samuel Tatelman opened a small furniture store in Waltham, Massachusetts. His son Edward became involved in the family business during the 1930s. By the 1950s, Edward's children, Barry and Eliot, were learning about furniture retailing first-hand as they helped out during busy periods. In the early 1970s, the two brothers jointly assumed responsibility for running the store, which then had eight employees.

The brothers then made two key decisions that dramatically altered the future course of the business. First, they decided to gear their merchandise and store decor to 18- to-34-year-olds because people in this age group need furniture when they settle down and start families. Second, they resolved to make the business fun for themselves, their customers, and their employees by adding a large element of entertainment to the shopping experience.

For example, the 110,000-square-foot store in Natick, Massachusetts, evokes the spirit of Bourbon Street in New Orleans, complete with steamboat and Mardi Gras festivities. One section of the store holds a 262-seat IMAX 3D theater, popcorn and all. The Reading, Massachusetts, store is home to Beantown, a series of jelly-bean creations depicting Boston landmarks, such as the left-field wall in Fenway Park, home of the Red Sox. Just as the Reading store is more than twice as large as the Natick store, its IMAX theater is also larger, roomy enough for an audience of 500 people.

The two-story Avon, Massachusetts, branch is home to the twenty-minute M.O.M., better known as the Motion Odyssey 3D Movie Ride, which draws children of all ages. Continuing the fun theme, visitors to the Nashua, New Hampshire, store are invited to munch on free fresh-baked chocolate chip cookies and sip coffee in the snack bar. And by the way, every one of the four stores also features a huge inventory of furniture for all tastes.

Ordinarily, customers shop for furniture only to fill a particular need. By making its stores exciting destinations for the entire family, Jordan's Furniture is out to change that behavior. When their children ask to visit the in-store IMAX theater, for instance, the parents may spot an entertainment unit or a chair they want to buy. "People come in here for fun," observes Eliot Tatelman. "They wind up having fun but also buying."

After Warren Buffett bought Jordan's Furniture, the brothers remained in charge to direct the chain's expansion. They also added a spiffy website and continued writing the funny television commercials for which the company was known throughout the Boston area. Eventually, they closed the original Waltham site to concentrate on the four stores built with entertainment in mind. By the time Barry left in 2006 to pursue a career as a Broadway producer, Eliot's two sons had followed family tradition and joined the company.

And that's how a small business founded as a sole proprietorship wound up as a corporation merged into a large conglomerate. Today, Jordan's Furniture is an established, profitable retail operation employing more than 1,200 people. It serves thousands of shoppers every day, and its sales average of $950 per square foot is considerably higher than that of the typical furniture store. But then, Jordan's Furniture is hardly a typical store, as its slogan suggests: "Not just a store, an experience!"[12]

For more information about this company, go to **www.jordans .com.**

Questions

1. Warren Buffett's Berkshire Hathaway owns three other furniture retailers in addition to Jordan's. Why do you think the conglomerate left the Tatelman family in charge of Jordan's after the merger?

2. What do you think Berkshire Hathaway and Jordan's have each gained from the merger?

3. How much influence are Berkshire Hathaway's stockholders likely to have (or want) over Jordan's management? Explain your answer.

BUILDING SKILLS FOR CAREER SUCCESS

1. Exploring the Internet

Arguments about mergers and acquisitions often come down to an evaluation of who benefits and by how much. Sometimes the benefits include access to new products, talented management, new customers, or new sources of capital. Often the debate is complicated by the involvement of firms based in different countries.

The Internet is a fertile environment for information and discussion about mergers. The firms involved will provide their view about who will benefit and why it is either a good thing or not. Journalists will report facts and offer commentary as to how they see the future result of any merger, and of course, chat rooms located on the websites of many journals promote discussion about the issues. Visit the text website for updates to this exercise.

Assignment

1. Using an Internet search engine such as Google or Yahoo!, locate two or three sites providing information about a recent merger (use a keyword such as *merger*).

2. After examining these sites and reading journal articles, report information about the merger, such as the dollar value, the reasons behind the merger, and so forth.

3. Based on your assessment of the information you have read, do you think the merger is a good idea or not for the firms involved, the employees, the investors, the industry, and society as a whole? Explain your reasoning.

2. Building Team Skills

Suppose that you have decided to quit your job as an insurance adjuster and open a bakery. Your business is now growing, and you have decided to add a full line of catering services. This means more work and responsibility. You will need someone to help you, but you are undecided about what to do. Should you hire an employee or find a partner? If you add a partner, what type of decisions should be made to create a partnership agreement?

Assignment

1. In a group, discuss the following questions:

    a. What are the advantages and disadvantages of adding a partner versus hiring an employee?

    b. How would you go about finding a partner?

2. As a group, prepare an articles-of-partnership agreement. Be prepared to discuss the pros and cons of your group's agreement with other groups from your class, as well as to examine their agreements.

3. Summarize your group's answers to these questions, and present them to your class.

3. Researching Different Careers

Many people spend their entire lives working in jobs that they do not enjoy. Why is this so? Often it is because they have taken the first job they were offered without giving it much thought. How can you avoid having this happen to you? First, you should determine your "personal profile" by identifying and analyzing your own strengths, weaknesses, things you enjoy, and things you dislike. Second, you should identify the types of jobs that fit your profile. Third, you should identify and research the companies that offer those jobs.

Assignment

1. Take two sheets of paper and draw a line down the middle of each sheet, forming two columns on each page. Label column 1 "Things I Enjoy or Like to Do," column 2 "Things I Do Not Like Doing," column 3 "My Strengths," and column 4 "My Weaknesses."

2. Record data in each column over a period of at least one week. You may find it helpful to have a relative or friend give you input.

3. Summarize the data, and write a profile of yourself.

Prepare for Class
Exploring the Internet

4. Take your profile to a career counselor at your college or to the public library and ask for help in identifying jobs that fit your profile. Your college may offer testing to assess your skills and personality. The Strong-Campbell Interest Inventory and the Myers-Briggs Personality Inventory can help you to assess the kind of work you may enjoy. The Internet is another resource.

5. Research the companies that offer the types of jobs that fit your profile.

6. Write a report on your findings.

CHAPTER 6

Small Business, Entrepreneurship, and Franchises

Your Guide to Success in Business

Why this chapter matters
America's small businesses drive the U.S. economy. Small businesses represent 99.7 percent of all employer firms, and there is a good probability that you will work for a small business or perhaps even start your own business. This chapter can help you to become a good employee or a successful entrepreneur.

LEARNING OBJECTIVES

1. Define what a small business is and recognize the fields in which small businesses are concentrated.

2. Identify the people who start small businesses and the reasons why some succeed and many fail.

3. Assess the contributions of small businesses to our economy.

4. Judge the advantages and disadvantages of operating a small business.

5. Explain how the Small Business Administration helps small businesses.

6. Appraise the concept and types of franchising.

7. Analyze the growth of franchising and list franchising's advantages and disadvantages.

Ladies Who Help Ladies Launch Their Dreams

"Breaking free of the traditional model of entrepreneurship" is the philosophy behind Ladies Who Launch, founded by Victoria Colligan and Beth Schoenfeldt. Colligan was living and working in New York when she observed that men seem to launch their business ideas differently than women—and with better support systems. So Colligan, who now lives in Cleveland, Ohio, teamed up with New York–based Schoenfeldt to form Ladies Who Launch, a business incubator and support group for women entrepreneurs.

Their Incubator Intensive programs are workshops in which ten to twelve women explore and expand on their business ideas in an encouraging, motivational atmosphere. Over time, the Incubator helps entrepreneurs to make business contacts, obtain financing, understand financial statements, and share ideas. Cofounder Colligan explains, "What we do with our Incubator program is try to put a structure around what women do well naturally."

After participants launch their new ventures, they can continue to tap Ladies Who Launch for advice and networking opportunities through its newsletters, special events, and online content. The entrepreneurs even can advertise their companies on the Ladies Who Launch website (**www.ladieswholaunch.com**). Many women have been able to launch their dreams after getting involved with Ladies Who Launch.

For example, Kate Richard learned how to turn her love of fashion into a series of profitable businesses through her Incubator participation. First, she opened a women's clothing store in her hometown of Detroit, Michigan, and then she went on to open a bridal fashion store, followed by a designer shoe store. Today, Richard shares her business experiences and expertise with other women entrepreneurs by leading the Detroit chapter of the Ladies Who Launch Incubator program.

When southern California designer Sarah Shaw decided to start a new business, she went directly to the Ladies Who Launch Incubator for assistance. "Just hearing the vision that other people had for my company was inspiring," she says. With the support system of Ladies Who Launch, Shaw started Simply Sarah (**www.simplysarahshaw.com**), a website that features handbags, gifts, and home accessories.[1]

Most small businesses that survive usually stay small. They provide a solid foundation for our economy—as employers, as suppliers and purchasers of goods and services, and as taxpayers.

> **DID YOU KNOW?**
>
> "Breaking free of the traditional model of entrepreneurship" is the philosophy behind Ladies Who Launch, founded by Victoria Colligan and Beth Schoenfeldt.

KEY TERMS

small business (180)
business plan (191)
Small Business Administration (SBA) (194)
Service Corps of Retired Executives (SCORE) (194)

small-business institutes (SBIs) (195)
small-business development centers (SBDCs) (196)
venture capital (197)

small-business investment companies (SBICs) (197)
franchise (197)
franchising (197)

franchisor (197)
franchisee (197)

ACE the Test
Crossword Puzzle
Flashcards

In this chapter, we will

* Define small business.
* Describe industries that often attract small businesses.
* Present profiles of some of the people who start small businesses.
* Consider the importance of small businesses in our economy.
* Present the advantages and disadvantages of smallness in business.
* Describe the services provided by the Small Business Administration.
* Discuss the pros and cons of franchising.

Small Business: A Profile

Learning Objective ❶

Define what a small business is and recognize the fields in which small businesses are concentrated.

small business one that is independently owned and operated for profit and is not dominant in its field

The Small Business Administration (SBA) defines a **small business** as "one which is independently owned and operated for profit and is not dominant in its field." How small must a firm be not to dominate its field? That depends on the particular industry it is in. The SBA has developed the specific "smallness" guidelines listed in Table 6.1 for the various industries.[2] The SBA periodically revises and simplifies its small-business size regulations.

Annual sales in the millions of dollars may not seem very small. However, for many firms, profit is only a small percentage of total sales. Thus a firm may earn only $40,000 or $50,000 on yearly sales of $1 million—and that is small in comparison with the profits earned by most medium-sized and large firms. Moreover, most small firms have annual sales well below the maximum limits in the SBA guidelines.

TABLE 6.1

Industry Group-Size Standards

Small business size standards are usually stated in number of employees or average annual sales. In the United States, 99.7 percent of all businesses are considered small.

Source: **www.sba.gov/size/summary-whatis.html**; accessed October 26, 2007.

INDUSTRY GROUP	SIZE STANDARD
Manufacturing	500 employees
Wholesale trade	100 employees
Agriculture	$750,000
Retail trade	$6.5 million
General & heavy construction (except dredging)	$31 million
Dredging	$18.5 million
Special trade contractors	$13 million
Travel agencies	$3.5 million (commissions & other income)
Business and personal services except • Architectural, engineering, surveying, and mapping services • Dry cleaning and carpet cleaning services	$6.5 million $4.5 million $4.5 million

	NUMBER OF PROCEDURES	TIME (DAYS)	COST (US$)	MINIMUM CAPITAL (% PER CAPITAL INCOME)
Australia	2	2	402	0
Belgium	7	56	2,633	75.1
Canada	2	3	127	0
Denmark	4	4	0	52.3
France	10	53	663	32.1
Germany	9	45	1,341	103.8
Greece	16	45	8,115	145.3
Ireland	3	12	2,473	0
Italy	9	23	4,565	49.6
Japan	11	31	3,518	71.3
Netherlands	7	11	3,276	70.7
New Zealand	3	3	28	0
Norway	4	24	1,460	33.1
Portugal	11	95	1,360	43.4
Spain	11	115	2,366	19.6
Sweden	3	16	190	41.4
Switzerland	6	20	3,228	33.8
United Kingdom	6	18	264	0
United States	5	4	210	0

TABLE 6.2

Establishing a Business Around the World

The entrepreneurial spirit provides the spark that enriches the U.S. economy. The growth will continue if lawmakers resist the urge to overregulate entrepreneurs and provide policies that foster free enterprise.

Source: World Bank (2004); as found in *Inside the Vault,* Federal Reserve Bank of St. Louis, Fall 2004, p. 1. Reprinted by permission.

The Small-Business Sector

In the United States, it typically takes four days and $210 to establish a business as a legal entity. The steps include registering the name of the business, applying for tax IDs, and setting up unemployment and workers' compensation insurance. In Japan, however, a typical entrepreneur spends more than $3,500 and thirty-one days to follow eleven different procedures (see Table 6.2).

A surprising number of Americans take advantage of their freedom to start a business. There are, in fact, about 26.8 million businesses in this country. Only just over 17,000 of these employ more than 500 workers—enough to be considered large.

Interest in owning or starting a small business has never been greater than it is today. During the last decade, the number of small businesses in the United States has increased 49 percent, and for the last few years, new-business formation in the United States has broken successive records, except during the 2001–2002 recession. Recently, nearly 649,700 new businesses were incorporated. Furthermore, part-time entrepreneurs have increased fivefold in recent years; they now account for one-third of all small businesses.[3]

Statistically, about 56 percent of new businesses can be expected to fail within their first four years.[4] The primary reason for these failures is mismanagement resulting from a lack of business know-how. The makeup of the small-business sector thus is constantly changing. Despite the high failure rate, many small businesses succeed modestly. Some, like Apple Computer, Inc., are extremely successful—to the point where they no longer can be considered small. Taken together, small businesses are also responsible for providing a high percentage of the jobs in the United States. According to some estimates, the figure is well over 50 percent.

Industries That Attract Small Businesses

Some industries, such as auto manufacturing, require huge investments in machinery and equipment. Businesses in such industries are big from the day they are started—if an entrepreneur or group of entrepreneurs can gather the capital required to start one.

By contrast, a number of other industries require only a low initial investment and some special skills or knowledge. It is these industries that tend to attract new businesses. Growing industries, such as outpatient-care facilities, are attractive because of their profit potential. However, knowledgeable entrepreneurs choose areas with which they are familiar, and these are most often the more established industries.

Small enterprise spans the gamut from corner newspaper vending to the development of optical fibers.

What Do Small-Business Owners Sell?

* The owners of small businesses sell gasoline, flowers, and coffee to go.
* They publish magazines, haul freight, teach languages, and program computers.
* They make wines, movies, and high-fashion clothes.
* They build new homes and restore old ones.
* They fix appliances, recycle metals, and sell used cars.
* They drive cabs and fly planes.
* They make us well when we are ill, and they sell us the products of corporate giants.
* In fact, 74 percent of real estate, rental, and leasing industries; 76 percent of the businesses in the arts, entertainment, and recreational services; and 90 percent of the construction industries are dominated by small businesses.[5] The various kinds of businesses generally fall into three broad categories of industry: distribution, service, and production.

Distribution Industries This category includes retailing, wholesaling, transportation, and communications—industries concerned with the movement of goods from producers to consumers. Distribution industries account for approximately 33 percent of all small businesses. Of these, almost three-quarters are involved in retailing, that is, the sale of goods directly to consumers. Clothing and jewelry stores, pet shops, bookstores, and grocery stores, for example, are all retailing firms. Slightly less than one-quarter of the small distribution firms are wholesalers. Wholesalers purchase products in quantity from manufacturers and then resell them to retailers.

Service Industries This category accounts for over 48 percent of all small businesses. Of these, about three-quarters provide such nonfinancial services as medical and dental care; watch, shoe, and TV repairs; haircutting and styling; restaurant meals; and dry cleaning. About 8 percent of the small service firms offer financial services, such as accounting, insurance, real estate,

CONCEPT CHECK Which two areas of business generally attract the most small business? Why are these areas attractive to small business?

and investment counseling. An increasing number of self-employed Americans are running service businesses from home.

Production Industries This last category includes the construction, mining, and manufacturing industries. Only about 19 percent of all small businesses are in this group, mainly because these industries require relatively large initial investments. Small firms that do venture into production generally make parts and subassemblies for larger manufacturing firms or supply special skills to larger construction firms.

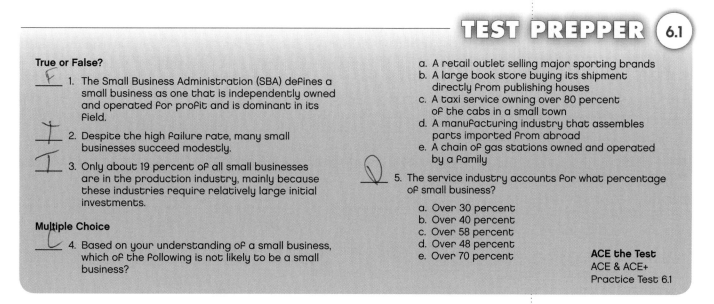

TEST PREPPER 6.1

True or False?

___F___ 1. The Small Business Administration (SBA) defines a small business as one that is independently owned and operated for profit and is dominant in its field.

___T___ 2. Despite the high failure rate, many small businesses succeed modestly.

___T___ 3. Only about 19 percent of all small businesses are in the production industry, mainly because these industries require relatively large initial investments.

Multiple Choice

___c___ 4. Based on your understanding of a small business, which of the following is not likely to be a small business?

a. A retail outlet selling major sporting brands
b. A large book store buying its shipment directly from publishing houses
c. A taxi service owning over 80 percent of the cabs in a small town
d. A manufacturing industry that assembles parts imported from abroad
e. A chain of gas stations owned and operated by a family

___d___ 5. The service industry accounts for what percentage of small business?

a. Over 30 percent
b. Over 40 percent
c. Over 58 percent
d. Over 48 percent
e. Over 70 percent

ACE the Test
ACE & ACE+
Practice Test 6.1

The People in Small Businesses: The Entrepreneurs

Learning Objective ②

Identify the people who start small businesses and the reasons why some succeed and many fail.

The entrepreneurial spirit is alive and well in the United States. A recent study revealed that the U.S. population is quite entrepreneurial when compared with those of other countries. More than 70 percent of Americans would prefer being an entrepreneur to working for someone else. This compares with 46 percent of adults in western Europe and 58 percent of adults in Canada. Another study on entrepreneurial activity for 2002 found that of thirty-six countries studied, the United States was in the top third in entrepreneurial activity and was the leader when compared with Japan, Canada, and western Europe.[6]

Small businesses typically are managed by the people who start and own them. Most of these people have held jobs with other firms and still could be so employed

Prepare for Class
Career Snapshot

if they wanted. Yet owners of small businesses would rather take the risk of starting and operating their own firms, even if the money they make is less than the salaries they otherwise might earn.

Researchers have suggested a variety of personal factors as reasons why people go into business for themselves. These are discussed below.

Characteristics of Entrepreneurs

Entrepreneurial spirit is the desire to create a new business. **EXAMPLE** Nikki Olyai always knew that she wanted to create and develop her own business. Her father, a successful businessman in Iran, was her role model. She came to the United States at the age of seventeen and lived with a host family in Salem, Oregon, attending high school there. Undergraduate and graduate degrees in computer science led her to start Innovision Technologies while she held two other jobs to keep the business going and took care of her four-year-old son. Recently, Nikki Olyai's business was honored by the Women's Business Enterprise National Council's "Salute to Women's Business Enterprises" as one of eleven top successful firms. For three consecutive years, her firm was selected as a "Future 50 of Greater Detroit Company."

Sweet Smell of Success.

Bill Gates, chairman and CEO of Microsoft Corp., believes that the true measure of the company success is not just in the power of its software, but in the potential it unleashes in us all. With great ideas—and great software—our future has no limits. In the past 30 years, Microsoft has grown from a small start-up to a Fortune 500 success story. Here, Mr. Gates meets with Chicago-area eighth graders at the Museum of Science and Industry.

ENTREPRENEURIAL CHALLENGE

More than a Good Idea

Entrepreneurs need more than a good idea to start a business. To be successful, they need to research their idea's viability, create a business plan to secure financing, and have a passion for their work. Here's how two sets of entrepreneurs turned good ideas into profitable businesses.

- *One-stop aquarium shopping.* When Cory Goldberg tried to buy aquarium supplies in Long Island, New York, he found no single store that stocked everything he needed. Instead, he found a business partner, Joseph Vivirito, a fish expert with management experience. They spent two years researching the market, writing a business plan,

and obtaining financing. Today they own and operate Suffolk County Fish & Reef, a store for fish hobbyists.
- *Helping underprivileged kids.* San Francisco businessmen Lee Zimmerman and Brian Anderluh wanted to help underprivileged kids. Learning that special funding was available for such a project, they prepared a business plan and received financing to buy Evergreen Lodge, a rustic resort where they provide staff internships for young adults aged 18 to 24. Their success is due to careful planning, persistence, and staying focused on their goals.

Sources: Based on information from Stacy Perman, "Where Entrepreneurs Find Inspiration," *Business-Week Online,* November 21, 2006, **www.businessweek.com**; Anne Field, "The Resort That Serves Its Staff," *FSB,* December 2006, p. 72; Adina Genn, "Entrepreneurs Open One-Stop-Shop Exclusively for Fish Owners," *Long Island Business News,* November 17, 2006, n.p.; Karen E. Spaeder, "How to Research Your Business Idea," *Entrepreneur,* November 29, 2006, **www.Entrepreneur.com**.

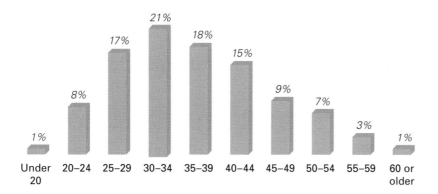

FIGURE 6.1

How Old Is the Average Entrepreneur?

People in all age groups become entrepreneurs, but more than 70 percent are between 24 and 44 years of age.

Source: Data developed and provided by the National Federation of Independent Business Foundation and sponsored by the American Express Travel Related Services Company, Inc.

Other Personal Factors

Other personal factors in small-business success include

* Independence

* A desire to determine one's own destiny

* A willingness to find and accept a challenge

* Family background (In particular, researchers think that people whose families have been in business, successfully or not, are most apt to start and run their own businesses.)

* Age (Those who start their own businesses also tend to cluster around certain ages—more than 70 percent are between 24 and 44 years of age; see Figure 6.1.)

Motivation

There must be some motivation to start a business. A person may decide that he or she simply has "had enough" of working and earning a profit for someone else. Another may lose his or her job for some reason and decide to start the business he or she has always wanted rather than to seek another job. Still another person may have an idea for a new product or a new way to sell an existing product. Or the opportunity to go into business may arise suddenly, perhaps as a result of a hobby. **EXAMPLE** Cheryl Strand started baking and decorating cakes from her home while working full time as a word processor at Clemson University. Her cakes became so popular that she soon found herself working through her lunch breaks and late into the night to meet customer demand.

Lighting Up the Cities with Lights.

Meet CEO Maryanne Cataldo who founded City Lights Electrical Company in 1989. A summa cum laude graduate of the University of Massachusetts and a master electrician, she started one of the state's first woman-owned electrical construction companies, while attending Harvard Business School to earn an MBA. Today, her company is New England's premier electrical company and is a recognized industry leader.

Women as Small Business Owners

* Women are 51 percent of the U.S. population, and according to the SBA, they owned at least 50 percent of all small businesses in 2005.

* Women already own 66 percent of the home-based businesses in this country, and the number of men in home-based businesses is growing rapidly.

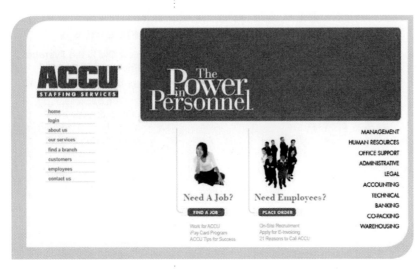

The Power in Personnel.

Doris M. Damm, president and CEO of ACCU Staffing Services of Delaware Valley, NJ, has been named one of the top 500 woman-owned companies in the United Sates, and one of the top 15 woman-owned staffing services in the nation. Starting her business in a small leased office, today her company spans 21 regional offices and provides staffing, consulting and corporate outplacement services to its clients.

* According to the SBA, 6.5 million women-owned businesses in the United States provide over 7.1 million jobs and generate $941 billion in sales and $174 billion in payroll annually.

* Women-owned businesses in the United States have proven that they are more successful; over 40 percent have been in business for twelve years or more.

* According to Dun and Bradstreet, women-owned businesses are financially sound and creditworthy, and their risk of failure is lower than average.

* Just over one-half of small businesses are home-based, and 91 percent have no employees. About 60 percent of home-based businesses are in service industries, 16 percent in construction, 14 percent in retail trade, and the rest in manufacturing, finance, transportation, communications, wholesaling, and other industries.[7]

In some people, the motivation to start a business develops slowly as they gain the knowledge and ability required for success as a business owner. Knowledge and ability—especially management ability—are probably the most important factors involved. A new firm is very much built around the entrepreneur. The owner must be able to manage the firm's finances, its personnel (if there are any employees), and its day-to-day operations. He or she must handle sales, advertising, purchasing, pricing, and a variety of other business functions. The knowledge and ability to do so are acquired most often through experience working for other firms in the same area of business.

Why Some Entrepreneurs and Small Businesses Fail

Small businesses are prone to failure. Key reasons for failure and survival are

* Capital
* Management
* Planning

Capital Businesses can experience a number of money-related problems. It may take several years before a business begins to show a profit. Entrepreneurs need to have not only the capital to open a business but also the money to operate it in its possibly lengthy start-up phase. One cash-flow obstacle often leads to others. And a series of cash-flow predicaments usually ends in a business failure. **EXAMPLE** In one month alone, Digital Entertainment Network shut its video-streaming site, clothing distributor boo.com closed after spending more than $100 million in only six months of business, and healthshop.com shut its doors completely after failing to meet its investors' expectations.[8]

CONCEPT CHECK

What are the major causes of small-business failure? Do these causes also apply to larger businesses?

Management and Planning Many entrepreneurs lack the management skills required to run a business. Money, time, personnel, and inventory all need to be managed effectively if a small business is to succeed. Starting a small business requires much more than optimism and a good idea.

Success and expansion sometimes lead to problems. Frequently, entrepreneurs with successful small businesses make the mistake of overexpansion. Fast growth often results in dramatic changes in a business. Thus the entrepreneur must plan carefully and adjust competently to new and potentially disruptive situations.

Every day and in every part of the country, people open new businesses. **EXAMPLE** Recently, 649,700 new businesses opened their doors, but at the same time, 564,900 businesses closed their business and 19,695 businesses declared bankruptcy.[9] Although many fail, others represent well-conceived ideas developed by entrepreneurs who have the expertise, resources, and determination to make their businesses succeed. As these well-prepared entrepreneurs pursue their individual goals, our society benefits in many ways from their work and creativity.

ACE the Test
ACE & ACE+
Practice Test 6.2

TEST PREPPER 6.2

True or False?

___T___ 1. More than 70 percent of Americans would prefer being an entrepreneur to working for someone else.

___T___ 2. The desire to determine one's own destiny is one of the personal factors affecting entrepreneurship.

___F___ 3. Many entrepreneurs lack the management skills required to run a business. This refers to the inability of entrepreneurs to earn enough money to open a business and keep it operational through its start-up phase.

___T___ 4. When well-prepared entrepreneurs pursue their individual goals, our society benefits in many ways from their work and creativity.

Multiple Choice

___C___ 5. According to many experts, women-owned businesses are more successful than their male counterparts. Which of the following best explains this phenomenon?

    a. Women own 66 percent of the home-based businesses in the United States.
    b. Women are 51 percent of the U.S. population.
    c. Women-owned businesses are financially sound and creditworthy.
    d. Since over one-half of small businesses are home-based, and women tend to be at home more often, they are better entrepreneurs.
    e. Most women belong to a prime entrepreneurial age, that is, the 24-and 44-year age group.

The Importance of Small Businesses in Our Economy

ACE the Test
Hangman

Learning Objective ③

Assess the contributions of small businesses to our economy.

This country's economic history abounds with stories of ambitious men and women who turned their ideas into business dynasties. The Ford Motor Company started as a one-man operation with an innovative method for industrial production. L. L. Bean, Inc., can trace its beginnings to a basement shop in Freeport, Maine.

Providing Technical Innovation

Invention and innovation are part of the foundations of our economy. The increases in productivity that have characterized the past 200 years of our history are all rooted in one principal source: new ways to do a job with less effort for less money. Studies show that the incidence of innovation among small-business workers is significantly higher than among workers in large businesses. Small firms produce two and a half times as many innovations as large firms relative to the number of persons employed. In fact, small firms employ 41 percent of all high-tech workers such as scientists, engineers, and computer specialists. No wonder small firms produce thirteen to fourteen times more patents per employee than large patenting firms.[10] According to the U.S. Office of Management and Budget, more than half the major technological advances of the twentieth century originated with individual inventors and small companies. Even just a sampling of those innovations is remarkable:

* Air conditioning
* Airplane
* Automatic transmission
* FM radio
* Heart valve
* Helicopter
* Instant camera
* Insulin
* Jet engine
* Penicillin
* Personal computer
* Power steering

Perhaps even more remarkable—and important—is that many of these inventions sparked major new U.S. industries or contributed to an established industry by adding some valuable service.

Providing Employment

Small firms traditionally have added more than their proportional share of new jobs to the economy. Recently, the U.S. economy created over three million new jobs. Seven of the ten industries that added the most new jobs were small-business-dominated industries. Small businesses creating the most new jobs recently included business services, leisure and hospitality services, and special trade contractors. Small firms hire a larger proportion of employees who are younger workers, older workers, women, and workers who prefer to work part time. Furthermore, small businesses provide 67 percent of workers with their first jobs and initial on-the-job training in basic skills. According to the SBA, small businesses represent 99.7 percent of all employers, employ about 50 percent of the private work force, and provide 60 to 80 percent of the net new jobs added to our economy.[11]

Providing Competition

Small businesses challenge larger, established firms in many ways, causing them to become more efficient and more responsive to consumer needs. A small business cannot, of course, compete with a large firm in all respects. But a number of small firms, each competing in its own particular area and its own particular way, together have the desired competitive effect. Thus several small janitorial companies together add up to reasonable competition for the no-longer-small ServiceMaster.

Filling Needs of Society and Other Businesses

By their nature, large firms must operate on a large scale. Many may be unwilling or unable to meet the special needs of smaller groups of consumers. Such groups create almost perfect markets for small companies, which can tailor their products to these groups and fill their needs profitably. **EXAMPLE** A firm that modifies automobile controls to accommodate handicapped drivers is a prime example.

Small firms also provide a variety of goods and services to each other and to much larger firms. Sears, Roebuck purchases merchandise from approximately 12,000 suppliers—and most of them are small businesses. **EXAMPLE** General Motors relies on more than 32,000 companies for parts and supplies and depends on more than 11,000 independent dealers to sell its automobiles and trucks. Large firms generally buy parts and assemblies from smaller firms for one very good reason: It is less expensive than manufacturing the parts in their own factories. This lower cost eventually is reflected in the price that consumers pay for their products.

It is clear that small businesses are a vital part of our economy and that, as consumers and as members of the labor force, we all benefit enormously from their existence. Now let us look at the situation from the viewpoint of the owners of small businesses.

> **CONCEPT CHECK**
> Briefly describe four contributions of small business to the American economy.

The Pros and Cons of Smallness

Learning Objective ④

Judge the advantages and disadvantages of operating a small business.

Do most owners of small businesses dream that their firms will grow into giant corporations—managed by professionals—while they serve only on the board of directors? Or would they rather stay small, in a firm where they have the opportunity (and the responsibility) to do everything that needs to be done? The answers depend on the personal characteristics and motivations of the individual owners. For many, the advantages of remaining small far outweigh the disadvantages.

Advantages of Small Business

Small-business owners with limited resources often must struggle to enter competitive new markets. They also have to deal with increasing international competition. However, they enjoy several unique advantages.

Personal Relationships with Customers and Employees For those who like dealing with people, small business is the place to be. The owners of retail shops get to know many of their customers by name and deal with them on a personal basis. Through such relationships, small-business owners often become involved in the social, cultural, and political life of the community.

Relationships between owner-managers and employees also tend to be closer in smaller businesses. In many cases, the owner is a friend and counselor as well as the boss. These personal relationships provide an important business advantage. The personal service small businesses offer to customers is a major competitive weapon—one that larger firms try to match but often cannot. In addition, close relationships with employees often help the small-business owner to keep effective workers who might earn more with a larger firm.

Ability to Adapt to Change Being his or her own boss, the owner-manager of a small business does not need anyone's permission to adapt to change. An owner may add or discontinue merchandise or services, change store hours, and experiment with various price strategies in response to changes in market conditions. And through personal relationships with customers, the owners of small businesses quickly become aware of changes in people's needs and interests, as well as in the activities of competing firms.

Simplified Record Keeping Many small firms need only a simple set of records. Record keeping might consist of a checkbook, a cash-receipts journal in which to record all sales, and a cash-disbursements journal in which to record all amounts paid out. Obviously, enough records must be kept to allow for producing and filing accurate tax returns.

Independence Small-business owners do not have to punch in and out, bid for vacation times, take orders from superiors, or worry about being fired or laid off. They are the masters of their own destinies—at least with regard to employment. For many people, this is the prime advantage of owning a small business.

Other Advantages According to the SBA, the most profitable companies in the United States are small firms that have been in business for more than ten years and employ fewer than twenty people. Small-business owners also enjoy all the advantages of sole proprietorships, which were discussed in Chapter 5. These include being able to keep all profits, the ease and low cost of going into business and (if necessary) going out of business, and being able to keep business information secret.

Disadvantages of Small Business

In contrast to all the advantages of owning a small business, there is the dark side that reflects problems unique to these firms.

Risk of Failure As we have noted, small businesses (especially new ones) run a heavy risk of going out of business—about two of three close their doors within the first six years. Older, well-established small firms can be hit hard by a business recession mainly because they do not have the financial resources to weather an extended difficult period.

Limited Potential Small businesses that survive do so with varying degrees of success. Many are simply the means

SPOTLIGHT

Small business bankruptcies

The number of small business bankruptcies has dramatically decreased over the past two decades.

71,549 — 1991
39,201 — Today

CLOSED

Source: U.S. Census Bureau, U.S. Department of Labor, Employment, and Training Administration, Administrative Office of the U.S. Courts, 2004. **www.sba.gov/advo/**, October 2005.

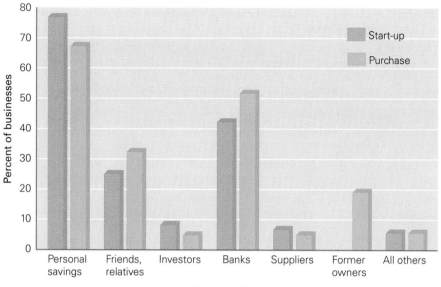

FIGURE 6.2

Sources of Capital for Entrepreneurs

Small businesses get financing from various sources; the most important is personal savings.

Source: Data developed and provided by the National Federation of Independent Business Foundation and sponsored by the American Express Travel Related Services Company, Inc.

of making a living for the owner and his or her family. **EXAMPLE** The owner may have some technical skill—such as a hair stylist or electrician—and may have started a business to put this skill to work. Such a business is unlikely to grow into big business. Also, employees' potential for advancement is limited.

Limited Ability to Raise Capital Small businesses typically have a limited ability to obtain capital. Figure 6.2 shows that most small-business financing comes out of the owner's pocket. Personal loans from lending institutions provide only about one-fourth of the capital required by small businesses. About 70 percent of all new firms begin with less than $25,000 in total capital, according to Census Bureau and Federal Reserve surveys. In fact, almost half of new firms begin with less than $10,000, usually provided by the owner or family members and friends.

Although every person who considers starting a small business should be aware of the hazards and pitfalls we have noted, a well-conceived business plan may help to avoid the risk of failure. The U.S. government is also dedicated to helping small businesses make it. It expresses this aim most actively through the SBA.

Advantages of Developing a Business Plan

Lack of planning can be as deadly as lack of money to a new small business. Planning is important to any business, large or small, and never should be overlooked or taken lightly. A **business plan** is a carefully constructed guide for the person starting a business. Consider it as a tool with three basic purposes: *communication, management*, and *planning*. As a communication tool, a business plan serves as a concise document that potential investors can examine to see if they would like to invest in or assist in financing a new venture. It shows whether a business has the potential to make a profit. As a management tool, the business plan helps to track, monitor, and evaluate progress. The business plan is a living document; it is modified as the entrepreneur gains knowledge and experience. It also serves to establish timelines

business plan a carefully constructed guide for the person starting a business

CONCEPT CHECK

What are the major components of a business plan? Why should an individual develop a business plan?

1. *Introduction.* Basic information such as the name, address, and phone number of the business; the date the plan was issued; and a statement of confidentiality to keep important information away from potential competitors.

2. *Executive summary.* A one- to two-page overview of the entire business plan, including a justification why the business will succeed.

3. *Benefits to the community.* Information on how the business will have an impact on economic development, community development, and human development.

4. *Company and industry.* The background of the company, choice of the legal business form, information on the products or services to be offered, and examination of the potential customers, current competitors, and the business's future.

5. *Management team.* Discussion of skills, talents, and job descriptions of management team, managerial compensation, management training needs, and professional assistance requirements.

6. *Manufacturing and operations plan.* Discussion of facilities needed, space requirements, capital equipment, labor force, inventory control, and purchasing requirement.

7. *Labor force.* Discussion of the quality of skilled workers available and the training, compensation, and motivation of workers.

8. *Marketing plan.* Discussion of markets, market trends, competition, market share, pricing, promotion, distribution, and service policy.

9. *Financial plan.* Summary of the investment needed, sales and cash-flow forecasts, breakeven analysis, and sources of funding.

10. *Exit strategy.* Discussion of a succession plan or going public. Who will take over the business?

11. *Critical risks and assumptions.* Evaluation of the weaknesses of the business and how the company plans to deal with these and other business problems.

12. *Appendix.* Supplementary information crucial to the plan, such as résumés of owners and principal managers, advertising samples, organization chart, and any related information.

TABLE 6.3

Components of a Business Plan

Source: Adapted from Timothy S. Hatten, *Small Business Management: Entrepreneurship and Beyond,* 3d ed. (Boston: Houghton Mifflin, 2006), pp. 108–120. Reprinted by permission.

and milestones and allows comparison of growth projections against actual accomplishments. Finally, as a planning tool, the business plan guides a business person through the various phases of business. For example, the plan helps to identify obstacles to avoid and to establish alternatives. According to Robert Krummer, Jr., chairman of First Business Bank in Los Angeles, "The business plan is a necessity. If the person who wants to start a small business can't put a business plan together, he or she is in trouble."

Components of a Business Plan

Table 6.3 shows the twelve sections that a business plan should include. Officials of financial institutions do not have the time to wade through pages of extraneous data. The business plan should answer the four questions banking officials and investors are most interested in: (1) What exactly is the nature and mission of the new venture? (2) Why is this new enterprise a good idea? (3) What are the business person's goals? (4) How much will the new venture cost?

The great amount of time and consideration that should go into creating a business plan probably will end up saving time later. For example, Sharon Burch, who was running a computer software business while earning a degree in business administration, had to write a business plan as part of one of her courses. Burch has said, "I wish I'd taken the class before I started my business. I see a lot of things I could have done differently. But it has helped me since because I've been using the business plan as a guide for my business." Table 6.4 provides a business plan checklist.

Accuracy and realistic expectations are crucial to an effective business plan. It is unethical to deceive loan officers, and it is unwise to deceive yourself.

1. Does the executive summary grab the reader's attention and highlight the major points of the business plan?

2. Does the business-concept section clearly describe the purpose of the business, the customers, the value proposition, and the distribution channel and convey a compelling story?

3. Do the industry and market analyses support acceptance and demand for the business concept in the marketplace and define a first customer in depth?

4. Does the management-team plan persuade the reader that the team could implement the business concept successfully? Does it assure the reader that an effective infrastructure is in place to facilitate the goals and operations of the company?

5. Does the product/service plan clearly provide details on the status of the product, the timeline for completion, and the intellectual property that will be acquired?

6. Does the operations plan prove that the product or service could be produced and distributed efficiently and effectively?

7. Does the marketing plan successfully demonstrate how the company will create customer awareness in the target market and deliver the benefit to the customer?

8. Does the financial plan convince the reader that the business model is sustainable—that it will provide a superior return on investment for the investor and sufficient cash flow to repay loans to potential lenders?

9. Does the growth plan convince the reader that the company has long-term growth potential and spin-off products and services?

10. Does the contingency and exit-strategy plan convince the reader that the risk associated with this venture can be mediated? Is there an exit strategy in place for investors?

TABLE 6.4

Business Plan Checklist

Source: Kathleen R. Allen, *Launching New Ventures: An Entrepreneurial Approach*, 4th ed. (Boston: Houghton Mifflin, 2006), p. 197. Reprinted by permission.

ACE the Test
ACE & ACE+
Practice Tests 6.3, 6.4

TEST PREPPER 6.3 6.4

True or False?

1. Small businesses, especially new ones, run a heavy risk of going out of business. However, older, well-established small firms rarely face difficulties once they have been operational for several years.

2. One of the components of a business plan is *company and industry.* This refers to the background of the company, choice of the legal business form, information on the products or services to be offered, and examination of the potential customers, current competitors, and the business's future.

Multiple Choice

3. A firm that modifies automobile controls to accommodate handicapped drivers essentially fulfills special needs of smaller groups of consumers who the larger firm is unwilling to service. This is a good example of which of the following characteristics of small businesses?

   a. Providing employment with flexible work hours to employees who are younger workers, older workers, women, or workers who prefer to work part time
   b. The ability to collectively challenge larger, established firms in many ways, causing them to become more efficient and more responsive to consumer needs
   c. Supplying parts and assemblies to large firms at a lower cost
   d. Hiring elite workers such as scientists, engineers, and computer specialists
   e. The innovative capacity to tailor mainstream products to special-needs groups and fill their needs profitably

4. The owners of retail shops get to know many of their customers by name and deal with them on a personal basis. Which of the following is one of the advantages of knowing your customers on a personal basis?

   a. It helps small-business owners to keep effective workers who might earn more with a larger firm.
   b. It enables personal service, a major competitive weapon.
   c. Small firms need only a simple set of records.
   d. It allows small-business owners independence by not having to take orders from superiors.
   e. It enables owners to be very perceptive to changes in market conditions, particularly in response to consumer demand.

5. Facilities needed, space requirements, capital equipment, labor force, inventory control, and purchasing requirement are all part of which component of a business statement?

   a. Financial plan
   b. Management team
   c. Labor force
   d. Management team
   e. Manufacturing and operations plan

The Small Business Administration

Learning Objective ⑤

Explain how the Small Business Administration helps small businesses.

Small Business Administration (SBA) a governmental agency that assists, counsels, and protects the interests of small businesses in the United States

The **Small Business Administration (SBA)**, created by Congress in 1953, is a governmental agency that assists, counsels, and protects the interests of small businesses in the United States. It helps people get into business and stay in business. The agency provides assistance to owners and managers of prospective, new, and established small businesses. Through more than 1,000 offices and resource centers throughout the nation, the SBA provides both financial assistance and management counseling. Recently, the SBA provided training, technical assistance, and education to over two million small businesses. It helps small firms to bid for and obtain government contracts, and it helps them to prepare to enter foreign markets.

Services Offered by the SBA

* Management assistance
* Management courses and workshops
* The Service Corps of Retired Executives (SCORE)
* Help for minority-owned businesses, especially those owned by women
* Small Business Institutes (SBIs)
* Small Business Development Centers (SBDCs)
* SBA publications
* SBA financial assitance
* Regular business loans
* Small Business Investment Companies (SBICs)

Management Services of the SBA

SBA Management Assistance Statistics show that most failures in small business are related to poor management. For this reason, the SBA places special emphasis on improving the management ability of the owners and managers of small businesses. The SBA's Management Assistance Program is extensive and diversified. It includes free individual counseling, courses, conferences, workshops, and a wide range of publications. Recently, the SBA provided management and technical assistance to nearly two million small businesses through its 950 Small Business Development Centers and 10,500 volunteers from the Service Corps of Retired Executives.[12]

Service Corps of Retired Executives (SCORE) a group of retired business people who volunteer their services to small businesses through the SBA

Management Courses and Workshops The management courses offered by the SBA cover all the functions, duties, and roles of managers. Instructors may be teachers from local colleges and universities or other professionals, such as management consultants, bankers, lawyers, and accountants. Fees for these courses are quite low. The SBA occasionally offers one-day conferences. These conferences are aimed at keeping owner-managers up-to-date on new management developments, tax laws, and the like.

The Small Business Training Network (SBTN) is an online training network consisting of eighty-three SBA-run courses, workshops, and resources. Recently, the SBA website (**www .sba.gov/training**) hosted more than one million visitors and trained nearly 2.5 million small-business owners.[13]

SCORE The Service Corps of Retired Executives (SCORE), created in 1964, is a group of more than 10,500 retired business people including over 2,000 women who volunteer their services to small businesses through the SBA. The collective experience of SCORE volunteers spans the full range of American enterprise. These volunteers have worked for such notable companies as Eastman Kodak, General Electric, IBM, and Procter & Gamble. Experts in areas of accounting, finance, marketing, engineering, and retailing provide counseling and mentoring to entrepreneurs.

A small-business owner who has a particular problem can request free counseling from SCORE. An assigned counselor visits the owner in his or her establishment and, through careful observation, analyzes the business situation and the problem. If the problem is complex, the counselor may call on other volunteer experts to assist. Finally, the counselor offers a plan for solving the problem and helping the owner through the critical period.

Consider the plight of Elizabeth Halvorsen, a mystery writer from Minneapolis. Her husband had built up the family advertising and graphic arts firm for seventeen years when he was called in 1991 to serve in the Persian Gulf War. The only one left behind who could run the business was Mrs. Halvorsen, who admittedly had no business experience. Enter SCORE. With a SCORE management expert at her side, she kept the business on track. Since 1964, SCORE volunteers have assisted more than 7.7 million small-business people like Mrs. Halvorsen.[14]

Help for Minority-Owned Small Businesses Americans who are members of minority groups have had difficulty entering the nation's economic mainstream. Raising money is a nagging problem for minority business owners, who also may lack adequate training. Members of minority groups are, of course, eligible for all SBA programs, but the SBA makes a special effort to assist those who want to start small businesses or expand existing ones. For example, the Minority Business Development Agency awards grants to develop and increase business opportunities for members of racial and ethnic minorities. Recently, over 4.1 million minority-owned firms in the United States provided over 4.8 million jobs and generated $694.1 billion in sales.[15] Helping women become entrepreneurs is also a special goal of the SBA.

Small-Business Institutes Small-business institutes (SBIs), created in 1972, are groups of senior and graduate students in business administration who provide management counseling to small businesses. SBIs have been set up on over 520 college campuses as another way to help business owners. The students work in small groups guided by faculty advisers and SBA management-assistance experts. Like SCORE volunteers, they analyze and help solve the problems of small-business owners at their business establishments.

Cool idea is a hot business.

Want a party for kids where parents can have fun too? Then go to a party at Little Scoops, and let the fun begin. Since 2001, Michelle Violetto and Tanya Ehrlich have hosted hundreds of parties and opened nine additions to their business. Both partners credit SCORE's volunteer counselors for their success. Violetto says, "We have lots of female friends who have started their own businesses. We refer them all to SCORE."

small-business institutes (SBIs) groups of senior and graduate students in business administration who provide management counseling to small businesses

small-business development centers (SBDCs) university-based groups that provide individual counseling and practical training to owners of small businesses

CONCEPT CHECK

Why does the SBA concentrate on providing management and financial assistance to small businesses?

Cleaning Up Katrina's Mess.

Following a disaster, through its Office of Disaster Assistance, the Small Business Administration provides affordable, timely and accessible financial assistance to businesses, homeowners and renters. Here, the SBA Administrator, Hector Barreto, answers questions concerning financial aid for Hurricane Katrina's victims.

Small-Business Development Centers Small-business development centers (SBDCs) are university-based groups that provide individual counseling and practical training to owners of small businesses. SBDCs draw from the resources of local, state, and federal governments, private businesses, and universities. These groups can provide managerial and technical help, data from research studies, and other types of specialized assistance of value to small businesses. Recently, there were over 1,100 SBDC locations, primarily at colleges and universities, assisting people such as Kathleen DuBois. After scribbling a list of her abilities and the names of potential clients on a napkin in a local restaurant, Kathleen DuBois decided to start her own marketing firm. Beth Thornton launched her engineering firm after a discussion with a colleague in the ladies room of the Marriott. These entrepreneurs took different routes in starting their new businesses in West Virginia, but they both turned to the West Virginia Small Business Development Center for the technical assistance to make their dreams become a reality.[16]

SBA Publications The SBA issues management, marketing, and technical publications dealing with hundreds of topics of interest to present and prospective managers of small firms. Most of these publications are available from the SBA free of charge. Others can be obtained for a small fee from the U.S. Government Printing Office.

Financial Services of the SBA

SBA Financial Assistance Small businesses seem to be constantly in need of money. An owner may have enough capital to start and operate the business. But then he or she may require more money to finance increased operations owing to different circumstances. **EXAMPLE** The Supplemental Terrorist Activity Relief (STAR) program has made $3.7 billion in loans to 8,202 small businesses harmed or disrupted by the September 11 terrorist attacks. In October 2005, the SBA guaranteed loans of up to $150,000 to small businesses affected by hurricanes Katrina and Rita.[17]

The SBA offers special financial-assistance programs that cover different situations. However, its primary financial function is to guarantee loans to eligible businesses.

Regular Business Loans Most of the SBA's business loans actually are made by private lenders such as banks, but repayment is partially guaranteed by the agency. That is, the SBA may guarantee that it will repay the lender up to 90 percent of the loan if the borrowing firm cannot repay it. Guaranteed loans approved on or after October 1, 2002, may be as large as $1.5 million (this loan limit may be increased in the future). The average size of an SBA-guaranteed business loan is about $300,000, and its average duration is about eight years. Recently, the SBA approved approximately $20 billion in guaranteed loans.[18]

Small-Business Investment Companies Venture capital is money that is invested in small (and sometimes struggling) firms that have the potential to become very successful. In many cases, only a lack of capital keeps these firms from rapid and solid growth. The people who invest in such firms expect that their investments will grow with the firms and become quite profitable.

The popularity of these investments has increased over the past twenty-five years, but most small firms still have difficulty obtaining venture capital. To help such businesses, the SBA licenses, regulates, and provides financial assistance to small-business investment companies (SBICs). An SBIC is a privately owned firm that provides venture capital to small enterprises that meet its investment standards. Such small firms as America Online, Apple Computer, Federal Express, Compaq Computer, Intel Corporation, Outback Steakhouse, and Staples, Inc., all were financed through SBICs during their initial growth period. SBICs are intended to be profit-making organizations. The aid the SBA offers allows them to invest in small businesses that otherwise would not attract venture capital. In 2006, SBICs financed 3,674 firms, providing them with $2.98 billion in capital. Since Congress created the program in 1958, SBICs have financed over 100,000 small businesses for a total of over $48 billion.[19]

Can one preserve one's independence as a business owner and still enjoy some of the benefits of "bigness"? Let's take a close look at franchising.

venture capital money that is invested in small (and sometimes struggling) firms that have the potential to become very successful

small-business investment companies (SBICs) privately owned firms that provide venture capital to small enterprises that meet their investment standards

TEST PREPPER 6.5

True or False?

_T_ 1. The SBA provides assistance to owners and managers of prospective, new, and established small businesses.

_T_ 2. Most of the SBA's business loans actually are made by public lenders such as banks, but repayment is partially guaranteed by the agency.

_F_ 3. Small-business development centers (SBDCs) are privately owned firms that provide venture capital to small enterprises that meet their investment standards.

_T_ 4. The Service Corps of Retired Executives (SCORE) is a group of retired business people who

volunteer their services to small businesses through the SBA.

Multiple Choice

_C_ 5. Which of the following is not one of the ways in which the SBA provides management assistance to small businesses?

   a. Provides free individual counseling
   b. Protects the interests of small businesses
   c. Provides all small firms with guaranteed government contracts
   d. Provides data from research studies
   e. Offers special financial-assistance programs

ACE the Test
ACE & ACE+
Practice Test 6.5

Franchising

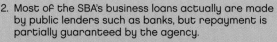

Learning Objective 6
Appraise the concept and types of franchising.

A **franchise** is a license to operate an individually owned business as if it were part of a chain of outlets or stores. Often the business itself is also called a *franchise*. Among the most familiar franchises are McDonald's, H & R Block, AAMCO Transmissions, GNC (General Nutrition Centers), and Dairy Queen. Many other franchises carry familiar names; this method of doing business has become very popular in the last thirty years or so. It is an attractive means of starting and operating a small business.

What Is Franchising?

Franchising is the actual granting of a franchise. A **franchisor** is an individual or organization granting a franchise. A **franchisee** is a person or organization

franchise a license to operate an individually owned business as though it were part of a chain of outlets or stores

franchising the actual granting of a franchise

franchisor an individual or organization granting a franchise

franchisee a person or organization purchasing a franchise

The Putt-Putt Fun.

When you purchase a Putt-Putt Fun Center franchise, you become a part of a 50-year tradition of family fun. The Fun Centers are mini amusement parks for children and adults. The new franchises include such attractions as go-karts, rock climbing, children's rides, a game room, snack bar, and make-your-own stuffed animal center.

TABLE 6.5

McDonald's Conventional Franchise Agreement as of October 2007

Source: McDonald's Corporation, Oak Brook, IL. Used with permission from McDonald's Corporation.

purchasing a franchise. The franchisor supplies a known and advertised business name, management skills, the required training and materials, and a method of doing business. The franchisee supplies labor and capital, operates the franchised business, and agrees to abide by the provisions of the franchise agreement. Table 6.5 lists some items that would be covered in a typical franchise agreement.

Types of Franchising

Franchising arrangements fall into three general categories.

Retail Franchising In the first approach, a manufacturer authorizes a number of retail stores to sell a certain brand-name item. This type of franchising arrangement, one of the oldest, is prevalent in sales of passenger cars and trucks, farm equipment, shoes, paint, earth-moving equipment, and petroleum. About 90 percent of all gasoline is sold through franchised, independent retail service stations, and franchised dealers handle virtually all sales of new cars and trucks.

License Franchising In the second type of franchising arrangement, a producer licenses distributors to sell a given product to retailers. This arrangement is common in the soft-drink industry. Most national manufacturers of soft-drink syrups—the

MCDONALD'S (FRANCHISOR) PROVIDES	INDIVIDUAL (FRANCHISEE) SUPPLIES
1. Nationally recognized trademarks and an established reputation for quality	1. Total investment of approximately $685,750 to $1,504,000, which includes initial franchise fee of $45,000
2. Designs and color schemes for restaurants, signs, and equipment	2. Approximate cash requirement of 40 percent of total investment; a minimum of $250,000 of nonborrowed personal funds
3. Specifications for certain food products	3. A monthly base rent or rent based on a percentage of monthly sales
4. Proven methods of inventory and operations control	4. A minimum of 4 percent of gross sales annually for marketing and advertising
5. Bookkeeping, accounting, and policies manuals specially geared toward a franchised restaurant	5. Payment of a service fee of 4 percent of monthly gross sales to McDonald's
6. A franchise term of up to twenty years	6. Payment of a variable rent percent of monthly gross sales to McDonald's based on McDonald's investment and/or sales
7. Formal training program completed on a part-time basis in approximately eighteen to twenty-four months in a McDonald's restaurant	7. Kitchen equipment, seating, decor, lighting, and signs in conformity with McDonald's standards (included in total investment figure)
8. Five weeks of classroom training, including two weeks at Hamburger University	8. Taxes, insurance, and maintenance costs on the restaurant building and land
9. Ongoing regional support services and field service staff	9. Commitment to ensuring high-quality standards and upholding the McDonald's reputation
10. Research and development of labor-saving equipment and methods	
11. Monthly bulletins, periodicals, or meetings to inform franchisees about management and marketing techniques	
12. Site selection (purchase or lease) and development, including building	

Coca-Cola Company, Dr. Pepper/Seven-Up Companies, PepsiCo, and Royal Crown Companies, Inc.—franchise independent bottlers who then serve retailers.

Service Franchising In a third form of franchising, a franchisor supplies brand names, techniques, or other services instead of a complete product. Although the franchisor may provide certain production and distribution services, its primary role is the careful development and control of marketing strategies. This approach to franchising, which is the most typical today, is used by Holiday Inns, Howard Johnson Company, AAMCO Transmissions, McDonald's, Dairy Queen, Avis, Hertz Corporation, KFC (Kentucky Fried Chicken), and SUBWAY, to name but a few.

Your Career

Franchising Starts with a Vision

Is your future in franchising? Two Washington state entrepreneurs started with a vision when launching Dream Dinners, now a nationwide franchise business. Stephanie Allen and Tina Kuna realized that families wanted healthy meals without the time and hassle of shopping, extensive food preparation, and cleanup. They dreamed up the concept of franchising assembly-line meal-preparation "parties." Each franchise location supplies exclusive recipes and fresh, ready-cut ingredients so that customers can quickly and conveniently put together a number of entrees to take home and freeze for future use.

Allen and Kuna were able to franchise their business with help from the SBA. Four years after founding Dream Dinners, they had sold 300 franchises—and expect to grow to 600 in the next year. If you're thinking about a career in franchising, you'll need what Allen and Kuna have

- A clear vision and goals for the company
- A well-written business plan
- A clear understanding of the costs, time, and dedication needed to succeed
- A track record of business experience

Sources: Based on information from Eileen Gunn, "Cranky Customer: A New Way to Get a Home-Cooked Meal," *Wall Street Journal*, February 2, 2006, p. D4; Brad Broberg, "Fast-Growing Franchisor's Entrée Came from SBA-Backed Loan," *Los Angeles Business Journal,* May 15, 2006, p. S12; Joe Matthews, Don DeBolt, and Deb Percival, "Setting Goals for Franchise Success," *Entrepreneur*, October 2, 2006, **www.Entrepreneur.com.**

The Growth of Franchising

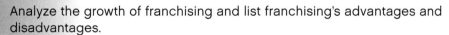

Learning Objective 7

Analyze the growth of franchising and list franchising's advantages and disadvantages.

CONCEPT CHECK

Explain the relationships among a franchise, the franchisor, and the franchisee.

Franchising, which began in the United States around the time of the Civil War, was used originally by large firms, such as the Singer Sewing Company, to distribute their products. Franchising has been increasing steadily in popularity since the early 1900s, primarily for filling stations and car dealerships; however, this retailing

RANK	FRANCHISE	TOTAL INVESTMENT	FRANCHISE FEE	ROYALTY FEE	NET-WORTH REQUIREMENT	CASH REQUIREMENT	COMMENTS
1	Subway	$74,900–$222,800	$15,000	8 %	$30,000–$90,000	$30,000–$90,000	20-year renewable term
2	Dunkin' Donuts	$179,000–$1,600,000	$40,000–$80,000	5.9 %	$1,500,000	$750,000	
3	Jackson Hewitt Tax Service	$48,600–$91,800	$25,000	15 %	Varies	$50,000	10-year renewable term
4	7-Eleven, Inc.	Varies	Varies	Varies	Varies	Varies	15-year renewable term
5	UPS Store/Mail Boxes, etc.	$153,950–$266,800	$29,950	5 %	$150,000	$60,000	10-year renewable term
6	Domino's Pizza, LLC	$141,400–$415,100	$15,000	5.5 %		$75,000	10-year renewable term
7	Jiffy Lube Int'l Inc.	$214,000–$273,000	$35,000	To 5 %	$450,000	$150,000	20-year renewable term; renewal fee $17,500
8	Sonic Drive-In Restaurants	$861,300	$30,000	1–5 %	$1,000,000	$500,000	20-year renewable term; renewal fee $6,000
9	McDonald's	$506,000–$1,600.000	$45,000	12.5 %+		$100,000	20-year renewable term; renewal fee $45,000
10	Papa John's Int'l Inc.	$250,000	$25,000	4 %	$185,000	$100,000	10-year renewable term; renewal fee $3,000

TABLE 6.6

Entrepreneur's top ten Franchises in 2007

Source: Reprinted with permission from *Entrepreneur* Magazine, **www.entrepreneur.com**; accessed August 25, 2007.

strategy has experienced enormous growth since the mid-1970s. A new franchise opens every eight minutes somewhere in the United States.[20] The franchise proliferation generally has paralleled the expansion of the fast-food industry. As Table 6.6 shows, six of *Entrepreneur* magazine's top-rated franchises for 2007 were in this category.

Of course, franchising is not limited to fast foods. Hair salons, tanning parlors, and dentists and lawyers are expected to participate in franchising arrangements in growing numbers. Franchised health clubs, pest exterminators, and campgrounds are already widespread, as are franchised tax preparers and travel agencies. The real estate industry also has experienced a rapid increase in franchising.

Also, franchising is attracting more women and minority business owners in the United States than ever before. One reason is that special outreach programs designed to encourage franchisee diversity have developed. **EXAMPLE** Consider Angela Trammel, a young mother of two. She had been laid off from her job at the Marriott after 9/11. Since she was a member of a Curves Fitness Center and liked the concept of empowering women to become physically fit, she began researching the cost of purchasing a Curves franchise and ways to finance the business. "I was online looking for financing, and I linked to Enterprise Development Group in Washington, D.C. I knew that they had diverse clients." The cost for the franchise was $19,500, but it took $60,000 to open the doors to her fitness center. "Applying for a loan to start the business was much harder than buying a house," said Trammel. Just three years later, Angela and her husband, Ernest, own three Curves

Fitness Centers with twelve employees. Recently, giving birth to her third child, she has found the financial freedom and flexibility needed to care for her busy family. In fact, within a three-year period, the Trammel's grew their annual household income from $80,000 to $250,000.[21] Franchisors such as Wendy's, McDonald's, Burger King, and Church's Chicken all have special corporate programs to attract minority and women franchisees. Just as important, successful women and minority franchisees are willing to get involved by offering advice and guidance to new franchisees.

Dual-branded franchises, in which two franchisors offer their products together, are a new small-business trend. For example, in 1993, pleased with the success of its first cobranded restaurant with Texaco in Beebe, Arkansas, McDonald's now has over 400 cobranded restaurants in the United States. Also, an agreement between franchisors Doctor's Associates, Inc., and TCBY Enterprises, Inc., now allows franchisees to sell SUBWAY sandwiches and TCBY yogurt in the same establishment.

Are Franchises Successful?

Franchising is designed to provide a tested formula for success, along with ongoing advice and training. The success rate for businesses owned and operated by franchisees is significantly higher than the success rate for other independently owned small businesses. In a recent nationwide Gallup poll of 944 franchise owners, 94 percent of franchisees indicated that they were very or somewhat successful, only 5 percent believed that they were very unsuccessful or somewhat unsuccessful, and 1 percent did not know. Despite these impressive statistics, franchising is not a guarantee of success for either franchisees or franchisors. Too rapid expansion, inadequate capital or management skills, and a host of other problems can cause failure for both franchisee and franchisor. **EXAMPLE** Thus, the Dizzy Dean's Beef and Burger franchise is no longer in business. Timothy Bates, a Wayne State University economist, warns, "Despite the hype that franchising is the safest way to go when starting a new business, the research just doesn't bear that out." Just consider Boston Chicken, which once had more than 1,200 restaurants before declaring bankruptcy in 1998.

Advantages of Franchising

Franchising plays a vital role in our economy and soon may become the dominant form of retailing. Why? Because franchising offers advantages to both the franchisor and the franchisee.

Brand Marriage Made in Heaven.

According to Chuck Rawley, president and chief operating officer of Kentucky Fried Chicken, "KFC/A&W brands merge well. Both have a strong signature product: KFC's fried chicken and A&W's root beer floats. There are a lot of similarities with both being established brands that are old yet contemporary."

To the Franchisor The franchisor benefits are as follows:

1. The franchisor gets fast and well-controlled distribution of its products without incurring the high cost of constructing and operating its own outlets.

2. Because of the preceding reason, the franchisor thus has more capital available to expand production and to use for advertising.

3. Through the franchise agreement, the franchisor makes sure that outlets are maintained and operated according to its own standards.

4. Usually a franchisee is a sole proprietor who is likely to be very highly motivated to succeed. The success of the franchise means more sales, which translate into higher royalties for the franchisor.

To the Franchisee The benefits for the franchisee are as follows:

1. The franchisee gets the opportunity to start a business with limited capital and to make use of the business experience of others.

2. The franchisee operates an outlet with a nationally advertised name, such as Radio Shack, McDonald's, or Century 21 Real Estate and has guaranteed customers as soon as it opens.

3. If business problems arise, the franchisor gives the franchisee guidance and advice. This counseling is primarily responsible for the very high degree of success enjoyed by franchises. In most cases, the franchisee does not pay for such help.

4. The franchisee also receives materials to use in local advertising and can take part in national promotional campaigns sponsored by the franchisor. McDonald's and its franchisees, for example, constitute one of the nation's top twenty purchasers of advertising.

5. Finally, the franchisee may be able to minimize the cost of advertising, supplies, and various business necessities by purchasing them in cooperation with other franchisees.

Disadvantages of Franchising

The main disadvantage of franchising affects the franchisee, and it arises because the *franchisor retains a great deal of control*. The franchisor's contract can dictate every aspect of the business: decor, design of employee uniforms, types of signs, and all the details of business operations. All Burger King French fries taste the same because all Burger King franchisees have to make them the same way.

Contract disputes are the cause of many lawsuits. **EXAMPLE** Rekha Gabhawala, a Dunkin' Donuts franchisee in Milwaukee, alleged that the franchisor was forcing her out of business so that the company could profit by reselling the downtown franchise to someone else; the company, on the other hand, alleged that Gabhawala breached the contract by not running the business according to company standards. Other franchisees claim that *contracts are unfairly tilted* toward the franchisors. Yet others have charged that they lost their franchise and inve stment because their *franchisor would not approve the sale* of the business when they found a buyer.

To arbitrate disputes between franchisors and franchisees, the National Franchise Mediation Program was established in 1993 by thirty member firms, including Burger

King Corporation, McDonald's Corporation, and Wendy's International, Inc. In 1997, to avoid government regulation, some of the largest franchisors proposed a new self-policing plan to the Federal Trade Commission.

In Table 6.6 you can see how much money a franchisee needs to start a new franchise for selected organizations. In some fields, franchise agreements are not uniform. One franchisee may pay more than another for the same services.

Sometimes a franchise is so successful that the franchisor opens its own outlet nearby, in direct competition—although franchisees may fight back. **EXAMPLE** A court recently ruled that Burger King could not enter into direct competition with the franchisee because the contract was not specific on the issue. Franchise operators work hard. They often put in ten- and twelve-hour days six days a week. The International Franchise Association advises prospective franchise purchasers to investigate before investing and to approach buying a franchise cautiously. Franchises vary widely in approach as well as in products. Some, such as Dunkin' Donuts and Baskin-Robbins, demand long hours. Others, such as Great Clips hair salons and Albert's Family Restaurants, are more appropriate for those who do not want to spend many hours at their stores.

Global Perspectives in Small Business

For small American businesses, the world is becoming smaller. National and international economies are growing more and more interdependent as political leadership and national economic directions change and trade barriers diminish or disappear. Globalization and instant worldwide communications are rapidly shrinking distances at the same time that they are expanding business opportunities. According to a recent study, the Internet is increasingly important to small-business strategic thinking, with more than 50 percent of those surveyed indicating that the Internet represented their most favored strategy for growth. This was more than double the next-favored choice, strategic alliances reflecting the opportunity to reach both global and domestic customers. The Internet and on-line payment systems enable even very small businesses to serve international customers. In fact, technology now gives small businesses the leverage and power to reach markets that were once limited solely to large corporations. No wonder the number of businesses exporting their goods and services has tripled since 1990, with two-thirds of that boom coming from companies with fewer than twenty employees.[22]

The SBA offers help to the nation's small-business owners who want to enter the world markets. The SBA's efforts include counseling small firms on how and where to market overseas, matching U.S. small-business executives with potential overseas customers, and helping exporters to secure financing. The agency brings small U.S. firms into direct contact with potential overseas buyers and partners. The U.S. Commercial Service, a Commerce Department division, aids small and medium-sized businesses in selling overseas.

CONCEPT CHECK
Would you rather own your own business independently or become a franchisee? Why?

International trade will become more important to small-business owners as they face unique challenges in the new century. Small businesses, which are expected to remain the dominant form of organization in this country, must be prepared to adapt to significant demographic and economic changes in the world marketplace.

ACE the Test
ACE & ACE+
Practice Tests 6.6, 6.7

TEST PREPPER 6.6 6.7

True or False?

 1. The franchisee supplies management skills and the required training, whereas the franchisor operates the franchised business.

 2. KFC's (Kentucky Fried Chicken) and SUBWAY's primary roles are the careful development and control of marketing strategies. They are therefore examples of service franchising.

Multiple Choice

 3. McDonald's, H & R Block, AAMCO Transmissions, and Dairy Queen are all examples of which type of small business?

   a. A partnership
   b. A home-based industry
   c. A sole proprietorship
   d. A franchise
   e. A leasing industry

 4. Which of the following is not an advantage to the franchisor for franchising?

a. Fast and well-controlled distribution of products
b. Lower distribution costs
c. The ability to ensure that outlets are maintained and operated according to certain standards
d. A high rate of success of the franchise, which leads to greater profits in royalties
e. The benefit of receiving guidance and advice

 5. Technology now gives small businesses the leverage and power to reach markets that were once limited solely to large corporations. What particular type of technology does this refer to?

   a. The use of the Internet as a marketing and sales tool
   b. Advances in manufacturing
   c. Gains in knowledge and information over the last two decades
   d. Freight and shipping capabilities of small businesses
   e. Support from the government in the form of the SBA

Prepare for Class
CL News Feeds
CL News Now

→ RETURN TO INSIDE BUSINESS

 Entrepreneurs face important professional and lifestyle choices when they launch a new business venture. Some want to leave the structure of a big corporation, some are seeking a better balance between work and home, and others are passionate about turning a favorite hobby or special interest into profit.

Victoria Colligan and Beth Schoenfeldt started Ladies Who Launch to help women turn their small business dreams into reality. Now they're going global with Incubator programs in Canada and South Africa. In addition, the cofounders are planning to offer Ladies Who Launch franchise opportunities. Colligan's advice to women entrepreneurs is, "Surround yourself with like-minded women, and do something really hard every day."

Questions

1. Would you advise Colligan and Schoenfeldt to offer an Incubator program for men who want to launch new businesses? Explain your answer.
2. What other assistance should Ladies Who Launch provide for women entrepreneurs?

LEARNING OBJECTIVES REVIEW

1 Define what a small business is and recognize the fields in which small businesses are concentrated.

- A small business is one that is independently owned and operated for profit and is not dominant in its field.
- There are over twenty-six million businesses in this country, and 99.7 percent of them are small businesses that employ more than half the nation's work force.
- More than half of all small businesses are in retailing and services.

2 Identify the people who start small businesses and the reasons why some succeed and many fail.

- Personal characteristics such as independence, desire to create a new enterprise, and willingness to accept a challenge may encourage individuals to start small businesses.
- Various external circumstances, such as special expertise or even the loss of a job, also can supply the motivation to strike out on one's own.
- Poor planning and lack of capital and management experience are the major causes of small-business failures.

3 Assess the contributions of small businesses to our economy.

- Small businesses have been responsible for a wide variety of inventions and innovations, some of which have given rise to new industries and they have mounted effective competition to larger firms.
- They provide things that society needs, act as suppliers to larger firms, and serve as customers of other businesses, both large and small.

4 Judge the advantages and disadvantages of operating a small business.

- *Advantages* of small business include
  - The opportunity to establish personal relationships with customers and employees
  - The ability to adapt to changes quickly
  - Independence
  - Simplified record keeping
- *Disadvantages* include
  - The high risk of failure
  - The limited potential for growth
  - The limited ability to raise capital

5 Explain how the Small Business Administration helps small businesses.

- The Small Business Administration (SBA) was created in 1953 to assist and counsel the nation's millions of small-business owners.
- The SBA offers management courses and workshops; managerial help, including one-to-one counseling through SCORE; various publications; and financial assistance through guaranteed loans and SBICs.
- The SBA places special emphasis on aid to minority-owned businesses, including those owned by women.

6 Appraise the concept and types of franchising.

- A franchise is a license to operate an individually owned business as though it were part of a chain.
- The franchisor provides a known business name, management skills, a method of doing business, and the training and required materials.
- The franchisee contributes labor and capital, operates the franchised business, and agrees to abide by the provisions of the franchise agreement.
- The three major categories of franchise arrangements are retail, license, and service arrangements.

7 Analyze the growth of franchising and list franchising's advantages and disadvantages.

- Franchising has grown tremendously since the mid-1970s.
- The franchisor's major advantage in franchising is fast and well-controlled distribution of products with minimal capital outlay.
- The franchisee has the opportunity to open a business with limited capital, to make use of the business experience of others, and to sell to an existing clientele.
- The franchisee usually must pay both an initial franchise fee and a continuing royalty based on sales.
- The franchisee must follow the dictates of the franchisor with regard to operation of the business.

Improve Your Grade
Audio Chapter Summary & Quiz

VIDEO CASE

No Funny Business at Newbury Comics

The two college students who started Newbury Comics have become serious business owners. Mike Dreese and John Brusger started Newbury Comics in 1978 with $2,000 and a valuable comic book collection. Their first store was actually a tiny apartment on Boston's popular Newbury Street, which they rented for $260 per month. Three decades later, the company operates twenty-seven stores in Connecticut, Massachusetts, Maine, New Hampshire, and Rhode Island. It still does business on Newbury Street—in a spacious storefront that rents for $23,000 per month.

How did Newbury Comics grow into a multimillion-dollar business? First, the owners identified a need that they could fill. They understood what kinds of comic books collectors were interested in buying, and they enjoyed dealing with these customers. They also realized that customer needs can change, which is why they have tested hundreds of new items over the years.

Second, Reese and Brusger thought of their business as a business. As much as they liked comics, they recognized the profit potential of carrying other products. Over time, they started stocking music and added movies, novelty items, and clothing accessories. They were among the first U.S. stores to import recordings by European groups such as U2. Today, comic books account for only a fraction of Newbury Comics' revenue, whereas CDs and DVDs account for about 70 percent of the revenue.

Third, the entrepreneurs didn't do everything themselves—they knew when to delegate to others. As Newbury Comics expanded beyond comics and opened new stores, the owners hired professionals to negotiate leases, make buying decisions, and select the exact merchandise assortment for each store. They also hired technology experts to design systems for tracking what was in stock, what had been sold, how much the company was spending, and how much each store was contributing to total sales. Now, if a new CD or DVD is selling particularly well, the buyer will know within three minutes—in plenty of time to reorder and satisfy customer demand.

Fourth, Reese and Brusger have paid close attention to Newbury Comics' financial situation. They're careful to pay

suppliers on time, and in exchange, they can get fast-selling products even when supplies are limited. Consider what happened during the Pokemon fad. Newbury Comics originally ordered a small quantity of cards, which quickly sold out. Every time it placed another order, it sent the supplier a check by express delivery. By the height of the fad, when demand was so high that the supplier could not fill every retailer's order, Newbury Comics still got its shipment. By the time the fad faded, the company had sold $4 million worth of Pokemon cards and made more than $2 million in profits.

Newbury Comics remains profitable, although Dreese notes that sales growth has slowed during the past few years. As a result, he says, "We have all had to grow up a little" and improve the way Newbury Comics operates. The company has formalized its store payroll budgets, assigned employees to check the quality of customer service at each store, and begun offering more products for sale online.

Despite the company's success, Dreese does not expect to expand beyond New England. He knows that a key strength is being able to restock quickly—and that means locating stores within a half-day's drive of the distribution center in Brighton, Massachusetts. Because Newbury Comics owns six trucks, it can resupply every store at least three times a week. Many competitors are far bigger, but no competitor knows its customers and its products better than the team at Newbury Comics.[23]

Questions

1. This chapter cites five advantages of small business. Which of these seem to apply to the owners' experience with Newbury Comics?
2. This chapter cites three disadvantages of small business. Based on what you know of Newbury Comics, which of these is likely to be the biggest problem in the coming years?
3. Newbury Comics was started without a formal business plan. If you were writing its plan today, what critical risks and assumptions would you examine—and why?

BUILDING SKILLS FOR CAREER SUCCESS

1. Exploring the Internet

Perhaps the most challenging difficulty for small businesses is operating with scarce resources, especially people and money. To provide information and point small-business operators in the right direction, many Internet sites offer helpful products and services. Although most are sponsored by advertising and may be free of charge, some charge a fee, and others are a combination of both. The SBA within the U.S. Department of Commerce provides a wide array of free information and resources. You can find your way to the SBA through **www.sbaonline.sba.gov** or **www.sba.gov**. Visit the text website for updates to this exercise.

Assignment

1. Describe the various services provided by the SBA site.
2. What sources of funding are there?
3. What service would you like to see improved? How?

2. Building Team Skills

A business plan is a written statement that documents the nature of a business and how that business intends to achieve its goals. Although entrepreneurs should prepare a business plan before starting a business, the plan also serves as an effective guide later on. The plan should concisely describe the business's mission, the amount of capital it requires, its target market, competition, resources, production plan, marketing plan, organizational plan, assessment of risk, and financial plan.

Assignment

1. Working in a team of four students, identify a company in your community that would benefit from using a business plan, or create a scenario in which a hypothetical entrepreneur wants to start a business.
2. Using the resources of the library or the Internet and/or interviews with business owners, write a business plan incorporating the information in Table 6.3
3. Present your business plan to the class.

3. Researching Different Careers

Many people dream of opening and operating their own businesses. Are you one of them? To be successful, entrepreneurs must have certain characteristics; their profiles generally differ from those of people who work for someone else. Do you know which personal characteristics make some entrepreneurs succeed and others fail? Do you fit the successful entrepreneur's profile? What is your potential for opening and operating a successful small business?

Assignment

1. Use the resources of the library or the Internet to establish what a successful entrepreneur's profile is and to determine whether your personal characteristics fit that profile. Internet addresses that can help you are **www.smartbiz.com/sbs/arts/ieb1.html** and **www.sba.gov** (see "Starting Your Business" and "FAQs"). These sites have quizzes online that can help you to assess your personal characteristics. The SBA also has helpful brochures.
2. Interview several small-business owners. Ask them to describe the characteristics they think are necessary for being a successful entrepreneur.
3. Using your findings, write a report that includes the following:
   a. A profile of a successful small-business owner
   b. A comparison of your personal characteristics with the profile of the successful entrepreneur
   c. A discussion of your potential as a successful small-business owner

Prepare for Class
Exploring the Internet

RUNNING A BUSINESS PART 2
Finagle A Bagel: A Fast-Growing Small Business

Finagle A Bagel, a fast-growing small business co-owned by Alan Litchman and Laura Trust, is at the forefront of one of the freshest concepts in the food-service business: fresh food. Each of the stores bakes a new batch of bagels every hour, and each receives new deliveries of cheeses, vegetables, fruits, and other ingredients every day. Rather than prepackage menu items, store employees make everything to order so that they can satisfy the specific needs of each *guest* (Finagle A Bagel's term for a customer). As a result, customers get fresh food prepared to their exact preferences—whether it's extra cheese on a bagel pizza or no onions in a salad—along with prompt, friendly service.

"Every sandwich, every salad is built to order, so there's a lot of communication between the customers and the cashiers, the customers and the sandwich makers, the customers and the managers," explains Trust. This allows Finagle A Bagel's store employees time to build customer relationships and encourage repeat business. Many, like Mirna Hernandez of the Tremont Street store in downtown Boston, are so familiar with what certain customers order that they spring into action when regulars enter the store. "We know what they want, and we just ring it in and take care of them," she says.

Some employees even know their customers by name and make conversation as they create a sandwich or fill a coffee container.

Financing a Small Business

Some small businesses achieve rapid growth through franchising. The entrepreneurs running Finagle A Bagel resisted franchising for a long time. "When you franchise, you gain a large influx of capital," says Trust, "but you begin to lose control over the people, the place, and the product." Since the beginning, the owners and their senior managers routinely popped into different Finagle A Bagel stores every day to check quality and service. Now the company says it will begin granting franchises in the near future and will institute a stringent quality-control regimen to maintain the highest standards wherever the brand name appears.

As a corporation, Finagle A Bagel could, as some other small businesses do, raise money for growth by selling corporate stock. The copresidents prefer not to transform their company into an open corporation at this time. "Going public is very tricky in the food-service business," Trust observes. "Some people have done it very successfully; others have not." The copresidents want to maintain total control over the pace and direction of growth rather than

feeling pressured to meet the growth expectations of securities analysts and shareholders.

Buying and Building the Business and Brand

What originally attracted Trust and Litchman to Finagle A Bagel was the combination of a strong local following and a favorable brand image. Looking back, Litchman says that he and his wife recognized that building a small business would require more than good business sense. "It has a lot to do with having a great brand and having great food, and reinforcing the brand every day," he remembers. "That's one of the key things that we bought."

To further reinforce the brand and reward customer loyalty, Finagle A Bagel created the Frequent Finagler card. The card costs $1 and is activated immediately at the store. Customers then receive one point for every dollar spent in a Finagle A Bagel store, and they can redeem accumulated points for coffee, juice, sandwiches, or other rewards.

To join, customers visit the company's website (**www.finagleabagel.com**) and complete a registration form asking for name, address, and other demographics. Once the account is set up, says Litchman, "It's a web-based program where customers can log on, check their points, and receive free gifts by mail. The Frequent Finagler is our big push right now to use technology as a means of generating store traffic." It's also an excellent way for the company to learn which menu items loyal customers buy, in which store, and at what time of day.

Bagels Online?

In the future, Litchman plans to expand the website so that customers can order food and catering services directly online. Although some competitors already invite online orders, Finagle A Bagel has a more extensive menu, and its fresh-food concept is not as easily adapted to e-commerce. "In our stores, all the food is prepared fresh, and it is very customized," Litchman notes. "This entails a fair amount of interaction between employees and customers: 'What kind of croutons do you want? What kind of dressing? What kind of mustard?' When we're ready to go in that direction,

it is going to be a fairly sizable technology venture for us to undertake."

Finagle A Bagel occasionally receives web or phone orders from customers hundreds or thousands of miles away. Still, the copresidents have no immediate plans to expand outside the Boston metropolitan area. Pointing to regional food-service firms that have profited by opening more stores in a wider geographic domain, Trust says, "We see that the most successful companies have really dominated their area first. Cheesecake Factory is an example of a company that's wildly successful right now, but they were a concept in California for decades before they moved beyond that area. In-and-Out Burger is an outstanding example of a food-service company in the West that's done what we're trying to do. They had seventeen stores at one time, and now they have hundreds of stores. They're very

successful, but they never left their backyard. That's kind of why we're staying where we are."

Questions

1. Why would Finagle A Bagel maintain a business-to-customer (B2C) website even before it's prepared to process online orders from individuals?

2. Do you agree with Finagle A Bagel's plan to franchise its fresh-food concept and brand name? Support your answer.

3. Although opening new stores is costly, the copresidents have chosen not to raise money by becoming an open corporation and selling stock. Do you agree with this decision? Discuss the advantages and disadvantages.

4. If you were writing the executive summary of Finagle A Bagel's business plan to show to lenders, what key points would you stress?

CHAPTER 7

Understanding the Management Process

Your Guide to Success in Business

Why this chapter matters

Most of the people who read this chapter will not spend much time at the bottom of organizations. They will advance upward and become managers. Thus an overview of the field of management is essential.

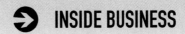

Campbell Soup's Key Ingredient

Campbell Soup's CEO believes that his company can do more than be profitable and competitive. He believes that it can nourish people's lives every day—and that nourishment starts within the company.

With the view that employees who are emotionally connected to their jobs are more productive, the CEO wants employees to "fall in love with your company's agenda." This insight has revitalized the company and led to leadership opportunities at every management level for its 24,000 employees.

Headquartered in Camden, New Jersey, Campbell's has been serving up innovative food products for nearly 140 years. It operates four divisions: U.S. Soup, Sauces, and Beverages; Baking and Snacking; International Soup and Sauces; and a division that distributes Campbell's products for resale. Soups account for more than half of Campbell's North American sales of $5.2 billion and international sales of $1.2 billion.

To keep Campbell competitive, top management has concentrated on planning for three aspects of its products: convenience, nutrition, and quality. Employees are also encouraged to suggest innovative ideas that will keep sales bubbling. For example, Campbell's employees have developed pop-top cans for more convenient use, lower-sodium soups for health-conscious consumers, and gourmet flavors such as Golden Butternut Squash.

Management planning extends to the way soup products are displayed in the supermarket. Now, when a shopper takes the first can of soup from the shelf, Campbell's automatic shelving system gently rolls the next can to the front. This shelving system also makes it easier for shoppers to find soups by category because soups such as Cream of Mushroom and Cream of Chicken are displayed together in the cooking area, whereas Chicken and Stars is displayed with soups for kids.

The CEO shows leadership with a personal touch, writing thank-you notes to employees and meeting with groups of employees during informal lunches. Just as important, he motivates managers and employees alike by communicating a sense of purpose and providing opportunities for advancement within the company.[1]

> **DID YOU KNOW?**
>
> Campbell Soup's CEO wants employees to "fall in love with your company's agenda."

K E Y   T E R M S

management (212)
planning (214)
mission (214)
strategic planning (214)
goal (214)
objective (214)
plan (215)
strategic plan (216)
tactical plan (216)
operational plan (216)

contingency plan (216)
organizing (216)
leading (217)
motivating (217)
directing (217)
controlling (217)
top manager (219)
middle manager (220)
first-line manager (220)
financial manager (220)

operations manager (221)
marketing manager (221)
human resources manager (221)
administrative manager (221)
technical skill (222)
conceptual skill (222)
interpersonal skill (223)
decisional role (223)
interpersonal role (223)
informational role (224)

leadership (224)
authoritarian leader (224)
laissez-faire leader (225)
democratic leader (225)
decision making (225)
problem (226)
total quality management
   (TQM) (229)

ACE the Test
Crossword Puzzle
Flashcards

The different leadership paths employed by the founders at Campbell's Soup illustrate that management can be one of the most exciting and rewarding professions available today. Depending on its size, a firm may employ a number of specialized managers who are responsible for particular areas of management, such as marketing, finance, and operations. That same organization also includes managers at several levels within the firm.

In this chapter, we

* Define *management* and describe the four basic management functions of planning, organizing, leading and motivating, and controlling.

* Focus on the types of managers with respect to levels of responsibility and areas of expertise and identify the skills of effective managers and the different roles managers must play.

* Examine several styles of leadership, explore the process by which managers make decisions, and describe how total quality management can improve customer satisfaction.

* Identify what it takes to be a successful manager today.

What Is Management?

Learning Objective

Define what management is.

management the process of coordinating people and other resources to achieve the goals of an organization

Management is the process of coordinating people and other resources to achieve the goals of an organization. As we saw in Chapter 1, most organizations make use of four kinds of resources: material, human, financial, and informational (see Figure 7.1).

MANAGEMENT

| Material resources | Human resources | Financial resources | Informational resources | → | Organizational goals |

FIGURE 7.1

The Four Main Resources of Management

Managers coordinate an organization's resources to achieve the goals of the organization.

1. *Material resources* are the tangible, physical resources an organization uses. **EXAMPLE** General Motors uses steel, glass, and fiberglass to produce cars and trucks on complex machine-driven assembly lines.

2. Perhaps the most important resources of any organization are its *human resources*—people. In fact, some firms live by the philosophy that their employees are their most important assets. One such firm is Southwest Airlines. Southwest treats its employees with the same respect and attention it gives its passengers. Southwest selectively seeks employees with upbeat attitudes and promotes from within 80 percent of the time. In decision making, everyone who will be affected is encouraged to get involved in the process. Unlike most airlines, Southwest keeps growing and making a profit because of its employees.

Many experts would agree with Southwest's emphasis on employees. Evidence suggests that the way employees are developed and managed may have more impact on an organization than other vital components such as marketing, sound financial decisions about large expenditures, production, or the use of technology.[2]

3. *Financial resources* are the funds an organization uses to meet its obligations to investors and creditors. **EXAMPLE** A 7-Eleven convenience store obtains money from customers at the check-out counters and uses a portion of that money to pay its suppliers.

4. Finally, many organizations increasingly find that they cannot afford to ignore *information*. External environmental conditions—including the economy, consumer markets, technology, politics, and cultural forces—are all changing so rapidly that a business that does not adapt probably will not survive. And to adapt to change, the business must know what is changing and how it is changing. Most companies gather information about their competitors to increase their knowledge about changes in their industry and to learn from other companies' failures and successes.

Human Resources.

In most organizations effective management of human resources is absolutely critical.

It is important to realize that these four types of resources are only general categories of resources. Within each category are hundreds or thousands of more specific resources. It is this complex mix of specific resources—and not simply "some of each" of the four general categories—that managers must coordinate to produce goods and services.

Another interesting way to look at management is in terms of the different functions managers perform. These functions have been identified as planning, organizing, leading and motivating employees, and controlling. We look at each of these management functions in the next section.

Basic Management Functions

ACE the Test
Hangman

Learning Objective ②

Describe the four basic management functions: planning, organizing, leading and motivating, and controlling.

A couple of years ago, AOL was struggling financially because it was losing significant market share to competitors such as Yahoo! and Google. At the time, AOL primarily was providing Internet service to dial-up customers. To turn the company around, top management had to make significant changes that included redesigning its format to offer a Yahoo!-like portal. In addition, this change forced AOL to provide customers with its rich content for free. These major changes have resulted in a turnaround for AOL. Now AOL is a financially sound organization.[3]

Management functions such as those just described do not occur according to some rigid, preset timetable. Managers do not plan in January, organize in February, lead

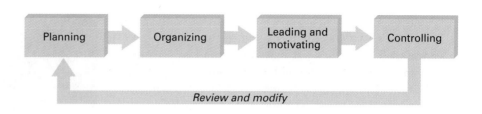

Review and modify

FIGURE 7.2

The Management Process

Note that management is not a step-by-step procedure but a process with a feedback loop that represents a flow.

planning establishing organizational goals and deciding how to accomplish them

mission a statement of the basic purpose that makes an organization different from others

strategic planning the process of establishing an organization's major goals and objectives and allocating the resources to achieve them

Mission Statement.

The mission statement at Microsoft is "We work to help people and businesses throughout the world realize their full potential."

goal an end result that an organization is expected to achieve over a one- to ten-year period

objective a specific statement detailing what an organization intends to accomplish over a shorter period of time

and motivate in March, and control in April. At any given time, managers may engage in a number of functions simultaneously. However, each function tends to lead naturally to others. Figure 7.2 provides a visual framework for a more detailed discussion of the four basic management functions. How well managers perform these key functions determines whether a business is successful.

Planning

Planning, in its simplest form, is establishing organizational goals and deciding how to accomplish them. It is often referred to as the "first" management function because all other management functions depend on planning. Organizations such as Nissan, Houston Community Colleges, and the U.S. Secret Service begin the planning process by developing a mission statement.

An organization's **mission** is a statement of the basic purpose that makes that organization different from others. **EXAMPLE** Google's mission statement is "to organize the

world's information and make it universally accessible and useful."[4] Once an organization's mission has been described in a mission statement, the next step is to develop organizational goals and objectives, usually through strategic planning. **Strategic planning** is the process of establishing an organization's major goals and objectives and allocating the resources to achieve them. **EXAMPLE** MinuteClinic, a quick-fix medical clinic, focuses on efficiency in treating minor ailments. MinuteClinic's strategic plan deals with the quick diagnosis and treatment of medical problems such as the flu, a sore throat, or an eye infection and does not allocate any resources to treating serious medical problems such as chest pain or broken bones.[5]

Establishing Goals and Objectives A **goal** is an end result that an organization is expected to achieve over a one- to ten-year period. **EXAMPLE** Daimler AG's goal in Europe is to sell 200,000 units by 2009.[6] An **objective** is a specific statement detailing what the organization intends to accomplish over a shorter period of time.

Goals and objectives can deal with a variety of factors, such as sales, company growth, costs, customer satisfaction, and employee morale. Whereas a small manufacturer may focus primarily on sales objectives for the next six months, a large firm may be more interested in goals for several years ahead.

EXAMPLE Under the leadership of CEO Will Manzer, Eastern Mountain Sports (EMS) has a goal to return to its roots as a hardcore sports gear provider. Over years of declining profits, EMS has blurred its image by shifting to "soft" merchandise that appeals to a broader market. The company's managers know that goals take time to achieve, and they are willing to invest to reach their goal of becoming the edgy outfitter they once were. They are taking action with objectives such as dropping all their soft merchandise, hiring hardcore sporting enthusiasts, and stocking gear for even the most fringe sports out there (e.g., kite skiing, ice climbing, and high-speed sledding).[7] Finally, goals are set at every level of an organization. Every member of an organization—the president of the company, the head of a department, and an operating employee at the lowest level—has a set of goals that he or she hopes to achieve.

The goals developed for these different levels must be consistent. However, it is likely that some conflict will arise. A production department, for example, may have a goal of minimizing costs. Marketing may have a goal of maximizing sales. As part of goal setting, the manager who is responsible for *both* departments must achieve some sort of balance between conflicting goals. This balancing process is called *optimization*.

Establishing Plans to Accomplish Goals and Objectives Once goals and objectives have been set for the organization, managers must develop plans for achieving them. A **plan** is an outline of the actions by which an organization intends to accomplish its goals and objectives. Just as it has different goals and objectives, the organization also develops several types of plans, as shown in Figure 7.3.

CONCEPT CHECK

What could be the mission of a neighborhood restaurant? Of the Salvation Army? What might be reasonable objectives for these organizations?

plan an outline of the actions by which an organization intends to accomplish its goals and objectives

FIGURE 7.3

Types of Plans

Managers develop and rely on several types of plans.

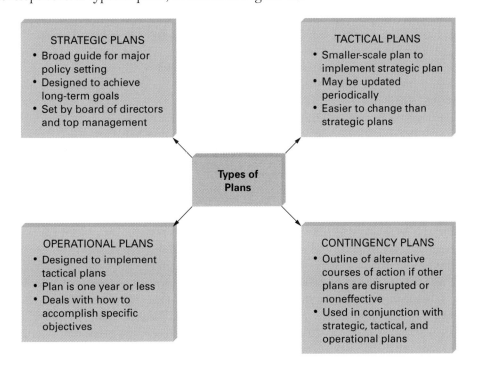

STRATEGIC PLANS
- Broad guide for major policy setting
- Designed to achieve long-term goals
- Set by board of directors and top management

TACTICAL PLANS
- Smaller-scale plan to implement strategic plan
- May be updated periodically
- Easier to change than strategic plans

Types of Plans

OPERATIONAL PLANS
- Designed to implement tactical plans
- Plan is one year or less
- Deals with how to accomplish specific objectives

CONTINGENCY PLANS
- Outline of alternative courses of action if other plans are disrupted or noneffective
- Used in conjunction with strategic, tactical, and operational plans

strategic plan an organization's broadest plan, developed as a guide for major policy setting and decision making

tactical plan a smaller-scale plan developed to implement a strategy

operational plan a type of plan designed to implement tactical plans

contingency plan a plan that outlines alternative courses of action that may be taken if an organization's other plans are disrupted or become ineffective

---

CONCEPT CHECK

How do a strategic plan, a tactical plan, and an operational plan differ? What do they all have in common?

---

organizing the grouping of resources and activities to accomplish some end result in an efficient and effective manner

Different Types of Plans

Resulting from the strategic planning process, an organization's **strategic plan** is its broadest plan, developed as a guide for major policy setting and decision making. Strategic plans are set by the board of directors and top management and generally are designed to achieve the long-term goals of the organization. Thus a firm's strategic plan defines what business the company is in or wants to be in and the kind of company it is or wants to be. **EXAMPLE** When the U.S. Surgeon General issued a report linking smoking and cancer, top management at Philip Morris Companies recognized that the company's survival was being threatened. Executives needed to develop a strategic plan to diversify into nontobacco products.

In addition to strategic plans, most organizations also employ several narrower kinds of plans. A **tactical plan** is a smaller-scale plan developed to implement a strategy. Most tactical plans cover a one- to three-year period. If a strategic plan will take five years to complete, the firm may develop five tactical plans, one covering each year. Tactical plans may be updated periodically as dictated by conditions and experience. Their more limited scope permits them to be changed more easily than strategies. **EXAMPLE** In an attempt to fulfill its diversification strategy, Philip Morris developed individual tactical plans to purchase several non-tobacco-related companies such as General Foods, Kraft Foods, and Miller Brewing.

An **operational plan** is a type of plan designed to implement tactical plans. Operational plans usually are established for one year or less and deal with how to accomplish the organization's specific objectives. **EXAMPLE** Assume that after Philip Morris purchased Kraft Foods, managers adopted the objective of increasing sales of Kraft's Cheez Whiz by 5 percent the first year. A sales increase this large does not just happen, however. Management must develop an operational plan that describes certain activities the firm can undertake over the next year to increase sales. Regardless of how hard managers try, sometimes business activities do not go as planned. Today, most corporations also develop contingency plans along with strategies, tactical plans, and operational plans. A **contingency plan** is a plan that outlines alternative courses of action that may be taken if an organization's other plans are disrupted or become ineffective. Remember that one reason for Philip Morris's purchase of Kraft was to diversify into nontobacco products. If it became impossible to purchase Kraft, Philip Morris could fall back on contingency plans to purchase other companies.

Organizing the Enterprise

After goal setting and planning, the second major function of the manager is organization. **Organizing** is the grouping of resources and activities to accomplish some end result in an efficient and effective manner. **EXAMPLE** Consider the case of an inventor who creates a new product and goes into business to sell it. At first, the inventor will do everything on his or her own—purchase raw materials, make the product, advertise it, sell it, and keep business records. Eventually, as business grows, the inventor will need help. To begin with, he or she might hire a professional sales representative and a part-time bookkeeper. Later, it also might be necessary to hire sales staff, people to assist with production, and an accountant. As the inventor hires new personnel, he or she must decide what each person will do, to whom each person will report, and how each

person can best take part in the organization's activities. We discuss these and other facets of the organizing function in much more detail in Chapter 8.

Leading and Motivating

The leading and motivating function is concerned with the human resources within an organization. Specifically, **leading** is the process of influencing people to work toward a common goal. **Motivating** is the process of providing reasons for people to work in the best interests of an organization. Together, leading and motivating are often referred to as **directing**.

We have already noted the importance of an organization's human resources. Because of this importance, leading and motivating are critical activities. Obviously, different people do things for different reasons—that is, they have different *motivations*. Some are interested primarily in earning as much money as they can. Others may be spurred on by opportunities to get promoted. Part of a manager's job, then, is to determine what factors motivate workers and to try to provide those incentives to encourage effective performance.

Controlling Ongoing Activities

Controlling is the process of evaluating and regulating ongoing activities to ensure that goals are achieved. To see how controlling works, consider a rocket launched by NASA to place a satellite in orbit. Do NASA personnel simply fire the rocket and then check back in a few days to find out whether the satellite is in place? Of course not. The rocket is monitored constantly, and its course is regulated and adjusted as needed to get the satellite to its destination. The control function includes three steps (see Figure 7.4).

1. *Setting standards* with which performance can be compared
2. *Measuring actual performance* and comparing it with the standard
3. *Taking corrective action* as necessary

leading the process of influencing people to work toward a common goal

motivating the process of providing reasons for people to work in the best interests of an organization

directing the combined processes of leading and motivating

controlling the process of evaluating and regulating ongoing activities to ensure that goals are achieved

BIZ TECH

Blogging: Managing the Tool

A growing number of companies see *blogs* (short for *web logs*, web-based journals) as a great way to share information both internally and externally. A blog can, for example, enhance communication between managers and employees, serve as an archive of company information, or add an important human element to an online dialogue with customers. As one media consultant states, "If you're not part of that conversation, you're missing out."

To manage this powerful communication tool, companies should have specific blogging policies in place and train employees who will be posting comments to the company blog. Before they log on and start to blog, employees need to

- Understand the company's policies on blogging
- Be aware of the legal issues associated with blogging
- Establish their goals for blogging
- Carefully assess the information to be posted
- Keep confidential or proprietary information off the blog

Sources: Based on information from "Beware the Pitfalls of a Blogging Boom," *Personnel Today*, October 24, 2006, n.p; Matt Villano, "Blogging the Hand That Feeds You," *New York Times*, September 27, 2006, p. G5; Paul Gillin, "The Unseen Blogosphere: Internal Blogs," *B to B*, November 13, 2006, p. 10; Jacqueline Klosek, "Corporate Blogs: Handle with Care," *BusinessWeek Online*, December 14, 2006, www.businessweek.com.

Notice that the control function is circular in nature. The steps in the control function must be repeated periodically until the goal is achieved. **EXAMPLE** Suppose that Southwest Airlines establishes a goal of increasing profits by 12 percent. To ensure that this goal is reached, Southwest's management might monitor its profit on a monthly basis. After three months, if profit has increased by 3 percent, management might be able to assume that plans are going according to schedule. Probably no action will be taken. However, if profit has increased by only 1 percent after three months, some corrective action would be needed to get the firm on track. The particular action that is required depends on the reason for the small increase in profit.

FIGURE 7.4

The Control Function

The control function includes three steps: setting standards, measuring actual performance, and taking corrective action.

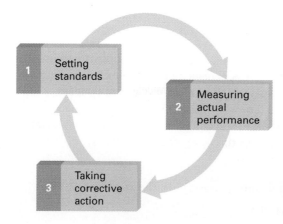

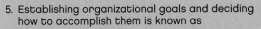

TEST PREPPER 7.1 7.2

True or False?

_T_ 1. Most companies gather information about their competitors to increase their knowledge about changes in their industry and to learn from other companies' failures and successes.

_F_ 2. Strategic plan is a plan that outlines alternative courses of action that may be taken if an organization's other plans are disrupted or become ineffective.

_T_ 3. Controlling is the process of evaluating and regulating ongoing activities to ensure that goals are achieved.

Multiple Choice

___ 4. External environmental conditions—including the economy, consumer markets, technology, politics, and cultural forces—are examples of

a. human resources.
b. informational resources.
c. material resources.
d. financial resources.
e. cultural resources

_A_ 5. Establishing organizational goals and deciding how to accomplish them is known as

a. planning.
b. the mission statement.
c. strategic planning.
d. developmental planning.
e. organizational planning.

ACE the Test
ACE & ACE+
Practice Tests 7.1, 7.2

Kinds of Managers

Learning Objective ③

Distinguish among the various kinds of managers in terms of both level and area of management.

Managers can be classified in two ways:

1. *According to their level within an organization*
2. *According to their area of management*

In this section we use both perspectives to explore the various types of managers based on both classifications.

Levels of Management

For the moment, think of an organization as a three-story structure (as illustrated in Figure 7.5). Each story corresponds to one of the three general levels of management: top managers, middle managers, and first-line managers.

Top Managers A **top manager** is an upper-level executive who guides and controls the overall fortunes of an organization. Top managers constitute a small group. In terms of planning, they are generally responsible for *developing the organization's mission*. They also determine *the firm's strategy*.

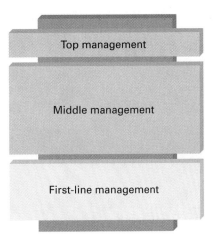

Top management

Middle management

First-line management

top manager an upper-level executive who guides and controls the overall fortunes of an organization

FIGURE 7.5

Management Levels Found in Most Companies

The coordinated effort of all three levels of managers is required to implement the goals of any company.

SPOTLIGHT

Would you like your manager's job?

Over 70% of workers do not wish to have their manager's job.

Yes 26%   3%   No 71%

Don't know

Manager

Source: Office Team Survey, **www.officeteam.com/PressRoom?LOBName=OT&releaseid=1564.**

middle manager a manager who implements the strategy and major policies developed by top management

first-line manager a manager who coordinates and supervises the activities of operating employees

Many analysts attribute Michael Dell's long-term success to the significant amount of time he spends with customers that helps him to make effective strategy and product decisions. Dell has continued to gain market share at a time when computer industry sales have decreased.[8] It takes years of hard work, long hours, and perseverance, as well as talent and no small share of good luck, to reach the ranks of top management in large companies. Common job titles associated with top managers are *president, vice president, chief executive officer* (CEO), and *chief operating officer* (COO).

Middle Managers Middle management probably makes up the largest group of managers in most organizations. A **middle manager** is a manager who implements the strategy and major policies developed by top management. Middle managers develop tactical plans and operational plans, and they coordinate and supervise the activities of first-line managers. Titles at the middle-management level include *division manager, department head, plant manager*, and *operations manager*.

First-Line Managers A **first-line manager** is a manager who coordinates and supervises the activities of operating employees. First-line managers spend most of their time working with and motivating their employees, answering questions, and solving day-to-day problems. Most first-line managers are former operating employees who, owing to their hard work and potential, were promoted into management. Many of today's middle and top managers began their careers on this first management level. Common titles for first-line managers include *office manager, supervisor*, and *foreman*.

Areas of Management Specialization

Organizational structure also can be divided into areas of management specialization (see Figure 7.6). The most common areas are finance, operations, marketing, human resources, and administration. Depending on its mission, goals, and objectives, an organization may include other areas as well—research and development (R&D), for example.

Financial Managers A **financial manager** is primarily responsible for an organization's financial resources. Accounting and investment are specialized areas within financial

Top Management.

J. W. Marriot, Jr., Chairman and CEO of Marriot Hotels, participates in the re-opening of the company's hotel in downtown New Orleans.

financial manager a manager who is primarily responsible for an organization's financial resources

| Finance | Operations | Marketing | Human resources | Administration | Other (e.g., research and development) |

FIGURE 7.6

Areas of Management Specialization

Other areas may have to be added, depending on the nature of the firm and the industry.

management. Because financing affects the operation of the entire firm, many of the CEOs and presidents of this country's largest companies are people who got their "basic training" as financial managers.

Operations Managers An operations manager manages the systems that convert resources into goods and services. Traditionally, operations management has been equated with manufacturing—the production of goods. However, in recent years, many of the techniques and procedures of operations management have been applied to the production of services and to a variety of nonbusiness activities. As with financial management, operations management has produced a large percentage of today's company CEOs and presidents.

Marketing Managers A marketing manager is responsible for facilitating the exchange of products between an organization and its customers or clients. Specific areas within marketing are marketing research, product management, advertising, promotion, sales, and distribution. A sizable number of today's company presidents have risen from the ranks of marketing management.

Human Resources Managers A human resources manager is charged with managing an organization's human resources programs. He or she engages in human resources planning; designs systems for hiring, training, and evaluating the performance of employees; and ensures that the organization follows government regulations concerning employment practices. Some human resources managers are making effective use of technology. For example, over one million job openings are posted on **Monster.com,** which attracts about eighteen million visitors monthly.[9]

Administrative Managers An administrative manager (also called a *general manager*) is not associated with any specific functional area but provides overall administrative guidance and leadership. A hospital administrator is an example of an administrative manager. He or she does not specialize in operations, finance, marketing, or human resources management but instead coordinates the activities of specialized managers in all these areas. In many respects, most top managers are really administrative managers.

Whatever their level in the organization and whatever area they specialize in, successful managers generally exhibit certain key skills and are able to play certain managerial roles. However, as we shall see, some skills are likely to be more critical at one level of management than at another.

Is holding down a lion a part of your job?

First line managers of the Henry Doorly Zoo in Omaha, Nebraska, hold down a sedated mountain lion while the zoo veterinarian performs minor surgery.

operations manager a manager who manages the systems that convert resources into goods and services

marketing manager a manager who is responsible for facilitating the exchange of products between an organization and its customers or clients

human resources manager a person charged with managing an organization's human resources programs

administrative manager a manager who is not associated with any specific functional area but who provides overall administrative guidance and leadership

TEST PREPPER 7.3

True or False?

_____ 1. Managers can be classified according to their level within an organization.

_____ 2. Middle managers develop tactical plans and operational plans, and they coordinate and supervise the activities of first-line managers.

_____ 3. A hospital administrator is an example of an administrative manager.

Multiple Choice

_____ 4. What do you call an upper-level executive who guides and controls the overall fortunes of an organization?

a. Middle manager
b. Top manager
c. First-line manager
d. Superior manager
e. Senior-most manager

_____ 5. This manager is responsible for facilitating the exchange of products between an organization and its customers or clients.

a. Human resources manager
b. Marketing manager
c. Materials manager
d. Financial manager
e. Facilitating manager

ACE the Test
ACE & ACE+
Practice Test 7.3

What Makes Effective Managers?

Learning Objective ❹

Identify the key management skills and managerial roles.

In general, effective managers are those who (1) possess certain important skills and (2) are able to use those skills in a number of managerial roles. Probably no manager is called on to use any particular skill *constantly* or to play a particular role *all the time*. However, these skills and abilities must be available when they are needed.

Key Management Skills

The skills that typify effective managers fall into three general categories: technical, conceptual, and interpersonal.

technical skill a specific skill needed to accomplish a specialized activity

Technical Skills A technical skill is a specific skill needed to accomplish a specialized activity. For example, the skills engineers and machinists need to do their jobs are technical skills. First-line managers (and, to a lesser extent, middle managers) need the technical skills relevant to the activities they manage. Although these managers may not perform the technical tasks themselves, they must be able to train subordinates, answer questions, and otherwise provide guidance and direction. **EXAMPLE** A first-line manager in the accounting department of the Hyatt Corporation, for example, must be able to perform computerized accounting transactions and help employees complete the same accounting task. In general, top managers do not rely on technical skills as heavily as managers at other levels. Still, understanding the technical side of a business is an aid to effective management at every level.

conceptual skill the ability to think in abstract terms

Conceptual Skills Conceptual skill is the ability to think in abstract terms. Conceptual skill allows a manager to see the "big picture" and understand how the various parts of an organization or idea can fit together. These skills are useful in a wide range of situations, including the optimization of goals described earlier. They are usually more useful for top managers than for middle or first-line managers.

Interpersonal Skills An interpersonal skill is the ability to deal effectively with other people, both inside and outside an organization. Examples of interpersonal skills are the ability to relate to people, understand their needs and motives, and show genuine compassion. **EXAMPLE** One reason why Mary Kay Ash, founder of Mary Kay Cosmetics, was so successful was her ability to motivate her employees. And although it is obvious that a CEO such as Mary Kay Ash must be able to work with employees throughout the organization, what is not so obvious is that middle and first-line managers also must possess interpersonal skills.

Managerial Roles

Research suggests that managers must, from time to time, act in ten different roles if they are to be successful.[10] (By *role*, we mean a set of expectations that one must fulfill.) These ten roles can be grouped into three broad categories: *decisional, interpersonal,* and *informational.*

Decisional Roles A decisional role involves various aspects of management decision making. The decisional role can be subdivided into the following four specific managerial roles:

1. *Entrpreneurial role.* In the role of an entrepreneur, the manager is the voluntary initiator of change. **EXAMPLE** The CEO of DuPont decided to put more financial resources into its Experimental Station, a large R&D center, to increase new products. This entrepreneurial emphasis on R&D led to the creation of Sorona, a synthetic fiber that could be used for clothing, car upholstery, and carpeting. DuPont hopes that these decisions will pay great dividends in the long run.[11]

2. *Disturbance handler.* A manager who settles a strike is handling a disturbance.

3. *Resource allocator.* In the role of resource allocator, a manager might have to decide which departmental budgets to cut and which expenditure requests to approve.

4. *Negotiator.* Being a negotiator might involve settling a dispute between a manager and a worker assigned to the manager's work group.

Interpersonal Roles Dealing with people is an integral part of the manager's job. An interpersonal role is a role in which the manager deals with people. Like the decisional role, the interpersonal role can be broken down according to three managerial functions.

5. *Figurehead.* The manager may be called on to serve as a figurehead perhaps by attending a ribbon-cutting ceremony or taking an important client to dinner.

6. *Liaison.* The manager also may have to play the role of liaison by serving as a go-between for two different groups. As a liaison, a manager might represent his or her firm at meetings of an industry-wide trade organization.

7. *Leader.* The manager often has to serve as a leader, which includes being an example for others in the organization as well as developing the skills, abilities, and motivation of employees.

interpersonal skill the ability to deal effectively with other people

decisional role a role that involves various aspects of management decision making

interpersonal role a role in which the manager deals with people

CONCEPT CHECK

In what ways are management skills related to the roles managers play? Provide a specific example to support your answer.

informational role a role in which the manager either gathers or provides information

Informational Roles An **informational role** is one in which the manager either gathers or provides information. The informational role can be subdivided as follows:

8. *Monitor.* In the role of monitor, a manager actively seeks information that may be of value to the organization. For example, a manager who hears about a good business opportunity is engaging in the role of monitor.

9. *Disseminator.* In the role of disseminator, a manager transmits key information to those who can use it. As a disseminator, the manager who heard about a good business opportunity would tell the appropriate marketing manager about it.

10. *Spokesperson.* In the role of spokesperson, a manager provides information to people outside the organization, such as the press, television reporters, and the public.

Leadership

Prepare for Class
Career Snapshot

> ### Learning Objective ⑤
> Explain the different types of leadership.

leadership the ability to influence others

Leadership has been defined broadly as the ability to influence others. A leader has power and can use it to affect the behavior of others. Leadership is different from management in that a leader strives for voluntary cooperation, whereas a manager may have to depend on coercion to change employee behavior.

Formal and Informal Leadership

Some experts make distinctions between formal leadership and informal leadership. Formal leaders have legitimate power of position. They have *authority* within an organization to influence others to work for the organization's objectives. Informal leaders usually have no such authority and may or may not exert their influence in support of the organization. Both formal and informal leaders make use of several kinds of power, including the ability to grant rewards or impose punishments, the possession of expert knowledge, and personal attraction or charisma. Informal leaders who identify with the organization's goals are a valuable asset to any organization. However, a business can be brought to its knees by informal leaders who turn work groups against management.

authoritarian leader one who holds all authority and responsibility, with communication usually moving from top to bottom

Styles of Leadership

For many years, leadership was viewed as a combination of personality traits, such as self-confidence, concern for people, intelligence, and dependability. Achieving a consensus on which traits were most important was difficult, however, and attention turned to styles of leadership behavior. In the last few decades, several styles of leadership have been identified: authoritarian, laissez-faire, and democratic.[12]

The **authoritarian leader** holds all authority and responsibility, with communication usually moving from top to bottom. This leader assigns workers to specific tasks and expects orderly, precise results. The leaders at United Parcel Service (UPS) employ authoritarian leadership.

> **CONCEPT CHECK**
>
> Which leadership style might be best suited to each of the three general levels of management within an organization?

The laissez-faire leader gives authority to employees. With the laissez-faire style, subordinates are allowed to work as they choose with a minimum of interference. Communication flows horizontally among group members. Leaders at Apple Computer employ a laissez-faire leadership style to give employees as much freedom as possible to develop new products.

The democratic leader holds final responsibility but also delegates authority to others, who determine work assignments. In this leadership style, communication is active upward and downward. Democratic leadership can motivate employees to work effectively because they are implementing *their own* decisions. However, the decision-making process in democratic leadership takes time that subordinates could be devoting to the work itself. **EXAMPLE** Managers for both Wal-Mart and Saturn have used democratic leadership to encourage employees to become more than just rank-and-file workers.

Which Managerial Leadership Style Is Best?

Today, most management experts agree that no "best" managerial leadership style exists. Each of the styles described—authoritarian, laissez-faire, and democratic—has advantages and disadvantages. The best leadership seems to occur when the leader's style matches the situation. Each of the leadership styles can be effective in the right situation. The *most* effective style depends on interaction among employees, characteristics of the work situation, and the manager's personality.

laissez-faire leader one who gives authority to employees and allows subordinates to work as they choose with a minimum of interference; communication flows horizontally among group members

democratic leader one who holds final responsibility but also delegates authority to others, who help to determine work assignments; communication is active upward and downward

ACE the Test
ACE & ACE+
Practice Tests 7.4, 7.5

TEST PREPPER 7.4 7.5

True or False?

___T___ 1. First-line managers (and, to a lesser extent, middle managers) need the technical skills relevant to the activities they manage.

___F___ 2. In the role of a negotiator, a manager might have to decide which departmental budgets to cut and which expenditure requests to approve.

___T___ 3. A democratic leader holds final responsibility but also delegates authority to others, who determine work assignments.

Multiple Choice

___b___ 4. These types of skills allow a manager to see the "big picture" and understand how the

various parts of an organization or idea can fit together.

   a. Interpersonal skills
   b. Conceptual skills
   c. Technical skills
   d. Management skills
   e. Decisional skills

___A___ 5. A leader who holds all authority and responsibility, with communication usually moving from top to bottom, is

   a. an authoritarian leader.
   b. a dictatorial leader.
   c. a laissez-faire leader.
   d. a transformational leader.
   e. a democratic leader.

Managerial Decision Making

Learning Objective 6

Discuss the steps in the managerial decision-making process.

Decision making is the act of choosing one alternative from a set of alternatives.[13] In ordinary situations, decisions are made casually and informally. We encounter a

decision making the act of choosing one alternative from a set of alternatives

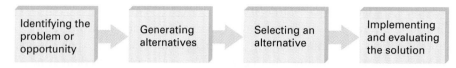

| Identifying the problem or opportunity | → | Generating alternatives | → | Selecting an alternative | → | Implementing and evaluating the solution |

FIGURE 7.7

Major Steps in the Managerial Decision-Making Process

Managers require a systematic method for solving problems in a variety of situations.

problem the discrepancy between an actual condition and a desired condition

problem, mull it over, settle on a solution, and go on. Managers, however, require a more systematic method for solving complex problems. As shown in Figure 7.7, managerial decision making involves four steps:

1. Identifying the problem or opportunity
2. Generating alternatives
3. Selecting an alternative
4. Implementing and evaluating the solution

Identifying the Problem or Opportunity

A **problem** is the discrepancy between an actual condition and a desired condition—the difference between what is occurring and what one wishes would occur. **EXAMPLE** A marketing manager at Campbell's Soup Company has a problem if sales revenues for Campbell's Hungry Man frozen dinners are declining (the actual condition). To solve this problem, the marketing manager must take steps to increase sales revenues (desired condition). Most people consider a problem to be "negative". However, a problem also can be "positive." A positive problem should be viewed as an *opportunity.*

Although accurate identification of a problem is essential before it can be solved or turned into an opportunity, this stage of decision making creates many difficulties for managers.

Your Career

Decision Making Isn't a Mystery

Are you able to make decisions? Using a mystery novel he wrote, Professor Hari Singh of Grand Valley State University in Grand Rapids, Michigan, helps his students practice the information-gathering and analytical strategies that are critical for good decision making. His novel follows two students who investigate a mysterious death and must make a variety of decisions as they solve the mystery.

Taking the mystery out of decision making means applying rules of decision making such as these:

• Know what your decision should accomplish.

• Allow enough time to make a decision; step back and gain perspective.
• When facing especially critical or complex decisions, "sleep on it."
• Ask the right questions; the solution will come.
• Seek other opinions; brainstorm and consider numerous options.
• Understand how much risk you and your organization are willing to take.
• Be aware of the resources you have to implement your decision.
• Obtain new information; incorporate feedback from others.

Sources: Based on information from Stefan Stern, "Approaching Strategy on a Case-by-Case Basis," *Los Angeles Times,* December 24, 2006, p. C2; Jan M. Rosen, "Taking the Mystery Out of Making Decisions," *New York Times,* September 12, 2006, p. G9; Benedict Carey, "The Unconscious Decision Maker," *New York Times,* February 21, 2006, p. F6.

Difficulties in Problem Identification

* Sometimes managers' preconceptions of the problem prevent them from seeing the actual situation. They produce an answer before the proper question has been asked.

* Managers overlook truly significant issues by focusing on unimportant matters.

* Managers may mistakenly analyze problems in terms of symptoms rather than underlying causes.

Steps for Effective Problem Identification

* Learn to look ahead so that they are prepared when decisions must be made.

* Clarify situations and examine the causes of problems, asking whether the presence or absence of certain variables alters a situation.

* Consider how individual behaviors and values affect the way problems or opportunities are defined.

Generating Alternatives

After a problem has been defined, the next task is to generate alternatives. The more important the decision, the more attention is devoted to this stage. Managers should be open to fresh, innovative ideas as well as obvious answers.

Certain techniques can aid in the generation of creative alternatives.

* *Brainstorming.* Commonly used in group discussions, brainstorming encourages participants to produce many new ideas. Other group members are not permitted to criticize or ridicule.

* *Blast! Then refine.* Another approach, developed by the U.S. Navy, is called "Blast! Then refine." Group members tackle a recurring problem by erasing all previous solutions and procedures. The group then re-evaluates its original objectives, modifies them if necessary, and devises new solutions.

* *Trial and error.* Other techniques—including trial and error—are also useful in this stage of decision making.

Selecting an Alternative

Final decisions are influenced by a number of considerations, including financial constraints, human and informational resources, time limits, legal obstacles, and political factors. Managers must select the alternative that will be most effective and practical. At times, two or more alternatives or some combination of alternatives will be equally appropriate. **EXAMPLE** After considering several alternatives to becoming more competitive, IBM management decided to outsource the manufacturing of more products such as disk drives and even low-end servers. Most recently, IBM decided to sell off its PC division to China's top PC maker, Lenovo.[14]

Managers may choose solutions to problems on several levels. The coined word "satisfice" describes solutions that are only adequate and not ideal, when time is of the essence. Whenever possible, managers should try to investigate alternatives carefully and select the ideal solution.

CONCEPT CHECK
Discuss what happens during each of the four steps of the managerial decision-making process.

Implementing and Evaluating the Solution

Implementation of a decision requires

* Time
* Planning
* Preparation of personnel
* Evaluation of results

The final step in managerial decision making entails evaluating the effectiveness of a decision. If the alternative that was chosen removes the difference between the actual condition and the desired condition, the decision is judged to be effective. If the problem still exists, managers may

* Decide to give the chosen alternative more time to work
* Adopt a different alternative
* Start the problem identification process all over again

Failure to evaluate decisions adequately may have negative consequences. Hewlett Packard's former CEO, Carly Fiorina, suffered negative consequences after the controversial merger with Compaq Computer did not help the company's earnings performance. Because Hewlett Packard's hardware units still were not highly competitive against the market leaders, Fiorina was replaced.[15]

TEST PREPPER 7.6

True or False?

 1. Generating alternatives is one of the steps involved in managerial decision making.

2. Most people consider a problem to be "negative"; however, a problem also can be "positive."

3. "Satisfice" describes solutions that are only adequate and not ideal.

Multiple Choice

4. Effective managers do not engage in which of the following behaviors?

    a. They believe in themselves.
    b. They are constantly studying the competition when solving a problem.
    c. They clarify situations and examine the causes of problems, asking whether the presence or absence of certain variables alters a situation.
    d. They are moral and ethical.
    e. They are fair with almost all employees.

 5. This method is commonly used in group discussions and encourages participants to produce many new ideas.

    a. Telling and selling
    b. Brainstorming
    c. The Delphi method
    d. Blast and then refine
    e. Trial and error

ACE the Test
ACE & ACE+
Practice Test 7.6

Managing Total Quality

Learning Objective 7

Describe how organizations benefit from total quality management.

The management of quality is a high priority in some organizations today. Major reasons for a greater focus on quality include foreign competition, more demanding customers, and poor financial performance resulting from reduced market share and higher costs. Over the last few years, several U.S. firms have lost the dominant competitive positions they had held for decades.

Total quality management is a much broader concept than just controlling the quality of the product itself (which is discussed in Chapter 9). **Total quality management (TQM)** is the coordination of efforts directed at improving customer satisfaction, increasing employee participation, strengthening supplier partnerships, and facilitating an organizational atmosphere of continuous quality improvement. For TQM programs to be effective, management must address each of the following components:

* *Customer satisfaction.* Ways to improve include producing higher-quality products, providing better customer service, and showing customers that the company cares.

* *Employee participation.* This can be increased by allowing employees to contribute to decisions, develop self-managed work teams, and assume responsibility for improving the quality of their work.

* *Strengthening supplier partnerships.* Developing good working relationships with suppliers can ensure that the right supplies and materials will be delivered on time at lower costs.

* *Continuous quality improvement.* This should not be viewed as achievable through one single program that has a target objective. A program based on continuous improvement has proven to be the most effective long-term approach.

Although many factors influence the effectiveness of a TQM program, two issues are crucial:

1. Top management must make a strong commitment to a TQM program by treating quality improvement as a top priority and giving it frequent attention. Firms that establish a TQM program but then focus on other priorities will find that their quality-improvement initiatives will fail.

2. Management must coordinate the specific elements of a TQM program so that they work in harmony with each other.

Although not all U.S. companies have TQM programs, these programs provide many benefits. Overall financial benefits include lower operating costs, higher return on sales and on investments, and an improved ability to use premium pricing rather than competitive pricing.

What It Takes to Become a Successful Manager Today

Learning Objective 8

Summarize what it takes to become a successful manager today.

Everyone hears stories about the corporate elite who make salaries in excess of $1 million a year, travel to and from work in chauffeur-driven limousines, and enjoy lucrative pension plans that provide for a luxurious lifestyle after they retire. Although management

total quality management (TQM) the coordination of efforts directed at improving customer satisfaction, increasing employee participation, strengthening supplier partnerships, and facilitating an organizational atmosphere of continuous quality improvement

obviously can be a rewarding career, what is not so obvious is the amount of time and hard work needed to achieve the impressive salaries and perks.

A Day in the Life of a Manager

Today's managers have demanding jobs. Managers spend a great deal of time talking with people on an individual basis. The purpose of these conversations is usually to obtain information or to resolve problems. In addition, a manager often spends time in meetings with other managers and employees. In most cases, the purpose of the meetings—some brief and some lengthy—is to resolve problems. And if the work is not completed by the end of the day, the manager usually packs his or her unfinished tasks in a briefcase.

Skills Required for Success

To be successful in today's competitive business environment, you must possess a number of skills. Some of these skills—technical, conceptual, and interpersonal skills—were discussed earlier in this chapter. However, you also need "personal" skills. Oral and written communication skills, computer skills, and critical-thinking skills may give you the edge in getting an entry-level management position.

* *Oral communication skills.* Because a large part of a manager's day is spent conversing with others, the ability to speak *and* listen is critical.
* *Written communication skills.* A manager's ability to prepare letters, e-mails, memos, reports, and other written documents may spell the difference between success and failure.
* *Computer skills.* Most employers expect managers to know how to use a computer to prepare written and statistical reports and to communicate with other employees.
* *Critical-thinking skills.* Employers expect managers to use critical-thinking skills to identify problems correctly, generate reasonable alternatives, and select the "best" alternatives to solve problems.

The Importance of Education and Experience

Although most experts agree that management skills must be learned on the job, the concepts that you learn in business courses lay the foundation for a successful career. In addition, successful completion of college courses or obtaining a degree can open doors to job interviews and career advancement.

There are methods you can use to "beef up" your résumé and to capitalize on your work experience.

First, obtain summer jobs that provide opportunities to learn about the field that interests you. Chosen carefully, part-time jobs can provide work experience that other job applicants may not have. Some colleges and universities sponsor cooperative work/school programs that give students college credit for job experience. Even with solid academics and work experience, many would-be managers find it difficult to land the "right" job. Often they start in an entry-level position to gain more experience.

In the next chapter we examine the organizing function of managers in some detail. We look specifically at various organizational forms that today's successful businesses use. As with many factors in management, how a business is organized depends on its goals, strategies, and personnel.

CONCEPT CHECK
What personal skills should a manager possess in order to be successful?

TEST PREPPER 7.7 7.8

True or False?

___T___ 1. One of the components of effective TQM is employee participation.

___T___ 2. Managers spend a great deal of time talking with people on an individual basis.

___F___ 3. Employers expect managers to use computer skills to identify problems correctly, generate reasonable alternatives, and select the "best" alternatives to solve problems.

Multiple Choice

___a___ 4. Which one of the following statements is correct about TQM?

    a. Top management must make a strong commitment to a TQM program by treating quality improvement as a top priority.

b. Employees should be aware of TQM movement, not necessarily involved in it.

c. Managers need to ask for input occasionally in order to practice TQM.

d. The top administration should appear to be interested in TQM.

e. In order for TQM to function effectively, you need a lot of resources.

___e___ 5. Because a large part of a manager's day is spent conversing with others, it is important for the manager to have

    a. written skills.
    b. people skills.
    c. idea skills.
    d. oral communication skills
    e. interpersonal skills.

ACE the Test
ACE & ACE+
Practice Tests 7.7, 7.8

Prepare for Class
CL News Feeds
CL News Now

→ RETURN TO INSIDE BUSINESS

Campbell Soup continues to thrive around the world because its top management plans carefully for the future and provides leadership with a personal touch. Sales are simmering now that the company has been reinvigorated by expanding to new markets. With Campbell's brands already established in North America, Europe, and Asia, management is planning to enter the Russian and Chinese markets—two countries where a lot of soup is consumed.

Campbell's management has integrated the company's purpose into every aspect of the organization and has created the Campbell Success Model to ensure that leadership opportunities are available to all employees. According to the CEO, Campbell's success will continue because "Great companies are the ones with both their heads and their hearts in the game. And only purpose can get you there."

Questions:

1. If you were developing a strategic plan for Campbell's Soup, what would you include?
2. What management challenges do you think Campbell's will face as it expands into the Russian and Chinese markets?

LEARNING OBJECTIVES REVIEW

1 Define what management is.

- Management is the process of coordinating people and other resources to achieve the goals of an organization.

- Managers are concerned with four types of resources—material, human, financial, and informational.

ER ACHIEVEMENT SERIES: **FOUNDATIONS OF BUSINESS**

2 Describe the four basic management functions: planning, organizing, leading and motivating, and controlling.

- Managers engage in planning—determining where the firm should be going and how best to get there.
  - Three types of plans are strategic plans, tactical plans, and operational plans.
- Managers also organize resources and activities to accomplish results in an efficient and effective manner.
- They lead and motivate others to work in the best interests of the organization.
- In addition, managers control ongoing activities to keep the organization on course.
  - There are three steps in the control function—setting standards, measuring actual performance, and taking corrective action.

3 Distinguish among the various kinds of managers in terms of both level and area of management.

- Level within the organization:
  - Top managers, who control the fortunes of the organization
  - Middle managers, who implement strategies and major policies
  - First-line managers, who supervise the activities of operating employees
- Area of management:
  - Finance
  - Operations
  - Marketing
  - Human resources
  - Administration

4 Identify the key management skills and managerial roles.

- Key management skills
  - Technical skills
  - Conceptual skills
  - Interpersonal skills
- Primary managerial roles
  - Decisional
  - Interpersonal
  - Informational

5 Explain the different types of leadership.

- Managers' effectiveness often depends on their styles of leadership—that is, their ability to influence others, either formally or informally.

- Leadership styles include
  - The authoritarian "do-it-my-way" style
  - The laissez-faire "do-it-your-way" style
  - The democratic "let's-do-it-together" style

6 Discuss the steps in the managerial decision-making process.

- Decision making is the process of developing a set of possible alternative solutions to a problem and choosing one alternative from among the set.
- Managerial decision making involves four steps:
  - Managers must accurately identify problems.
  - Managers must generate several possible solutions.
  - Managers must choose the solution that will be most effective under the circumstances.
  - Managers must implement and evaluate the chosen course of action.

7 Describe how organizations benefit from total quality management.

- Total quality management (TQM) is the coordination of efforts directed at
  - Improving customer satisfaction
  - Increasing employee participation
  - Strengthening supplier partnerships
  - Facilitating an organizational atmosphere of continuous quality improvement
- To have an effective TQM program, top management
  - Must make a strong, sustained commitment to the effort
  - Must be able to coordinate all the program's elements so that they work in harmony
- Overall financial benefits of TQM include
  - Lower operating costs
  - Higher return on sales and on investment
  - An improved ability to use premium pricing rather than competitive pricing

8 Summarize what it takes to become a successful manager today.

- Personal skills (oral and written communication skills, computer skills, and critical-thinking skills)
- An academic background that provides a foundation for a management career
- Practical work experience

Improve Your Grade
Audio Chapter Summary & Quiz

Developing Leaders at Accenture

With 133,000 employees and $17 billion in annual sales, Accenture is a global giant in consulting, technology, and outsourcing. Accenture's services are as diverse as its customer base. Over the years, its experts have provided a variety of services for banks, government agencies, entertainment firms, telecommunications companies, energy firms, automotive manufacturers, and businesses in many other industries.

As an example, Accenture designed a data management system that allows Fairmont Hotels and Resorts to capture, store, and analyze information about guest inquiries, reservations, and preferences. For Radio Shack, Accenture created a comprehensive inventory management system to track and resupply the 15,000 items offered in each store. For Microsoft, the company installed state-of-the-art sales software to enhance the productivity of Microsoft's 10,000 salespeople worldwide. And Kimberly-Clark hired Accenture to handle all the administrative details of human relations functions such as recruiting, payroll, and training.

Running an organization of this size and complexity requires top-notch leadership skills. Gill Rider, Accenture's first chief leadership officer, was a pioneer in formalizing leadership training for the company's 11,000 senior managers worldwide. Reporting directly to the CEO, the chief leadership officer is an important link between the corporation's strategy and its workforce. Just as the chief financial officer is responsible for managing Accenture's financial resources, the chief leadership officer is responsible for managing Accenture's human resources ("human capital," in Rider's words).

Leadership training is expected to contribute to Accenture's success in three ways. First, it must create value for the business and its clients. Second, it must develop the capabilities of Accenture's workforce. And third, it must help make the company's global operations more effective and more efficient. In addition, Accenture's management believes that today's leaders have a responsibility to teach tomorrow's leaders.

Gill Rider and her successor, Pierre Nanterme, have traveled the world to fulfill these goals—and to serve as good role models for Accenture's exacting leadership standards. Every month the company holds a leadership training meeting somewhere in the world to bring together top managers with groups of up-and-coming managers. These meetings keep everyone informed and involved, as well as providing opportunities for developing the managers' conceptual and interpersonal skills. Because the company has offices in 150 cities, managers in each area are likely to have different personal styles. Yet, because of Accenture's leadership training, these managers understand and can apply the corporation's fundamental leadership principles regardless of location.

In fact, Accenture's ongoing success depends, to a large extent, on its ability to recruit, develop, and retain a steady stream of employees and managers with leadership potential. One way Accenture makes itself even more attractive as an employer (while developing future leaders) is by offering top performers time off from their regular jobs to consult for a nonprofit organization in a developing country. Employees and managers are eligible to apply after they've worked at Accenture for at least two years, and only those with outstanding performance reviews are considered. Although hundreds of Accenture personnel apply every year, only a few dozen are chosen to be "loaned" to nonprofits.

Nicola Locke says this program "was one of the reasons I joined Accenture in the first place." She was loaned to an Indonesian nonprofit group working on large-scale strategies for rebuilding homes destroyed by a devastating tsunami. Stephanie Runyan found the experience so rewarding the first time around that she applied and was accepted a second time. She recently spent six months helping a nonprofit organization in Nairobi create a training program for local nurses. Like other Accenture participants, Runyan and Locke were paid only half their regular salary while on loan, yet they confirm that programs like this make Accenture an especially appealing place to work. This is exactly how the company hopes top performers—its future leaders—will see things, too.[16]

Questions

1. Why should Accenture's leadership training be geared toward helping managers develop their capabilities in all four management functions, not just leading and motivating? Be specific.
2. Which of the three key management skills does Accenture appear to be emphasizing in its leadership training program? How do you know?
3. Do you agree with Accenture's decision to allow only top performers to be loaned to nonprofit groups? Explain your answer.

BUILDING SKILLS FOR CAREER SUCCESS

1. Exploring the Internet

Most large companies call on a management consulting firm for a variety of services, including employee training, help in selecting an expensive purchase such as a computer system, recruitment of employees, and direction in reorganization and strategic planning.

Large consulting firms generally operate globally and provide information to companies considering entry into foreign countries or business alliances with foreign firms. They use their websites, along with magazine-style articles, to celebrate achievements and present their credentials to clients. Business students can acquire an enormous amount of up-to-date information in the field of management by perusing these sites.

Assignment

1. Explore each of the following websites:

   Accenture: **www.accenture.com**

   BearingPoint (formerly KPMG Consulting): **www.bearingpoint.com**

   Cap Gemini Ernst & Young: **www.capgemini .com**

   Visit the text website for updates to this exercise.

2. Judging from the articles and notices posted, what are the current areas of activities of one of these firms?

3. Explore one of these areas in more detail by comparing postings from each firm's site. For instance, if "global business opportunities" appears to be a popular area of management consulting, how has each firm distinguished itself in this area? Who would you call first for advice?

4. Given that consulting firms are always trying to fill positions for their clients and to meet their own recruitment needs, it is little wonder that employment postings are a popular area on their sites. Examine these in detail. Based on your examination of the site and the registration format, what sort of recruit are they interested in?

2. Building Team Skills

Over the past few years, an increasing number of employees, stockholders, and customers have been demanding to know what their companies are about. As a result, more companies have been taking the time to analyze their operations and to prepare mission statements that focus on the purpose of the company. The mission statement is becoming a critical planning tool for successful companies. To make effective decisions, employees must understand the purpose of their company.

Assignment

1. Divide into teams and write a mission statement for one of the following types of businesses:
   a. Food service, restaurant
   b. Banking
   c. Airline
   d. Auto repair
   e. Cabinet manufacturing

2. Discuss your mission statement with other teams. How did the other teams interpret the purpose of your company? What is the mission statement saying about the company?

3. Write a one-page report on what you learned about developing mission statements.

3. Researching Different Careers

A successful career requires planning. Without a plan, or roadmap, you will find it very difficult, if not impossible, to reach your desired career destination. The first step in planning is to establish what your career goal is. You then must set objectives and develop plans for accomplishing those objectives. This kind of planning takes time, but it will pay off later.

Assignment

Complete the following statements:

1. My career goal is to

   _____.

Prepare for Class
Exploring the Internet

This statement should encapsulate what you want to accomplish over the long run. It may include the type of job you want and the type of business or industry you want to work in. Examples include

- My career goal is to work as a top manager in the food industry.
- My career goal is to supervise aircraft mechanics.
- My career goal is to win the top achievement award in the advertising industry.

2. My career objectives are to

_____.

Objectives are benchmarks along the route to a career destination. They are more specific than a career goal. A statement about a career objective should specify what you want to accomplish, when you will complete it, and any other details that will serve as criteria against which you can measure your progress. Examples include

- My objective is to be promoted to supervisor by January 1, 20xx.
- My objective is to enroll in a management course at Main College in the spring semester 20xx.
- My objective is to earn an A in the management course at Main College in the spring semester 20xx.
- My objective is to prepare a status report by September 30 covering the last quarter's

activities by asking Charlie in Quality Control to teach me the procedures.

3. Exchange your goal and objectives statements with another class member. Can your partner interpret your objectives correctly? Are the objectives concise and complete? Do they include criteria against which you can measure your progress? If not, discuss the problem and rewrite the objective.

Skills Assessment	BELOW AVERAGE	AVERAGE	ABOVE AVERAGE	SPECIFIC EXAMPLES
Personal skills				
Oral communication skills				
Written communication skills				
Computer skills				
Critical-thinking skills				
Managerial skills				
Conceptual skills				
Technical skills				
Interpersonal skills				
Decision-making skills				

CHAPTER 8

Creating A Flexible Organization

Your Guide to Success in Business

Why this chapter matters

To operate a business at an acceptable level of profit-ability, those in charge must create an organization that not only operates efficiently but also is able to attract resources, such as employees, and to develop long-term relationships with customers.

LEARNING OBJECTIVES

1. Understand what an organization is and identify its characteristics.

2. Explain why job specialization is important.

3. Identify the various bases for departmentalization.

4. Explain how decentralization follows from delegation.

5. Understand how the span of management affects the organizational structure.

6. Understand how the chain of command is established by using line and staff management.

7. Describe the four basic forms of organizational structure: bureaucratic, matrix, cluster, and network.

8. Explain how corporate culture, intrapreneurship, committees, coordination techniques, and informal groups affect organizational structure.

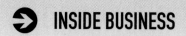

W.L. Gore & Associates

For five decades, W.L. Gore & Associates has encouraged employee innovation, satisfaction, and retention through a unique "flat lattice" organization where everybody works in teams. Although the president and CEO hold those titles as required by law, employees carry the title of *associate*, and middle managers are called *sponsors*.

With worldwide sales of $1.9 billion and 7,500 employees in forty-five locations, Delaware-based Gore has prospered by stressing teamwork to speed up creativity and communication. The company is best known for its Gore-Tex line of clothes, but it also makes a wide range of other products, including medical supplies (implants and membranes), filtration systems, sealants, guitar strings, and even a premium-quality dental floss.

Founder Bill Gore built his company on four core principles:

- Fairness
- Encouraging employee growth
- Honoring commitments
- Consulting with others before making decisions

Gore's philosophy is explained by the president and CEO, "We work hard at maximizing individual potential, maintaining an emphasis on product integrity, and cultivating an environment where creativity can flourish."

Once associates' core responsibilities to their teams are fulfilled, they're encouraged to develop new ideas and work on their own projects. Associates are accountable to their peers, and those with good management skills become sponsors and are allowed to form their own teams. Having few management layers enables Gore to develop and launch new products quickly. For example, the idea for Gore's successful shred-resistant dental floss came from an associate who wondered whether the firm's industrial-strength fibers could be used for teeth cleaning.

Gore associates are encouraged to move within the company as they gain knowledge and develop new skills. Sponsors meet regularly to discuss associates' skill sets and determine how best to use their talents and expertise within the company. In addition, associates can use the company's intranet to search for internal positions that provide new responsibilities and new challenges. Thus, as Gore grows, associates and sponsors gain more opportunities for professional growth.[1]

DID YOU KNOW?

Gore's CEO states, "We work hard at maximizing individual potential, maintaining an emphasis on product integrity, and cultivating an environment where creativity can flourish."

KEY TERMS

organization (238)
organization chart (238)
chain of command (239)
job specialization (241)
job rotation (242)
departmentalization (243)
departmentalization by function (243)
departmentalization by product (243)
departmentalization by location (244)

departmentalization by customer (245)
delegation (246)
responsibility (246)
authority (246)
accountability (246)
decentralized organization (247)
centralized organization (247)
span of management (or span of control) (248)

organizational height (249)
line management position (250)
staff management position (250)
bureaucratic structure (252)
matrix structure (252)
cross-functional team (253)
cluster structure (254)
network structure (254)
corporate culture (255)

intrapreneur (257)
ad hoc committee (258)
standing committee (258)
task force (258)
managerial hierarchy (258)
informal organization (258)
informal group (259)
grapevine (259)

ACE the Test
Crossword Puzzle
Flashcards

To survive and to grow, companies such as W.L. Gore & Associates must constantly look for ways to improve their methods of doing business. Managers at W.L. Gore & Associates, like those at many other organizations, deliberately reorganized the company to achieve its goals and objectives and to create satisfying products that foster long-term customer relationships.

When firms are organized, or reorganized, the focus is sometimes on achieving low operating costs. Other firms, such as Nike, emphasize providing high-quality products to ensure customer satisfaction. A firm's organization influences its performance. Thus the issue of organization is important.

We begin this chapter by

* Examining the business organization—what it is and how it functions in today's business environment.

* Focusing one by one on five characteristics that shape an organization's structure:
    * Job specialization within a company
    * Grouping of jobs into manageable units or departments
    * Delegation of power from management to workers
    * The span of management
    * Establishment of a chain of command
* Examining the four approaches to organizational structure:
    * The bureaucratic structure
    * The matrix structure
    * The cluster structure
    * The network structure
* Looking at the network of social interactions—the informal organization—that operates within the formal business structure.

What Is an Organization?

Learning Objective 1

Understand what an organization is and identify its characteristics.

We used the term *organization* throughout Chapter 7 without really defining it mainly because its everyday meaning is close to its business meaning. Here, however, let us agree that an **organization** is a group of two or more people working together to achieve a common set of goals. **EXAMPLE** A neighborhood dry cleaner owned and operated by a husband-and-wife team is an organization. IBM and Home Depot, which employ thousands of workers worldwide, are also organizations in the same sense. Although each corporation's organizational structure is more complex than the dry-cleaning establishment, all must be organized to achieve their goals.

An inventor who goes into business to produce and market a new invention hires people, decides what each will do, determines who will report to whom, and so on. These activities are the essence of organizing, or creating, the organization. One way to create this "picture" is to create an organization chart.

organization a group of two or more people working together to achieve a common set of goals

organization chart a diagram that represents the positions and relationships within an organization

Developing Organization Charts

An **organization chart** is a diagram that represents the positions and relationships within an organization. An example of an organization chart is shown in Figure 8.1. Each rectangle represents a particular position or person in the organization. At the top is the president; at the next level are the vice presidents. The solid vertical lines connecting the vice presidents to the president indicate that the vice presidents are in the chain of command. The **chain of command** is the line of authority that extends from the highest to the lowest levels of the organization. The chain of command can be short or long. **EXAMPLE** At Royer's Roundtop Café, an independent restaurant in Roundtop, Texas, the chain of command is very short. Bud Royer, the owner, is responsible only to himself and can alter his hours or change his menu quickly. On the other hand, the chain of command at McDonald's is long. Before making certain types of changes, a McDonald's franchisee seeks permission from regional management, which, in turn, seeks approval from corporate headquarters.

Chain of command the line of authority that extends from the highest to the lowest levels of an organization

In the chart, the connections to the directors of legal services, public affairs, and human resources are shown as broken lines; these people are not part of the direct chain of command. Instead, they hold *advisory*, or *staff*, positions.

Most smaller organizations find organization charts useful. They clarify positions and reporting relationships for everyone in the organization, and they help managers to track growth and change in the organizational structure.

However, many large organizations, such as ExxonMobil, Kellogg, and Procter & Gamble, do not maintain complete, detailed charts for the following reasons:

1. It is difficult to chart even a few dozen positions accurately, much less the thousands that characterize larger firms.
2. Larger organizations are almost always changing parts of their structure.

Technology is helping large companies implement up-to-date organization charts. **EXAMPLE** Workstream, Inc., is a provider of enterprise

workforce management software and has signed big-name clients. Carol Caruso, an organizational design specialist at Mercedes-Benz USA, reported that the software saves time and effort in communicating organizational structure. Aside from providing organization charts, the software also will support human resources processes such as workflow approval and succession planning.[2]

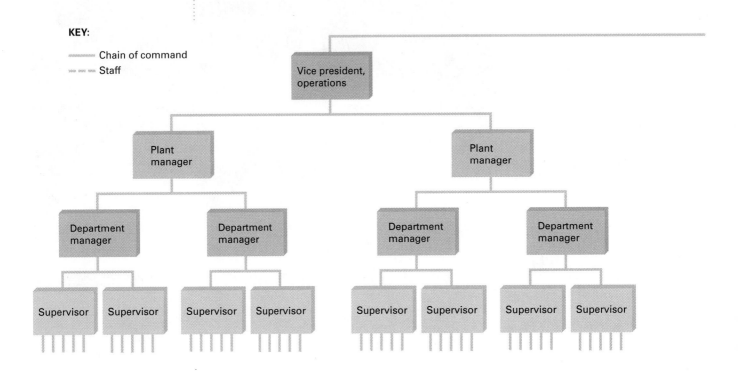

KEY:

——— Chain of command
— — — Staff

FIGURE 8.1

A Typical Corporate Organization Chart

A company's organization chart represents the positions and relationships within the organization and shows the managerial chains of command.

Five Steps for Organizing a Business

When a firm is started, management must decide how to organize the firm. These decisions are all part of five major steps that sum up the organizing process. The five steps are

1. *Job design.* Divide the work that is to be done by the entire organization into separate parts, and assign those parts to positions within the organization.
2. *Departmentalization.* Group the various positions into manageable units or departments.
3. *Delegation.* Distribute responsibility and authority within the organization.
4. *Span of management.* Determine the number of subordinates who will report to each manager.
5. *Chain of command.* Establish the organization's chain of command by designating the positions with direct authority and those that are support positions.

In the next several sections we discuss major issues associated with these steps.

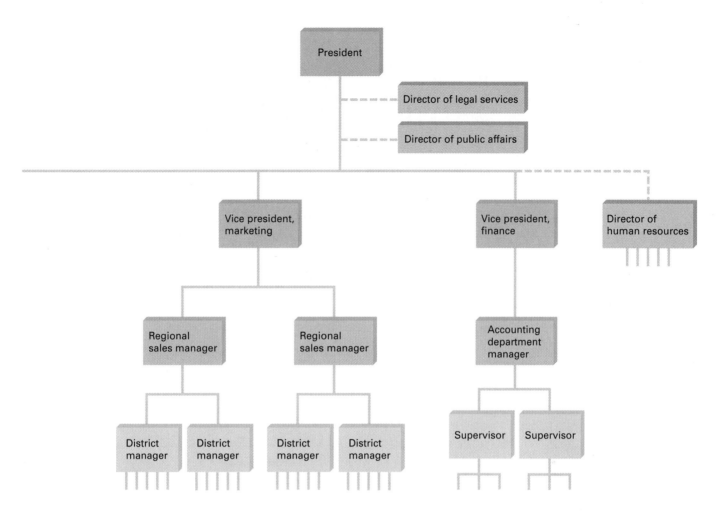

Job Design

Learning Objective ②

Explain why job specialization is important.

In Chapter 1 we defined *specialization* as the separation of a manufacturing process into distinct tasks and the assignment of different tasks to different people. Here we are extending that concept to *all* the activities performed within an organization.

Job Specialization

Job specialization is the separation of all organizational activities into distinct tasks and the assignment of different tasks to different people. Adam Smith, the eighteenth-century economist whose theories gave rise to capitalism, was the first to emphasize the power of specialization in his book, *The Wealth of Nations*. According

CONCEPT CHECK

Explain how the five steps of the organizing process determine the characteristics of the resulting organization. Which steps are most important?

job specialization
the separation of all organizational activities into distinct tasks and the assignment of different tasks to different people

Job Specialization.

Yum? A part of these product developers' job specialization is to taste potential flavors that may become commercialized products for Ben and Jerry's.

to Smith, the various tasks in a particular pin factory were arranged so that one worker drew the wire for the pins, another straightened the wire, a third cut it, a fourth ground the point, and a fifth attached the head. Smith claimed that ten men were able to produce 48,000 pins per day. Before specialization, they could produce only 200 pins per day because each worker had to perform all five tasks!

The Rationale for Specialization

For a number of reasons, some job specialization is necessary in every organization.

* The "job" of most organizations is too large for one person to handle. In a firm such as Daimler AG, thousands of people are needed to manufacture automobiles. Others are needed to sell the cars, control the firm's finances, and so on.

* When a worker has to learn one specific, highly specialized task, that individual should be able to learn it very efficiently.

* A worker repeating the same job does not lose time changing from operations, as the pin workers did when producing complete pins.

* The more specialized the job, the easier it is to design specialized equipment.

* The more specialized the job, the easier is the job training.

CONCEPT CHECK

What determines the degree of specialization within an organization?

Unfortunately, specialization can have negative consequences as well. The most significant drawback is the boredom and dissatisfaction employees may feel when repeating the same job. Bored employees may be absent from work frequently, may not put much effort into their work, and may even sabotage the company's efforts to produce quality products.

Alternatives to Job Specialization

To combat the problems of specialization, managers often turn to job rotation. Job rotation is the systematic shifting of employees from one job to another. For example, a worker may be assigned a different job every week for a four-week period and then return to the first job in the fifth week. Job rotation provides a variety of tasks so that workers are less likely to become bored and dissatisfied.

Two other approaches—*job enlargement* and *job enrichment*—also can provide solutions to the problems caused by job specialization. These topics, along with other methods used to motivate employees, are discussed in Chapter 11.

job rotation the systematic shifting of employees from one job to another

TEST PREPPER 8.1 8.2

True or False?

 1. A football team would be considered a group. *organization*

 2. Span of management is determining how wide of a geographic span a manager has under him or her.

F 3. For the most part, there are no negatives associated with job specialization.

Multiple Choice

C 4. Many larger organizations do not maintain complete, detailed organizational charts. One of the reasons for this is that

    a. most organizations are not very clear about the chain of command.

b. organizations typically do not follow organization charts.

c. it is difficult to plot the thousands of positions that characterize an organization.

d. organizations find it expensive to make these charts.

e. organizations find plotting the charts is a waste of time.

5. Who was the first to recognize the power of specialization?

    a. Karl Marx
    b. Max Weber
    c. John Kenneth Galbraith
    d. Adam Smith
    e. Thomas Friedman

ACE the Test
ACE & ACE+
Practice Tests 8.1, 8.2

Departmentalization

Learning Objective

Identify the various bases for departmentalization.

After jobs are designed, they must be grouped together into "working units," or departments. This process is called *departmentalization*. More specifically, **departmentalization** is the process of grouping jobs into manageable units. Several departmentalization bases are used commonly. In fact, most firms use more than one. Today, the most common bases for organizing a business into effective departments are

    * By function   * By location

    * By product   * By customer

departmentalization the process of grouping jobs into manageable units

By Function

Departmentalization by function groups jobs that relate to the same organizational activity. Under this scheme, all marketing personnel are grouped together in the marketing department, all production personnel in the production department, and so on. Most smaller and newer organizations departmentalize by function. Supervision is simplified because everyone is involved in the same activities, and coordination is easy. The disadvantages of this method of grouping jobs are that it can lead to slow decision making and that it tends to emphasize the department over the whole organization.

departmentalization by function grouping jobs that relate to the same organizational activity

By Product

Departmentalization by product groups activities related to a particular product or service. This approach is used often by older and larger firms that produce and sell a variety of products. Each department handles its own marketing, production,

departmentalization by product grouping activities related to a particular product or service

Your Career

Are You Flexible Enough for a Flexible Organization?

With today's mergers and acquisitions, global competition, and the pressures associated with maintaining a healthy bottom line, companies are looking for managers and employees who can adapt quickly when market demands shift unexpectedly. As you plan your next career move, think about how your background, experience, and attitude can help an employer make the most of its flexible organization structure.

Ask yourself:

- Are you the right person at the right time to help the company compete effectively?

- What additional skills will make you even more valuable to employers?
- How readily can you adapt to rapid changes in the business environment?
- Can you further your career by accepting a temporary position or a job created during a period of peak production?
- Do you have the knowledge, capabilities, and drive to work as an independent on contract terms for a company?

Sources: Based on information from Stephen Coco, "Creating (and Maintaining) a Nimble and Flexible Organization," *CIO Update*, July 13, 2006, **www .cioupdate.com**; "Hiring of Temporary Workers Pushes G.M. Shares Up 8%," *New York Times*, May 25, 2006, p. C3; Diane Stafford and Randolph Heaster, "1 in 4 Workers Not on Permanent Payrolls," *Boston Globe*, September 10, 2006, p. G16.

departmentalization by location grouping activities according to the defined geographic area in which they are performed

financial management, and human resources activities. Departmentalization by product makes decision making easier and provides for the integration of all activities associated with each product. However, it causes some duplication of specialized activities—such as finance—from department to department. And the emphasis is placed on the product rather than on the whole organization.

By Location

Departmentalization by location groups activities according to the defined geographic area in which they are performed. Departmental areas may range from whole countries (for international firms) to regions within countries (for national firms) to areas of several city blocks (for police departments organized into precincts). Departmentalization by location allows the organization to respond readily to the unique demands or requirements of different locations. Nevertheless, a large administrative staff and an elaborate control system may be needed to coordinate operations in many locations.

By Customer

Departmentalization by customer groups activities according to the needs of various customer populations. A local Chevrolet dealership, for example, may have one sales staff to deal with individual consumers and a different sales staff to work with corporate fleet buyers. The obvious advantage of this approach is that it allows the firm to deal efficiently with unique customers or customer groups. The biggest drawback is that a larger-than-usual administrative staff is needed.

departmentalization by customer grouping activities according to the needs of various customer populations

Combinations of Bases

Many organizations use more than one of these departmentalization bases. Take a moment to examine Figure 8.2. Notice that departmentalization by customer is used to organize New-Wave Fashions, Inc., into three major divisions: men's, women's, and children's clothing. Then functional departmentalization is used to distinguish the firm's production and marketing activities. Finally, location is used to organize the firm's marketing efforts.

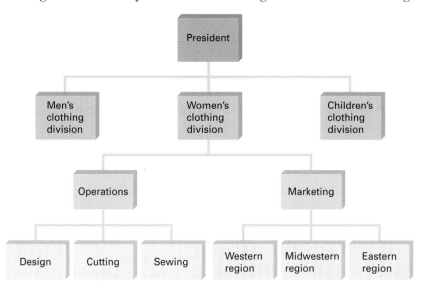

FIGURE 8.2

Multibase Departmentalization for New-Wave Fashions, Inc.

Most firms use more than one basis for departmentalization to improve efficiency and to avoid overlapping positions.

TEST PREPPER 8.3

True or False?

_T_ 1. One of the most common bases of departmentalization is by type of product produced.

_F_ 2. When organizing by customer, you do not necessarily need a large staff.

_T_ 3. Most companies use several bases of departmentalization to improve efficiency.

Multiple Choice

_A_ 4. Most smaller and newer organizations organize by
   a. function.
   b. product.
   c. customer.
   d. location.
   e. managerial preference.

_B_ 5. Older and larger firms that produce and sell a variety of products organize by
   a. location.
   b. product.
   c. customer.
   d. function.
   e. executive decisions.

ACE the Test
ACE & ACE+
Practice Test 8.3

Delegation, Decentralization, and Centralization

Learning Objective ④

Explain how decentralization follows from delegation.

delegation assigning part of a manager's work and power to other workers

responsibility the duty to do a job or perform a task

authority the power, within an organization, to accomplish an assigned job or task

accountability the obligation of a worker to accomplish an assigned job or task

The third major step in the organizing process is to distribute power in the organization. Delegation assigns part of a manager's work and power to other workers. The degree of centralization or decentralization of authority is determined by the overall pattern of delegation within the organization.

Delegation of Authority

Because no manager can do everything, delegation is vital to completion of a manager's work. Delegation is also important in developing the skills and abilities of subordinates. It allows those who are being groomed for higher-level positions to play increasingly important roles in decision making.

Steps in Delegation The delegation process generally involves three steps (see Figure 8.3). First, the manager must *assign responsibility.* Responsibility is the duty to do a job or perform a task. In most job settings, a manager simply gives the worker a job to do. Typical job assignments might range from having a worker prepare a report on the status of a new quality control program to placing the person in charge of a task force. Second, the manager must *grant authority.* Authority is the power, within the organization, to accomplish an assigned job or task. This might include the power to obtain specific information, order supplies, authorize relevant expenditures, or make certain decisions. Finally, the manager must *create accountability.* Accountability is the obligation of a worker to accomplish an assigned job or task.

Note that accountability is created, but it cannot be delegated. **EXAMPLE** Suppose that you are an operations manager for Target and are responsible for performing a specific task. You, in turn, delegate this task to someone else. You nonetheless remain accountable to your immediate supervisor for getting the task done properly. If the other person fails to complete the assignment, you—not the person to whom you delegated the task—will be held accountable.

Barriers to Delegation For several reasons, managers may be unwilling to delegate work. These reasons may be because

* They want to be sure that the work gets done.
* The manager fears that the worker will do the work well and attract the approving notice of higher-level managers.
* They are so disorganized that they simply are not able to plan and assign work effectively.

Decentralization of Authority

The pattern of delegation throughout an organization determines the extent to which that organization is decentralized or centralized. In a **decentralized organization**, management consciously attempts to spread authority widely across various organization levels. A **centralized organization**, on the other hand, systematically works to concentrate authority at the upper levels. For example, many publishers of college-level textbooks are centralized organizations, with authority concentrated at the top. Large organizations may have characteristics of both decentralized and centralized organizations. **EXAMPLE** Wal-Mart centralizes its operations in Bentonville, Arkansas, but usually permits tremendous independence in stocking the stores with items local customers want. The top-management team in Bentonville focuses primarily on the top 20 percent and bottom 20 percent of its stores and tends to leave the rest alone.[3]

Factors Affecting Decentralization

* *Nature of the external environment.* The more complex and unpredictable this environment, the more likely it is that top management will let lower-level managers make important decisions. After all, lower-level managers are closer to the problems.
* *Nature of the decision itself.* The riskier or more important the decision, the greater is the tendency to centralize decision making.
* *Ability of low-level managers.* If these managers do not have strong decision-making skills, top managers will be reluctant to decentralize. In contrast, strong lower-level decision-making skills encourage decentralization.
* *History of decision making.* Finally, a firm that traditionally has practiced centralization or decentralization is likely to maintain that posture in the future.

In principle, neither decentralization nor centralization is right or wrong. What works for one organization may or may not work for another. Kmart Corporation and McDonald's are very successful—and both practice centralization. But decentralization has worked very well for General Electric and Sears. Every organization must assess its own situation and then choose the level of centralization or decentralization that will work best.

THE DELEGATION PROCESS

Manager
1 Assign responsibility
2 Grant authority
3 Assign accountability
Worker

FIGURE 8.3

Steps in the Delegation Process

To be successful, a manager must learn how to delegate. No one can do everything alone.

decentralized organization an organization in which management consciously attempts to spread authority widely in the lower levels of the organization

centralized organization an organization that systematically works to concentrate authority at the upper levels of the organization

CONCEPT CHECK

How does a firm's top management influence its degree of centralization?

The Span of Management

> **Learning Objective** ⑤
>
> Understand how the span of management affects the organizational structure.

span of management (or span of control) the number of workers who report directly to one manager

The fourth major step in organizing a business is establishing the **span of management** (or **span of control**), which is the number of workers who report directly to one manager. For hundreds of years, theorists have searched for an ideal span of management. When it became apparent that there is no perfect number of subordinates for a manager to supervise, they turned their attention to the general issue of whether the span should be wide or narrow. This issue is complicated because the span of management may change by department within the same organization. **EXAMPLE** The span of management at FedEx varies within the company. Departments in which workers do the same tasks on a regular basis—customer-service agents, handlers and sorters, and couriers—usually have a span of management of fifteen to twenty employees per manager. Groups performing multiple and different tasks are more likely to have smaller spans of management consisting of five or six employees.[4] Thus FedEx uses a wide span of control in some departments and a narrower one in others.

Wide and Narrow Spans of Control

A *wide* span of management exists when a manager has a larger number of subordinates. A *narrow* span exists when the manager has only a few subordinates. Several factors determine the span that is better for a particular manager (see Figure 8.4).

Generally, the span of control may be *wide* when

1. The manager and the subordinates are very competent.
2. The organization has a well-established set of standard operating procedures.
3. Few new problems are expected to arise.

FIGURE 8.4

The Span of Management

Several criteria determine whether a firm uses a wide span of management, in which a larger number of workers report to one manager, or a narrow span, in which a manager supervises only a few workers.

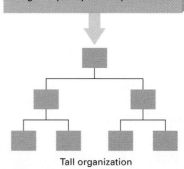

WIDE SPAN
- High level of competence in managers and workers
- Standard operating procedures
- Few new problems

Flat organization

NARROW SPAN
- Physical dispersion of subordinates
- Manager has additional tasks
- High level of interaction required between manager and workers
- High frequency of new problems

Tall organization

The span should be *narrow* when

1. Workers are physically located far from one another.
2. The manager has much work to do in addition to supervising workers.
3. A great deal of interaction is required between supervisor and workers.
4. New problems arise frequently.

Organizational Height

The span of management has an obvious impact on relations between managers and workers. It has a more subtle but equally important impact on the height of the organization. **Organizational height** is the number of layers, or levels, of management in a firm. The span of management plays a direct role in determining the height of the organization, as shown in Figure 8.4. If spans of management are wider, fewer levels are needed, and the organization is *flat*. If spans of management generally are narrow, more levels are needed, and the resulting organization is *tall*.

organizational height
the number of layers, or levels, of management in a firm

Pros and Cons of Flatter Versus Taller Organization

* In a taller organization, administrative costs are higher because more managers are needed. Communication among levels may become distorted because information has to pass up and down through more people.

* When companies are cutting costs, one option is to decrease organizational height in order to reduce related administrative expenses. **EXAMPLE** When Raytheon, a high-tech defense supplier, needed to reduce its enormous cost structure, the CEO decided to eliminate an entire layer of management, resulting in a flatter organization.[5]

* Although flat organizations avoid these problems, their managers may perform more administrative duties simply because there are fewer managers.

* Wide spans of management also may require managers to spend considerably more time supervising and working with subordinates.

ACE the Test
ACE & ACE+
Practice Tests 8.4, 8.5

TEST PREPPER 8.4 8.5

True or False?

__T__ 1. A manager can delegate successfully by assigning responsibility, not necessarily authority.

__F__ 2. *Span of management* refers to the number of workers who report directly to more than one manager.

__T__ 3. In a taller organization, administrative costs are higher because more managers are needed.

Multiple Choice

__e__ 4. Many managers are reluctant to delegate. Which one of the following is *not* one of the reasons they are reluctant to do so?

    a. They want to be sure that the work gets done.
    b. They fear that workers will do the work well and attract the approving notice of higher-level managers.

c. They are so disorganized that they simply are not able to plan and assign work.
d. Most managers are workaholics.
e. Most subordinates are reluctant to accept delegated tasks.

__A__ 5. The span of control can be wide for several reasons. Which of the following is one of the reasons why it can be so?

a. The organization has a well-established set of standard operating procedures.
b. The organization has several competent managers.
c. The organization has several locations.
d. The organization has a well-defined organization chart.
e. The organization is an older, established one.

Chain of Command: Line and Staff Management

Learning Objective ⑥

Understand how the chain of command is established by using line and staff management.

line management position a position that is part of the chain of command and that includes direct responsibility for achieving the goals of the organization

staff management position a position created to provide support, advice, and expertise within an organization

Establishing the chain of command is another step in organizing a business. It reaches from the highest to the lowest levels of management. A **line management position** is part of the chain of command; it is a position in which a person makes decisions and gives orders to subordinates to achieve the goals of the organization. A **staff management position**, by contrast, is a position created to provide support, advice, and expertise to someone in the chain of command. Staff managers are not part of the chain of command but do have authority over their assistants (see Figure 8.5).

Line and Staff Positions Compared

Both line and staff managers are needed for effective management, but the two positions differ in important ways. The basic difference is in terms of authority. Line managers have *line authority*, which means that they can make decisions and issue directives relating to the organization's goals.

Staff managers seldom have this kind of authority. Instead, they usually have either advisory authority or functional authority. *Advisory authority* is the expectation that line managers will consult the appropriate staff manager when making decisions.

FIGURE 8.5

Line and Staff Management

A line manager has direct responsibility for achieving the company's goals and is in the direct chain of command. A staff manager supports and advises the line managers.

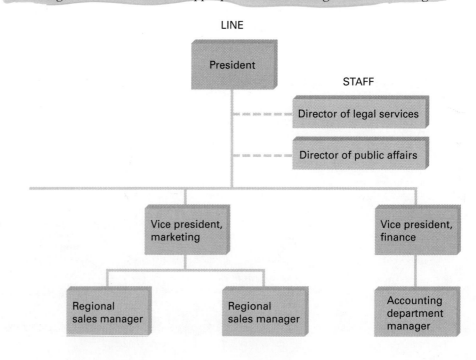

Functional authority is stronger. *Functional authority* is the authority of staff managers to make decisions and issue directives about their areas of expertise. For example, a legal adviser for Nike can decide whether to retain a particular clause in a contract but not product pricing.

Line-Staff Conflict

For a variety of reasons, conflict between line managers and staff managers is fairly common in businesses. Staff managers often have more formal education and sometimes are younger (and perhaps more ambitious) than line managers. Line managers may perceive staff managers as a threat to their own authority and thus may resent them. For their part, staff managers may become annoyed or angry if their expert recommendations—in public relations or human resources management, for example—are not adopted by line management.

Fortunately, there are several ways to minimize the likelihood of such conflict. One way is to integrate line and staff managers into one team. Another is to ensure that the areas of responsibility of line and staff managers are clearly defined. Finally, line and staff managers both can be held accountable for the results of their activities.

Before studying the next topic—forms of organizational structure—you may want to review the five organization-shaping characteristics that we have just discussed. See Table 8.1 for a summary.

Line and Staff Positions.

Ronald McDonald occupies a staff position and does not have direct authority over other employees at McDonalds. The other individuals shown here occupy line positions and do have direct authority over some of the other McDonald employees.

DIMENSION	PURPOSE
Job design	To divide the work performed by an organization into parts and assign each part a position within the organization.
Departmentalization	To group various positions in an organization into manageable units. Departmentalization may be based on function, product, location, customer, or a combination of these bases.
Delegation	To distribute part of a manager's work and power to other workers. A deliberate concentration of authority at the upper levels of the organization creates a centralized structure. A wide distribution of authority into the lower levels of the organization creates a decentralized structure.
Span of management	To set the number of workers who report directly to one manager. A narrow span has only a few workers reporting to one manager. A wide span has a large number of workers reporting to one manager.
Line and staff management	To distinguish between those positions that are part of the chain of command and those that provide support, advice, or expertise to those in the chain of command.

TABLE 8.1

Five Characteristics of Organizational Structure

Forms of Organizational Structure

bureaucratic structure
a management system
based on a formal frame-
work of authority that is
outlined carefully and
followed precisely

matrix structure an
organizational structure
that combines vertical
and horizontal lines of
authority, usually by
superimposing product
departmentalization
on a functionally
departmentalized
organization

**Bureaucratic
Structure.**

Bureaucratic structures,
like the Department of
Veteran Affairs, can
become so mired in
policies and procedures
that it becomes
dysfunctional, thus
losing its effectiveness.

Learning Objective 7

Describe the four basic forms of organizational structure: bureaucratic, matrix, cluster, and network.

Up to this point we have focused our attention on the major characteristics of organizational structure. In many ways this is like discussing the parts of a jigsaw puzzle one by one. It is time to put the puzzle together. In particular, we discuss four basic forms of organizational structure: *bureaucratic, matrix, cluster, and network.*

The Bureaucratic Structure

The term *bureaucracy* is used often in an unfavorable context to suggest rigidity and red tape. This image may be negative, but it does capture some of the essence of the bureaucratic structure.

A **bureaucratic structure** is a management system based on a formal framework of authority that is outlined carefully and followed precisely. A bureaucracy is likely to have the following characteristics:

1. A high level of job specialization
2. Departmentalization by function
3. Formal patterns of delegation
4. A high degree of centralization
5. Narrow spans of management, resulting in a tall organization
6. Clearly defined line and staff positions with formal relationships between the two

Perhaps the best examples of contemporary bureaucracies are government agencies and colleges and universities. Consider the very rigid college entrance and registration procedures. The reason for such procedures is to ensure that the organization is able to deal with large numbers of people in an equitable and fair manner. We may not enjoy them, but regulations and standard operating procedures guarantee uniform treatment.

The biggest drawback to the bureaucratic structure is lack of flexibility. A bureaucracy has trouble adjusting to change and coping with the unexpected. Because today's business environment is dynamic and complex, many firms have found that the bureaucratic structure is not an appropriate organizational structure.

The Matrix Structure

When the matrix structure is used, individuals report to more than one superior at the same time. The **matrix structure** combines vertical and horizontal lines of authority. The matrix structure occurs when product departmentalization is superimposed on a functionally departmentalized organization. In a matrix organization, authority flows both down and across.

To understand the structure of a matrix organization, consider combining the functional arrangement of departments such as engineering, finance, and marketing with a special group that is working on a new project as a team. This team is called a

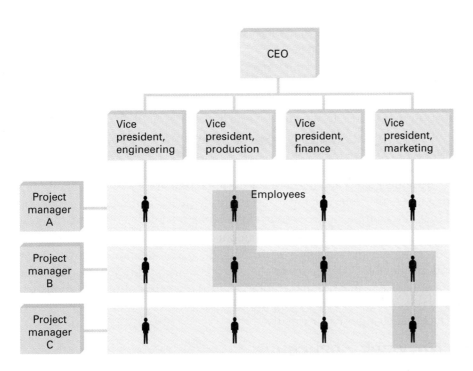

FIGURE 8.6

A Matrix Structure

A matrix is usually the result of combining product departmentalization with function departmentalization. It is a complex structure in which employees have more than one supervisor.

Source: Ricky W. Griffin, *Management*, 9th ed. Copyright © 2008 by Houghton Mifflin Company. Adapted with permission.

cross-functional team. Frequently, cross-functional teams are charged with the responsibility of developing new products. **EXAMPLE** Ford Motor Company assembled a special project team to design and manufacture its cars. The manager in charge of a team is usually called a *project manager.* Any individual who is working with the team reports to *both* the project manager and the individual's superior in the functional department (see Figure 8.6).

cross-functional team a group of employees from different departments who work together on a specific project

Characteristics of the Cross-Functional Team

* Prospective cross-functional team members may receive special training because effective teamwork can require different skills.
* To be successful, team members must be given specific information on the job each performs. The team also must develop a sense of cohesiveness and maintain good communications among its members.
* Added flexibility is probably the most obvious advantage of this structure over other structures.
* The matrix structure also can increase productivity, raise morale, and nurture creativity and innovation. In addition, employees experience personal development by doing a variety of jobs.

Disadvantages of the Matrix Structure

* Having employees report to more than one supervisor can cause confusion about who is in charge.
* Teams may take longer to resolve problems and issues than individuals working alone.
* Other difficulties include personality clashes, poor communication, undefined individual roles, unclear responsibilities, and finding ways to reward individual and team performance simultaneously.

CONCEPT CHECK

Contrast the bureaucratic and matrix forms of organizational structure.

* Because more managers and support staff may be needed, a matrix structure may be more expensive to maintain.

The Cluster Structure

cluster structure an organization that consists primarily of teams with no or very few underlying departments

Characteristics of the Cluster Structure A cluster structure is a type of business that consists primarily of teams with no or very few underlying departments. This type of structure is also called *team* or *collaborative.* In this type of organization, team members work together on a project until it is finished, and then the team may remain intact and be assigned another project, or team members may be reassigned to different teams, depending on their skills and the needs of the organization. In a cluster organization, the operating unit is the team, and it remains relatively small. If a team becomes too large, it can be split into multiple teams, or individuals can be assigned to other existing teams.

Pros and Cons of the Cluster Structure The cluster organizational structure has both strengths and weaknesses. Keeping the teams small provides the organization with the flexibility necessary to change directions quickly, to try new techniques, and to explore new ideas. Some employees in these types of organizations express concerns regarding job security and the increased amount of stress that arises owing to the fact that changes occur rapidly.[6]

The Network Structure

network structure an organization in which administration is the primary function, and most other functions are contracted out to other firms

In a network structure (sometimes called a *virtual organization*), administration is the primary function performed, and other functions such as engineering, production, marketing, and finance are contracted out to other organizations. Frequently, a network organization does not manufacture the products it sells.

Pros and Cons of the Network Structure An obvious strength of the network structure is flexibility that allows the organization to adjust quickly to changes. Some of the challenges faced by managers in network-structured organizations include controlling the quality of work performed by other organizations, low morale and high turnover among hourly workers, and the vulnerability associated with relying on outside contractors.

ACE the Test
ACE & ACE+
Practice Tests 8.6, 8.7

TEST PREPPER 8.6 8.7

True or False?

___F___ 1. A line position is created to provide support, advice, and expertise within an organization.

___T___ 2. The basic difference between line and staff positions is in terms of authority.

___F___ 3. A network organization manufactures the products it sells.

Multiple Choice

___B___ 4. Which of the following statements is *incorrect* about bureaucracy?

    a. Departmentalization by function
    b. Informal patterns of delegation
    c. A high degree of centralization
    d. Narrow spans of management, resulting in a tall organization
    e. Clearly defined line and staff positions with formal relationships between the two

___e___ 5. Which of the following is *not* one of the characteristics of cross-functional teams?

    a. Cross-functional teams can be temporary.
    b. Prospective cross-functional team members may receive special training.
    c. Team members must be given specific information.
    d. Added flexibility is probably the most obvious advantage of working in cross-functional teams.
    e. Cross-functional teams in a matrix structure are characterized by lack of productivity and lower employee morale.

Additional Factors That Influence an Organization

ACE the Test
Hangman

Learning Objective 8

Explain how corporate culture, intrapreneurship, committees, coordination techniques, and informal groups affect organizational structure.

As you might expect, other factors in addition to those already covered in this chapter affect the way a large corporation operates on a day-to-day basis. To get a "true picture" of the organizational structure of a huge corporation such as Marriott, for example, which employs over 150,000 people,[7] you need to consider the topics discussed in this section.

BIZ TECH

Meet the Avatars

How can you go to a meeting without leaving your desk? As the pace of business gets faster and travel becomes more expensive, a growing number of companies are calling meetings on the Internet. Sites such as Second Life (www.secondlife.com) offer affordable online meeting "spaces" and cutting-edge digital tools to make communication fast, easy, and out of the ordinary.

Second Life is a virtual world inhabited by computer-generated three-dimensional images called *avatars*, each customized to represent a particular person. To attend a meeting in Second Life, employees log on from anywhere and navigate their personal avatars to the meeting space—which may even be a virtual replica of the firm's actual conference room. Attendees sit in their real-world offices and converse by instant messaging text or, in some cases, Internet phone calls supplemented by web-cam video. Companies also gain from the hands-on experience with cutting-edge technologies. "To explore the new world, you have to live in it," observes an executive at the advertising agency Leo Burnett Worldwide, which holds Second Life meetings with employees worldwide.

Sources: Based on information from Emily Steel, "Avatars at the Office," *Wall Street Journal*, November 13, 2006, p. B1; Andrew Adam Newman, "The Reporter Is Real, but the World He Covers Isn't," *New York Times*, October 16, 2006, p. C6; www.secondlife.com; Richard Siklos, "A Virtual World but Real Money," *New York Times*, October 19, 2006, p. C1.

Corporate Culture

Most managers function within a corporate culture. A **corporate culture** is generally defined as the inner rites, rituals, heroes, and values of a firm. An organization's culture has a powerful influence on how employees think and act. It also can determine public perception of the organization.

corporate culture the inner rites, rituals, heroes, and values of a firm

Corporate Culture.

The corporate culture at Google includes informality and a playful atmosphere.

Corporate culture generally is thought to have a very strong influence on a firm's performance over time. Hence it is useful to be able to assess a firm's corporate culture. Common indicators include the physical setting (building, office layouts), what the company says about its corporate culture (in advertising and news releases), how the company greets guests (does it have formal or informal reception areas?), and how employees spend their time (working alone in an office or working with others).

Goffee and Jones have identified four distinct types of corporate cultures (see Figure 8.7):

* *Networked culture* is characterized by a base of trust and friendship among employees, a strong commitment to the organization, and an informal environment.

* *Mercenary culture* embodies the feelings of passion, energy, sense of purpose, and excitement for one's work. It does not imply that employees are motivated to work only for the money, but this is part of it. In this culture, employees are very intense, focused, and determined to win.

* *Fragmented culture* is characterized by employees who do not become friends, and they work "at" the organization, not "for" it. Employees have a high degree of autonomy, flexibility, and equality.

* *Communal culture* combines the positive traits of the networked culture and the mercenary culture—those of friendship, commitment, high focus on performance, and high energy. People's lives revolve around the product in this culture, and success by anyone in the organization is celebrated by all.[8]

Some experts believe that cultural change is needed when a company's environment changes, when the industry becomes more competitive, when the company's performance is mediocre, and when the company is growing or is about to become a truly large organization. **EXAMPLE** The PC industry has become highly competitive as PC sales have stagnated. Fast growth used to be Dell's top concern, but now Michael Dell and other executives are focusing on developing the company's culture. "The Soul of Dell" is the computer giant's guide to corporate culture and ethics, and management hopes that a strong culture will increase employee loyalty

SP☉TLIGHT

Should coworkers date?

About half say *yes*, and about half say *no*.

Yes 45%

5% Don't know

No 50%

Source: Maritz poll.

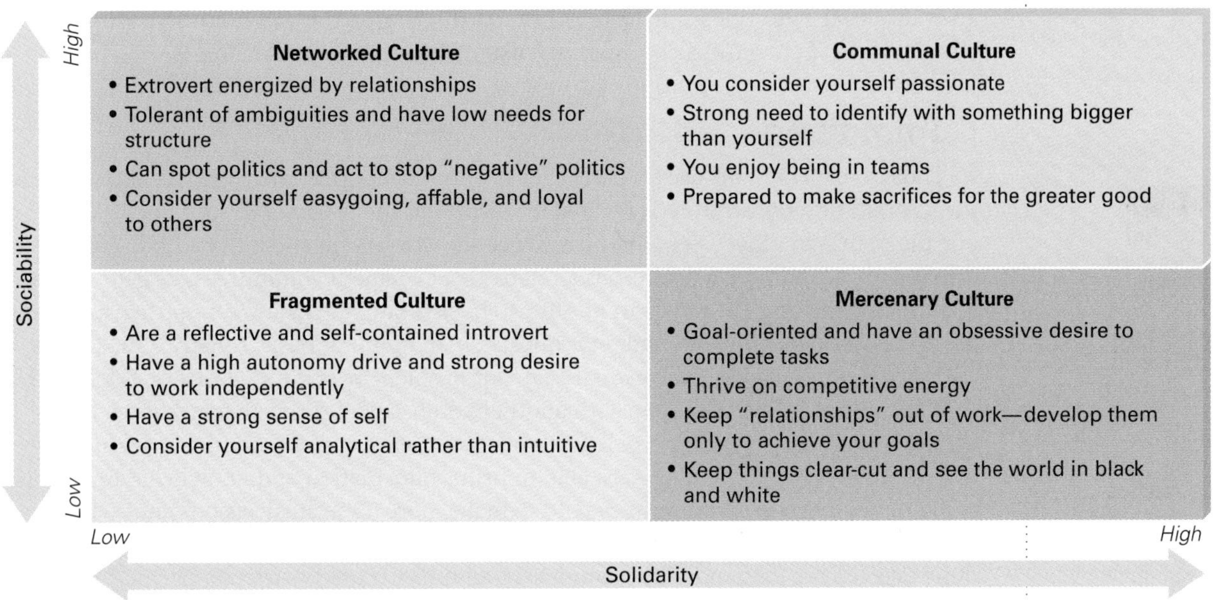

Networked Culture
- Extrovert energized by relationships
- Tolerant of ambiguities and have low needs for structure
- Can spot politics and act to stop "negative" politics
- Consider yourself easygoing, affable, and loyal to others

Communal Culture
- You consider yourself passionate
- Strong need to identify with something bigger than yourself
- You enjoy being in teams
- Prepared to make sacrifices for the greater good

Fragmented Culture
- Are a reflective and self-contained introvert
- Have a high autonomy drive and strong desire to work independently
- Have a strong sense of self
- Consider yourself analytical rather than intuitive

Mercenary Culture
- Goal-oriented and have an obsessive desire to complete tasks
- Thrive on competitive energy
- Keep "relationships" out of work—develop them only to achieve your goals
- Keep things clear-cut and see the world in black and white

High / *Low* — Sociability

Low — *High* — Solidarity

FIGURE 8.7

Types of Corporate Cultures

Which corporate culture would you choose?

Source: "Types of Corporate Culture," in Rob Goffee and Gareth Jones, *The Character of a Corporation* (New York: HarperCollins, 1998). Copyright © 1998 by Rob Goffee and Gareth Jones. Reprinted by permission.

and the success of the company.[9] Creating a culture of trust in an organization can lead to increases in growth, profit, productivity, and job satisfaction. A culture of trust can retain the best people, inspire customer loyalty, develop new markets, and increase creativity.

Business leaders often cite the role of corporate cultures in the integration process as one of the primary factors affecting the success of a merger or acquisition. Experts note that corporate culture is a way of conducting business both within the company and externally. If two merging companies do not address differences in corporate culture, they are setting themselves up for missed expectations and possibly failure.[10]

Intrapreneurship

Since innovations and new-product development are important to companies, and since entrepreneurs are innova- tive people, it seems almost natural that an entrepreneurial charac- ter would surface prominently in many of today's larger organ- izations. An **intrapreneur** is an employee who takes responsibility for push- ing an innovative idea, product, or process through an organi- zation.[11] An intra- preneur possesses the confidence and drive of an entrepre- neur but is allowed to use organizational re- sources for idea develop- ment. For example, Art Fry, inventor of the colorful Post-it-Notes that Americans can't live without, is a devoted advocate of intrapreneurship. Fry indicates that an *intrapreneur* is

Urgent!

intrapreneur an employee who pushes an innovative idea, product, or process through an organization an individual who does not have all the skills to get the job done and thus has to work within an organization, making use of its skills and attributes.

Committees

Today, business firms use several types of committees that affect organizational structure. An **ad hoc committee** is created for a specific short-term purpose, such as reviewing the firm's employee benefits plan. Once its work is finished, the ad hoc committee disbands. A **standing committee** is a relatively permanent committee charged with performing a recurring task. A firm might establish a budget review committee, for example, to review departmental budget requests on an ongoing basis. Finally, a **task force** is a committee established to investigate a major problem or pending decision. **EXAMPLE** A firm contemplating a merger with another company might form a task force to assess the pros and cons of the merger. Committees offer some advantages over individual action. Their several members are able to bring information and knowledge to the task at hand. Furthermore, committees tend to make more accurate decisions and to transmit their results through the organization more effectively. However, committee deliberations take longer than individual actions. In addition, unnecessary compromise may take place within the committee. Or the opposite may occur as one person dominates (and thus negates) the committee process.

Coordination Techniques

A large organization is forced to coordinate organizational resources to minimize duplication and to maximize effectiveness. One technique is simply to make use of the **managerial hierarchy,** which is the arrangement that provides increasing authority at higher levels of management. One manager is placed in charge of all the resources being coordinated. That person is able to coordinate them by virtue of the authority accompanying his or her position.

Resources also can be coordinated through rules and procedures. For example, a rule can govern how a firm's travel budget is allocated. This particular resource, then, would be coordinated in terms of that rule.

In complex situations, more sophisticated coordination techniques may be called for. One approach is to establish a liaison. A *liaison* is a go-between—a person who coordinates the activities of two groups. Finally, for *very* complex coordination needs, a committee could be established. **EXAMPLE** Suppose that General Motors is in the process of purchasing the steering-wheel supplier. In this case, a committee might be appointed to integrate the new firm into General Motors' larger organizational structure.

The Informal Organization

There is another kind of organization besides the formal organization that does not show up on any chart. We define this **informal organization** as the pattern of behavior and interaction that stems from personal rather than official relationships. Firmly

---

ad hoc committee a committee created for a specific short-term purpose

standing committee a relatively permanent committee charged with performing some recurring task

task force a committee established to investigate a major problem or pending decision

managerial hierarchy the arrangement that provides increasing authority at higher levels of management

CONCEPT CHECK

How do decisions concerning span of management, the use of committees, and coordination techniques affect organizational structure?

informal organization the pattern of behavior and interaction that stems from personal rather than official relationships embedded within every informal organization are informal groups and the notorious grapevine.

Informal Groups An informal group is created by the group members themselves to accomplish goals that may or may not be relevant to the organization. Workers may create an informal group to go bowling, form a union, get a particular manager fired or transferred, or for lunch. The group may last for several years or a few hours.

Informal groups can be powerful forces in organizations. They can restrict output, or they can help managers through tight spots. They can cause disagreement and conflict, or they can help to boost morale and job satisfaction. They can show new people how to contribute to the organization, or they can help people to get away with substandard performance. Clearly, managers should be aware of these informal groups. Those who make the mistake of fighting the informal organization have a major obstacle to overcome.

The Grapevine The grapevine is the informal communications network within an organization. It is completely separate from—and sometimes much faster than—the organization's formal channels of communication. Formal communications usually follow a path that parallels the organizational chain of command. Information can be transmitted through the grapevine in any direction—up, down, diagonally, or horizontally across the organizational structure. Subordinates may pass information to their bosses, an executive may relay something to a maintenance worker, or there may be an exchange of information between people who work in totally unrelated departments. Grapevine information may be concerned with topics ranging from the latest management decisions to gossip.

How should managers treat the grapevine? Certainly it would be a mistake to try to eliminate it. People working together, day in and day out, are going to communicate. A more rational approach is to recognize its existence. For example, managers should respond promptly and aggressively to inaccurate grapevine information to minimize the damage that such misinformation might do. Moreover, the grapevine can come in handy when managers are on the receiving end of important communications from the informal organization.

Informal Groups.

Informal groups, such as these employees at Midway Home Entertainment, can be a source of information and camaraderie for participants. Although informal groups can sometimes create problems for an organization, they can also provide significant benefits.

informal group a group created by the members themselves to accomplish goals that may or may not be relevant to an organization

grapevine the informal communications network within an organization

TEST PREPPER 8.8

True or False?

_T_ 1. Mariott Hotel's corporate culture can be known by the company's advertisements.

_F_ 2. An advantage of working in a committee is that necessary compromise takes place within the committee.

_T_ 3. Informal groups can be powerful forces in organizations.

Multiple Choice

_C_ 4. A culture characterized as one where employees do not become friends and work "at" the organization is a

a. networked culture.
b. mercenary culture.
c. fragmented culture.
d. communal culture.
e. hostile culture.

_B_ 5. A relatively permanent committee charged with performing some recurring task is called

a. an ad hoc committee.
b. a standing committee.
c. a task force.
d. a managerial committee.
e. a permanent committee.

ACE the Test
ACE & ACE+
Practice Test 8.8

Prepare for Class
CL News Feeds
CL News Now

 **RETURN TO INSIDE BUSINESS**

Finding just the right people to fit into the corporate culture of W.L. Gore & Associates is not always easy. Employees have to be dedicated, adapt well to the flat structure, and be willing to share ideas and information. Although Gore receives more than 38,000 job applications each year, it hires only a few highly motivated individuals who can work effectively within the small-team model.

As Gore has grown nationally and internationally, it has had to adjust and formalize its flat-lattice team structure to coordinate internal activities without losing the spirit of intrapreneurship that has made the company so successful. In the words of Gore associate Jackie Brinton, "It's a challenge to get bigger while staying small."

Questions

1. Into what form of organizational structure does Gore most closely fit? Explain your answer.
2. How would you describe Gore's span of management? Do you consider this span appropriate for a company of Gore's size? Why?

LEARNING OBJECTIVES REVIEW

1 Understand what an organization is and identify its characteristics.

- An organization is a group of two or more people working together to achieve a common set of goals.

- The relationships among positions within an organization can be illustrated by means of an organization chart.

- Five specific characteristics—job design, departmentalization, delegation, span of management, and chain of command—help to determine what an organization chart and the organization itself look like.

2 Explain why job specialization is important.

- Job specialization is the separation of all the activities within an organization into smaller components and the assignment of those different components to different people.

- Several factors combine to make specialization a useful technique for designing jobs.

- High levels of specialization may cause employee dissatisfaction and boredom. One technique for overcoming these problems is job rotation.

3 Identify the various bases for departmentalization.

- Departmentalization is the grouping of jobs into manageable units.

- Typical bases for departmentalization are by function, product, location, or customer.

- Because each of these bases provides particular advantages, most firms—especially larger ones—use a combination of different bases in different organizational situations.

4 Explain how decentralization follows from delegation.

- Delegation is the assigning of part of a manager's work to other workers.

- It involves the following three steps:
  - Assigning responsibility
  - Granting authority
  - Creating accountability

- A decentralized firm is one that delegates as much power as possible to people in the lower management levels.

- In a centralized firm, on the other hand, power is systematically retained at the upper levels.

5 Understand how the span of management affects the organizational structure.

- The span of management is the number of workers who report directly to a manager.

- Spans generally are characterized as wide (many workers per manager) or narrow (few workers per manager).

- Wide spans generally result in flat organizations (few layers of management).

- Narrow spans generally result in tall organizations (many layers of management).

6 Understand how the chain of command is established by using line and staff management.

- A line position is one that is in the organization's chain of command or line of authority.

- A manager in a line position makes decisions and gives orders to workers to achieve the goals of the organization.

- A manager in a staff position provides support, advice, and expertise to someone in the chain of command.

- Staff positions may carry some authority, but it usually applies only within staff areas of expertise.

7 Describe the four basic forms of organizational structure: bureaucratic, matrix, cluster, and network.

- The bureaucratic structure is characterized by formality and rigidity. With the bureaucratic structure, rules and procedures are used to ensure uniformity.

- The matrix structure may be visualized as product departmentalization superimposed on functional departmentalization. With the matrix structure, an employee on a cross-functional team reports to both the project manager and the individual's supervisor in a functional department.

Improve Your Grade
Audio Chapter Summary & Quiz

- The cluster structure is an organization that consists primarily of teams with very few underlying functional departments.

- In an organization with a network structure, the primary function performed internally is administration, and other functions are contracted out to other firms.

8 Explain how corporate culture, intrapreneurship, committees, coordination techniques, and informal groups affect organizational structure.

- Corporate culture—the inner rites, rituals, heroes, and values of a firm—is thought to have a very strong influence on a firm's performance over time.

- An intrapreneur is an employee in an organizational environment who takes responsibility for pushing an innovative idea, product, or process through the organization.

- Additional elements that influence an organization include the use of committees and the development of techniques for achieving coordination among various groups within the organization.

- Finally, both informal groups created by group members and an informal communication network called the grapevine may affect an organization and its performance.

VIDEO CASE

Organizing for Success at Green Mountain Coffee Roasters

Even with a work force of 600, Green Mountain Coffee Roasters, based in Waterbury, Vermont, stays as entrepreneurial as when Bob Stiller founded the company in 1981 with one coffee shop and a handful of employees. The original plan was to open a series of coffee shops throughout New England. By the time Green Mountain Coffee had grown to twelve shops, profitability was struggling, so Stiller switched to importing, roasting, and wholesaling high-quality coffee beans to stores, food-service professionals, and restaurants around the country. Today his company brews up profits from $225 million in annual sales to Aramark Food Service, McDonald's New England outlets, Wild Oats Market groceries, Publix supermarkets, and 7,000 other businesses.

Jobs at Green Mountain Coffee are departmentalized into six functions: sales and marketing, operations, human resources, finance, information systems, and social responsibility. The organization chart shows how specialized jobs are linked by a distinct chain of command leading to CEO Bob Stiller at the top. What the chart doesn't show, however, is how collaboration and communication among all levels—rather than strict hierarchy—give the company a decision-making edge.

This is a flat organization, with only four levels between a corporate salesperson and the CEO. In line with the company's collaborative culture, decisions are made by inviting people from different functions and different levels to offer their input. Decisions may take a little more time under this system, but they're more informed and usually yield a better solution to the problem than if handled by a single manager or a tiny group.

For a particularly challenging decision, Green Mountain Coffee relies on a "constellation" of communication to collect ideas from around the organization. Managers frequently post decision data on the corporate computer system and ask coworkers for comments. They also exchange a blizzard of e-mail messages and call cross-functional meetings, when necessary, to share information and opinions. Ultimately, the manager closest to the situation is responsible for evaluating all the data and making the decision, guided by the company's values.

Green Mountain Coffee's values are revealed in its mission statement: "We create the ultimate coffee experience in every life we touch from tree to cup—transforming the way the world understands business." Because the company buys from hundreds of coffee growers and sells to thousands of businesses as well as thousands of consumers who order by mail or online, it touches a lot of lives. Social responsibility ranks high on Green Mountain Coffee's corporate agenda. It is known for donating considerable cash, coffee, and volunteer time to the communities it serves in the United States and in coffee-producing nations.

Every year the company flies dozens of employees to Central America to see how coffee beans are grown, meet the growers, and learn about the farming communities. "The effect is profound," says Stephen Sabol, vice president of development. "The knowledge of the care that goes into the coffee is important, but when [employees] see the social part of it, and how dependent these growers are on us being a quality partner, it hits right home—the obligation we have to do well." After one of these "Coffee Source Trips," employees come back to work with renewed energy and dedication.

Green Mountain Coffee Roasters not only has been cited as one of the fastest-growing companies in the United States, but it also has been named among the most socially responsible. The CEO recognizes that his company must do well in order to do good. "To help the world, we have to be successful," Stiller says. "If we help the world and go out of business, we're not going to help anybody."[12]

For more information about this company, go to **www .greenmountaincoffee.com.**

Questions

1. How is Green Mountain Coffee's "constellation" of communication likely to affect the informal organization?
2. Does Green Mountain Coffee appear to have a networked, communal, mercenary, or fragmented culture? Support your answer.
3. Is Green Mountain Coffee a centralized or decentralized organization? How do you know?

BUILDING SKILLS FOR CAREER SUCCESS

1. Exploring the Internet

After studying the various organizational structures described in this chapter and the reasons for employing them, you may be interested in learning about the organizational structures in place at large firms. As noted in the chapter, departmentalization typically is based on function, product, location, and customer. Many large firms use a combination of these organizational strategies successfully. You can gain a good sense of which organizational theme prevails in an industry by looking at several corporate websites.

Assignment

1. Explore the website of any large firm that you believe is representative of its industry, and find its organization chart or a description of its organization. Create a brief organization chart from the information you have found. (You may choose one of the consulting firms listed in the Internet exercise for Chapter 7.)

2. Describe the bases on which this firm is departmentalized.

2. Building Team Skills

An organization chart is a diagram showing how employees and tasks are grouped and how the lines of communication and authority flow within an organization. These charts can look very different depending on a number of factors, including the nature and size of the business, the way it is departmentalized, its patterns of delegating authority, and its span of management.

Assignment

1. Working in a team, use the following information to draw an organization chart: The KDS Design Center works closely with two home-construction companies, Amex and Highmass. KDS's role is to help customers select materials for their new homes and to ensure that their selections are communicated accurately to the builders. The company is also a retailer of wallpaper, blinds, and drapery. The retail department, the Amex accounts, and the

Highmass accounts make up KDS's three departments. The company has the following positions:

Prepare for Class
Exploring the Internet

President

Executive vice president

Managers, two

Appointment coordinators, two

Amex coordinators, two

Highmass coordinators, two

Consultants/designers for the Amex and Highmass accounts, fifteen

Retail positions, four

Payroll and billing personnel, one

2. After your team has drawn the organization chart, discuss the following:

   a. What type of organizational structure does your chart depict? Is it a bureaucratic, matrix, cluster, or network structure? Why?

   b. How does KDS use departmentalization?

   c. To what extent is authority in the company centralized or decentralized?

   d. What is the span of management within KDS?

   e. Which positions are line positions and which are staff? Why?

3. Prepare a three-page report summarizing what the chart revealed about relationships and tasks at the KDS Design Center and what your team learned about the value of organization charts. Include your chart in your report.

3. Researching Different Careers

In the past, company loyalty and ability to assume increasing job responsibility usually ensured advancement within an organization. While the reasons for seeking advancement (the desire for a better-paying position, more prestige, and job satisfaction) have not changed, the qualifications for career advancement have. In today's business environment, climbing the corporate ladder requires packaging and marketing yourself. To be promoted within your company or to be considered for employment with another company, it is wise to improve your skills continually. By taking workshops and seminars or enrolling in community college courses, you can keep up with the changing technology in your industry. Networking with people in your business or community can help you to find a new job. Most jobs are filled through personal contacts. Who you know can be important.

A list of your accomplishments on the job can reveal your strengths and weaknesses. Setting goals for improvement helps to increase your self-confidence.

Be sure to recognize the signs of job dissatisfaction. It may be time to move to another position or company.

Assignment

Are you prepared to climb the corporate ladder? Do a self-assessment by analyzing the following areas, and summarize the results in a two-page report.

1. Skills
   - What are your most valuable skills?
   - What skills do you lack?
   - Describe your plan for acquiring new skills and improving your skills.
2. Networking
   - How effective are you at using a mentor?
   - Are you a member of a professional organization?
   - In which community, civic, or church groups are you participating?
   - Whom have you added to your contact list in the last six weeks?
3. Accomplishments
   - What achievements have you reached in your job?
   - What would you like to accomplish? What will it take for you to reach your goal?
4. Promotion or new job
   - What is your likelihood of getting a promotion?
   - Are you ready for a change? What are you doing or willing to do to find another job?

CHAPTER 9

CONGRATULATIONS ASSOCIATES!

1,000,000th

Alabama-Built Honda

November 3, 2006

HONDA | Honda Manufacturing of Alabama, LLC

Producing Quality Goods and Services

Your Guide to Success in Business

Why this chapter matters
Think for a moment about the products and services you bought in the past week. If it weren't for the production activities described in this chapter, those products and services would not be available.

LEARNING OBJECTIVES

1. Understand the nature of production by examining operations management and the characteristics of a successful operations manager.

2. Understand production by outlining how the conversion process transforms raw materials, labor, and other resources into finished products or services.

3. Describe how research and development lead to new products and services.

4. Discuss the components involved in planning the production process.

5. Explain how purchasing, inventory control, scheduling, and quality control affect production.

6. Summarize how productivity and technology are related.

Motorola Meets the Quality Challenge

Motorola's world-famous focus on quality has saved the Illinois-based company more than $17 billion over twenty years. That's a lot of money even for a multinational with $37 billion in annual revenue from cutting-edge products such as wireless networking equipment and multifunction cell phones. Because Motorola's products are based on fast-changing technology, they must be designed, tested, produced, and brought to market quickly. How does Motorola do it?

Motorola introduced the first commercially available cell phone in the early 1980s. Since that time, the company has captured more than 22 percent of the global cell phone market despite intense competition from Nokia, which leads the industry. Today, Motorola makes stylish cell phones such as the RAZR that are smaller, slimmer, and more sophisticated than the bulkier units of the past. They're also both reliable and profitable, thanks to Motorola's obsession with quality improvement.

Quality experts are involved in every aspect of new product design, development, and production at Motorola. Every new phone or networking device must be designed to satisfy customers' needs and must meet stringent performance standards. Motorola's quality experts have fine-tuned the manufacturing process to near-perfect level, with fewer than four defects per million items produced.

In addition to these internal quality requirements, Motorola's phones must pass the demanding quality tests of telecommunications carriers such as T-Mobile, which sell the phones to its customers. Despite Motorola's rigorous controls, a product occasionally falls short in one test or another. Not long ago, T-Mobile tested a metallic-colored version of Motorola's PEBL cell phone but wasn't satisfied with the case material. "The results showed it wasn't ready for prime time," said a T-Mobile official. The carrier agreed to offer its customers green, orange, and blue PEBL phones—but not the metallic-colored ones.

Motorola has earned such a reputation for quality that other companies will pay to send their employees to Motorola University for quality control education. Motorola also coaches its suppliers and its business customers on how to achieve near-perfect quality products and processes. How far can quality take Motorola as it battles international competition and seeks ever-higher sales and profits?[1]

DID YOU KNOW?

Motorola has saved more than $17 billion over twenty years by involving its quality experts in every aspect of product design, development, and production.

KEY TERMS

operations management (268)
mass production (270)
analytical process (270)
synthetic process (270)
utility (271)
form utility (271)
service economy (273)
research and development (R&D) (274)
design planning (276)
product line (276)

product design (276)
capacity (277)
labor-intensive technology (278)
capital-intensive technology (278)
plant layout (278)
planning horizon (280)
purchasing (281)
inventory control (282)
materials requirements planning (MRP) (283)
just-in-time inventory system (283)

scheduling (283)
Malcolm Baldrige National Quality Award (283)
quality control (284)
inspection (284)
quality circle (284)
productivity (286)
automation (287)
robotics (287)
computer-aided design (CAD) (287)

computer-aided manufacturing (CAM) (288)
computer-integrated manufacturing (CIM) (288)
continuous process (288)
flexible manufacturing system (FMS) (288)
intermittent process (288)

ACE the Test
Crossword Puzzle
Flashcards

Can Motorola continue to increase cell phone sales in the very competitive electronics industry? Good question! Certainly the company has established a reputation for quality and cutting-edge products. And yet it must constantly look for ways to improve its methods of doing business to improve not only quality but also manufacturing productivity. The fact is that no company illustrates this chapter's content—the production of quality goods and services—better than Motorola. Manufacturers, such as Motorola, take all kinds of raw materials and components and transform them into fine-tuned electronic products that are sold to demanding customers around the globe. Today people expect more when purchasing a cell phone, and now Motorola is working to produce a product that people want.

In this chapter, we

* Examine a brief overview of operations management—the activities required to produce products and services that meet the needs of customers.

* Discuss competition in the global marketplace and careers in operations management.

* Describe the conversion process that transforms raw materials, labor, and other resources into finished products.

* Note the growing role of services in our economy.

* Examine more closely three important aspects of operations management—developing ideas for new products and services, planning for production, and effectively controlling operations after production has begun.

* Look at productivity trends and ways that productivity can be improved through the use of technology.

What Is Production?

Learning Objective

Understand the nature of production by examining operations management and the characteristics of a successful operations manager.

Have you ever wondered where a new pair of Levi jeans comes from? Or a new Mitsubishi flat-screen color television, or Izod pullover sweater? In fact, these goods and services and millions of others like them would not exist if it weren't for production activities.

Let's begin this chapter by reviewing what an operating manager does. In Chapter 7 we described an *operations manager* as a person who manages the systems that convert resources into goods and services. This area of management is usually referred to as **operations management**, which consists of all the activities managers engage in to produce goods and services.

operations management
all the activities managers engage in to produce goods and services

To produce a product or service successfully, a business must perform a number of specific activities. **EXAMPLE** Suppose that an organization such as General Motors has an idea for a new Pontiac Solstice convertible that will cost in excess of $22,000. *Marketing research* must determine not only if customers are willing to pay the price for this product but also what special features they want. Then General Motor's *operations managers* must turn the concept into reality.

General Motors managers cannot just push the "start button" and immediately begin producing the new automobile. Production must be planned. As you will see, planning takes place both *before* anything is produced and *during* the production process.

Managers also must concern themselves with the *control of operations* to ensure that the organization's goals are achieved. For a product such as the Pontiac Solstice, control involves a number of important issues, including product quality, performance standards, the amount of inventory of both raw materials and finished products, and production costs.

We discuss each of the major activities of operations management later in this chapter. First, however, let's take a closer look at American manufacturers and how they compete in the global marketplace.

Competition in the Global Marketplace

After World War II, the United States became the most productive country in the world. For almost thirty years, until the late 1970s, its leadership was never threatened. By then, however, manufacturers in Japan, Germany, the United Kingdom, Taiwan, Canada, Korea, and other industrialized nations were offering U.S. firms increasing competition. And now the Chinese are manufacturing everything from sophisticated electronic equipment and automobiles to less expensive everyday items—often for lower cost than the same goods can be manufactured in other countries. As a result, the goods Americans purchase may have been manufactured in the United States or in other countries around the globe and shipped to the United States. Competition has never been fiercer, and in some ways, the world has never been smaller.

In an attempt to regain a competitive edge on foreign manufacturers, U.S. firms have taken another look at the importance of improving quality and meeting the needs of their customers. The most successful U.S. firms also have focused on the following:

1. Motivating employees to cooperate with management and improve productivity
2. Reducing production costs by selecting suppliers that offer higher-quality raw materials and components at reasonable prices
3. Replacing outdated equipment with state-of-the-art manufacturing equipment
4. Using computer-aided and flexible manufacturing systems that allow a higher degree of customization

A global game that Microsoft wants to win.

For Microsoft, the Xbox requires a major investment in order to produce products that will enable the firm to increase sales in the very competitive electronic video game industry. To meet consumer demand, the latest electronic game consoles are produced in its Tokyo manufacturing facility. Once manufactured, Xboxes are distributed to retail outlets in both North and South America, Europe, Asia, and around the globe.

SPOTLIGHT

Career outlook in manufacturing

Between now and 2014, the need for employees in the manufacturing sector of the economy is expected to decrease as manufacturers find ways to become more productive.

Total number of employees for each year (in millions)
17.0   14.3   13.6
1994   2004   2014

Source: "2002–12 Employment Projections," U.S. Bureau of Labor Statistics website: www.bls.gov.

mass production a manufacturing process that lowers the cost required to produce a large number of identical or similar products over a long period of time

analytical process a process in operations management in which raw materials are broken into different component parts

synthetic process a process in operations management in which raw materials or components are combined to create a finished product

CONCEPT CHECK

What is the difference between an analytical and a synthetic manufacturing process? Give an example of each type of process.

5. Improving control procedures to help lower manufacturing costs and improve product quality
6. Building new manufacturing facilities in foreign countries where labor costs are lower

Although competing in the global economy is a major challenge, it is a worthwhile pursuit. For most firms, competing in the global marketplace is not only profitable, but it is also an essential activity that requires the cooperation of everyone within the organization.

Careers in Operations Management

Although it is hard to provide information about specific career opportunities in operations management, some generalizations do apply to this management area. First you must appreciate the manufacturing process and the steps required to produce a product or service. A basic understanding of mass production and the difference between an analytical process and a synthetic process is essential. **Mass production** is a manufacturing process that lowers the cost required to produce a large number of identical or similar products over a long period of time. An **analytical process** breaks raw materials into different component parts. **EXAMPLE** A barrel of crude oil refined by Marathon Oil Corporation—a Texas-based oil and chemical refiner—can be broken down into gasoline, oil and lubricants, and many other petroleum by-products. A **synthetic process** is just the opposite of an analytical process. The synthetic process combines raw materials or components to create a finished product. **EXAMPLE** Black & Decker, for instance, uses a synthetic process when it combines plastic, steel, rechargeable batteries, and other components to produce a cordless drill.

Once you understand that operations managers are responsible for producing tangible products or services that customers want, you must determine how you fit into the production process. Today's successful operations managers must

1. Be able to motivate and lead people
2. Understand how technology can make a manufacturer more productive and efficient
3. Appreciate the control processes that help lower production costs and improve product quality
4. Understand the relationship between the customer, the marketing of a product, and the production of a product

If operations management seems like an area you might be interested in, why not do more career exploration? You could take an operations management course if your college or university offers one, or you could obtain a part-time job during the school year or a summer job in a manufacturing company.

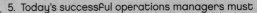

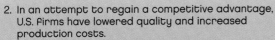
TEST PREPPER 9.1

True or False?

___T___ 1. Operations management consists of all the activities managers engage in to produce goods and services.

___F___ 2. In an attempt to regain a competitive advantage, U.S. firms have lowered quality and increased production costs.

___T___ 3. Mass production is a process used to lower the costs required to produce a large number of identical or similar products over a long period of time.

Multiple Choice

___B___ 4. When an analytical process is used, manufacturers

　　a. combine raw materials and components into finished products.

　　b. break down materials into different component parts.
　　c. use technology to improve productivity.
　　d. use the cheapest resources available.
　　e. employ non-skilled workers to assemble finished products.

___E___ 5. Today's successful operations managers must

　　a. be able to motivate and lead people.
　　b. understand how technology can make a manufacturer more productive.
　　c. appreciate the control processes that help lower production costs.
　　d. understand the relationship between the customer, the marketing of a product, and the production of a product.
　　e. All of the above

ACE the Test
ACE & ACE+
Practice Test 9.1

The Conversion Process

Learning Objective ②

Understand production by outlining how the conversion process transforms raw materials, labor, and other resources into finished products or services.

To have something to sell, a business must convert resources into goods and services. The resources are materials, finances, people, and information—the same resources discussed in Chapters 1 and 7. The goods and services are varied, ranging from consumer products to heavy manufacturing equipment. The purpose of this conversion of resources into goods and services is to provide utility to customers. **Utility** is the ability of a good or service to satisfy a human need. Although there are four types of utility—form, place, time, and possession—operations management focuses primarily on form utility. **Form utility** is created by converting raw materials, people, finances, and information into finished goods or services. The other types of utility—place, time, and possession—are discussed in Chapter 12.

But how does the conversion take place? How does Kellogg convert wheat, corn, sugar, salt, and other ingredients; money from previous sales and stockholders' investments; production workers and managers; and economic and marketing forecasts into cereal products? They do so through the use of a conversion process like the one illustrated in Figure 9.1.

INPUTS
- Concept for a new good or service
- Financial, material, human, and information resources

↓

CONVERSION
- Develop specifications to convert an idea to a good or service
↓
- Planning for production
↓
- Actual production

↓

OUTPUTS
- Completed good or service

utility the ability of a good or service to satisfy a human need

form utility utility created by converting raw materials, people, finances, and information into finished goods or services

---

FIGURE 9.1

The Conversion Process

The conversion process converts resources such as people, materials, finances, and information into useful goods, services, and ideas. The ability to produce goods, services, and ideas is a crucial step in the economic development of any nation.

EXAMINING ETHICS

Can Remanufacturing Save the Planet?

Most factories are designed to assemble products; Caterpillar's plant in Corinth, Mississippi, was designed to disassemble them. The 600 employees spend their days taking old diesel engines apart, sorting the components, repairing and cleaning what can be salvaged, and then reassembling the parts into engines for heavy equipment. "It's oily, greasy, heavy work," comments one Caterpillar worker—but the overhauled engines work well and cost much less than new ones.

Operating fourteen plants like the one in Corinth, including one in China, Caterpillar has built remanufacturing into a $1 billion business. The engines coming out of these plants may not look as shiny as new ones, but they're earth-friendly in several ways:

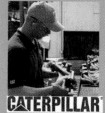

- They conserve raw materials by recycling usable parts.
- They incorporate parts that otherwise would clog the world's landfills.
- They run more efficiently, which saves fuel.

Caterpillar's remanufacturing plants put less strain on the environment because, according to one executive, "the only thing we send to the landfill from Corinth is food scraps from our cafeteria."

Sources: Based on information from Brian Hindo, "Everything Old Is New Again," *BusinessWeek*, September 25, 2006, pp. 64–70; Jim Johnson, "Caterpillar Leads the Way with Remanufacturing in China," *Waste News*, September 25, 2006, p. 18; Michael Arndt, "Cat Sinks Its Claws into Services," *BusinessWeek*, December 5, 2005, p. 56.

Manufacturing Using a Conversion Process

The conversion of resources into goods and services can be described in several ways. We limit our discussion here to three:

* The *focus*, or major resource, used in the conversion process
* Its *magnitude of change*
* The *number of production processes* employed

Focus   By the *focus* of a conversion process, we mean the resource or resources that make up the major or most important *input*. **EXAMPLE** For a bank such as Citibank, financial resources are the major resource. A chemical and energy company such as Chevron concentrates on material resources. A college or university is concerned primarily with information. And a temporary employment service focuses on the use of human resources. *Note:* While one resource may be the focus of a conversion process, other resources are still needed. Even though its focus is financial, Citibank still needs people, information, and material resources.

Magnitude of Change   The *magnitude* of a conversion process is the degree to which the resources are physically changed. **EXAMPLE** At one extreme lie such processes as the one by which the Glad Products Company, a division of the Clorox Corporation, produces Glad Cling Wrap. Various chemicals in liquid or powder form are combined to form long, thin sheets of plastic Glad Cling Wrap. Here, the original resources are totally unrecognizable in the finished product. At the other extreme, Southwest Airlines produces *no* physical change in its original resources. The airline simply provides a service and transports people from one place to another.

Number of Production Processes A single firm may employ one production process or many. In general, larger firms that make a variety of products use multiple production processes. **EXAMPLE** General Electric manufactures some of its own products, buys other merchandise from suppliers, and operates a consumer credit division, a commercial insurance division, an entertainment division, and a medical equipment division. Smaller firms, by contrast, may use one production process.

Operations Management in the Service Industry

The application of the basic principles of operations management to the production of services has coincided with a dramatic growth in the number and diversity of service businesses. In 1900, only 28 percent of American workers were employed in service firms. By 1950, this figure had grown to 40 percent, and by October 2006, it had risen to 83 percent.[2] In fact, the American economy is now characterized as a **service economy** (see Figure 9.2). A service economy is one in which more effort is devoted to the production of services than to the production of goods.

Today, the managers of restaurants, dry cleaners, real estate agencies, banks, movie theaters, airlines, and other service firms have realized that they can benefit from the experience of manufacturers. And yet the production of services is very different from the production of manufactured goods in the following four ways:

1. Services are consumed immediately and, unlike manufactured goods, cannot be stored. For example, a hair stylist cannot store completed haircuts.
2. Services are provided when and where the customer desires the service. In many cases customers will not travel far to obtain a service.
3. Services are usually labor-intensive because the human resource is often the most important resource used in the production of services.

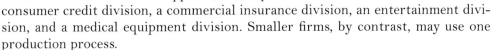

Percent of American workers employed by service industries

1975	72%
1985	76%
1995	80%
Today	83%

Coffee and a breakfast sandwich.

Starbucks, known for high-end coffee drinks, now offers breakfast sandwiches. While it's a logical extension of the company's business operations, Starbucks must now convert raw materials—bacon, eggs, cheese, and biscuits—into the finished product.

service economy an economy in which more effort is devoted to the production of services than to the production of goods

FIGURE 9.2

Service Industries

The growth of service firms has increased so dramatically that we live in what is now referred to as a service economy.

Source: U.S. Bureau of Labor Statistics website at **www.bls.gov;** accessed August 31, 2007.

4. Services are intangible, and it is therefore more difficult to evaluate customer satisfaction.[3]

Although it is often more difficult to measure customer satisfaction, today's successful service firms work hard at providing the services customers want. Compared with manufacturers, service firms often listen more carefully to customers and respond more quickly to the market's changing needs. Now that we understand something about the production process that is used to transform resources into goods and services, we can consider three major activities involved in operations management. These are new product development, planning for production, and operations control.

TEST PREPPER 9.2

True or False?

 1. When a hungry customer buys a Big Mac, he or she is in essence satisfying a need and therefore has utility for the Big Mac.

 2. There are four types of utility: form, price, functional, and possession,

 3. Larger firms that make a variety of products use multiple production processes.

Multiple Choice

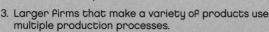

4. The focus of the conversion process for Burger King is

   a. timely service.
   b. food products.

c. satisfied customers.
d. higher revenues.
e. bigger market share.

 5. Which of the following statements is not true?

   a. Service firms employ approximately 83 percent of American workers.
   b. Services are consumed immediately.
   c. Service firms are always more profitable than manufacturing firms.
   d. Services are provided when and where the customer desires the service.
   e. Services are usually labor intensive.

ACE the Test
ACE & ACE+
Practice Test 9.2

Where Do New Products and Services Come From?

Learning Objective 3

Describe how research and development lead to new products and services.

No firm can produce a product or service until it has an idea. In other words, someone first must come up with a new way to satisfy a need—a new product or an improvement in an existing product. **EXAMPLE** Apple's iPod, SanDisk's USB Flash Drive, and Yamaha's Jet Ski began as an idea. While no one can predict with 100 percent accuracy what types of products will be available in the next five years, it is safe to say that companies will continue to introduce new products that will change the way we take care of ourselves, interact with others, and find the information and services we need.

Research and Development

How did we get notebook computers and portable DVD players? We got them the same way we got light bulbs and automobile tires—from people working with new ideas. Thomas Edison created the first light bulb, and Charles Goodyear discovered the vulcanization process that led to tires. In the same way, scientists and researchers working in businesses and universities have produced many of the newer products we already take for granted.

These activities generally are referred to as *research and development*. For our purposes, **research and development (R&D)** are a set of activities intended to identify new ideas that have the potential to result in new goods and services.

Today, business firms use three general types of R&D activities:

* *Basic research* consists of activities aimed at uncovering new knowledge. The goal of basic research is scientific advancement, without regard for its potential use in the development of goods and services.

* *Applied research*, in contrast, consists of activities geared toward discovering new knowledge with some potential use.

* *Development and implementation* are research activities undertaken specifically to put new or existing knowledge to use in producing goods and services. **EXAMPLE** The 3M Company has always been known for its development and implementation research activities. Today, the company has more than 6,500 researchers worldwide and invests more than $1 billion a year in developing new products designed to make people's lives easier. Does a company like 3M quit innovating because it has developed successful products? No, not at all! Just recently the 3M company used development and implementation when it created a new line of goggles for personal eye protection that are more comfortable, lightweight, and incorporate antiscratch and antifog features.[4]

CONCEPT CHECK

Describe how different types of research and development activities lead to new products or the extension and refinement of existing products.

Product Extension and Refinement

When a brand-new product is first marketed, its sales are zero and slowly increase from that point. If the product is successful, annual sales increase more and more rapidly until they reach some peak. Then, as time passes, annual sales begin to decline, and they continue to decline until it is no longer profitable to manufacture the product. (This rise-and-decline pattern, called the *product life cycle*, is discussed in more detail in Chapter 13.)

If a firm sells only one product, when that product reaches the end of its life cycle, the firm will die too. To stay in business, the firm must, at the very least, find ways to refine or extend the want-satisfying capability of its product. **EXAMPLE** Since television sets were introduced in the late 1930s, they have been constantly *refined* so that they now provide clearer, sharper pictures with less dial adjusting. During the same time, television sets also were *extended*. There are color sets, television-only sets, and others that include VCR and DVD players. There

McDonald's has gone fishing.

For McDonald's Holding Company, the Japanese subsidiary of U.S. based McDonald's Corporation, Fish McDippers are a logical product extension of McDonald's popular fish sandwiches. Similar to the fast-food giant's Chicken McNuggets, McDonald's Japanese unit added more fish items to its menus in order to combat consumer concerns about mad cow disease and the spread of bird flu in Japan.

are even television sets that allow their owners to access the Internet. And the latest development—high-definition (HD) television—is already available.

TEST PREPPER 9.3

True or False?

___I___ 1. Applied research consists of activities geared toward discovering new knowledge with some potential use.

___T___ 2. It is safe to say that VCRs are at the end of their product life cycle.

Multiple Choice

___D___ 3. The type of research activities aimed at uncovering new knowledge without regard for potential use is referred to as

   a. development research.
   b. implementation.
   c. application.
   d. basic research.
   e. adaptations.

___b___ 4. When 3M employees invested the time and effort to develop a new line of goggles for personal eye protection, they were using

   a. applied research.
   b. development and implementation.
   c. cost-benefit analysis.
   d. basic research.
   e. scientific theory.

___b___ 5. The rise-and-decline pattern of sales and profits for a product is referred to as

   a. the sales life cycle.
   b. product life cycle.
   c. pattern of diminished returns.
   d. product decline pattern.
   e. product planning cycle.

ACE the Test
ACE & ACE+
Practice Test 9.3

How Do Managers Plan for Production?

Learning Objective ❹

Discuss the components involved in planning the production process.

Only a few of the many ideas for new products, refinements, and extensions ever reach the production stage. For those ideas that do, however, the next step is planning for production. Once a new product idea has been identified, planning for production involves three major phases:

* *Design planning*

* *Site selection and facilities planning*

* *Operational planning* (see Figure 9.3)

Design Planning

When the R&D staff at Apple Computer recommended to top management that the firm produce and market an iPod, the company could not simply swing into production the next day. Instead, a great deal of time and energy had to be invested in determining what the new iPod would look like, where and how it would be produced, and what options would be included.

design planning the development of a plan for converting a product idea into an actual product or service

product line a group of similar products that differ only in relatively minor characteristics

product design the process of creating a set of specifications from which a product can be produced

These decisions are a part of design planning. **Design planning** is the development of a plan for converting a product idea into an actual product or service. The major decisions involved in design planning deal with

* *Product line*
* *Required production capacity*
* *Use of technology*

Product Line A **product line** is a group of similar products that differ only in relatively minor characteristics. During the design-planning stage, a manufacturer such as Apple needs to determine how many different models to produce and what major options to offer. A restaurant chain such as Pizza Hut must decide how many menu items to offer.

An important issue in deciding on the product line is to balance customer preferences and production requirements. For this reason, marketing managers play an important role in making product-line decisions. Typically, marketing personnel want a "long" product line that offers customers many options. The production personnel generally want a "short" product line because products are easier to produce. The actual choice between a long and short product line involves balancing customer preferences with the cost and problems associated with a more complex production process.

Once the product line has been determined, each product within the product line must be designed. **Product design** is the process of creating a set of specifications from which a product can be produced. When designing a new product, specifications are extremely important. **EXAMPLE** Product engineers for Whirlpool Corporation must make sure that a new frost-free refrigerator keeps food frozen in the freezer compartment. At the same time, they must make sure that lettuce and tomatoes do not freeze in the crisper section of the refrigerator. The need for a complete product design is fairly obvious; products that work cannot be manufactured without it. But services should be designed carefully as well—and *for the same reason.*

Required Production Capacity Capacity is the amount of products or services that an organization can produce in a given period of time. **EXAMPLE** The capacity of a Saab automobile assembly plant might be 300,000 cars per year. Operations managers—again working with the firm's marketing managers—must determine the required capacity. Capacity means about the

FIGURE 9.3

Planning for Production

Once research and development have identified an idea that meets customers' needs, manufacturers use three additional phases to convert the idea to an actual product or service.

1 Research and development identifies a new idea.

2 Design planning develops a plan to convert an idea into a good or service.

3 Facilities planning identifies a site where the good or service can be manufactured.

4 Operational planning decides on the amount of goods or services that will be produced within a specific time period.

capacity the amount of products or services that an organization can produce in a given time

Would you buy an iPod from this man?

The answer is yes. Steve Jobs, co-founder and chief executive officer for Apple Computer was part of the driving force behind the creation of the iPod. But Mr. Jobs would be the first to tell you that it took many people to turn the idea into reality. In fact, Apple employees had to design the product, determine the product line, estimate production capacity, and create a production facility to manufacture the product—all important activities described in this chapter.

same thing to service businesses. **EXAMPLE** The capacity of a restaurant such as the Hard Rock Cafe in Orlando, Florida, is the number of customers it can serve at one time.

Use of Technology During the design-planning stage, management must determine the degree to which *automation* will be used to produce a product or service. Here, there is a tradeoff between high initial costs and low operating costs (for automation) and low initial costs and high operating costs (for human labor). Ultimately, management must choose between a labor-intensive technology and a capital-intensive technology. A **labor-intensive technology** is a process in which people must do most of the work. **EXAMPLE** Housecleaning services and the New York Yankees baseball team, are labor-intensive. A **capital-intensive technology** is a process in which machines and equipment do most of the work. **EXAMPLE** A Motorola automated assembly plant is capital-intensive.

Site Selection and Facilities Planning

Once initial decisions have been made about a new product line, required capacity, and the use of technology, it is time to determine where the products or services are going to be produced. Generally, a business will choose to produce a new product in an existing factory as long as (1) the existing factory has enough capacity to handle customer demand for both the new product and established products and (2) the cost of refurbishing an existing factory is less than the cost of building a new one.

After exploring the capacity of existing factories, management may decide to build a new production facility. Once again, a number of decisions must be made. Should all the organization's production capacity be placed in one or two large facilities? Or should it be divided among several smaller facilities? Generally firms that manufacture a wide variety of products find it more economical to have a number of smaller facilities. Firms that produce only a small number of products tend to have fewer but larger facilities.

In determining where to locate new production facilities, management must consider a number of variables that include location of customers and suppliers, cost of land and building a new facility, environmental regulations and zoning laws, and local and state taxes. In fact, the choice of a location often involves balancing the most important variables for each production facility. Before making a final decision about where a proposed plant will be located and how it will be organized, two other factors—human resources and plant layout—should be examined.

Human Resources Several issues involved in facilities planning and site selection require that human resources and operations managers work closely together. **EXAMPLE** Suppose that a U.S. firm such as Reebok International wants to lower labor costs by constructing a sophisticated production plant in China. The human resources manager will have to recruit managers and employees with the appropriate skills who are willing to relocate to a foreign country or develop training programs for local Chinese workers or both.

Plant Layout **Plant layout** is the arrangement of machinery, equipment, and personnel within a production facility. Three general types of plant layout are used (see Figure 9.4):

---

labor-intensive technology a process in which people must do most of the work

capital-intensive technology a process in which machines and equipment do most of the work

CONCEPT CHECK
What factors should be considered when selecting a site for a new manufacturing facility?

plant layout the arrangement of machinery, equipment, and personnel within a production facility

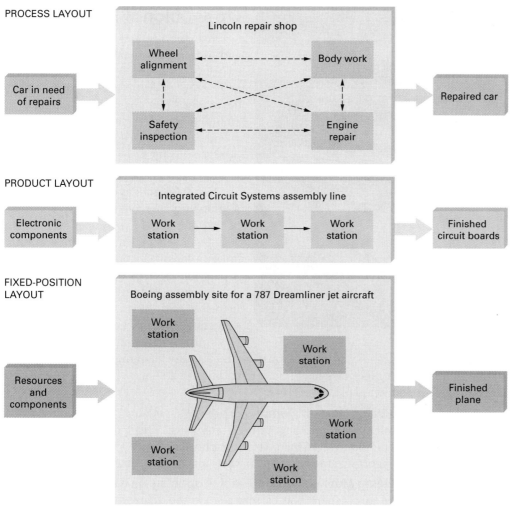

PROCESS LAYOUT

PRODUCT LAYOUT

FIXED-POSITION LAYOUT

FIGURE 9.4

Facilities Planning

The process layout is used when small batches of different products are created or when working on different parts of a product. The product layout (assembly line) is used when all products undergo the same operations in the same sequence. The fixed-position layout is used in producing a product too large to move.

* *Process layout* is used when different operations are required for creating small batches of different products or working on different parts of a product. The plant is arranged so that each operation is performed in its own particular area. **EXAMPLE** An auto repair facility at a local automobile dealership provides an example of a process layout. The various operations may be engine repair, body work, wheel alignment, and safety inspection. Each operation is performed in a different area. If you take your Lincoln Navigator for a wheel alignment, your car "visits" only the area where alignments are performed.

* *Product layout* (sometimes referred to as an *assembly line*) is used when all products undergo the same operations in the same sequence. Workstations are arranged to match the sequence of operations, and work flows from station to station. An assembly line is the best example of a product layout.

* *Fixed-position layout* is used when a very large product is produced. **EXAMPLE** Aircraft manufacturers and shipbuilders apply this method because of the difficulty of moving a large product such as an airliner or a ship. The product remains stationary, and people and machines are moved as needed to assemble the product.

planning horizon the time period during which an operational plan will be in effect

Operational Planning

Once the product has been designed and a decision has been made to use an existing production facility or build a new one, operational plans must be developed. The objective of operational planning is to decide on the amount of products or services each facility will produce during a specific period of time. Four steps are required.

Step 1: Selecting a Planning Horizon
A planning horizon is simply the time period during which an operational plan will be in effect. A common planning horizon for production plans is one year. A planning horizon of one year generally is long enough to average out seasonal increases and decreases in sales. At the same time, it is short enough for planners to adjust production to accommodate long-range sales trends. Firms that operate in a rapidly changing business environment with many competitors may find it best to select a shorter planning horizon to keep their production planning current.

Step 2: Estimating Market Demand The *market demand* for a product is the quantity that customers will purchase at the going price. This quantity must be estimated for the time period covered by the planning horizon. Sales projections developed by marketing managers are the basis for market-demand estimates.

Step 3: Comparing Market Demand with Capacity The third step in operational planning is to compare the estimated market demand with the facility's capacity to satisfy that demand. (Remember that capacity is the amount of products or services that an organization can produce in a given time.) One of three outcomes may result: Demand may exceed capacity, capacity may exceed demand, or capacity and demand may be equal. If they are equal, the facility should be operated at full capacity. However, if market demand and capacity are not equal, adjustments may be necessary.

Step 4: Adjusting Products or Services to Meet Demand The biggest reason for changes to a firm's production schedule is changes in the amount of products or services that a company sells to its customers. **EXAMPLE** Indiana-based Berry Plastics uses an injection-molded manufacturing process to produce all kinds of plastic products. One particularly successful product line for Berry Plastics is drink cups that can be screen-printed to promote a company or the company's products or services.[5] If Berry Plastics obtains a large contract to provide promotional mugs to a large fast-food chain such as Whataburger or McDonald's, the company may need to work three shifts a day, seven days a week until the contract is fulfilled. Unfortunately, the reverse is also true.

True or False?

___T___ 1. The product line represents a group of products that differ only in relatively minor characteristics.

___F___ 2. When a capital-intensive technology is used, people do most of the work.

___F___ 3. Popularity of the product is the basis for market-demand estimates.

Multiple Choice

___E___ 4. The development of a plan for converting a product idea into an actual product or service is referred to as

a. technology planning.
b. strategic production planning.
c. basic planning.
d. matrix planning.
e. design planning.

___A___ 5. The best type of plant layout suitable for producing a limited edition of unique dolls would be a

a. product layout.
b. process layout.
c. fixed-position layout.
d. unique layout.
e. small-batch layout.

ACE the Test
ACE & ACE+
Practice Test 9.4

Operations Control

Learning Objective 5

Explain how purchasing, inventory control, scheduling, and quality control affect production.

We have discussed the development of an idea for a product or service and the planning that translates that idea into the reality. Now we are ready to push the "start button" to begin the production process and examine four important areas of operations control: purchasing, inventory control, scheduling, and quality control (see Figure 9.5).

Purchasing

Purchasing consists of all the activities involved in obtaining required materials, supplies, components (or subassemblies), and parts from other firms. **EXAMPLE** Levi Strauss must purchase denim cloth, thread, and zippers before it can produce a single pair of jeans. For all firms, the purchasing function is far from routine, and its importance should not be underestimated. For some products, purchased materials make up more than 50 percent of their wholesale costs.

The objective of purchasing is to ensure that required materials are available when they are needed, in the proper amounts, and at minimum cost. Generally, the company with purchasing needs and suppliers must develop a working relationship built on trust.

Purchasing personnel should be on the lookout constantly for new or backup suppliers, even when their needs are being met by their present suppliers, because

OPERATIONS CONTROL

| Purchasing | Inventory control | Scheduling | Quality control |

FIGURE 9.5

Four Aspects of Operations Control

Implementing the operations control system in any business requires the effective use of purchasing, inventory control, scheduling, and quality control.

purchasing all the activities involved in obtaining required materials, supplies, components, and parts from other firms

problems such as strikes and equipment breakdowns can cut off the flow of purchased materials from a primary supplier at any time. The choice of suppliers should result from careful analysis of a number of factors. The following are especially critical:

* *Price.* Comparing prices offered by different suppliers is always an essential part of selecting a supplier. Even tiny differences in price add up to enormous sums when large quantities are purchased.

* *Quality.* Purchasing specialists always try to buy materials at a level of quality in keeping with the type of product being manufactured. The minimum acceptable quality usually is specified by product designers.

* *Reliability.* An agreement to purchase high-quality materials at a low price is the purchaser's dream. But such an agreement becomes a nightmare if the supplier does not deliver.

* *Credit terms.* Purchasing specialists should determine if the supplier demands immediate payment or will extend credit. Also, does the supplier offer a cash discount or reduction in price for prompt payment?

* *Shipping costs.* One of the most overlooked factors in purchasing is the geographic location of the supplier. Low prices and favorable credit terms offered by a distant supplier can be wiped out when the buyer must pay the shipping costs. Above all, the question of who pays the shipping costs should be answered before any supplier is chosen.

Inventory Control

Can you imagine what would happen if a Coca-Cola manufacturing plant ran out of the company's familiar red and white aluminum cans? It would be impossible to complete the manufacturing process and ship the cases of Coke to retailers. Management would be forced to shut the assembly line down until the next shipment of cans arrived from a supplier. In reality, operations managers for Coca-Cola realize the disasters that a shortage of needed materials can cause and will avoid this type of problem if at all possible.

Operations managers are concerned with three types of inventories:

inventory control the process of managing inventories in such a way as to minimize inventory costs, including both holding costs and potential stock-out costs

Sometimes inventory is pretty.

For a product like poinsettias, timing is everything. The goal for North Carolina based Metrolina Greenhouses is to make sure that the flowers that arrive at retailer locations across the nation are not only beautiful and healthy, but also just in time for the holiday season.

* *Raw-materials inventory* consists of materials that will become part of the product during the production process.

* *Work-in-process inventory* consists of partially completed products.

* *Finished-goods inventory* consists of completed goods.

Associated with each type of inventory are a *holding cost*, or storage cost, and a *stock-out cost*, the cost of running out of inventory. **Inventory control** is the process of managing inventories in such a way as to minimize inventory costs, including both holding costs and potential stock-out costs.

Today, computer systems are being used to keep track of inventories, provide periodic inventory reports, and alert managers to impending stock-outs. One of the most sophisticated methods of inventory control used today is materials requirements planning. **Materials requirements planning (MRP)** is a computerized system that integrates production planning and inventory control. One of the great advantages of an MRP system is its ability to juggle delivery schedules and lead times effectively. For a complex product such as an automobile or airplane, it is virtually impossible for individual managers to oversee the hundreds of parts that go into the finished product. However, a manager using an MRP system can arrange both order and delivery schedules so that materials, parts, and supplies arrive when they are needed.

Because many firms can incur huge inventory costs, a just-in-time inventory system can be used to control inventory. A **just-in-time inventory system** is designed to ensure that materials or supplies arrive at a facility just when they are needed so that storage and holding costs are minimized. The customer must specify what will be needed, when, and in what amounts. The supplier must be sure that the right supplies arrive at the agreed-on time and location. **EXAMPLE** Managers using a just-in-time inventory system at a Toyota assembly plant determine the number of automobiles that will be assembled in a specified time period. Then Toyota purchasing personnel order *just* the parts needed to produce those automobiles. In turn, suppliers deliver the parts *in time* or when they are needed on the assembly line.

Scheduling

Scheduling is the process of ensuring that materials and other resources are at the right place at the right time. The materials and resources may be moved from a warehouse to the workstations, they may move from station to station along an assembly line, or they may arrive at workstations "just in time" to be made part of the work in process there.

As our definition implies, both place and time are important to scheduling. The *routing* of materials is the sequence of workstations that the materials will follow. **EXAMPLE** Assume that Drexel-Heritage—one of America's largest and oldest furniture manufacturers—is scheduling production of an oval coffee table made from cherry wood. Operations managers would route the needed materials (wood, screws, packaging materials, and so on) through a series of individual workstations along an assembly line. At each workstation, a specific task would be performed, and then the partially finished coffee table would move to the next workstation.

When scheduling production, managers also are concerned with timing. The *timing* function specifies when the materials will arrive at each station and how long they will remain there. **EXAMPLE** For a cherry coffee table, it may take workers thirty minutes to cut the table top and legs and an hour to drill the holes and assemble the table. Before packaging the coffee table for shipment, it must be finished with cherry stain and allowed to dry. This last step may take as long as three days depending on weather conditions and humidity.

Quality Control

As mentioned earlier in this chapter, American business firms that compete in the very competitive global marketplace have taken another look at the importance of improving quality. Today there is even a national quality award. The **Malcolm Baldrige National Quality Award** is given by the president of the United States to organizations that apply and are judged to be outstanding in specific

materials requirements planning (MRP) a computerized system that integrates production planning and inventory control

just-in-time inventory system a system designed to ensure that materials or supplies arrive at a facility just when they are needed so that storage and holding costs are minimized

scheduling the process of ensuring that materials and other resources are at the right place at the right time

Malcolm Baldrige National Quality Award an award given by the president of the United States to organizations that apply and are judged to be outstanding in specific managerial tasks that lead to improved quality for both products and services

managerial tasks that lead to improved quality for both products and services. For many organizations, using the Baldrige criteria results in

* Better employee relations
* Higher productivity
* Greater customer satisfaction
* Increased market share
* Improved profitability[6]

While winning the Baldrige can mean prestige and lots of free media coverage, the winners all have one factor in common: They use quality control to improve their firm's products or services.

Quality control is the process of ensuring that goods and services are produced in accordance with design specifications. The major objective of quality control is to see that the organization lives up to the standards it has set for itself on quality. Some firms, such as Mercedes-Benz and Neiman Marcus, have built their reputations on quality. Customers pay more for their products in return for assurances of high quality. Other firms adopt a strategy of emphasizing lower prices along with reasonable (but not particularly high) quality.

Inspections Increased effort is also being devoted to **inspection,** which is the examination of the quality of work in process. Inspections are performed at various times during production. Purchased materials may be inspected when they arrive at the production facility. Subassemblies and manufactured parts may be inspected before they become part of a finished product. And finished goods may be inspected before they are shipped to customers. Items that are within design specifications continue on their way. Those that are not within design specifications are removed from production.

Improving Quality Through Employee Participation Over the years, more and more managers have realized that quality is an essential "ingredient" of the good or service being provided. This view of quality provides several benefits. The number of defects decreases, which causes profits to increase. Making products right the first time reduces many of the rejects and much of the rework. And making employees responsible for quality often eliminates the need for inspection. An employee is indoctrinated to accept full responsibility for the quality of his or her work.

The use of a **quality circle,** a team of employees who meet on company time to solve problems of product quality, is another way manufacturers are achieving better quality at the operations level. **EXAMPLE** Quality circles have been used successfully in such companies as IBM, Northrop Grumman Corporation, and Compaq Computers.

Because of increased global competition, many American manufacturers have adopted a goal that calls for better quality in their products. As noted in Chapter 7, a *total quality management* (TQM) program coordinates

---

quality control the process of ensuring that goods and services are produced in accordance with design specifications

inspection the examination of the quality of work in process

CONCEPT CHECK

How are the areas of purchasing, inventory control, scheduling, and quality interrelated?

quality circle a team of employees who meet on company time to solve problems of product quality

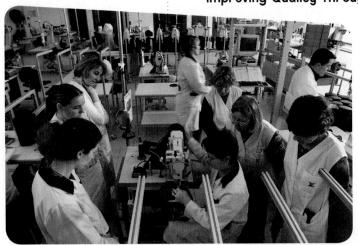

▲
Sometimes quality is a team effort.

Customers who purchase Louis Vuitton leather goods expect high-quality products that are both stylish and worth the price. To ensure that its products are high quality, Louis Vuitton employees are trained to inspect both work in process and all finished products before they leave the firm's manufacturing facility in Ducey, France.

the efforts directed at improving customer satisfaction, increasing employee participation, strengthening supplier partnerships, and facilitating an organizational atmosphere of continuous quality improvement. **EXAMPLE** Firms such as American
Express, AT&T, Motorola, and Hewlett Packard all have used TQM to improve
product quality and, ultimately, customer satisfaction.

Your Career

What Color Is Your Belt?

Whether you plan to work in manufacturing, medical care, or another industry, watch for an opportunity to be trained in Six Sigma. Earning a Six Sigma "belt" will give you an understanding of how performance is improved when quality is improved. Just as important, it will teach you a structured process for analyzing quality problems, planning changes, and measuring the results.

Six Sigma belts come in three colors:

- The white belt entails intensive, short-term training for small-scale or localized quality projects.
- The green belt provides extensive training in quality-improvement methods for more complex or department-wide projects.

- The black belt involves long-term training plus hands-on experience and is often a requirement for leading projects involving multiple depart-ments or divisions.

Jack Bolick, who heads a division of Honeywell, is among the growing number of senior managers who have moved up in management thanks to black-belt expertise. At John Crane, an Illinois manufacturing firm, the entire top-management team has attended black-belt training. And in Des Moines, Iowa, green- and black-belt employees of Mercy Medical Center have saved the hospital $10 million annually while improving patient care—a definite career booster for all. For more information about Six Sigma, go to **www.isixsigma.com.**

Sources: Based on information from "Mercy Saves with Six Sigma," *Business Record* (Des Moines, IA), July 10, 2006, p. 9; Marilyn Fischbach, "Organically Grown Quality," *Industrial Engineer*, January 2006, pp. 41+; Bob Vavra, "Honeywell's Jack Bolick," *Plant Engineering*, June 2006, pp. 60+; John W. Matthews III, "Six Sigma: How It Works in Motorola and What It Can Do for the U.S. Army," *Armed Forces Comptroller*, Spring 2006, pp. 35+.

TEST PREPPER 9.5

True or False?

___F___ 1. Work-in-process inventory consists of materials that will become part of the product during the production process.

___T___ 2. Materials requirements planning (MRP) is a tech-nique that enables managers to use a computer to plan production and inventory control.

___F___ 3. The major objective of quality control is to see that the organization lives up to the standards of its competitors.

Multiple Choice

___E___ 4. Which one of the following is *not* one of the factors to be considered in the choice of suppliers?

  a. Price
  b. Quality
  c. Reliability
  d. Credit terms
  e. Reputation

___C___ 5. The process of ensuring that materials and other resources are at the right place at the right time is called

  a. quality control.
  b. inventory management.
  c. scheduling.
  d. just-in-time inventory management.
  e. purchasing.

ACE the Test
ACE & ACE+
Practice Test 9.5

Management of Productivity and Technology

Learning Objective 6

Summarize how productivity and technology are related.

No coverage of production and operations management would be complete without a discussion of productivity. Productivity concerns all managers, but it is especially important to operations managers, the people who must oversee the creation of a firm's goods or services. We define **productivity** as the average level of output per worker per hour. Hence, if each worker at plant A produces seventy-five units per day and each worker at plant B produces only seventy units per day, the workers at plant A are more productive. If one bank teller serves twenty-five customers per hour and another serves twenty-eight per hour, the second teller is more productive.

productivity the average level of output per worker per hour

Productivity Trends

According to Ben Bernanke, Chairman of the Federal Reserve Board, "Productivity remains strong today and bodes well for the future of the U.S. economy."[7] More specifically, manufacturing in 2005 increased 5.1 percent. (*Note*: At the time of publication, 2005 was the last year that complete statistics were available.) Our productivity growth rate was ranked the fifth-largest increase among the fifteen countries for which comparable data are available—the United States, Canada, Japan, Korea, Taiwan, Australia, and nine European countries. Our *rate of productivity growth* is lagging behind the productivity growth rates of such countries as Korea, Taiwan, Canada, and Germany.[8] While many people think of the productivity growth rate as just another economic statistic, it is a very important statistic because it is the main determinant of changes in our standard of living. (Remember, *standard of living* was defined in Chapter 1 as a loose, subjective measure of how well off an individual or a society is mainly in terms of want satisfaction through goods and services.)

Improving Productivity Growth Rates

Several techniques and strategies have been suggested to improve current productivity growth rates:

* Government policies that may be hindering productivity could be eliminated or at least modified.

* Increased cooperation between management and labor could be fostered to improve productivity.

* Unions and management working together quite often can result in improved productivity.

* Increased employee motivation and participation can enhance productivity.

* Changing the incentives for work, by changing the reward system so that people are paid for what they contribute rather than for the time they put in, may motivate employees to produce at higher levels.

* Investing more money in facilities, equipment, and employee training. There is hard evidence that investments in technological innovations are linked to job growth, higher employee wages, new products, *and* increased productivity. While building a new factory or purchasing new equipment does not guarantee that a firm's productivity will increase, many companies such as Ford Motor Company, Honeywell International, Deere & Company, and IBM have experienced dramatic increases in productivity when employees can use state-of-the-art equipment.

The Impact of Computers and Robotics on Production

Automation, a development that has been revolutionizing the workplace, is the total or near-total use of machines to do work. The rapid increase in automated procedures has been made possible by the microprocessor, a silicon chip that led to the production of desktop computers for businesses, homes, and schools. In factories, microprocessors are used in robotics and in computer manufacturing systems.

Robotics **Robotics** is the use of programmable machines to perform a variety of tasks by manipulating materials and tools. Robots work quickly, accurately, and steadily. **EXAMPLE** Illumina, Inc., a San Diego company, uses robots to screen blood samples and identify DNA quirks that cause diseases. The information then is sold to some of the world's largest pharmaceutical companies, where it is used to alter existing prescription drugs, develop new drug therapies, and customize diagnoses and treatments for all kinds of serious diseases. As an added bonus, Illumina's robots can work 24 hours a day at much lower costs than if human lab workers performed the same tests.[9] Robots are especially effective in tedious, repetitive assembly-line jobs such as this, as well as in handling hazardous materials. They are also useful as artificial "eyes" that can check the quality of products as they are being processed on the assembly lines. To date, the automotive industry has made the most extensive use of robotics, but robots also have been used to mine coal, inspect the inner surfaces of pipes, assemble computer components, provide certain kinds of patient care in hospitals, and clean and guard buildings at night.

Computer Manufacturing Systems People are quick to point out how computers have changed their everyday lives, but most people do not realize the impact computers have had on manufacturing. In simple terms, the factory of the future has already arrived. For most manufacturers, the changeover began with the use of computer-aided design and computer-aided manufacturing. **Computer-aided design (CAD)** is the use of computers to aid in the development of products. **EXAMPLE** Using CAD, Ford speeds up car design, Canon designs new cameras and photocopiers, and American Greetings creates new birthday

automation the total or near-total use of machines to do work

robotics the use of programmable machines to perform a variety of tasks by manipulating materials and tools

computer-aided design (CAD) the use of computers to aid in the development of products

computer-aided manufacturing (CAM) the use of computers to plan and control manufacturing processes

computer-integrated manufacturing (CIM) a computer system that not only helps to design products but also controls the machinery needed to produce the finished product

continuous process a manufacturing process in which a firm produces the same product(s) over a long period of time

flexible manufacturing system (FMS) a single production system that combines robotics and computer-integrated manufacturing

intermittent process a manufacturing process in which a firm's manufacturing machines and equipment are changed to produce different products

cards. **Computer-aided manufacturing (CAM)** is the use of computers to plan and control manufacturing processes. A well-designed CAM system allows manufacturers to become much more productive. Not only are a greater number of products produced, but speed and quality also increase. **EXAMPLE** Toyota, Hasbro, Oneida, and Apple Computer all have used CAM to increase productivity.

If you are thinking that the next logical step is to combine the CAD and CAM computer systems, you are right. Today, the most successful manufacturers use CAD and CAM together to form a computer-integrated manufacturing system. Specifically, **computer-integrated manufacturing (CIM)** is a computer system that not only helps to design products but also controls the machinery needed to produce the finished product. **EXAMPLE** Liz Claiborne, Inc., uses CIM to design clothing, to establish patterns for new fashions, and then to cut the cloth needed to produce the finished product. Other advantages of using CIM include improved flexibility, more efficient scheduling, and higher product quality—all factors that make a production facility more competitive *and* productive in today's global economy.

Flexible Manufacturing Systems Manufacturers have known for a number of years that the old-style, traditional assembly lines used to manufacture products present a number of problems. For example, although traditional assembly lines turn out extremely large numbers of identical products economically, the system requires expensive, time-consuming retooling of equipment whenever a new product is to be manufactured. This type of manufacturing is often referred to as a continuous process. **Continuous process** is a manufacturing process in which a firm produces the same product(s) over a long period of time. Now it is possible to use flexible manufacturing systems to solve such problems. A **flexible manufacturing system (FMS)** combines robotics and computer-integrated manufacturing in a single production system. Instead of having to spend vast amounts of time and effort to retool the traditional mechanical equipment on an assembly line for each new product, an FMS is rearranged simply by reprogramming electronic machines. Because FMSs require less time and expense to reprogram, manufacturers can produce smaller batches of a variety of products without raising the production cost. Flexible manufacturing is sometimes referred to as an *intermittent process*. An **intermittent process** is a manufacturing process in which a firm's manufacturing machines and equipment are changed to produce different products. When compared with the continuous process (longer production runs), an intermittent process has a shorter production run.

For most manufacturers, the driving force behind flexible manufacturing systems is the customer. In fact, the term *customer-driven production* is often used by operations managers to describe a manufacturing system that is driven by customer needs and what customers want to buy. **EXAMPLE** Advanced software and a flexible manufacturing system have enabled Dell Computer to change to a more customer-driven manufacturing process. The process starts when a customer phones a sales representative on a toll-free line or accesses Dell's website. Then the representative or the customer enters the specifications for the new product directly into a computer. The order then is sent to a Dell manufacturing plant. Once the order is received, a team of employees with the help of a reprogrammable assembly line can build the product just the way the customer wants it. Products include desktops computers, notebook computers, and other Dell equipment.[10] Although the costs of designing and installing an FMS such as this are high, the electronic equipment is used more efficiently than the machinery on a traditional assembly line.

Technological Displacement Automation is increasing productivity by cutting manufacturing time, reducing error, and simplifying retooling procedures. Many of the robots being developed for use in manufacturing will not replace human employees. Rather, these robots will work with employees in making their jobs easier and help to prevent accidents. No one knows, however, what the effect will be on the work force. Some experts estimate that automation will bring new changes to more than half of all jobs within the next ten years. Total unemployment may not increase, but many workers will be faced with the choice of retraining for new jobs or seeking jobs in other sectors of the economy. Government, business, and education will have to cooperate to prepare workers for new roles in an automated workplace.

The next chapter discusses many of the issues caused by technological displacement. In addition, a number of major components of human resources management are described, and we see how managers use various reward systems to boost motivation, productivity, and morale.

> **CONCEPT CHECK**
> How can CAD, CAM, CIM, and FMS help a manufacturer to produce products?

TEST PREPPER 9.6

True or False?

___ 1. If one bank teller serves twenty-five customers per hour and another serves twenty-eight per hour, the second teller is more productive.

___ 2. The U.S. rate of productivity growth is ahead of the productivity growth rates of such countries as Korea, Taiwan, Canada, and Germany.

___ 3. Computer-aided design is the use of computers to aid in the development of new products.

Multiple Choice

___ 4. Which of the following statements does *not* correctly characterize robotics?

    a. Robots work quickly, accurately, and steadily.

    b. Robots are especially effective in tedious, repetitive assembly-line jobs.

    c. Robots are useful as artificial "eyes" that can check the quality of products.

    d. The automotive industry has made the least use of robotics.

    e. Robots have been used to mine coal, inspect the inner surfaces of pipes, and assemble computer components.

___ 5. For most manufacturers, the driving force behind flexible manufacturing systems is

    a. the cost.

    b. the customer.

    c. competition.

    d. technological advancement.

    e. profit motives.

ACE the Test
ACE & ACE+
Practice Test 9.6

Prepare for Class
CL News Feeds
CL News Now

→ **RETURN TO INSIDE BUSINESS**

Back in 1986, Motorola began its search for new methods to improve product quality. Today, according to many experts in the consumer electronics industry, Motorola is so proficient that hundreds of companies have sent employees to Motorola University for quality training. By paying close attention to quality in every area of operations, Motorola has reduced waste, improved productivity, and boosted product reliability. Quality also has helped Motorola control costs and bring its gross profit margin above 31 percent—higher than rival Nokia's gross margin of 29 percent.

Now, armed with decades of experience in quality improvement, the company is working toward an ambitious new goal. It wants to make its products and processes 100 percent perfect. Can Motorola meet this latest quality challenge?

Questions

1. Motorola has extended its efforts to improve quality to product design and to nonmanufacturing departments such as human resources. What benefits might Motorola expect to gain from improving quality in these areas?

2. How do you think Motorola's drive for perfection is likely to affect its market share and its profitability?

Learning Objectives Review

Improve Your Grade
Audio Chapter Review & Quiz

1 Understand the nature of production by examining operations management and the characteristics of a successful operations manager.

- Operations management consists of all the activities that managers engage in to create goods and services.

- Operations are as relevant to service organizations as to manufacturing firms.

- Generally, three major activities are involved in producing goods or services:
  - Product development
  - Planning for production
  - Operations control

- Competing in the global economy for U.S. firms is not only profitable but also an essential activity that requires the cooperation of everyone within an organization.

- Successful operations managers must
  - Be able to motivate and lead people
  - Understand how technology can make a manufacturer more productive and efficient
  - Appreciate the control processes that help to lower production costs and improve product quality
  - Understand the relationship between the customer, the marketing of a product, and the production of a product

2 Understand production by outlining how the conversion process transforms raw materials, labor, and other resources into finished products or services.

- A business transforms resources into goods and services in order to provide utility to customers. Utility is the ability of a good or service to satisfy a human need.

- Form utility is created by converting raw materials, people, finances, and information into finished products.

- Conversion processes vary in terms of the major resources used to produce goods and services (focus), the degree to which resources are changed (magnitude), and the number of production processes that a business uses.

- The application of the basic principles of operations management to the production of services has coincided with the growth and importance of service businesses in the United States.

3 Describe how research and development lead to new products and services.

- Operations management often begins with product research and development (R&D).

- The results of R&D may be entirely new products or extensions and refinements of existing products.

- R&D activities are classified as
  - Basic research (aimed at uncovering new knowledge)
  - Applied research (discovering new knowledge with some potential use)
  - Development and implementation (using new or existing knowledge to produce goods and services)

- If a firm sells only one product, when that product reaches the end of its life cycle, the firm will die. To stay in business, the firm must, at the very least, find ways to refine or extend the want-satisfying capability of its product.

4 Discuss the components involved in planning the production process.

- Planning for production involves three major phases:
  - Design planning
  - Site selection and facilities planning
  - Operational planning

- Design planning is undertaken to address questions related to the product line, product design, required production capacity, and the use of technology.

- Site selection, production facilities, human resources, and plant layout then must be considered.

- Operational planning focuses on the use of production facilities and resources.

- The steps for operational planning include
  - Selecting a planning horizon
  - Estimating market demand
  - Comparing market demand with capacity
  - Adjusting production of products or services to meet demand

5 Explain how purchasing, inventory control, scheduling, and quality control affect production.

- The major areas of operations control are purchasing, inventory control, scheduling, and quality control.

- Purchasing involves selecting suppliers. The choice of suppliers should result from careful analysis of a number of factors, including price, quality, reliability, credit terms, and shipping costs.

- Inventory control is the management of stocks of raw materials, work in process, and finished goods to minimize the total inventory cost.

- Today, most firms use a computerized system to maintain inventory records. In addition, many firms use a just-in-time inventory system, in which materials or supplies arrive at a facility just when they are needed so that storage and holding costs are minimized.

- Scheduling ensures that materials and other resources are at the right place at the right time—for use within the facility or for shipment to customers.

- Quality control is the process of ensuring that goods and services are produced in accordance with design specifications.

- The major objective of quality control is to see that the organization lives up to the standards it has set for itself on quality.

6 Summarize how productivity and technology are related.

- Several suggestions to improve productivity include less government regulation, increased cooperation between management, labor, and unions, increased employee motivation and participation, new incentives for work, and additional investment by business to fund new or renovated facilities, equipment, employee training, and the use of technology.

- Automation, the total or near-total use of machines to do work, has for some years been changing the way work is done in U.S. factories.

- A growing number of industries are using programmable machines called robots to perform tasks that are tedious or hazardous to human beings.

- Computer-aided design, computer-aided manufacturing, and computer-integrated manufacturing use computers to help design and manufacture products.

- The flexible manufacturing system combines robotics and computer-integrated manufacturing to produce smaller batches of products more efficiently than on the traditional assembly line.

- FMSs require less time and expense to reprogram, and manufacturers can produce smaller batches of a variety of products without raising the production cost.

The Ins and Outs of Inputs and Outputs: Managing Production and Quality

When Finagle A Bagel makes bagels, when New Balance makes sneakers, when Bakers' Best makes meals, and when Stonyfield Farm makes yogurt, they use completely different raw materials and processes. Yet all four companies manage production very carefully to achieve the same result: a quality product.

Imagine the challenge of mixing, shaping, baking, and packing 10,000 bagels in just eight hours. Now imagine perfecting the production process so that every bagel turns out fresh, tasty, and inviting—every day, all year long. This is the way that Finagle A Bagel has built its business. The company operates a chain of bagel cafés and a catering business in New England; it also sells its bagels to supermarkets and other resellers nationwide.

Finagle A Bagel produces bagels in huge batches using electronic equipment to weigh and measure ingredients and to keep the assembly line running smoothly. Depending on the flavor of bagel being produced, the conversion process requires flour, water, and additional ingredients such as spices, chocolate chips, or bits of fruit. Even the temperature of the water in which the bagels are boiled is monitored and adjusted constantly to ensure that the bagels have the proper consistency and crust. The factory sends baked bagels to wholesale customers but sends raw dough to Finagle A Bagel cafés so that bagels can be baked fresh daily on the premises. As a final check on quality, the copresidents visit the stores, sample the bagels, and weigh sandwich ingredients to be sure portion sizes are correct.

New Balance faces a different set of production challenges as it makes athletic shoes in its U.S. factories. Each shoe goes through the hands of at least twenty (sometimes as many as thirty) workers in the course of being cut, stitched, shaped, finished, and packed. First, a worker stacks sheets of sole material in the cutting room and, using a template, cuts the layers in the precise size and shape for a particular model of shoe. After a worker applies cosmetic touches, a computerized machine stitches the sole to the upper part of the shoe. Next, the product is shaped into shoe form and reinforced. Finally, workers add laces, tag each

pair, box and label the shoes, and add them to inventory, ready to be shipped to stores. The production process is particularly important because New Balance sets itself apart from competitors on the basis of its commitment to "made in America" quality and its ability to get new styles to market quickly.

For Bakers' Best, scheduling is a key production challenge. When Michael Baker opened his first Baker's Best take-out food store in 1984, the specialty was turkey sandwiches. Today, Baker's Best consists of four Boston-area food businesses: a daytime café, an evening restaurant, full-service catering, and corporate catering. The executive chef is in charge of scheduling more than forty cooks to staff these kitchens. He assigns each cook a specific task and provides supervision to ensure that dishes are prepared properly and on time—and that they look as good as they taste. No detail is too small. For example, the caterers check that tablecloths and napkins are delivered with every meal.

At Stonyfield Farm, which makes yogurts and other dairy products, quality control is a central concern. Because the company's organic yogurts use certified organic ingredients, the diet and living conditions of the cows that provide the milk must be carefully inspected. Pesticides, herbicides, and hormones are not allowed, and the cows must be treated humanely. Thanks to stringent quality control and an earth-friendly production process, the company has reduced waste, is reusing materials where possible, and has arranged to recycle old yogurt cups into useful items such as toothbrushes and razors.[11]

1. Is Finagle A Bagel using a process, product, or fixed-position layout? Why is its layout appropriate for producing bagels?
2. In terms of operational planning, why is New Balance's made-in-America production a competitive advantage in an industry where most rivals produce athletic shoes overseas?
3. Imagine that Bakers' Best is catering a corporate party three weeks from today and wants to begin scheduling important tasks. What types of activities would you expect to see planned for the first week? For the last week?

BUILDING SKILLS FOR CAREER SUCCESS

1. Exploring the Internet

Improvements in the quality of products and services is an ever-popular theme in business management. Besides the obvious increase to profitability to be gained by such improvements, a company's demonstration of its continuous search for ways to improve operations can be a powerful statement to customers, suppliers, and investors. Two of the larger schools of thought in this field are Six Sigma and the European-based International Organization for Standardization. Visit the text website for updates to this exercise.

Assignment

1. Use Internet search engines to find more information about each of these topics.

2. From the information on the Internet, can you tell whether there is any real difference between these two approaches?

3. Describe one success story of a firm that realized improvement by adopting either approach.

2. Building Team Skills

Suppose that you are planning to build a house in the country. It will be a brick, one-story structure of approximately 2,000 square feet, centrally heated and cooled. It will have three bedrooms, two bathrooms, a family room, a dining room, a kitchen with a breakfast nook, a study, a utility room, an entry foyer, a two-car garage, a covered patio, and a fireplace. Appliances will operate on electricity and propane fuel. You have received approval and can be connected to the cooperative water system at any time. Public sewerage services are not available; therefore, you must rely on a septic system. You want to know how long it will take to build the house.

Assignment

1. Working in a group, list the major activities involved in the project, and sequence them in the proper order.

2. Estimate the time required for each activity, and establish the critical path.

3. Present your list of construction activities to the class, and ask for comments and suggestions.

3. Researching Different Careers

Because service businesses are now such a dominant part of our economy, job seekers sometimes overlook the employment opportunities available in production plants. Two positions often found in these plants are quality control inspector and purchasing agent.

Assignment

1. Using the *Occupational Outlook Handbook* at your local library or on the Internet (**http://stats.bls.gov/oco/home.htm**), find the following information for the jobs of quality control inspector and purchasing agent:
   a. Job description, including main activities and responsibilities
   b. Job outlook
   c. Earnings and working conditions
   d. Training and qualifications

2. Look for other production jobs that may interest you, and compile the same sort of information about them.

3. Summarize in a two-page report the key things you learned about jobs in production plants.

Prepare for Class
Exploring the Internet

RUNNING A BUSINESS PART 3
Finagle A Bagel's Management, Organization, and Production Finesse

"We don't have a traditional corporate organizational chart," states Heather Robertson, Finagle A Bagel's director of marketing, human resources, and research and development. When she hires new employees, Robertson draws the usual type of organization chart showing the copresidents on the top and the store employees on the bottom. Then she turns it upside down, explaining, "The most important people in our stores are the crew members, and the store manager's role is to support those crew members. Middle management's role is to support the store managers. And the copresidents' responsibility is to support us," referring to herself and her middle-management colleagues.

In short, the copresidents and all the people in corporate headquarters work as a team to help the general managers (who run the stores) and their crew members. Every store strives to achieve preset sales goals within budget guidelines. Higher-level managers are available to help any general manager whose store's performance falls outside the expected ranges. Moreover, each general manager is empowered to make decisions that will boost sales and make the most of opportunities to build positive relationships with local businesses and community organizations. "We want our general managers to view the store as their business," copresident Laura Trust emphasizes. "If a general manager wants to do something that will alleviate a store problem or increase sales, we give him the leeway to do it."

Many Bagels, One Factory

Although the copresidents decentralized authority for many store-level decisions, they achieved more efficiency by centralizing the authority and responsibility for food procurement and preparation. For example, headquarters handles payroll, invoices, and many other time-consuming activities on behalf of all the stores. This reduces the paperwork burden on general managers and frees them to concentrate on managing store-level food service to satisfy customers.

Finagle A Bagel also decided to centralize production and supply functions in its Newton headquarters, where the factory has enough capacity to supply up to 100 stores. "We outgrew our old facility and we wanted to find some place we could expand our operations," copresident Laura Trust explains. Production employees prepare and shape dough for 100,000 bagels and mix 2,000 pounds of flavored cream cheese spreads every day. In addition, they slice 1,500 pounds of fruit every week. Then they gather whatever each store needs—raw dough, salad fixings, packages of condiments, or plastic bowls—and load it on the truck for daily delivery.

Baking Bagels and More

Once the raw dough reaches a store, crew members follow the traditional New York–style method of boiling and baking bagels in various varieties, ranging from year-round favorites such as sesame to seasonal offerings such as pumpkin raisin. In line with Finagle A Bagel's fresh-food concept, the stores bake bagels every hour and tumble them into a line of bins near the front counter. Each store has a unique piece of equipment, dubbed the "bagel buzz saw," to slice and move bagels to the sandwich counter after customers have placed their orders. This equipment not only helps prevent employee accidents and speeds food preparation, but it also entertains customers as they wait for their sandwiches.

Finagle A Bagel is constantly introducing new menu items to bring customers back throughout the day. One item the company has perfected is the bagel pizza. Earlier bagel pizzas turned out soggy, but the newest breakfast pizzas are both crunchy and tasty. The central production facility starts by mixing egg bagel dough, forms it into individual flat breads, grills the rounds, and ships them to the stores. There, a crew member tops each round with the customer's choice of ingredients, heats it, and serves it toasty fresh.

Managing a Bagel Restaurant

Finagle A Bagel's general managers stay busy from the early morning, when they open the store and help crew members to get ready for customers, to the time they close the store at night after one last look to see whether everything is in order for the next day. General managers such as Paulo Pereira, who runs the Harvard Square Finagle A Bagel in Cambridge, must have the technical skills required to run a fast-paced food-service operation.

They also need good conceptual skills so that they can look beyond each individual employee and task to see how everything should fit together. One way Pereira does this is by putting himself in the customer's shoes. He is constantly evaluating how customers would judge the in-store experience, from courteous, attentive counter service to availability of fresh foods, clean tables, and well-stocked condiment containers.

Just as important, Pereira—like other Finagle A Bagel general managers—must have excellent interpersonal skills to work effectively with customers, crew members, colleagues, and higher-level managers. Pereira knows that he can't be successful without being able to work well with other people, especially those he supervises. "You need to have a good crew behind you to help you every single hour of the day," he says. "Every employee

needs to feel special and appreciated. I try to treat employees as fairly as possible, and I try to accommodate their needs."

Questions

1. What does Finagle A Bagel's upside-down organization chart suggest about the delegation of authority and coordination techniques within the company?
2. Is Finagle A Bagel a tall or flat organization? How do you know?
3. What values seem to permeate Finagle A Bagel's corporate culture?
4. Why would Finagle A Bagel build a dough factory that has more capacity than the company needs to supply its stores and its wholesale customers?

CHAPTER 10

Attracting and Retaining the Best Employees

Your Guide to Success in Business

Why this chapter matters
Being able to understand how to attract and keep the right people is crucial. Also, you can better understand about your own interactions with your coworkers.

LEARNING OBJECTIVES

1. Describe the major components of human resources management.

2. Identify the steps in human resources planning.

3. Describe cultural diversity and understand some of the challenges and opportunities associated with it.

4. Explain the objectives and uses of job analysis.

5. Describe the importance of recruiting, employee selection, and orientation in the acquisition phase of human resources management.

6. Discuss the primary elements of employee compensation and benefits.

7. Explain the purposes and techniques of employee training, development, and performance appraisal.

8. Outline the major legislation affecting human resources management.

Valero Energy Corporation— Maintaining a Culture of Respect

"Care more about your employees than you care about yourself" is the philosophy of Valero Energy Corp.'s CEO, who views the work force as one of his company's most valuable assets. Based in San Antonio, Texas, Valero specializes in energy products such as gasoline, jet fuel, kerosene, home heating oil, asphalt, propane, and octane. With annual revenues exceeding $80 billion, the company employs 22,000 people, can refine 3.3 million barrels of oil a day, and operates more than 5,000 gas stations across the United States. Valero attracts skilled employees with top-notch compensation and benefits packages, challenging job responsibilities, and a diverse work environment.

Because Valero has a healthy pipeline of mergers and acquisitions, retaining employees is particularly important. "What we do in each acquisition is to make certain that we do more for the employees than the previous owner," notes the CEO. Right after an acquisition, Valero's human resources personnel start assessing the current salaries and benefits of the affected employees. Once they develop improved compensation packages, they share this information with the new employees and explain how Valero's employee recognition programs work.

This careful attention to detail ensures a smooth transition during each Valero acquisition—which, in turn, keeps employees satisfied, motivated, and dedicated. Valero has never had a layoff, which also helps to fuel employee satisfaction. In addition, the company has established a Safe Fund to provide money to employees in need—a fund that has been especially valuable for employees working in the hurricane-prone Gulf Coast region. And as a good corporate citizen, Valero sponsors a Volunteer Council that encourages employees and managers to give back to their communities, with the idea that caring about the community equates to caring about the company.

Valero's CEO statement that "the more you do for the employees, then the more they will do for the company" demonstrates his respect for his work force and his belief in their value to the company. No wonder Valero makes frequent appearances on *Fortune* magazine's annual list of the "100 Best Companies to Work For."[1]

> **DID YOU KNOW?**
>
> The philosophy of Valero's CEO is "Care more about your employees than you care about yourself."

KEY TERMS

human resources management (HRM) (298)
human resources planning (300)
cultural (workplace) diversity (303)
job analysis (305)
job description (305)
job specification (306)

recruiting (307)
external recruiting (307)
internal recruiting (307)
selection (308)
orientation (311)
compensation (312)
compensation system (312)

wage survey (312)
job evaluation (312)
comparable worth (313)
hourly wage (313)
salary (313)
commission (313)
incentive payment (314)

lump-sum salary increase (314)
profit sharing (314)
employee benefit (314)
flexible benefit plan (315)
employee training (316)
management development (316)
performance appraisal (318)

ACE the Test
Crossword Puzzle
Flashcards

Valero Energy Corporation encourages the hiring and training of employees with diverse ethnic backgrounds. Hiring a diverse mix of employees helps the company to serve a diverse customer base. For many companies, these are important factors to consider when attracting, motivating, and retaining the appropriate mix of human resources.

We begin our study of human resources management (HRM) with an

* Overview of how businesses acquire, maintain, and develop their human resources
* Examination of the steps by which firms match their human resources needs with the supply available
* Exploration of several dimensions of cultural diversity
* Examination of the concept of job analysis
* Emphasis on a firm's recruiting, selection, and orientation procedures as the means of acquiring employees
* Exploration of the forms of employee compensation that motivate employees to remain with a firm and to work effectively
* Examination of the methods of employee training, management development, and performance appraisal
* Overview of legislation that affects HRM practices

Human Resources Management: An Overview

Learning Objective ❶

Describe the major components of human resources management.

The human resource is not only unique and valuable, but it is also an organization's most important resource. It seems logical that an organization would expend a great deal of effort to acquire and make full use of such a resource. This effort is known as *human resources management* (HRM). It also has been called *staffing* and *personnel management*.

human resources management (HRM) all the activities involved in acquiring, maintaining, and developing an organization's human resources

Human resources management (HRM) consists of all the activities involved in acquiring, maintaining, and developing an organization's human resources. As the definition implies, HRM begins with acquisition—getting people to work for the organization. The acquisition process can be quite competitive for certain types of qualified employees. **EXAMPLE** Brokerage houses such as JPMorgan, Citigroup, and Merrill Lynch are building their specialized algorithmic trading teams by recruiting experienced employees from other brokerage firms.[2] Next, steps must be taken to keep these valuable resources. (After all, they are the only business resources that can leave an organization.) Finally, the human resources should be developed to their full capacity.

HRM Activities

Each of the three phases of HRM—acquiring, maintaining, and developing human resources—consists of a number of related activities. Acquisition, for example, includes planning, as well as the various activities that lead to hiring new personnel. Altogether, this phase of HRM includes five separate activities.

Acquisition Activities

* *Human resources planning*—determining the firm's future human resources needs

* *Job analysis*—determining the exact nature of the positions

* *Recruiting*—attracting people to apply for positions

* *Selection*—choosing and hiring the most qualified applicants

* *Orientation*—acquainting new employees with the firm

Maintenance Activities Maintaining human resources consists primarily of encouraging employees to remain with the firm and to work effectively by using a variety of HRM programs, including

* *Employee relations*—increasing employee job satisfaction through satisfaction surveys, employee communication programs, exit interviews, and fair treatment

* *Compensation*—rewarding employee effort through monetary payments

* *Benefits*—providing rewards to ensure employee well-being

Development Activities The development phase of HRM is concerned with improving employees' skills and expanding their capabilities. The two important activities within this phase are

* *Training and development*—teaching employees new skills, new jobs, and more effective ways of doing their present jobs

* *Performance appraisal*—assessing employees' current and potential performance levels

These activities are discussed in more detail shortly, when we have completed this overview of HRM.

Responsibility for HRM

In general, HRM is a shared responsibility of line managers and staff HRM specialists. In very small organizations, the owner handles all or most HRM activities. As a firm grows in size, a human resources manager is hired to take over staff responsibilities. **EXAMPLE** In firms as large as Disney, HRM activities tend to be very highly specialized. There are separate groups to deal with compensation, benefits, training and development, and other staff activities.

Specific HRM activities are assigned to those who are in the best position to perform them.

* Human resources planning and job analysis usually are done by staff specialists, with input from line managers.

* Recruiting and selection are handled by staff experts, although line managers are involved in hiring decisions.

* Orientation programs are devised by staff specialists and carried out by both staff specialists and line managers.

* Compensation systems (including benefits) most often are developed and administered by the HRM staff. However, line managers recommend pay increases and promotions.

* Training and development activities are the joint responsibility of staff and line managers. Performance appraisal is the job of the line manager, although HRM personnel design the firm's appraisal system in many organizations.

TEST PREPPER 10.1

Multiple Choice

1. Valero Energy Corp. retains its employees by making certain that "we do more for the employees than the previous owner." Which of the following best describes benefits that attempt to ease workers of acquired companies into their new roles?

    a. Compensation package
    b. Employee satisfaction
    c. Pay raise
    d. Layoff
    e. Hiring and training of employees

2. Which of the following is the term used to describe a process by which managers determine a firm's future human resources needs?

    a. Job analysis
    b. Human resources planning
    c. Selection
    d. Recruiting
    e. Orientation

3. Which of the following is the best way to describe "employee relations"?

    a. Attracting the best people to apply for positions

    b. Using satisfaction surveys and employee communication programs
    c. Recruiting experienced employees from other firms
    d. Providing rewards to ensure employee well-being
    e. Improving employees' skills and expanding their capabilities

4. Which of the following is *least likely* to be the responsibility of a line manager?

    a. Developing a compensation system
    b. Implementing an orientation program
    c. Job analysis
    d. Recommending a promotion
    e. Hiring employees

5. Which of the following best describes the process of teaching employees new skills and more effective ways of doing their present jobs?

    a. Performance appraisal
    b. Compensation
    c. Benefits
    d. Human resource planning
    e. Training and development

ACE the Test
ACE & ACE+
Practice Test 10.1

human resources planning the development of strategies to meet a firm's future human resources needs

Human Resources Planning

Learning Objective 2

Identify the steps in human resources planning.

Human resources planning is the development of strategies to meet a firm's future human resources needs.

* The starting point is the organization's overall strategic plan.

* From this, human resources planners can forecast future demand for human resources.

* Next, the planners must determine whether the needed human resources will be available.

* Finally, they have to take steps to match supply with demand.

Cultural Diversity in Human Resources

Learning Objective

Describe cultural diversity and understand some of the challenges and opportunities associated with it.

Today's work force is made up of many types of people. Firms can no longer assume that every employee has similar beliefs or expectations. Whereas North American white males may believe in challenging authority, Asians tend to respect and defer to it. In Hispanic cultures, people often bring music, food, and family members to work, a custom that U.S. businesses traditionally have not allowed. A job applicant who will not make eye contact during an interview may be rejected for being unapproachable, when, according to his or her culture, he or she was just being polite.

Since a larger number of women, minorities, and immigrants have entered the U.S. work force, the workplace is more diverse. It is estimated that women make up about 46 percent of the U.S. work force, and African Americans and Hispanics each account for about 11 percent.[4]

Cultural (workplace) diversity refers to the differences among people in a work force owing to race, ethnicity, and gender. Increasing cultural diversity is forcing managers to learn to supervise and motivate people with a broader range of value systems. The flood of women into the work force, combined with a new emphasis on participative parenting by men, has brought many family-related issues to the workplace. Today's more educated employees also want greater independence and flexibility. In return for their efforts, they want both compensation and a better quality of life.

Although cultural diversity presents a challenge, managers should view it as an opportunity rather than a limitation. When managed properly, cultural diversity can provide competitive advantages for an organization. Table 10.1 shows several benefits that creative management of cultural diversity can offer.

Because cultural diversity creates challenges along with advantages, it is important for an organization's employees to understand it. To accomplish this goal, numerous U.S. firms have trained their managers to respect and manage diversity. Diversity training programs may include recruiting minorities, training minorities to be managers, training managers to view diversity positively, teaching English as a second language, and facilitating support groups for immigrants.

cultural (workplace) diversity differences among people in a work force owing to race, ethnicity, and gender

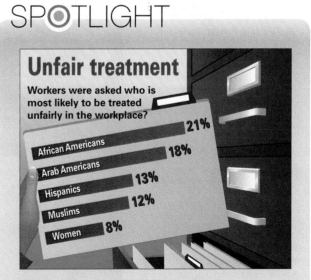

SP⊙TLIGHT

Unfair treatment

Workers were asked who is most likely to be treated unfairly in the workplace?

African Americans — 21%
Arab Americans — 18%
Hispanics — 13%
Muslims — 12%
Women — 8%

Source: USA Today, April 10, 2002, p. B1.

Cost	As organizations become more diverse, the cost of a poor job in integrating workers will increase. Companies that handle this well thus can create cost advantages over those that do a poor job. In addition, companies also experience cost savings by hiring people with knowledge of various cultures as opposed to having to train Americans, for example, about how German people do business.
Resource acquisition	Companies develop reputations as being favorable or unfavorable prospective employers for women and ethnic minorities. Those with the best reputations for managing diversity will win the competition for the best personnel.
Marketing edge	For multinational organizations, the insight and cultural sensitivity that members with roots in other countries bring to marketing efforts should improve these efforts in important ways. The same rationale applies to marketing subpopulations domestically.
Flexibility	Culturally diverse employees often are open to a wider array of positions within a company and are more likely to move up the corporate ladder more rapidly, given excellent performance.
Creativity	Diversity of perspectives and less emphasis on conformity to norms of the past should improve the level of creativity.
Problem solving	Differences within decision-making and problem-solving groups potentially produce better decisions through a wider range of perspectives and more thorough critical analysis of issues.
Bilingual skills	Cultural diversity in the workplace brings with it bilingual and bicultural skills, which are very advantageous to the ever-growing global marketplace. Employees with knowledge about how other cultures work not only can speak to them in their language but also can prevent their company from making embarrassing moves owing to a lack of cultural sophistication. Thus companies seek job applicants with perhaps a background in cultures in which the company does business.

TABLE 10.1

Competitive Advantages of Cultural Diversity

Sources: Taylor H. Cox and Stacy Blake, "Managing Cultural Diversity: Implications for Organizational Competitiveness," *Academy of Management Executive* 5(3):46, 1991; Graciela Kenig, "Yo Soy Ingeniero: The Advantages of Being Bilingual in Technical Professions," *Diversity Monthly*, February 28, 1999, p. 13; and "Dialogue Skills in the Multicultural Workplace," *North American Post*, March 19, 1999, p. 2.

A diversity program will be successful only if it is systematic and ongoing and has a strong, sustained commitment from top leadership. Cultural diversity is here to stay. Its impact on organizations is widespread and will continue to grow within corporations. Management must learn to overcome the obstacles and capitalize on the advantages associated with culturally diverse human resources.

CONCEPT CHECK

What are the major challenges and benefits associated with a culturally diverse workforce?

TEST PREPPER 10.3

True or False?

___ 1. Hiring people with knowledge of various cultures as opposed to having to train them in diverse business practices is one advantage of a culturally diverse work force.

___ 2. Employees with knowledge about how other cultures work not only can speak to them in their language but also can prevent their company from making embarrassing moves owing to a lack of cultural sophistication. Therefore, employees who have bilingual skills are an asset to a company.

Multiple Choice

___ 3. Companies develop reputations as being favorable or unfavorable prospective employers for women and ethnic minorities. Based on this understanding of company reputation, what advantage do companies that have a good record for managing diversity have over others?
   a. Resource acquisition
   b. Flexibility
   c. Bilingual skills
   d. Cost saving
   e. Creativity

___ 4. Which of the following is the best description of the term *marketing edge*?
   a. Culturally diverse employees often are open to a wider array of positions within a company.
   b. Companies that handle integrating workers well thus can create cost advantages over those that do a poor job.
   c. Diversity of perspectives and less emphasis on conformity to norms of the past should improve the level of creativity.
   d. Employees with roots in other countries bring insight and cultural sensitivity to advertising efforts.
   e. Differences within decision-making and problem-solving groups potentially produce better decisions through a wider range of perspectives.

___ 5. Which of the following is the term used to describe a process of "recruiting minorities, training minorities to be managers, training managers to view diversity positively, and teaching English as a second language"?
   a. Problem solving
   b. Flexibility
   c. Resource acquisition
   d. Diversity training
   e. Acquiring bilingual skills

ACE the Test
ACE & ACE+
Practice Test 10.3

Job Analysis

Learning Objective 4

Explain the objectives and uses of job analysis.

There is no sense in hiring people unless we know what we are hiring them for. In other words, we need to know the nature of a job before we can find the right person to do it.

Job analysis is a systematic procedure for studying jobs to determine their various elements and requirements. **EXAMPLE** Consider the position of clerk. In a large corporation, there may be fifty kinds of clerk positions. They all may be called "clerks," but each position may differ from the others in the activities to be performed, the level of proficiency required for each activity, and the particular set of qualifications that the position demands. These distinctions are the focus of job analysis. Some companies, such as ManTech International, specialize in developing job-analysis materials and conducting the analyses for companies and government entities alike; in fact, ManTech won a contract worth $76 million to provide its services to the U.S. Navy.[5]

The job analysis for a particular position typically consists of two parts—a job description and a job specification. A **job description** is a list of the elements that

job analysis a systematic procedure for studying jobs to determine their various elements and requirements

job description a list of the elements that make up a particular job

This job description explains the job of sales coordinator and lists the responsibilities of the position. The job specification is contained in the last paragraph.

CENGAGE LEARNING COMPANY
JOB DESCRIPTION

TITLE: Georgia Sales Coordinator   **DATE:** 3/25/05

DEPARTMENT: College, Sales   **GRADE:** 12

REPORTS TO: Regional Manager   **EXEMPT/NON-EXEMPT:** Exempt

BRIEF SUMMARY:

Supervise one other Georgia-based sales representative to gain supervisory experience. Captain the 4 members of the outside sales rep team that are assigned to territories consisting of colleges and universities in Georgia. Oversee, coordinate, advise, and make decisions regarding Georgia sales activities. Based upon broad contact with customers across the state and communication with administrators of schools, the person will make recommendations regarding issues specific to the needs of higher education in the state of Georgia such as distance learning, conversion to the semester system, potential statewide adoptions, and faculty training.

PRINCIPLE ACCOUNTABILITIES:

1. Supervises/manages/trains one other Atlanta-based sales rep.
2. Advises two other sales reps regarding the Georgia schools in their territories.
3. Increases overall sales in Georgia as well as individual sales territory.
4. Assists regional manager in planning and coordinating regional meetings and Atlanta conferences.
5. Initiates a dialogue with campus administrators, particularly in the areas of the semester conversion, distance learning, and faculty development.

DIMENSIONS:

This position will have one direct report in addition to the leadership role played within the region. Revenue most directly impacted will be within the individually assigned territory, the supervised territory, and the overall sales for the state of Georgia.

KNOWLEDGE AND SKILLS:

Must have displayed a history of consistently outstanding sales in personal territory. Must demonstrate clear teamwork and leadership skills and be willing to extend beyond the individual territory goals. Should have a clear understanding of the company's systems and product offerings in order to train and lead other sales representatives. Must have the communication skills and presence to communicate articulately with higher education administrators and to serve as a bridge between the company and higher education in the state.

make up a particular job. It includes the duties to be performed, the working conditions, responsibilities, and the tools and equipment that must be used on the job (see Figure 10.1).

A **job specification** is a list of the qualifications required to perform a particular job. Included are the skills, abilities, education, and experience the jobholder must have. **EXAMPLE** When attempting to hire a financial analyst, Bank of America used the following job specification:

* "Requires 8–10 years of financial experience,
* a broad-based financial background, strong customer focus,
* the ability to work confidently with the client's management team,
* strong analytical skills. Must have strong Excel and Word skills.

job specification a list of the qualifications required to perform a particular job

* Personal characteristics should include strong desire to succeed, impact performer (individually and as a member of a team), positive attitude, high energy level and ability to influence others."[6]

The job analysis is not only the basis for recruiting and selecting new employees, but it is also used in other areas of HRM, including evaluation and the determination of equitable compensation levels.

Recruiting, Selection, and Orientation

Learning Objective 5

Describe the importance of recruiting, employee selection, and orientation in the acquisition phase of human resources management.

In an organization with jobs waiting to be filled, HRM personnel need to (1) find candidates for those jobs and (2) match the right candidate with each job. Three activities are involved: recruiting, selection, and (for new employees) orientation.

Recruiting

Recruiting is the process of attracting qualified job applicants. Because it is a vital link in a costly process (the cost of hiring an employee can be several thousand dollars), recruiting needs to be a systematic process. One goal of recruiters is to attract the "right number" of applicants. The right number is enough to allow a good match between applicants and open positions but not so many that matching them requires too much time and effort.

Recruiters may seek applicants outside the firm, within the firm, or both. The source used depends on the nature of the position, the situation within the firm, and sometimes the firm's established or traditional recruitment policies.

External Recruiting External recruiting is the attempt to attract job applicants from outside an organization. External recruiting may include newspaper advertising, employment agencies, recruiting on college campuses, soliciting recommendations from present employees, conducting "open houses," and online. The biggest of the online job-search sites is Monster.com, which has as clients about 490 of the *Fortune* 500 companies.[7] In addition, many people simply apply at a firm's employment office.

The primary advantage of external recruiting is that it brings in people with new perspectives and varied business backgrounds. A disadvantage of external recruiting is that it is often expensive, especially if private employment agencies must be used. External recruiting also may provoke resentment among present employees.

Internal Recruiting Internal recruiting means considering present employees as applicants for available positions. Generally, current employees are considered for *promotion* to higher-level positions. However, employees may be considered for *transfer* from one position to another at the same level. Among leading companies, 85 percent

recruiting the process of attracting qualified job applicants

external recruiting the attempt to attract job applicants from outside an organization

internal recruiting considering present employees as applicants for available positions

Recruiting at Job Fairs.

At job fairs, such as the one advertised here, recruiters and job applicants can meet to discuss job opportunities and applicants' qualifications.

Before China Beckons

Fast-growing local and multinational Chinese companies increasingly are competing with U.S. companies for Western-trained managers. As the country becomes more cosmopolitan and its economy expands, a growing number of bilingual managers see career benefits in going East. Although working for a company in China can be exciting and lucrative, keep these issues in mind:

- *Cultural differences.* Patience is needed because many middle managers in Chinese companies find it difficult to adjust to Western-style management.
- *Language barriers.* Although English-language fluency is spreading, the most sought-after managers are those who know Mandarin and other Chinese dialects, so polish your language skills now.
- *Business customs.* Some local business practices may seem questionable by Western standards. Learn as much as you can before you go.
- *Living conditions.* Because of pollution and other issues, be aware that your daily life will be different, especially if you are assigned to a rural area.

Sources: Based on information from "Go East, My Son," *The Economist,* August 12, 2006, p. 53; "Apply Within," *The Economist,* September 23, 2006, p. 74; Alex Halperin, "All the World's an Office," *BusinessWeek Online,* September 27, 2006, **www.businessweek.com**; Diane Brady and Dexter Roberts, "Management Grab: In Fast-Growing China, Multinationals Are Scrambling to Attract and Retain Smart, Bilingual Executives," *BusinessWeek,* August 21, 2006, p. 88.

selection the process of gathering information about applicants for a position and then using that information to choose the most appropriate applicant

of CEOs are promoted from within. In the companies that hire CEOs from outside, 40 percent of the CEOs are gone after eighteen months.[8]

Promoting from within provides strong motivation for current employees and helps the firm to retain quality personnel. General Electric, Exxon, and Eastman Kodak are companies dedicated to promoting from within. The practice of *job posting*, or informing current employees of upcoming openings, may be a company policy or required by union contract. The primary disadvantage of internal recruiting is that promoting a current employee leaves another position to be filled. Not only does the firm still incur recruiting and selection costs, but it also must train two employees instead of one.

In many situations it may be impossible to recruit internally. For example, a new position may be such that no current employee is qualified. Or the firm may be growing so rapidly that there is no time to reassign positions that promotion or transfer requires.

Selection

Selection is the process of gathering information about applicants for a position and then using that information to choose the most appropriate applicant. Note the use of the word *appropriate*. In selection, the idea is not to hire the person with the *most* qualifications but rather the applicant who is *most appropriate*. The selection of an applicant is made by line managers responsible for the position. However, HRM personnel usually help by developing a pool of applicants and by expediting the assessment of these applicants. Common means of obtaining information about applicants' qualifications are

* Employment applications
* References
* Interviews
* Assessment centers

Employment Applications An employment application is useful in collecting factual information on a candidate's education, work experience, and personal history (see Figure 10.2). The data obtained from applications usually are used for two purposes:

1. To identify applicants who are worthy of further scrutiny
2. To familiarize interviewers with their backgrounds

Many job candidates submit résumés, and some firms require them. A résumé may be sent to a firm to request consideration for available jobs, or it may be submitted along with an employment application.

To improve the usefulness of information, HRM specialists ask current employees about factors in their backgrounds most related to their current jobs. Then these factors are included on the applications and may be weighted more heavily when evaluating new applicants' qualifications.

Employment Tests Tests administered to job candidates usually focus on aptitudes, skills, abilities, or knowledge relevant to the job. Such tests (basic computer skills tests, for example) indicate how well the applicant will do the job. Occasionally, companies use general intelligence or personality tests, but these are seldom helpful in predicting specific job performance. However, *Fortune* 500 companies, as well as an increasing number of medium- and small-sized companies, are using predictive-behavior personality tests as administration costs decrease. **EXAMPLE** Darden Restaurants, parent company of The Olive Garden and Red Lobster, uses a work-style inventory in its hiring process for all positions, whereas firms such as Disney and Hampton Inn use similar tests for management positions.[9]

A firm must be able to prove that a test is not discriminatory by demonstrating that it accurately measures one's ability to perform. Applicants who believe that they have been discriminated against through an invalid test may file a complaint with the Equal Employment Opportunity Commission (EEOC).

Interviews The interview is perhaps the most widely used selection technique. Job candidates are interviewed by at least one member of the HRM staff and by the person for whom they will be working. Candidates for higher-level jobs may meet with a department head or vice president over several interviews.

Pros of Interviews

* Interviews provide an opportunity for applicants and the firm to learn more about each other.
* Interviewers can pose problems to test the candidate's abilities, probe employment history, and learn something about the candidate's attitudes and motivation.
* The candidate has a chance to find out more about the job and potential co-workers.

CONCEPT CHECK

In your opinion, what are the two best techniques for gathering information about job candidates?

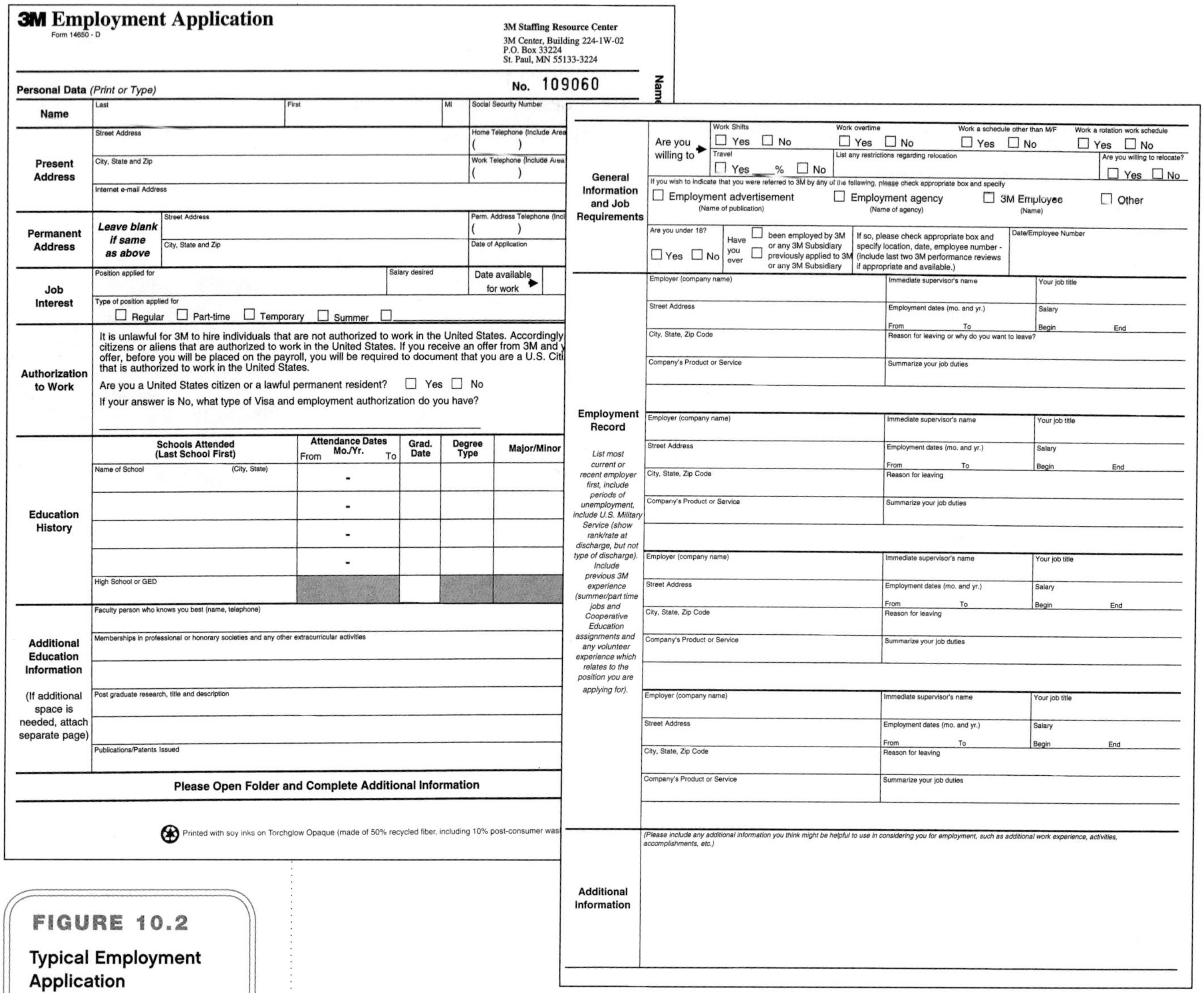

3M Employment Application
Form 14650 - D

3M Staffing Resource Center
3M Center, Building 224-1W-02
P.O. Box 33224
St. Paul, MN 55133-3224

Personal Data (Print or Type) No. 109060

Name: Last / First / MI / Social Security Number

Present Address: Street Address / Home Telephone (Include Area) / City, State and Zip / Work Telephone (Include Area) / Internet e-mail Address

Permanent Address: Leave blank if same as above / Street Address / Perm. Address Telephone / City, State and Zip / Date of Application

Job Interest: Position applied for / Salary desired / Date available for work / Type of position applied for: ☐ Regular ☐ Part-time ☐ Temporary ☐ Summer ☐

Authorization to Work: It is unlawful for 3M to hire individuals that are not authorized to work in the United States. Accordingly citizens or aliens that are authorized to work in the United States. If you receive an offer from 3M and offer, before you will be placed on the payroll, you will be required to document that you are a U.S. Citi that is authorized to work in the United States.
Are you a United States citizen or a lawful permanent resident? ☐ Yes ☐ No
If your answer is No, what type of Visa and employment authorization do you have?

Education History					
Schools Attended (Last School First)	Attendance Dates Mo./Yr. From To	Grad. Date	Degree Type	Major/Minor
Name of School (City, State)	-			
	-			
	-			
	-			
High School or GED				

Additional Education Information (If additional space is needed, attach separate page): Faculty person who knows you best (name, telephone) / Memberships in professional or honorary societies and any other extracurricular activities / Post graduate research, title and description / Publications/Patents Issued

Please Open Folder and Complete Additional Information

Printed with soy inks on Torchglow Opaque (made of 50% recycled fiber, including 10% post-consumer was

General Information and Job Requirements: Are you willing to ▸ Work Shifts ☐ Yes ☐ No / Work overtime ☐ Yes ☐ No / Work a schedule other than M/F ☐ Yes ☐ No / Work a rotation work schedule ☐ Yes ☐ No / Travel ☐ Yes ___% ☐ No / List any restrictions regarding relocation / Are you willing to relocate? ☐ Yes ☐ No
If you wish to indicate that you were referred to 3M by any of the following, please check appropriate box and specify: ☐ Employment advertisement (Name of publication) ☐ Employment agency (Name of agency) ☐ 3M Employee (Name) ☐ Other
Are you under 18? ☐ Yes ☐ No / Have you ever ☐ been employed by 3M or any 3M Subsidiary ☐ previously applied to 3M or any 3M Subsidiary / If so, please check appropriate box and specify location, date, employee number - (include last two 3M performance reviews if appropriate and available.) / Date/Employee Number

Employment Record: List most current or recent employer first, include periods of unemployment, include U.S. Military Service (show rank/rate at discharge, but not type of discharge). Include previous 3M experience (summer/part time jobs and Cooperative Education assignments and any volunteer experience which relates to the position you are applying for).
Employer (company name) / Immediate supervisor's name / Your job title / Street Address / Employment dates (mo. and yr.) From To / Salary Begin End / City, State, Zip Code / Reason for leaving or why do you want to leave? / Company's Product or Service / Summarize your job duties

Additional Information: (Please include any additional information you think might be helpful to use in considering you for employment, such as additional work experience, activities, accomplishments, etc.)

FIGURE 10.2

Typical Employment Application

Employers use applications to collect factual information on a candidate's education, work experience, and personal history.

Source: Courtesy of 3M.

Cons of Interviews

* Interviewing may be the stage at which discrimination begins. **EXAMPLE** Suppose that a female applicant mentions that she is the mother of small children. Her interviewer may assume that she would not be available for job-related travel.
* Interviewers may be unduly influenced by such factors as appearance.
* Interviewers may ask different questions of different applicants so that it becomes impossible to compare candidates' qualifications.

Some of these problems can be solved through better interviewer training and use of structured interviews. In a *structured interview,* the interviewer asks only a prepared set of job-related questions. The firm also may consider using several different interviewers for each applicant, but this is likely to be costly.

References A job candidate generally is asked to furnish the names of *references*—people who can verify background information and provide personal evaluations. Naturally, applicants tend to list only references who are likely to say good things. Thus personal evaluations obtained from references may not be of much value. However, references are often contacted to verify such information as previous job responsibilities and the reason an applicant left a former job.

Assessment Centers An assessment center is used primarily to select current employees for promotion to higher-level positions. Typically, a group of employees is sent to the center for a few days. While there they participate in activities designed to simulate the management environment and to predict managerial effectiveness. Trained observers make recommendations regarding promotion possibilities. Although this technique is gaining popularity, the expense involved limits its use.

Orientation

Once all information about job candidates has been collected and analyzed, a job offer is extended. If it is accepted, the candidate becomes an employee.

Soon after a candidate joins a firm, he or she goes through the firm's orientation program. Orientation is the process of acquainting new employees with an organization. Orientation topics range from the location of the company cafeteria to career paths within the firm. The orientation itself may consist of a half-hour informal presentation by a human resources manager. Or it may be an elaborate program involving dozens of people and lasting several days or weeks.

orientation the process of acquainting new employees with an organization

TEST PREPPER 10.4 10.5

True or False?

_____ 1. A job description is a systematic procedure for studying jobs to determine their various elements and requirements.
   a. True
   b. False

_____ 2. Job specification is a list of the qualifications required to perform a particular job.
   a. True
   b. False

_____ 3. Internal recruiting is when companies consider present employees as applicants for available positions, usually in the form of a promotion.
   a. True
   b. False

_____ 4. Interviewers ask different questions of different applicants, which is always one of the major advantages of taking interviews.
   a. True
   b. False

Multiple Choice

_____ 5. Which of the following terms describes the process of attracting qualified job applicants?
   a. External recruiting
   b. Recruiting
   c. Internal recruiting
   d. Selection
   e. Promotion

_____ 6. Which of the following terms describes the attempt to attract job applicants from outside an organization?
   a. Transfer
   b. Job posting
   c. External recruiting
   d. Selection
   e. Promotion

_____ 7. Which of the following is *not* a common means of obtaining information about applicants' qualifications?
   a. Employment applications
   b. Interviews
   c. References
   d. Employment tests
   e. The SAT Reasoning Test

ACE the Test
ACE & ACE+
Practice Tests 10.4, 10.5

Compensation and Benefits

Learning Objective 6

Discuss the primary elements of employee compensation and benefits.

An effective employee compensation system must
1. Enable employees to satisfy basic needs
2. Provide rewards comparable with those offered by other firms
3. Be distributed fairly within the organization
4. Recognize that different people have different needs

A firm's compensation system can be structured to meet the first three of these requirements. The fourth is more difficult because it must account for many variables. Most firms offer a number of benefits that, taken together, generally help to provide for employees' varying needs.

Compensation Decisions

compensation the payment employees receive in return for their labor

compensation system the policies and strategies that determine employee compensation

Compensation is the payment employees receive in return for their labor. Its importance to employees is obvious. And because compensation may account for up to 80 percent of a firm's operating costs, it is equally important to management. The firm's **compensation system**, the policies and strategies that determine employee compensation, therefore must be designed carefully to provide for employee needs while keeping labor costs within reasonable limits. For most firms, designing an effective compensation system requires three separate management decisions—wage level, wage structure, and individual wages.

Wage Level Management first must position the firm's general pay level relative to pay levels of comparable firms. Most firms choose a pay level near the industry average. A firm that is not in good financial shape may pay less than average, and large, prosperous organizations may pay more than average. To determine what the average is, the firm may use wage surveys. A **wage survey** is a collection of data on prevailing wage rates within an industry or a geographic area. Such surveys are compiled by industry associations, local governments, personnel associations, and (occasionally) individual firms.

wage survey a collection of data on prevailing wage rates within an industry or a geographic area

Wage Structure Next, management must decide on relative pay levels for all the positions within the firm. Will managers be paid more than secretaries? Will secretaries be paid more than custodians? The result of this set of decisions is often called the firm's *wage structure*.

job evaluation the process of determining the relative worth of the various jobs within a firm

The wage structure almost always is developed on the basis of a job evaluation. **Job evaluation** is the process of determining the relative worth of the various jobs within a firm. Most observers probably would agree that a secretary should make more money than a custodian, but how much more? Job evaluation should provide the answer to this question.

Individual Wages Finally, the specific payments individual employees will receive must be determined. Consider the case of two administrative assistants working side by side. Job evaluation has been used to determine the relative level of pay within the firm's wage structure. However, suppose that one administrative assistant has fifteen years of experience and can type eighty words per minute accurately. The other has two years of experience and can type only fifty-five words per minute. In most firms these two people would not receive the same pay. Instead, a wage range would be established for the administrative assistant position. In this case, the range might be $7 to $9.50 per hour. The more experienced and proficient administrative assistant then would be paid an amount near the top of the range (say, $8.90 per hour); the less experienced administrative assistant would receive an amount that is lower but still within the range (say, $7.75 per hour).

Two wage decisions come into play here. First, the employee's initial rate must be established. It is based on experience, other qualifications, and expected performance. Later, the employee may be given pay increases based on seniority and performance.

Comparable Worth

One reason women in the work force are paid less may be that a proportion of women occupy female-dominated jobs—nurses, administrative assistants, and medical records analysts, for example—that require education, skills, and training equal to higher-paid positions but are undervalued. Comparable worth is a concept that seeks equal compensation for jobs that require about the same level of education, training, and skills. Several states have enacted laws requiring equal pay for comparable work in government positions.

Types of Compensation

Compensation can be paid in a variety of forms. Most forms of compensation fall into the following categories: hourly wage, weekly or monthly salary, commissions, incentive payments, lump-sum salary increases, and profit sharing.

Hourly Wage An hourly wage is a specific amount of money paid for each hour of work. People who earn wages are paid their hourly wage for the first forty hours worked in any week. They are then paid one and one-half times their hourly wage for time worked in excess of forty hours. (That is, they are paid "time and a half" for overtime.) Workers in retailing and fast-food chains, on assembly lines, and in clerical positions usually are paid an hourly wage.

Weekly or Monthly Salary A salary is a specific amount of money paid for an employee's work during a set calendar period, regardless of the actual number of hours worked. Salaried employees receive no overtime pay, but they do not lose pay when they are absent from work. Most professional and managerial positions are salaried.

Commissions A commission is a payment that is a percentage of sales revenue. Sales representatives and sales managers often are paid entirely through commissions or through a combination of commissions and salary.

CONCEPT CHECK
Explain how the three wage-related decisions result in a compensation system.

comparable worth a concept that seeks equal compensation for jobs requiring about the same level of education, training, and skills

ACE the Test
Hangman

hourly wage a specific amount of money paid for each hour of work

salary a specific amount of money paid for an employee's work during a set calendar period, regardless of the actual number of hours worked

commission a payment that is a percentage of sales revenue

Incentive Payments   An incentive payment is a payment in addition to wages, salary, or commissions. Incentive payments are really extra rewards for outstanding job performance. They may be distributed to all employees or only to certain employees.

To avoid yearly across-the-board salary increases, some organizations reward outstanding workers individually through *merit pay.* This pay-for-performance approach allows management to control labor costs while encouraging employees to work more efficiently. An employee's merit pay depends on his or her achievements relative to those of others.

Lump-Sum Salary Increases   In traditional reward systems, an employee who receives an annual pay increase is given part of the increase in each pay period. Companies that offer a lump-sum salary increase give the employee the option of taking the entire pay raise in one lump sum. The employee then draws his or her "regular" pay for the rest of the year. The lump-sum payment typically is treated as an interest-free loan that must be repaid if the employee leaves the firm during the year.

Profit Sharing   Profit sharing is the distribution of a percentage of a firm's profit among its employees. The idea is to motivate employees to work effectively by giving them a stake in the company's financial success. Some firms—including Sears, Roebuck—have linked their profit-sharing plans to employee retirement programs; that is, employees receive their profit-sharing distributions, with interest, when they retire.

Employee Benefits

An employee benefit is a reward in addition to regular compensation that is provided indirectly to employees. Employee benefits consist mainly of services (such as insurance) that are paid for partially or totally by employers and employee expenses (such as college tuition) that are reimbursed by employers. Currently, the average cost of these benefits is 28 percent of an employee's total compensation, which includes wages plus benefits. Thus a person who received total compensation (including benefits) of $40,000 a year earned $28,000 in wages and received an additional $11,200 in benefits.[10] A recent online survey conducted by TrueCareers found that 84 percent of employees would rather receive better benefits than higher salaries. These findings are significant to employers as they try to attract and retain good employees. Increased desire for benefits is partially the result of increasing health care insurance costs.[11]

Types of Benefits   Employee benefits take a variety of forms. *Pay for time not worked* covers such absences as vacation time, holidays, and sick leave. *Insurance packages* may include health, life, and dental insurance for employees and their families. Some firms pay the entire cost of the insurance package, and others share the cost with the employee. The costs of *pension and retirement programs* also may be borne entirely by the firm or shared with the employee.

Some benefits are required by law. For example, employers must maintain *workers' compensation insurance,* which pays medical bills for injuries that occur on the job and provides income for employees who are disabled by job-related injuries. Employers also must pay for *unemployment insurance* and contribute to each employee's federal *Social Security* account.

Other benefits provided by employers include tuition-reimbursement plans, credit unions, child care, company cafeterias, exercise rooms, and broad stock-option plans available to all employees. Some companies offer special benefits to U.S. military reservists who are called up for active duty. IBM offers to make up the difference between a reservist's military pay and his or her regular pay so that overall pay remains at the IBM level. In addition, normal benefits still are given when reservists are called, and employees can continue to contribute to their 401(k) plans and receive contributions from IBM. When reservists return from active duty, they come back to their same positions, and their active-duty time counts toward their years of service with IBM.[12]

Flexible Benefit Plans   Through a **flexible benefit plan**, an employee receives a predetermined amount of benefit dollars and may allocate those dollars to various categories of benefits in the mix that best fits his or her needs. Some flexible benefit plans offer a broad array of benefit options, including health care, dental care, life insurance, accidental death and dismemberment coverage for both the worker and dependents, long-term disability coverage, vacation benefits, retirement savings, and dependent-care benefits. Other firms offer limited options, primarily in health and life insurance and retirement plans.

Although the cost of administering flexible plans is high, a number of organizations, including Quaker Oats and Coca-Cola, have implemented this option for several reasons. Because employees' needs are so diverse, flexible plans help firms to offer benefit packages that more specifically meet their employees' needs. Flexible plans can, in the long run, help a company to contain costs because a specified amount is allocated to cover the benefits of each employee. Furthermore, organizations that offer flexible plans with many choices may be perceived as being employee-friendly. Thus they are in a better position to attract and retain qualified employees.

flexible benefit plan compensation plan whereby an employee receives a predetermined amount of benefit dollars to spend on a package of benefits he or she has selected to meet individual needs

TEST PREPPER 10.6

True or False?

_____ 1. A firm's wage structure is the relative pay levels for all the positions within the firm.

_____ 2. A compensation plan whereby an employee receives a predetermined amount of benefit dollars to spend on a package of benefits that he or she has selected to meet individual needs is known as a flexible benefit plan.

Multiple Choice

_____ 3. Which of the following is *not* usually characteristic of an effective employee-compensation system?

    a. Enable employees to satisfy basic needs
    b. Restricted to monetary compensation
    c. Provide competitive salaries
    d. Be distributed fairly within the organization
    e. Recognize that different people have different needs

_____ 4. Which of the following is the best definition of comparable worth?

    a. Wage differentiation on the basis of experience, other qualifications, and expected performance
    b. The process of determining the relative worth of the various jobs within a firm
    c. Seeking equal compensation for jobs requiring about the same level of education, training, and skills
    d. Positioning the firm's general pay level relative to pay levels of comparable firms
    e. The policies and strategies that determine employee compensation

_____ 5. Which of the following is the term used to describe a payment that is a percentage of sales revenue?

    a. A commission
    b. A weekly salary
    c. Incentive payments
    d. Lump-sum increments
    e. Profit sharing

ACE the Test
ACE & ACE+
Practice Test 10.6

Training and Development

employee training the process of teaching operations and technical employees how to do their present jobs more effectively and efficiently

management development the process of preparing managers and other professionals to assume increased responsibility in both present and future positions

Learning Objective 7

Explain the purposes and techniques of employee training, development, and performance appraisal.

Both training and development are aimed at improving employees' skills and abilities. However, the two are usually differentiated as either employee training or management development. **Employee training** is the process of teaching operations and technical employees how to do their present jobs more effectively and efficiently. **Management development** is the process of preparing managers and other professionals to assume increased responsibility in both present and future positions. Thus training and development differ in who is being taught and the purpose of the teaching. Both are necessary for personal and organizational growth.

Companies that hope to stay competitive typically make huge commitments to employee training and development. **EXAMPLE** Edward Jones, the stockbroker with nearly 8,000 branches, spends 3.8 percent of its payroll on training. These expenditures average out to be 146 hours per year for each employee, with new hires receiving about four times this amount of training. This dedication to its employees has helped Edward Jones claim the rating as the best company to work for by *Fortune* magazine for two consecutive years.[13] Internet-based e-learning is growing. Driven by cost, travel, and time savings, online learning alone and in conjunction with face-to-face situations is a strong alternative strategy. Development of a training program usually has three components:

Training.

Airlines use flight simulators to train pilots.

* Analysis of needs
* Determination of training and development methods
* Creation of an evaluation system to assess the program's effectiveness

Analysis of Training Needs

When thinking about developing a training program, managers first must determine if training is needed and, if so, what types of training needs exist. At times, what at first appears to be a need for training is actually, on assessment, a need for motivation. Training needs can vary considerably. For example, some employees may need training to improve their technical skills, or they may need training about organizational procedures. Training also may focus on business ethics, product information, or customer service. Because training is expensive, it is critical that the correct training needs be identified.

Your Career

Do You Need a Career Coach?

Whether you're looking for a new job, thinking about starting your own business, or want a change within your current company, you may need a career coach. A career coach is someone inside or outside the company who helps you develop career goals and take steps to achieve them. Consider a career coach for help

- *Landing your first job.* A job search can be less daunting with a career coach to guide you in developing a résumé and practicing interview techniques.

- *Starting a business.* Some entrepreneurs seek out career coaches for assistance in setting goals and getting better organized. "Working with a coach gives you the opportunity to discuss issues and brainstorm," says career coach Michelle Payne.
- *Changing jobs within your company.* Accounting firm Deloitte and Touche provides employees with confidential career coaching opportunities through its Deloitte Career Connections program. Thanks to this program, the company has retained over 650 employees who would have left the firm otherwise.

Sources: Based on information in Jack Gordon, "The Coach Approach Career Counseling Is on the Money at Deloitte," *Training Magazine*, October 2006, p. 26; Eilene Zimmerman, "Hoping to Get on the Fast Track, Students Turn to Career Coaches," *New York Times*, May 21, 2006, sec. 10, p. 1; Cyndia Zwahlen, "A Coach May Improve Your Game;" *Los Angeles Times*, October 11, 2006, p. C9.

Training and Development Methods

A number of methods are available for employee training and management development. Some of these methods may be more suitable for one or the other, but most can be applied to both.

- *On-the-job methods.* The trainee learns by doing the work under the supervision of an experienced employee.

- *Simulations.* The work situation is simulated in a separate area so that learning takes place away from the day-to-day pressures of work.

- *Classroom teaching and lectures.* You probably already know these methods quite well.

- *Conferences and seminars.* Experts and learners meet to discuss problems and exchange ideas.

- *Role playing.* Participants act out the roles of others in the organization for better understanding of those roles (primarily a management development tool).

Evaluation of Training and Development

Training and development are very expensive. The training itself costs quite a bit, and employees usually are not working—or are working at a reduced load and pace—during training sessions. To ensure that training and development are cost-effective, the managers responsible should evaluate the company's efforts periodically.

The starting point for this evaluation is a set of verifiable objectives that are developed *before* the training is undertaken. Suppose that a training program is expected to improve the skills of machinists. The objective of the program might be

Prepare for Class
Career Snapshot

CONCEPT CHECK

What is the difference between the objective of employee training and the objective of management development?

stated as follows: "At the end of the training period, each machinist should be able to process thirty parts per hour with no more than one defective part per ninety parts completed." This objective clearly specifies what is expected and how training results may be measured or verified. Evaluation then consists of measuring machinists' output and the ratio of defective parts produced after the training.

The results of training evaluations should be made known to all those involved in the program—including trainees and upper management. For trainees, the results of evaluations can enhance motivation and learning. For upper management, the results may be the basis for making decisions about the training program itself.

Performance Appraisal

performance appraisal
the evaluation of employees' current and potential levels of performance to allow managers to make objective human resources decisions

Performance appraisal is the evaluation of employees' current and potential levels of performance to allow managers to make objective human resources decisions. The process has three main objectives.

* Managers use performance appraisals to let workers know how well they are doing and how they can do better in the future.

* A performance appraisal provides an effective basis for distributing rewards, such as pay raises and promotions.

* Performance appraisal helps the organization monitor its employee selection, training, and development activities.

If large numbers of employees continually perform below expectations, the firm may need to revise its selection process or strengthen its training and development activities.

Common Evaluation Techniques

The various techniques and methods for appraising employee performance are either objective or judgmental in nature.

Objective Methods   Objective appraisal methods use some measurable quantity as the basis for assessing performance. Units of output, dollar volume of sales, number of defective products, and number of insurance claims processed are all objective, measurable quantities. Thus an employee who processes an average of twenty-six insurance claims per week is given a higher evaluation than one whose average is nineteen claims per week.

Judgmental Methods   Judgmental appraisal methods are used much more frequently than objective methods. They require that the manager judge or estimate the employee's performance level. However, judgmental methods are not capricious. These methods are based on employee ranking or rating scales. When ranking is used, the manager ranks subordinates from best to worst. This approach has a number of drawbacks, including the lack of any absolute standard. Rating scales are the most popular judgmental appraisal technique. A *rating scale* consists of a number of statements; each employee is rated on the degree to which the statement applies (see Figure 10.3). For example, one statement might be, "This employee always does high-quality work." The supervisor would give the employee a rating, from 5 down to 1, corresponding to gradations ranging from "strongly agree" to "strongly disagree." The ratings on all the statements are added to obtain the employee's total evaluation.

3M **Contribution and Development Summary**
FORM 37450 - B

Employee Name	Employee Number	Job Title
Department		Location
Coach/Supervisor(s) Name(s)		Review Period From : To :

Major Job Responsibilities

Goals/Expectations	Contributions/Results

Contribution (To be completed by coach/supervisor)

☐ Good Level of Contribution for this year   ☐ Exceptional Level of Contribut...

☐ Unsatisfactory Level of Contribution for this year

Development Summary

Areas of Strength	Development Priorities

Career Interests

Next job	Longer Range

Current Mobility

☐ 0 - Currently Unable to Relocate   ☐ 3 - Position Within O.U.S. Area (ex: Europe, Asia)
☐ 1 - Position In Home Country Only (Use if Home Country is Outside U.S.)   ☐ 4 - Position In U.S.
☐ 2 - Position Within O.U.S. Region (e: Nordic, SEA...)   ☐ 5 - Position Anywhere In The World

Development

☐ W - Well placed. Development plans achievable in current role for at least the next year   ☐ X - Not well placed. Action required to resolve placement issues.
☐ C - Ready now for a move to a different job for career broadening experience   **Comments on Development**
☐ I - Ready now for a move to a different job involving increased responsibility

Employee Comments

Coach/Supervisor Comments	Other Supervisor (if applicable) and/or Reviewer

Signatures

Coach/Supervisor	Date	Other Coach/Supervisor or Reviewer	Date
Employee			Date

page 4

Avoiding Appraisal Errors Managers must be cautious if they are to avoid making mistakes when appraising employees.

* It is common to overuse one portion of an evaluation instrument, thus overemphasizing some issues and underemphasizing others.

* A manager must guard against allowing an employee's poor performance on one activity to influence his or her judgment of that subordinate's work on other activities.

* Similarly, putting too much weight on recent performance distorts an employee's evaluation.

* Finally, a manager must guard against discrimination on the basis of race, age, gender, religion, national origin, or sexual orientation.

FIGURE 10.3

Performance Appraisal

Judgmental appraisal methods are used much more often than objective methods. Using judgmental methods requires the manager to estimate the employee's performance level relative to some standard.

Source: Courtesy of 3M.

Performance Feedback

No matter which appraisal technique is used, the results should be discussed with the employee soon after the evaluation is completed. The manager should explain the basis for present rewards and should let the employee know what he or she can do to be recognized as a better performer in the future. The information provided to an employee in such discussions is called a *performance feedback,* and the process is known as a *performance feedback interview.*

We should note that many managers find it difficult to discuss the negative aspects of an appraisal. Unfortunately, they may ignore performance feedback altogether or provide it in a very weak and ineffectual manner. In truth, though, most employees have strengths that can be emphasized to soften the discussion of their weaknesses. An employee may not even be aware of weaknesses and their consequences. If such weaknesses are not pointed out through performance feedback, they cannot possibly be eliminated. Only through tactful, honest communication can the results of an appraisal be fully used.

TEST PREPPER 10.7

True or False?

 1. "Employee training" refers to the process of preparing managers and other professionals to assume increased responsibility in both present and future positions.

 2. A performance appraisal is a set of verifiable objectives that are developed *before* the training is undertaken in order to ensure that training and development are cost-effective.

 3. During a performance feedback interview, managers should avoid discussing an employee's weaknesses and focus on his or her strengths to let the employee know what he or she can do to be recognized as a better performer in the future.

Multiple Choice

 4. Which of the following is not typically a training method used for employee training and management development?

a. Interviews and aptitude tests
b. On-the-job methods
c. Simulations
d. Seminars
e. Role playing

 5. Which of the following is a good example of the "judgmental method" of evaluation?

a. Each employee is rated on the degree to which the statement applies.
b. The number of insurance claims processed is evaluated.
c. The units of output per employee are calculated.
d. An employee's dollar volume of sales per week is assessed.
e. The number of defective products an employee produces, on average, is counted.

ACE the Test
ACE & ACE+
Practice Test 10.7

The Legal Environment of HRM

Learning Objective 8

Outline the major legislation affecting human resources management.

Legislation regarding HRM practices has been passed mainly to protect the rights of employees, to promote job safety, and to eliminate discrimination in the workplace. The major federal laws affecting HRM are described in Table 10.2.

LAW	PURPOSE
National Labor Relations Act (1935)	Established a collective-bargaining process in labor-management relations as well as the National Labor Relations Board (NLRB)
Fair Labor Standards Act (1938)	Established a minimum wage and an overtime pay rate for employees working more than forty hours per week
Labor-Management Relations Act (1947)	Provided a balance between union power and management power; also known as the Taft-Hartley Act
Equal Pay Act (1963)	Specified that men and women who do equal jobs must be paid the same wage
Title VII of the Civil Rights Act (1964)	Outlawed discrimination in employment practices based on sex, race, color, religion, or national origin
Age Discrimination in Employment Act (1967–1986)	Outlawed personnel practices that discriminate against people aged 40 and older; the 1986 amendment eliminated a mandatory retirement age
Occupational Safety and Health Act (1970)	Regulated the degree to which employees can be exposed to hazardous substances and specified the safety equipment that the employer must provide
Employment Retirement Income Security Act (1974)	Regulated company retirement programs and provided a federal insurance program for retirement plans that go bankrupt
Worker Adjustment and Retraining Notification (WARN) Act (1988)	Required employers to give employees sixty days notice regarding plant closure or layoff of fifty or more employees
Americans with Disabilities Act (1990)	Prohibited discrimination against qualified individuals with disabilities in all employment practices, including job-application procedures, hiring, firing, advancement, compensation, training, and other terms, conditions, and privileges of employment
Civil Rights Act (1991)	Facilitated employees' suing employers for sexual discrimination and collecting punitive damages
Family and Medical Leave Act (1993)	Required an organization with fifty or more employees to provide up to twelve weeks of leave without pay on the birth (or adoption) of an employee's child or if an employee or his or her spouse, child, or parent is seriously ill

TABLE 10.2
Federal Legislation Affecting Human Resources Management

National Labor Relations Act and Labor-Management Relations Act

These laws are concerned with dealings between business firms and labor unions. This general area is, in concept, a part of HRM. However, because of its importance, it is often treated as a separate set of activities. We discuss both labor-management relations and these two acts in detail in Chapter 12.

Fair Labor Standards Act

This act, passed in 1938 and amended many times since, applies primarily to wages. It established minimum wages and overtime pay rates. Many managers and other professionals, however, are exempt from this law. Managers, for example, seldom get paid overtime when they work more than forty hours a week.

Equal Pay Act

Passed in 1963, this law overlaps somewhat with Title VII of the Civil Rights Act (see below). The Equal Pay Act specifies that men and women who are doing equal jobs must be paid the same wage. Equal jobs are jobs that demand equal effort, skill, and responsibility and that are performed under the same conditions. Differences in pay are legal if they can be attributed to differences in seniority, qualifications, or performance. However, women cannot be paid less (or more) for the same work solely because they are women.

Civil Rights Acts

Title VII of the Civil Rights Act of 1964 applies directly to selection and promotion. It forbids organizations with fifteen or more employees to discriminate in those areas on the basis of sex, race, color, religion, or national origin. The purpose of Title VII is to ensure that employers make personnel decisions on the basis of employee qualifications only. As a result of this act, discrimination in employment (especially against African Americans) has been reduced in this country.

The Equal Employment Opportunity Commission (EEOC) is charged with enforcing Title VII. A person who believes that he or she has been discriminated against can file a complaint with the EEOC. The EEOC investigates the complaint, and if it finds that the person has, in fact, been the victim of discrimination, the commission can take legal action on his or her behalf.

The Civil Rights Act of 1991 facilitates an employee's suing and collecting punitive damages for sexual discrimination. Discriminatory promotion and termination decisions as well as on-the-job issues, such as sexual harassment, are covered by this act.

Age Discrimination in Employment Act

The general purpose of this act, which was passed in 1967 and amended in 1986, is the same as that of Title VII—to eliminate discrimination. However, as the name implies, the Age Discrimination in Employment Act is concerned only with discrimination based on age. It applies to companies with twenty or more employees. In particular, it outlaws personnel practices that discriminate against people aged 40 or older. (No federal law forbids discrimination against people younger than age 40, but several states have adopted age discrimination laws that apply to a variety of age groups.) Also outlawed are company policies that specify a mandatory retirement age.

Occupational Safety and Health Act

Passed in 1970, this act is concerned mainly with issues of employee health and safety. For example, the act regulates the degree to which employees can be exposed to hazardous substances. It also specifies the safety equipment that the employer must provide.

Protecting workers.

This OSHA poster affirms the right of workers to a safe and healthful workplace. Employers are expected to post this sign in a location visible to employees.

Employee Retirement Income Security Act

This act was passed in 1974 to protect the retirement benefits of employees. It does not require that firms provide a retirement plan. However, it does specify that *if* a retirement plan is provided, it must be managed in such a way that the interests of employees are protected. It also provides federal insurance for retirement plans that go bankrupt.

Affirmative Action

Affirmative action is not one act but a series of executive orders issued by the president of the United States. These orders established the requirement for affirmative action in personnel practices. This stipulation applies to all employers with fifty or more employees holding federal contracts in excess of $50,000. It prescribes that such employers (1) actively encourage job applications from members of minority groups and (2) hire qualified employees from minority groups not fully represented in their organizations. Many firms that do not hold government contracts voluntarily take part in this affirmative action program.

Americans with Disabilities Act

The Americans with Disabilities Act (ADA) prohibits discrimination against qualified individuals with disabilities in all employment practices—including job-application procedures, hiring, firing, advancement, compensation, training, and other terms and conditions of employment. All private employers and government agencies with fifteen or more employees are covered by the ADA. Defining who is a qualified individual with a disability is, of course, difficult. Depending on how *qualified individual with a disability* is interpreted, up to forty-three million Americans can be included under this law. This law also mandates that all businesses that serve the public must make their facilities accessible to people with disabilities.

Not only are individuals with obvious physical disabilities protected under the ADA, but also safeguarded are those with less visible conditions such as heart disease, diabetes, epilepsy, cancer, AIDS, and emotional illnesses. Because of this law, many organizations no longer require job applicants to pass physical examinations as a condition of employment.

Employers are required to provide disabled employees with reasonable accommodation. *Reasonable accommodation* is any modification or adjustment to a job or work environment that will enable a qualified employee with a disability to perform a central job function. **EXAMPLE** Making existing facilities readily accessible to and usable by an individual confined to a wheelchair is a reasonable accommodation. Reasonable accommodation also might mean restructuring a job, modifying work schedules, acquiring or modifying equipment, providing qualified readers or inter-

Accommodation of Disabled Employees.

The Americans with Disabilities Act requires all employers to provide disabled employees with reasonable accommodation. This blind employee at Southern California Edison is permitted to have a guide dog accompany her at her work station.

TEST PREPPER (10.8)

True or False?

 1. The Age Discrimination in Employment Act particularly outlaws personnel practices that discriminate against people aged 40 or older.

Multiple Choice

 2. Larry was hurt while playing football in his senior year in high school. Since then, he has been confined to a wheel chair. After receiving his college diploma, he applied for a supervision job in a local warehouse. Under ADA, the employer must provide *reasonable accommodation* for disabled employees. Which activity will not legally cover Larry?

   a. Providing adequate home medical care
   b. Making existing facilities accessible
   c. Modifying work schedules
   d. Providing qualified readers
   e. Changing examinations

 3. What is the umbrella term for laws that are concerned with dealings between business firms and labor unions?

   a. Equal Pay Act
   b. National Labor Relations Act and Labor-Management Relations Act

   c. Fair Labor Standards Act
   d. Worker Adjustment and Retraining Notification (WARN) Act
   e. Fair Labor Standards Act

 4. Susan files a complaint against her employer with the EEOC on the charge of sexual harassment. Which of the following acts does the EEOC cover?

   a. The Age Discrimination in Employment Act of 1986
   b. Title VII of the Civil Rights Act of 1964
   c. The Employee Retirement Income Security Act
   d. The Occupational Safety and Health Act of 1970
   e. Equal Pay Act (1963)

 5. The legal order(s) that require employers in certain industries to actively encourage job applications from members of minority groups and hire qualified employees from minority groups not fully represented in their organizations is known as

   a. affirmative action.
   b. the ADA.
   c. the civil rights acts.
   d. fair labor standards.
   e. labor-management relations.

ACE the Test
ACE & ACE+
Practice Test 10.8

Prepare for Class
CL News Feeds
CL News Now

➲ RETURN TO INSIDE BUSINESS

Valero Energy Corporation prides itself on a culture of commitment and community involvement, a culture carried through by careful recruitment to find just the right person for each position. Because the energy industry can change quickly, Valero's human resources experts have developed computerized analytical tools to monitor key trends and project the company's future labor needs. This drastically reduces the time Valero needs to recruit and hire new employees, which has accelerated Valero's growth.

Attracting talented people and offering competitive compensation packages are only two aspects of Valero's effective management of human resources. Its top executives meet regularly with managers at different levels to discuss Valero's plans for profitable growth—based on their confidence in the work force as the company's most valuable asset.

Questions

1. Why is Valero so concerned about retaining the employees of the companies it acquires?
2. Explain how Valero's human resources activities reflect the CEO's statement that "The more you do for the employees, then the more they will do for the company."

LEARNING OBJECTIVES REVIEW

1 Describe the major components of human resources management.

- Human resources management (HRM) is the set of activities involved in acquiring, maintaining, and developing an organization's human resources.
- Responsibility for HRM is shared by specialized staff and line managers.
- HRM activities include human resources planning, job analysis, recruiting, selection, orientation, compensation, benefits, training and development, and performance appraisal.

2 Identify the steps in human resources planning.

- Human resources planning consists of forecasting the human resources that a firm will need and those that it will have available and then planning a course of action to match supply with demand.
- Layoffs, attrition, early retirement, and (as a last resort) firing are ways to reduce the size of the work force.
- Supply is increased through hiring.

3 Describe cultural diversity and understand some of the challenges and opportunities associated with it.

- Cultural diversity refers to the differences among people in a work force owing to race, ethnicity, and gender.
- With an increasing number of women, minorities, and immigrants entering the U.S. work force, management is faced with both challenges and competitive advantages.
- Organizations are implementing diversity-related training programs and working to make the most of cultural diversity.
- With the proper guidance and management, a culturally diverse organization can prove beneficial to all involved.

4 Explain the objectives and uses of job analysis.

- Job analysis provides a job description and a job specification for each position within a firm.
- A job description is a list of the elements that make up a particular job.
- A job specification is a list of qualifications required to perform a particular job.

- Job analysis is used in evaluation and in determining compensation levels and serves as the basis for recruiting and selecting new employees.

5 Describe the importance of recruiting, employee selection, and orientation in the acquisition phase of human resources management.

- Recruiting is the process of attracting qualified job applicants.
- Candidates for open positions may be recruited from within or outside a firm.
- In the selection process, information about candidates is obtained from applications, résumés, tests, interviews, references, or assessment centers. This information then is used to select the most appropriate candidate for the job.
- Newly hired employees then will go through a formal or informal orientation program to acquaint them with the firm.

6 Discuss the primary elements of employee compensation and benefits.

- Compensation is the payment employees receive in return for their labor.
- Management must decide on the firm's general wage level (relative to other firms), the wage structure within the firm, and individual wages. Wage surveys and job analyses are useful in making these decisions.
- Employees may be paid hourly wages, salaries, or commissions or receive incentive payments, lump-sum salary increases, or profit-sharing payments.
- Employee benefits, which are non-monetary rewards to employees, add about 28 percent to the cost of compensation.

7 Explain the purposes and techniques of employee training, development, and performance appraisal.

- Employee training and management-development programs enhance the ability of employees to contribute to a firm.
- Training is expensive, so an organization should evaluate the effectiveness of its training programs periodically.

- Performance appraisal, or evaluation, is used to provide employees with performance feedback, to serve as a basis for distributing rewards, and to monitor selection and training activities. Both objective and judgmental appraisal techniques are used.

8 **Outline the major legislation affecting human resources management.**

- A number of laws have been passed that affect HRM practices and that protect the rights and safety of employees. Some of these are
  - The National Labor Relations Act of 1935
  - The Labor-Management Relations Act of 1947

- The Fair Labor Standards Act of 1938
- The Equal Pay Act of 1963
- Title VII of the Civil Rights Act of 1964
- The Age Discrimination in Employment Acts of 1967 and 1986
- The Occupational Safety and Health Act of 1970
- The Employment Retirement Income Security Act of 1974
- The Worker Adjustment and Retraining Notification Act of 1988
- The Americans with Disabilities Act of 1990
- The Civil Rights Act of 1991
- The Family and Medical Leave Act of 1993

Improve Your Grade
Audio Chapter Review & Quiz

VIDEO CASE

People Make the Difference at the New England Aquarium

From porpoises and penguins to seals and sea turtles, the nonprofit New England Aquarium houses an incredibly diverse array of the world's sea life. The aquarium's official mission statement is "To present, promote, and protect the world of water." It also wants to appeal to the broadest possible audience and build a work force of paid and unpaid staff that reflects the diversity of the Boston community.

Volunteers are a major resource for the New England Aquarium. Its staff of 1,000 volunteers—one of the nonprofit world's largest—contributes 100,000 hours of service yearly. Many high school and college students volunteer to try out possible career choices. Adults with and without specialized college degrees (in fields such as marine biology and environmental affairs) volunteer their time as well. And the New England Aquarium's internships offer college students and recent graduates hands-on experience in veterinary services, communications, and other key areas.

Maureen C. Hentz, director of volunteer programs, is a champion of workplace diversity. Most organizations "are good at putting diversity in their mission statements and talking about it, but not actually accomplishing it," she observes. In contrast, she and her New England Aquarium colleagues aggressively reach out to recruit volunteers, interns, and employees of different races, ethnicities, socioeconomic levels, physical abilities, and ages. In addition, they welcome people of diverse educational backgrounds, personalities, and viewpoints because of the new ideas these differences can bring to the organization's opportunities and challenges.

One reason the New England Aquarium needs to constantly recruit and train new volunteers (and employees) is that it attracts more visitors every year. Also, like most nonprofits, the New England Aquarium has a very limited budget and must manage its payroll expenses carefully. Therefore, Hentz is always looking for volunteers to assist paid staff in various departments, including education, administration, and animal rescue.

The New England Aquarium must plan for employees, volunteers, or interns to handle certain tasks whenever the facility is open. For example, it needs cashiers to collect admission fees during daytime, evening, and weekend hours. Volunteers are often available to work during weekend hours, but filling daytime positions can be difficult. This is another reason why Hentz and her staff attend community meetings and find other ways to encourage volunteerism.

The web is an important and cost-effective recruiting tool for the New England Aquarium. Prospective volunteers can browse its website (**www.neaq.org**) to find open positions, read job descriptions and specifications, and download an application form to complete and submit. Hentz and her staff members read all the applications and ask those who seem the most qualified to come in for a personal interview. Once the final selections are made, volunteers are notified about their assignments and working hours. They receive training in the organization's procedures and learn their specific duties before they start their jobs.

Candidates for internships must send a letter expressing interest in working as an intern and include a résumé plus two academic or professional references. As an option, candidates can send a letter of reference and a college transcript to support the application letter. The New England Aquarium's internship coordinators interview the most promising candidates and make

the final selections. Interns, like volunteers, gain valuable experience and can list their New England Aquarium positions on their résumés when looking for future employment.

Paid employees receive a full package of valuable benefits, including paid holidays and sick days, insurance, and tuition reimbursement. Just as important, employees gain an opportunity to make a difference. When hired, they become part of an organization that protects the underwater environment, educates the public, and saves the lives of whales and other marine life.

For more information about this organization, go to **www .neaq.org**.[14]

Questions

1. Why would the New England Aquarium require people to apply in writing for unpaid volunteer and internship positions?
2. In addition to using the web and attending community meetings, what other external recruiting techniques would you suggest that Hentz use? Why?
3. Do you think that the New England Aquarium should evaluate the performance of its volunteers periodically? Support your answer.

BUILDING SKILLS FOR CAREER SUCCESS

1. Exploring the Internet

Although you may believe that your formal learning will end when you graduate and enter the working world, it won't. Companies both large and small spend billions of dollars annually on training employees and updating their knowledge and skills. Besides supporting employees who attend accredited continuing-education programs, companies also may provide more specialized in-house course work on new technologies, products, and markets for strategic planning. The Internet is an excellent search tool to find out about course work offered by private training organizations, as well as by traditional academic institutions. Learning online over the Internet is a fast-growing alternative, especially for busy employees requiring updates to skills in the information technology (IT) field, where software knowledge must be refreshed continuously. Visit the text website for updates to this exercise.

Assignment

1. Visit the websites of several academic institutions and examine their course work offerings. Also examine the offerings of some of the following private consulting firms:
   Learning Tree International: **www.learningtree.com**
   Accenture: **www.accenture.com**
   KPMG: **www.kpmg.com**
   Ernst & Young: **www.ey.com/global**
2. What professional continuing-education training and services are provided by one of the academic institutions whose site you visited?
3. What sort of training is offered by one of the preceding consulting firms?
4. From the company's point of view, what is the total real cost of a day's worth of employee training? What is the money value of one day of study for a full-time college student? Can you explain why firms are willing to pay higher starting salaries for employees with higher levels of education?

5. The American Society for Training and Development (**www.astd.org/**) and the Society for Human Resource Management (**www.shrm.org/**) are two good sources for information about online training programs. Describe what you found out at these and other sites providing online learning solutions.

2. Building Team Skills

The New Therapy Company is soliciting a contract to provide five nursing homes with physical, occupational, speech, and respiratory therapy. The therapists will float among the five nursing homes. The therapists have not yet been hired, but the nursing homes expect them to be fully trained and ready to go to work in three months. The previous therapy company lost its contract because of high staff turnover owing to "burnout" (a common problem in this type of work), high costs, and low-quality care. The nursing homes want a plan specifying how the New Therapy Company will meet staffing needs, keep costs low, and provide high-quality care.

Assignment

1. Working in a group, discuss how the New Therapy Company can meet the three-month deadline and still ensure that the care its therapists provide is of high quality. Also discuss the following:
   a. How many of each type of therapist will the company need?
   b. How will it prevent therapists from "burning out"?
   c. How can it retain experienced staff and still limit costs?
   d. Are promotions available for any of the staff? What is the career ladder?
   e. How will the company manage therapists at five different locations? How will it keep in touch with them (computer, voice mail, monthly meetings)? Would it make more sense to have therapists work permanently at each location rather than rotate among them?

f. How will the company justify the travel costs? What other expenses might it expect?

2. Prepare a plan for the New Therapy Company to present to the nursing homes.

3. Researching Different Careers

A résumé provides a summary of your skills, abilities, and achievements. It also may include a description of the type of job you want. A well-prepared résumé indicates that you know what your career objectives are, shows that you have given serious thought to your career, and tells a potential employer what you are qualified to do. The way a résumé is prepared can make a difference in whether you are considered for a job.

Assignment

1. Prepare a résumé for a job that you want.

   a. First, determine what your skills are and decide which skills are needed to do this particular job.

   b. Decide which type of format—chronological or functional—would be most effective in presenting your skills and experience.

   c. Keep the résumé to one page, if possible (definitely no more than two pages). (Note that portfolio items may be attached for certain types of jobs, such as artwork.)

2. Have several people review the résumé for accuracy.

3. Ask your instructor to comment on your résumé.

Prepare For Class
Exploring the Internet

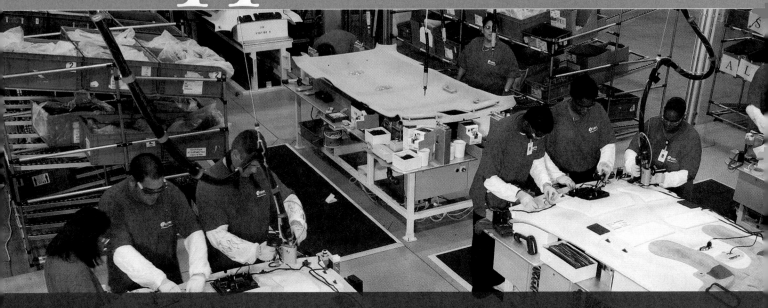

CHAPTER 11

Motivating and Satisfying Employees and Teams

Your Guide to Success in Business

Why this chapter matters

As you move up into management positions or operate your own business, you will need to understand what motivates others in an organization.

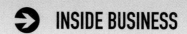

Genentech

It isn't the free cappuccino, Friday night "ho-ho" parties, onsite day care, or even the convenience of a company store that motivates Genentech's employees. What really excites them is Genentech's policy of hiring people with a passion for making a difference and allowing them the freedom to work on their own projects. Doing work that matters is Genentech's mission as it develops products to treat diseases such as cancer, asthma, and heart disease.

Founded in 1976, San Francisco–based Genentech has $6.6 billion in annual revenues and a work force of 9,500 people with a passion for saving lives through biotechnology. The company's spacious corporate campus is nestled alongside the Bay Area's top innovative companies, cutting-edge firms such as Google and Apple.

Genentech's prescription for employee satisfaction is a unique corporate culture in which milestones and successes are celebrated with parties and commemorative T-shirts. After six years on the job, each employee can apply for a six-week sabbatical, which helps to prevent burnout. To find just the right people for its nonhierarchical structure, the company has a stringent hiring process in which a candidate is interviewed as many as twenty times before the job is offered. Genentech retains and motivates its highly skilled personnel by encouraging scientists and engineers to devote at least 20 percent of their work week to pet projects.

For example, scientist Napoleone Ferrara came to Genentech to continue work on a special project that he had pursued for seventeen years—uncovering the key to blood vessel formation. His discovery, VEGF, allowed Genentech to develop an antibody that affects the blood supply to certain tumors. Now Ferrara's pet project has fueled the development of two important drugs for Genentech: Avastin for cancer treatment and Lucentis for age-related blindness. Because of the importance of innovative work such as that of Dr. Ferrara, Genentech's CEO reinvests 50 percent of the company's revenues into funding research. "At the end of the day we want to make drugs that really matter," the CEO explains.[1]

DID YOU KNOW?

"At the end of the day we want to make drugs that really matter," states Genentech's CEO.

• • •

KEY TERMS

motivation (332)
morale (332)
scientific management (333)
piece-rate system (334)
need (335)
Maslow's hierarchy of needs (335)
physiological needs (336)
safety needs (336)
social needs (337)
esteem needs (337)

self-actualization needs (338)
motivation-hygiene theory (338)
motivation factors (339)
hygiene factors (339)
Theory X (339)
Theory Y (339)
Theory Z (341)
reinforcement theory (342)
equity theory (343)
expectancy theory (344)

goal-setting theory (345)
management by objectives (MBO) (346)
job enrichment (347)
job enlargement (347)
job redesign (348)
behavior modification (348)
flextime (349)
part-time work (350)
job sharing (350)

telecommuting (350)
empowerment (351)
employee ownership (352)
team (353)
problem-solving team (354)
virtuoso team (354)
self-managed teams (354)
cross-functional team (354)
virtual team (355)

ACE the Test
Crossword Puzzle
Flashcards

To achieve its goals, any organization—whether it's Genentech, Four Seasons Hotels, Wegmans, or a local convenience store—must be sure that its employees have more than the right raw materials, adequate facilities, and equipment that works. The organization also must ensure that its employees are *motivated*. To some extent, a high level of employee motivation derives from effective management practices.

In this chapter

* We explain what motivation is.

* We present several views of motivation that have influenced management practices over the years: Taylor's ideas of scientific management, Mayo's Hawthorne studies, Maslow's hierarchy of needs, Herzberg's motivation-hygiene theory, McGregor's Theory X and Theory Y, Ouchi's Theory Z, and reinforcement theory.

* We examine contemporary ideas about motivation, including equity theory, expectancy theory, and goal-setting theory.

* We discuss specific techniques managers can use to foster employee motivation and satisfaction.

What Is Motivation?

Learning Objective ❶

Explain what motivation is.

motivation the individual internal process that energizes, directs, and sustains behavior; the personal "force" that causes you or me to behave in a particular way

morale an employee's attitude or feelings about his or her job, about superiors, and about the firm itself

A *motive* is something that causes a person to act. A successful athlete is said to be "highly motivated." A student who avoids work is said to be "unmotivated." We define **motivation** as the individual internal process that energizes, directs, and sustains behavior. **EXAMPLE** Job rotation may increase your job satisfaction and your enthusiasm for your work so that you devote more energy to it, but perhaps job rotation would not have the same impact on me.

Morale is an employee's attitude or feelings about his or her job, about superiors, and about the firm itself. To achieve organizational goals effectively, employees need more than the right raw materials, adequate facilities, and equipment that works. High morale results mainly from the satisfaction of needs on the job or as a result of the job. One need that might be satisfied on the job is the need *to be recognized* as an important contributor to the organization. A need satisfied as a result of the job is the need for *financial security*. High morale, in turn, leads to dedication and loyalty, as well as to the desire to do the job well. Low morale can lead to shoddy work, absenteeism, and high turnover rates as employees leave to seek more satisfying jobs with other firms. **EXAMPLE** A study conducted by the Society for Human Resource Management (SHRM) showed that 75 percent of all employees are actively or passively seeking new employment opportunities. To offset this turnover trend, companies are creating retention plans focused on employee morale.[2] Sometimes creative solutions are needed to motivate people and boost morale. This is especially true where barriers to change are deeply rooted in cultural stereotypes of the job and in the industry.

Motivation, morale, and the satisfaction of employees' needs thus are intertwined. Along with productivity, they have been the subject of much study since the end of the nineteenth century. Some landmarks of that early research are discussed in the next section.

Historical Perspectives on Motivation

Learning Objective ②

Understand the major theories of motivation and how they influence management practices.

Researchers often begin a study with a fairly narrow goal in mind. After they develop an understanding of their subject, however, they realize that both their goal and their research should be broadened. This is exactly what happened when early research into productivity blossomed into the more modern study of employee motivation. Some of the major historical theories are

* Scientific management
* The Hawthorne studies
* Maslow's hierarchy of needs
* Herzberg's motivation-hygiene theory
* Theory X and Theory Y
* Reinforcement theory

Scientific Management

Toward the end of the nineteenth century, Frederick W. Taylor became interested in improving the efficiency of individual workers. This interest stemmed from his own experiences in manufacturing plants. It eventually led to **scientific management,** the application of scientific principles to management of work and workers.

One of Taylor's first jobs was with the Midvale Steel Company in Philadelphia, where he developed a strong distaste for waste and inefficiency. He also observed a practice he called "soldiering." Workers "soldiered," or worked slowly, because they feared that if they worked faster, they would run out of work and lose their jobs. Taylor realized that

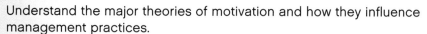

scientific management
the application of scientific principles to management of work and workers

◀

Motivating Employees.

Whether 100 years ago or today, employee motivation sometimes occurs through direct supervision.

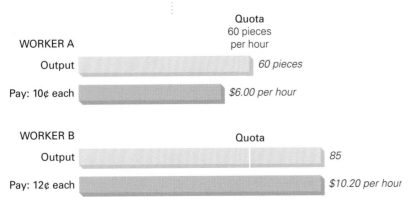

WORKER A

	Quota 60 pieces per hour
Output	60 pieces
Pay: 10¢ each	$6.00 per hour

WORKER B

	Quota
Output	85
Pay: 12¢ each	$10.20 per hour

FIGURE 11.1

Taylor's Piece-Rate System

Workers who exceeded their quota were rewarded by being paid at a higher rate per piece for all the pieces they produced.

piece-rate system a compensation system under which employees are paid a certain amount for each unit of output they produce

ACE the Test
Hangman

managers were not aware of this practice because they had no idea what the workers' productivity levels *should* be.

Later, at Bethlehem Steel, Taylor made his most significant contribution. In particular, he suggested that

* Each job should be broken down into separate tasks.
* Then management should determine
    * The best way to perform these tasks.
    * The job output to expect when the tasks were performed properly.
* Next, management should carefully choose the best person for each job and train that person to do the job properly.
* Finally, management should cooperate with workers to ensure that jobs are performed as planned.

Taylor also developed the idea that most people work only to earn money. He therefore reasoned that pay should be tied directly to output. The more a person produced, the more he or she should be paid. This gave rise to the **piece-rate system**, under which employees are paid a certain amount for each unit of output they produce. Under Taylor's piece-rate system, each employee was assigned an output quota. Those exceeding the quota were paid a higher per-unit rate for *all* units they produced (see Figure 11.1). Today, the piece-rate system is still used by some manufacturers and by farmers who grow crops that are harvested by farm laborers.

Taylor's revolutionary ideas had a profound impact on management practice. Ultimately, Taylor's view of motivation was recognized as overly simplistic and narrow. Simply increasing a person's pay may not increase that person's motivation or productivity.

The Hawthorne Studies

Between 1927 and 1932, Elton Mayo conducted two experiments at the Hawthorne plant of the Western Electric Company in Chicago. The original objective of these studies, now referred to as the *Hawthorne studies*, was to determine the effects of the work environment on employee productivity.

In the first set of experiments,

* Lighting in the workplace was varied for one group of workers but not for a second group.
* Productivity of both groups was measured to determine the effect of the light.
* Productivity increased for *both* groups.
* In the group whose lighting was varied, productivity remained high until the light was reduced to the level of moonlight!

In the second set of experiments,

* The focus was on the effectiveness of the piece-rate system in increasing the output of *groups* of workers.

* Researchers expected that output would increase because faster workers would put pressure on slower workers to produce more.

* Results were not as expected.

* Output remained constant no matter what "standard" rates management set.

Conclusions of the Hawthorne Studies

* *Human factors* were responsible for the results of the two experiments.

* In the lighting experiments, researchers had given both groups of workers a *sense of involvement* in their jobs merely by asking them to participate in the research.

* In the piece-rate experiments, each group of workers informally set the acceptable rate of output for the group. To gain or retain the *social acceptance* of the group, each worker had to produce at that rate. Slower or faster workers were pressured to maintain the group's pace.

* The Hawthorne studies showed that such human factors are at least as important to motivation as pay rates.

* From these and other studies, the *human relations movement* in management was born.

* Its premise was simple: Employees who are happy and satisfied with their work are motivated to perform better.

* Hence management would do best to provide a work environment that maximizes employee satisfaction.

Maslow's Hierarchy of Needs

Abraham Maslow, an American psychologist whose best-known works were published in the 1960s and 1970s, developed a theory of motivation based on a hierarchy of needs. A **need** is a personal requirement. Maslow assumed that humans are "wanting" beings who seek to fulfill a variety of needs. He observed that these needs can be arranged according to their importance in a sequence now known as **Maslow's hierarchy of needs** (see Figure 11.2).

At the most basic level are **physiological needs**, the things we require to survive. They include food and water, clothing, shelter, and sleep. In the employment context, these needs usually are satisfied through adequate wages.

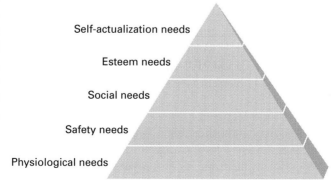

Self-actualization needs

Esteem needs

Social needs

Safety needs

Physiological needs

CONCEPT CHECK
How did the results of the Hawthorne Studies influence researchers' thinking about employee motivation?

need a personal requirement

Maslow's hierarchy of needs a sequence of human needs in the order of their importance

physiological needs the things we require for survival

FIGURE 11.2

Maslow's Hierarchy of Needs

Maslow believed that people act to fulfill five categories of needs.

—Examining ethicS—
Beware of the Yes Man

There's danger ahead when managers get out of touch with their employees, customers, or competitors. Most of the time, executives work hard to stay informed about employee concerns through site visits, work force surveys, and town hall meetings. Knowing that management is listening is a morale booster for employees as well.

But what should you do if some managers in your company prefer "yes men," people who simply agree with their bosses and conceal or minimize problems? Managers who don't want to hear the truth may steer the company in the wrong direction and, in the process, hurt employee motivation. So try these steps to get your boss to hear you out:

- Use logic and reasoning, stating and documenting the facts.
- Tactfully point out the implications of the situation.
- Explain why, in this instance, the boss's expectations might not be met.

Sources: Based on information from Carol Hymowitz, "Executives Who Build Truth-Telling Cultures Learn Fast What Works," *Wall Street Journal*, June 12, 2006, p. B1; Jared Sandberg, "How Do You Say No to a Yes Man? Often Unsuccessfully," *Wall Street Journal*, July 25, 2006, p. B1.

---

safety needs the things we require for physical and emotional security

At the next level are **safety needs**, the things we require for physical and emotional security. Safety needs may be satisfied through job security, health insurance, pension plans, and safe working conditions. During a time of falling corporate profits, many companies are facing increasing insurance premiums for employee health care. **EXAMPLE** Both General Electric (GE) and Hershey recently endured strikes centered on the issue of increased health care costs. Reduced health care coverage is a threat to employees' need for safety. Some companies are trying to find unique solutions. For example, SAS, a software company, maintains its own health care center that offers free physical examinations, emergency treatment, immunizations, and care for chronic illnesses.[3]

social needs the human requirements for love and affection and a sense of belonging

Next are the **social needs**, the human requirements for love and affection and a sense of belonging. To an extent, these needs can be satisfied through relationships in the work environment and the informal organization. However, social networks beyond the workplace—with family and friends, for example—usually are needed too. **EXAMPLE** Casino operator Isle of Capri Casinos, Inc., uses unique methods to help employees meet their social needs. The company holds an annual retreat for managers that is fun and exciting. The latest retreat was called "Isle Survive" and featured a *Survivor*-like game where employees were teamed up and given money and other resources and sent on a sort of scavenger hunt. This is just one of the ways Isle of Capri motivates its workers, and the company seems to be successful in meeting its employees' needs, as evidenced by the lowest employee turnover in the industry.[4]

At the level of **esteem needs** we require respect and recognition from others and a sense of our own accomplishment and worth (self-esteem). These needs may be satisfied through personal accomplishment, promotion to more responsible jobs, various honors and awards, and other forms of recognition.

At the top of the hierarchy are our **self-actualization needs**, the need to grow and develop and to become all that we are capable of being. These are the most difficult needs to satisfy, and the means of satisfying them tend to vary with the individual. For some people, learning a new skill, starting a new career after retirement, or becoming "the best there is" at some endeavor may be the way to realize self-actualization.

Esteem needs.

Employee recognition helps to satisfy esteem needs. Recognition of this type shows respect for an individual and his or her accomplishments.

Overview of Maslow's Hierarchy

* Maslow suggested that people work to satisfy their physiological needs first, then their safety needs, and so on up the "needs ladder."

* In general, they are motivated by the needs at the lowest level that remain unsatisfied.

* Needs at one level do not have to be satisfied completely before needs at the next-higher level come into play.

* If the majority of a person's physiological and safety needs are satisfied, that person will be motivated primarily by social needs. But any physiological and safety needs that remain unsatisfied also will be important.

* By and large, American business has been able to satisfy workers' basic needs, but the higher-order needs present more of a challenge. These needs are not satisfied in a simple manner, and the means of satisfaction vary from one employee to another.

esteem needs our need for respect, recognition, and a sense of our own accomplishment and worth

self-actualization needs the need to grow and develop and to become all that we are capable of being

Herzberg's Motivation-Hygiene Theory

In the late 1950s, Frederick Herzberg interviewed approximately two hundred accountants and engineers in Pittsburgh. During the interviews, he asked them to think of a time when they had felt especially good about their jobs and their work. Then he asked them to describe the factor or factors that had caused them to feel that way. Next, he did the same regarding a time when they had felt especially bad about their work. He was surprised to find that feeling good and feeling bad resulted from entirely different sets of factors; that is, low pay may have made a particular person feel bad, but it was not high pay that had made that person feel good. Instead, it was some completely different factor.

What motivates this team?

For many situations, more than one motivation theory can be used to explain what motivates people.

motivation-hygiene theory the idea that satisfaction and dissatisfaction are separate and distinct dimensions

motivation factors job factors that increase motivation but whose absence does not necessarily result in dissatisfaction

FIGURE 11.3

Herzberg's Motivation-Hygiene Theory

Herzberg's theory takes into account that there are different dimensions to job satisfaction and dissatisfaction and that these factors do not overlap.

Satisfaction and Dissatisfaction Before Herzberg's interviews, the general assumption was that employee satisfaction and dissatisfaction lay at opposite ends of the same scale. People felt satisfied, dissatisfied, or somewhere in between. But Herzberg's interviews convinced him that satisfaction and dissatisfaction may be different dimensions altogether. One dimension might range from satisfaction to no satisfaction, and the other might range from dissatisfaction to no dissatisfaction. In other words, the opposite of satisfaction is not dissatisfaction. The idea that satisfaction and dissatisfaction are separate and distinct dimensions is referred to as the **motivation-hygiene theory** (see Figure 11.3).

Job Factors Associated with Satisfaction

* Achievement
* Recognition
* Responsibility
* Advancement
* Growth
* The work itself

These factors generally are referred to as **motivation factors** because their presence increases motivation. When motivation factors are present, they act as *satisfiers*.

Job Factors Associated with Dissatisfaction

* Supervision
* Working conditions
* Interpersonal relationships

MOTIVATION FACTORS	HYGIENE FACTORS
• Achievement • Recognition • Responsibility • Advancement • Growth • The work itself	• Supervision • Working conditions • Interpersonal relationships • Pay • Job security • Company policies and administration
Satisfaction *No satisfaction*	*Dissatisfaction* *No dissatisfaction*

* Pay
* Job security
* Company policies and administration

These factors, called **hygiene factors**, reduce dissatisfaction when they are present to an acceptable degree. However, they do not necessarily result in high levels of motivation. When hygiene factors are absent, they act as *dissatisfiers*.

Managerial Application of Herzberg's Motivation-Hygiene Theory Herzberg provides explicit guidelines for using the motivation-hygiene theory of employee motivation. He suggests that

* Hygiene factors must be present to ensure that a worker can function comfortably.

* A state of *no dissatisfaction* never exists. In any situation, people always will be dissatisfied with something.

* Managers should make hygiene as positive as possible but then should expect only short-term, not long-term, improvement in motivation.

* Managers must focus on providing those motivation factors that presumably *will* enhance motivation and long-term effort.

* Pay provides only short-term change and not true motivation. In many organizations, pay constitutes a form of recognition and reward for achievement—and recognition and achievement are both motivation factors. If a pay increase does not depend on performance (as in across-the-board or cost-of-living raises), it may not motivate people. However, if pay is increased as a form of recognition (as in bonuses or incentives), it may play a powerful role in motivating employees to higher performance.

Theory X and Theory Y

The concepts of Theory X and Theory Y were advanced by Douglas McGregor in his book, *The Human Side of Enterprise.*[5] They are, in essence, sets of assumptions that underlie management's attitudes and beliefs regarding worker behavior.

Theory X is a concept of employee motivation generally consistent with Taylor's scientific management. Theory X assumes that employees dislike work and will function effectively only in a highly controlled work environment. According to Theory X,

1. People dislike work and try to avoid it.
2. Because people dislike work, managers must coerce, control, and frequently threaten employees to achieve organizational goals.
3. People generally must be led because they have little ambition and will not seek responsibility; they are concerned mainly with security.

The logical outcome of such assumptions will be a highly controlled work environment—one in which managers make all the decisions and employees take all the orders.

On the other hand, **Theory Y** is a concept of employee motivation generally consistent with the ideas of the human relations movement. Theory Y assumes that employees

hygiene factors job factors that reduce dissatisfaction when present to an acceptable degree but that do not necessarily result in high levels of motivation

Theory X a concept of employee motivation generally consistent with Taylor's scientific management; assumes that employees dislike work and will function only in a highly controlled work environment

Theory Y a concept of employee motivation generally consistent with the ideas of the human relations movement; assumes that employees accept responsibility and work toward organizational goals if by so doing they also achieve personal rewards

accept responsibility and work toward organizational goals if by so doing they also achieve personal rewards. According to Theory Y,

1. People do not naturally dislike work; in fact, work is an important part of their lives.
2. People will work toward goals to which they are committed.
3. People become committed to goals when it is clear that accomplishing the goals will bring personal rewards.
4. People often seek out and willingly accept responsibility.
5. Employees have the potential to help accomplish organizational goals.
6. Organizations generally do not make full use of their human resources.

Obviously, this view is quite different from—and much more positive than—that of Theory X. McGregor argued that most managers behave in accordance with Theory X. But he maintained that Theory Y is more appropriate and effective as a guide for managerial action (see Table 11.1).

TABLE 11.1

Theory X and Theory Y Contrasted

AREA	THEORY X	THEORY Y
Attitude toward work	Dislike	Involvement
Control systems	External	Internal
Supervision	Direct	Indirect
Level of commitment	Low	High
Employee potential	Ignored	Identified
Use of human resources	Limited	Not limited

The human relations movement and Theories X and Y increased managers' awareness of the importance of social factors in the workplace. A number of factors must be considered in any attempt to increase motivation.

Theory Z

William Ouchi, a management professor at UCLA, studied business practices in American and Japanese firms. He concluded that different types of management systems dominate in these two countries.[6] In Japan, Ouchi found what he calls "type J" firms.

Characteristics of Type J Firms

* Lifetime employment for employees
* Collective (or group) decision making
* Collective responsibility for the outcomes of decisions
* Slow evaluation and promotion
* Implied control mechanisms
* Nonspecialized career paths
* A holistic concern for employees as people

American industry is dominated by what Ouchi calls "type A" firms, which follow a different pattern.

Characteristics of Type A Firms

* Emphasis on short-term employment
* Individual decision making
* Individual responsibility for the outcomes of decisions
* Rapid evaluation and promotion
* Explicit control mechanisms
* Specialized career paths
* A segmented concern for employees only as employees

A few very successful American firms represent a blend of the type J and type A patterns. These firms, called "type Z" organizations, blend the two points of view.

Characteristics of Type Z Firms

* Emphasis on long-term employment
* Collective decision making
* Individual responsibility for the outcomes of decisions
* Slow evaluation and promotion
* Informal control along with some formalized measures
* Moderately specialized career paths
* A holistic concern for employees

Ouchi's **Theory Z** is the belief that some middle ground between his type A and type J practices is best for American business (see Figure 11.4). A major part of Theory Z is the emphasis on participative decision making. The focus is on "we" rather than on "us versus them." Theory Z employees and managers view the organization as a family. This participative spirit fosters cooperation and the dissemination of information and organizational values.

Theory Z the belief that some middle ground between Ouchi's type A and type J practices is best for American business

FIGURE 11.4

The Features of Theory Z

The best aspects of Japanese and American management theories are combined to form the nucleus of Theory Z.

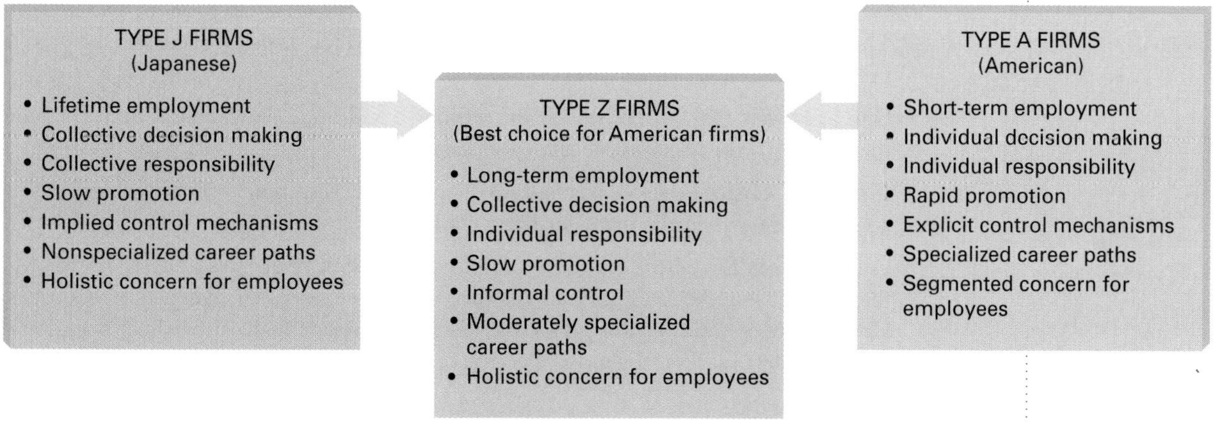

TYPE J FIRMS
(Japanese)

* Lifetime employment
* Collective decision making
* Collective responsibility
* Slow promotion
* Implied control mechanisms
* Nonspecialized career paths
* Holistic concern for employees

TYPE Z FIRMS
(Best choice for American firms)

* Long-term employment
* Collective decision making
* Individual responsibility
* Slow promotion
* Informal control
* Moderately specialized career paths
* Holistic concern for employees

TYPE A FIRMS
(American)

* Short-term employment
* Individual decision making
* Individual responsibility
* Rapid promotion
* Explicit control mechanisms
* Specialized career paths
* Segmented concern for employees

Reinforcement Theory

Reinforcement theory is based on the premise that behavior that is rewarded is likely to be repeated, whereas behavior that is punished is less likely to recur. A *reinforcement* is an action that follows directly from a particular behavior. It may be a pay raise following a particularly large sale to a new customer or a reprimand for coming to work late.

Reinforcements can take a variety of forms and can be used in a number of ways. A *positive reinforcement* is one that strengthens desired behavior by providing a reward. **EXAMPLE** For example, many employees respond well to praise; recognition from their supervisors for a job well done increases (strengthens) their willingness to perform well in the future. A *negative reinforcement* strengthens desired behavior by eliminating an undesirable task or situation. **EXAMPLE** Suppose that a machine shop must be cleaned thoroughly every month—a dirty, miserable task. During one particular month when the workers do a less-than-satisfactory job at their normal work assignments, the boss requires the workers to clean the factory rather than bringing in the usual private maintenance service. The employees will be motivated to work harder the next month to avoid the unpleasant cleanup duty again.

Punishment is an undesired consequence of undesirable behavior. Common forms of punishment used in organizations include reprimands, reduced pay, disciplinary layoffs, and termination (firing). Punishment often does more harm than good. It tends to create an unpleasant environment, fosters hostility and resentment, and suppresses undesirable behavior only until the supervisor's back is turned.

Managers who rely on *extinction* hope to eliminate undesirable behavior by not responding to it. The idea is that the behavior eventually will become "extinct." **EXAMPLE** Suppose that an employee has a habit of writing memo after memo to his or her manager about insignificant events. If the manager does not respond to any of these memos, the employee probably will stop writing them, and the behavior will have been squelched.

Conclusions on Reinforcement Theory

* The effectiveness of reinforcement depends on which type is used and how it is timed.

* One approach may work best under certain conditions, but some situations lend themselves to the use of more than one approach.

* Generally, positive reinforcement is considered the most effective, and it is recommended when the manager has a choice.

* Continual reinforcement can become tedious for both managers and employees. At the start, it may be necessary to reinforce a desired behavior every time it occurs. However, once a desired behavior has become more or less established, occasional reinforcement seems to be most effective.

---

reinforcement theory
a theory of motivation based on the premise that behavior that is rewarded is likely to be repeated, whereas behavior that is punished is less likely to recur

---

CONCEPT CHECK

What is the fundamental premise of reinforcement theory?

TEST PREPPER 11.1 11.2

True or False?

_F_ 1. Morale is defined as the individual internal process that energizes, directs, and sustains behavior.

_F_ 2. Maslow's higher-level needs are the easiest to satisfy.

_T_ 3. The Hawthorne studies concluded that human factors were responsible for the results.

Multiple Choice

_E_ 4. According to Theory Y, which of the following behaviors would a supervisor expect from an employee?

a. Delegates most of the work to others
b. Avoids working too hard
c. Spends time discussing job security
d. Asks to leave early several times a month
e. Seeks opportunities to learn new skills

_D_ 5. The idea that satisfaction and dissatisfaction are separate and distinct dimensions comes from which of the following theories?

a. Maslow's hierarchy of needs
b. Frederick Taylor's scientific management
c. Reinforcement theory
d. Frederick Herzberg's motivation-hygiene theory
e. Hawthorne studies

ACE the Test
ACE & ACE+
Practice Tests 11.1, 11.2

Contemporary Views on Motivation

Learning Objective 3

Describe the three views of why and how motivation works: equity theory, expectancy theory, and goal-setting theory.

Maslow's hierarchy of needs and Herzberg's motivation-hygiene theory attempt to specify *what* motivates people, but neither explains *why* or *how* motivation develops or is sustained over time. In recent years, managers have begun to explore three other models that take a more dynamic view of motivation. These are equity theory, expectancy theory, and goal-setting theory.

equity theory a theory of motivation based on the premise that people are motivated to obtain and preserve equitable treatment for themselves

Equity Theory

The **equity theory** of motivation is based on the premise that people are motivated to obtain and preserve equitable treatment for themselves. As used here, *equity is the distribution of rewards in direct proportion to the contribution of each employee to the organization.* Everyone need not receive the *same* rewards, but the rewards should be in accordance with individual contributions.

According to this theory, we tend to implement the idea of equity in the following ways:

* First, we develop our own input-to-outcome ratio. *Inputs* are the time, effort, skills, education, experience, and so on that we contribute to the organization. *Outcomes* are the rewards we get from the organization, such as pay, benefits, recognition, and promotions.

* Next, we compare this ratio with what we perceive as the input-to-outcome ratio for some other person. It might be a coworker, a friend who works for another firm, or even an average of all the people in our organization. This person is called

the *comparison other.* Note that our perception of this person's input-to-outcome ratio may be absolutely correct or completely wrong. However, we believe that it is correct.

* If the two ratios are roughly the same, we feel that the organization is treating us equitably. In this case we are motivated to leave things as they are. However, if our ratio is the higher of the two, we feel under-rewarded and are motivated to make changes.

* We may (1) decrease our own inputs by not working so hard, (2) try to increase our total outcome by asking for a raise in pay, (3) try to get the comparison other to increase some inputs or receive decreased outcomes, (4) leave the work situation, or (5) do a new comparison with a different comparison other.

* Equity theory is most relevant to pay as an outcome.

* Managers can try to avoid problems arising from inequity by making sure that rewards are distributed on the basis of performance and that everyone clearly understands the basis for his or her own pay.

Expectancy Theory

expectancy theory a model of motivation based on the assumption that motivation depends on how much we want something and on how likely we think we are to get it

Expectancy theory, developed by Victor Vroom, is a very complex model of motivation based on a deceptively simple assumption. According to expectancy theory, motivation depends on how much we want something and on how likely we think we are to get it (see Figure 11.5). **EXAMPLE** Consider the case of three sales representatives who are candidates for promotion to one sales manager's job. Bill has had a very good sales year and always gets good performance evaluations. However, he isn't sure that he wants the job because it involves a great deal of travel, long working hours, and much stress and pressure. Paul wants the job badly but doesn't think he has much chance of getting it. He has had a terrible sales year and gets only mediocre performance evaluations from his present boss. Susan wants the job as much as Paul, and she thinks that she has a pretty good shot at it. Her sales have improved significantly this past year, and her evaluations are the best in the company.

Expectancy theory would predict that Bill and Paul are not very motivated to seek the promotion. Bill doesn't really want it, and Paul doesn't think that he has much of a chance of getting it. Susan, however, is very motivated to seek the promotion because she wants it *and* thinks that she can get it.

CONCEPT CHECK

According to expectancy theory, what two variables determine motivation?

Expectancy theory is complex because each action we take is likely to lead to several different outcomes; some we may want, and others we may not want. For example, a person who works hard and puts in many extra hours may get a pay raise, be promoted, and gain valuable new job skills. However, that person also may be forced to spend less time with his or her family and be forced to cut back on his or her social life.

FIGURE 11.5

Expectancy Theory

Vroom's theory is based on the idea that motivation depends on how much people want something and on how likely they think they are to get it.

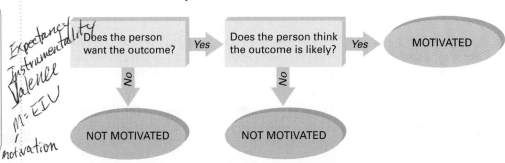

For one person, the promotion may be paramount, the pay raise and new skills fairly important, and the loss of family and social life of negligible importance. For someone else, the family and social life may be most important, the pay raise of moderate importance, the new skills unimportant, and the promotion undesirable because of the additional hours it would require. The first person would be motivated to work hard and put in the extra hours, whereas the second person would not be at all motivated to do so. In other words, it is the entire bundle of outcomes—and the individual's evaluation of the importance of each outcome—that determines motivation.

Expectancy theory is difficult to apply, but it does provide several useful guidelines for managers. It suggests that managers must recognize that

1. Employees work for a variety of reasons.
2. These reasons, or expected outcomes, may change over time.
3. It is necessary to clearly show employees how they can attain the outcomes they desire.

Goal-Setting Theory

Goal-setting theory suggests that employees are motivated to achieve goals that they and their managers establish together.

Attributes of the Goal-Setting Theory

* The goal should be very specific, moderately difficult, and one the employee will be committed to achieve.[7]

* Rewards should be tied directly to goal achievement.

* Using goal-setting theory, a manager can design rewards that fit employee needs, clarify expectations, maintain equity, and provide reinforcement.

* A major benefit of this theory is that it provides a good understanding of the goal the employee is to achieve and the rewards that will accrue to the employee if the goal is accomplished.

goal-setting theory a theory of motivation suggesting that employees are motivated to achieve goals that they and their managers establish together

ACE the Test
ACE & ACE+
Practice Test 11.3

TEST PREPPER 11.3

True or False?

___ 1. According to the equity theory, everyone need not receive the same rewards, but the rewards should be in accordance with individual contributions.

___ 2. According to the goal-setting theory, the goal should be very specific, moderately difficult, and one the employee will be committed to achieve.

___ 3. Expectancy theory is complex because each action we take is likely to lead to several different outcomes.

Multiple Choice

___ 4. Developing an input-to-output ratio is the basis of the _____ theory.

a. equity
b. expectancy
c. reward
d. reinforcement
e. quality circle

___ 5. Expectancy theory is difficult to apply, but it does provide several useful guidelines for managers. One such outcome that managers must realize is that

a. everyone expects the same things.
b. employees expect to be financially rewarded for hard work.
c. employees work for a variety of reasons.
d. most employees tend to be unreasonable in their expectations.
e. managers need to use the authoritarian style to get tasks accomplished.

Key Motivation Techniques

Learning Objective ❹

Explain several techniques for increasing employee motivation.

Today, it takes more than a generous salary to motivate employees. Increasingly, companies are trying to provide motivation by satisfying employees' less tangible needs. In this section we discuss several specific—and somewhat more orthodox—techniques that help managers to boost employee motivation and job satisfaction.

Management by Objectives

Management by objectives (MBO) is a motivation technique in which managers and employees collaborate in setting goals. The primary purpose of MBO is to clarify the roles employees are expected to play in reaching the organization's goals. **EXAMPLE** Daymark Solutions has put MBO to use by establishing short-term goals for every employee. These quarterly objectives may be achieving a high level of customer satisfaction or receiving specific certifications. These smaller goals correlate directly with the larger company objectives, such as cost containment or revenue goals.[8] By allowing individuals to participate in goal setting and performance evaluation, MBO increases their motivation. Most MBO programs consist of a series of five steps.

management by objectives (MBO) a motivation technique in which managers and employees collaborate in setting goals

Five Steps Involved in Developing MBO

1. The first step in setting up an MBO program is to secure the acceptance of top management.
2. Next, preliminary goals must be established. Top management also plays a major role in this activity because the preliminary goals reflect the firm's mission and strategy. The intent of an MBO program is to have these goals filter down through the organization.
3. The third step, which actually consists of several smaller steps, is the heart of MBO:
   * The manager explains to each employee that he or she has accepted certain goals for the group (the manager as well as the employees) and asks the individual to think about how he or she can help to achieve these goals.
   * The manager later meets with each employee individually. Together they establish goals for the employee. Whenever possible, the goals should be measurable and should specify the time frame for completion (usually one year).
   * The manager and the employee decide what resources the employee will need to accomplish his or her goals.
4. In the fourth step, the manager and each employee meet periodically to review the employee's progress. They may agree to modify certain goals during these meetings if circumstances have changed.

5. The fifth step is evaluation. At the end of the designated time period, the manager and each employee meet again to determine which of the individual's goals were met, which were not met, and why. The employee's reward (in the form of a pay raise, praise, or promotion) is based primarily on the degree of goal attainment.

Advantages of MBO

* MBO can motivate employees by involving them actively in the life of the firm.
* The collaboration on goal setting and performance appraisal improves communication and makes employees feel that they are an important part of the organization.
* Periodic review of progress also enhances control within an organization.

Disadvantages of MBO

* A major problem with MBO is that it does not work unless the process begins at the top of an organization.
* A manager may not like sitting down and working out goals with subordinates and may instead just assign them goals.
* MBO programs prove difficult to implement unless goals are quantifiable.

Job Enrichment

job enrichment a motivation technique that provides employees with more variety and responsibility in their jobs

job enlargement expanding a worker's assignments to include additional but similar tasks

Job enrichment is a method of motivating employees by providing them with variety in their tasks while giving them some responsibility for and control over their jobs. At the same time, employees gain new skills and acquire a broader perspective about how their individual work contributes to the goals of the organization. **EXAMPLE** Employees at 3M get to spend 15 percent of their time at work on whatever projects they choose regardless of the relationship of these "pet projects" to the employees' regular duties. This type of enrichment can motivate employees and create a variety of benefits for the company.[9] At times, **job enlargement**, expanding a worker's assignments to include additional but similar tasks, can lead to job enrichment. Job enlargement might mean that a worker on an assembly line who used to connect three wires to components moving down the line now connects five wires. Unfortunately, the added tasks often are just as routine as those the worker performed before the change. In such cases, enlargement may not be effective.

Why Job Enrichment Works

* It provides workers with both more tasks to do and more control over how they perform them. In particular, job enrichment removes many controls from jobs, gives workers more authority, and assigns work in complete, natural units.

Job enrichment.

Employees at this New Balance plant are enrolled in a job enrichment program. Each person on this work team has been cross-trained to do other team members' jobs.

* Employees frequently are given fresh and challenging job assignments.

* By blending more planning and decision making into jobs, job enrichment gives work more depth and complexity.

job redesign a type of job enrichment in which work is restructured to cultivate the worker-job match

Job redesign is a type of job enrichment in which work is restructured in ways that cultivate the worker-job match. Job redesign can be achieved by combining tasks, forming work groups, or establishing closer customer relationships.

Why Job Redesign Works

* Employees often are more motivated when jobs are combined because the increased variety of tasks presents more challenge and therefore more reward.

* Work groups motivate employees by showing them how their jobs fit within the organization as a whole and how they contribute to its success.

* Establishing client relationships allows employees to interact directly with customers.

* Not only does this type of redesign add a personal dimension to employment, but it also provides workers with immediate and relevant feedback about how they are doing their jobs.

Critical Analysis of Job Enrichment as a Motivational Technique

* Job enrichment works best when employees seek more challenging work. Employees must desire personal growth and have the skills and knowledge to perform enriched jobs. Lack of self-confidence, fear of failure, or distrust of management's intentions are likely to lead to ineffective performance on enriched jobs.

* Some workers do not view their jobs as routine and boring, and others even prefer routine jobs because they find them satisfying.

* Companies that use job enrichment as an alternative to specialization also face extra expenses, such as the cost of retraining.

behavior modification a systematic program of reinforcement to encourage desirable behavior

* A job redesign that carefully matches worker to job can prevent stress-related injuries, which constitute about 60 to 80 percent of all work-related injuries. The reduced stress also creates greater motivation.[10]

Behavior Modification

Behavior modification is a systematic program of reinforcement to encourage desirable behavior. Behavior modification involves both rewards to encourage desirable actions and punishments to discourage undesirable actions. However, studies have shown that rewards, such as compliments and expressions of appreciation, are much more effective behavior modifiers than punishments, such as reprimands and scorn.

When applied to management, behavior modification strives to encourage desirable organizational behavior. Use of this technique begins with identification of a *target behavior*—the behavior that is to be changed. (It might be low production levels or a high rate of absenteeism, for example.) Existing levels of this behavior then are

SP⊙TLIGHT

Causes of job stress

Seven out of ten employees say they feel "moderate" to "great" stress on the job.

Demands of the job — 54%

Co-workers — 20%

The boss — 10%

Layoff fears — 8%

The four top causes of stress

Source: *USA Today*, October 29, 2002, p. A1.

measured. Next, managers provide positive reinforcement in the form of a reward when employees exhibit the *desired behavior* (such as increased production or less absenteeism). The reward might be praise or a more tangible form of recognition, such as a gift, meal, or trip. Finally, the levels of the target behavior are measured again to determine whether the desired changes have been achieved. If they have, the reinforcement is maintained. However, if the target behavior has not changed significantly in the desired direction, the reward system must be changed to one that is likely to be more effective. John Kotter, a renowned Harvard Business School professor, states that this is difficult because the kind of emotional persuasion needed for these changes is not taught in business schools and is not often properly considered in many business settings.[11]

Flextime

To most people, a work schedule means the standard nine-to-five, forty-hour work-week. In reality, though, many people have work schedules that are quite different from this. Police officers, firefighters, restaurant personnel, airline employees, and medical personnel usually have work schedules that are far from standard. Some manufacturers also rotate personnel from shift to shift. And many professional people—such as managers, artists, and lawyers—need more than forty hours each week to get their work done.

Flextime is a system in which employees set their own work hours within certain limits determined by employers. Typically, the firm establishes two bands of time: the *core time*, when all employees must be at work, and the *flexible time*, when employees may choose whether to be at work. The only condition is that every employee must work a total of eight hours each day. For example, the hours between 9 and 11 a.m. and 1 and 3 p.m. might be core time, and the hours between 6 and 9 a.m., between 11 a.m. and 1 p.m., and between 3 and 6 p.m. might be flexible time. This would give employees the option of coming in early and getting off early, coming in later and leaving later, or taking an extralong lunch break. But flextime also ensures that everyone is present at certain times, when conferences with supervisors and department meetings can be scheduled. Another type of flextime allows employees to work a forty-hour work week in four days instead of five. Workers who put in ten hours a day instead of eight get an extra day off each week. According to a survey conducted by the Society for Human Resource Management, approximately 56 percent of firms offer flextime.[12] At times, smaller firms use flextime to attract and retain employees, especially when they cannot match the salaries and benefit package provided by larger companies. **EXAMPLE** Independent accounting firm Jefferson Wells uses flexible schedules as an incentive when recruiting high-quality candidates. By offering a customized work schedule and part-time positions with full-time benefits, the firm is able to remain competitive with larger companies.[13]

flextime a system in which employees set their own work hours within employer-determined limits

Advantages and Disadvantages of Flextime

* The sense of independence and autonomy employees gain from having a say in what hours they work can be a motivating factor.

* Employees who have enough time to deal with nonwork issues often work more productively and with greater satisfaction when they are on the job. Approximately

29 percent of U.S. workers participate in determining their own work schedules, thus experiencing some form of flextime.[14]

* Two common problems associated with using flextime are (1) supervisors sometimes find their jobs complicated by having employees who come and go at different times, and (2) employees without flextime sometimes resent coworkers who have it.

Part-Time Work and Job Sharing

Part-time work is permanent employment in which individuals work less than a standard work week. The specific number of hours worked varies, but part-time jobs are structured so that all responsibilities can be completed in the number of hours an employee works. Part-time work is of special interest to parents who want more time with their children and people who simply desire more leisure time. One disadvantage of part-time work is that it often does not provide the benefits that come with a full-time position. **EXAMPLE** This is not, however, the case at Starbucks, where approximately 80 percent of its employees work part time. Starbucks does not treat its part-time employees any differently from its full-time employees; all receive the same access to numerous benefits, which even include a free pound of coffee every week.[15]

part-time work permanent employment in which individuals work less than a standard work week

Part-time work.

At Starbucks, part-time employees receive the same level of benefits as full-time employees.

Job sharing (sometimes referred to as *work sharing*) is an arrangement whereby two people share one full-time position. One job sharer may work from 8 a.m. to noon, and the other may work from 1 to 5 p.m., or they may alternate work days. **EXAMPLE** At the BBC, two women share the same job. By communicating daily through telephone, voice mail, and fax machines, these announcers are able to handle a challenging administrative position and still have time for their families. Through their partnership at work, they have been able to share a position for more than six years.[16] Job sharing combines the security of a full-time position with the flexibility of a part-time job. Among the "100 Best Companies for Working Mothers," ninety-four offer job sharing because it allows these companies to retain highly talented professionals.[17]

Advantages and Disadvantages of Job Sharing

* For firms, job sharing provides a unique opportunity to attract highly skilled employees who might not be available on a full-time basis.

* Companies can save on expenses by reducing the cost of benefits and avoiding the disruptions of employee turnover.

* For employees, opting for the flexibility of job sharing may mean giving up some of the benefits received for full-time work.

* Job sharing is difficult if tasks are not easily divisible or if two people do not work or communicate well with each other.

job sharing an arrangement whereby two people share one full-time position

telecommuting working at home all the time or for a portion of the work week

Telecommuting

A growing number of companies allow **telecommuting**, working at home all the time or for a portion of the work week. Personal computers, modems, fax machines, voice mail, cellular phones, and overnight couriers all facilitate the work-at-home trend. Working at home means that individuals can set their own hours and have more time with their families. Even the federal government is recognizing the benefits of telecommuting in that 90 percent of the U.S. Treasury Inspector General for Tax Administration (TIGTA) workers and over 100 lawyers for the U.S. Trademark Office telecommute at least three days a week.[18]

Advantages and Disadvantages of Telecommuting

* Companies that allow telecommuting experience several benefits, including increased productivity, lower real estate and travel costs, reduced employee absenteeism and turnover, increased work/life balance and improved morale, and access to additional labor pools.

* Pitney Bowes reports that an additional benefit gained when employees work from home is the company's image as a good corporate citizen because the program helps to decrease pollution and traffic congestion.[19]

* Disadvantages to telecommuting are feelings of isolation, putting in longer hours, and being distracted by family or household responsibilities.

* Some supervisors have difficulty monitoring productivity. Although most bosses say that they trust their staff to work from home, many think that home workers are work-shy and less productive than office-based staff. A survey conducted in the United Kingdom found that up to 38 percent of managers surveyed believe that home workers are less productive, and 22 percent think that working from home is an excuse for time off.[20]

Employee Empowerment

Many companies are increasing employee motivation and satisfaction through the use of empowerment. **Empowerment** means making employees more involved in their jobs and in the operations of the organization by increasing their participation in decision making. With empowerment, control no longer flows exclusively from the top levels of the organization downward. Empowered employees have a voice in what they do and how and when they do it. **EXAMPLE** At Wegmans grocery stores, employees are empowered to ensure that the store achieves its primary objective: "No customer leaves unhappy." Employees are allowed to make any concessions or decisions necessary to provide a good shopping experience. Anything is possible—from baking a family's Thanksgiving turkey in the store's oven to traveling to a customer's home to fix a botched order. Not only are Wegmans employees empowered to make on-the-spot customer-service decisions, but they also receive extensive training in the products they sell so as to guarantee that they can answer customers' questions about recipes, exotic items, and even food preparation.[21]

For empowerment to work effectively, management must be involved. Managers should set expectations, communicate standards, institute periodic evaluations, and guarantee follow-up. Effectively implemented, empowerment can lead to increased job satisfaction, improved job performance, higher-self esteem, and increased organizational commitment. Obstacles to empowerment include resistance on the part of management, distrust of management on the part of workers, insufficient training, and poor communication between management and employees.

Prepare for Class
Career Snapshot

empowerment making employees more involved in their jobs by increasing their participation in decision making

CONCEPT CHECK

What combination of motivational techniques do you think would result in the best overall motivation and reward system?

Employee Ownership

employee ownership
a situation in which employees own the company they work for by virtue of being stockholders

Some organizations are discovering that a highly effective technique for motivating employees is **employee ownership**— that is, employees own the company they work for by virtue of being stockholders. Employee-owned businesses reward employees directly for success. When the company enjoys increased sales or lower costs, employees benefit directly. The National Center for Employee Ownership, an organization that studies employee-owned American businesses, reports that employee stock ownership plans (ESOPs) provide considerable employee incentive and increase employee involvement and commitment. In the United States today, about 8.5 million employees participate in 11,500 ESOPs and stock bonus plans.[22] As a means to motivate top executives and, frequently, middle-ranking managers who are working long days for what are generally considered poor salaries, some firms provide stock options as part of the employee compensation package. The option is simply the right to buy shares of the firm within a prescribed time at a set price. If the firm does well and its stock price rises past the set price (presumably because of all the work being done by the employee), the employee can exercise the option and immediately sell the stock and cash in on the company's success.

The difficulties of such companies as United Airlines have damaged the idea of employee ownership. United's ESOP has failed to solve problems between employees and management. In addition, Lowe's, the home-improvement retailer, recently stopped its long-running and mostly successful ESOP and transferred remaining money into 401(k) plans.[23]

TEST PREPPER 11.4

True or False?

 1. The primary purpose of MBO is to clarify the roles employees are expected to play in reaching the organization's goals.

 2. Studies have shown that rewards, such as compliments and expressions of appreciation, are less effective behavior modifiers than punishments, such as reprimands and scorn.

 3. In the United States today, about 8.5 million employees participate in 11,500 ESOPs and stock bonus plans.

Multiple Choice

 4. Which of the following is a motivation technique that provides employees with more variety and responsibility in their jobs?

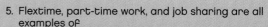

a. Job rotation
b. Job enrichment
c. Job redesign
d. Flextime
e. Telecommuting

5. Flextime, part-time work, and job sharing are all examples of
   a. different work schedules that are being demanded by employees.
   b. unsuccessful work arrangements.
   c. motivational techniques applied by firms.
   d. work schedules used mostly in large firms.
   e. work schedules used mostly by multinational firms.

ACE the Test
ACE & ACE+
Practice Test 11.4

Teams and Teamwork

Learning Objective ⑤
Understand the types, development, and uses of teams.

The concepts of teams and teamwork may be most commonly associated with sports, but they also are integral parts of business organizations. This organizational structure is popular because it encourages employees to participate more fully in business decisions.

America Funds has been using the team structure since 1958. This mutual fund company employs a team of managers and a team of analysts that each handles a portion of the fund's investments. This approach prevents egotism and fad stocks from damaging a fund's performance.[24]

Your Career

Go To the Head of the Team

Do you have what it takes to be a team leader? To assume a leadership role in a teamwork situation, you should be able to

- Influence and inspire your team members
- Build trust and a sense of purpose
- Communicate clearly and facilitate discussion
- Help members to achieve consensus
- Set goals and respect deadlines
- Lead by example

Search firm executive Anthony Palumbo has an unusual way of leading by example and inspiring his employees. On Friday afternoons, he and his staff take off early for a team ride along the New Jersey shoreline. Palumbo says cycling keeps him focused and helps team members "prove to themselves that they can do more than they think."

Sources: Based on information from "How To? Leadership Qualities of Team Leaders," *Personnel Today*, July 4, 2006; Adina Genn, "Owner Peddles Biking as Team-Building Exercise," *Long Island Business News*, September 29, 2006; Nancy Hatch Woodward, "Make the Most of Team Building," *HR Magazine*, September 2006, pp. 72+.

What Is a Team?

In a business organization, a **team** is a group of workers functioning together as a unit to complete a common goal or purpose. A team may be assigned any number of tasks or goals, from development of a new product to selling that product.[25] **EXAMPLE** Jones Walker, a New Orleans–based law firm, recently assembled a team of business students, alumni, and faculty advisors from Harvard University to assist Mayor C. Ray Nagin's Bring New Orleans Back Commission.[26] While teamwork may seem like a simple concept learned on soccer or football fields, since teams function as a microcosm of the larger organization, it is important to understand the types, development, and general nature of teams.

team a group of workers functioning together as a unit to complete a common goal or purpose

Types of Teams

There are several types of teams within businesses that function in specific ways to achieve different purposes, including problem-solving teams, self-managed teams, cross-functional teams, and virtual teams.

Problem-Solving Teams The most common type of team in business organizations is the problem-solving team. It is generally used temporarily in order to bring knowledgeable employees together to tackle a specific problem. Once the problem is solved, the team typically is disbanded. **EXAMPLE** When General Motors (GM) announced its plans to close an assembly plant in Wilmington, Delaware, employees formed problem-solving teams with managers to improve quality control and reduce costs. The changes suggested by the teams were so effective that within two years the factory became the lowest-cost producer of all GM factories. This prompted GM to keep the plant open, and the employees' jobs were saved.[27]

In some extraordinary cases, an expert team may be needed to generate groundbreaking ideas. A virtuoso team consists of exceptionally highly skilled and talented individuals brought together to produce significant change. As with other kinds of problem-solving teams, virtuoso teams usually are assembled on a temporary basis. Instead of being task-oriented, they focus on producing ideas and provoking change that could have an impact on the company and its industry. Because of the high skill level of their members, virtuoso teams can be difficult to manage. And unlike traditional teams, virtuoso teams place an emphasis on individuality over teamwork, which can cause further conflict. However, their conflicts usually are viewed as competitive and therefore productive in generating the most substantial ideas.[28]

Self-Managed Work Teams Self-managed teams are groups of employees with the authority and skills to manage themselves. Experts suggest that workers on self-managed teams are more motivated and satisfied because they have more task variety and job control. On many work teams, members rotate through all the jobs for which the team is responsible. Some organizations cross-train the entire team so that everyone can perform everyone else's job. In a traditional business structure, management is responsible for hiring and firing employees, establishing budgets, purchasing supplies, conducting performance reviews, and taking corrective action. When self-managed teams are in place, they take over some or all of these management functions. **EXAMPLE** At its factory, Ferrari uses work teams designed to let each team perform a variety of tasks for about an hour and a half before the vehicle moves on to the next team. Employees learn more job skills, are more interested in their work, and develop a greater sense of pride in and loyalty to Ferrari.[29] The major advantages and disadvantages of self-managed teams are listed in Figure 11.6.

Cross-Functional Teams Traditionally, businesses have organized employees into departments based on a common function or specialty. However, increasingly, business organizations are faced with projects that require a diversity of skills not available within a single department. A cross-functional team consists of individuals with varying specialties, expertise, and skills who are brought together to achieve a common task. **EXAMPLE** A purchasing agent might create a cross-functional team with representatives from various departments to gain insight into useful purchases for the company. This structure avoids departmental separation and allows greater efficiency when there is a single goal. Although cross-functional teams aren't necessarily self-managed, most

---

problem-solving team a team of knowledgeable employees brought together to tackle a specific problem

virtuoso team a team of exceptionally highly skilled and talented individuals brought together to produce significant change

self-managed teams groups of employees with the authority and skills to manage themselves

CONCEPT CHECK

What are the major benefits and limitations associated with the use of self-managed teams?

cross-functional team a team of individuals with varying specialties, expertise, and skills who are brought together to achieve a common task

self-managed teams are cross-functional. Owing to their speed, flexibility, and increased employee satisfaction, it is likely that the use of cross-functional teams will increase.

Virtual Teams With the advent of sophisticated communications technology, it is no longer necessary for teams to be geographically close. A **virtual team** consists of members who are geographically dispersed but communicate electronically. In fact, team members may never meet in person but rely solely on e-mail, teleconferences, faxes, voice mail, and other technologic interactions. In the modern global environment, virtual teams connect employees on a common task across continents, oceans, time zones, and organizations. **EXAMPLE** Oracle recruited former U.S. Army Lieutenant General Keith Kellogg to lead a virtual team to develop technology to address homeland security solutions.[30] In some cases, the physical distances between participants and the lack of face-to-face interaction can be difficult when deadlines approach or communication is not clear.

ADVANTAGES	DISADVANTAGES
• Boosts employee morale • Increases productivity • Aids innovation • Reduces employee boredom	• Additional training costs • Teams may be disorganized • Conflicts may arise • Leadership role may be unclear

FIGURE 11.6

Advantages and Disadvantages of Self-Managed Teams

While self-managed teams provide benefits, managers must recognize their limitations.

virtual team a team consisting of members who are geographically dispersed but communicate electronically

Developing and Using Effective Teams

When a team is first developed, it takes time for the members to establish roles, relationships, delegation of duties, and other attributes of an effective team. As a team matures, it passes through five stages of development, as shown in Figure 11.7.

Forming In the first stage, *forming*, team members are introduced to one another and begin to develop a social dynamic. The members of the team are still unsure how to relate to one another, what behaviors are considered acceptable, and what the ground rules for the team are. Through group member interaction over time, team members become more comfortable, and a group dynamic begins to emerge.

Storming During the *storming* stage, the interaction may be volatile, and the team may lack unity. Because the team is still relatively new, this is the stage at which goals and objectives begin to develop. Team members will brainstorm to develop ideas and plans and establish a broad-ranging agenda. It is important at this stage for team members to grow more comfortable around the others so that they can contribute openly. At this time, the leadership role likely will be formally undefined. A team member may emerge as the informal leader. The success or failure of the ideas in storming determines how long until the team reaches the next stage.

Norming After storming and the first large burst of activity, the team begins to stabilize during the *norming* stage. During this process, each person's role within the

FORMING
The team is new. Members get to know each other.

STORMING
The team may be volatile. Goals and objectives are developed.

NORMING
The team stabilizes. Roles and duties are accepted and recognized.

PERFORMING
The team is dynamic. Everyone makes a focused effort to accomplish goals.

ADJOURNING
The team is finished. The goals have been accomplished and the team is disbanded.

FIGURE 11.7

Stages of Team Development

When attempting to develop teams, managers must understand that multiple stages generally are required.

group starts to become apparent, and members begin to recognize the roles of others. A sense of unity will become stronger. If it hasn't already occurred, an identified leader will emerge. The group still may be somewhat volatile at this point and may regress back to the second stage if any conflict, especially over the leadership role, occurs.

Performing The fourth stage, *performing*, is when the team achieves its full potential. It is usually slow to develop and occurs when the team begins to focus strongly on the assigned task and away from team-development issues. The members of the team work in harmony under the established roles to accomplish the necessary goals.

Adjourning In the final stage, *adjourning*, the team is disbanded because the project has been completed. Team members may be reassigned to other teams or tasks. This stage does not always occur if the team is placed together for a task with no specific date of completion. **EXAMPLE** A marketing team for Best Buy may continue to develop promotional efforts for a store even after a specific promotional task has been accomplished. This stage is especially common in problem-solving teams that are dismantled after the assigned problem has been resolved.

Roles Within a Team

Within any team, each member has a role to play in helping the team attain its objectives. Each of these roles adds important dimensions to team member interactions.

* The group member who pushes forward toward goals and places the objective first is playing the *task-specialist role*. On a cross-functional team, this might be the person with the most expertise relating to the current task.

* The *socioemotional role* is played by the individual who supports and encourages the emotional needs of the other members. This person places the team members' personal needs over the task of the team. While this may sound unimportant, the socioemotional member's dedication to team cohesiveness will lead to greater unity and higher productivity.

* The leader of the team, and possibly others as well, will play a *dual role*. This dual role is a combination of both the socioemotional and task-specialist roles because this individual focuses on both the task and the team.

* Sometimes an individual assumes the *nonparticipant role*. This role behavior is characterized by a person who does not contribute to accomplishing the task and does not provide favorable input with respect to team members' socioemotional needs.

Team Cohesiveness

Developing a unit from a diverse group of personalities, specialties, backgrounds, and work styles can be challenging and complicated. In a cohesive team, the members get along and are able to accomplish their tasks effectively.

Factors Affecting Team Cohesiveness

* Teams generally are ideal when they contain five to twelve people. Fewer than five people is too few to accomplish tasks and generate a variety of ideas. More than twelve is too large because members do not develop relationships, may feel intimidated to speak, or may disconnect.

* It also may be beneficial to have team members introduce themselves and describe their past work experiences. This activity will foster familiarity and shared experiences.

* One of the most reliable ways to build cohesiveness within a team is through competition with other teams. When two teams are competing for a single prize or recognition, they are forced to put aside conflict and accomplish their goal.

* A favorable appraisal from an outsider may strengthen team cohesiveness. Since the team is being praised as a group, team members recognize their contribution as a unit.

* Teams are also more successful when goals have become agreed on. A team that is clear about its objective will focus more on accomplishing it.

* Frequent interaction also builds cohesiveness as relationships strengthen and familiarity increases.

Team Conflict and How to Resolve It

Conflict occurs when a disagreement arises between two or more team members. Conflict traditionally has been viewed as negative, but if handled properly, conflict can work to improve a team. For example, if two team members disagree about a certain decision, both may analyze the situation more closely to determine the best choice. As long as conflict is handled in a respectful and professional manner, it can improve the quality of work produced. If conflict turns hostile and affects the work environment, then steps must be taken to arrive at a suitable compromise. Compromises can be difficult in a business organization because neither party ends up getting everything he or she wants. The best solution is a middle-ground alternative in which each party is satisfied to some degree. It is best to avoid attempting to minimize or ignore conflicts within a group because this may cause the conflict to grow as members concentrate on the problem instead of the task. However the conflict is resolved, it is important to remember that conflict must be acknowledged if it is to be either resolved or serve a constructive purpose.

CONCEPT CHECK

In what ways are team cohesiveness and team conflict related?

Benefits and Limitations of Teams

* Teamwork has been credited as a key to reducing turnover and costs and increasing production, quality, and customer service.

* There is also evidence that working in teams leads to higher levels of job satisfaction among employees and a harmonious work environment.

* The process of reorganizing into teams can be stressful and time-consuming with no guarantee that the team will develop effectively.

* If a team lacks cohesiveness and is unable to resolve conflict, the company may experience lower productivity.

Team-building exercises.

Employees at AT&T participate in team-building exercises that will help them improve their overall abilities to engage in productive teamwork.

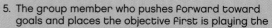

TEST PREPPER 11.5

True or False?

_T_ 1. The difference between a problem-solving team and a virtuoso team is that instead of being task-oriented, a virtuoso team focuses on producing ideas and provoking change.

_T_ 2. Conflict traditionally has been viewed as negative, but if handled properly, conflict can work to improve a team.

_F_ 3. Ideal team size is between six and fifteen people.

Multiple Choice

_C_ 4. What stage of a team is usually slow to develop and occurs when the team begins to focus

strongly on the assigned task and away from team-development issues?

   a. Norming
   b. Storming
   c. Performing
   d. Adjourning
   e. Unifying

_A_ 5. The group member who pushes forward toward goals and places the objective first is playing the

   a. task-specialist role.
   b. socioemotional role.
   c. nonparticipant role.
   d. pusher role.
   e. aggressive role.

ACE the Test
ACE & ACE+
Practice Test 11.5

Prepare for Class
CL News Feeds
CL News Now

→ RETURN TO INSIDE BUSINESS

For five years in a row, _Science_ magazine has named Genentech the top (and the most admired) employer. _Fortune_ magazine also has put Genentech on its annual list of the "100 Best Companies to Work For." How does Genentech do it?

The company starts by recruiting highly talented people and giving them the best tools, a safe and pleasant work environment, recognition for their accomplishments, and the freedom to pursue their own scientific interests. New employees attend orientation sessions to become immersed in the company's culture, mission, goals, and history. Management uses weekly work force polls to monitor employee satisfaction and check on progress toward meeting goals. The CEO sums up Genentech's mission this way: "We commit ourselves to high standards of integrity in contributing to the best interests of patients, the medical profession, our employees, and our communities."

Questions

1. Which of Maslow's hierarchy of needs does Genentech appear to be using to motivate its work force? Why are these effective for the company?

2. Would highly qualified job candidates be likely to react positively or negatively to Genentech's stringent hiring procedures? What effect would their reactions have on the company's ability to attract and retain the best employees?

LEARNING OBJECTIVES REVIEW

1 Explain what motivation is.

- Motivation is the individual internal process that energizes, directs, and sustains behavior. Motivation is affected by employee morale—that is, the employee's feelings about the job, superiors, and the firm itself.
- Motivation, morale, and job satisfaction are closely related.

2 Understand the major theories of motivation and how they influence management practices.

- Frederick Taylor's scientific management is the application of scientific principles to the management of work and workers. He believed that employees work only for money and that they must be closely supervised and managed, which led to the piece-rate system.
- The Hawthorne studies attempted to determine the effects of the work environment on productivity. Results of these studies indicated that human factors affect productivity more than do physical aspects of the workplace.
- Maslow's hierarchy of needs suggests that people are motivated by five sets of needs. These motivators are physiological, safety, social, esteem, and self-actualization needs. People are motivated by the lowest set of needs that remains unfulfilled, and as needs at one level are satisfied, people try to satisfy needs at the next level.
- Frederick Herzberg found that job satisfaction and dissatisfaction are influenced by two distinct sets of factors: motivation factors and hygiene factors.
- Theory X is a concept of motivation in which managers must coerce, control, and threaten employees. This theory generally is consistent with Taylor's scientific management.
- Theory Y suggests that employees can be motivated to behave as responsible members of the organization.
- Theory Z emphasizes long-term employment, collective decision making, individual responsibility for the outcomes of decisions, informal control, and a holistic concern for employees.
- Reinforcement theory is based on the idea that people will repeat behavior that is rewarded and will avoid behavior that is punished.

3 Describe the three views why and how motivation works: equity theory, expectancy theory, and goal-setting theory.

- Equity theory maintains that people are motivated to obtain and preserve equitable treatment for themselves.

- Expectancy theory suggests that our motivation depends on how much we want something and how likely we think we are to get it.
- Goal-setting theory suggests that employees are motivated to achieve a goal that they and their managers establish together.

4 Explain several techniques for increasing employee motivation.

- Management by objectives (MBO) is a motivation technique in which managers and employees collaborate in setting goals.
- Job enrichment seeks to motivate employees by varying their tasks and giving them more responsibility for and control over their jobs.
  - Job enlargement, expanding a worker's assignments to include additional tasks, is one aspect of job enrichment.
  - Job redesign is a type of job enrichment in which work is restructured to improve the worker-job match.
- Flextime, employee empowerment, self-managed work teams, and employee ownership are also techniques that boost employee motivation.

5 Understand the types, development, and uses of teams.

- In a business organization, a team is a group of workers functioning together as a unit to complete a common goal or purpose.
- There are several types of teams within businesses that function in specific ways to achieve different purposes.
  - A problem-solving team is a team of knowledgeable employees brought together to tackle a specific problem.
  - A virtuoso team is a team of highly skilled and talented individuals brought together to produce significant change.
  - A cross-functional team is a team of individuals with varying specialties, expertise, and skills.
  - A virtual team is a team consisting of members who are geographically dispersed but communicate electronically.
- The five stages of team development are forming, storming, norming, performing, and adjourning.
- The four roles within teams are
  - Task specialist
  - Dual
  - Socioemotional
  - Nonparticipative

Improve Your Grade
Audio Chapter Review
& Quiz

VIDEO CASE

American Flatbread Fires up Employees

George Schenk's passion is making work meaningful, sustainable, and personal. He learned about wood-fired cooking from his grandmother in Vermont and, years later, rekindled his love of cooking with fire when he founded the American Flatbread Company. His company produces frozen wood-fired flatbread pizzas from all-natural, locally grown ingredients, hand-made by 100 employees in Waitsfield and Middlebury, Vermont.

On Mondays, Tuesdays, Wednesdays, and Thursdays, two shifts of employees stoke the bakeries' wood-fired ovens to a temperature of 800°F and prepare the flatbreads. After the products are baked, frozen, and wrapped, they are shipped to grocery and specialty stores such as Whole Foods supermarkets. Both bakeries are transformed into casual pizza restaurants on Friday and Saturday nights, where diners sit in view of the gigantic ovens to enjoy salads and flatbreads. Schenk also has licensed American Flatbread's brand and wood-fired cooking methods to bakeries and restaurants in New England, California, and Virginia. One-third of American Flatbread's annual revenue comes from the licensing deals and restaurant receipts, whereas the wholesale frozen pizza operation contributes the remaining two-thirds.

Schenk's enthusiasm for wood-fired cooking is matched by his enthusiasm for building a business in which the work has long-term significance to the employees and the community. Among American Flatbread's goals are to "create a pleasant, fulfilling, sustainable, and secure workplace" and "to trust one another and practice respectful relationships with everyone involved in this work."

Another goal mentioned in the mission statement is to be grateful, respectful, and forgiving—and to encourage the same in others. In line with this goal, Schenk has worked hard to avoid what he calls "founder's syndrome," the notion that the founder can do nothing wrong. Because Schenk is quick to admit that he's not perfect, his managers and employees know they can speak up about their mistakes and not lose the opportunity to try new things.

Jennifer Moffroid, the company's director of marketing, stresses that the founder has created an environment in which employees can do work that is in keeping with what they want for their lives. Making the workday fun is one of Schenk's priorities, as is making the workplace an inviting place to be. Moffroid also notes that Schenk not only delegates, but he also "empowers employees and celebrates their work." The company's seven senior managers are involved in decision making, and every suggestion is evaluated on its merit, not on its source. "We're all in this together," Schenk says.

Since the beginning, American Flatbread has supported local food producers and given back to the community in a variety of ways. For example, the restaurants hold "benefit bakes" to raise money for causes such as public health clinics and habitat preservation. In turn, the community has come to the company's aid on more than one occasion. When flood waters inundated American Flatbread's bakery, people came from miles around to clean and rebuild the facility. Thanks to this outpouring of support, the bakery was able to reopen in only seven days. Without the help of the community, Schenk observes, the company might well have failed.

Today, the Vermont bakeries turn out 10,000 flatbreads every week; the California bakery produces another 4,000 for distribution in western states. Schenk keeps the company's values in the spotlight by writing a dedication for each week's menu. These dedications focus employees on what's important and provide "food for thought" for restaurant customers. Sharing values, being "a good neighbor," and building trusting, respectful relationships with stakeholders have enabled American Flatbread to keep employees happy and productive, minimize turnover, and strengthen financial performance.

For more information about this company, go to **www.americanflatbread.com**.[31]

Questions

1. Does George Schenk manage American Flatbread as a type A or a type Z firm? Support your answer.
2. Would you recommend that American Flatbread offer bakery and restaurant employees flextime arrangements? Explain.
3. How has George Schenk paved the way for empowerment at his company?

BUILDING SKILLS FOR CAREER SUCCESS

1. Exploring the Internet

There are few employee incentives as motivating as owning "a piece of the action." Either through profit sharing or equity, many firms realize that the opportunity to share in the wealth generated by their effort is a primary force to drive employees toward better performance and a sense of ownership. The Foundation for Enterprise Development (**www.fed.org/**) is a nonprofit organization dedicated to helping entrepreneurs and executives use employee ownership and equity compensation as a fair and effective means of motivating the work force and improving corporate performance. You can learn more about this approach at the foundation's website. Visit the text website for updates to this exercise.

Assignment

1. Describe the content and services provided by the Foundation for Enterprise Development through its website.
2. Do you agree with this orientation toward motivation of employees/owners, or does it seem contrived to you? Discuss.
3. How else might employees be motivated to improve their performance?

2. Building Team Skills

By increasing employees' participation in decision making, empowerment makes workers feel more involved in their jobs and the operations of the organization. While empowerment may seem like a commonsense idea, it is a concept not found universally in the workplace. If you had empowerment in your job, how would you describe it?

Assignment

1. Use brainstorming to explore the concept of empowerment.
   a. Write each letter of the word *empowerment* in a vertical column on a sheet of paper or on the classroom chalkboard.
   b. Think of several words that begin with each letter.
   c. Write the words next to the appropriate letter.

2. Formulate a statement by choosing one word from each letter that best describes what empowerment means to you.
3. Analyze the statement.
   a. How relevant is the statement for you in terms of empowerment? Or empowerment in your workplace?
   b. What changes must occur in your workplace for you to have empowerment?
   c. How would you describe yourself as an empowered employee?
   d. What opportunities would empowerment give to you in your workplace?
4. Prepare a report of your findings.

3. Researching Different Careers

Because a manager's job varies from department to department within firms, as well as among firms, it is virtually impossible to write a generic description of a manager's job. If you are contemplating becoming a manager, you may find it very helpful to spend time on the job with several managers learning first hand what they do.

Assignment

1. Make an appointment with managers in three firms, preferably firms of different sizes. When you make the appointments, request a tour of the facilities.
2. Ask the managers the following questions:
   a. What do you do in your job?
   b. What do you like most and least about your job? Why?
   c. What skills do you need in your job?
   d. How much education does your job require?
   e. What advice do you have for someone thinking about pursuing a career in management?
3. Summarize your findings in a two-page report. Include answers to these questions:
   a. Is management a realistic field of study for you? Why?
   b. What might be a better career choice? Why?

Prepare for Class
Exploring the Internet

RUNNING A BUSINESS PART 4
Inside the People Business at Finagle A Bagel

People are a vital ingredient in Finagle A Bagel's recipe for success. As a quick-serve business, the company strives for high turnover in food, not employees. In fact, careful attention to HRM has enabled Finagle A Bagel to continue expanding its market share without spending money on advertising. Low work force turnover means less money and time spent on recruiting and training—an important financial consideration for a fast-growing business. It also means that Finagle A Bagel has the human resources strength to combine super service with fresh food for a distinctive competitive advantage in a crowded marketplace.

The Right People in the Right Place

"We depend on our crew at the store level—who are interacting with our guests every day—to know their jobs, to understand the company mission, and to communicate with the guests," says Heather Robertson, who directs the company's marketing, human resources, and research and development. "And once we get them on board, people don't leave our company. They just stay. They realize that it can be a career for them."

A sizable number of Finagle A Bagel's managers and employees (including Robertson) were hired years ago and became so excited about the product, the company, and the customers that they stayed. Many remain with Finagle A Bagel because they prefer the more personal atmosphere of a 320-employee business over the relatively faceless anonymity of a gigantic corporation. "It's really unusual to have one-on-one interaction on a daily basis with the president of the company or any senior executive member of the company," Robertson states. "Our cashiers, our café attendants, our bakers, and our managers know they can pick up the phone at any point and call anybody here and say, 'Here's my problem. How do I fix it?' or 'I need your help.' The size of our company allows us to do that, and the culture of the company encourages that."

Because bagels are an integral part of every menu item, employees who join Finagle A Bagel must "love" bagels, regardless of any other skills or experiences they bring to their jobs. When Robertson advertises to fill an open position in Finagle A Bagel's headquarters, for example, she always mentions this requirement. As résumés come in, she sorts them according to whether the candidates indicate a fondness for bagels. Those who fail to mention it are automatically disqualified from consideration.

Different Kinds of Managers for Different Locations

Alan Litchman, Finagle A Bagel's copresident, says that selecting a candidate to manage one of the Boston stores is easier than selecting one for a suburban store. Given the inner-city location of the company's support center, he or another executive can get to the Boston stores more quickly if a problem arises. Moreover, the city stores compete by providing speedy, accurate service to busy customers who have little time to waste waiting in line. Paulo Pereira, general manager of one of the Cambridge stores, has become an expert in squeezing inefficiencies from the city stores so that customers are in and out more quickly. By increasing the number of customers served each day and slashing the number of bagels left over at closing, Pereira boosts both sales revenues and profits.

When selecting a manager for a suburban store, Litchman looks for people with an "owner-operator mentality" who have the drive, initiative, and know-how to build business locally. His message to a potential general manager is: "If you want to be a franchisee but don't have the capital, or if you want to own your own business, we're going to put you in business. You don't have to give us any money to do that. And if your store achieves more than a certain level of sales or profits, we'll start splitting the bottom line with you in a bonus program." Consider Nick Cochran, who worked his way up from assistant manager to general manager of the store in Wayland, an affluent Boston suburb. Cochran's enthusiasm for quality and service has drawn a highly loyal customer following and contributed to the Wayland store's success.

Hiring and Motivating Store Personnel

General managers such as Cochran and Pereira are responsible for recruiting, interviewing, hiring, training, motivating, and evaluating store-level personnel. They assign job responsibilities according to the skills and strengths of each manager and employee, but they also expect everyone to work as a team during extremely busy periods. In addition to motivating general managers by offering bonuses based on meeting revenue and profit goals, Finagle A Bagel encourages crew members to take advantage of extra training and internal promotions.

"In a company our size," stresses copresident Laura Trust, "there is always opportunity. You just have to find the right fit for the individual." In fact, says her husband, "The best

supervisors, coordinators, assistant managers, or managers in any unit—by far—are the ones who have started with us at a lower level and worked their way up."

Diverse Work Force, Family Business

Finagle A Bagel has an extremely diverse work force made up of people originally from Latin America, Europe, western Africa, and many other areas. Over the years, the company has served as a sponsor for new Americans who need government-issued work permits so that they can legally remain in the United States for work reasons. Despite diversity's many advantages—including creativity, flexibility, and the ability to relate to a broader customer base—it also can create communications challenges when English is not an employee's native language. To avoid confusion, Litchman and Trust insist that employees speak only in English when addressing customers.

As a small, family-run business, Finagle A Bagel sees its work force as a group of unique individuals, not interchangeable cogs in an impersonal corporate machine. Trust feels strongly that "there's a responsibility that you have to your

employees and to your colleagues. These people work for you—they work hard to try and move your company forward—and their efforts need to be recognized." Because the business is still small, she adds, "the people who have become a part of the management team are very much like family to Alan and me. If you run your company that way, then you'll be successful because everybody believes that you care about not only the work they do but everything they do, and every part of their lives affects their job."

Questions
1. What effect has diversity had on Finagle A Bagel?
2. If you were the general manager of a downtown Finagle A Bagel store, what job description and job specification would you prepare for a cashier? Based on these, what kinds of questions would you ask when interviewing candidates for this position?
3. Which of Herzberg's motivation factors are Trust and Litchman emphasizing for general managers?
4. Would it be feasible for Finagle A Bagel to apply the concept of flextime to store employees? To senior managers at the headquarters facility? Explain.

CHAPTER 12

Building Customer Relationships Through Effective Marketing

Your Guide to Success in Business

Why this chapter matters
Marketers are concerned about building long-term customer relationships. To develop competitive product offerings, business people must identify acceptable target customer groups and understand their behavior.

LEARNING OBJECTIVES

1. Understand the meaning of *marketing* and the importance of management of customer relationships.

2. Explain how marketing adds value by creating several forms of utility.

3. Trace the development of the marketing concept and understand how it is implemented.

4. Understand what markets are and how they are classified.

5. Identify the four elements of the marketing mix and their importance in developing a marketing strategy.

6. Explain how the marketing environment affects strategic market planning.

7. Understand the major components of a marketing plan.

8. Describe how market measurement helps in determining sales forecasts.

9. Distinguish between a marketing information system and marketing research.

10. Explain the importance of studying buying behavior and its major classifications.

Applebee's Stirs Up Its Marketing Mix

Applebee's Neighborhood Grill & Bar is moving into more neighborhoods around the world, offering a casual dining experience tailored to local tastes. Headquartered in Overland Park, Kansas, Applebee's was founded in 1983. Now, with 1,900 outlets—most operated by franchisees—the chain has grown into a global player in the restaurant business.

The company's recipe for success starts with a large dose of customer knowledge. Each restaurant is decorated to reflect the neighborhood, with photos and items commemorating local schools, events, history, and celebrities. This gives each restaurant a distinctive yet informal look that captures the essence of the area, an important competitive element in an industry where chain restaurants usually look alike.

Applebee's marketers also recognized that consumers with busy lifestyles put a high value on convenience. In response, they introduced Carside to Go. Here's how it works: The customer calls in an order on his or her cell phone, along with a brief description of the car. When the meal is ready, an Applebee's employee watches the parking lot and brings the food directly to that customer's car. Many Applebee's employees also carry wireless devices to scan the customer's credit card for payment on the spot. Promoted through ad campaigns targeting busy adults, this curbside service has increased Applebee's takeout sales by $430 million over the past three years.

Applebee's also pays close attention to quality. It recently upgraded the ingredients in all its recipes and fine-tuned the seasonings to give each dish just the right taste. And it hires creative chefs to cook up new signature dishes in the company's state-of-the-art test kitchen.

For example, celebrity chef Tyler Florence has created dishes such as the pesto-topped Bruschetta Burger, dishes that are constantly being added to the menu alongside perennial favorites. In addition, the menu features healthy drinks such as smoothies and energy-juice blends plus tasty Weight Watchers selections for customers watching their waistlines. Now every time customers open the menu at an Applebee's, "they're seeing new news," explains the senior vice president of menu development.[1]

DID YOU KNOW?

Because Applebee's is always adding new dishes, every time customers open the menu, "they're seeing new news," says the senior vice president of menu development.

KEY TERMS

marketing (366)
relationship marketing (367)
customer relationship management (CRM) (367)
customer lifetime value (368)
utility (368)
form utility (368)

place utility (368)
time utility (368)
possession utility (368)
marketing concept (369)
market (371)
marketing strategy (373)

marketing mix (373)
target market (373)
undifferentiated approach (374)
market segment (375)
market segmentation (375)
marketing plan (379)

sales forecast (381)
marketing information system (381)
marketing research (382)
buying behavior (385)
consumer buying behavior (385)
business buying behavior (385)

ACE the Test
Crossword Puzzle
Flashcards

TABLE 12.1

Major Marketing
Functions

EXCHANGE FUNCTIONS: ALL COMPANIES—MANUFACTURERS, WHOLESALERS, AND RETAILERS—BUY AND SELL TO MARKET THEIR MERCHANDISE.
1. *Buying* includes obtaining raw materials to make products, knowing how much merchandise to keep on hand, and selecting suppliers.
2. *Selling* creates possession utility by transferring the title of a product from seller to customer.
PHYSICAL DISTRIBUTION FUNCTIONS: THESE FUNCTIONS INVOLVE THE FLOW OF GOODS FROM PRODUCERS TO CUSTOMERS. TRANSPORTATION AND STORAGE PROVIDE TIME UTILITY AND PLACE UTILITY AND REQUIRE CAREFUL MANAGEMENT OF INVENTORY.
3. *Transporting* involves selecting a mode of transport that provides an acceptable delivery schedule at an acceptable price.
4. *Storing* goods is often necessary to sell them at the best selling time.
FACILITATING FUNCTIONS: THESE FUNCTIONS HELP THE OTHER FUNCTIONS TAKE PLACE.
5. *Financing* helps at all stages of marketing. To buy raw materials, manufacturers often borrow from banks or receive credit from suppliers. Wholesalers may be financed by manufacturers, and retailers may receive financing from the wholesaler or manufacturer. Finally, retailers often provide financing to customers.
6. *Standardizing* sets uniform specifications for products or services. *Grading* classifies products by size and quality, usually through a sorting process. Together, standardization and grading facilitate production, transportation, storage, and selling.
7. *Risk taking*—even though competent management and insurance can minimize risks—is a constant reality of marketing because of such losses as bad-debt expense, obsolescence of products, theft by employees, and product-liability lawsuits.
8. *Gathering market information* is necessary for making all marketing decisions.

marketing an organizational function and a set of processes for creating, communicating, and delivering value to customers and for managing customer relationships in ways that benefit the organization and its stakeholders

Marketing efforts are directed toward providing customer satisfaction. Understanding customers' needs, such as "what's cool," is crucial to providing customer satisfaction. Although marketing encompasses a diverse set of decisions and activities performed by individuals and by both business and nonbusiness organizations, marketing always begins and ends with the customer. The American Marketing Association defines **marketing** as "an organizational function and a set of processes for creating, communicating, and delivering value to customers and for managing customer relationships in ways that benefit the organization and its stakeholders."[2] The marketing process involves eight major functions and numerous related activities (see Table 12.1). All these functions are essential if the marketing process is to be effective.

In this chapter,

* We examine marketing activities that add value to products.
* We trace the evolution of the marketing concept and describe how organizations practice it.
* We discuss market classifications and marketing strategy.
* We analyze the four elements of a marketing mix and also discuss uncontrollable factors in the marketing environment.
* We examine the major components of a marketing plan.
* We consider tools for strategic market planning, including market measurement, sales forecasts, marketing information systems, and marketing research.
* We look at the forces that influence consumer and organizational buying behavior.

Marketing and the Management of Customer Relationships

Learning Objective

Understand the meaning of *marketing* and the importance of management of customer relationships.

Marketing relationships with customers are the lifeblood of all businesses. Maintaining positive relationships with customers is an important goal for marketers. The term **relationship marketing** refers to establishing "long-term, mutually beneficial arrangements in which both the buyer and seller focus on value enhancement through the creation of more satisfying exchanges."[3] Successful marketers respond to customer needs and strive to continually increase value to buyers over time. Eventually, this interaction becomes a solid relationship that allows for cooperation and mutual dependency. **EXAMPLE** Customers depend on the Coca-Cola Company to provide a standardized, reliable, satisfying soft drink or beverage anyplace in the world. Owing to its efforts to expand distribution to every possible location, Coca-Cola sells 33 percent of its volume in Europe and the Middle East, 31 percent in North America, 22 percent in the Asian/Pacific region, 10 percent in Latin America, and 5 percent in Africa.[4] The company continues to introduce new products, expand distribution, and maintain high-quality products. Coca-Cola is also a good "corporate citizen," donating millions of dollars to education, health and human services, and disaster-plagued regions each year.

To build long-term customer relationships, marketers increasingly are turning to marketing research and information technology. **Customer relationship management (CRM)** focuses on using information about customers to create marketing strategies that develop and sustain desirable customer relationships. By increasing customer value over time, organizations try to retain and increase long-term profitability through customer loyalty.[5]

Managing customer relationships requires identifying patterns of buying behavior and using that information to focus on the most promising and profitable customers.[6] In some instances it may be more profitable for a company to focus on satisfying a valuable existing customer than to attempt to attract a new one who may never develop the same level of loyalty. This involves determining how much the customer will spend over his or her

relationship marketing
establishing long-term, mutually satisfying buyer-seller relationships

customer relationship management (CRM)
using information about customers to create marketing strategies that develop and sustain desirable customer relationships

◄

Relationship marketing.

Opteum Financial Services indicates in its advertisements that it wants to develop long-term relationships with customers based on trust. Opteum advertises that it lives by the promises it makes.

Opteum.
FINANCIAL SERVICES

A Promise is a Promise.

WE PROMISE YOU A FIVE-STAR MORTGAGE EXPERIENCE.
IF YOU CLOSE YOUR LOAN WITH US
AND WE DON'T DELIVER, WE'LL PAY YOU $500.

customer lifetime value a combination of purchase frequency, average value of purchases, and brand-switching patterns over the entire span of a customer's relationship with a company

utility the ability of a good or service to satisfy a human need

form utility utility created by converting production inputs into finished products

place utility utility created by making a product available at a location where customers wish to purchase it

time utility utility created by making a product available when customers wish to purchase it

possession utility utility created by transferring title (or ownership) of a product to a buyer

lifetime. The **customer lifetime value** is a combination of purchase frequency, average value of purchases, and brand-switching patterns over the entire span of a customer's relationship with a company.[7] However, there are also intangible benefits of retaining lifetime-value customers, such as their ability to provide feedback to a company and refer new customers of similar value. The amount of money a company is willing to spend to retain such customers is also a factor. In general, when marketers focus on customers chosen for their lifetime value, they earn higher profits in future periods than when they focus on customers selected for other reasons.[8] Because the loss of a potential lifetime customer can result in lower profits, managing customer relationships has become a major focus of marketers.

Utility: The Value Added by Marketing

Learning Objective ②

Explain how marketing adds value by creating several forms of utility.

As defined in Chapter 9, **utility** is the ability of a good or service to satisfy a human need. A lunch at a Pizza Hut, an overnight stay at a Holiday Inn, and a Mercedes S500L all satisfy human needs. Thus each possesses utility. There are four kinds of utility.

Form utility is created by converting production inputs into finished products. Marketing efforts may influence form utility indirectly because the data gathered as part of marketing research frequently are used to determine the size, shape, and features of a product.

The three kinds of utility that are created directly by marketing are place, time, and possession utility. **Place utility** is created by making a product available at a location where customers wish to purchase it. A pair of shoes is given place utility when it is shipped from a factory to a department store.

Time utility is created by making a product available when customers wish to purchase it. For example, Halloween costumes may be manufactured in April but not displayed until late September, when consumers start buying them. By storing the costumes until they are wanted, the manufacturer or retailer provides time utility.

Possession utility is created by transferring title (or ownership) of a product to a buyer. For a product as simple as a pair of shoes, ownership usually is transferred by means of a sales slip or receipt. For such products as automobiles and homes, the transfer of title is a more complex process. Along with the title to its products, the seller transfers the right to use that product to satisfy a need (see Figure 12.1).

Place, time, and possession utility have real value in terms of both money and convenience. This value is created and added to goods and services through a wide variety of marketing activities—from research

Wanted: One pair of size 8 shoes in Duluth, immediately. Will pay $50.	CAN SATISFY THE NEED WITH:	BUT CANNOT SATISFY THE NEED WITH:
Form utility	Size 8 shoes	Size 10 shoes
Place utility	Size 8 shoes in Duluth	Size 8 shoes in Los Angeles
Time utility	Size 8 shoes in Duluth available now	Size 8 shoes in Duluth available next month
Possession utility	Size 8 shoes in Duluth available now for $50	Size 8 shoes in Duluth available now for $80

FIGURE 12.1

Types of Utility

Form utility is created by the production process, but marketing creates place, time, and possession utility.

CONCEPT CHECK

How, specifically, does marketing create place, time and possession utility?

indicating what customers want to product warranties ensuring that customers get what they pay for.

Place, time, and possession utility are only the most fundamental applications of marketing activities. In recent years, marketing activities have been influenced by a broad business philosophy known as the *marketing concept*.

TEST PREPPER 12.1 12.2

True or False?

_T_ 1. In some instances it may be more profitable for a company to focus on satisfying a valuable existing customer than to attempt to attract a new one who may never develop the same level of loyalty.

_T_ 2. Companies offering discounts for referring friends is an example of retaining lifetime-value customers.

_F_ 3. Place, time, and possession utility have no real value in terms of both money and convenience.

Multiple Choice

_A_ 4. When Campbell Soup Company provides the same product in smaller packages for single people, this is an example of providing

    a. form utility.
    b. place utility.
    c. distribution utility.
    d. package utility.
    e. efficient utility.

_B_ 5. 7-Eleven stays open 24 hours for its customers. This is an example of

    a. place utility.
    b. time utility.
    c. convenience utility.
    d. form utility.
    e. area utility.

ACE the Test
ACE & ACE+
Practice Tests 12.1, 12.2

The Marketing Concept

Learning Objective ❸

Trace the development of the marketing concept and understand how it is implemented.

The **marketing concept** is a business philosophy that a firm should provide goods and services that satisfy customers' needs through a coordinated set of activities that allows the firm to achieve its objectives.

marketing concept a business philosophy that a firm should provide goods and services that satisfy customers' needs through a coordinated set of activities that allows the firm to achieve its objectives

Steps Involved in the Marketing Concept

1. Initially, the firm must communicate with potential customers to assess their product needs.
2. Then the firm must develop a good or service to satisfy those needs.
3. Finally, the firm must continue to seek ways to provide customer satisfaction.

EXAMPLE Ben & Jerry's, for example, constantly assesses customer demand for ice cream and sorbet. On its website, it maintains a "flavor graveyard" listing combinations that were tried and ultimately failed. It also notes its top ten flavors each month. Thus the marketing concept emphasizes that marketing begins and ends with customers.

Evolution of the Marketing Concept

From the start of the Industrial Revolution until the early twentieth century, business effort was directed mainly toward the production of goods. Consumer demand for manufactured products was so great that manufacturers could almost bank on selling everything they produced. Business had a strong *production orientation*, in which emphasis was placed on increased output and production efficiency. Marketing was limited to taking orders and distributing finished goods.

In the 1920s, production caught up with and began to exceed demand. Now producers had to direct their efforts toward selling goods rather than just producing goods that consumers readily bought. This new *sales orientation* was characterized by increased advertising, enlarged sales forces, and occasionally, high-pressure selling techniques. Manufacturers produced the goods they expected consumers to want, and marketing consisted primarily of promoting products through personal selling and advertising, taking orders, and delivering goods.

During the 1950s, however, business people started to realize that even enormous advertising expenditures and the most thoroughly proven sales techniques were not enough. Marketers realized that the best approach was to adopt a customer orientation—in other words, the organization had to first determine what customers need and then develop goods and services to fill those particular needs (see Table 12.2).

All functional areas—research and development (R&D), production, finance, human resources, and of course, marketing—are viewed as playing a role in providing customer satisfaction.

TABLE 12.2

Evolution of Customer Orientation

Business managers recognized that they were not primarily producers or sellers but rather were in the business of satisfying customers' needs.

PRODUCTION ORIENTATION	SALES ORIENTATION	CUSTOMER ORIENTATION
Take orders	Increase advertising	Determine customer needs
Distribute goods	Enlarge sales force	Develop products to fill these needs
	Intensify sales techniques	Achieve the organization's goals

Implementing the Marketing Concept

The marketing concept has been adopted by many of the most successful business firms. Some firms, such as Ford Motor Company and Apple Computer, have gone through minor or major reorganizations in the process.

Steps Involved in Implementing the Marketing Concept

1. A firm first must obtain information about its present and potential customers.

2. The firm must determine not only what customers' needs are but also how well those needs are being satisfied by products currently on the market—both its own products and those of competitors.

3. The firm must ascertain how its products might be improved and what opinions customers have about the firm and its marketing efforts.

4. The firm then must use this information to pinpoint the specific needs and potential customers toward which it will direct its marketing activities and resources.

5. Next, the firm must mobilize its marketing resources to

  * Provide a product that will satisfy its customers.
  * Price the product at a level that is acceptable to buyers and that will yield an acceptable profit.
  * Promote the product so that potential customers will be aware of its existence and its ability to satisfy their needs.
  * Ensure that the product is distributed so that it is available to customers where and when needed.

6. Finally, the firm again must obtain marketing information—this time regarding the effectiveness of its efforts. The firm must be ready to modify any or all of its marketing activities based on information about its customers and competitors.

EXAMPLE Toyota has taken the lead in the American automotive industry through its promise of high-quality yet sensible cars. But Toyota isn't satisfied with producing practical cars and is launching a new campaign to make consumers passionate about its products. Toyota is revamping its relationship with customers by forgoing traditional advertising and bringing its cars straight to the consumer. The Toyota Camry, the number one selling car in America, has been redesigned to integrate a flashier grill and a sportier body to add fun to its proven quality. When the hybrid version of the new Camry debuted, Toyota teamed up with medical doctors to promote the vehicle as asthma-friendly. Toyota tested out its new FJ Cruiser sport-utility vehicle (SUV) at off-road and trail events instead of using more traditional television advertising. As for its truck line, Toyota focused on fishing and hunting events.[9]

Markets and Their Classification

Learning Objective 4

Understand what markets are and how they are classified.

A **market** is a group of individuals or organizations, or both, that needs products in a given category and that has the ability, willingness, and authority to purchase such products.

market a group of individuals or organizations, or both, that needs products in a given category and that has the ability, willingness, and authority to purchase such products

Markets are broadly classified as consumer or business-to-business markets. These classifications are based on the characteristics of the individuals and organizations within each market.

* *Consumer markets* consist of purchasers and/or household members who intend to consume or benefit from the purchased products and who do not buy products to make profits.

* *Business-to-business markets*, also called *industrial markets*, are grouped broadly into producer, reseller, governmental, and institutional categories. These markets purchase specific kinds of products for use in making other products for resale or for day-to-day operations.

* *Producer markets* consist of individuals and business organizations that buy certain products to use in the manufacture of other products.

* *Reseller markets* consist of intermediaries such as wholesalers and retailers that buy finished products and sell them for a profit.

* *Governmental markets* consist of federal, state, county, and local governments. They buy goods and services to maintain internal operations and to provide citizens with such products as highways, education, water, energy, and national defense. Governmental purchases total billions of dollars each year.

* *Institutional markets* include churches, not-for-profit private schools and hospitals, civic clubs, fraternities and sororities, charitable organizations, and foundations. Their goals are different from such typical business goals as profit, market share, or return on investment.

BUSINESS AROUND THE WORLD

OXO Comes to Grips with Global Markets

OXO's best-known products are the Good Grips line of kitchen tools, designed to fit the hand and please the eye. Targeting seniors whose grip strength or manual dexterity has declined, OXO's Good Grips are popular in the U.S. market but flopped when first introduced in Japan. After months of meticulous marketing research, however, OXO was able to improve its target marketing and create products especially for Japanese consumers.

It turns out that U.S. and Japanese consumers use kitchen tools differently. "Most Westerners hold a spatula like a ten-  nis racket when they stir, flip, or cook," says OXO's CEO. "But the Japanese women we observed cooking all held it like a pen." After OXO rede- signed the tools and made them smaller for compact Japanese kitchens, sales soared. In an unexpected twist, a smaller salad spinner that became OXO's top seller in Japan has caught on with U.S. consumers who prefer space-saving devices.

Sources: Based on information in Helen Walters, "OXO: Remade in Japan," *BusinessWeek Online*, December 8, 2006, **www .businessweek.com**; Dalia Fahmy, "Making Necessities Stylish and Getting a Higher Price," *New York Times*, March 9, 2006, p. C7.

Developing a Marketing Strategy

Learning Objective 5

Identify the four elements of the marketing mix and their importance in developing a marketing strategy.

A marketing strategy is a plan that will enable an organization to make the best use of its resources and advantages to meet its objectives. A marketing strategy consists of (1) the selection and analysis of a target market and (2) the creation and maintenance of an appropriate marketing mix, a combination of product, price, distribution, and promotion developed to satisfy a particular target market.

Target-Market Selection and Evaluation

A target market is a group of individuals or organizations, or both, for which a firm develops and maintains a marketing mix suitable for the specific needs and preferences of that group. In selecting a target market, marketing managers examine potential markets for their possible effects on the firm's sales, costs, and profits. Marketing managers may define a target market as a vast number of people or a relatively small group. **EXAMPLE** Rolls-Royce targets its

Our Readers Spend $5.5 Billion Improving Their Homes

HOME IMPROVEMENT & REMODELING

HOUSEHOLD FURNISHINGS	$1.5 BILLION
PAINT & STAIN	$495 MILLION
FLOORING	$660 MILLION
WINDOWS	$215 MILLION
DECKING	$488 MILLION
LIGHTING	$115 MILLION
CARPETING	$398 MILLION
ROOM ADDITIONS	$827 MILLION
PLUMBING FIXTURE/FAUCETS	$258 MILLION
LANDSCAPING/GARDEN MAINTENANCE	$330 MILLION

Are you getting your share?

Family Handyman
Turning houses into homes.

marketing strategy a plan that will enable an organization to make the best use of its resources and advantages to meet its objectives

marketing mix a combination of product, price, distribution, and promotion developed to satisfy a particular target market

target market a group of individuals or organizations, or both, for which a firm develops and maintains a marketing mix suitable for the specific needs and preferences of that group

◄ **Reaching a target market.**

A company's marketing efforts for a brand or product group are aimed at a specific target market. This advertisement for *Family Handyman* magazine indicates that the magazine can help a company reach a target market of customers who do their home improvement projects.

automobiles toward a small, very exclusive market: wealthy people who want the ultimate in prestige in an automobile. Other companies target multiple markets with different products, prices, distribution systems, and promotion for each one.

Undifferentiated Approach A company that designs a single marketing mix and directs it at the entire market for a particular product is using an **undifferentiated approach** (see Figure 12.2). This approach assumes that individual customers in the target market for a specific kind of product have similar needs and that the organization therefore can satisfy most customers with a single marketing mix. This single marketing mix consists of one type of product with little or no variation, one price, one promotional program aimed at everyone, and one distribution system to reach all customers in the total market. Products that can be marketed successfully with the undifferentiated approach include staple food items, such as sugar and salt, and certain kinds of farm produce. An undifferentiated approach is useful in only a limited number of situations because for most product categories, buyers have different needs. When customers' needs vary, a company should use the market-segmentation approach.

Market-Segmentation Approach A firm that is marketing forty-foot yachts would not direct its marketing effort toward every person in the total boat market. Some might want a sailboat or a canoe. Others might want a speedboat or an outboard-powered fishing boat. Still others might be looking for something resembling a small ocean liner. Marketing efforts directed toward such boat buyers would be wasted. Instead, the firm would direct its attention toward a particular portion, or *segment*, of the total market for boats. A **market segment** is a group of individuals or organizations within a market that shares one or more common characteristics. The process of dividing a market into segments is called **market segmentation**. As shown in Figure 12.2, there are two types of market-segmentation approaches: concentrated and differentiated. When an organization uses *concentrated* market segmentation, a single marketing mix is directed at a single market segment. If *differentiated* market segmentation is employed, multiple marketing mixes are focused on multiple market segments.

In our boat example, one common characteristic, or *basis*, for segmentation might be "end use of a boat." The firm would be interested primarily in that market segment whose uses for a boat could lead to the purchase of a forty-foot yacht. Another basis for segmentation might be income; still another might be geographic location. Each of these variables can affect the type of boat an individual might purchase. When choosing a

Undifferentiated Approach.

The producer of Morton Salt uses an undifferentiated approach because people's need for salt is homogenous.

undifferentiated approach directing a single marketing mix at the entire market for a particular product

Is this ad aimed at all women?

The maker of RoC Retinol Correxion is not aiming its products at all women, but it is using market segmentation. This product is targeted to women aged 40 and older.

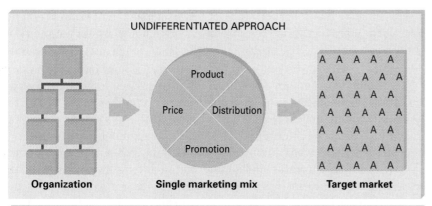

UNDIFFERENTIATED APPROACH

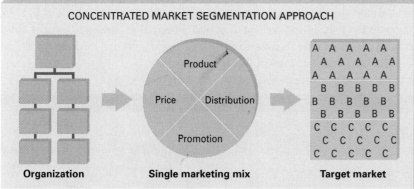

CONCENTRATED MARKET SEGMENTATION APPROACH

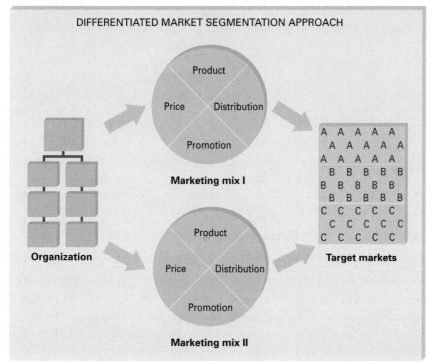

DIFFERENTIATED MARKET SEGMENTATION APPROACH

NOTE: The letters in each target market represent potential customers. Customers that have the same letters have similar characteristics and similar product needs.

FIGURE 12.2

General Approaches for Selecting Target Markets

The undifferentiated approach assumes that individual customers have similar needs and that most customers can be satisfied with a single marketing mix. When customers' needs vary, the market-segmentation approach—either concentrated or differentiated—should be used.

Source: William M. Pride and O. C. Ferrell, *Marketing: Concepts and Strategies* (Boston: Houghton Mifflin, 2006). Copyright © 2006 by Houghton Mifflin Company. Adapted with permission.

market segment a group of individuals or organizations within a market that shares one or more common characteristics

market segmentation the process of dividing a market into segments and directing a marketing mix at a particular segment or segments rather than at the total market

CONCEPT CHECK

What is the purpose of market segmentation? What is the relationship between market segmentation and the selection of target markets?

TABLE 12.3

Common Bases of Market Segmentation

Source: William M. Pride and O. C. Ferrell, *Marketing: Concepts and Strategies* (Boston: Houghton Mifflin, 2006). Copyright © 2006 by Houghton Mifflin Company. Adapted with permission.

ACE the Test
Hangman

basis for segmentation, it is important to select a characteristic that relates to differences in people's needs for a product. The yacht producer, for example, would not use religion to segment the boat market because people's needs for boats do not vary based on religion.

Marketers use a wide variety of segmentation bases. Those bases most commonly applied to consumer markets are shown in Table 12.3. Each may be used as a single basis for market segmentation or in combination with other bases. **EXAMPLE** Vertu, a part of mobile phone maker Nokia, has segmented the market for cellular phones and is using a concentrated targeting strategy. The segment Vertu is after is very wealthy customers who want luxurious, social-status possessions. The company's mobile phones are made from precious materials, including gold, platinum, and sapphire crystal. The phones include a button that connects the owner to a personal assistant twenty-four hours a day. To reach its wealthy target market, Vertu sells its phones in private suites in select large cities (e.g., New York, London, Paris, Tokyo, and of course, Beverly Hills) and at Nieman Marcus department stores for a price ranging from just under $5,000 to almost $20,000 per phone. Such stars as Gwyneth Paltrow and Madonna are some of Vertu's customers.[10]

DEMOGRAPHIC	PSYCHOGRAPHIC	GEOGRAPHIC	BEHAVIORISTIC
Age	Personality attributes	Region	Volume usage
Gender	Motives	Urban, suburban,	End use
Race	Lifestyles	Rural	Benefit expectations
Ethnicity		Market density	Brand loyalty
Income		Climate	Price sensitivity
Education		Terrain	
Occupation		City size	
Family size		County size	
Family life cycle		State size	
Religion			
Social class			

Creating a Marketing Mix

A business firm controls four important elements of marketing that it combines in a way that reaches the firm's target market. These four elements are

* Product   * Distribution
* Price   * Promotion

When combined, these four elements form a marketing mix (see Figure 12.3).

A firm can vary its marketing mix by changing any one or more of these ingredients. Thus a firm may use one marketing mix to reach one target market and a second, somewhat different marketing mix to reach another target market. **EXAMPLE** Toyota's marketing research about Generation Y drivers found that they practically live in their cars and that many even keep a change of clothes handy in their vehicles. As a result of this research, Toyota designed its Scion as a "home on wheels," with a 15-volt outlet for plugging in a computer, reclining front seats for napping, and a powerful audio system for listening to MP3 music files, all for a $12,500 price tag.[11]

The *product* ingredient of the marketing mix includes decisions about the product's design, brand name, packaging, warranties, and the like. **EXAMPLE** When McDonald's decides on brand names, package designs, sizes of orders, flavors of sauces, and recipes, these choices are all part of the product ingredient.

The *pricing* ingredient is concerned with both base prices and discounts of various kinds. Pricing decisions are intended to achieve particular goals, such as to maximize profit or even to make room for new models. The rebates offered by automobile manufacturers are a pricing strategy developed to boost low auto sales. Product and pricing are discussed in detail in Chapter 14.

■ Marketing mix

■ Marketing environment

The *distribution* ingredient involves not only transportation and storage but also the selection of intermediaries. How many levels of intermediaries should be used in the distribution of a particular product? Should the product be distributed as widely as possible? Or should distribution be restricted to a few specialized outlets in each area? These and other questions related to distribution are considered in Chapter 15.

The *promotion* ingredient focuses on providing information to target markets. The major forms of promotion are advertising, personal selling, sales promotion, and public relations. These four forms are discussed in Chapter 14.

These ingredients of the marketing mix are controllable elements. A firm can vary each of them to suit its organizational goals, marketing goals, and target markets. As we extend our discussion of marketing strategy, we will see that the marketing environment includes a number of *uncontrollable* elements.

FIGURE 12.3

The Marketing Mix and the Marketing Environment

The marketing mix consists of elements that the firm controls—product, price, distribution, and promotion. The firm generally has no control over forces in the marketing environment.

Source: William M. Pride and O. C. Ferrell, *Marketing: Concepts and Strategies* (Boston: Houghton Mifflin, 2006). Copyright © 2006 by Houghton Mifflin Company. Adapted with permission.

TEST PREPPER 12.5

True or False?

____ 1. An undifferentiated approach is useful in only a limited number of situations because for most product categories, buyers have different needs.

____ 2. A firm that is marketing a luxury automobile would not direct its marketing efforts toward every person in the automotive market.

____ 3. Vertu, a part of Nokia, is after very wealthy customers who want luxurious, social-status possessions.

Multiple Choice

 4. When Coca-Cola uses different marketing campaigns for Coke than for Dasani for different target markets, it is engaging in

    a. market segmentation.
    b. marketing mix.
    c. target marketing.
    d. beverage marketing.
    e. differentiated marketing.

ACE the Test
ACE & ACE+
Practice Test 12.5

Marketing Strategy and the Marketing Environment

Learning Objective ⑥

Explain how the marketing environment affects strategic market planning.

CONCEPT CHECK

Describe the forces in the marketing environment that affect an organization's marketing decisions

The marketing mix consists of elements that a firm controls and uses to reach its target market. In addition, the firm has control over such organizational resources as finances and information. These resources, too, may be used to accomplish marketing goals. However, the firm's marketing activities are also affected by a number of external—and generally uncontrollable—forces. As Figure 12.3 illustrates, the forces that make up the external *marketing environment* are

* *Economic forces*—the effects of economic conditions on customers' ability and willingness to buy

* *Sociocultural forces*—influences in a society and its culture that result in changes in attitudes, beliefs, norms, customs, and lifestyles

* *Political forces*—influences that arise through the actions of elected and appointed officials

BIZ TECH

Leaping from Virtual to Reality

When some people saw the Internet as the end of the greeting card business, Hallmark took it as a new beginning. The company has integrated its online and offline marketing efforts to build customer relationships, launch new products, and keep profits growing.

"If you get customers to interact with you both online and in the stores, they're better customers," states Hallmark's marketing manager. This is the idea behind Hallmark's free e-cards, electronic greeting cards that customers can personalize and e-mail to friends and relatives. Customers who come to the Hallmark site to send e-cards also see other Hallmark products.

What's more, e-cards are a good way to test new product ideas. Hallmark's talking cartoon dogs, Hoops and YoYo, became so popular on e-cards that Hallmark put them on nonvirtual products such as T-shirts, dolls, wallets, wristwatches, and even a CD—sold online and in Hallmark stores.

Sources: Information based on Chris Batchik, "Integration: Bridging the Online/Offline Gap," *B to B*, March 13, 2006, p. 12; Bob Tedeschi, "The Resurgence of E-Cards," *New York Times*, January 30, 2006, p. C6; "Online Marketing: Trust and the Blogging Stranger," *Marketing Week*, November 23, 2006, p. 38.

* *Competitive forces*—the actions of competitors, who are in the process of implementing their own marketing plans
* *Legal and regulatory forces*—laws that protect consumers and competition and government regulations that affect marketing
* *Technological forces*—technological changes that, on the one hand, can create new marketing opportunities or, on the other, can cause products to become obsolete almost overnight

These forces influence decisions about marketing-mix ingredients. Changes in the environment can have a major impact on existing marketing strategies. In addition, changes in environmental forces may lead to abrupt shifts in customers' needs. **EXAMPLE** Technological forces, for example, are having a major impact at Intel, the world's largest producer of computer microchips. With competition from iPods, Blackberrys, cell phones, and other handheld devices, the PC industry is slowing, and Intel is revamping its focus and its brand in an effort to remain relevant. Intel is launching more new products than at any time in the company's history. The Viiv will be a new chip designed to replace your TiVo, stereo, and potentially, cable or satellite box. It can download first-run movies, music, and games. In addition to its expanding product range, Intel is hiring software developers, sociologists, ethnographers, and even doctors for product development.[12]

Developing a Marketing Plan

Learning Objective 7

Understand the major components of a marketing plan.

A **marketing plan** is a written document that specifies an organization's resources, objectives, marketing strategy, and implementation and control efforts to be used in marketing a specific product or product group.

The marketing plan

* Describes the firm's current position or situation
* Establishes marketing objectives for the product
* Specifies how the organization will attempt to achieve these objectives

Marketing plans vary with respect to the time period involved. Short-range plans are for one year or less, medium-range plans cover from over one year up to five years, and long-range plans cover periods of more than five years.

Why a Well-Written Marketing Plan Is Important

* The plan will be used for communication among the firm's employees.
* It covers the assignment of responsibilities, tasks, and schedules for implementation.
* It specifies how resources are to be allocated to achieve marketing objectives.
* It helps marketing managers monitor and evaluate the performance of the marketing strategy.

marketing plan a written document that specifies an organization's resources, objectives, strategy, and implementation and control efforts to be used in marketing a specific product or product group

Because the forces of the marketing environment are subject to change, marketing plans have to be updated frequently. **EXAMPLE** Disney recently made changes to its marketing plans by combining all activities and licensing associated with the Power Rangers, Winnie the Pooh, and Disney Princess into one marketing plan with a $500 million budget. The primary goal is to send consistent messages about branding to customers. As the new marketing plan is implemented, Disney will have to respond quickly to customers' reactions and make adjustments to the plan.[13] The major components of a marketing plan are shown in Table 12.4.

TABLE 12.4

Components of the Marketing Plan

Source: William M. Pride and O. C. Ferrell, *Marketing: Concepts and Strategies* (Boston: Houghton Mifflin, 2006). Copyright © 2006 by Houghton Mifflin Company. Reprinted with permission.

PLAN COMPONENT	COMPONENT SUMMARY	HIGHLIGHTS
Executive summary	One- to two-page synopsis of the entire marketing plan	
Environmental analysis	Information about the company's current situation with respect to the marketing environment	1. Assessment of marketing environment factors 2. Assessment of target market(s) 3. Assessment of current marketing objectives and performance
SWOT analysis	Assessment of the organization's strengths, weaknesses, opportunities, and threats	1. *Strengths* 2. *Weaknesses* 3. *Opportunities* 4. *Threats*
Marketing objectives	Specification of the firm's marketing objectives	Qualitative measures of what is to be accomplished
Marketing strategies	Outline of how the firm will achieve its objectives	1. Target market(s) 2. Marketing mix
Marketing implementation	Outline of how the firm will implement its marketing strategies	1. Marketing organization 2. Activities and responsibilities 3. Implementation timetable
Evaluation and control	Explanation of how the firm will measure and evaluate the results of the implemented plan	1. Performance standards 2. Financial controls 3. Monitoring procedures (audits)

TEST PREPPER 12.6 12.7

True or False?

T 1. Changes in environmental forces may lead to abrupt shifts in customers' needs.

T 2. One of the reasons that a marketing plan is important is because the plan will be used for communication among the firm's employees.

F 3. Conducting a SWOT analysis is not part of the marketing plan.

Multiple Choice

A 4. McDonald's, Wendy's, and Burger King all compete for children's meals with similar toys. In the marketing world, this would be an example of

a. competitive force.
b. sociocultural force.
c. economic force.
d. legal force.
e. technological force.

ACE the Test
ACE & ACE+
Practice Tests 12.6, 12.7

Market Measurement and Sales Forecasting

Learning Objective ⑧

Describe how market measurement helps in determining sales forecasts.

Measuring the sales potential of specific types of market segments helps an organization to make some important decisions. It can evaluate the feasibility of entering new segments. The organization also can decide how best to allocate its marketing resources and activities among market segments in which it is already active. All such estimates should identify the relevant time frame. As with marketing plans, these estimates may be short range, covering periods of less than one year; medium range, covering one to five years; or long range, covering more than five years. The estimates also should define the geographic boundaries of the forecast. For example, sales potential can be estimated for a city, county, state, or group of nations. Finally, analysts should indicate whether their estimates are for a specific product item, a product line, or an entire product category.

A **sales forecast** is an estimate of the amount of a product that an organization expects to sell during a certain period of time based on a specified level of marketing effort. Managers in different divisions of an organization rely on sales forecasts when they purchase raw materials, schedule production, secure financial resources, consider plant or equipment purchases, hire personnel, and plan inventory levels. Because the accuracy of a sales forecast is so important, organizations often use several forecasting methods, including executive judgments, surveys of buyers or sales personnel, time-series analyses, correlation analyses, and market tests. The specific methods used depend on the costs involved, type of product, characteristics of the market, time span of the forecast, purposes for which the forecast is used, stability of historical sales data, availability of the required information, and expertise and experience of forecasters.

sales forecast an estimate of the amount of a product that an organization expects to sell during a certain period of time based on a specified level of marketing effort

CONCEPT CHECK
What major issues should be specified before conducting a sales forecast?

Marketing Information

Learning Objective ⑨

Distinguish between a marketing information system and marketing research.

The availability and use of accurate and timely information are critical to making effective marketing decisions. A wealth of marketing information is obtainable. There are two general ways to obtain it: through a marketing information system and through marketing research.

Marketing Information Systems

A **marketing information system** is a system for managing marketing information that is gathered continually from internal and external sources. Most such systems

marketing information system a system for managing marketing information that is gathered continually from internal and external sources

are computer-based because of the amount of data the system must accept, store, sort, and retrieve. *Continual* collection of data is essential if the system is to incorporate the most up-to-date information.

How the Marketing Information System Works

* Data from a variety of sources are fed into the system.
* Data from *internal* sources include sales figures, product and marketing costs, inventory levels, and activities of the sales force.
* Data from *external* sources relate to the organization's suppliers, intermediaries, and customers; competitors' marketing activities; and economic conditions.
* All these data are stored and processed within the marketing information system.
* Its output is a flow of information in the form that is most useful for making marketing decisions. This information might include daily sales reports by territory and product, forecasts of sales or buying trends, and reports on changes in market share for the major brands in a specific industry.

Marketing Research

Marketing research is the process of systematically gathering, recording, and analyzing data concerning a particular marketing problem. Thus marketing research is used in specific situations to obtain information not otherwise available to decision makers. It is an intermittent, rather than a continual, source of marketing information. **EXAMPLE** With the help of a new software company, Dunkin' Donuts is using marketing research to remain competitive against Krispy Kreme and Starbucks, as well as McDonald's, which recently entered the espresso-drink market. A survey of Dunkin' Donuts customers revealed that they welcomed menu changes such as iced beverages, espresso drinks, and scrambled eggs and cheese on a bagel. The firm's research also suggested that it should continue its strategy of targeting workday on-the-go customers and not taking on Starbucks directly.[14]

Table 12.5 outlines a six-step procedure for conducting marketing research. This procedure is particularly well suited to testing new products, determining various

---

CONCEPT CHECK

What new information technologies are changing the ways that marketers keep track of business trends and customers?

---

marketing research the process of systematically gathering, recording, and analyzing data concerning a particular marketing problem

---

TABLE 12.5

The Six Steps of Marketing Research

1. Define the problem	In this step, the problem is stated clearly and accurately to determine what issues are involved in the research, what questions to ask, and what types of solutions are needed. This is a crucial step that should not be rushed.
2. Make a preliminary investigation	The objective of preliminary investigation is to develop both a sharper definition of the problem and a set of tentative answers. The tentative answers are developed by examining internal information and published data and by talking with persons who have some experience with the problem. These answers will be tested by further research.
3. Plan the research	At this stage, researchers know what facts are needed to resolve the identified problem and what facts are available. They make plans on how to gather needed but missing data.
4. Gather factual information	Once the basic research plan has been completed, the needed information can be collected by mail, telephone, or personal interviews; by observation; or from commercial or government data sources. The choice depends on the plan and the available sources of information.
5. Interpret the information	Facts by themselves do not always provide a sound solution to a marketing problem. They must be interpreted and analyzed to determine the choices available to management.
6. Reach a conclusion	Sometimes the conclusion or recommendation becomes obvious when the facts are interpreted. However, in other cases, reaching a conclusion may not be so easy because of gaps in the information or intangible factors that are difficult to evaluate. If and when the evidence is less than complete, it is important to say so.

characteristics of consumer markets, and evaluating promotional activities. Food-processing companies, such as Kraft Foods and Kellogg's, use a variety of marketing research methods to avoid costly mistakes in introducing the wrong products or products in the wrong way or at the wrong time. They have been particularly interested in using marketing research to learn more about the African-American and Hispanic markets. Understanding of the food preferences, loyalties, and purchase motivators of these groups enables these companies to serve them better.

Using Technology to Gather and Analyze Marketing Information

Technology is making information for marketing decisions increasingly accessible. The integration of telecommunications with computing technology provides marketers with access to accurate information not only about customers and competitors but also about industry forecasts and business trends.

Communication Tools Used to Obtain Marketing Information

* *Databases.* A *database* is a collection of information arranged for easy access and retrieval. Using databases, marketers tap into internal sales reports, newspaper articles, company news releases, government economic reports, bibliographies, and more. Many marketers use commercial databases, such as LEXIS-NEXIS, to obtain useful information for marketing decisions. Many of these commercial databases are available in printed form (for a fee), online (for a fee), or on purchasable CD-ROMs. Other marketers develop their own databases in-house. Some firms sell their databases to other organizations. **EXAMPLE** *Reader's Digest*, for example, markets a database that provides information on 100 million households.

* *Online information services.* Online information services offer subscribers access to e-mail, websites, files for downloading (such as with Acrobat Reader), news, databases, and research materials. By subscribing to mailing lists, marketers can receive electronic newsletters and participate in online discussions with other network users. This ability to communicate online with customers, suppliers, and employees improves the capability of a firm's marketing information system and helps the company track its customers' changing desires and buying habits.

* *Internet.* The Internet has evolved as a powerful communication medium, linking customers and companies around the world via computer networks with e-mail,

Marketing research.

Marketing research service companies, such as AC Nielsen, provide a variety of marketing research services to organizations that have information needs.

SPOTLIGHT

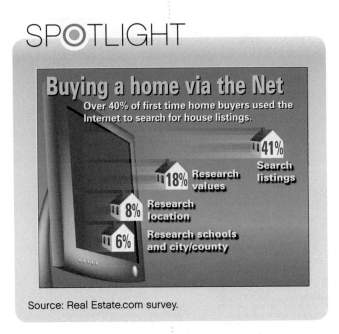

Buying a home via the Net

Over 40% of first time home buyers used the Internet to search for house listings.

41% Search listings

18% Research values

8% Research location

6% Research schools and city/county

Source: Real Estate.com survey.

forums, web pages, and more. Growth in Internet use has given rise to an entire industry that makes marketing information easily accessible to both companies and customers. **EXAMPLE** Among the many web pages useful for marketing research are the home pages of Nielsen marketing research and *Advertising Age*.

Table 12.6 lists a number of websites that may serve as valuable resources for marketing research. The Bureau of the Census, for example, uses the Internet to disseminate information that may be useful to marketing researchers, particularly through the *Statistical Abstract of the United States* and data from the most recent Census. The "Census Lookup" option allows marketing researchers to create their own customized information. With this online tool, researchers can select tables by clicking boxes to select a state and then, within the state, the county, place, and urbanized area or metropolitan statistical area to be examined.

TABLE 12.6

Internet Sources of Marketing Information

Source: William M. Pride and O. C. Ferrell, *Marketing: Concepts and Strategies* (Boston: Houghton Mifflin, 2006). Copyright © 2006 by Houghton Mifflin Company. Reprinted with permission.

GOVERNMENT SOURCES	COMMERCIAL SOURCES	PERIODICALS AND BOOKS
census.gov	acnielsen.com	adage.com
state.gov	Infores.com	salesandmarketing.com
fedworld.gov	gallup.com	Fortune.com
	arbitron.com	inc.com
	chamber-of-commerce.com	businessweek.com
		bloomberg.com

TEST PREPPER (12.8 12.9)

True or False?

 1. One reason that market measurement is important is because an organization can decide how best to allocate its marketing resources and activities among market segments in which it is already active.

2. *Reader's Digest* markets a database that provides information on 10 million households.

3. Growth in Internet use has given rise to an entire industry that makes marketing information easily accessible to both companies and customers.

Multiple Choice

 4. The difference between a marketing information system (MIS) and market research is

 a. market research is continual, whereas an MIS is for a specific problem.

 b. market research is for a specific problem, whereas an MIS is continual.
 c. market research is cheaper to conduct than the cost of an MIS.
 d. market research is complex, whereas an MIS is simple.
 e. market research deals with advertisement, and MIS does not.

5. What is (are) a collection of information arranged for easy access and retrieval.

 a. A database
 b. Online services
 c. The Internet
 d. A marketing plan
 e. The marketing mix

ACE the Test
ACE & ACE+
Practice Tests 12.8, 12.9

Types of Buying Behavior

Learning Objective ⑩

Explain the importance of studying buying behavior and its major classifications.

Buying behavior may be defined as the decisions and actions of people involved in buying and using products.[15]

Consumer buying behavior refers to the purchasing of products for personal or household use, not for business purposes. **Business buying behavior** is the purchasing of products by producers, resellers, governmental units, and institutions. Since a firm's success depends greatly on buyers' reactions to a particular marketing strategy, it is important to understand buying behavior. Marketing managers are better able to predict customer responses to marketing strategies and to develop a satisfying marketing mix if they are aware of the factors that affect buying behavior.

Consumer Buying Behavior

Consumers' buying behaviors differ when they buy different types of products. For frequently purchased, low-cost items, a consumer employs routine response behavior involving very little search or decision-making effort. When buying an unfamiliar, expensive item or one that is seldom purchased, the consumer engages in extensive decision making.

A person deciding on a purchase goes through some or all of the steps shown in Figure 12.4.

* First, the consumer acknowledges that a problem exists. A problem is usually the lack of a product or service that is desired or needed.

* Then the buyer looks for information, which may include brand names, product characteristics, warranties, and other features.

* Next, the buyer weighs the various alternatives he or she has discovered and then finally makes a choice and acquires the item.

* In the after-purchase stage, the consumer evaluates the suitability of the product. This judgment

buying behavior the decisions and actions of people involved in buying and using products

consumer buying behavior the purchasing of products for personal or household use, not for business purposes

business buying behavior the purchasing of products by producers, resellers, governmental units, and institutions

Recognizing a problem.

Some advertisements, such as this one used for uni-ball pens, are aimed to a particular stage of the consumer's buying-decision process. This uni-ball pen ad is meant to simulate the problem-recognition stage of the buying-decision process.

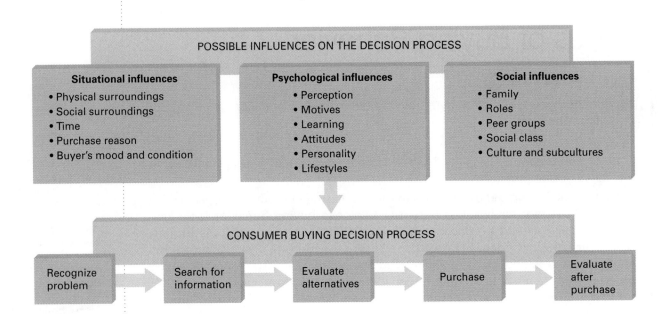

POSSIBLE INFLUENCES ON THE DECISION PROCESS

Situational influences
- Physical surroundings
- Social surroundings
- Time
- Purchase reason
- Buyer's mood and condition

Psychological influences
- Perception
- Motives
- Learning
- Attitudes
- Personality
- Lifestyles

Social influences
- Family
- Roles
- Peer groups
- Social class
- Culture and subcultures

CONSUMER BUYING DECISION PROCESS

Recognize problem → Search for information → Evaluate alternatives → Purchase → Evaluate after purchase

FIGURE 12.4

Consumer Buying Decision Process and Possible Influences on the Process

A buyer goes through some or all of these steps when making a purchase.

Source: William M. Pride and O. C. Ferrell, *Marketing: Concepts and Strategies* (Boston: Houghton Mifflin, 2006). Copyright © 2006 by Houghton Mifflin Company. Adapted with permission.

personal income the income an individual receives from all sources *less* the Social Security taxes the individual must pay

disposable income personal income *less* all additional personal taxes

discretionary income disposable income *less* savings and expenditures on food, clothing, and housing

will affect future purchases. As Figure 12.4 shows, the buying process is influenced by situational factors (physical surroundings, social surroundings, time, purchase reason, and buyer's mood and condition), psychological factors (perception, motives, learning, attitudes, personality, and lifestyle), and social factors (family, roles, peer groups, social class, and culture and subcultures).

Consumer buying behavior is also affected by ability to buy, or *buying power*, which is largely determined by income. As every taxpayer knows, not all income is available for spending. For this reason, marketers consider income in three different ways. **Personal income** is the income an individual receives from all sources *less* the Social Security taxes the individual must pay. **Disposable income** is personal income *less* all additional personal taxes. These taxes include income, estate, gift, and property taxes levied by local, state, and federal governments. About 3 percent of all disposable income is saved. **Discretionary income** is disposable income *less* savings and expenditures on food, clothing, and housing. Discretionary income is of particular interest to marketers because consumers have the most choice in spending it. Consumers use their discretionary income to purchase items ranging from automobiles and vacations to movies and pet food.

Business Buying Behavior

Business buyers consider a product's quality, its price, and the service provided by suppliers. **EXAMPLE** Marketers at GraniteRock Company understand the value of customer service and thus concentrate their efforts on on-time delivery to distinguish GraniteRock from its competitors.[16] Business buyers usually are better informed than consumers about products and generally buy in larger quantities. In a business, a committee or group of people, rather than single individuals, often decides on purchases. Committee members must consider the organization's objectives, purchasing policies, resources, and personnel. Business buying occurs through description, inspection, sampling, or negotiation. A number of organizations buy a variety of products online.

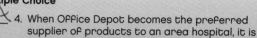

TEST PREPPER 12.10

True or False?

___ 1. Buying behavior can be classified in three broad categories.

___ 2. When buying an unfamiliar, expensive item or one that is seldom purchased, the consumer does not engage in extensive decision making.

___ 3. Consumer buying behavior is also affected by ability to buy, or buying power, which is largely determined by income.

Multiple Choice

___ 4. When Office Depot becomes the preferred supplier of products to an area hospital, it is important to know

   a. business buying behavior.
   b. consumer buying behavior.
   c. bulk buying behavior.
   d. institutional buying behavior.
   e. not-for-profit buying behavior.

ACE the Test
ACE & ACE+
Practice Test 12.10

Prepare for Class
CL News Feeds
CL News Now

➔ RETURN TO INSIDE BUSINESS

Applebee's marketers know that the casual dining industry is highly competitive. They never stop researching when, where, why, and how often customers dine out so that they can cook up an appropriate marketing mix. Innovations such as Carside to Go and special signature dishes are intended to keep customers coming back for more—and to set Applebee's apart from the competition.

At the same time, Applebee's is careful to retain the marketing-mix elements that have strengthened relationships with regular customers. For instance, it emphasizes the "neighborhood" nature of its business by customizing the decor for each restaurant. Value is another key element in Applebee's marketing mix. In the words of one Applebee's executive, the chain is "bringing affordable dishes to a new level of excellence for mainstream America."

Questions

1. Why does Applebee's often add new menu items?
2. What forces in the marketing environment appear to be affecting Applebee's marketing mix?

LEARNING OBJECTIVES REVIEW

1 Understand the meaning of *marketing* and the importance of management of customer relationships.

- Marketing is an organizational function and a set of processes for creating, communicating, and delivering value to customers and for managing customer relationships in ways that benefit the organization and its stakeholders.

- Maintaining positive relationships with customers is crucial.

- Relationship marketing is establishing long-term, mutually satisfying buyer-seller relationships. Customer relationship management uses information about customers to create marketing strategies that develop and sustain desirable customer relationships.

- Managing customer relationships requires identifying patterns of buying behavior and focusing on the most profitable customers.

- Customer lifetime value is a combination of purchase frequency, average value of purchases, and brand-switching patterns over the entire span of a customer's relationship with a company.

2 Explain how marketing adds value by creating several forms of utility.

- Marketing adds value in the form of utility, or the power of a product or service to satisfy a need.

- It creates place utility by making products available where customers want them, time utility by making products available when customers want them, and possession utility by transferring ownership of products to buyers.

3 Trace the development of the marketing concept and understand how it is implemented.

- From the Industrial Revolution until the early twentieth century, business people focused on the production of goods.

- From the 1920s to the 1950s, the emphasis moved to the selling of goods.

- During the 1950s, business people recognized the importance of selling products and satisfying customers' needs.

- They began to implement the marketing concept, a business philosophy that involves the entire organization in the dual processes of meeting the customers' needs and achieving the organization's goals.

- Implementation of the marketing concept begins and ends with customers—first to determine what customers' needs are and later to evaluate how well the firm is meeting those needs.

4 Understand what markets are and how they are classified.

- A market consists of people with needs, the ability to buy, and the desire and authority to purchase.

- Markets are classified as consumer and industrial (producer, reseller, governmental, and institutional) markets.

5 Identify the four elements of the marketing mix and their importance in developing a marketing strategy.

- The four elements of a firm's marketing mix are product, price, distribution, and promotion.
  - The product ingredient includes decisions about the product's design, brand name, packaging, and warranties.
  - The pricing ingredient is concerned with both base prices and various types of discounts.
  - Distribution involves not only transportation and storage but also the selection of intermediaries.
  - Promotion focuses on providing information to target markets.

- The elements of the marketing mix can be varied to suit broad organizational goals, marketing objectives, and target markets.

- A marketing strategy is a plan for the best use of an organization's resources to meet its objectives.

- Developing a marketing strategy involves selecting and analyzing a target market and creating and maintaining a marketing mix that will satisfy that target market.

Improve Your Grade
Audio Chapter Summary & Quiz

- A target market is chosen through either the undifferentiated approach or the market-segmentation approach.

- A market segment is a group of individuals or organizations within a market that has similar characteristics and needs.

- Businesses that use an undifferentiated approach design a single marketing mix and direct it at the entire market for a particular product.

- The market-segmentation approach directs a marketing mix at a segment of a market.

6 **Explain how the marketing environment affects strategic market planning.**

- To achieve a firm's marketing objectives, marketing-mix strategies must begin with an assessment of the marketing environment, which, in turn, will influence decisions about marketing-mix ingredients.

- Marketing activities are affected by a number of external forces that make up the marketing environment. These forces include
  - Economic forces
  - Sociocultural forces
  - Political forces
  - Competitive forces
  - Legal and regulatory forces
  - Technological forces

7 **Understand the major components of a marketing plan.**

- A marketing plan is a written document that specifies an organization's resources, objectives, strategy, and implementation and control efforts to be used in marketing a specific product or product group.

- Marketing plans can be short range, covering one year or less; medium range, covering two to five years; or long range, covering periods of more than five years.

8 **Describe how market measurement helps in determining sales forecasts.**

- Market measurement and sales forecasting are used to estimate sales potential and predict product sales in specific market segments.

9 **Distinguish between a marketing information system and marketing research.**

- Strategies are monitored and evaluated through marketing research and the marketing information system that stores and processes internal and external data in a form that aids marketing decision making.

- A marketing information system is a system for managing marketing information that is gathered continually from internal and external sources.

- Marketing research is the process of systematically gathering, recording, and analyzing data concerning a particular marketing problem. It is an intermittent rather than a continual source of marketing information.

- Technology is making information for marketing decisions more accessible.

- Information technologies that are changing the way marketers obtain and use information are databases, online information services, and the Internet.

10 **Explain the importance of studying buying behavior and its major classifications**

- Buying behavior consists of the decisions and actions of people involved in buying and using products.

- Consumer buying behavior refers to the purchase of products for personal or household use. Organizational buying behavior is the purchase of products by producers, resellers, governments, and institutions.

- Understanding buying behavior helps marketers to predict how buyers will respond to marketing strategies.

- The consumer buying decision process consists of five steps, including recognizing the problem, searching for information, evaluating alternatives, purchasing, and evaluating after purchase. Factors affecting the consumer buying decision process fall into three categories: situational influences, psychological influences, and social influences.

VIDEO CASE

New Balance Races for Customer Relationships

New Balance is racing to build relationships with consumers who are less interested in superstar endorsements than in superperformance shoes. The brand is, as company ads proclaim, "endorsed by no one," which sets it apart from competitors that sign high-profile sports stars to promote their athletic shoes. Yet New Balance regularly racks up $1.5 billion in annual sales and is speeding along to gain ground on much larger competitors such as Nike and Reebok.

Rather than chase the teen market, New Balance appeals to a variety of segments of 21- to 55-year-old adults who want to achieve their personal best. Its marketers begin by studying customer needs in a specific category—for instance, running—and ask questions such as: For what type of runner will the shoe be designed? How many miles is that person likely to run every day or week? What is the runner's body makeup? The company also hires an outside firm to prepare a marketing brief with more details about the target customer, special features the shoe should have, estimated sales forecasts, and potential profit levels.

Next, marketing experts start adding up the costs of producing each new product so that they can estimate the retail price. Upscale high-performance shoes may contain more expensive materials and technology and thus sell for higher prices. Lower-end products may employ less technology and use different materials that perform at a different level. By varying both materials and technology, New Balance can offer a variety of products at different prices for various segments in each sports category, such as running shoes or basketball sneakers. Still, most New Balance shoes are priced at $60 and above, reinforcing the brand's reputation for high quality and high performance.

When New Balance is developing an $80 cushioning shoe, its marketers examine $80 cushioning shoes from competitors, comparing features as well as appearance and color. They often buy competing shoes to see what else is on the market and how New Balance products match up. Then the company will either make a prototype in one of its New England plants or, if the shoe is to be manufactured abroad, have one of the overseas factories make a prototype. This gives marketers a more realistic picture of costs so that they can determine the actual selling price and the expected profit.

Now New Balance is expanding beyond athletic shoes to target other markets. For example, it makes women's shoes under the Aravon brand. The Office line of Aravon shoes targets women who want fashion footwear, the Sandals line targets women who want casual footwear, and the Everyday line targets women who want comfortable footwear. All Aravon shoes use the foot-cushioning technology that New Balance builds into its sports shoes. In addition, New Balance markets high-performance sports apparel for men and women and has licensed its brand for parkas, jackets, and other outerwear apparel.

New Balance's decision to continue producing shoes in the United States is a smart competitive move for two reasons. First, the company has modernized and reorganized its U.S. factories to cut the production cycle from eight days to just eight hours. This means that it can get by with much less inventory. More important, it can start production immediately when retailers order or reorder merchandise. Second, New Balance has the manufacturing flexibility to fill special orders for unusual sizes and widths quickly. This strengthens its relationships with retailers, who are key players in the company's marketing mix. Because purchasing patterns can and do change at any time, New Balance has to be fast on its feet to stay ahead of the trends and win the race for customer relationships.[17]

For more information about this company, go to **www .newbalance.com.**

Questions
1. Is there evidence that New Balance is applying the marketing concept? Support your answer.
2. Is New Balance using an undifferentiated approach, a concentrated approach, or a differentiated approach to selecting target markets?
3. Why does New Balance pay close attention when retailers reorder a particular item?

BUILDING SKILLS FOR CAREER SUCCESS

1. Exploring the Internet

Consumer products companies with a variety of famous brand names known around the world are making their presence known on the Internet through websites and online banner advertising. The giants in consumer products include U.S.-based Procter & Gamble (**www.pg.com/**), Swiss-based Nestlé (**www.nestle.com/**), and British-based Unilever (**www.unilever.com/**).

According to a spokesperson for the Unilever Interactive Brand Center in New York, the firm is committed to making the Internet part of its marketing strategy. The center carries out research and development (R&D) and serves as a model for others now in operation in the Netherlands and Singapore. Information is shared with interactive marketers assigned to specific business units. Eventually, centers will be established globally, reflecting the fact that most of Unilever's $52 billion in sales takes place in about 100 countries around the world.

Unilever's view that online consumer product sales are the way of the future was indicated by online alliances established with Microsoft Network, America Online, and NetGrocer.com. Creating an online dialogue with consumers on a global scale is no simple task. Cultural differences often are subtle and difficult to explain but nonetheless are perceived by the viewers interacting with a site. Unilever's website, which is its connection to customers all over the world, has a global feel to it. The question is whether or not it is satisfactory to each target audience.[18] Visit the text website for updates to this exercise.

Assignment

1. Examine the Unilever, Procter & Gamble, and Nestlé sites and describe the features that you think would be most interesting to consumers.
2. Describe those features you do not like and explain why.
3. Do you think that the sites can contribute to better consumer buyer behavior? Explain your thinking.

2. Building Team Skills

Review the text definitions of *market* and *target market*. Markets can be classified as consumer or industrial.

Buyer behavior consists of the decisions and actions of those involved in buying and using products or services. By examining aspects of a company's products, you usually can determine the company's target market and the characteristics important to members of that target market.

Assignment

1. Working in teams of three to five, identify a company and its major products.
2. List and discuss characteristics that customers may find important. These factors may include price, quality, brand name, variety of services, salespeople, customer service, special offers, promotional campaign, packaging, convenience of use, convenience of purchase, location, guarantees, store/office decor, and payment terms.
3. Write a description of the company's primary customer (target market).

3. Researching Different Careers

Before interviewing for a job, you should learn all you can about the company. With this information, you will be prepared to ask meaningful questions about the firm during the interview, and the interviewer no doubt will be impressed with your knowledge of the business and your interest in it. To find out about a company, you can conduct some market research.

Assignment

1. Choose at least two local companies for which you might like to work.
2. Contact your local Chamber of Commerce. (The Chamber of Commerce collects information about local businesses, and most of its services are free.) Ask for information about the companies.
3. Call the Better Business Bureau in your community and ask if there are any complaints against the companies.
4. Prepare a report summarizing your findings.

Prepare for Class
Exploring the Internet

CHAPTER *13*

Creating and Pricing Products That Satisfy Customers

Your Guide to Success in Business

Why this chapter matters
To be successful, a business person must understand how to develop and manage a mix of appropriately priced products and to change the mix of products as customers' needs change.

LEARNING OBJECTIVES

1. Explain what a product is and how products are classified.
2. Discuss the product life cycle.
3. Define *product line* and *product mix*.
4. Identify the methods available for changing a product mix.
5. Explain the uses and importance of branding.
6. Explain the uses and importance of labeling and packaging.
7. Describe the economic basis of pricing and the means by which sellers can influence prices and buyers' perceptions of prices.
8. Identify the major pricing objectives used by businesses.
9. Examine the three major pricing methods that firms employ.
10. Explain the different types of pricing strategies.
11. Describe three major types of pricing for business products.

PCs for All: The Final Computer Frontier

Is it possible to create, produce, and distribute a laptop computer—let alone one equipped for wireless Internet access—priced as low as $150? As surprising as it may seem, a number of organizations are doing just that to get affordable PCs into the hands of children in developing countries.

For example, the nonprofit One Laptop Per Child initiative has developed the $150 XO laptop, powered by a small pull-cord generator rather than electricity or a battery. The XO's small (7.5-inch) screen uses very little power but displays only one program or document at a time. A wireless network connection is built into every laptop so that the young users can stay in touch, even if they live in remote rural areas. "I think of digital access for kids as a human right," says the founder of One Laptop Per Child, the former head of the MIT Media Lab, who expects to ship 50 million XO laptops to Africa, Latin America, and Asia within two years.

The giant chipmaker Intel has its own affordable PC programs. For example, the Community PC is designed to be the entire village rather than a single user. It runs on either electricity or car batteries, and if the software crashes, a one-touch "recover" button gets it going again. The price, in India, is about $550. Another Intel product, the Low Cost Full Featured PC, is a smaller version of the familiar desktop PC. Intel sells this low-cost version for less than $350 in Mexico.

Taiwan-based VIA Technologies is creating $230 PCs for use in Africa, with sand-resistant cases and the ability to run on either solar power or car batteries. In contrast to traditional PCs, which typically are assembled from readily available components, VIA's computers had to be designed from the ground up, part by part. The executive in charge of the design group notes that developing a low-price PC "is much more difficult than doing the high end. It's like building a Nissan to drive at the same speed as a Porsche."[1]

DID YOU KNOW?

The designer of VIA's low-price PC says developing this type of product is "much more difficult than doing the high end. It's like building a Nissan to drive at the same speed as a Porsche."

KEY TERMS

product (394)
consumer product (394)
business product (394)
convenience product (395)
shopping product (395)
specialty product (395)
raw material (396)
major equipment (396)
accessory equipment (396)
component part (396)
process material (396)
supply (396)
business service (396)
product life cycle (397)
product line (400)
product mix (400)
product modification (401)

line extension (402)
product deletion (402)
brand (406)
brand name (406)
brand mark (406)
trademark (406)
trade name (406)
manufacturer (or producer) brand (407)
store (or private) brand (407)
generic product (or brand) (407)
brand loyalty (408)
brand equity (408)
individual branding (409)
family branding (409)
brand extension (409)
packaging (410)

labeling (412)
express warranty (412)
price (413)
supply (413)
demand (413)
price competition (414)
nonprice competition (414)
product differentiation (414)
markup (417)
breakeven quantity (417)
total revenue (417)
fixed cost (417)
variable cost (417)
total cost (417)
price skimming (419)
penetration pricing (420)
negotiated pricing (420)

secondary-market pricing (420)
periodic discounting (421)
random discounting (421)
odd-number pricing (421)
multiple-unit pricing (421)
reference pricing (421)
bundle pricing (421)
everyday low prices (EDLPs) (422)
customary pricing (422)
captive pricing (422)
premium pricing (422)
price lining (422)
price leaders (423)
special-event pricing (423)
comparison discounting (423)
transfer pricing (424)
discount (424)

ACE the Test
Crossword Puzzle
Flashcards

product everything one receives in an exchange, including all tangible and intangible attributes and expected benefits; it may be a good, service, or idea

consumer product a product purchased to satisfy personal and family needs

business product a product bought for resale, for making other products, or for use in a firm's operations

CONCEPT CHECK

What are the products of (a) a bank, (b) an insurance company, and (c) a university?

Developing and managing products effectively are crucial to an organization's ability to maintain successful marketing mixes.

In this chapter we

* Define what a product is.

* Examine product classifications and describe the four stages, or life cycle, through which every product moves.

* Illustrate how firms manage products effectively by modifying or deleting existing products and by developing new products.

* Discuss branding, packaging, and labeling of products.

* Focus on pricing.

* Explain competitive factors that influence sellers' pricing decisions and also explore buyers' perceptions of prices.

* Consider organizational objectives that can be accomplished through pricing.

* Outline several methods for setting prices.

* Describe pricing strategies by which sellers can reach target markets successfully.

Classification of Products

Learning Objective

Explain what a product is and how products are classified.

A **product** is everything one receives in an exchange, including all tangible and intangible attributes and expected benefits. A car includes a warranty, an owner's manual, and perhaps free emergency road service for a year. Some of the intangibles that may go with an automobile include the status associated with ownership and the memories generated from past rides.

A product may be a good, a service, or an idea.

* A *good* is a real, physical thing that we can touch, such as a Classic Sport football.

* A *service* is a change we pay others to make for us. A real estate agent's services result in a change in the ownership of real property.

* An *idea* may take the form of philosophies, lessons, concepts, or advice. Thus we might buy a book (a good) that provides ideas on how to lose weight. Or we might join Weight Watchers for ideas on how to lose weight and for help (services) in doing so.

Different classes of products are directed at particular target markets. A product's classification largely determines what kinds of distribution, promotion, and pricing are appropriate in marketing the product.

Products can be grouped into two general categories: consumer and business (also called *business-to-business* or *industrial products*). A product purchased to satisfy personal and family needs is a **consumer product**. A product bought for resale, for making other products, or for use in a firm's operations is a **business product**. The buyer's use of the product determines the classification of an item. Note that a single item can be both a consumer and a business product. **EXAMPLE** A broom is a consumer product if you use it in your home. However, the same broom is a business product if you use it in the maintenance of your business.

Consumer Product Classifications

The traditional and most widely accepted system of classifying consumer products consists of three categories: convenience, shopping, and specialty products. These groupings are based primarily on characteristics of buyers' purchasing behavior.

A **convenience product** is a relatively inexpensive, frequently purchased item for which buyers want to exert only minimal effort. Examples include bread, gasoline, newspapers, soft drinks, and chewing gum. The buyer spends little time in planning the purchase of a convenience item or in comparing available brands or sellers.

A **shopping product** is an item for which buyers are willing to expend considerable effort on planning and making the purchase. Buyers allocate ample time for comparing stores and brands with respect to prices, product features, qualities, services, and perhaps warranties. Appliances, upholstered furniture, men's suits, bicycles, and cellular phones are examples of shopping products. These products are expected to last for a fairly long time and thus are purchased less frequently than convenience items.

A **specialty product** possesses one or more unique characteristics for which a group of buyers is willing to expend considerable purchasing effort. Buyers actually plan the purchase of a specialty product; they know exactly what they want and will not accept a substitute. In searching for specialty products, purchasers do not compare alternatives. Examples include unique sports cars, a specific type of antique dining table, a rare imported beer, or perhaps special handcrafted stereo speakers.

Business Product Classifications

Based on their characteristics and intended uses, business products can be classified into the following categories: raw materials,

convenience product a relatively inexpensive, frequently purchased item for which buyers want to exert only minimal effort

shopping product an item for which buyers are willing to expend considerable effort on planning and making the purchase

specialty product an item that possesses one or more unique characteristics for which a group of buyers is willing to expend considerable purchasing effort

◀

Shopping products.

Most brands of watches are shopping products. However, very expensive watches that are sold in few outlets across the U.S. are classified as specialty products.

raw material a basic material that actually becomes part of a physical product; usually comes from mines, forests, oceans, or recycled solid wastes

major equipment large tools and machines used for production purposes

accessory equipment standardized equipment used in a firm's production or office activities

component part an item that becomes part of a physical product and is either a finished item ready for assembly or a product that needs little processing before assembly

process material a material that is used directly in the production of another product but is not readily identifiable in the finished product

supply an item that facilitates production and operations but does not become part of a finished product

business service an intangible product that an organization uses in its operations

major equipment, accessory equipment, component parts, process materials, supplies, and services.

A **raw material** is a basic material that actually becomes part of a physical product. It usually comes from mines, forests, oceans, or recycled solid wastes. Raw materials usually are bought and sold according to grades and specifications.

Major equipment includes large tools and machines used for production purposes. Examples of major equipment are lathes, cranes, and stamping machines. Some major equipment is custom-made for a particular organization, but other items are standardized products that perform one or several tasks for many types of organizations.

Accessory equipment is standardized equipment used in a firm's production or office activities. Examples include hand tools, fax machines, fractional-horsepower motors, and calculators. Compared with major equipment, accessory items are usually much less expensive and are purchased routinely with less negotiation.

A **component part** becomes part of a physical product and is either a finished item ready for assembly or a product that needs little processing before assembly. Although it becomes part of a larger product, a component part often can be identified easily. Clocks, tires, computer chips, and switches are examples of component parts.

A **process material** is used directly in the production of another product. Unlike a component part, however, a process material is not readily identifiable in the finished product. Like component parts, process materials are purchased according to industry standards or the specifications of the individual purchaser. Examples include industrial glue and food preservatives.

A **supply** facilitates production and operations but does not become part of a finished product. Paper, pencils, oils, and cleaning agents are examples.

A **business service** is an intangible product that an organization uses in its operations. Examples include financial, legal, online, janitorial, and marketing research services. Purchasers must decide whether to provide their own services internally or to hire them from outside the organization.

TEST PREPPER 13.1

True or False?

 1. Basically, a product may be classified as a good or a service.

 2. An item that becomes part of a physical product and is either a finished item ready for assembly or a product that needs little processing before assembly is called a component part.

 3. Use of the accounting services of KBMG by T-Mobile would be considered the purchase of a business service.

Multiple Choice

 4. Stephen Chambers has just returned from the store having bought a quart of his favorite ice cream. This can best be classified as a purchase of a

  a. consumer product.
  b. business product.
  c. convenience product.
  d. specialty product.
  e. shopping product.

 5. Johnson County Community College recently replaced all its fax machines. This can best be classified as a purchase of

  a. major equipment.
  b. a business product.
  c. accessory equipment.
  d. a business service.
  e. a specialty product.

ACE the Test
ACE & ACE+
Practice Test 13.1

The Product Life Cycle

Learning Objective

Discuss the product life cycle.

In a way, products are like people. They are born, they live, and they die. Every product progresses through a **product life cycle**, a series of stages in which a product's sales revenue and profit increase, reach a peak, and then decline. A firm must be able to launch, modify, and delete products from its offering of products in response to changes in product life cycles. Otherwise, the firm's profits will disappear, and the firm will fail. Depending on the product, life-cycle stages will vary in length. In this section we discuss the stages of the life cycle and how marketers can use this information.

Stages of the Product Life Cycle

Generally, the product life cycle is assumed to be composed of four stages—introduction, growth, maturity, and decline—as shown in Figure 13.1. Some products progress through these stages rapidly, in a few weeks or months. Others may take years to go through each stage. The Rubik's Cube had a relatively short life cycle. Parker Brothers' Monopoly game, which was introduced over seventy years ago, is still going strong.

Introduction In the *introduction stage,* customer awareness and acceptance of the product are low. Sales rise gradually as a result of promotion and distribution activities, but initially, high development and marketing costs result in low profit or even in a loss. There are relatively few competitors. The price is sometimes high, and purchasers are primarily people who want to be "the first" to own the new product. The marketing challenge at this stage is to make potential customers aware of the product's existence and its features, benefits, and uses.

> **product life cycle** a series of stages in which a product's sales revenue and profit increase, reach a peak, and then decline

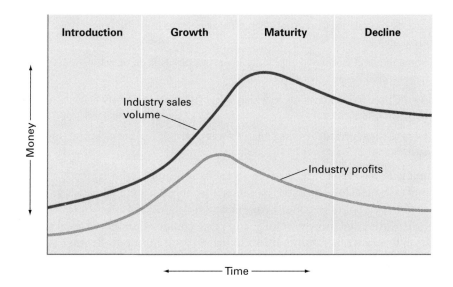

FIGURE 13.1

Product Life Cycle

The graph shows sales volume and profits during the life cycle of a product.

Source: William M. Pride and O. C. Ferrell, *Marketing: Concepts and Strategies* (Boston: Houghton Mifflin, 2006). Copyright © 2006 by Houghton Mifflin Company. Adapted with permission.

Marketing During the Introduction Stage

* Marketers must watch early buying patterns carefully and be prepared to modify the new product promptly if necessary.

* The product should be priced to attract the particular market segment that has the greatest desire and ability to buy the product.

* Plans for distribution and promotion should suit the targeted market segment.

* As with the product itself, the initial price, distribution channels, and promotional efforts may need to be adjusted quickly to maintain sales growth during the introduction stage.

Growth In the *growth stage,* sales increase rapidly as the product becomes well known. Other firms probably have begun to market competing products. The competition and lower unit costs (owing to mass production) result in a lower price, which reduces the profit per unit. Note that industry profits reach a peak and begin to decline during this stage. To meet the needs of the growing market, the originating firm offers modified versions of its product and expands its distribution. **EXAMPLE** The 3M Company, the maker of Post-it Notes, has developed a variety of sizes, colors, and designs.

Marketing During the Growth Stage

* Management's goal in the growth stage is to stabilize and strengthen the product's position by encouraging brand loyalty.

* To beat the competition, the company may further improve the product or expand the product line to appeal to additional market segments. **EXAMPLE** Apple, for example, has introduced several variations on its wildly popular iPod MP3 player. The iPod Mini is a smaller, more colorful device, and the iPod Shuffle is a more affordable version. The iPod Nano is a pencil-thin device that weighs barely over 1 ounce. The Video iPod can store and play movies, television shows, and music videos. Apple has expanded its iTunes Music Store to include downloadable versions of popular shows such as *Saturday Night Live, Desperate Housewives,* and *Lost,* as well as exclusive music videos from artists such as U2. Continuous product innovation and service expansion have helped to expand Apple's market penetration in the competitive MP3 player industry.[2]

* Management also may compete by lowering prices if increased production efficiency has resulted in savings for the company.

* As the product becomes more widely accepted, marketers may be able to broaden the network of distributors.

* During this period, promotional efforts attempt to build brand loyalty among customers.

Maturity Sales are still increasing at the beginning of the *maturity stage,* but the rate of increase has slowed. Later in this stage, the sales curve peaks and begins to decline. Industry profits decline throughout this stage. Product lines are simplified, markets are segmented more carefully, and price competition increases. The increased competition forces weaker competitors to leave the industry. Refinements and extensions of the original product continue to appear on the market.

Marketing During the Maturity Stage

* During a product's maturity stage, its market share may be strengthened by redesigned packaging or style changes.

* Consumers may be encouraged to use the product more often or in new ways.

* Pricing strategies are flexible during this stage.

* Marketers may offer incentives and assistance of various kinds to dealers to encourage them to support mature products, especially in the face of competition from private-label brands.

* New promotional efforts and aggressive personal selling may be necessary during this period of intense competition.

Decline During the *decline stage*, sales volume decreases sharply. Profits continue to fall. The number of competing firms declines, and the only survivors in the market-place are firms that specialize in marketing the product. Production and marketing costs become the most important determinant of profit.

When a product adds to the success of the overall product line, the company may retain it; otherwise, management must determine when to eliminate the product. A product usually declines because of technological advances or environmental factors or because consumers have switched to competing brands. Therefore, few changes are made in the product itself during this stage.

Marketing During the Decline Stage

* Management may raise the price to cover costs, reprice to maintain market share, or lower the price to reduce inventory.

* Management will narrow distribution of the declining product to the most profitable existing markets.

* During this period, the company probably will not spend heavily on promotion, although it may use some advertising and sales incentives to slow the product's decline.

* The company may choose to eliminate less profitable versions of the product from the product line or may decide to drop the product entirely.

Using the Product Life Cycle

Marketers should be aware of the life-cycle stage of each product for which they are responsible. And they should try to estimate how long the product is expected to remain in that stage. Both must be taken into account in making decisions about the marketing strategy for a product. If a product is expected to remain in the maturity stage for a long time, a replacement product might be introduced later in the ma-turity stage. If the maturity stage is expected to be short, however, a new product should be introduced much earlier. **EXAMPLE** Logitech, a leading manufacturer of computer mice, faces a short product life cycle with its technology-driven accessories. In an industry with powerful competitors such as Microsoft, Logitech must introduce new products frequently with the current trend toward everything wireless. Logitech also has introduced its Laser Mouse, engineered specifically for use in gaming. The company has made strides against the competition with significant growth in sales in recent years.[3]

CONCEPT CHECK

What factors might determine how long a product remains in each stage of the product life cycle? What can a firm do to prolong each stage?

TEST PREPPER 13.2

True or False?

_____ 1. Consumers may be encouraged to use the product more often or in new ways. This is a strategy for goods in the maturity stage of the product life cycle.

_____ 2. If a product is expected to remain in the maturity stage for a long time, a replacement product might be introduced sooner in the maturity stage.

_____ 3. During the maturity stage, promotional efforts attempt to build brand loyalty among customers.

Multiple Choice

_____ 4. Sales rise gradually as a result of promotion and distribution activities, but initially, high

development and marketing costs result in low profit or even in a loss. This best describes which stage of the product life cycle?

    a. Maturity
    b. Introduction
    c. Decline
    d. Growth
    e. Steady

_____ 5. The Arm and Hammer company keeps coming up with newer uses for their baking soda, a good that is in its

    a. maturity stage.
    b. introduction stage.
    c. decline stage.
    d. growth stage.
    e. newer stage.

ACE the Test
ACE & ACE+
Practice Test 13.2

Product Line and Product Mix

> **Learning Objective** ❸
>
> Define _product line_ and _product mix_.

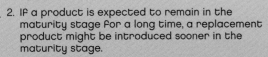
product line a group of similar products that differ only in relatively minor characteristics

A **product line** is a group of similar products that differ only in relatively minor characteristics. Generally, the products within a product line are related to each other in the way they are produced, marketed, or used. **EXAMPLE** Procter & Gamble, for example, manufactures and markets several shampoos, including Prell, Head & Shoulders, Pert Plus, and Ivory.

Many organizations tend to introduce new products within existing product lines. This permits them to apply the experience and knowledge they have acquired to the production and marketing of new products. Other firms develop entirely new product lines.

product mix all the products a firm offers for sale

An organization's **product mix** consists of all the products the firm offers for sale. For example, Procter & Gamble, which recently acquired Gillette, has over 300 brands that fall into one of twenty-two product lines ranging from deodorants to paper products.[4] Two "dimensions" are often applied to a firm's product mix. The _width_ of the mix is the number of product lines it contains. The _depth_ of the mix is the average number of individual products within each line. These are general measures; we speak of a _broad_ or a _narrow_ mix rather than a mix of exactly three or five product lines. Some organizations provide broad product mixes to be competitive. **EXAMPLE** For example, GE Financial Network (GEFN), a comprehensive Internet-based consumer-friendly financial services resource, provides an extensive product mix of financial services, including home mortgages, mutual funds, stock price quotes, annuities, life insurance, auto insurance, long-term care insurance, credit cards, and auto warranty plans.[5]

Managing the Product Mix

Learning Objective 4

Identify the methods available for changing a product mix.

To provide products that satisfy people in a firm's target market or markets and that also achieve the organization's objectives, a marketer must develop, adjust, and maintain an effective product mix.

Methods of Changing a Product Mix

* Altering its product mix to adapt to competition.

* Eliminating a product from the mix because one or more competitors dominate that product's specific market segment.

* Introducing a new product or modifying an existing one to compete more effectively.

* Expanding the firm's product mix to take advantage of excess marketing and production capacity. **EXAMPLE** Both Coca-Cola and Pepsi have expanded their lines by adding the bottled-water brands Dasani and Aquafina. More recently, they have launched berry- and citrus-flavored waters. The bottled-water category leader, Nestle, is planning to release its own four-flavor line of water called Pure Life Splash in direct response to Coca-Cola and Pepsi's latest line extensions.[6]

There are three major ways to improve a product mix:

* Change an existing product.

* Delete a product.

* Develop a new product.

Managing Existing Products

A product mix can be changed by deriving additional products from existing ones. This can be accomplished through product modifications and by line extensions.

Product Modifications **Product modification** refers to changing one or more of a product's characteristics. For this approach to be effective, several conditions must be met:

* The product must be modifiable.

* Existing customers must be able to perceive that a modification has been made, assuming that the modified item is still directed at the same target market.

* The modification should make the product more consistent with customers' desires so that it provides greater satisfaction. **EXAMPLE** Ford modified its popular F-150 pickup by adding more interior room, better safety features, and an optional DVD

Prepare for Class
Career Snapshot

CONCEPT CHECK
What is the difference between a product line and a product mix? Give an example of each.

product modification the process of changing one or more of a product's characteristics

player built in. The company designed these modifications for 80 percent of its F-150 customers who use the truck as family transportation.[7]

Existing products can be altered in three primary ways: in quality, function, and aesthetics:

* *Quality modifications* are changes that relate to a product's dependability and durability and usually are achieved by alterations in the materials or production process.

* *Functional modifications* affect a product's versatility, effectiveness, convenience, or safety; they usually require redesign of the product.

* *Aesthetic modifications* are directed at changing the sensory appeal of a product by altering its taste, texture, sound, smell, or visual characteristics.

Line Extensions A line extension is the development of a product closely related to one or more products in the existing product line but designed specifically to meet somewhat different customer needs. **EXAMPLE** Nabisco extended its cookie line to include Reduced Fat Oreos and Double Stuf Oreos.

Line extensions are more common than new products because they are a less expensive, lower-risk alternative for increasing sales. Line extensions are also used to take market share from competitors.

Deleting Products

To maintain an effective product mix, an organization often has to eliminate some products. This is called product deletion. A weak product costs a firm time, money, and resources that could be used to modify other products or develop new ones. Also, when a weak product generates an unfavorable image among customers, the negative image may rub off on other products sold by the firm.

Most organizations find it difficult to delete a product. Some firms drop weak products only after they have become severe financial burdens. A better approach is some form of systematic review of the product's impact on the overall effectiveness of a firm's product mix.

line extension development of a new product that is closely related to one or more products in the existing product line but designed specifically to meet somewhat different customer needs

product deletion the elimination of one or more products from a product line

Line extensions.

Gatorade Endurance Formula products are line extensions. These products are available in three ready-to-drink flavors and instant mixes.

Developing New Products

Developing and introducing new products are frequently time-consuming, expensive, and risky. Thousands of new products are introduced annually. Depending on how we define it, the failure rate for new products ranges between 60 and 75 percent. Although developing new products is risky, failing to introduce new products can be just as hazardous. New products generally are grouped into three categories on the basis of their degree of similarity to existing products:

* *Imitations* are products designed to be similar to—and to compete with—existing products

of other firms. Examples include the various brands of whitening toothpastes that were developed to compete with Rembrandt.

* *Adaptations* are variations of existing products that are intended for an established market. **EXAMPLE** With increasing concerns nationwide about health issues such as diabetes and obesity, Hershey decided to introduce product adaptations with the launching of its sugar-free versions of twenty-four of its major chocolate brands in conjunction with a partnership with the American Diabetes Association. Instead of sugar, these candy bars contain Splenda.[8] Product refinements and extensions are the adaptations considered most often, although imitative products also may include some refinement and extension.

* *Innovations* are entirely new products. They may give rise to a new industry or revolutionize an existing one. **EXAMPLE** The introduction of CDs, for example, has brought major changes to the recording industry. Innovative products take considerable time, effort, and money to develop. They are therefore less common than adaptations and imitations. As shown in Figure 13.2, the process of developing a new product consists of seven phases.

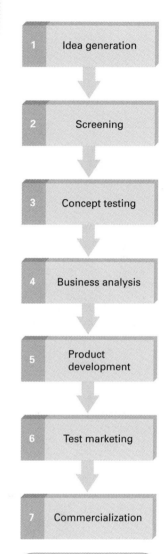

FIGURE 13.2

Phases of New Product Development

Generally, marketers follow these seven steps to develop a new product.

Source: William M. Pride and O. C. Ferrell, *Marketing: Concepts and Strategies* (Boston: Houghton Mifflin, 2006). Copyright © 2006 by Houghton Mifflin Company. Adapted with permission.

BUSINESS AROUND THE WORLD

Carl Zeiss Makes New Products Pay Off

Just a decade ago, Carl Zeiss, the German maker of precision optical products such as microscopes and camera lenses, was in serious financial trouble. Today, however, it's a profitable $2.8 billion company, with two-thirds of its sales from products introduced within the past five years. Based on close attention to customers' needs and changing market conditions, Zeiss makes its rigorous new product development pay off. Here's how:

1. Hold an annual innovation conference where hundreds of employees present their new product ideas.
2. Select the most promising twenty to thirty ideas for evaluation by a special "ideas board."
3. Allow six months to analyze the challenges and opportunities of the best ideas.
4. Based on this analysis, assign teams to create prototypes for the top two or three product ideas.
5. Test the prototypes and put the winner into production.

"Innovation is about more than invention," says CEO Dieter Kurz. "It is about creating something that gives the company an advantage."

Sources: Based on information in Jens Meyer, "Priming the R&D Machine," *Business 2.0,* September 2006, p. 60; "Zeiss Microscopy Unit Undergoes Change," *R&D,* March 2006, p. 13.

Steps in Developing New Products

As shown in Figure 13.2, the process of developing a new product consists of seven phases:

1. Idea generation
2. Screening
3. Concept testing
4. Business analysis
5. Product development
6. Test marketing
7. Commercialization

Idea Generation *Idea generation* involves looking for product ideas that will help a firm to achieve its objectives. Although some organizations get their ideas almost by chance, firms trying to maximize product-mix effectiveness usually develop systematic approaches for generating new product ideas. Ideas may come from managers, researchers, engineers, competitors, advertising agencies, management consultants, private research organizations, customers, salespersons, or top executives.

Screening During *screening,* ideas that do not match organizational resources and objectives are rejected. In this phase, a firm's managers consider whether the organization has personnel with the expertise to develop and market the proposed product. Management may reject a good idea because the company lacks the necessary skills and abilities. The largest number of product ideas are rejected during the screening phase.

Concept Testing *Concept testing* is a phase in which a product idea is presented to a small sample of potential buyers through a written or oral description (and perhaps a few drawings) to determine their attitudes and initial buying intentions regarding the product. Concept testing is a low-cost means for an organization to determine consumers' initial reactions to a product idea before investing considerable resources in product research and development (R&D). Product development personnel can use the results of concept testing to improve product attributes and product benefits that are most important to potential customers.

Business Analysis *Business analysis* provides tentative ideas about a potential product's financial performance, including its probable profitability. During this stage, the firm considers how the new product, if it were introduced, would affect the firm's sales, costs, and profits. Marketing personnel usually work up preliminary sales and cost projections at this point, with the help of R&D and production managers.

Product Development *Product development* is the phase in which the company must find out first if it is technically feasible to produce the product and then if the product can be made at a low enough cost to justify a reasonable price. If a product idea makes it to this point, it is transformed into a working model, or *prototype.*

Test Marketing *Test marketing* is the limited introduction of a product in several towns or cities chosen to be representative of the intended target market. Its aim is to determine buyers' probable reactions. The product is left in the test markets long

COMPANY	PRODUCT
Orajel	Toddler training toothpaste
3M	Floptical storage disk
IncrEdibles Breakaway Foods	Push n' Eat
General Mills	Betty Crocker MicroRave Singles
Adams (Pfizer)	Body Smarts nutritional bars
General Motors Corp.	Cadillac Allante luxury sedan
Anheuser-Busch Companies	Bud Dry and Michelob Dry beers
Coca-Cola	Surge Citrus drink
Heinz	Ketchup Salsa
Noxema	Noxema Skin Fitness

TABLE 13.1

Examples of Product Failures

Sources: **www .newproductworks.com;** accessed January 23, 2006; Robert M. McMath, "Copycat Cupcakes Don't Cut It," *American Demographics*, January 1997, p. 60; Eric Berggren and Thomas Nacher, "Why Good Ideas Go Bust," *Management Review*, February 2000, pp. 32–36.

enough to give buyers a chance to repurchase the product if they are so inclined. Marketers can experiment with advertising, pricing, and packaging in different test areas and can measure the extent of brand awareness, brand switching, and repeat purchases that result from alterations in the marketing mix.

Commercialization During *commercialization,* plans for full-scale manufacturing and marketing must be refined and completed, and budgets for the project must be prepared. In the early part of the commercialization phase, marketing management analyzes the results of test marketing to find out what changes in the marketing mix are needed before the product is introduced. Most new products are marketed in stages, beginning in selected geographic areas and expanding into adjacent areas over a period of time.

Why Do Products Fail? Despite this rigorous process for developing product ideas, most new products end up as failures. In fact, many well-known companies have produced market failures (see Table 13.1). Some of the reasons why products fail are

* The product and its marketing program are not planned and tested as completely as they should be.

* To save on development costs, a firm may test-market its product but not its entire marketing mix.

* A firm may market a new product before all the "bugs" have been worked out.

* A firm may try to recover its product development costs by pushing ahead with full-scale marketing anyway even when problems show up in the testing stage.

* Some firms try to market new products with inadequate financing.

Will this product succeed?

Developing a new product involves considerable risk, because a significant portion of new products fail. However, failure to create new products is also very risky.

TEST PREPPER 13.3 13.4

True or False?

___T___ 1. Width and depth are two dimensions applied to plan for the product mix.

___T___ 2. Cosmetic companies keep introducing new fragrances with minor modifications. This would be an example of aesthetic modification, which is one of the three ways to change an existing product.

___T___ 3. To save on development costs, a firm may test-market its product but not its entire marketing mix. This describes one of the reasons why products fail.

Multiple Choice

___A___ 4. Which one of the following is one of the major ways to manage the product mix?

a. Develop new products.
b. Discover international markets.
c. Have an appropriate mix of different products.
d. Stop introducing new products.
e. Reintroduce the same products.

___B___ 5. The largest number of product ideas are rejected during this phase.

a. Concept testing
b. Screening
c. Test marketing
d. Idea generation
e. Business analysis

ACE the Test
ACE & ACE+
Practice Tests 13.3, 13.4

Branding

> **Learning Objective** 5
>
> Explain the uses and importance of branding.

 brand a name, term, symbol, design, or any combination of these that identifies a seller's products as distinct from those of other sellers

brand name the part of a brand that can be spoken

brand mark the part of a brand that is a symbol or distinctive design

trademark a brand name or brand mark that is registered with the U.S. Patent and Trademark Office and thus is legally protected from use by anyone except its owner

trade name the complete and legal name of an organization

Three important features of a product (particularly a consumer product) are its *brand*, *package*, and *label*. These features may be used to associate a product with a successful product line or to distinguish it from existing products. They may be designed to attract customers at the point of sale or to provide information to potential purchasers. Because the brand, package, and label are very real parts of the product, they deserve careful attention during product planning.

What Is a Brand?

A **brand** is a name, term, symbol, design, or any combination of these that identifies a seller's products as distinct from those of other sellers.[9] A **brand name** is the part of a brand that can be spoken. It may include letters, words, numbers, or pronounceable symbols, such as the ampersand in *Procter & Gamble*. A **brand mark**, on the other hand, is the part of a brand that is a symbol or distinctive design, such as the Nike "swoosh." A **trademark** is a brand name or brand mark that is registered with the U.S. Patent and Trademark Office and thus is legally protected from use by anyone except its owner. A **trade name** is the complete and legal name of an organization, such as Pizza Hut or Cengage Learning Company (the publisher of this text).

Types of Brands

Brands often are classified according to who owns them: manufacturers or stores. A **manufacturer** (or **producer**) **brand**, as the name implies, is a brand that is owned by a manufacturer. **EXAMPLE** Many foods (Frosted Flakes), major appliances (Whirlpool), gasolines (Exxon), automobiles (Honda), and clothing (Levis) are sold as manufacturer brands. Some consumers prefer manufacturer brands because they usually are nationally known, offer consistent quality, and are widely available.

A **store** (or **private**) **brand** is a brand that is owned by an individual wholesaler or retailer. **EXAMPLE** Among the better-known store brands are Kenmore and Craftsman, both owned by Sears, Roebuck. Owners of store brands claim that they can offer lower prices, earn greater profits, and improve customer loyalty with their own brands. Some companies that manufacture private brands also produce their own manufacturer brands. They often find such operations profitable because they can use excess capacity and at the same time avoid most marketing costs. Many private-branded grocery products are produced by companies that specialize in making private-label products. About 20 percent of products sold in supermarkets are private-branded items.[10]

Consumer confidence is the most important element in the success of a branded product, whether the brand is owned by a producer or by a retailer. In supermarkets, the products most likely to keep their shelf space are the brands with large market shares and strong customer loyalty.

A **generic product** (sometimes called a **generic brand**) is a product with no brand at all. Its plain package carries only the name of the product—applesauce, peanut butter, potato chips, or whatever. Generic products, available in supermarkets since 1977, sometimes are made by the major producers that manufacture name brands. Even though generic brands may have accounted for as much as 10 percent of all grocery sales several years ago, they currently represent less than one-half of 1 percent.

Benefits of Branding

Both buyers and sellers benefit from branding. The following are some of the benefits of branding:

* Because brands are easily recognizable, they reduce the amount of time buyers must spend shopping.

* Choosing particular brands, such as Nike, can be a way of expressing oneself.

* When buyers are unable to evaluate a product's characteristics, brands can help them to judge the quality of the product.

* Brands can symbolize a certain quality level to a customer, allowing that perception of quality to represent the actual quality of the item.

* Customers may receive a psychological reward that comes from owning a brand that symbolizes status, such as owning a Lexus.

* Branding helps a firm to introduce a new product that carries the same brand name because buyers are already familiar with a firm's existing brands. **EXAMPLE** Unilever, the company that produces the Dove brand, as well as many others, has continued to expand its Dove product line. Originally, Dove made bar soap and then

manufacturer (or **producer**) **brand** a brand that is owned by a manufacturer

store (or **private**) **brand** a brand that is owned by an individual wholesaler or retailer

generic product (or **brand**) a product with no brand at all

extended to deodorant, facial cleansing products, and body soap. The latest additions are Dove shampoos and conditioners. Unilever hopes to gain market share quickly because of customers' favorable perceptions of Dove products.[11]

* Branding aids sellers in their promotional efforts because promotion of each branded product indirectly promotes other products of the same brand. **EXAMPLE** H.G. Heinz, for example, markets many products with the Heinz brand name, such as ketchup, vinegar, vegetarian beans, gravies, barbecue sauce, and steak sauce. Promotion of one Heinz product indirectly promotes the others.

brand loyalty extent to which a customer is favorable toward buying a specific brand

brand equity marketing and financial value associated with a brand's strength in a market

One chief benefit of branding is the creation of **brand loyalty**, the extent to which a customer is favorable toward buying a specific brand. The stronger the brand loyalty, the greater is the likelihood that buyers will consistently choose the brand.

There are three levels of brand loyalty: recognition, preference, and insistence. *Brand recognition* is the level of loyalty at which customers are aware that the brand exists and will purchase it if their preferred brands are unavailable or if they are unfamiliar with available brands. This is the weakest form of brand loyalty. *Brand preference* is the level of brand loyalty at which a customer prefers one brand over competing brands. However, if the preferred brand is unavailable, the customer is willing to substitute another brand. *Brand insistence* is the strongest level of brand loyalty. Brand-insistent customers strongly prefer a specific brand and will not buy substitutes. Brand insistence is the least common type of brand loyalty. Partly owing to marketers' increased dependence on discounted prices, coupons, and other short-term promotions, and partly because of the enormous array of new products with similar characteristics, brand loyalty in general seems to be declining.

Brand equity is the marketing and financial value associated with a brand's strength in a market. Although difficult to measure, brand equity represents the value of a brand to an organization. Some of the world's most valuable brands include Coca-Cola, Microsoft, IBM, General Electric, and Intel.[12]

The four major factors that contribute to brand equity are

* *Brand awareness.* This leads to brand familiarity, and buyers are more likely to select a familiar brand than an unfamiliar one.

* *Brand associations.* Linked to a brand such as Starbucks, these can connect a personality type or lifestyle with a particular brand.

* *Perceived brand quality.* When consumers are unable to judge for themselves the quality of a product, they may rely on their perception of the quality of the product's brand.

* *Brand loyalty.* This is a valued element of brand equity because it reduces both a brand's vulnerability to competitors and the need to spend tremendous resources to attract new customers; it also provides brand visibility and encourages retailers to carry the brand.

Trade Characters.

The Michelin Man is a trade character. Companies employ trade characters to elicit positive brand associations in consumers' minds.

Choosing and Protecting a Brand

A number of issues should be considered when selecting a brand name.

* The name should be easy for customers to say, spell, and recall. Short, one-syllable names such as *Tide* often satisfy this requirement.

* The brand name should suggest, in a positive way, the product's uses, special characteristics, and major benefits and should be distinctive enough to set it apart from competing brands.

* It is important that a firm select a brand that can be protected through registration, reserving it for exclusive use by that firm. To protect its exclusive right to the brand, the company must ensure that the selected brand will not be considered an infringement on any existing brand already registered with the U.S. Patent and Trademark Office. This task may be complicated by the fact that infringement is determined by the courts, which base their decisions on whether a brand causes consumers to be confused, mistaken, or deceived about the source of the product. **EXAMPLE** Starbucks, the Seattle-based coffee company, recently took legal action against companies using similar brand names, including Sambuck's Coffeehouse, Black Bear's Charbucks Blend, and A&D Café's Warbucks coffee.[13]

* A firm must guard against a brand name's becoming a generic term that refers to a general product category. Generic terms cannot be protected legally as exclusive brand names. **EXAMPLE** Names such as *yo-yo, aspirin, escalator,* and *thermos*—all exclusively brand names at one time—eventually were declared generic terms that refer to product categories. As such, they could no longer be protected.

CONCEPT CHECK
What is the difference between manufacturer brands and store brands? Between family branding and individual branding?

Branding Strategies

The basic branding decision for any firm is whether to brand its products. A producer may market its products under its own brands, private brands, or both. A retail store may carry only producer brands, its own brands, or both. Once either type of firm decides to brand, it chooses one of two branding strategies: individual branding or family branding.

Individual branding is the strategy in which a firm uses a different brand for each of its products. **EXAMPLE** Procter & Gamble uses individual branding for its line of bar soaps, which includes Ivory, Camay, Zest, Safeguard, Coast, and Oil of Olay. Individual branding offers two major advantages:

1. A problem with one product will not affect the good name of the firm's other products.
2. The different brands can be directed toward different market segments. **EXAMPLE** Marriotts' Fairfield Inns are directed toward budget-minded travelers and Marriott Hotels toward upscale customers.

Family branding is the strategy in which a firm uses the same brand for all or most of its products. Sony, Dell, IBM, and Xerox use family branding for their entire product mixes. A major advantage of family branding is that the promotion of any one item that carries the family brand tends to help all other products with the same brand name. In addition, a new product has a head start when its brand name is already known and accepted by customers.

Brand Extensions A **brand extension** occurs when an organization uses one of its existing brands to brand a new product in a different product category. **EXAMPLE** Procter & Gamble employed a brand extension when it named a new product Ivory Body Wash. A brand extension should not be confused with a line extension. A *line extension* refers to using an existing brand on a new product in the same product

individual branding the strategy in which a firm uses a different brand for each of its products

family branding the strategy in which a firm uses the same brand for all or most of its products

brand extension using an existing brand to brand a new product in a different product category

category, such as a new flavor or new sizes. For example, when the makers of Tylenol introduced Extra Strength Tylenol PM, the new product was a line extension because it was in the same product category. One thing marketers must be careful of, however, is extending a brand too many times or extending too far outside the original product category, which may weaken the brand.

TEST PREPPER 13.5

True or False?

 1. Liz Clairborne Clothing is an example of manufacturer (or producer) brand.

2. When the Coca-Cola Company uses different names for its beverages, such as Dasani or Sprite, it demonstrates the importance of family branding.

3. Apple has introduced several variations on its wildly popular iPod MP3 player. The iPod Mini is a smaller, more colorful device, and the iPod Shuffle is a more affordable version. The iPod Nano is a pencil-thin device that weighs barely over 1 ounce. This is an example of brand extension.

Multiple Choice

4. The name Godfather's Pizza is an example of a

   a. trademark.
   b. trade name.
   c. brand name.
   d. brand equity.
   e. brand extension.

5. A customer who consistently buys Sony television whenever he or she needs to replace his or her TV set demonstrates

   a. the importance of trademarks.
   b. the importance of trade names.
   c. the importance of brand awareness.
   d. brand loyalty.
   e. brand equity.

ACE the Test
ACE & ACE+
Practice Test 13.5

Packaging and Labeling

> **Learning Objective 6**
>
> Explain the uses and importance of labeling and packaging.

 packaging all the activities involved in developing and providing a container with graphics for a product

Packaging consists of all the activities involved in developing and providing a container with graphics for a product. The package is a vital part of the product. It can make the product more versatile, safer, or easier to use. Through its shape, appearance, and printed message, a package can influence purchasing decisions.

Packaging Functions

Effective packaging means more than simply putting products in containers and covering them with wrappers. The basic function of packaging materials is to *protect the product and maintain its functional form.* Fluids such as milk, orange juice, and hair spray need packages that preserve and protect them; the packaging should prevent damage that could affect the product's usefulness and increase costs.

Another function of packaging is to offer *consumer convenience.* For example, small, aseptic packages—individual-serving boxes or plastic bags that contain liquids and do not require refrigeration—appeal strongly to children and young adults with active lifestyles. A third function of packaging is to *promote a product* by communicating its features, uses, benefits, and image. Sometimes a firm develops a reusable package to make its product more desirable. **EXAMPLE** The Cool Whip package doubles as a food-storage container.

Package Design Considerations

Many factors must be weighed when developing packages. Obviously, one major consideration is cost. Marketers also must decide whether to package the product in single or multiple units. Multiple-unit packaging can increase demand by increasing the amount of the product available at the point of consumption (in the home, for example). However, multiple-unit packaging does not work for infrequently used products because buyers do not like to tie up their dollars in an excess supply or to store those products for a long time. However, multiple-unit packaging can make storage and handling easier (as in the case of six-packs used for soft drinks); it also can facilitate special price offers, such as two-for-one sales. In addition, multiple-unit packaging may increase consumer acceptance of a product by encouraging the buyer to try it several times. On the other hand, customers may hesitate to try the product at all if they do not have the option to buy just one.

Marketers should consider how much consistency is desirable among an organization's package designs. To promote an overall company image, a firm may decide that all packages must be similar or include one major element of the design. This approach, called *family packaging*, is sometimes used only for lines of products, as with Campbell's soups, Weight Watchers entrees, and Planters nuts.

Packages also play an important promotional role. Through verbal and nonverbal symbols, the package can inform potential buyers about the product's content, uses, features, advantages, and hazards. Firms can create desirable images and associations by choosing particular colors, designs, shapes, and textures. Many cosmetics manufacturers, for example, design their packages to create impressions of richness, luxury, and exclusiveness. The package performs another promotional function when it is designed to be safer or more convenient to use if such features help to stimulate demand.

Packaging also must meet the *needs of intermediaries.* Wholesalers and retailers consider whether a package facilitates transportation, handling, and storage. Resellers may refuse to carry certain products if their packages are cumbersome.

Finally, firms must consider the issue of *environmental responsibility* when developing packages. Companies must balance consumers' desires for convenience against the need to preserve the environment. About one-half of all garbage consists of discarded plastic packaging, such as plastic soft-drink bottles and carryout bags.

Package design.

McDonald's has changed its package designs, which now feature images of people enjoying life's simple pleasures. One of McDonald's goals is to do a better job of connecting with customers worldwide.

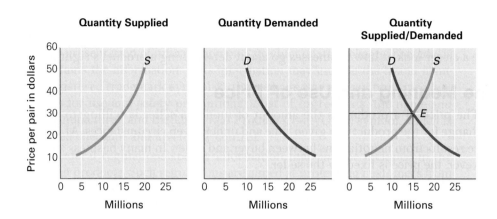

Quantity Supplied   **Quantity Demanded**   **Quantity Supplied/Demanded**

FIGURE 13.3

Supply and Demand Curves

Supply curve (*left*): The upward slope means that producers will supply more jeans at higher prices. Demand curve (*center*): The downward slope (to the right) means that buyers will purchase fewer jeans at higher prices. Supply and demand curves together (*right*): Point *E* indicates equilibrium in quantity and price for both sellers and buyers.

---

price competition an emphasis on setting a price equal to or lower than competitors' prices to gain sales or market share

nonprice competition competition based on factors other than price

product differentiation the process of developing and promoting differences between one's product and all similar products

---

Price competition.

Sam's Club engages in price competition for its Soy Infant Formula.

Price competition occurs when a seller emphasizes the low price of a product and sets a price that equals or beats competitors' prices. To use this approach most effectively, a seller must have the flexibility to change prices often and must do so rapidly and aggressively whenever competitors change their prices. The Internet makes price comparison relatively easy for users. This ease of price comparison helps to drive competition. Examples of websites where customers can compare prices include **mysimon.com, pricescan.com, bizrate.com, pricegrabber.com, pricecomparison.com, shopping.yahoo.com, nextag.com,** and **froogle.google.com.**

Nonprice competition is competition based on factors other than price. It is used most effectively when a seller can make its product stand out from the competition by distinctive product quality, customer service, promotion, packaging, or other features. Buyers must be able to perceive these distinguishing characteristics and consider them desirable. Once customers have chosen a brand for nonprice reasons, they may not be attracted as easily to competing firms and brands. In this way, a seller can build customer loyalty to its brand. A method of nonprice competition is **product differentiation**, which is the process of developing and promoting differences between one's product and all similar products.

Buyers' Perceptions of Price

In setting prices, managers should consider the price sensitivity of people in the target market. Members of one market segment may be more influenced by price than members of another. For a particular product, the price may be a bigger factor to some buyers than to others. For example, buyers may be more sensitive to price when purchasing gasoline than when purchasing running shoes.

Buyers will accept different ranges of prices for different products; that is, they will tolerate a narrow range for certain items and a wider range for others. Consider the wide range of prices that consumers pay for soft drinks—from

15 cents per ounce at the movies down to 1.5 cents per ounce on sale at the grocery store. Management should be aware of these limits of acceptability and the products to which they apply. The firm also should take note of buyers' perceptions of a given product in relation to competing products.

Sometimes buyers relate price to quality. They may consider a higher price to be an indicator of higher quality. Managers involved in pricing decisions should determine whether this outlook is widespread in the target market. If it is, a higher price may improve the image of a product and, in turn, make the product more desirable. **EXAMPLE** German automobile manufacturer Porsche has always worked to keep its quality and image as a luxury sports car maker. In addition to its traditional 911 model and more recently the Boxster model, Porsche recently added a new model called the Cayenne. Porsche hopes this SUV-like vehicle will be very desirable to customers, equally for those who are willing to pay the $88,900.[14]

Nonprice competition.

Tums competes with Prilosec on the basis of product attributes. There is no mention of price in this advertisement.

CONCEPT CHECK
Under what conditions would a firm be most likely to use nonprice competition?

BIZ TECH

Personalized Products Are Priceless

Thanks to technology, big brands can offer personalized products and packaging at premium prices. Smaller companies are also cashing in on the public's appetite for personalization. Here are just a few examples:

• *Candy.* Consumers and businesses pay extra for M&Ms with special messages and packed in commemorative tins or boxes (see **www.myms.com**). The company says that personalized M&Ms will be a $100 million business by 2010.

• *Condiments.* Heinz invites buyers to personalize the labels of its ketchup or mustard bottles with a greeting, name, or other wording (see **myheinz.com**). "Consumers want products designed for themselves," observes a senior brand manager: "This gives them a personal connection with the brand."

• *Soft drinks.* Choose a flavor, write a saying, upload a digital image, and click to buy—that's how buyers personalize labels on bottles of Jones Soda (see **myjones.com**). The minimum order is a twelve-bottle case, priced at about $49 including shipping and handling.

Sources: Based on information in Renee Enna, "Off the Shelf: Personalized Condiments, Recipe Box, Wine Bags," *Chicago Tribune*, October 2, 2006, www.chicagotribune.com; Joan Johnson, "Manufacturers Are Letting Consumers Personalize Their Purchases," *Colorado Springs Business Journal*, August 18, 2006.

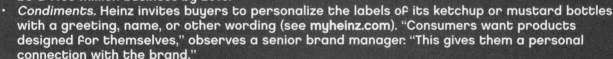

TEST PREPPER 13.7

True or False?

T 1. From an economic point of view, price serves the function of allocator.

F 2. A seller does not necessarily need to have the flexibility to change prices often in order to engage in price competition.

T 3. Nonprice competition is competition based on factors other than price.

Multiple Choice

D 4. When there is a shortage of citrus fruit, the economic forces of supply and demand would suggest that

   a. price will not be affected.
   b. price will decrease.
   c. price will stay constant.
   d. price, all things remaining equal, will increase.
   e. it will take a long time before the shortage is felt in the market.

A 5. In setting prices, managers should consider the _____ of people in the target market.

   a. price sensitivity
   b. demand
   c. incomes
   d. feelings
   e. taste

ACE the Test
ACE & ACE+
Practice Test 13.7

Pricing Objectives

Learning Objective 8

Identify the major pricing objectives used by businesses.

Before setting prices for a firm's products, management must decide what it expects to accomplish through pricing. That is, management must set pricing objectives that are in line with both organizational and marketing objectives. Of course, one objective of pricing is to make a profit, but this may not be a firm's primary objective. One or more of the following factors may be just as important.

Survival

A firm may have to price its products to survive—either as an organization or as a player in a particular market. This usually means that the firm will cut its price to attract customers, even if it then must operate at a loss. Obviously, such a goal hardly can be pursued on a long-term basis, for consistent losses would cause the business to fail.

Profit Maximization

Many firms may state that their goal is to maximize profit, but this goal is impossible to define (and thus impossible to achieve). What, exactly, is the *maximum* profit? How does a firm know when it has been reached? Firms that wish to set profit goals should express them as either specific dollar amounts or percentage increases over previous profits.

Target Return on Investment

The *return on investment* (ROI) is the amount earned as a result of that investment. Some firms set an annual percentage ROI as their pricing goal. **EXAMPLE** ConAgra, the company that produces Healthy Choice meals and a multitude of other products, has a target after-tax ROI of 20 percent.

Market-Share Goals

A firm's *market share* is its proportion of total industry sales. Some firms attempt, through pricing, to maintain or increase their share of the market. **EXAMPLE** To gain market share, Netzero priced unlimited hours of service for $6.95.[15]

Status-Quo Pricing

In pricing their products, some firms are guided by a desire to avoid "making waves," or to maintain the status quo. This is especially true in industries that depend on price stability. If such a firm can maintain its profit or market share simply by meeting the competition—charging about the same price as competitors for similar products—then it will do so.

Pricing Methods

Learning Objective ⑨
Examine the three major pricing methods that firms employ.

Once a firm has developed its pricing objectives, it must select a pricing method to reach that goal. Two factors are important to every firm engaged in setting prices:

1. Recognition that the market, and not the firm's costs, ultimately determines the price at which a product will sell.
2. Awareness that costs and expected sales can be used only to establish some sort of *price floor*, the minimum price at which the firm can sell its product without incurring a loss.

In this section we look at three kinds of pricing methods: cost-based, demand-based, and competition-based pricing.

Cost-Based Pricing

Using the simplest method of pricing, *cost-based pricing*, the seller first determines the total cost of producing (or purchasing) one unit of the product. The seller then adds an amount to cover additional costs (such as insurance or interest) and profit. The amount that is added is called the **markup**. The total of the cost plus the markup is the selling price of the product. A firm's management can calculate markup as a percentage of its total costs. Suppose, for example, that the total cost of manufacturing and marketing 1,000 DVD players is $100,000, or $100 per unit. If the manufacturer wants a markup that is 20 percent above its costs, the selling price will be $100 plus 20 percent of $100, or $120 per unit.

Cost-based pricing also can be facilitated through the use of breakeven analysis. For any product, the **breakeven quantity** is the number of units that must be sold for the total revenue (from all units sold) to equal the total cost (of all units sold). **Total revenue** is the total amount received from the sales of a product. We can

markup the amount a seller adds to the cost of a product to determine its basic selling price

breakeven quantity the number of units that must be sold for the total revenue (from all units sold) to equal the total cost (of all units sold)

total revenue the total amount received from sales of a product

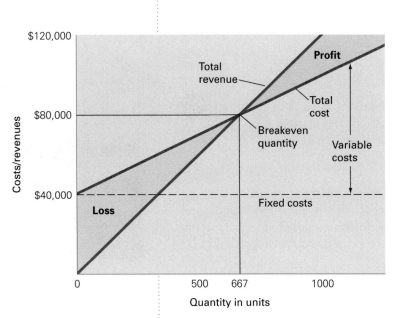

FIGURE 13.4

Breakeven Analysis

Breakeven analysis answers the question, "What is the lowest level of production and sales at which a company can break even on a particular product?"

fixed cost a cost incurred no matter how many units of a product are produced or sold

variable cost a cost that depends on the number of units produced

total cost the sum of the fixed costs and the variable costs attributable to a product

estimate projected total revenue as the selling price multiplied by the number of units sold.

The costs involved in operating a business can be broadly classified as either fixed or variable costs. A **fixed cost** is a cost incurred no matter how many units of a product are produced or sold. Rent, for example, is a fixed cost; it remains the same whether 1 or 1,000 units are produced. A **variable cost** is a cost that depends on the number of units produced. The cost of fabricating parts for a DVD player is a variable cost. The more units produced, the higher is the cost of parts. The **total cost** of producing a certain number of units is the sum of the fixed costs and the variable costs attributed to those units.

Figure 13.4 shows the total revenue and the total cost incurred by the sale of various quantities of a product. To find the breakeven quantity, first deduct the variable cost from the selling price to determine how much money the sale of one unit contributes to offsetting the fixed cost. Then divide that contribution into the total fixed cost to arrive at the breakeven quantity. If fixed costs are $40,000, variable costs are $60 per unit, and the selling price is $120, the breakeven quantity is 667 units.

Demand-Based Pricing

Rather than basing the price of a product on its cost, companies sometimes use a pricing method based on the level of demand for the product: *demand-based pricing*. This method results in a high price when product demand is strong and a low price when demand is weak. **EXAMPLE** Some long-distance telephone companies use demand-based pricing. Buyers of new cars that are in high demand, such as Hummer H3, Pontiac Solstice, Dodge Charger, Ford Mustang GT, and Toyota Prius, pay sticker prices plus a premium. Obviously, the effectiveness of this method depends on the firm's ability to estimate demand accurately.

Competition-Based Pricing

In using *competition-based pricing*, an organization considers costs and revenue secondary to competitors' prices. The importance of this method increases if competing products are quite similar and the organization is serving markets in which price is the crucial variable of the marketing strategy. A firm that uses competition-based pricing may choose to be below competitors' prices, slightly above competitors' prices, or at the same level. The price that your bookstore paid to the publishing company of this text was determined using competition-based pricing. Competition-based pricing can help to attain a pricing objective to increase sales or market share. Competition-based pricing may be combined with other cost approaches to arrive at profitable levels.

TEST PREPPER (13.8 13.9)

True or False?

___ 1. The primary objective of the firm in pricing its product is to make a profit.

___ 2. Demand-based pricing is the method that results in a high price when product demand is strong and a low price when demand is weak.

___ 3. A firm may favor a competition-based pricing method called *price differentiation* if it wants to use more than one price in the marketing of a specific product.

Multiple Choice

___ 4. A firm wanting to establish its presence more than likely will focus on this factor when considering pricing.

a. Target
b. Survival
c. Profit maximization
d. Status-quo pricing
e. Market-share goals

___ 5. The importance of _____ increases if competing products are quite similar and the organization is serving markets in which price is the crucial variable of the marketing strategy.

a. competition-based pricing
b. demand-based pricing
c. cost-based pricing
d. status-quo pricing
e. market-based pricing

ACE the Test
ACE & ACE+
Practice Tests 13.8, 13.9

Pricing Strategies

Learning Objective 10

Explain the different types of pricing strategies.

A *pricing strategy* is a course of action designed to achieve pricing objectives. Generally, pricing strategies help marketers to solve the practical problems of setting prices. The extent to which a business uses any of the following strategies depends on

* Its pricing and marketing objectives
* The markets for its products
* The degree of product differentiation
* The life-cycle stage of the product

Figure 13.5 contains a list of the major types of pricing strategies. We discuss these strategies in the remainder of this section.

New Product Strategies

The two primary types of new product pricing strategies are price skimming and penetration pricing. An organization can use either one or even both over a period of time.

Price Skimming Some consumers are willing to pay a high price for an innovative product either because of its novelty or because of the prestige or status that ownership confers. **Price skimming** is the strategy of charging the highest possible price for

price skimming the strategy of charging the highest possible price for a product during the introduction stage of its life cycle

PRICING STRATEGIES				
New-Product Pricing	**Differential Pricing**	**Psychological Pricing**	**Product-Line Pricing**	**Promotional Pricing**
• Price skimming • Penetration pricing	• Negotiated pricing • Secondary-market pricing • Periodic discounting • Random discounting	• Odd-number pricing • Multiple-unit pricing • Reference pricing • Bundle pricing • Everyday low prices • Customary pricing	• Captive pricing • Premium pricing • Price lining	• Price leaders • Special-event pricing • Comparison discounting

FIGURE 13.5

Types of Pricing Strategies

Companies have a variety of pricing strategies available to them.

CONCEPT CHECK

What are the major disadvantages of price skimming?

penetration pricing the strategy of setting a low price for a new product

negotiated pricing establishing a final price through bargaining

secondary-market pricing setting one price for the primary target market and a different price for another market

a product during the introduction stage of its life cycle. The seller essentially "skims the cream" off the market, which helps to recover the high costs of R&D more quickly. Also, a skimming policy may hold down demand for the product, which is helpful if the firm's production capacity is limited during the introduction stage. The greatest disadvantage is that a skimming price may make the product appear lucrative to potential competitors, who then may attempt to enter that market.

Penetration Pricing At the opposite extreme, **penetration pricing** is the strategy of setting a low price for a new product. The main purpose of setting a low price is to build market share for the product quickly. The seller hopes that the building of a large market share quickly will discourage competitors from entering the market. If the low price stimulates sales, the firm also may be able to order longer production runs, which result in lower production costs per unit. A disadvantage of penetration pricing is that it places a firm in a less flexible position. It is more difficult to raise prices significantly than it is to lower them.

Differential Pricing

An important issue in pricing decisions is whether to use a single price or different prices for the same product. *Differential pricing* means charging different prices to different buyers for the same quality and quantity of product. For differential pricing to be effective, the market must consist of multiple segments with different price sensitivities. When this method is employed, caution should be used to avoid confusing or antagonizing customers. Differential pricing can occur in several ways, including negotiated pricing, secondary-market pricing, periodic discounting, and random discounting.

Negotiated Pricing Negotiated pricing occurs when the final price is established through bargaining between the seller and the customer. Negotiated pricing occurs in a number of industries and at all levels of distribution. Consumers commonly negotiate prices for houses, cars, and used equipment.

Secondary-Market Pricing Secondary-market pricing means setting one price for the primary target market and a different price for another market. Often the price charged in the secondary market is lower. Examples of secondary markets include a geographically isolated domestic market, a market in a foreign country, and a segment willing to purchase a product during off-peak times (such as "early bird" diners at restaurants and off-peak users of cellular phones).

Periodic Discounting Periodic discounting is the temporary reduction of prices on a patterned or systematic basis. For example, many retailers have annual holiday sales, and some women's apparel stores have two seasonal sales each year—a winter sale in the last two weeks of January and a summer sale in the first two weeks of July. From the marketer's point of view, a major problem with periodic discounting is that customers can predict when the reductions will occur and may delay their purchases until they can take advantage of the lower prices.

Random Discounting To alleviate the problem of customers' knowing when discounting will occur, some organizations employ random discounting. That is, they reduce their prices temporarily on a nonsystematic basis. When price reductions of a product occur randomly, current users of that brand are not likely to be able to predict when the reductions will occur and so will not delay their purchases in anticipation of buying the product at a lower price. Marketers also use random discounting to attract new customers.

Psychological Pricing Strategies

Psychological pricing strategies encourage purchases based on emotional responses rather than on economically rational responses. These strategies are used primarily for consumer products rather than business products.

Odd-Number Pricing Many retailers believe that consumers respond more positively to odd-number prices such as $4.99 than to whole-dollar prices such as $5. Odd-number pricing is the strategy of setting prices using odd numbers that are slightly below whole-dollar amounts. Nine and five are the most popular ending figures for odd-number prices.

Multiple-Unit Pricing Many retailers (and especially supermarkets) practice multiple-unit pricing, setting a single price for two or more units, such as two cans for 99 cents rather than 50 cents per can. Especially for frequently purchased products, this strategy can increase sales.

Reference Pricing Reference pricing means pricing a product at a moderate level and positioning it next to a more expensive model or brand in the hope that the customer will use the higher price as a reference price (i.e., a comparison price). Because of the comparison, the customer is expected to view the moderate price favorably. When you go to Sears to buy a DVD recorder, a moderately priced DVD recorder may appear especially attractive because it offers most of the important attributes of the more expensive alternatives on display and at a lower price.

Bundle Pricing Bundle pricing is the packaging together of two or more products, usually of a complementary nature, to be sold for a single price. Bundle pricing is used commonly for banking and travel services, computers, and automobiles with option packages. Bundle pricing can help to increase customer satisfaction. **EXAMPLE** Verizon is offering the Verizon Freedom Package plan that gives customers unlimited local, long-distance, wireless, DSL, and Direct TV for a bundled price of about $112 per month.[16]

Everyday Low Prices (EDLPs) To reduce or eliminate the use of frequent short-term price reductions, some organizations use an approach referred to as

periodic discounting temporary reduction of prices on a patterned or systematic basis

random discounting temporary reduction of prices on an unsystematic basis

odd-number pricing the strategy of setting prices using odd numbers that are slightly below whole-dollar amounts

multiple-unit pricing the strategy of setting a single price for two or more units

reference pricing pricing a product at a moderate level and positioning it next to a more expensive model or brand

bundle pricing packaging together two or more complementary products and selling them for a single price

everyday low prices (EDLPs) setting a low price for products on a consistent basis

customary pricing pricing on the basis of tradition

captive pricing pricing the basic product in a product line low, but pricing related items at a higher level

premium pricing pricing the highest-quality or most-versatile products higher than other models in the product line

price lining the strategy of selling goods only at certain predetermined prices that reflect definite price breaks

everyday low prices (EDLPs). When EDLPs are used, a marketer sets a low price for its products on a consistent basis rather than setting higher prices and frequently discounting them. EDLPs, though not deeply discounted, are set far enough below competitors' prices to make customers feel confident that they are receiving a fair price. EDLPs are employed by retailers such as Wal-Mart and by manufacturers such as Procter & Gamble. A company that uses EDLPs benefits from reduced promotional costs, reduced losses from frequent mark downs, and more stability in its sales. A major problem with this approach is that customers have mixed responses to it. In some instances, customers simply do not believe that EDLPs are what they say they are but are instead a marketing gimmick.

Customary Pricing In customary pricing, certain goods are priced primarily on the basis of tradition. Examples of customary, or traditional, prices would be those set for candy bars and chewing gum.

Product-Line Pricing

Rather than considering products on an item-by-item basis when determining pricing strategies, some marketers employ product-line pricing. *Product-line pricing* means establishing and adjusting the prices of multiple products within a product line. Product-line pricing can provide marketers with flexibility in price setting. For example, marketers can set prices so that one product is quite profitable, whereas another increases market share by virtue of having a lower price than competing products.

When marketers employ product-line pricing, they have several strategies from which to choose. These include captive pricing, premium pricing, and price lining.

Captive Pricing When captive pricing is used, the basic product in a product line is priced low, but the price on the items required to operate or enhance it are set at a higher level. For example, a manufacturer of cameras and film may price a camera at a low level to attract customers but price the film at a relatively high level because customers must continue to purchase film in order to use their cameras.

Premium Pricing Premium pricing occurs when the highest-quality product or the most-versatile version of similar products in a product line is given the highest price. Other products in the line are priced to appeal to price-sensitive shoppers or to those who seek product-specific features. Marketers that use premium pricing often realize a significant portion of their profits from premium-priced products. Examples of product categories in which premium pricing is common are small kitchen appliances, beer, ice cream, and television cable service.

Price Lining Price lining is the strategy of selling goods only at certain predetermined prices that reflect definite price breaks. For example, a shop may sell men's ties only at $22 and $37. This strategy is used widely in clothing and accessory stores. It eliminates minor price differences from the buying decision—both for customers and for managers who buy merchandise to sell in these stores.

Promotional Pricing

Price, as an ingredient in the marketing mix, often is coordinated with promotion. The two variables sometimes are so interrelated that the pricing policy is promotion-oriented. Examples of promotional pricing include price leaders, special-event pricing, and comparison discounting.

Price Leaders Sometimes a firm prices a few products below the usual markup, near cost, or below cost, which results in prices known as price leaders. This type of pricing is used most often in supermarkets and restaurants to attract customers by giving them especially low prices on a few items. Management hopes that sales of regularly priced products will more than offset the reduced revenues from the price leaders.

Special-Event Pricing To increase sales volume, many organizations coordinate price with advertising or sales promotions for seasonal or special situations. Special-event pricing involves advertised sales or price cutting linked to a holiday, season, or event. If the pricing objective is survival, then special sales events may be designed to generate the necessary operating capital.

Comparison Discounting Comparison discounting sets the price of a product at a specific level and simultaneously compares it with a higher price. The higher price may be the product's previous price, the price of a competing brand, the product's price at another retail outlet, or a manufacturer's suggested retail price. Customers may find comparative discounting informative, and it can have a significant impact on them. However, because this pricing strategy on occasion has led to deceptive pricing practices, the Federal Trade Commission has established guidelines for comparison discounting. If the higher price against which the comparison is made is the price formerly charged for the product, sellers must have made the previous price available to customers for a reasonable period of time. If sellers present the higher price as the one charged by other retailers in the same trade area, they must be able to demonstrate that this claim is true. When they present the higher price as the manufacturer's suggested retail price, then the higher price must be similar to the price at which a reasonable proportion of the product was sold. Some manufacturers' suggested retail prices are so high that very few products actually are sold at those prices. In such cases, it would be deceptive to use comparison discounting.

---

price leaders products priced below the usual markup, near cost, or below cost

special-event pricing advertised sales or price cutting linked to a holiday, season, or event

comparison discounting setting a price at a specific level and comparing it with a higher price

---

TEST PREPPER 13.10

True or False?

___F___ 1. Price penetration is one of the strategies used when dealing with products that have been around for a number of years.

___T___ 2. Time Warner prices Internet, telephone, and cable TV services all in one package. This is an example of bundle pricing.

___F___ 3. A President's Day sale is an example of customary pricing.

Multiple Choice

___E___ 4. Which one of the following is *not* one of the factors a business would consider when designing its pricing strategy?

    a. Its pricing and marketing objectives
    b. The markets for its products
    c. The degree of product differentiation
    d. The life-cycle stage of the product
    e. The exact cost basis

___C___ 5. Like many other food establishments, Denny's offers senior citizen's discount. This is an example of

    a. periodic discounting.
    b. random discounting.
    c. differential pricing.
    d. negotiated pricing.
    e. senior market pricing.

ACE the Test
ACE & ACE+
Practice Test 13.10

Pricing Business Products

Learning Objective 11
Describe three major types of pricing for business products.

Many of the pricing issues discussed thus far in this chapter deal with pricing in general. Setting prices for business products can be different from setting prices for consumer products owing to several factors, such as size of purchases, transportation considerations, and geographic issues. We examine three types of pricing associated with business products, including geographic pricing, transfer pricing, and discounting.

Geographic Pricing

Geographic pricing strategies deal with delivery costs. The pricing strategy that requires the buyer to pay the delivery costs is called *FOB origin pricing*. It stands for "free on board at the point of origin," which means that the price does not include freight charges, and thus the buyer must pay the transportation costs from the seller's warehouse to the buyer's place of business. *FOB destination* indicates that the price does include freight charges, and thus the seller pays these charges.

Transfer Pricing

transfer pricing prices charged in sales between an organization's units

When one unit in an organization sells a product to another unit, **transfer pricing** occurs. The price is determined by calculating the cost of the product. A transfer price can vary depending on the types of costs included in the calculations. The choice of the costs to include when calculating the transfer price depends on the company's management strategy and the nature of the units' interaction. An organization also must ensure that transfer pricing is fair to all units involved in the purchases.

Discounting

discount a deduction from the price of an item

A **discount** is a deduction from the price of an item. Producers and sellers offer a wide variety of discounts to their customers, including the following:

* *Trade discounts* are discounts from the list prices that are offered to marketing intermediaries, or middlemen. A furniture retailer, for example, may receive a 40 percent discount from the manufacturer. The retailer then would pay $60 for a lamp carrying a list price of $100.

* *Quantity discounts* are discounts given to customers who buy in large quantities. The seller's per-unit selling cost is lower for larger purchases. The quantity discount is a way of passing part of these savings on to the buyer.

* *Cash discounts* are discounts offered for prompt payment. A seller may offer a discount of "2/10, net 30," meaning that the buyer may take a 2 percent discount if the bill is paid within ten days and that the bill must be paid in full within thirty days.

* A *seasonal discount* is a price reduction to buyers who purchase out of season. This discount lets the seller maintain steadier production during the year.

CONCEPT CHECK

Identify and describe the main types of discounts that are used in the pricing of business products.

* An *allowance* is a reduction in price to achieve a desired goal. Trade-in allowances, for example, are price reductions granted for turning in used equipment when purchasing new equipment.

TEST PREPPER 13.11

True or False?

___T___ 1. The pricing strategy that requires the buyer to pay the delivery costs is called FOB origin pricing.

___T___ 2. Retail giants such as Wal-Mart more than likely receive quantity discounts.

___F___ 3. When customers buy deeply discounted winter clothing out of season, they are taking advantage of a retailer discount.

Multiple Choice

___A___ 4. The choice of the costs to include when calculating the transfer price depends on

    a. the company's management strategy and the nature of the units' interaction.

    b. how much profit each unit wants to show.

    c. the company's traditional transfer pricing model.

    d. the quarterly targets the managers have agreed on.

    e. the nature of the units' interaction only.

___A___ 5. When a retail paint shop such as Sherwin Williams receives a discount from a paint manufacturer, it is called a

    a. trade discount.

    b. quantity discount.

    c. seasonal discount.

    d. retailer discount.

    e. cash discount.

ACE the Test
ACE & ACE+
Practice Test 13.11

Prepare for Class
CL News Feeds
CL News Now

→ RETURN TO INSIDE BUSINESS

Despite the low, low prices of PCs designed specifically for use in developing countries, companies can profit from such products. Quanta Computer, which is headquartered in Taiwan, will see profits once it is fully geared up to produce the XO laptop in high volume. In fact, the cost to manufacture XOs will drop drastically as the quantity produced goes up. Ultimately, One Laptop Per Child expects to lower the price to about $100 per laptop.

Microsoft has been testing a different approach to making affordable PCs for consumers in South America, Asia, and Eastern Europe. Its FlexGo is a "pay as you go" PC. After an initial down payment, the buyer pays by the hour as the PC is used until the full price (less than $600) has been paid off.

Questions

1. Are Microsoft, Intel, and VIA Technologies using price or nonprice competition? Explain your answer.

2. Where in the product life cycle does the PC appear to be? Why do less expensive PCs make sense at this stage of the life cycle?

LEARNING OBJECTIVES REVIEW

1 Explain what a product is and how products are classified.

- A product is everything one receives in an exchange, including all attributes and expected benefits. The product may be a manufactured item, a service, an idea, or some combination of these.

- Products are classified according to their ultimate use.

- Classification affects a product's distribution, promotion, and pricing.

- Consumer products, which include convenience, shopping, and specialty products, are purchased to satisfy personal and family needs.

- Business products are purchased for resale, for making other products, or for use in a firm's operations.

- Business products can be classified as raw materials, major equipment, accessory equipment, component parts, process materials, supplies, and services.

2 Discuss the product life cycle.

- Every product moves through a series of four stages—introduction, growth, maturity, and decline—which together form the product life cycle.

- As the product progresses through these stages, its sales and profitability increase, peak, and then decline.

- Marketers keep track of the life-cycle stage of products in order to estimate when a new product should be introduced to replace a declining one.

3 Define *product* line and *product* mix.

- A product line is a group of similar products marketed by a firm.

- The products in a product line are related to each other in the way they are produced, marketed, and used.

- A firm's product mix includes all the products it offers for sale.

- The width of a product mix is the number of product lines it contains.

- The depth of a product mix is the average number of individual products within each line.

Improve Your Grade
Audio Chapter Summary & Quiz

4 Identify the methods available for changing a product mix.

- Customer satisfaction and organizational objectives require marketers to develop, adjust, and maintain an effective product mix.

- Marketers may improve a product mix by changing existing products, deleting products, and developing new products.

- New products are developed through a series of seven steps:
  1. Idea generation involves the accumulation of a pool of possible product ideas.
  2. Screening removes from consideration product ideas that do not mesh with organizational goals or resources.
  3. Concept testing is a phase in which a small sample of potential buyers is exposed to a proposed product through a written or oral description in order to determine their initial reaction and buying intentions.
  4. Business analysis generates information about the potential sales, costs, and profits.
  5. Development occurs when the product idea is transformed into mock-ups and actual proto-types to determine if the product is technically feasible to build and can be produced at a reasonable cost.
  6. Test marketing is an actual launch of the product in several selected cities.
  7. Commercialization occurs when plans for full-scale production and marketing are refined and implemented. Most product failures result from inadequate product planning and development.

5 Explain the uses and importance of branding.

- A brand is a name, term, symbol, design, or any combination of these that identifies a seller's products as distinct from those of other sellers.

- Brands can be classified as manufacturer brands, store brands, or generic brands.

- A firm can choose between two branding strategies—individual branding or family branding. Branding strategies are used to associate (or not associate) particular products with existing products, producers, or intermediaries.

6 Explain the uses and importance of labeling and packaging.

- Labeling provides customers with product information, some of which is required by law.

- Packaging protects goods, offers consumer convenience, and enhances marketing efforts by communicating product features, uses, benefits, and image.

7 Describe the economic basis of pricing and the means by which sellers can influence prices and buyers' perceptions of prices.

- Prices are determined by the workings of supply and demand.

- Sellers exert some control, primarily through product differentiation. Product differentiation is the process of developing and promoting differences between one's product and all similar products.

- Firms also attempt to gain some control over pricing through advertising.

- A few large sellers have considerable control over prices because each controls a large proportion of the total supply of the product.

- Firms must consider the relative importance of price to buyers in the target market before setting prices.

- Buyers' perceptions of prices are affected by the importance of the product to them, the range of prices they consider acceptable, their perceptions of competing products, and their association of quality with price.

8 Identify the major pricing objectives used by businesses.

- Objectives of pricing include survival, profit maximization, target return on investment, achieving market goals, and maintaining the status quo.

- Firms sometimes have to price products to survive, which usually requires cutting prices to attract customers.

- Return on investment (ROI) is the amount earned as a result of the investment in developing and marketing the product. The firm sets an annual percentage ROI as the pricing goal.

- Some firms use pricing to maintain or increase their market share.

- In industries in which price stability is important, firms often price their products by charging about the same as competitors.

9 Examine the three major pricing methods that firms employ.

- The three major pricing methods are cost-based pricing, demand-based pricing, and competition-based pricing.

- When cost-based pricing is employed, a proportion of the cost is added to the total cost to determine the selling price.

- When demand-based pricing is used, the price will be higher when demand is higher, and the price will be lower when demand is lower.

- A firm that uses competition-based pricing may choose to price below competitors' prices, at the same level as competitors' prices, or slightly above competitors' prices.

10 Explain the different types of pricing strategies.

- Pricing strategies fall into five categories: new product pricing, differential pricing, psychological pricing, product-line pricing, and promotional pricing.

- Price skimming and penetration pricing are two strategies used for pricing new products. Differential pricing can be accomplished through negotiated pricing, secondary-market pricing, periodic discounting, and random discounting.

- The types of psychological pricing strategies are odd-number pricing, multiple-unit pricing, reference pricing, bundle pricing, everyday low prices, and customary pricing.

11 Describe three major types of pricing for business products.

- Setting prices for business products can be different from setting prices for consumer products as a result of several factors, such as size of purchases, transportation considerations, and geographic issues.

- The three types of pricing associated with the pricing of business products are geographic pricing, transfer pricing, and discounting.

VIDEO CASE

Flying High with Low Prices at JetBlue

How long can JetBlue Airways stay in the black while offering low airfares, lots of flights, and lots of legroom? Founded by David Neeleman, a savvy entrepreneur who sold his regional airline to Southwest Airlines in 1994, JetBlue sent its first flight into the skies in 2000. The airline quickly attained profitability and built a loyal customer base on the winning combination of customer-friendly service and low airfares. In recent years, however, JetBlue's high-flying profitability has lost a little altitude owing to high fuel costs.

CEO Neeleman knows that price is one of the top considerations for travelers. Major carriers typically quote dozens of fares between two locations depending on time of day and other factors. By comparison, JetBlue's everyday pricing structure is generally lower and far simpler and avoids complicated requirements such as Saturday-night stayovers. The CEO says that the fares are based on demand and that JetBlue uses pricing to equalize the loads on the flights so that no jet takes off empty while another is completely full. Thus fares for Sunday-night flights tend to be higher because of higher demand, whereas Tuesday-night flights may be priced lower owing to lower demand. Whenever the airline inaugurates a new route, it grabs travelers' attention with even lower promotional fares.

Price is not the only way that JetBlue sets itself apart from competing airlines. Whereas many new carriers buy used jets, JetBlue flies new Airbus A320 and Embraer 190 jets with seat-back video screens showing satellite television programming. Rather than squeeze in the maximum 180 seats that A320s can hold, JetBlue flies with only 156 seats, giving passengers more legroom. In addition, the jets are outfitted with roomier leather seats, which cost twice as much as ordinary seats but last twice as long and make passengers feel pampered.

Another advantage of new jets is higher fuel efficiency. A320s can operate on 60 percent of the amount of fuel burned by an equivalent jet built decades before. Even so, JetBlue's profit margin drops when fuel costs skyrocket. "It's all about the fuel,"

the CEO says. Nonetheless, the airline's total cost of 6.5 cents per mile remains well below the per-mile costs of most major competitors. In part, this is so because JetBlue's technicians work on only two types of jets, which means they gain proficiency at maintenance tasks and therefore save the airline time and money. Also, newer jets are under warranty, which keeps maintenance expenses down.

CEO Neeleman decided to base his airline in New York City for two main reasons. First, he knew that New York travelers departing from nearby LaGuardia Airport faced crowds and delays unless they were willing to venture eight miles farther to fly from John F. Kennedy (JFK) International Airport. Second, JFK was not a regional hub for major airlines or for low-fare carriers such as Southwest. Seizing an opportunity to trade off a slightly less convenient location for lower competition and better on-time performance, Neeleman secured enough space to accommodate JetBlue's growth for years to come.

From its first day of operation, JetBlue has relied on Internet bookings to minimize sales costs. Travelers who buy tickets directly through the company's website (**www.jetblue.com**) get a special discount and are also eligible for online specials. JetBlue books about half its fares on the web and saves about $5 in transaction costs for each ticket booked online. Now, as Neeleman accepts delivery of one new jet every three weeks and hires 1,700 new employees per year, he must keep travelers coming back, rein in costs, and keep JetBlue's prices competitive without grounding profits.

For more information about this company, go to **www .jetblue.com**.[22]

Questions

1. In an industry where pricing has driven many firms out of business or into bankruptcy protection, why does JetBlue compete so successfully on the basis of price?
2. How would you use the airplane and other physical aspects of the business to build the JetBlue brand?
3. How does JetBlue use pricing to deal with demand fluctuations?

BUILDING SKILLS FOR CAREER SUCCESS

1. Exploring the Internet

The Internet has quickly taken comparison shopping to a new level. Several websites such as **bizrate.com, pricescan.com,** and **mysimon.com** have emerged boasting that they can find the consumer the best deal on any product. From computers to watches, these sites offer unbiased price and product information to compare virtually any product. Users may read reviews about products as well as provide their own input from personal experience. Some of these sites also offer special promotions and incentives in exchange for user information. Visit the text website for updates to this exercise.

Assignment

1. Search all three of the websites listed above for the same product.
2. Did you notice any significant differences between the sites and the information they provide?
3. What percentage of searches do you think lead to purchases as opposed to browsing? Explain your answer.
4. Which site are you most likely to use on a regular basis? Why?
5. In what ways do these websites contribute to price competition?

2. Building Team Skills

In his book, *The Post-Industrial Society,* Peter Drucker wrote

> Society, community, and family are all conserving institutions. They try to maintain stability and to prevent, or at least slow down, change. But the organization of the post-capitalist society of organizations is a destabilizer. Because its function is to put knowledge to work—on tools, processes, and products; on work; on knowledge itself—it must be organized for constant change. It must be organized for innovation.

New product development is important in this process of systematically abandoning the past and building a future. Current customers can be sources of ideas for new products and services and ways of improving existing ones.

Prepare for Class
Exploring the Internet

Assignment

1. Working in teams of five to seven, brainstorm ideas for new products or services for your college.
2. Construct questions to ask currently enrolled students (your customers). Sample questions might include
    a. Why did you choose this college?
    b. How can this college be improved?
    c. What products or services do you wish were available?
3. Conduct the survey and review the results.
4. Prepare a list of improvements and/or new products or services for your college.

3. Researching Different Careers

Standard & Poor's Industry Surveys, designed for investors, provides insight into various industries and the companies that compete within those industries. The "Basic Analysis" section gives overviews of industry trends and issues. The other sections define some basic industry terms, report the latest revenues and earnings of more than 1,000 companies, and occasionally list major reference books and trade associations.

Assignment

1. Identify an industry in which you might like to work.
2. Find the industry in *Standard & Poor's.* (*Note: Standard & Poor's* uses broad categories of industry. For example, an apparel or home-furnishings store would be included under "Retail" or "Textiles.")
3. Identify the following:
    a. Trends and issues in the industry
    b. Opportunities and/or problems that might arise in the industry in the next five years
    c. Major competitors within the industry (These companies are your potential employers.)
4. Prepare a report of your findings.

CHAPTER 14

ELECTRONICS

Distributing and Promoting Products

Your Guide to Success in Business

Why this chapter matters
Not only is it important to create and maintain a mix of products that satisfies customers but also to make these products available at the *right place* and *time* and to communicate with customers effectively.

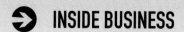

Treasure Hunt at Costco

Costco has no flashy advertising, no fancy store displays, and no cushy carpeting. Yet the company, founded in 1983, is now the fourth largest U.S. retailer. It rings up nearly $60 billion in annual sales and operates an online division as well as 495 gigantic stores, some topping 200,000 square feet. What's more, 48 million members pay an annual fee ($50 for consumers and small businesses, $100 for executives) just to be able to shop at Costco. And shop they do; members visit local Costco stores an average of twenty-two times every year.

Why do customers flock to Costco?

1. *To find bargains.* The company buys in huge quantities and passes the savings along to shoppers. It never marks merchandise up more than 14 percent above what the items cost. In contrast, prices at discount stores are often 30 percent above merchandise cost—and prices at department stores are 50 percent above merchandise cost and sometimes higher.

2. *To find treasure-hunts.* Shoppers return again and again because they never know exactly what they'll find as they browse the aisles. About one-quarter of the roughly 4,000 items in each Costco store are what the CEO calls "treasure-hunt stuff that's always changing. It's the type of item customers know they better buy because it will not be there next time, like Waterford crystal. We try to get that sense of urgency in our customers."[1]

DID YOU KNOW?

About 1,000 of the 4,000 items in each cavernous Costco store are what the CEO calls "treasure-hunt stuff that's always changing."

● ● ●

K E Y   T E R M S

Some companies, like Costco, use a particular approach to distribution and marketing channels that gives them a sustainable competitive advantage. More than two million firms in the United States help to move products from producers to consumers. Store chains such as Dollar General Stores, Starbucks, Sears, and Wal-Mart operate retail outlets where consumers make purchases. Some retailers, such as Avon Products and Amway, send their salespeople to the homes of customers. Other retailers, such as Lands' End and L. L. Bean, sell online, through catalogs, or both. Still others, such as Amazon, sell online to customers.

This chapter examines

* Various channels of distribution that products follow as they move from producer to ultimate user.

* Wholesalers and retailers within these channels.

* The types of shopping centers.

* The physical distribution functions.

* The four promotional methods and their importance in a marketing plan.

Channels of Distribution

Learning Objective

Identify the various channels of distribution and explain the concept of market coverage.

A **channel of distribution**, or **marketing channel**, is a sequence of marketing organizations that directs a product from the producer to the ultimate user. Every marketing channel begins with the producer and ends with either the consumer or the business user.

A marketing organization that links a producer and user within a marketing channel is called a **middleman**, or **marketing intermediary**. For the most part, middlemen are concerned with the transfer of *ownership* of products.

Two Types of Middlemen

1. A **merchant middleman** (or, more simply, a *merchant*) is a middleman that actually takes title to products by buying them.

2. A **functional middleman**, on the other hand, helps in the transfer of ownership of products but does not take title to the products.

Commonly Used Channels for Consumer Products

The four most commonly used channels for consumer products are illustrated in Figure 14.1.

---

channel of distribution (or marketing channel) a sequence of marketing organizations that directs a product from the producer to the ultimate user

middleman (or marketing intermediary) a marketing organization that links a producer and user within a marketing channel

merchant middleman a middleman that actually takes title to products by buying them

functional middleman a middleman that helps in the transfer of ownership of products but does not take title to the products

CONSUMER PRODUCTS

Producer					Consumer
Producer				Retailer	Consumer
Producer		Wholesaler		Retailer	Consumer
Producer	Agent	Wholesaler		Retailer	Consumer

FIGURE 14.1

Distribution Channels

Producers use various channels to distribute their products.

Producer to Consumer This channel, often called the *direct channel*, includes no marketing intermediaries. Practically all services and a few consumer goods are distributed through a direct channel. **EXAMPLE** Marketers that sell goods directly to consumers include Dell Computer, Mary Kay Cosmetics, and Avon Products. Producers sell directly to consumers for several reasons. They can better control the quality and price of their products. They do not have to pay (through discounts) for the services of intermediaries. And they can maintain closer ties with customers.

Producer to Retailer to Consumer A **retailer** is a middleman that buys from producers or other middlemen and sells to consumers. Producers sell directly to retailers when retailers (such as Wal-Mart) can buy in large quantities. **EXAMPLE** This channel is used most often for products that are bulky, such as furniture and automobiles, for which additional handling would increase selling costs. It is also the usual channel for perishable products, such as fruits and vegetables, and for high-fashion products that must reach the consumer in the shortest possible time.

Producer to Wholesaler to Retailer to Consumer This channel is known as the *traditional channel* because many consumer goods (especially convenience goods) pass through wholesalers to retailers. A **wholesaler** is a middleman that sells products to other firms. These firms may be retailers, industrial users, or other wholesalers. A producer uses wholesalers when its products are carried by so many retailers that the producer cannot deal with all of them. **EXAMPLE** The maker of Wrigley's gum uses this type of channel.

Producer to Agent to Wholesaler to Retailer to Consumer Producers may use agents to reach wholesalers. Agents are functional middlemen that do not take title to products and that are compensated by commissions paid by producers. Often these products are inexpensive, frequently purchased items. **EXAMPLE** To reach a large number of potential customers, a small manufacturer of gas-powered lawn edgers might choose to use agents to market its product to wholesalers, which, in turn, sell the lawn edgers to a large number of retailers. This channel is also used for highly seasonal products (such as Christmas tree ornaments) and by producers that do not have their own sales forces.

CONCEPT CHECK

What are the most common marketing channels for consumer products?

retailer a middleman that buys from producers or other middlemen and sells to consumers

wholesaler a middleman that sells products to other firms

Multiple Channels for Consumer Products Often a manufacturer uses different distribution channels to reach different market segments. For example, candy bars are sold through channels containing wholesalers and retailers as well as channels in which the producer sells them directly through large retailers. Multiple channels are also used to increase sales or to capture a larger share of the market with the goal of selling as much merchandise as possible. **EXAMPLE** Firestone markets its tires through its own retail outlets as well as through independent dealers.

Levels of Market Coverage

The *level* of market coverage refers to the number of outlets used at the wholesale level or retail level in a distribution channel. The three major levels of market coverage are intensive, selective, and exclusive distribution.

Intensive distribution is the use of all available outlets for a product. The producer that wants to give its product the widest possible exposure in the marketplace chooses intensive distribution. **EXAMPLE** Many convenience goods, including candy, gum, and soft drinks, are distributed intensively.

Selective distribution is the use of only a portion of the available outlets for a product in each geographic area. **EXAMPLE** Manufacturers of goods such as furniture, major home appliances, and clothing typically prefer selective distribution.

Exclusive distribution is the use of only a single retail outlet for a product in a large geographic area. Exclusive distribution usually is limited to very prestigious products. **EXAMPLE** This is appropriate, for instance, for specialty goods such as upscale pianos, fine china, and expensive jewelry. The producer usually places many requirements (such as inventory levels, sales training, service quality, and warranty procedures) on exclusive dealers.

intensive distribution the use of all available outlets for a product

selective distribution the use of only a portion of the available outlets for a product in each geographic area

exclusive distribution the use of only a single retail outlet for a product in a large geographic area

Selective Distribution.

Home appliances, such as those manufactured by Whirlpool, are usually distributed through selective distribution.

TEST PREPPER 14.1

True or False?

_____ 1. Every market channel begins with the producer and ends with the consumer or business user.

_____ 2. When the same product is sold to consumers and business customers, a manufacturer uses multiple channels.

Multiple Choice

_____ 3. Which one of the channels listed below is one of the channels of distribution?

    a. Producer to retailer
    b. Consumer to producer

    c. Producer to retailer to wholesaler
    d. Producer to wholesaler to retailer to consumer
    e. Wholesaler to retailer to consumer

_____ 4. A women's apparel manufacturer most likely will use

    a. intensive distribution.
    b. selective distribution.
    c. exclusive distribution.
    d. high-style distribution.
    e. popular-style distribution.

ACE the Test
ACE & ACE+
Practice Test 14.1

Partnering Through Supply-Chain Management

Learning Objective 2

Explain partnering through supply-chain management.

Supply-chain management is a long-term partnership among channel members working together to create a distribution system that reduces inefficiencies, costs, and redundancies while creating a competitive advantage and satisfying customers. Supply-chain management requires cooperation throughout the entire marketing channel, including manufacturing, research, sales, advertising, and shipping. Supply chains focus not only on producers, wholesalers, retailers, and customers, but also on component-parts suppliers, shipping companies, communication companies, and other organizations that participate in product distribution. Suppliers are having a greater impact on determining what items retail stores carry. This phenomenon, called _category management,_ is becoming common for mass merchandisers, supermarkets, and convenience stores. Through category management, the retailer asks a supplier in a particular category how to stock the shelves. **EXAMPLE** Borders asked publisher HarperCollins what books it should sell, which includes both HarperCollins' books and competitors' books. Many retailers and suppliers claim this process delivers maximum efficiency.[2]

Traditionally, buyers and sellers have been adversarial when negotiating purchases. Supply-chain management, however, encourages cooperation among buyers and sellers by

* Reducing the costs of inventory, transportation, administration, and handling.
* Speeding order-cycle times.
* Increasing profits for all channel members.

When buyers, sellers, marketing intermediaries, and facilitating agencies work together, customers' needs regarding delivery, scheduling, packaging, and other requirements

supply-chain management long-term partnership among channel members working together to create a distribution system that reduces inefficiencies, costs, and redundancies while creating a competitive advantage and satisfying customers

are better met. **EXAMPLE** Home Depot, North America's largest home-improvement retailer, is working to help its suppliers improve productivity and thereby supply Home Depot with better-quality products at lower costs. The company has even suggested a cooperative partnership with its competitors so that regional trucking companies making deliveries to all these organizations can provide faster, more efficient delivery.

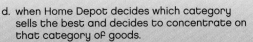

TEST PREPPER 14.2

True or False?

___ 1. According to the text, a supply-chain partnership creates a distribution system that reduces inefficiencies, costs, and redundancies.

___ 2. Supply chains do not focus on suppliers and shipping companies.

Multiple Choice

___ 3. Category management is

    a. a producer deciding which category to concentrate on for the next season.
    b. a retailer asking the supplier in a particular category on how to stock the shelves.
    c. when suppliers tell the manufacturer which category to produce more of.

    d. when Home Depot decides which category sells the best and decides to concentrate on that category of goods.
    e. the combined efforts of producers and wholesalers to manage the wholesaler's inventory.

___ 4. One of the reasons that Home Depot has become the largest home-improvement retailer is because

    a. it works with suppliers to improve productivity and thereby reduce costs.
    b. it only stocks superior-quality merchandise.
    c. it has a large product line.
    d. it has superior customer service compared with other retailers.
    e. it exerts pressure on suppliers to cut suppliers' prices.

ACE the Test
ACE & ACE+
Practice Test 14.2

Marketing Intermediaries: Wholesalers

Learning Objective 3

Discuss the need for wholesalers, describe the services they provide, and identify the major types of wholesalers.

Wholesalers may be the most misunderstood of marketing intermediaries. Producers sometimes try to eliminate them from distribution channels by dealing directly with retailers or consumers. Yet wholesalers provide a variety of essential marketing services. Although wholesalers can be eliminated, their functions cannot be eliminated; these functions *must* be performed by other channel members or by the consumer or ultimate user. Eliminating a wholesaler may or may not cut distribution costs.

Wholesalers Provide Services to Retailers and Manufacturers

Wholesalers help retailers

    * By buying in large quantities and then selling to retailers in smaller quantities and by delivering goods to retailers.

* By stocking in one place the variety of goods that retailers otherwise would have to buy from many producers.

* By providing assistance in other vital areas, including promotion, market information, and financial aid.

Wholesalers help manufacturers by

* Performing functions similar to those provided to retailers.

* Providing a sales force, reducing inventory costs, assuming credit risks, and furnishing market information.

Types of Wholesalers

Wholesalers generally fall into two categories: merchant wholesalers; agents and brokers. Of these, merchant wholesalers constitute the largest portion. They account for about four-fifths of all wholesale establishments and employees.

Merchant Wholesalers A merchant wholesaler is a middleman that purchases goods in large quantities and then sells them to other wholesalers or retailers and to institutional, farm, government, professional, or industrial users.

Characteristics of a Merchant Wholesaler

* Merchant wholesalers usually operate one or more warehouses at which they receive, take title to, and store goods. These wholesalers are sometimes called *distributors* or *jobbers*.

* Most merchant wholesalers are businesses composed of salespeople, order takers, receiving and shipping clerks, inventory managers, and office personnel.

* The successful merchant wholesaler must analyze available products and market needs. It must be able to adapt the type, variety, and quality of its products to changing market conditions.

* Merchant wholesalers may be classified as full-service or limited-service wholesalers depending on the number of services they provide. A full-service wholesaler performs the entire range of wholesaler functions described earlier in this section. These functions include delivering goods, supplying warehousing, arranging for credit, supporting promotional activities, and providing general customer assistance.

* A full-service wholesaler can be of three different types:

    * A general-merchandise wholesaler deals in a wide variety of products, such as drugs, hardware, nonperishable foods, cosmetics, detergents, and tobacco.

    * A limited-line wholesaler stocks only a few product lines but carries numerous product items within each line.

    * A specialty-line wholesaler carries a select group of products within a single line. Food delicacies such as shellfish represent the kind of product handled by this type of wholesaler.

Agents and Brokers Agents and brokers are functional middlemen. Functional middlemen do not take title to products. They perform a small number of marketing activities and are paid a commission that is a percentage of the sales price.

An agent is a middleman that expedites exchanges, represents a buyer or a seller, and often is hired permanently on a commission basis. When agents represent producers, they are known as *sales agents* or *manufacturer's agents*. As long as the

merchant wholesaler a middleman that purchases goods in large quantities and then sells them to other wholesalers or retailers and to institutional, farm, government, professional, or industrial users

full-service wholesaler a middleman that performs the entire range of wholesaler functions

general-merchandise wholesaler a middleman that deals in a wide variety of products

limited-line wholesaler a middleman that stocks only a few product lines but carries numerous product items within each line

specialty-line wholesaler a middleman that carries a select group of products within a single line

agent a middleman that expedites exchanges, represents a buyer or a seller, and often is hired permanently on a commission basis

broker a middleman that specializes in a particular commodity, represents either a buyer or a seller, and is likely to be hired on a temporary basis

products represented do not compete, a sales agent may represent one or several manufacturers on a commission basis. The agent solicits orders for the manufacturers within a specific territory. As a rule, the manufacturers ship the merchandise and bill the customers directly. The manufacturers also set the prices and other conditions of the sales.

Question: What do the manufacturers gain by using a sales agent?

Answer: The sales agent provides immediate entry into a territory, regular calls on customers, selling experience, and a known, predetermined selling expense (a commission that is a percentage of sales revenue).

A **broker** is a middleman that specializes in a particular commodity, represents either a buyer or a seller, and is likely to be hired on a temporary basis. However, food brokers, which sell grocery products to resellers, generally have long-term relationships with their clients. Brokers may perform only the selling function or both buying and selling using established contacts or special knowledge of their fields.

TEST PREPPER 14.3

True or False?

1. Wholesalers help retailers by buying in large quantities and selling to retailers in smaller quantities.
2. A full-service wholesaler is a type of merchant wholesaler.
3. General-merchandise wholesalers, limited-line wholesalers, and specialty-line wholesalers all fall under the category of full-service wholesalers.

Multiple Choice

4. Merchant wholesalers constitute what portion of all wholesale establishments and employees?

   a. Three-quarters
   b. Two-thirds
   c. One-third
   d. Four-fifths
   e. One-half

ACE the Test
ACE & ACE+
Practice Test 14.3

Marketing Intermediaries: Retailers

Learning Objective 4

Distinguish among the major types of retailers and shopping centers.

Retailers are the final link between producers and consumers. Retailers may buy from either wholesalers or producers. They sell not only goods but also such services as auto repairs, haircuts, and dry cleaning. Some retailers sell both. **EXAMPLE** Sears, Roebuck sells consumer goods, financial services, and repair services for home appliances bought at Sears.

Of approximately 2.6 million retail firms in the United States, about 90 percent have annual sales of less than $1 million. On the other hand, some large retail organizations realize well over $1 million in sales revenue per day. Table 14.1 lists the ten largest retail organizations and their approximate sales revenues and yearly profits.

RANK	COMPANY	ANNUAL SALES (000)	ANNUAL PROFITS (000)	NUMBER OF STORES
1	Wal-Mart, Inc.	$348,650	$11,284	6,779
2	The Home Depot	90,837	5,761	2,147
3	Kroger	66,111	1,115	3,659
4	Costco	60,151	1,103	488
5	Target	59,490	2,787	1,487
6	Sears Holdings	53,012	858	3,835
7	Walgreen's	47,409	1,751	5,461
8	Lowe's	46,927	3,105	1,375
9	CVS	43,814	1,355	6,202
10	Safeway	40,185	871	1,761

TABLE 14.1

The Ten Largest Retail Firms in the United States

Source: 2007 Top 100 Retailers, www.stores.org; accessed July, 18 2007.

Types of Retail Stores

One way to classify retailers is by the number of stores owned and operated by the firm.

1. An **independent retailer** is a firm that operates only one retail outlet. Approximately three-fourths of retailers are independent. One-store operators, like all small businesses, generally provide personal service and a convenient location.

2. A **chain retailer** is a company that operates more than one retail outlet. By adding outlets, chain retailers attempt to reach new geographic markets. As sales increase, chains usually buy merchandise in larger quantities and thus take advantage of quantity discounts. They also wield more power in their dealings with suppliers. About one-fourth of retail organizations operate chains.

Another way to classify retail stores is by store size and the kind and number of products carried. Let's take a closer look at store types based on these dimensions.

Department Stores These large retail establishments consist of several sections, or departments, that sell a wide assortment of products. According to the U.S. Bureau of the Census, a **department store** is a retail store that (1) employs twenty-five or more persons and (2) sells at least home furnishings, appliances, family apparel, and household linens and dry goods, each in a different part of the store. **EXAMPLE** Marshall Field's in Chicago (and several other cities), Harrods in London, and Au Printemps in Paris are examples of large department stores. Sears, Roebuck and JCPenney are also department stores. Traditionally, department stores have been service-oriented. Along with the goods they sell, these retailers provide credit, delivery, personal assistance, liberal return policies, and pleasant shopping atmospheres.

Discount Stores A **discount store** is a self-service general-merchandise outlet that sells products at lower-than-usual prices. These stores can offer lower prices by operating on smaller markups and by offering minimal customer services. To keep prices low, discount stores operate on the basic principle of high turnover of such items as appliances, toys, clothing, automotive products, and sports equipment. **EXAMPLE** Popular discount stores include KMart, Wal-Mart, Dollar General, and Target.

independent retailer a firm that operates only one retail outlet

chain retailer a company that operates more than one retail outlet

department store a retail store that (1) employs twenty-five or more persons and (2) sells at least home furnishings, appliances, family apparel, and household linens and dry goods, each in a different part of the store

discount store a self-service general-merchandise outlet that sells products at lower-than-usual prices

warehouse showroom
a retail facility in a large, low-cost building with a large, on-premises inventory and minimal service

convenience store a small food store that sells a limited variety of products but remains open well beyond normal business hours

supermarket a large self-service store that sells primarily food and household products

superstore a large retail store that carries not only food and nonfood products ordinarily found in supermarkets but also additional product lines

warehouse club a large-scale members-only establishment that combines features of cash-and-carry wholesaling with discount retailing

traditional specialty store a store that carries a narrow product mix with deep product lines

Warehouse Showrooms A warehouse showroom is a retail facility with five basic characteristics: (1) a large, low-cost building, (2) warehouse materials-handling technology, (3) vertical merchandise displays, (4) a large, on-premises inventory, and (5) minimal service. Some of the best-known showrooms are operated by big furniture retailers. These operations employ few personnel and offer few services. Most customers carry away purchases in the manufacturer's carton, although some warehouse showrooms will deliver for a fee.

Convenience Stores A convenience store is a small food store that sells a limited variety of products but remains open well beyond normal business hours. Almost 70 percent of convenience store customers live within a mile of the store. **EXAMPLE** White Hen Pantry, 7-Eleven, Circle K, and Open Pantry stores, for example, are found in some areas, as are independent convenience stores. Convenience stores are the fastest-growing category of retailer, with a 5.8 percent growth in sales over the past year compared with an 8 percent decline in overall retail sales.[3]

Supermarkets A supermarket is a large self-service store that sells primarily food and household products. It stocks canned, fresh, frozen, and processed foods; paper products; and cleaning supplies. Supermarkets also may sell such items as housewares, toiletries, toys and games, drugs, stationery, books and magazines, plants and flowers, and a few clothing items. Supermarkets are large-scale operations that emphasize low prices and one-stop shopping for household needs.

Superstores A superstore is a large retail store that carries not only food and nonfood products ordinarily found in supermarkets but also additional product lines—housewares, hardware, small appliances, clothing, personal-care products, garden products, and automotive merchandise. Superstores also provide a number of services to entice customers. Typically, these include automotive repair, snack bars and restaurants, film developing, and banking.

Warehouse Clubs The warehouse club is a large-scale members-only establishment that combines features of cash-and-carry wholesaling with discount retailing. For a nominal annual fee (about $25), small retailers may purchase products at wholesale prices for business use or for resale. Warehouse clubs also sell to ultimate consumers. Individual purchasers usually can choose to pay yearly dues for membership cards that allow them to avoid the 5 percent additional charge.

Because their product lines are shallow and sales volumes are high, warehouse clubs can offer a broad range of merchandise, including perishable and nonperishable foods, beverages, books, appliances, housewares, automotive parts, hardware, furniture, and sundries.

Traditional Specialty Stores A traditional specialty store carries a narrow product mix with deep product lines. Traditional specialty stores are sometimes called *limited-line retailers*. If they carry depth in one particular product category, they may be called *single-line retailers*. Specialty stores usually sell such products as clothing, jewelry, sporting goods, fabrics, computers, flowers, baked goods, books, and pet supplies. Specialty stores usually offer deeper product mixes than department stores. They attract customers by emphasizing service, atmosphere, and location. Consumers who are dissatisfied with the impersonal atmosphere of large retailers often find the attention offered by small specialty stores appealing. **EXAMPLE** Specialty stores include the Gap, Radio Shack, Bath and Body Works, and Foot Locker.

Off-Price Retailers An **off-price retailer** is a store that buys manufacturers' seconds, overruns, returns, and off-season merchandise at below-wholesale prices and sells them to consumers at deep discounts. Off-price retailers sell limited lines of national-brand and designer merchandise, usually clothing, shoes, or housewares. **EXAMPLE** Off-price retailers include T.J. Maxx, Burlington Coat Factory, and Marshalls. Off-price stores charge up to 50 percent less than department stores do for comparable merchandise but offer few customer services. They often include community dressing rooms and central checkout counters, and some off-price retailers have a no-returns, no-exchanges policy.

Traditional Specialty Stores.

Swatch store is an example of a traditional specialty store.

CONCEPT CHECK
What types of retail outlets are best suited to intensive distribution? To selective distribution? To exclusive distribution? Explain your answer in each case.

Category Killers A **category killer** is a very large specialty store that concentrates on a single product line and competes by offering low prices and an enormous number of products. These stores are called *category killers* because they take business away from smaller, high-cost retail stores. **EXAMPLE** Category killers include Home Depot (building materials), Office Depot (office supplies and equipment), and Best Buy (electronics), all of which are leaders in their niche. Some experts are predicting a decrease in the number of large-scale category killers in the not so distant future owing to other stores focusing on even smaller niches.[4]

Types of Nonstore Selling

Nonstore retailing is selling that does not take place in conventional store facilities; consumers purchase products without visiting a store. This form of retailing accounts for an increasing percentage of total retail sales. Nonstore retailers use direct selling, direct marketing, and vending machines.

Direct Selling **Direct selling** is the marketing of products to customers through face-to-face sales presentations at home or in the workplace. Traditionally called *door-to-door selling*, direct selling in the United States began with peddlers more than a century ago and has grown to about $30 billion in U.S. sales annually.[5] Instead of the door-to-door approach, many companies today—such as Mary Kay, Kirby, Amway, and Avon—use other approaches. They identify customers by mail, telephone, the Internet, or at shopping malls and then set up appointments. Direct selling sometimes involves the "party plan," which can occur in the customer's home or workplace. Direct selling through the party plan requires effective salespeople who can identify potential hosts and provide encouragement and incentives for them to organize a gathering of friends and associates. **EXAMPLE** Companies that commonly use the party plan are Tupperware, Stanley Home Products, Pampered Chef, and Sarah Coventry.

off-price retailer a store that buys manufacturers' seconds, overruns, returns, and off-season merchandise for resale to consumers at deep discounts

category killer a very large specialty store that concentrates on a single product line and competes on the basis of low prices and product availability

nonstore retailing a type of retailing whereby consumers purchase products without visiting a store

direct selling the marketing of products to customers through face-to-face sales presentations at home or in the workplace

direct marketing the use of the telephone, Internet, and nonpersonal media to introduce products to customers, who then can purchase them via mail, telephone, or the Internet

catalog marketing a type of marketing in which an organization provides a catalog from which customers make selections and place orders by mail, telephone, or the Internet

direct-response marketing a type of marketing in which a retailer advertises a product and makes it available through mail, telephone, or online orders

telemarketing the performance of marketing-related activities by telephone

television home shopping a form of selling in which products are presented to television viewers, who can buy them by calling a toll-free number and paying with a credit card

Direct Marketing **Direct marketing** is the use of the telephone, Internet, and nonpersonal media to communicate product and organizational information to customers, who then can purchase products via mail, telephone, or the Internet. Direct marketing is one type of nonstore retailing. Direct marketing can occur through

* Catalog marketing
* Direct-response marketing
* Telemarketing
* Television home shopping
* Online retailing

In **catalog marketing**, an organization provides a catalog from which customers make selections and place orders by mail, telephone, or the Internet. Catalog marketing began in 1872 when Montgomery Ward issued its first catalog to rural families. Today, there are more than 7,000 catalog marketing companies in the United States, as well as a number of retail stores, such as JCPenney, that engage in catalog marketing. Some organizations, including Spiegel and JCPenney, offer a broad array of products spread over multiple product lines. **EXAMPLE** Catalog companies such as Lands' End, Pottery Barn, and J. Crew offer considerable depth in one major line of products. Still other catalog companies specialize in only a few products within a single line. The advantages of catalog marketing include efficiency and convenience for customers. The retailer benefits by being able to locate in remote, low-cost areas, save on expensive store fixtures, and reduce both personal selling and store operating expenses. Disadvantages, on the other hand, are that catalog marketing is inflexible, provides limited service, and is most effective for only a selected set of products.

Direct-response marketing occurs when a retailer advertises a product and makes it available through mail, telephone, or online orders. **EXAMPLE** Direct-response marketing includes a television commercial offering a recording artist's musical collection, a newspaper or magazine advertisement for a series of children's books, and even a billboard promoting floral services available by calling 1-800-Flowers. Direct-response marketing is also conducted by sending letters, samples, brochures, or booklets to prospects on a mailing list and asking that they order the advertised products by mail, telephone, or online.

Telemarketing is the performance of marketing-related activities by telephone. Some organizations use a prescreened list of prospective clients. Telemarketing has many advantages such as generating sales leads, improving customer service, speeding up payments on past-due accounts, raising funds for nonprofit organizations, and gathering market data.

Currently, the laws and regulations regarding telemarketing, while in a state of flux, are becoming more restrictive. On October 1, 2003, the U.S. Congress implemented a national do-not-call registry for consumers who do not want to receive telemarketing calls. After two years, the do-not-call registry listed over 100 million phone numbers. Regulations associated with the national do-not-call registry are enforced by the Federal Trade Commission (FTC). Companies are subject to fines of up to $12,000 for each call made to consumers listed on the national do-not-call registry.[6] For example, DirecTV recently was ordered to pay $5.3 million in fines by the FTC for violating the do-not-call list.[7] Certain exceptions apply to no-call lists. A company still can use telemarketing to communicate with existing customers. In addition, charitable, political, and telephone survey organizations are not restricted by the national registry.

Television home shopping presents products to television viewers, encouraging them to order through toll-free numbers and pay with credit cards. Home Shopping Network (HSN) originated and popularized this format. The most popular products sold through television home shopping are jewelry (40 percent of total sales), clothing, housewares, and electronics. Home shopping channels have grown so rapidly in recent years that more than 60 percent of U.S. households have access to home shopping programs. **EXAMPLE** HSN and QVC are two of the largest home shopping networks. Approximately 60 percent of home shopping sales revenues come from repeat purchasers.

Online retailing makes products available to buyers through computer connections. Most bricks-and-mortar retailers have websites to sell products, provide information about their company, or distribute coupons. **EXAMPLE** Netflix has changed the video rental industry by offering its completely online movie rental service. Customers pay a monthly fee for unlimited rentals and browse the Netflix site to compose a list of

SP☉TLIGHT

Benefits of online marketing

Researchers report that the four major advantages of online marketing are increased revenue, greater visibility, cost savings, and reaching new customers.

Increased revenue ▶ 73%

Greater visibility ▶ 58%

Cost savings ▶ 56%

Reaching new customers ▶ 54%

Search [_____] GO   Clothing   Footwear   Accessories   Home

Source: Multichannel Marketing 2005 Report, DMA.

online retailing retailing that makes products available to buyers through computer connections

BIZ TECH

Apple's iTunes Becomes a Major Entertainment Success

Apple's online iTunes Store has revolutionized entertainment retailing by selling downloadable music, television shows, feature films, games, audio books, and more. Launched in 2003 to support sales of Apple's iPod media player, iTunes has captured a whopping 72 percent of the online-music market and is now the fourth-largest retailer of music in any form, anywhere. In addition, iTunes has done well with downloadable movies. Walt Disney, the first studio to retail its movies through iTunes, sold 125,000 downloads worth $1 million in revenue during the first week alone.

However, iTunes faces increasingly aggressive competition from deep-pocketed rivals. Amazon.com, an online retailing pioneer, began selling movie downloads one week before iTunes got into the business, and both Wal-Mart and Blockbuster are moving into movie downloads. Also, Microsoft is heavily promoting its own digital media players and online entertainment store, Zune Marketplace. Can iTunes stay on top?

Sources: Based on information in Jennifer Netherby, "Paid Downloads Slow to Catch On," *Video Business*, January 1, 2007, p. 1; "Wal-Mart Adds Net Offer," *Los Angeles Times*, November 29, 2006, p. C3; "Disney Posts $1 Million in Movie Sales on iTunes," *Los Angeles Times*, September 20, 2006, p. C9; Ethan Smith, "Can Anybody Catch iTunes?" *Wall Street Journal*, November 27, 2006. p. R.1.

videos they want to rent. Selections are mailed to their home, and customers are free to keep the rental as long as they want without the late fees typically charged by traditional stores.[8] Although online retailing represents a major retailing venue, security remains an issue. In a recent survey conducted by the Business Software Alliance, some Internet users still expressed concerns about shopping online. The major problems are identity theft and credit-card theft.

automatic vending the use of machines to dispense products

Automatic vending is the use of machines to dispense products. It accounts for less than 2 percent of all retail sales. Video game machines provide an entertainment service, and many banks offer automatic teller machines (ATMs), which dispense cash and perform other services.

Automatic vending is one of the most impersonal forms of retailing. Small, standardized, routinely purchased products (e.g., chewing gum, candy, newspapers, cigarettes, soft drinks, and coffee) can be sold in machines because consumers usually buy them at the nearest available location. Machines in areas of heavy traffic provide efficient and continuous service to consumers. Such high-volume areas may have more diverse product availability—for example, hot and cold sandwiches, DVD rentals, or even iPods (yes, $200 iPods are available in machines with coin slots). **EXAMPLE** San Francisco–based Zoom Systems has expanded its vending machine offerings from snacks to digital cameras. Its number one seller, though, is the iPod vending machine that offers Apple's popular MP3 players as well as accessories such as headphones, speakers, and battery chargers.[9]

Types of Shopping Centers

lifestyle shopping center an open-air-environment shopping center with upscale chain specialty stores

The *planned shopping center* is a self-contained retail facility constructed by independent owners and consisting of various stores. Shopping centers are designed and promoted to serve diverse groups of customers with widely differing needs. The management of a shopping center strives for a coordinated mix of stores, a comfortable atmosphere, adequate parking, pleasant landscaping, and special events to attract customers. The convenience of shopping for most family and household needs in a single location is an important part of shopping-center appeal.

A planned shopping center is one of four types: lifestyle, neighborhood, community, or regional. Although shopping centers vary, each offers a complementary mix of stores for the purpose of generating consumer traffic.

Lifestyle Shopping Centers A **lifestyle shopping center** is a shopping center that has an open-air configuration and is occupied by upscale national chain specialty stores.

Lifestyle shopping centers.

The Village of Rochester Hills shopping center is one example of a lifestyle shopping center.

The lifestyle center is more convenient than a traditional enclosed mall but offers the same quality of upscale retail and department stores, movie theaters, and dining. A strong emphasis is placed on the architecture of the center and creating a pleasant and "hip" shopping environment. Most lifestyle centers are found in affluent neighborhoods.[10]

Neighborhood Shopping Centers A neighborhood shopping center typically consists of several small convenience and specialty stores. Businesses in neighborhood shopping centers might include small grocery stores, drugstores, gas stations, and fast-food restaurants. These retailers serve consumers who live less than ten minutes away, usually within a two- to three-mile radius of the stores. Because most purchases in the neighborhood shopping center are based on convenience or personal contact, these retailers generally make only limited efforts to coordinate promotional activities among stores in the shopping center.

Community Shopping Centers A community shopping center includes one or two department stores and some specialty stores, along with convenience stores. It attracts consumers from a wider geographic area who will drive longer distances to find products and specialty items unavailable in neighborhood shopping centers. Community shopping centers, which are carefully planned and coordinated, generate traffic with special events such as art exhibits, automobile shows, and sidewalk sales. The management of a community shopping center maintains a balance of tenants so that the center can offer wide product mixes and deep product lines.

Regional Shopping Centers A regional shopping center usually has large department stores, numerous specialty stores, restaurants, movie theaters, and sometimes even hotels. It carries most of the merchandise offered by a downtown shopping district. Downtown merchants, in fact, often have renovated their stores and enlarged their parking facilities to meet the competition of successful regional shopping centers. Urban expressways and improved public transportation also have helped many downtown shopping areas to remain vigorous.

Regional shopping centers carefully coordinate management and marketing activities to reach the 150,000 or more customers in their target market. These large centers usually advertise, hold special events, and provide transportation to certain groups of customers. They also maintain a suitable mix of stores. National chain stores can gain leases in regional shopping centers more easily than small independent stores because they are better able to meet the centers' financial requirements.

neighborhood shopping center a planned shopping center consisting of several small convenience and specialty stores

community shopping center a planned shopping center that includes one or two department stores and some specialty stores, along with convenience stores

regional shopping center a planned shopping center containing large department stores, numerous specialty stores, restaurants, movie theaters, and sometimes even hotels

TEST PREPPER 14.4

True or False?

___T___ 1. One way to classify retailers is by the number of stores owned and operated by the firm.

___F___ 2. About half of retail organizations operate chains.

___T___ 3. Wal-Mart would be a good example of a discount store.

___T___ 4. The most common forms of nonstore retailing are direct selling, direct marketing, and vending machines.

Multiple Choice

___C___ 5. Which one of the following is an example of a category killer?
   a. KMart
   b. 7-Eleven stores
   c. Home Depot
   d. Burlington Coat Factory
   e. Macy's

ACE the Test
ACE & ACE+
Practice Test 14.4

Physical Distribution

Learning Objective 5

Explain the five most important physical distribution activities.

Physical distribution is all those activities concerned with the efficient movement of products from the producer to the ultimate user. Physical distribution therefore is the movement of the products themselves—both goods and services—through their channels of distribution. It is a combination of several interrelated business functions. The most important of these are inventory management, order processing, warehousing, materials handling, and transportation. These functions and their costs are highly interrelated. For example, using expensive air freight may reduce warehousing and inventory costs. Because of such interrelationships, marketers view physical distribution as an integrated effort that supports other important marketing activities, such as getting the right product to the right place at the right time and at minimal total cost.

Inventory Management

In Chapter 9 we discussed inventory management from the standpoint of operations. We defined **inventory management** as the process of managing inventories in such a way as to minimize inventory costs, including both holding costs and potential stock-out costs. Both the definition and the objective of inventory control apply here as well.

Holding costs are the costs of storing products until they are purchased or shipped to customers. *Stock-out costs* are the costs of sales lost when items are not in inventory. Of course, holding costs can be reduced by minimizing inventories, but then stock-out costs could be financially threatening to the organization. And stock-out costs can be minimized by carrying very large inventories, but then holding costs would be enormous.

Inventory management therefore is a sort of balancing act between stock-out costs and holding costs. The latter include the cost of money invested in inventory, the cost of storage space, insurance costs, and inventory taxes. Often even a relatively small reduction in inventory investment can provide a relatively large increase in working capital. And sometimes this reduction can best be accomplished through a willingness to incur a reasonable level of stock-out costs. Companies frequently rely on technology and software to help manage inventory on a regular basis.

Order Processing

Order processing consists of activities involved in receiving and filling customers' purchase orders. It may include not only the means by which customers order products but also procedures for billing and for granting credit.

Fast, efficient order processing is an important marketing service—one that can provide a dramatic competitive edge. The people who purchase goods for intermediaries are especially concerned with their suppliers' promptness and reliability in order processing. To them, promptness and reliability mean minimal inventory costs as well as the ability to order goods when they are needed rather than weeks in advance. The Internet is providing new opportunities for improving services associated with order processing.

Warehousing

Warehousing is the set of activities involved in receiving and storing goods and preparing them for reshipment. Goods are stored to create time utility; that is, they are held until they are needed for use or sale. Warehousing includes the following activities:

* *Receiving goods.* The warehouse accepts delivered goods and assumes responsibility for them.
* *Identifying goods.* Records are made of the quantity of each item received. Items may be marked, coded, or tagged for identification.
* *Sorting goods.* Delivered goods may have to be sorted before being stored.
* *Dispatching goods to storage.* Items must be moved to specific storage areas, where they can be found later.
* *Holding goods.* The goods are kept in storage under proper protection until needed.
* *Recalling, picking, and assembling goods.* Items that are to leave the warehouse must be selected from storage and assembled efficiently.
* *Dispatching shipments.* Each shipment is packaged suitably and directed to the proper transport vehicle. Shipping and accounting documents are prepared.

A firm may use its own private warehouses or rent space in public warehouses. A *private warehouse*, owned and operated by a particular firm, can be designed to serve the firm's specific needs. However, the organization must take on the task of financing the facility, determining the best location for it, and ensuring that it is used fully. Generally, only companies that deal in large quantities of goods can justify private warehouses. *Public warehouses* offer their services to all individuals and firms. Most are huge, one-story structures on the outskirts of cities, where rail and truck transportation is easily available. They provide storage facilities, areas for sorting and assembling shipments, and office and display spaces for wholesalers and retailers. Public warehouses also will hold—and issue receipts for—goods used as collateral for borrowed funds.

Materials Handling

Materials handling is the actual physical handling of goods—in warehouses as well as during transportation. Proper materials-handling procedures and techniques can increase the usable capacity of a warehouse or that of any means of transportation. Proper handling can reduce breakage and spoilage as well.

Modern materials handling attempts to reduce the number of times a product is handled. One method is called *unit loading.* Several smaller cartons, barrels, or boxes are combined into a single standard-size load that can be handled efficiently by forklift, conveyer, or truck.

warehousing the set of activities involved in receiving and storing goods and preparing them for reshipment

materials handling the actual physical handling of goods, in warehouses as well as during transportation

transportation the shipment of products to customers

carrier a firm that offers transportation services

Transportation

As a part of physical distribution, **transportation** is simply the shipment of products to customers. The greater the distance between seller and purchaser, the more important is the choice of the means of transportation and the particular carrier.

A firm that offers transportation services is called a **carrier**. A *common carrier* is a transportation firm whose services are available to all shippers. Railroads, airlines, and most long-distance trucking firms are common carriers. A *contract carrier* is available for hire by one or several shippers. Contract carriers do not serve the general public. Moreover, the number of firms they can handle at any one time is limited by law. A *private carrier* is owned and operated by the shipper.

In addition, a shipper can hire agents called *freight forwarders* to handle its transportation. Freight forwarders pick up shipments from the shipper, ensure that the goods are loaded on selected carriers, and assume responsibility for safe delivery of the shipments to their destinations. Freight forwarders often can group a number of small shipments into one large load (which is carried at a lower rate). This, of course, saves money for shippers.

The six major criteria used for selecting transportation modes are compared in Table 14.2. These six criteria are

1. Cost
2. Speed
3. Dependability
4. Load flexibility
5. Accessibility
6. Frequency

Obviously, the *cost* of a transportation mode is important to marketers. At times, marketers choose higher-cost modes of transportation because of the benefits they provide. *Speed* is measured by the total time that a carrier possesses the products,

TABLE 14.2

Characteristics of Transportation Modes

Source: U.S. Bureau of Transportation Statistics, *National Transportation Statistics 2005*, **www.bts.gov**; accessed July 12, 2006.

SELECTION CRITERIA	MODE OF TRANSPORTATION				
	RAILROADS	TRUCKS	PIPELINES	WATERWAYS	AIRPLANES
Cost	Moderate	High	Low	Very low	Very high
Speed	Average	Fast	Slow	Very slow	Very fast
Dependability	Average	High	High	Average	High
Load flexibility	High	Average	Very low	Very high	Low
Accessibilty	High	Very high	Very limited	Limited	Average
Frequency	Low	High	Very high	Very low	Average
Percent of use	36.8%	29.0%	19.9%	13.9%	0.3%
Products carried	Coal, grain, lumber, heavy equipment, paper and pulp products, chemicals	Clothing, computers, books, groceries and produce, livestock	Oil, processed coal, natural gas, wood chips	Chemicals, bauxite, grain, motor vehicles, agricultural implements	Flowers, food (highly perishable), technical instruments, emergency parts and equipment, overnight mail

including time required for pickup and delivery, handling, and movement between point of origin and destination. Usually there is a direct relationship between cost and speed; that is, faster modes of transportation are more expensive. A transportation mode's *dependability* is determined by the consistency of service provided by that mode. *Load flexibility* is the degree to which a transportation mode can provide appropriate equipment and conditions for moving specific kinds of products and can be adapted for moving other kinds of products. For example, certain types of products may need controlled temperatures or humidity levels. *Accessibility* refers to a transportation mode's ability to move goods over a specific route or network. *Frequency* refers to how often a marketer can ship products by a specific transportation mode. Whereas pipelines provide continuous shipments, railroads and waterways follow specific schedules for moving products from one location to another. In Table 14.2, each transportation mode is rated on a relative basis for these six selection criteria and the percentage of use (ton-miles) for each mode.

Railroads In terms of total freight carried, railroads are America's most important mode of transportation. They are also the least expensive for many products. Almost all railroads are common carriers, although a few coal-mining companies operate their own lines. Many commodities carried by railroads could not be transported easily by any other means.

Trucks The trucking industry consists of common, contract, and private carriers. Trucks can move goods to suburban and rural areas not served by railroads. They can handle freight quickly and economically, and they carry a wide range of shipments. Many shippers favor this mode of transportation because it offers door-to-door service, less stringent packaging requirements than ships and airplanes, and flexible delivery schedules. Railroad and truck carriers have teamed up to provide a form of transportation called *piggyback.* Truck trailers are carried from city to city on specially equipped railroad flatcars. Within each city, the trailers are then pulled in the usual way by truck tractors.

Airplanes Air transport is the fastest but most expensive means of transportation. All certified airlines are common carriers. Supplemental or charter lines are contract carriers. Because of the high cost, lack of airport facilities in many areas, and reliance on weather conditions, airlines carry less than 1 percent of all intercity freight. Only high-value, perishable items or goods that are needed immediately usually are shipped by air.

Waterways Cargo ships and barges offer the least expensive but slowest form of transportation. They are used mainly for bulky, nonperishable goods such as iron ore, bulk wheat, motor vehicles, and agricultural implements. Of course, shipment by water is limited to cities located on navigable waterways.

Pipelines Pipelines are a highly specialized mode of transportation. They are used primarily to carry petroleum and natural gas. Pipelines have become more important as the nation's need for petroleum products has increased. Such products as semiliquid coal and wood chips also can be shipped through pipelines continuously, reliably, and with minimal handling.

True or False?

 1. Branding goods is also one of the activities of warehousing.

 2. Organizations design warehouses to be cost-efficient as well as to provide excellent customer service.

Multiple Choice

3. Which activity combines inventory management, order processing, warehousing, materials handling, and transportation?

    a. Marketing
    b. Merchandising
    c. Warehousing
    d. Physical distribution
    e. Transporting

 4. Which one of the following is not one of the criteria for selecting transportation modes?

    a. Cost
    b. Design
    c. Dependability
    d. Load flexibility
    e. Accessibility

 5. Which one of the following is the fastest but most expensive means of transportation?

    a. Airplanes
    b. Waterways
    c. Railroads
    d. Trucks
    e. Pipelines

ACE the Test
ACE & ACE+
Practice Test 14.5

What Is Integrated Marketing Communications?

 Learning Objective 6

Explain how integrated marketing communications works to have the maximum impact on the customer.

integrated marketing communications
coordination of promotion efforts to ensure maximal informational and persuasive impact on customers

Integrated marketing communications is the coordination of promotion efforts to ensure maximal informational and persuasive impact on customers. A major goal of integrated marketing communications is to send a consistent message to customers. Integrated marketing communications provides an organization with a way to coordinate and manage its promotional efforts to ensure that customers do receive consistent messages. This approach fosters not only long-term customer relationships but also the efficient use of promotional resources.

The concept of integrated marketing communications has been increasingly accepted for several reasons:

1. Mass-media advertising, a very popular promotional method in the past, is used less today because of its high costs and less predictable audience sizes. Marketers now can take advantage of more precisely targeted promotional tools, such as cable TV, direct mail, DVDs, the Internet, special-interest magazines, and podcasts.

2. Database marketing is also allowing marketers to be more precise in targeting individual customers.

3. Until recently, suppliers of marketing communications were specialists. Advertising agencies provided advertising campaigns, sales promotion companies

provided sales promotion activities and materials, and public-relations organizations engaged in public-relations efforts. Today, a number of promotion-related companies provide one-stop shopping to the client seeking advertising, sales promotion, and public relations, thus reducing coordination problems for the sponsoring company.

4. Because the overall costs of marketing communications are significant, management demands systematic evaluations of communications efforts to ensure that promotional resources are being used efficiently. Although the fundamental role of promotion is not changing, the specific communication vehicles employed and the precision with which they are used are changing.

The Promotion Mix: An Overview

Learning Objective 7

Describe the basic concept of the promotion mix.

Promotion is communication about an organization and its products that is intended to inform, persuade, or remind target-market members. The promotion with which we are most familiar—advertising—is intended to inform, persuade, or remind us to buy particular products. But there is more to promotion than advertising, and it is used for other purposes as well. **EXAMPLE** Charities use promotion to inform us of their need for donations, to persuade us to give, and to remind us to do so in case we have forgotten. Even the Internal Revenue Service uses promotion (in the form of publicity) to remind us of its April 15 deadline for filing tax returns.

A **promotion mix** (sometimes called a *marketing-communications mix*) is the particular combination of promotion methods a firm uses to reach a target market. The makeup of a mix depends on many factors, including the firm's promotional resources and objectives, the nature of the target market, the product characteristics, and the feasibility of various promotional methods.

The four major elements in an organization's mix are

* Advertising
* Personal selling
* Sales promotion
* Public relations (see Figure 14.2)

While it is possible that one ingredient may be used, it is likely that two, three, or four of these ingredients will be used in a promotion mix depending on the type of product and target market involved.

promotion communication about an organization and its products that is intended to inform, persuade, or remind target-market members

promotion mix the particular combination of promotion methods a firm uses to reach a target market

─ EXAMINING ETHIC**S** ─
Who's Behind the Blog Buzz?

I s it ethical to have a product mentioned in a blog (an online journal) without clearly identifying that a company is behind the attempt to build buzz? Here are two recent examples that caused controversy:

- *Wal-Mart.* The "Wal-Marting Across America" blog seemed to be written by two ordinary people who drove their RV to Wal-Mart parking lots and chatted with happy employees and customers. The blog included a banner from "Working Families for Wal-Mart" but never mentioned that funding came from Wal-Mart—a fact first revealed by *BusinessWeek* magazine.
- *Nokia.* When David Ponce of the **OhGizmo.com** blog reviewed a $600 multifunction Nokia cell phone, he wrote that although "some features lack a little polish . . . the phone is worth its weight in gold." Only careful readers of OhGizmo would notice a statement that reviewers accept free samples of products for review. Yet Ponce told *Smart Money* magazine that the Nokia was a great music player but not a very good phone.

So should bloggers and companies be required to disclose any connections they may have?

Sources: Based on information in Anne Kadet, "Romancing the Bloggers," *SmartMoney*, November 2006, pp. 92+; Pallavi Gogoi, "Wal-Mart vs. the Blogosphere," *BusinessWeek*, October 17, 2006, **www.businessweek.com;** Pallavi Gogoi, "Wal-Mart's Jim and Laura: The Real Story," *BusinessWeek*, October 8, 2006, **www.businessweek.com;** Howard Kurtz, "Post Photographer Repays Group for Trip Expenses," *Washington Post*, October 12, 2006, p. C2.

advertising a paid nonpersonal message communicated to a select audience through a mass medium

personal selling personal communication aimed at informing customers and persuading them to buy a firm's products

sales promotion the use of activities or materials as direct inducements to customers or salespersons

public relations communication activities used to create and maintain favorable relationships between an organization and various public groups, both internal and external

Advertising is a paid nonpersonal message communicated to a select audience through a mass medium. Advertising is flexible enough that it can reach a very large target group or a small, carefully chosen one.

Personal selling is personal communication aimed at informing customers and persuading them to buy a firm's products. It is more expensive to reach a consumer through personal selling than through advertising, but this method provides immediate feedback and often is more persuasive than advertising.

Sales promotion is the use of activities or materials as direct inducements to customers or salespersons. It adds extra value to the product or increases the customer's incentive to buy the product.

Public relations is a broad set of communication activities used to create and maintain favorable relationships between an organization and various public groups, both internal and external. Public-relations activities are numerous and varied and can be a very effective form of promotion.

TEST PREPPER 14.6 14.7

True or False?

___1. One of the reasons that integrated marketing communications is being increasingly accepted is because of mass-media advertising.

2. Personal selling is more expensive than advertising.

3. Sales promotion does not add extra value to the product being sold.

Advertising

Learning Objective ⑧

Explain the three types of advertising and describe the major steps of developing an advertising campaign.

In 2005, organizations spent $276 billion on advertising in the United States.[11] Figure 14.3 shows how advertising expenditures and employment in advertising have increased since 1982.

Types of Advertising by Purpose

Depending on its purpose and message, advertising may be classified into one of three groups: primary demand, selective demand, or institutional.

Primary-Demand Advertising Primary-demand advertising is advertising aimed at increasing the demand for *all* brands of a product within a specific industry. **EXAMPLE** Trade and industry associations, such as the California Milk Processor Board ("got milk?"), are the major users of primary-demand advertising. Their advertisements promote broad product categories, such as beef, milk, pork, potatoes, and prunes, without mentioning specific brands.

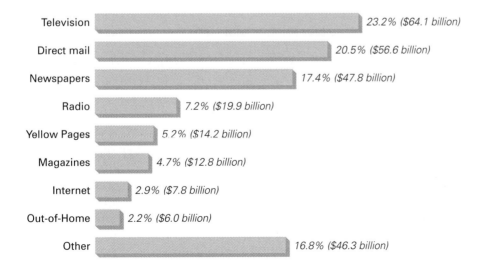

Media	Percentage (Amount)
Television	23.2% ($64.1 billion)
Direct mail	20.5% ($56.6 billion)
Newspapers	17.4% ($47.8 billion)
Radio	7.2% ($19.9 billion)
Yellow Pages	5.2% ($14.2 billion)
Magazines	4.7% ($12.8 billion)
Internet	2.9% ($7.8 billion)
Out-of-Home	2.2% ($6.0 billion)
Other	16.8% ($46.3 billion)

ACE the Test
ACE & ACE+
Practice Tests 14.6, 14.7

CONCEPT CHECK
A number of companies have shifted a portion of their promotion dollars from advertising to trade sales promotion methods. Why?

primary-demand advertising advertising whose purpose is to increase the demand for *all* brands of a product within a specific industry

FIGURE 14.3

Percentage Advertising Spending on Types of Media

Over the last twenty years, television advertising has become the number one advertising medium, and newspaper advertising has slipped to number three.

Source: "Ad Spending Totals by Types of Media," *Advertising Age*, June 27, 2005, p. S-21.

selective-demand (or brand) advertising advertising that is used to sell a particular brand of product

institutional advertising advertising designed to enhance a firm's image or reputation

Selective-Demand Advertising Selective-demand (or brand) advertising is advertising that is used to sell a particular brand of product. It is by far the most common type of advertising, and it accounts for the lion's share of advertising expenditures. Producers use brand-oriented advertising to convince us to buy everything from Bubble Yum to Buicks.

Selective-demand advertising that aims at persuading consumers to make purchases within a short time is called *immediate-response advertising*. Most local advertising is of this type. Often local advertisers promote products with immediate appeal. Selective advertising aimed at keeping a firm's name or product before the public is called *reminder advertising*.

Comparative advertising compares the sponsored brand with one or more identified competing brands. Of course, the comparison shows the sponsored brand to be as good as or better than the other identified competing brands.

Institutional Advertising Institutional advertising is advertising designed to enhance a firm's image or reputation. Many public utilities and larger firms use part of their advertising dollars to build goodwill rather than to stimulate sales directly. A positive public image helps an organization to attract customers, employees, and investors.

Major Steps in Developing an Advertising Campaign

An advertising campaign is developed in several stages. These stages may vary in number and the order in which they are implemented depending on the company's resources, products, and audiences. The development of a campaign in any organization, however, will include the following steps in some form:

1. Identify and Analyze the Target Audience The target audience is the group of people toward which a firm's advertisements are directed. To pinpoint the organization's target audience and develop an effective campaign, marketers must analyze such information as the geographic distribution of potential customers; their age, sex, race, income, and education; and their attitudes toward both the advertiser's product and competing products. How marketers use this information will be influenced by the features of the product to be advertised and the nature of the competition. Precise identification of the target audience is crucial to the proper development of subsequent stages and, ultimately, to the success of the campaign itself.

2. Define the Advertising Objectives The goals of an advertising campaign should be stated precisely and in measurable terms. The objectives should include the current position of the firm, indicate how far and in what direction from that original reference point the company wishes to move, and specify a definite period of time for the achievement of the goals. Advertising objectives that focus on sales will stress increasing sales by a certain percentage or dollar amount or expanding the firm's market share. Communication objectives will emphasize increasing product or brand awareness, improving consumer attitudes, or conveying product information.

3. Create the Advertising Platform An advertising platform includes the important selling points or features that an advertiser wishes to incorporate into the advertising campaign. These features should be important to customers in their selection and use of a product, and if possible, they should be features that competing products lack. Although research into what consumers view as important issues is expensive, it is the most productive way to determine which issues to include in an advertising platform.

4. Determine the Advertising Appropriation The advertising appropriation is the total amount of money designated for advertising in a given period. This stage is critical to the success of the campaign because advertising efforts based on an inadequate budget will understimulate customer demand, and a budget too large will waste a company's resources. Advertising appropriations may be based on last year's (or next year's forecasted) sales, on what competitors spend on advertising, or on executive judgment.

5. Develop the Media Plan A media plan specifies exactly which media will be used in the campaign and when advertisements will appear. Although cost-effectiveness is not easy to measure, the primary concern of the media planner is to reach the largest number of persons in the target audience for each dollar spent. In addition to cost, media planners must consider the location and demographics of people in the advertising target, the content of the message, and the characteristics of the audiences reached by various media. The media planner begins with general media decisions, selects subclasses within each medium, and finally chooses particular media vehicles for the campaign. The advantages and disadvantages (and the proportion of ad spending) of the major media classes are shown in Table 14.3.

6. Create the Advertising Message The content and form of a message are influenced by the product's features, the characteristics of people in the target audience, the objectives of the campaign, and the choice of media. An advertiser must consider these factors to choose words and illustrations that will be meaningful and appealing to persons in the advertising target. The copy, or words, of an advertisement will vary depending on the media choice but should attempt to move the audience through attention, interest, desire, and action. Artwork and visuals should complement copy by attracting the audience's attention and communicating an idea quickly. **EXAMPLE** Creating a cohesive advertising message is especially difficult for a company such as eBay that offers such a broad mix of products. eBay developed a "whatever it is" campaign that features a variety of consumers of every age using a variety of products (a car, a television, a dress, and a laptop) all shaped like the letters *it*. The tagline, "Whatever *it* is, you can get it on eBay," emphasizes the massive range of products available from the site and showcases the service that the company provides effectively.

Target audience—Is this ad aimed at everyone?

Most advertisements are not aimed at everyone. This Harlequin Enterprises advertisements asks women: "Is your man too good to be true? Hot, gorgeous, and romantic?" Then the company indicates that he could be a Harlequin Blaze cover model or win prizes.

MEDIUM	PERCENT OF TOTAL*	ADVANTAGES	DISADVANTAGES
Television	25.1%	Reaches large audiences; high frequency available; dual impact of audio and video; highly visible; high prestige; geographic and demographic selectivity; difficult to ignore	Very expensive; highly perishable message; size of audience not guaranteed; amount of prime time limited; lack of selectivity in target market
Direct mail	20.4%	Little wasted circulation; highly selective; circulation controlled by advertiser; few distractions; personal; stimulates actions; use of novelty; relatively easy to measure performance; hidden from competitors	Very expensive; lacks editorial content to attract readers; often thrown away unread as junk mail; criticized as invasion of privacy; consumers must choose to read the ad
Newspapers	17.4%	Reaches large audience; purchased to be read; geographic flexibility; short lead time; frequent publication; favorable for cooperative advertising; merchandising services	Not selective for socioeconomic groups or target market; short life; limited reproduction capabilities; large advertising volume limits exposure to any one advertisement
Radio	7.2%	Reaches 95 percent of consumers; highly mobile and flexible; very low relative costs; ad can be changed quickly; high level of geographic and demographic selectivity; encourages use of imagination	Lacks visual imagery; short life of message; listeners' attention limited because of other activities; market fragmentation; difficult buying procedures; limited media and audience research
Yellow Pages	5.2%	Wide availability; action and product category oriented; low relative costs; ad frequency and longevity; nonintrusive	Market fragmentation; extremely localized; slow updating; lack of creativity; long lead times; requires large space to be noticed
Magazines	4.7%	Demographic selectivity; good reproduction; long life; prestige; geographic selectivity when regional issues are available; read in leisurely manner	High costs; 30- to 90-day average lead time; high level of competition; limited reach; communicates less frequently
Internet	2.9%	Immediate response; potential to reach a precisely targeted audience; ability to track customers and build databases; highly interactive medium	Costs of precise targeting are high; inappropriate ad placement; effects difficult to measure; concerns about security and privacy
Outdoor	2.3%	Allows for frequent repetition; low cost; message can be placed close to point of sale; geographic selectivity; operable 24 hours a day; high creativity and effectiveness	Message must be short and simple; no demographic selectivity; seldom attracts readers' full attention; criticized as traffic hazard and blight on countryside; much wasted coverage; limited capabilities

*Spending on miscellaneous advertising accounts for 13.2% of total expenditures.

TABLE 14.3

Percent Use and Advantages and Disadvantages of Major Media Classes

Sources: William F. Arens, *Contemporary Advertising* (Burr Ridge, IL: Irwin/McGraw-Hill, 2004); George E. Belch and Michael Belch, *Advertising and Promotion* (Burr Ridge, IL: Irwin/McGraw-Hill, 2004); "Ad Spending Totals by Media," *Advertising Age*, June 26, 2006, p. S-8.

7. Execute the Campaign Execution of an advertising campaign requires extensive planning, scheduling, and coordinating because many tasks must be completed on time. The efforts of many people and firms are involved. Production companies, research organizations, media firms, printers, photoengravers, and commercial artists are just a few of the people and firms that may contribute to a campaign. Advertising managers constantly must assess the quality of the work and take corrective action when necessary. In some instances, advertisers make changes during the campaign to meet objectives more effectively.

8. Evaluate Advertising Effectiveness A campaign's success should be measured in terms of its original objectives before, during, and/or after the campaign. An advertiser should at least be able to estimate whether sales or market share went up because of the campaign or whether any change occurred in customer attitudes or brand awareness. Data from past and current sales and responses to coupon offers and customer surveys administered by research organizations are some of the ways in which advertising effectiveness can be evaluated.

Advertising Agencies

Advertisers can plan and produce their own advertising with help from media personnel, or they can hire advertising agencies. An **advertising agency** is an independent firm that plans, produces, and places advertising for its clients. Many large ad agencies offer help with sales promotion and public relations as well. The media usually pay a commission of 15 percent to advertising agencies. Thus the cost to the agency's client can be quite moderate. The client may be asked to pay for selected services that the agency performs. Other methods for compensating agencies are also used.

Firms that do a lot of advertising may use both an in-house advertising department and an independent agency. This approach gives the firm the advantage of being able to call on the agency's expertise in particular areas of advertising. An agency also can bring a fresh viewpoint to a firm's products and advertising plans.

Social and Legal Considerations in Advertising

Critics of U.S. advertising have two main complaints—that it is wasteful and that it can be deceptive. Although advertising (like any other activity) can be performed inefficiently, it is far from wasteful. Let's look at the evidence:

* Advertising is the most effective and least expensive means of communicating product information to a large number of individuals and organizations.

* Advertising encourages competition and is, in fact, a means of competition. It thus leads to the development of new and improved products, wider product choices, and lower prices.

* Advertising revenues support our mass-communications media—newspapers, magazines, radio, and television. This means that advertising pays for much of our news coverage and entertainment programming.

* Advertising provides job opportunities in fields ranging from sales to film production.

A number of government and private agencies scrutinize advertising for false or misleading claims or offers. At the national level, the Federal Trade Commission (FTC), the Food and Drug Administration (FDA), and the Federal Communications Commission (FCC) oversee advertising practices. The FDA conducted a survey of doctors about the impact of direct-to-consumer advertising for prescription drugs and found that 92 percent could recall a patient initiating conversation about a drug he or she had seen advertised. Direct-to-consumer prescription ads, a controversial type of advertising, make patients more aware of potential treatments according to 72 percent of the physicians surveyed, and they also caused 47 percent of these doctors to feel pressured into prescribing a particular drug.[12] Advertising also may be monitored by state and local agencies, better business bureaus, and industry associations.

advertising agency an independent firm that plans, produces, and places advertising for its clients

TEST PREPPER 14.8

True or False?

_T_ 1. Primary-demand, selective-demand, and institutional-demand advertising are types of advertising based on purpose of advertising.

_T_ 2. Advertising provides jobs in fields ranging from sales to film production.

Multiple Choice

_B_ 3. Selective-demand advertising that aims at persuading customers to make purchases within a short time is called

    a. frequency advertising.
    b. immediate-response advertising.
    c. right-now advertising.
    d. comparative advertising.
    e. institutional advertising.

_C_ 4. Choose the correct order of the following three of the eight steps in developing an advertising campaign.

    a. Create the advertising platform; identify and analyze the target audience; define the advertising objectives.
    b. Identify and analyze the target audience; create the advertising platform; define the advertising objectives.

    c. Identify and analyze the target audience; define the advertising objectives; create the advertising platform.
    d. Define the advertising objectives; identify and analyze the target audience; create the advertising platform.
    e. Define the advertising objectives; create the advertising platform; identify and analyze the target audience.

_A_ 5. Critics of advertising are most likely to be concerned that:

    a. Advertising is deceptive and wasteful.
    b. Advertising does not promote job growth and is inefficient.
    c. Advertising makes money for both manufacturers and retailers.
    d. Advertising does not lead to the development of new products and ideas.
    e. Advertising brings revenues to dishonest firms.

_A_ 6. Which type of advertising accounts for the lion's share of advertising?

    a. Selective-demand advertising
    b. Primary-demand advertising
    c. Target advertising
    d. Institutional advertising
    e. Foreign advertising

ACE the Test
ACE & ACE+
Practice Test 14.8

Personal Selling

Learning Objective 9

Recognize the kinds of salespersons, the steps in the personal-selling process, and the major sales management tasks.

Personal selling is the most adaptable of all promotional methods because the person who is presenting the message can modify it to suit the individual buyer. However, personal selling is also the most expensive method of promotion. Most successful salespeople are able to communicate with others on a one-to-one basis and are strongly motivated. They strive to have a thorough knowledge of the products they offer for sale. And they are willing and able to deal with the details involved in handling and processing orders. Sales managers tend to emphasize these qualities when recruiting and hiring. Many selling situations demand the face-to-face contact and adaptability of personal selling. This is especially true of industrial sales, in which a single purchase may amount to millions of dollars. Obviously, sales of that size must be based on carefully planned sales presentations, personal contact with customers, and thorough negotiations.

Kinds of Salespersons

Because most businesses employ different salespersons to perform different functions, marketing managers must select the kinds of sales personnel that will be most effective in selling the firm's products. Salespersons may be identified as order getters, order takers, and support personnel. A single individual can, and often does, perform all three functions.

Order Getters An order getter is responsible for what is sometimes called creative selling—selling a firm's products to new customers and increasing sales to current customers. An order getter must perceive buyers' needs, supply customers with information about the firm's product, and persuade them to buy the product. Some order-getters focus on current customers, whereas others focus on new customers.

Order Takers An order taker handles repeat sales in ways that maintain positive relationships with customers. An order taker sees that customers have products when and where they are needed and in the proper amounts. *Inside order takers* receive incoming mail and telephone orders in some businesses; salespersons in retail stores are also inside order takers. *Outside* (or *field*) *order takers* travel to customers. Often the buyer and the field salesperson develop a mutually beneficial relationship of placing, receiving, and delivering orders. Both inside and outside order takers are active salespersons and often produce most of their companies' sales.

Support Personnel Sales support personnel aid in selling but are more involved in locating *prospects* (likely first-time customers), educating customers, building goodwill for the firm, and providing follow-up service. The most common categories of support personnel are missionary, trade, and technical salespersons.

A missionary salesperson, who usually works for a manufacturer, visits retailers to persuade them to buy the manufacturer's products. If the retailers agree, they buy the products from wholesalers, who are the manufacturer's actual customers.

A trade salesperson, who generally works for a food producer or processor, assists customers in promoting products, especially in retail stores. A trade salesperson may obtain additional shelf space for the products, restock shelves, set up displays, and distribute samples. Because trade salespersons usually are order takers as well, they are not strictly support personnel.

A technical salesperson assists a company's current customers in technical matters. He or she may explain how to use a product, how it is made, how to install it, or how a system is designed. A technical salesperson should be formally educated in science or engineering.

Marketers usually need sales personnel from several of these categories. Factors that affect hiring and other personnel decisions include the number of customers and their characteristics; the product's attributes, complexity, and price; the distribution channels used by the company; and the company's approach to advertising.

The Personal-Selling Process

No two selling situations are exactly alike, and no two salespeople perform their jobs in exactly the same way. Most salespeople, however, follow the six-step procedure illustrated in Figure 14.4.

order getter a salesperson who is responsible for selling a firm's products to new customers and increasing sales to present customers

creative selling selling products to new customers and increasing sales to present customers

order taker a salesperson who handles repeat sales in ways that maintain positive relationships with customers

sales support personnel employees who aid in selling but are more involved in locating prospects, educating customers, building goodwill for the firm, and providing follow-up service

missionary salesperson a salesperson—generally employed by a manufacturer—who visits retailers to persuade them to buy the manufacturer's products

trade salesperson a salesperson—generally employed by a food producer or processor—who assists customers in promoting products, especially in retail stores

technical salesperson a salesperson who assists a company's current customers in technical matters

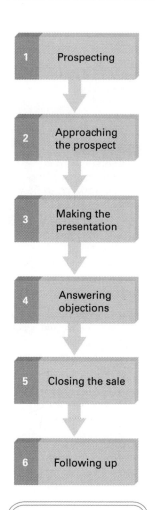

FIGURE 14.4

The Six Steps of the Personal-Selling Process

Personal selling is not only the most adaptable of all promotional methods but also the most expensive.

Source: William M. Pride and O. C. Ferrell, *Marketing: Concepts and Strategies* (Boston: Houghton Mifflin, 2006). Copyright © 2006 by Houghton Mifflin Company. Adapted with permission.

Prospecting The first step in personal selling is to research potential buyers and choose the most likely customers, or prospects. Sources of prospects include business associates and customers, public records, telephone and trade-association directories, and company files. The salesperson concentrates on those prospects who have the financial resources, willingness, and authority to buy the product.

Approaching the Prospect First impressions are often lasting impressions. Thus the salesperson's first contact with the prospect is crucial to successful selling. The best approach is one based on knowledge of the product, of the prospect's needs, and of how the product can meet those needs. Salespeople who understand each customer's particular situation are likely to make a good first impression—and to make a sale.

Making the Presentation The next step is actual delivery of the sales presentation. In many cases this includes demonstrating the product. The salesperson points out the product's features, its benefits, and how it is superior to competitors' merchandise. If the product has been used successfully by other firms, the salesperson may mention this as part of the presentation.

During a demonstration, the salesperson may suggest that the prospect try out the product personally. The demonstration and product trial should underscore specific points made during the presentation.

Answering Objections The prospect is likely to raise objections or ask questions at any time. This gives the salesperson a chance to eliminate objections that might prevent a sale, to point out additional features, or to mention special services the company offers.

Closing the Sale To close the sale, the salesperson asks the prospect to buy the product. This is considered the critical point in the selling process. Many experienced salespeople make use of a *trial closing*, in which they ask questions based on the assumption that the customer is going to buy the product. The questions "When would you want delivery?" and "Do you want the standard model or the one with the special options package?" are typical of trial closings. They allow the reluctant prospect to make a purchase without having to say, "I'll take it."

Following Up The salesperson must follow up after the sale to ensure that the product is delivered on time, in the right quantity, and in proper operating condition. During follow-up, the salesperson also makes it clear that he or she is available in case problems develop. Follow-up leaves a good impression and eases the way toward future sales. Hence it is essential to the selling process. The salesperson's job does not end with a sale. It continues as long as the seller and the customer maintain a working relationship.

Major Sales Management Tasks

A firm's success often hinges on the competent management of its sales force. Although some companies operate efficiently without a sales force, most firms rely on a strong sales force—and the sales revenue it brings in—for their success.

Responsibilities of Sales Managers

* Sales managers must set sales objectives in concrete, quantifiable terms and specify a certain period of time and a certain geographic area.

* Sales managers must adjust the size of the sales force to meet changes in the firm's marketing plan and the marketing environment.

* Sales managers must attract and hire effective salespersons. **EXAMPLE** Guitar Center, the largest musical instrument chain in the United States, has only one requirement for members of its sales force—that they be able to play a musical instrument. The company believes that a rocking sales force will care more deeply about the product and sell it more effectively to customers.[13]

* Sales managers must develop a training program and decide where, when, how, and for whom to conduct the training.

* Sales managers must formulate a fair and adequate compensation plan to keep qualified employees.

* Sales managers must motivate salespersons to boost their productivity.

* Sales managers must define sales territories and determine scheduling and routing of the sales force.

* Finally, sales managers must evaluate the operation as a whole through sales reports, communications with customers, and invoices.

CONCEPT CHECK

Explain how each step in the personal-selling process leads to the next step.

TEST PREPPER 14.9

True or False?

___ 1. Most successful salespeople are able to communicate with others on a one-to-one basis and are strongly motivated.

___ 2. A missionary salesperson generally is employed by a manufacturer.

Multiple Choice

___ 3. Salespeople may be identified as

    a. experts, order makers, and support personnel.
    b. order preparers, order takers, and order receivers.

    c. order getters, order takers, and support personnel.
    d. order getters, order makers, and order receivers.
    e. order getters, order dictators, and support personnel.

___ 4. Order takers can be further subdivided into these two categories:

    a. expert and novice order takers.
    b. foreign and domestic order takers.
    c. local and regional order takers.
    d. inside and outside order takers.
    e. seasonal and continuous order takers.

ACE the Test
ACE & ACE+
Practice Test 14.9

Sales Promotion

Learning Objective 10

Describe sales promotion objectives and methods.

Sales promotion consists of activities or materials that are direct inducements to customers or salespersons. Are you a member of an airline frequent-flyer program? Did you recently receive a free sample in the mail or at a supermarket? Have you recently received a rebate from a manufacturer? Do you use coupons? All these are examples of sales promotion efforts. Sales promotion techniques often are used to enhance and supplement other promotional methods. They can have a significant impact on sales.

The dramatic increase in spending for sales promotion shows that marketers have recognized the potential of this promotional method. Many firms now include numerous sales promotion efforts as part of their overall promotion mix.

Prepare for Class
Career Snapshot

Sales Promotion Objectives

Sales promotion activities may be used singly or in combination, both offensively and defensively, to achieve one goal or a set of goals. Marketers use sales promotion activities and materials for a number of purposes, including

1. To attract new customers
2. To encourage trial of a new product
3. To invigorate the sales of a mature brand
4. To boost sales to current customers
5. To reinforce advertising
6. To increase traffic in retail stores
7. To steady irregular sales patterns
8. To build up reseller inventories
9. To neutralize competitive promotional efforts
10. To improve shelf space and displays[14]

Any sales promotion objectives should be consistent with the organization's general goals and with its marketing and promotional objectives.

Sales Promotion Methods

Most sales promotion methods can be classified as promotional techniques for either consumer sales or trade sales.

A **consumer sales promotion method** attracts consumers to particular retail stores and motivates them to purchase certain new or established products.

A **trade sales promotion method** encourages wholesalers and retailers to stock and actively promote a manufacturer's product. Incentives such as money, merchandise, marketing assistance, and gifts are commonly awarded to resellers who buy products or respond positively in other ways. Of the combined dollars spent on sales promotion and advertising last year, about one-half was spent on trade promotions, one-fourth on consumer promotions, and one-fourth on advertising.

Selection of Sales Promotion Methods

Several factors affect the choice of sales promotion methods to be used. Of greatest importance are

1. The objectives of the promotional effort
2. Product characteristics—size, weight, cost, durability, uses, features, and hazards
3. Target-market profiles—age, gender, income, location, density, usage rate, and buying patterns
4. Distribution channels and availability of appropriate resellers
5. The competitive and regulatory forces in the environment

Rebates   A **rebate** is a return of part of the purchase price of a product. Usually the refund is offered by the producer to consumers who send in a coupon along with a specific proof of purchase. Rebating is a relatively low-cost promotional method.

consumer sales promotion method a sales promotion method designed to attract consumers to particular retail stores and to motivate them to purchase certain new or established products

trade sales promotion method a sales promotion method designed to encourage wholesalers and retailers to stock and actively promote a manufacturer's product

rebate a return of part of the purchase price of a product

One problem with rebates is that many people perceive the redemption process as too complicated. Only about half of individuals who purchase rebated products actually apply for the rebates.

Coupons A coupon reduces the retail price of a particular item by a stated amount at the time of purchase. Coupons may be worth anywhere from a few cents to a few dollars. They are made available to customers through newspapers, magazines, direct mail, online, and shelf dispensers in stores. Some coupons are precisely targeted at customers. **EXAMPLE** All Online Coupons is an Internet site that provides visitors with links to all online coupons currently being offered. Customers can find coupons by category or store name. Other companies, such as Old Navy and The Gap, offer coupons on their websites that can be used online or in stores. Billions of coupons are distributed annually. Of these, just under 2 percent are redeemed by consumers. Still, 73 percent of consumers say that coupons save them a lot of money.[15]

Samples A sample is a free product given to customers to encourage trial and purchase. Marketers use free samples to stimulate trial of a product, increase sales volume in the early stages of a product's life cycle, and obtain desirable distribution. Samples may be offered via online coupons, direct mail, or in stores. Many customers prefer to receive their samples by mail. It is the most expensive sales promotion technique, and while it is used often to promote new products, it can be used to promote established brands, too, such as cosmetics companies that use samples to attract customers. In designing a free sample, organizations must consider such factors as seasonal demand for the product, market characteristics, and prior advertising.

Premiums A premium is a gift that a producer offers a customer in return for buying its product. They are used to attract competitors' customers, introduce different sizes of established products, add variety to other promotional efforts, and stimulate consumer loyalty. Creativity is essential when using premiums; to stand out and achieve a significant number of redemptions, the premium must match both the target audience and the brand's image. Premiums also must be easily recognizable and desirable. Premiums are placed on or inside packages and also can be distributed through retailers or through the mail.

Frequent-User Incentives A frequent-user incentive is a program developed to reward customers who engage in repeat (frequent) purchases. Such programs are used commonly by service businesses such as airlines, hotels, and auto rental agencies. Frequent-user incentives foster customer loyalty to a specific company or group of cooperating companies because the customer is given an additional reason to continue patronizing the business.

Point-of-Purchase Displays A point-of-purchase display is promotional material placed within a retail store. The display is usually located near the product being promoted. It actually may hold merchandise (as do L'eggs hosiery displays) or inform customers about what the product offers and encourage them to buy it. Most point-of-purchase displays are prepared and set up by manufacturers and wholesalers.

Trade Shows A trade show is an industry-wide exhibit at which many sellers display their products. Some trade shows are organized exclusively for dealers—to

Handing out samples.

In this photo, NBA stars hand out free samples of McDonald's chicken strip products.

coupon reduces the retail price of a particular item by a stated amount at the time of purchase

sample a free product given to customers to encourage trial and purchase

premium a gift that a producer offers a customer in return for buying its product

frequent-user incentive a program developed to reward customers who engage in repeat (frequent) purchases

point-of-purchase display promotional material placed within a retail store

trade show an industry-wide exhibit at which many sellers display their products

permit manufacturers and wholesalers to show their latest lines to retailers. Others are promotions designed to stimulate consumer awareness and interest. Among the latter are boat shows, home shows, and flower shows put on each year in large cities.

Buying Allowances A buying allowance is a temporary price reduction to resellers for purchasing specified quantities of a product. **EXAMPLE** A laundry detergent manufacturer might give retailers $1 for each case of detergent purchased. A buying allowance may serve as an incentive to resellers to handle new products and may stimulate purchase of items in large quantities. While the buying allowance is simple, straightforward, and easily administered, competitors can respond quickly by offering a better buying allowance.

Cooperative Advertising Cooperative advertising is an arrangement whereby a manufacturer agrees to pay a certain amount of a retailer's media cost for advertising the manufacturer's products. To be reimbursed, a retailer must show proof that the advertisements actually did appear. A large percentage of all cooperative advertising dollars are spent on newspaper advertisements. Not all retailers take advantage of available cooperative advertising offers because they cannot afford to advertise or do not choose to do so.

buying allowance
a temporary price reduction to resellers for purchasing specified quantities of a product

cooperative advertising
an arrangement whereby a manufacturer agrees to pay a certain amount of a retailer's media cost for advertising the manufacturer's products

---

TEST PREPPER 14.10

True or False?

_T_ 1. In order to manage a sales force effectively, a sales manager should monitor the operation through accurate sales reports.

_T_ 2. It is not enough to have a good product; it is crucial to have an effective sales force.

Multiple Choice

_B_ 3. The first step in the personal selling process is

    a. product display.
    b. prospecting.

    c. approaching the prospect.
    d. organizing the sales pitch.
    e. making the presentation.

_B_ 4. Which one of the following questions reflects a trial closing?

    a. Why do you not like this design?
    b. When would you want delivery?
    c. What can I do to make you buy this product?
    d. What are some of your thoughts about this product line?
    e. Have you seen this product through other vendors?

ACE the Test
ACE & ACE+
Practice Test 14.10

Public Relations

 Learning Objective 11

Understand the types and uses of public relations.

As noted earlier, public relations is a broad set of communication activities used to create and maintain favorable relationships between an organization and various public groups, both internal and external. These groups can include customers, employees, stockholders, suppliers, educators, the media, government officials, and society in general.

Types of Public-Relations Tools

Organizations use a variety of public-relations tools to convey messages and to create images. Public-relations professionals prepare written materials such as brochures, newsletters, company magazines, annual reports, and news releases. They also create corporate-identity materials such as logos, business cards, signs, and stationery. Speeches are another public-relations tool. Speeches can affect an organization's image and therefore must convey the desired message clearly.

Another public-relations tool is event sponsorship, in which a company pays for all or part of a special event such as a concert, sports competition, festival, or play. Sponsoring special events is an effective way for organizations to increase brand recognition and receive media coverage with comparatively little investment. **EXAMPLE** Pharmaceutical company Bristol-Myers Squibb sponsored the Tour of Hope, a nine-day bike trek from San Diego, California, to Washington, D.C., to raise money for cancer research. Bristol-Myers spokesman, seven-time Tour de France winner and cancer survivor Lance Armstrong, led twenty-four other bikers on the tour.[16]

Some public-relations tools traditionally have been associated specifically with publicity, which is a part of public relations. Publicity is communication in news-story form about an organization, its products, or both. Publicity is transmitted through a mass medium, such as newspapers or radio, at no charge. Organizations use publicity to provide information about products; to announce new product launches, expansions, or research; and to strengthen the company's image. Public-relations personnel sometimes organize events, such as grand openings with prizes and celebrities, to create news stories about a company.

The most widely used type of publicity is the news release. It is generally one typed page of about 300 words provided by an organization to the media as a form of publicity. The release includes the firm's name, address, phone number, and contact person. There are also several other kinds of publicity-based public-relations tools. A feature article, which may run as long as 3,000 words, is usually written for inclusion in a particular publication. For example, a software firm might send an article about its new product to a computer magazine. A captioned photograph, a picture accompanied by a brief explanation, is an effective way to illustrate a new or improved product. A press conference allows invited media personnel to hear important news announcements and to receive supplementary textual materials and photographs. Finally, letters to the editor, special newspaper or magazine editorials, films, and tapes may be prepared and distributed to appropriate media for possible use.

Uses of Public Relations

Public relations can be used to promote people, places, activities, ideas, and even countries. Public relations focuses on enhancing the reputation of the total organization by making people aware of a company's products, brands, or activities and by creating specific company images such as that of innovativeness or dependability. **EXAMPLE** Ice-cream maker Ben and Jerry's uses news stories and other public-relations efforts to reinforce its reputation as a socially responsible company. By getting the media to report on a firm's accomplishments, public relations helps a company to maintain positive public visibility. Effective management of public-relations efforts also can reduce the unfavorable effects of negative events.

publicity communication in news-story form about an organization, its products, or both

news release a typed page of about 300 words provided by an organization to the media as a form of publicity

feature article a piece (of up to 3,000 words) prepared by an organization for inclusion in a particular publication

captioned photograph a picture accompanied by a brief explanation

press conference a meeting at which invited media personnel hear important news announcements and receive supplementary textual materials and photographs

CONCEPT CHECK
How can public-relations efforts aimed at the general public help an organization?

TEST PREPPER (14.11)

True or False?

1. Event sponsorship is a public-relations tool.

2. Public relations focuses on enhancing the reputation of the total organization not just its product lines.

3. A news release is a type of public-relations tool and is generally around two pages, or about 1,000 words.

Multiple Choice

4. Which one of the following is *not* a public-relations tool?

    a. Captioned photograph
    b. Press conference
    c. Feature article

    d. Cooperative advertising
    e. News release

5. Which one of the following is *not* one of the uses of public relations?

    a. Public relations helps a company maintain a positive visibility with the help of the media.
    b. Public relations helps in enhancing the reputation of the total organization by making people aware of the company's products.
    c. Public relations counteracts the unfavorable effects of negative events.
    d. Public relations can be used to cut down production costs.
    e. Public relations can be used to promote people, places, activities, ideas, and even countries.

ACE the Test
ACE & ACE+
Practice Test 14.11

Prepare for Class
CL News Feeds
CL News Now

➔ RETURN TO INSIDE BUSINESS

    Costco, the most successful warehouse club in a shrinking retail category, buys in bulk and sells at low prices. Although a typical discount store carries up to 60,000 items, each Costco outlet stocks a limited selection of about 4,000 items. Rather than display two, three, or more sizes and variations of products such as aspirin or napkins, Costco generally carries only one: either a low-priced, single-family-sized package or a heavily discounted multipack.

    To maintain its profits and keep growing, Costco has to make its stores as productive as possible. Outdoing even upscale retailers such as Nordstrom, Costco stores currently generate an average of $918 in sales per square foot. However, management never stops looking for ways to lower both costs and prices. "Our business can only succeed if we are efficient," notes the CEO.

Questions

1. How has Costco's expertise in inventory management contributed to its success?

2. Although more than twenty warehouse club companies once dotted the U.S. retail landscape, only a handful are still in business. Why do you think so few warehouse clubs remain?

LEARNING OBJECTIVES REVIEW

 Identify the various channels of distribution and explain the concept of market coverage.

- A marketing channel is a sequence of marketing organizations that directs a product from producer to ultimate user. The marketing channel for a particular product is concerned with the transfer of ownership of that product.

- The channels used for consumer products include
  - The direct channel from producer to consumer
  - The channel from producer to retailer to consumer
  - The channel from producer to wholesaler to retailer to consumer
  - The channel from producer to agent to wholesaler to retailer to consumer

Improve Your Grade
Audio Chapter Summary & Quiz

- Market coverage
  - Intensive distribution is the use of all available outlets for a product, providing the widest market coverage.
  - Selective distribution uses only a portion of the available outlets in an area.
  - Exclusive distribution uses only a single retail outlet for a product in a large geographic area.

2 Explain partnering through supply-chain management.

- Supply-chain management is a long-term partnership among channel members working together to create a distribution system that reduces inefficiencies, costs, and redundancies while creating a competitive advantage and satisfying customers.
- Cooperation is required among all channel members, including manufacturing, research, sales, advertising, and shipping. When all channel partners work together, delivery, scheduling, packaging, and other customer requirements are better met.
- Technology, such as bar coding and electronic data interchange (EDI), makes supply-chain management easier to implement.

3 Discuss the need for wholesalers, describe the services they provide, and identify the major types of wholesalers.

- Wholesalers are intermediaries that purchase from producers or other intermediaries and sell to industrial users, retailers, or other wholesalers.
- If wholesalers are eliminated from the distribution channel, other channel members— such as the producer or retailers—must perform these functions.
- Wholesalers provide retailers with help in promoting products, collecting information, and financing. They provide manufacturers with sales help, reduce their inventory costs, furnish market information, and extend credit to retailers.
- Merchant wholesalers buy and then sell products. Agents do not take title to the goods they distribute.

4 Distinguish among the major types of retailers and shopping centers.

- Retailers are intermediaries that buy from producers or wholesalers and sell to consumers.

- In-store retailers include department stores, discount stores, warehouse showrooms, convenience stores, supermarkets, superstores, warehouse clubs, traditional specialty stores, off-price retailers, and category killers.
- Nonstore retailers do not sell in conventional store facilities. Instead, they use direct selling, direct marketing, and automatic vending.
- Types of direct marketing include catalog marketing, direct-response marketing, telemarketing, television home shopping, and online retailing.
- There are three major types of shopping centers: neighborhood, community, and regional. A center fits one of these categories based on its mix of stores and the size of the geographic area it serves.

5 Explain the five most important physical distribution activities.

- Physical distribution consists of activities designed to move products from producers to ultimate users. Its five major functions are
  - Inventory management
  - Order processing
  - Warehousing
  - Materials handling
  - Transportation
- These interrelated functions are integrated into the marketing effort.

6 Explain how integrated marketing communications works to have the maximum impact on the customer.

- Integrated marketing communications is the coordination of promotion efforts to achieve maximum informational and persuasive impact on customers.
- Integrated marketing has been increasingly accepted for the following reasons:
  - Mass media advertising is used less today because of its high costs.
  - Marketers now can take advantage of more precisely targeted promotional tools.
  - Database marketing is allowing marketers to be more precise in targeting individual customers.
  - Promotion-related companies provide one-stop shopping to the client.
  - There are greater demands for systematic evaluations of communication efforts from the management owing to high overall marketing costs.

7 **Describe the basic concept of the promotion mix.**

- Promotion mix is sometimes called marketing communications mix and consists of the particular combination of promotional methods a firm uses to reach a target market. The makeup of the mix depends on
  - The firm's promotional resources and objectives
  - The nature of the target market
  - Product characteristics
  - The feasibility of various promotional methods

8 **Explain the three types of advertising and describe the major steps of developing an advertising campaign.**

- Advertising is a paid nonpersonal message communicated to a specific audience through a mass medium.
- Primary-demand advertising promotes the products of an entire industry rather than just a single brand.
- Selective-demand advertising promotes a particular brand of product.
- Institutional advertising is image-building advertising for a firm.
- An advertising campaign is developed in several stages.
  - A firm's first task is to identify and analyze its advertising target.
  - The goals of the campaign also must be clearly defined.
  - Then the firm must develop the advertising platform, or statement of important selling points, and determine the size of the advertising budget.
  - The next steps are to develop a media plan, to create the advertising message, and to execute the campaign.
  - Finally, promotion managers must evaluate the effectiveness of the advertising efforts before, during, and/or after the campaign.

9 **Recognize the kinds of salespersons, the steps in the personal-selling process, and the major sales management tasks.**

- Personal selling is personal communication aimed at informing customers and persuading them to buy a firm's products. It is the most adaptable promotional method because the salesperson can modify the message to fit each buyer.

- Three major kinds of salespersons are order getters, order takers, and support personnel.
- The six steps in the personal-selling process are
  - Prospecting
  - Approaching the prospect
  - Making the presentation
  - Answering objections
  - Closing the sale
  - Following up
- Sales managers are involved directly in setting sales force objectives; recruiting, selecting, and training salespersons; compensating and motivating sales personnel; creating sales territories; and evaluating sales performance.

10 **Describe sales promotion objectives and methods.**

- Sales promotion is the use of activities and materials as direct inducements to customers and salespersons. The primary objective of sales promotion methods is to enhance and supplement other promotional methods.
- Methods of sales promotion include:
  - Rebates, coupons, samples, premiums, frequent-user incentives, point-of-purchase displays, trade shows, buying allowances, and cooperative advertising.

11 **Understand the types and uses of public relations.**

- Public relations is a broad set of communication activities used to create and maintain favorable relationships between an organization and various public groups, both internal and external.
- Organizations use a variety of public-relations tools to convey messages and create images.
  - Brochures, newsletters, company magazines, and annual reports are written public-relations tools.
  - Speeches, event sponsorship, and publicity are other public-relations tools.
- Publicity is communication in news-story form about an organization, its products, or both.
  - Types of publicity include news releases, feature articles, captioned photographs, and press conferences.
- Public relations can be used to promote people, places, activities, ideas, and even countries. It can be used to enhance the reputation of an organization and also to reduce the unfavorable effects of negative events.

VIDEO CASE

REI: The Great Indoors

Few retailers allow customers to test ride mountain bikes on special indoor trails or let them pour water through different filtration devices before they decide which model to purchase. An open invitation to "try it before you buy it" is just one reason why Recreational Equipment, Inc. (REI), stands out in the world of retailing.

REI was founded in 1938 by twenty-five mountain climbers who pooled their buying power to get a better deal on ice axes and other climbing gear. From the start, REI was a consumer cooperative: a retail business that shares some of its profits with members. Today, the retailer sells a vast array of outdoor sporting goods and apparel through more than eighty stores in twenty-seven states, a printed catalog, and a website, as well as by telephone.

The in-store shopping experience is an adventure in itself. Every REI store contains a two-story climbing wall where customers can try gear before buying. For example, the store in Sandy, Utah, features a twenty-two-foot-high climbing wall modeled after the granite walls of a local canyon. Like other stores in the chain, the Sandy store has demonstration areas devoted to camp stoves, water-filter testing, and hiking boots. Surrounding these special areas are acres and acres of items that one employee calls "grown-up toys," from kayaks and canteens to snow shoes and sleeping bags.

REI's retail website features page after page of details about 50,000 products in stock, as well as how-to articles about outdoor sports and equipment. Customers can shop the site from home or order from Internet kiosks set up in each store. More than one-third of **REI.com's** customers arrange to pick up their online orders at a nearby REI store, which eliminates shipping fees. And when customers pick up their orders in the store, they keep shopping—spending as much as $85 more per visit.

Customers can become members of the REI cooperative by paying a one-time fee of $15. They are then eligible for refund vouchers of up to 10 percent on their total annual purchases from REI stores, catalogs, and websites. They also pay lower prices for equipment rented or repaired in REI stores.

One of REI's core values is its ongoing commitment to protecting the natural environment by donating to nature centers, open-space projects, youth recreation programs, land conservation, and related activities in local communities. Moreover, as REI's president notes, store employees invest a great deal of "sweat equity" in the local community by volunteering their time to maintain hiking trails, clean up rivers, and preserve the environment in many other ways.

The market for outdoor sporting goods and apparel is highly competitive. One key rival is Bass Pro Shops, which targets customers who like fishing, hunting, and boating. Another is Eastern Mountain Sports (EMS), which operates eighty stores in eastern and midwestern states. In addition, REI competes with many independent stores and chain retailers that carry clothing and gear for the active lifestyle.

REI now generates more than $885 million in revenue and serves 2.8 million customers yearly. Its eighty stores range in size from 10,000 to 95,000 square feet, so no two stores carry exactly the same merchandise. "Even though we don't have a lot of stores, we have a lot of variety in our stores," says REI's inventory planning manager, "and that creates merchandising challenges for us." REI's solution: Analyze the profitability and sales per square foot of each product category in each store, and then eliminate the weakest categories to make room for the strongest. This helps the retailer to manage inventory more efficiently and choose the most profitable assortment for each store.

For more information about this company, go to **www.rei. com.31**

Questions

1. Knowing that it incurs transportation costs to ship merchandise to each store, what are the advantages and disadvantages of REI waiving shipping fees for merchandise ordered online that is picked up in a store?

2. How would you classify REI as an in-store retailer? Support your answer.

3. REI opens a handful of new stores every year. Would you recommend that the company invest more heavily in online retailing than in-store retailing? Why?

BUILDING SKILLS FOR CAREER SUCCESS

1. Exploring the Internet

One reason the Internet has generated so much excitement and interest among both buyers and distributors of products is that it is a highly effective method of direct marketing. Already a multibillion dollar industry, e-commerce is growing as more businesses recognize the power of the Internet to reach customers twenty-four hours a day anywhere in the world. In addition to using the Internet to provide product information to potential customers, businesses can use it to process orders and accept payment from customers. Quick delivery from warehouses or stores by couriers such as UPS and FedEx adds to the convenience of Internet shopping.

Businesses whose products traditionally have sold well through catalogs are clear leaders in the electronic marketplace. Books, CDs, clothing, and other frequently purchased, relatively low-cost items sell well through both the Internet and catalogs. As a result, many successful catalog companies are including the Internet as a means of communicating about products. And many of their customers are finding that they prefer the more dynamic online versions of the catalogs.

Assignment

1. Explore the websites listed below, or just enter "shopping" on one of the web search engines—then stand back! Also visit the text website for updates to this exercise.
   www.llbean.com
   www.jcpenney.com
   www.sears.com
   www.landsend.com
   www.barnesandnoble.com
   www.amazon.com
2. Which website does the best job of marketing merchandise? Explain your answer.
3. Find a product that you would be willing to buy over the Internet, and explain why you would buy it. Name the website and describe the product.
4. Find a product that you would be unwilling to buy over the Internet, and again, explain your reasoning. Name the website and describe the product.

2. Building Team Skills

Surveys are a commonly used tool in marketing research. The information they provide can reduce business risk and facilitate decision making. Retail outlets often survey their customers' wants and needs by distributing comment cards or questionnaires. The customer survey (on p. 471) is an example of a survey that a local photography shop might distribute to its customers.

Assignment

1. Working in teams of three to five, choose a local retailer.
2. Classify the retailer according to the major types of retailers.
3. Design a survey to help the retailer to improve customer service. (You may find it beneficial to work with the retailer and actually administer the survey to the retailer's customers. Prepare a report of the survey results for the retailer.)
4. Present your findings to the class.

3. Researching Different Careers

Most public libraries maintain relatively up-to-date collections of occupational or career materials. Begin your library search by looking at the computer listings under "vocations" or "careers" and then under specific fields. Check the library's periodicals section, where you will find trade and professional magazines and journals about specific occupations and industries. (*Business Periodicals Index,* published by H. W. Wilson, is an index to articles in major business publications. Arranged alphabetically, it is easy to use.) Familiarize yourself with the concerns and activities of potential employers by skimming their annual reports and other information they distribute to the public. You also can find occupational information on videocassettes, in kits, and through computerized information systems.

Assignment

1. Choose a specific occupation.
2. Conduct a library search of the occupation.
3. Prepare an annotated bibliography for the occupation.

Customer Survey

To help us to serve you better, please take a few minutes while your photographs are being developed to answer the following questions. Your opinions are important to us.

1. Do you live/work in the area? (Circle one or both if they apply.)

2. Why did you choose us? (Circle all that apply.)
   Close to home
   Close to work
   Convenience
   Good service
   Quality
   Full-service photography shop
   Other

3. How did you learn about us? (Circle one.)
   Newspaper
   Flyer/coupon
   Passing by
   Recommended by someone
   Other

4. How frequently do you have film developed? (Please estimate.)
   _____ Times per month
   _____ Times per year

5. Which aspects of our photography shop do you think need improvement?

6. Our operating hours are from 8:00 A.M. to 7:00 P.M. weekdays and Saturdays from 9:30 A.M. to 6:00 P.M. We are closed on Sundays and legal holidays. If changes in our operating hours would serve you better, please specify how you would like them changed.

7. Age (Circle one.)
   Under 25
   26–39
   40–59
   Over 60
   Comments:

Prepare for Class
Exploring the Internet

RUNNING A BUSINESS PART 5
Finagle A Bagel's Approach to Marketing

Round, flat, seeded, plain, crowned with cheese, or cut into croutons, bagels form the basis of every menu item at Finagle A Bagel. "So many other shops will just grab onto whatever is hot, whatever is trendy, in a 'me-too' strategy," observes Heather Robertson, the director of marketing, human resources, and research and development. In contrast, she says, "We do bagels—that's what we do best. And any menu item in our stores really needs to reaffirm that as our core concept."

In addition to its retailing activities, the company wholesales its bagels in bulk to hospitals, schools, and other organizations. It also wholesales a line of Finagle A Bagel–branded bagels for resale in Shaw's Market stores. Whether selling wholesale or retail, the company is always hunting for new product ideas involving bagels.

Product Development: Mix, Bake, Bite, and Try Again

To identify a new product idea, Robertson and her colleagues conduct informal research by talking with both customers and employees. They also browse food magazines and cookbooks for ideas about out-of-the-ordinary flavors, taste combinations, and preparation methods. When developing a new bagel variety, for example, Robertson looks for ideas that are uncommon and innovative yet appealing: "If

someone else has a sun-dried tomato bagel, that's all the more reason for me not to do it. People look at Finagle A Bagel as kind of the trendsetter."

The next step is to write up a formula or recipe, go into the dough factory, and mix up a test batch. Through trial and error, Robertson and her team refine the idea until they like the way the bagel or sandwich looks and tastes. Occasionally, they have to put an idea on hold until they can find just the right ingredients.

For example, when Robertson was working on a bagel with jalapeno peppers and cheddar cheese, she had difficulty finding a cheese that would melt but not dissolve and disappear into the batter when baked. Ultimately, she found a supplier willing to cook up cheese formulas especially for Finagle A Bagel. The supplier would send a batch of cheese overnight for Robertson to incorporate into the next day's test batch of bagels. After baking, Robertson would send some of the bagels overnight to the supplier so that the two of them could discuss the flavor, consistency, and other details.

The cheeses and bagels flew back and forth for eight months until Finagle A Bagel found a suitable recipe. "When we finally got it done," Robertson says, "we shipped test batches to our stores, three stores at a time. And we just gave

the product away. We'd make several batches during the week, and guess who would come back wanting to buy dozens of these bagels?" That's when she knew the new product was going to be successful. Today, plain bagels remain the best-selling flavor, followed by sesame. A cocoa bagel, introduced during baseball season to honor the Boston Red Sox, also has been a big hit.

Samples and Coupons Spark Word-of-Mouth Communication

Many quick-serve food companies use television and radio commercials, newspaper advertisements, and other mass-media messages to build brand awareness, promote products, and attract customers. Not Finagle A Bagel. Robertson and her colleagues believe that the best way to build the brand and whet customers' appetites for a new menu item is to give them a free taste.

Consider what happened when Finagle A Bagel used samples and coupons to build lunchtime sales of bagel sandwiches in one of its suburban stores. Instead of advertising in the local newspaper, Robertson and her staff went to the store and prepared 100 sandwiches. They cut each in half and wrapped the halves individually. Then they set up 200 Finagle A Bagel bags, put a half-sandwich into each, and added a coupon for a free bagel sandwich. They piled all the bags into a big basket, attached a sign reading, "Free Bagel Sandwiches," and headed to a large intersection just a block from the store.

"Every time the light turned red, we would run out into the middle of the street and throw a bag through someone's car window," Robertson recalls. "We got a lot of strange looks. A few people would roll up their car windows . . . but a lot of people just thought it was hysterically funny. They would be motioning, waving us over, saying, 'What have you got?' And then they'd go back to their office and tell their coworkers, 'Hey, you know what happened to me today? Some crazy lady threw a bagel through my car window, and it was great. You should check it out.'" The entire effort cost $100—and convinced a large number of customers to look around the store, try a sandwich risk-free, and talk up the experience to other people.

The popular Finagle A Bagel headquarters tour has become an effective public-relations tool. Community groups, students, and bagel lovers of all ages can browse exhibits representing the company's successes and mistakes. In the factory area, visitors watch through a huge window as hundreds of pounds of dough are mixed, cut, and shaped into bagels.

Buy a Branded Bagel—Again and Again

Although some restaurant companies want each unit to look distinctly different, Finagle A Bagel uses consistency to reinforce the brand image—another of its marketing rules. "We believe the stores should have a very similar look and feel so that you can walk into any Finagle A Bagel and know what to expect," says copresident Alan Litchman. For example, every Finagle A Bagel store sports an eye-catching burgundy-and-yellow sign featuring an oversized bagel with a few bites taken out. This bagel icon is repeated on posters highlighting menu items as well as on other store decorations.

Still, the suburban stores are not exactly like the downtown stores. Many of the suburban stores have children's furniture and cushiony chairs so that families can sit and relax. In contrast, the city stores have no children's furniture because they cater to busy working people who want to be in and out in a hurry.

Pricing a Bagel

Pricing is an important consideration in the competitive world of quick-serve food. Yet, regardless of cost, Finagle A Bagel will not compromise quality. Therefore, the first step in pricing a new product is to find the best possible ingredients. After thinking about what customers might expect to pay for such a menu item, analyzing the costs, shopping the competition, and then talking with customers, the company settles on a price that represents "a great product for a fair value," says Robertson.

Although Finagle A Bagel's rental costs vary, the copresidents price menu items the same in higher-rent stores as in lower-rent stores. "We have considered adjusting prices based upon the location of the store, but we haven't done it because it can backfire in a very significant way," copresident Laura Trust explains. "People expect to be treated fairly, regardless of where they live."

Questions

1. Does Finagle A Bagel apply all seven phases of the new product development process when working on a new menu item such as the jalapeno-and-cheese bagel? Explain.

2. Do you agree with Laura Trust's assessment that adjusting prices based on store location can backfire? What arguments can you offer for and against Finagle A Bagel raising prices in higher-rent stores?

3. Finagle A Bagel is both a wholesaler and a retailer. Which of these two marketing intermediary roles do you think the company should develop more aggressively in the next few years? Why?

4. Should Finagle A Bagel continue to rely primarily on sales promotion techniques such as samples and coupons instead of investing in expensive advertising campaigns?

CHAPTER 15

Using Accounting Information

Your Guide to Success in Business

Why this chapter matters
Although lenders, suppliers, stockholders, and government agencies all rely on the information generated by a firm's accounting system, the primary users of accounting information are managers and employees.

LEARNING OBJECTIVES

1 Explain why accurate accounting information and audited financial statements are important.

2 Identify the people who use accounting information and possible careers in the accounting industry.

3 Discuss the accounting process.

4 Read and interpret a balance sheet.

5 Read and interpret an income statement.

6 Describe business activities that affect a firm's cash flow.

7 Summarize how managers evaluate the financial health of a business.

Beyond the Basics: Annual Reports

Accounting is at the heart of the annual reports that public corporations have, since 1934, been legally required to prepare. The original intent was to keep stockholders informed about a company's financial performance. Today, however, many annual reports go well beyond the basics. More and more aim to show investors, prospective investors, employees, customers, banks, brokers, financial analysts, and community groups not only how well a company is doing but also what it stands for, where it's going, and why.

For example, Sears Holdings Corporation reaches out to several audiences through its annual report, available in print and online. Chairman Edward S. Lampert's letter in a recent annual report explained that Sears was not going to follow the usual growth strategy of aggressively opening new stores. Instead, the company is emphasizing higher profits over higher revenues to build a solid foundation for long-term financial health.

Although stockholders and lenders would find this explanation helpful, Lampert also was anticipating the concerns of financial analysts who expect retailers to grow, grow, grow. Knowing that what analysts say can affect the investment decisions of many stockholders, Lampert used the annual report to communicate why Sears wasn't planning to open as many stores as its competitors—yet. Then there's the human side of Sears, which the annual report reveals by featuring exemplary employees and mentioning community connections, topics of special interest to the work force and to many customers.

GB&T Bancshares of Gainesville, Georgia, uses its annual report to supplement the required financial information with a "peek behind the numbers," according to Michael Banks, the bank's vice president of marketing. "Your numbers are important, but the narrative shows what makes you successful." For GB&T, "it's our people and our customers," he adds. The annual report is addressed "to stockholders, customers, and friends" and includes testimonials from satisfied customers. GB&T's report is especially appealing to large investors, Banks says, because they're "looking for something that tells your company story."[1]

DID YOU KNOW?

In an annual report, "your numbers are important, but the narrative shows what makes you successful," notes a GB&T Bancshares executive.

KEY TERMS

accounting (476)
audit (478)
generally accepted accounting principles (GAAPs) (478)
managerial accounting (482)
financial accounting (482)
certified public accountant (CPA) (483)
certified management accountant (CMA) (484)
assets (485)

liabilities (485)
owners' equity (485)
accounting equation (485)
double-entry bookkeeping (485)
trial balance (486)
annual report (486)
balance sheet (or statement of financial position) (486)
liquidity (488)
current assets (488)

fixed assets (490)
depreciation (490)
intangible assets (490)
current liabilities (491)
long-term liabilities (491)
retained earnings (491)
income statement (492)
revenues (492)
gross sales (492)
net sales (493)

cost of goods sold (493)
gross profit (493)
operating expenses (494)
net income (495)
net loss (495)
statement of cash flows (496)
financial ratio (498)

ACE the Test
Crossword Puzzle
Flashcards

How important is a firm's annual report and its accounting system? The answer is simple: Real Important! Most everyone remembers the accounting scandals that occurred in the past few years—a situation so bad that the government stepped in and passed the Sarbanes-Oxley Act in 2002 in order to improve accounting standards. Now—more than five years after the act was enacted—corporate accountants and independent auditors are working harder than ever to make sure a company's annual report reports accurate financial information and a firm's accounting records are above suspicion. And as pointed out in the Inside Business feature for this chapter, these same corporations use their annual reports to tell a "story" about what the company is all about. While all companies want to report an increase in sales and profits, many also want their stakeholders—investors, customers, suppliers, lenders, and the government—to know the company is more than just a profit-making machine.

We begin this chapter by looking at

* Why accounting information is important.
* The recent problems in the accounting industry and attempts to improve financial reporting.
* How managers, employees, individuals, and groups outside a firm use accounting information.
* Different types of accountants and career opportunities in the accounting industry.
* The accounting process and the basics of an accounting system.
* The three most important financial statements: the balance sheet, the income statement, and the statement of cash flows.
* How ratios are used to measure specific aspects of a firm's financial health.

Why Accounting Information Is Important

Learning Objective ❶

Explain why accurate accounting information and audited financial statements are important.

accounting the process of systematically collecting, analyzing, and reporting financial information

Accounting is the process of systematically collecting, analyzing, and reporting financial information. Today it is impossible to manage a business without accurate and up-to-date information supplied by the firm's accountants. Just for a moment, think about the following three questions:

1. How much profit did a business earn last year?
2. How much tax does a business owe the Internal Revenue Service?
3. How much cash does a business have on hand?

In each case, the firm's accountants and its accounting system provide the answers to these questions and many others. And while accounting information can be used to answer questions about what has happened in the past, it also can be used to help make decisions about the future. For these reasons, accounting is one of the most important areas within a business organization.

Because the information provided by a firm's accountants and its accounting system is so important, managers and other groups interested in a business firm's financial records must be able to "trust the numbers." Unfortunately, a large number of accounting scandals have caused people to doubt not only the numbers but also the accounting industry.

Recent Accounting Problems for Corporations and Their Auditors

Today, much of the pressure on corporate executives to "cook" the books is driven by the *desire to look good* to Wall Street analysts and investors. Every three months, companies report their revenues, expenses, profits, and projections for the future. If a company meets or exceeds "the street's" expectations, everything is usually fine. However, if a company reports financial numbers that are lower than expected, the company's stock value can drop dramatically. An earnings report that is lower by even a few pennies per share than what is expected can cause a company's stock value to drop immediately by as much as 30 to 40 percent or more.

Greed—especially when salary and bonuses are tied to a company's stock value—is another factor that can lead some corporate executives to use questionable accounting methods to inflate a firm's financial performance. Lower-level managers may go along with dubious accounting schemes because they stand to profit from cooperating, because they fear retaliation from senior executives, or because they worry about losing their jobs—especially when new employment opportunities are scarce.

In a perfect world, the accountants who inspect the corporate books would catch mistakes and disclose questionable accounting practices. Unfortunately, we do not live in a perfect world. **EXAMPLE** Consider the part that auditors for the accounting firm Arthur Andersen played in the Enron meltdown. When the Securities and Exchange Commission (SEC) launched its inquiry into Enron's financial affairs, Andersen employees shredded the documents related to the audit. As a result, both the SEC and the Department of Justice began to investigate Andersen's role in the failure of Enron. Eventually, Andersen was convicted of obstruction of justice and was forced to cease auditing public companies. Simply put, Andersen—the once-proud accounting firm—was found guilty.[2] Less than a month after admitting accounting errors that inflated earnings by almost $600 million since 1994, Enron filed for bankruptcy.[3] Other high-profile companies, including Adelphia, Quest Communications, and Tyco International, have been hauled into court to explain their accounting practices. And more accounting firms—including KPMG and PricewaterhouseCoopers—have been targeted by trial lawyers, government regulators, and in some cases the Internal Revenue Service (IRS) for providing questionable audit work for major corporate clients.[4] Make no mistake, the penalties for what some critics call "executive crime" are real. Consider the following:

* Bernard Ebbers, WorldCom CEO, was sentenced to twenty-five years in prison for his part in defrauding investors, employees, pension holders, and other groups that lost money on WorldCom stock.[5]

Accounting problems at Enron.

For employees like Meredith Stewart, the accounting problems at Enron reached a personal level when they lost their jobs. In addition to those who lost their jobs when the one-time energy giant failed, investors, retirees, and creditors also lost millions of dollars.

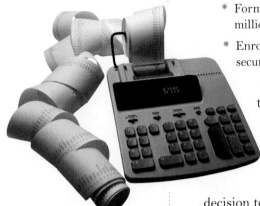

* Former Tyco CEO Dennis Kozlowski was found guilty of looting more than $600 million from the company.[6]

* Enron executives Ken Lay and Jeff Skilling were convicted of conspiracy to commit securities and wire fraud in May 2006.[7]

While there will be appeals for each of these individuals, the cases show that corporate executives can't escape responsibility for reporting inaccurate or misleading accounting information. Unfortunately, the ones hurt often are not the high-paid corporate executives. In many cases it's the employees who lose their jobs and often the money they invested in the company's retirement program and investors, lenders, and suppliers who relied on fraudulent accounting information in order to make a decision to invest in or lend money to the company.

In an indirect way, the recent accounting scandals underscore how important accurate accounting information is for a corporation. To see how the auditing process can improve accounting information, read the next section.

Why Audited Financial Statements Are Important

Assume that you are a bank officer responsible for evaluating loan applications. How do you make a decision to approve or reject a loan request? In this situation, most bank officers rely on the information contained in the firm's balance sheet, income statement, and statement of cash flows, along with other information provided by the prospective borrower. In fact, most lenders insist that these financial statements be audited by a certified public accountant (CPA).

An **audit** is an examination of a company's financial statements and the accounting practices that produced them. The purpose of an audit is to make sure that a firm's financial statements have been prepared in accordance with generally accepted accounting principles. Today, **generally accepted accounting principles (GAAPs)** have been developed to provide an accepted set of guidelines and practices for companies reporting financial information and the accounting profession. Today, three organizations—the Financial Accounting Standards Board (FASB), the American Institute of Certified Public Accountants (AICPA), and the International Accounting Standards Board (IASB)—have greatly influenced the methods used by the accounting profession.

If an accountant determines that a firm's financial statements present financial information fairly and conform to GAAPs, then he or she will issue the following statement: "In our opinion, the financial statements. . . present fairly, in all material respects . . . in conformity with generally accepted accounting principles."

While an audit and the resulting report do not *guarantee* that a company has not "cooked" the books, it does imply that, on the whole, the company has followed GAAPs. Bankers, creditors, investors, and government agencies are willing to rely on an auditor's opinion because of the historically ethical reputation and independence of auditors and accounting firms. Finally, it should be noted that without the

CONCEPT CHECK

Why do you think there have been so many accounting scandals involving public companies in recent years?

audit an examination of a company's financial statements and the accounting practices that produced them

generally accepted accounting principles (GAAPs) an accepted set of guidelines and practices for companies reporting financial information and for the accounting profession

BUSINESS AROUND THE WORLD

China's Answer to GAAP: CASS

Accounting changes are sweeping through China. Why? "To become an economic superpower, China needs capital to fund growth," observes the CEO of the Hong Kong Institute of Certified Public Accountants, "and it will help if its companies speak the same business language as the rest of the world." So the country has been changing the accounting standards for the 1,100 public companies traded on the Shanghai and Shenzhen stock exchanges.

The goal is to make the China Accounting Standards System (CASS) consistent with the generally accepted accounting practices (GAAPs) that apply in Western countries. This will give investors a clearer picture of each company's financial performance. More than 150 Chinese companies listed on foreign stock exchanges already use international accounting standards. Huaneng Power International, for instance, is listed on the Shanghai and Hong Kong exchanges and therefore must prepare two sets of financial statements. The switch to CASS goes well beyond numbers: It's also creating thousands of new jobs for accounting professionals.

Sources: Based on information in James T. Areddy, "Adding Up Chinese Data," *Wall Street Journal*, February 27, 2006, p. C10; Nisha Gopalan, "Mainland-Listed Chinese Firms to Follow Global Accounting Rules," *Wall Street Journal*, July 19, 2006, n.p.

audit function and GAAPs, there would be very little oversight or supervision. The validity of a firm's financial statements and its accounting records would drop quickly, and firms would find it difficult to obtain debt financing, acquire goods and services from suppliers, find investor financing, or prepare documents requested by government agencies.

Reform: The Sarbanes-Oxley Act of 2002

According to John Bogle, founder of Vanguard Mutual Funds, "Investing is an act of faith. Without that faith—that reported numbers reflect reality, that companies are being run honestly, that Wall Street is playing it straight, and that investors aren't being hoodwinked—our capital markets simply can't function."[8] In reality, what Mr. Bogle says is true. To help ensure that corporate financial information is accurate and in response to the many accounting scandals that surfaced in the last part of the 1990s and the first part of the twenty-first century, Congress enacted the Sarbanes-Oxley Act. Key components include the following:

* The SEC is required to establish a full-time five-member federal oversight board that will police the accounting industry.

* Chief executives and financial officers are required to certify periodic financial reports and may be subject to criminal penalties for violations of securities reporting requirements.

* Accounting firms are prohibited from providing many types of nonaudit and consulting services to the companies they audit.

* Auditors must maintain financial documents and audit work papers for five years.

* Auditors, accountants, and employees can be imprisoned for up to twenty years for destroying financial documents and willful violations of the securities laws.

* A public corporation must change its lead auditing firm every five years.

* There is added protection for whistle-blowers who report violations of the Sarbanes-Oxley Act.

While most people welcome the Sarbanes-Oxley Act, complex rules make compliance more expensive and time-consuming for corporate management and more difficult for accounting firms. And yet, most people agree that the cost of compliance is justified. As you read the next section, you will see just how important accurate accounting information is.

 TEST PREPPER (15.1)

True or False?

___T___ 1. Greed—especially when salary and bonuses are tied to a company's stock value—is another factor that can lead some corporate executives to use questionable accounting methods.

___F___ 2. The 2002 act that improved accounting practices for public companies operating in the United States is the Securities and Exchange Act.

___T___ 3. Three organizations—the Financial Accounting Standards Board (FASB), the American Institute of Certified Public Accountants (AICPA), and the International Accounting Standards Board (IASB)—have greatly influenced the methods used by the accounting profession.

Multiple Choice

___B___ 4. One of the reasons for recent accounting fiascos such as the Enron scandal is

a. the pressure from the international shareholders of companies.
b. the desire to look good on the part of executives.
c. the fact that all major firms are involved.
d. the pressure from customers on the CEOs of companies.
e. the desire to gain a footing in international markets.

___A___ 5. _____, WorldCom CEO, was sentenced to twenty-five years in prison for his part in defrauding investors, employees, pension holders, and other groups that lost money on WorldCom stock.

a. Bernard Ebbers
b. Ken Lay
c. John Bogle
d. Jeff Skilling
e. Dennis Kozlowski

ACE the Test
ACE & ACE+
Practice Test 15.1

Who Uses Accounting Information

Learning Objective 2

Identify the people who use accounting information and possible careers in the accounting industry.

Managers and employees, lenders, suppliers, stockholders, and government agencies all rely on the information contained in three financial statements, each no more than one page in length. These three reports—the *balance sheet*, the *income statement*, and the *statement of cash flows*—are concise summaries of a firm's activities during a specific time period. Together they represent the results of perhaps tens of thousands of transactions that have occurred during the accounting period. Moreover, the form of the financial statements is pretty much the same for all businesses, from a neighborhood video store or small dry cleaner to giant conglomerates such as Home Depot, Boeing, and Bank of America. This information has a variety of uses both within the firm and outside it. However, first and foremost, accounting information is management information.

The People Who Use Accounting Information

The primary users of accounting information are *managers* and *employees*. The firm's accounting system provides information that can be compiled for the entire firm and for each product, sales territory, store, or salesperson; for each division or department; and generally in any way that will help those who manage the organization. **EXAMPLE** At a company such as Kraft Foods, financial information is gathered for all its hundreds of food products: Maxwell House Coffee, A1 Steak Sauce, Post Cereals, Jell-O Desserts, Kool Aid, and so on. The president of the company would be interested in total sales for all these products. The vice president for marketing may be interested in national sales for Post Cereals and Jell-O Desserts. The northeastern sales manager might want to look at sales figures for Kool Aid in New England. For a large, complex organization like Kraft, the accounting system must enable managers to get the information they need.

Much of this accounting information is *proprietary;* it is not divulged to anyone outside the firm. This type of information is used by a firm's managers and employees to plan and set goals, organize, lead, motivate, and control—all the management functions that were described in Chapter 7.

In addition to proprietary information used inside the firm, certain financial information must be supplied to lenders, suppliers, stockholders and potential investors, and government agencies (see Table 15.1). An important function of accountants is to ensure that such information is accurate and thorough enough to satisfy these outside groups.

How did he get so rich?

Although there are many reasons why Warren Buffet, chairman of the board of Berkshire Hathaway, has become one of the wealthiest people in America, his ability to understand accounting information has enabled him to identify investments that are extremely profitable. The same appreciation for numbers is one reason why Berkshire Hathaway subsidiary companies are known to have lower operating costs and larger bottom-line profits than their competitors.

MANAGEMENT	LENDERS AND SUPPLIERS	STOCKHOLDERS AND POTENTIAL INVESTORS	GOVERNMENT AGENCIES
Plan and set goals, organize, lead and motivate, and control—all management functions described in Chapter 7.	Evaluate financial statements and credit risks before committing to short- or long-term loans or extending credit for raw materials, parts, or finished goods the firm needs to operate.	Evaluate the financial health of the firm before making a decision to retain or purchase stocks or bonds issued by the firm.	Confirm tax liabilities, confirm payroll deductions, and approve new issues of stocks and bonds before they are issued.

Different Types of Accounting

While many people think that all accountants do the same tasks, there are special areas of expertise within the accounting industry. In fact, accounting usually is broken down into two broad categories: managerial and financial.

Managerial accounting provides managers and employees with the information needed to make decisions about a firm's *financing*, *investing*, and *operating activities*. By using managerial accounting information, both managers and employees can evaluate how well they have done in the past and what they can expect in the future. **Financial accounting**, on the other hand, generates financial statements and reports for interested people outside of an organization. Typically, stockholders, financial analysts, bankers, lenders, suppliers, government agencies, and other interested groups use the information provided by financial accounting to determine how well a business firm has achieved its goals. In addition to managerial and financial accounting, additional special areas of accounting include the following:

* *Cost accounting*—determining the cost of producing specific products or services.

* *Government accounting*—providing basic accounting services to ensure that tax revenues are collected and used to meet the goals of state, local, and federal agencies.

* *Not-for-profit accounting*—helping not-for-profit organizations to account for all donations and expenditures.

* *Tax accounting*—planning tax strategy and preparing tax returns for the firm.

Careers in Accounting

Want a job? Positions in the accounting and auditing field increasingly are becoming available to those with the required training. According to the *Occupational Outlook Handbook*, published by the Department of Labor, job opportunities for accountants, auditors, and managers in the accounting area are expected to grow faster than average between now and the year 2014.[9]

Many people have the idea that accountants spend their day working with endless columns of numbers in a small office locked away from other people. In fact, accountants do spend a lot of time at their desks, but their job entails far more than just adding or subtracting numbers. Accountants are expected to share their ideas and the information they possess with people who need the information.

Accounting can be an exciting and rewarding career—one that offers higher-than-average starting salaries.

Characteristics of Successful Accountants

* Accountants must be responsible, honest, and ethical.

* Accountants must have a strong background in financial management.

* Accountants must know how to use a computer and software to process data into accounting information.

* Accountants must be able to communicate with people who need accounting information.

Today, accountants generally are classified as either private accountants or public accountants. A *private accountant* is employed by a specific organization. A medium-sized or large firm may employ one or more private accountants to design its accounting information system, manage its accounting department, and provide managers with advice and assistance.

Individuals, self-employed business owners, and smaller firms that do not require their own full-time private accountants can hire the services of public accountants. A *public accountant* works on a fee basis for clients and may be self-employed or be the employee of an accounting firm. Accounting firms range in size from one-person operations to huge international firms with hundreds of accounting partners and thousands of employees. Today, the largest accounting firms, sometimes referred to as the "Big Four," are PricewaterhouseCoopers, Ernst & Young, KPMG, and Deloitte Touche Tohmatsu.

Typically, public accounting firms include on their staffs at least one **certified public accountant (CPA)**, an individual who has met state requirements for accounting education and experience and has passed a rigorous accounting examination prepared by the AICPA. The AICPA uniform CPA examination covers four areas:

* Ethics, taxation, business law, and professional responsibilities

* Auditing

* Business environment and concepts

* Financial accounting and reporting

More information about general requirements and the CPA profession can be obtained by contacting the AICPA at **www.aicpa.org**.[10]

Once an individual becomes a CPA, he or she must participate in continuing-education programs to maintain state certification. These specialized programs are

Accounting information you can use.

The website for the American Institute of Certified Public Accountants (AICPA) provides a wealth of career information for people who are interested in becoming certified public accountants (CPAs). Why not check it out at **www.aicpa.org**?

certified public accountant (CPA) an individual who has met state requirements for accounting education and experience and has passed a rigorous accounting examination prepared by the AICPA

SPOTLIGHT

Salaries for accountants and auditors

Accountant and auditor salaries depend on the amount of experience, area of the country, and qualifications.

Top 10% of accountants and auditors
$88,610

Bachelor's degree— starting salary
$43,269

Master's degree— starting salary
$46,251

Median— all accountants and auditors
$50,770

Source: The Bureau of Labor Statistics website: **www.bls.gov**; accessed November 11, 2006.

designed to provide the current training needed in today's changing business environment. CPAs also must take an ethics course to satisfy the continuing-education requirement.

Certification as a CPA brings both status and responsibility. In addition to auditing a corporation's financial statements, typical services performed by CPAs include

* Planning and preparing tax returns

* Determining the true cost of producing and marketing a firm's goods or services

* Compiling the financial information needed to make major management decisions

Fees for the services provided by CPAs generally range from $50 to $300 an hour.

In addition to certified public accountants, there are also certified management accountants. A **certified management accountant (CMA)** is an accountant who has met the requirements for education and experience, passed a rigorous exam, and is certified by the Institute of Management Accountants. The CMA exam is designed to develop and measure not only accounting skills but also decision-making and critical-thinking skills. For more information about the CMA exam, visit the Institute of Management Accountants website at **www.imanet.org.** While both CPAs and CMAs can work for the public, a CMA is more likely to work within a large organization. Also, both types of accountants are excellent career choices.

certified management accountant (CMA) an accountant who has met the requirements for education and experience, passed a rigorous exam, and is certified by the Institute of Management Accountants

TEST PREPPER 15.2

True or False?

___ 1. The form of financial statements is pretty different for all businesses.

___ 2. Financial accounting provides managers and employees with the information needed to make decisions about a firm's financing, investing, and operating activities.

___ 3. Typically, public accounting firms include on their staffs at least one certified public accountant (CPA).

Multiple Choice

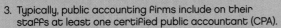 4. The president of a company would be most interested in

    a. total sales figures of all the products.
    b. regional sales figures.

    c. the cost-of-products figure.
    d. national sales figures of the company's popular brands.
    e. The president of a company does not view accounting information per se.

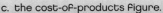 5. Which one of the following is *not* one of the characteristics of successful accountants?

    a. Be responsible, honest, and ethical
    b. Have a strong background in financial management.
    c. Know how to use a computer and software to process data into accounting information.
    d. Be able to communicate with people who need accounting information.
    e. Be able to speak different languages.

ACE the Test
ACE & ACE+
Practice Test 15.2

The Accounting Process

Learning Objective

Discuss the accounting process.

In Chapter 4, *information* was defined as data presented in a form that is useful for a specific purpose. In this section we examine accounting as the system for transforming raw financial *data* into useful financial *information*. Then, in the next sections we describe the three most important financial statements provided by the accounting process.

The Accounting Equation

The accounting equation is a simple statement that forms the basis for the accounting process. This important equation shows the relationship between a firm's assets, liabilities, and owners' equity.

* **Assets** are the resources a business owns—cash, inventory, equipment, and real estate.

* **Liabilities** are the firm's debts—what it owes to others.

* **Owners' equity** is the difference between total assets and total liabilities—what would be left for the owners if the firm's assets were sold and the money used to pay off its liabilities.

The relationship between assets, liabilities, and owners' equity is shown by the following **accounting equation:**

Assets = liabilities + owners' equity

Whether a business is a small corner grocery store or a giant corporation such as General Motors, its assets must equal the sum of its liabilities and owners' equity. To use this equation, a firm's accountants must record raw data—that is, the firm's day-to-day financial transactions—using the double-entry system of bookkeeping. The **double-entry bookkeeping system** is a system in which each financial transaction is recorded as two separate accounting entries to maintain the balance shown in the accounting equation. With the double-entry system, an accountant can use the steps in the accounting cycle to generate accounting information and financial statements.

The Accounting Cycle

In the typical accounting system, raw data are transformed into financial statements in five steps. The first three—*analyzing, recording,* and *posting*—are performed on a regular basis throughout the accounting period. The last two—*preparation of the trial balance* and *preparation of the financial statements and closing the books*—are performed at the end of the accounting period.

Analyzing Source Documents Basic accounting data are contained in *source documents,* the receipts, invoices, sales slips, and other documents that show the dollar amounts of day-to-day business transactions. The accounting cycle begins with the analysis of each of these documents. The purpose of the analysis is to determine which accounts are affected by the documents and how they are affected.

assets the resources that a business owns

liabilities a firm's debts and obligations

owners' equity the difference between a firm's assets and its liabilities

accounting equation the basis for the accounting process: *assets = liabilities + owners' equity*

double-entry bookkeeping system a system in which each financial transaction is recorded as two separate accounting entries to maintain the balance shown in the accounting equation

trial balance a summary of the balances of all general ledger accounts at the end of the accounting period

annual report a report distributed to stockholders and other interested parties that describes a firm's operating activities and its financial condition

Recording Transactions Every financial transaction then is recorded in a journal—a process called *journalizing*. Transactions must be recorded in the firm's general journal or in specialized journals. The *general journal* is a book of original entry in which typical transactions are recorded in order of their occurrence. An accounting system also may include *specialized journals* for specific types of transactions that occur frequently. Thus a retail store might have journals for cash receipts, cash disbursements, purchases, and sales in addition to its general journal.

Posting Transactions After the information is recorded in the general journal and specialized journals, it is transferred to the general ledger. The *general ledger* is a book of accounts containing a separate sheet or section for each account. Today, most businesses use a computer and software to post accounting entries from the general journal or specialized journals to the general ledger.

Preparing the Trial Balance A **trial balance** is a summary of the balances of all general ledger accounts at the end of the accounting period. To prepare a trial balance, the accountant determines and lists the balances for all ledger accounts. If the trial balance totals are correct and the accounting equation is still in balance, the accountant can prepare the financial statements. If not, a mistake has occurred somewhere, and the accountant must find it and correct it before proceeding.

Preparing Financial Statements and Closing the Books The firm's financial statements are prepared from the information contained in the trial balance. This information is presented in a standardized format to make the statements as accessible as possible to the various people who may be interested in the firm's financial affairs—managers, employees, lenders, suppliers, stockholders, potential investors, and government agencies. A firm's financial statements are prepared at least once a year and included in the firm's annual report. An **annual report** is a report distributed to stockholders and other interested parties that describes a firm's operating activities and its financial condition. Most firms also have financial statements prepared semi-annually, quarterly, or monthly.

Once these statements have been prepared and checked, the firm's books are "closed" for the accounting period, and a *postclosing* trial balance is prepared, although, like the trial balance just described, the postclosing trial balance generally is prepared after *all* accounting work is completed for one accounting period. If the postclosing trial balance totals agree, the accounting equation is still in balance at the end of the cycle. Only then can a new accounting cycle begin for the next accounting period.

With this brief information about the steps of the accounting cycle in mind, let's now examine the three most important financial statements generated by the accounting process: the *balance sheet*, the *income statement*, and the *statement of cash flows*.

CONCEPT CHECK

Briefly describe the five steps of the accounting cycle in order.

balance sheet (or **statement of financial position**) a summary of the dollar amounts of a firm's assets, liabilities, and owners' equity accounts at the end of a specific accounting period

TEST PREPPER 15.3

True or False?

____ 1. The difference between total assets and total liabilities is called the net difference.

____ 2. Regardless of the size of a firm, its assets must equal the sum of its liabilities and owners' equity.

____ 3. Recording transactions is the first step in the accounting cycle.

Multiple Choice

____ 4. In the typical accounting system, raw data are transformed into financial statements in _____ steps.

a. seven
b. five
c. eight
d. ten
e. six

____ 5. A firm's financial statements are prepared from the information contained in the

a. balance sheet.
b. source documents.
c. general journal.
d. special journal.
e. trial balance.

ACE the Test
ACE & ACE+
Practice Test 15.3

The Balance Sheet

Learning Objective ④

Read and interpret a balance sheet.

Question: Where could you find the total amount of assets, liabilities, and owners' equity for Hershey Foods Corporation?

Answer: The firm's balance sheet.

A **balance sheet** (sometimes referred to as a **statement of financial position**) is a summary of the dollar amounts of a firm's assets, liabilities, and owners' equity accounts at the end of a specific accounting period. The balance sheet must demonstrate that assets are equal to liabilities plus owners' equity. Most people think of a balance sheet as a statement that reports the financial condition of a business firm such as Hershey Foods Corporation, but balance sheets apply to individuals, too. **EXAMPLE** Marty Campbell graduated from college three years ago and obtained a position as a sales representative for an office supply firm. After going to work, he established a checking and savings account and purchased an automobile, stereo, television, and a few pieces of furniture. Marty paid cash for some purchases, but he had to borrow money to pay for the larger ones. Figure 15.1 shows Marty's current personal balance sheet.

Marty Campbell's assets total $26,500, and his liabilities amount to $10,000. While the difference between total assets and total liabilities is referred to as *owners' equity* or *stockholders' equity* for a business, it is normally called *net worth* for an individual. As

Marty Campbell
Personal Balance Sheet
December 31, 20XX

ASSETS		
Cash	$ 2,500	
Savings account	5,000	
Automobile	15,000	
Stereo	1,000	
Television	500	
Furniture	2,500	
TOTAL ASSETS		$26,500
LIABILITIES		
Automobile loan	$ 9,500	
Credit card balance	500	
TOTAL LIABILITIES		$10,000
NET WORTH (Owner's Equity)		16,500
TOTAL LIABILITIES AND NET WORTH		$26,500

FIGURE 15.1

Personal Balance Sheet

Even individuals can determine their net worth, or owner's equity, by subtracting the value of their debts from the value of their assets.

ENTREPRENEURIAL CHALLENGE

Open-Book Management

Why would an entrepreneur consider opening the company's financial details to all employees, a practice known as *open-book management*? Proponents say that it's a good way to show employees how their activities actually affect profit performance. However, not everyone is open to open-book management. Here are some of the advantages and disadvantages:

Advantages. Helping employees understand the company's finances can involve them more deeply in their jobs, encourage initiative, and foster closer cooperation. **EXAMPLE** At Ankrom Moisan Associated Architects, key financial data (except salaries) is available to employees as well as to other stakeholders. As a result, "it's a wildly

entrepreneurial place" that empowers people, says the firm's director of business development.

Disadvantages. "Full disclosure has its own degree of misunderstanding," notes the founder of a restaurant design firm, who believes that employees need education and training to understand a company's accounting data. Another potential problem: Employees may become overwhelmed by all the details or discouraged when they see profits dropping. Therefore, entrepreneurs should explain exactly what the numbers mean and what makes profits go up and down.

Sources: Based on information in Rachel Long, "Owner's Inc.," *Hospitality Design,* April 2006, p. 54; David Drickhamer, "By the Numbers," *Material Handling Management,* January 2006, pp. 229+.

ACE the Test
Hangman

reported on Marty's personal balance sheet, net worth is $16,500. The total assets ($26,500) and the total liabilities *plus* net worth ($26,500) are equal.

Figure 15.2 shows the balance sheet for Northeast Art Supply, a small corporation that sells picture frames, paints, canvases, and other artists' supplies to retailers in New England. Note that assets are reported at the top of the statement, followed by liabilities and stockholders' equity. Let's work through the different accounts in Figure 15.2 from top to bottom.

Assets

liquidity the ease with which an asset can be converted into cash

current assets assets that can be converted quickly into cash or that will be used in one year or less

On a balance sheet, assets are listed in order from the *most liquid* to the *least liquid.* The liquidity of an asset is the ease with which it can be converted into cash.

Current Assets Current assets are assets that can be converted quickly into cash or that will be used in one year or less. Because cash is the most liquid asset, it is listed

NORTHEAST ART SUPPLY, INC.

Balance Sheet
December 31, 20XX

ASSETS

Current assets

Cash		$ 59,000
Marketable securities		10,000
Accounts receivable	$ 40,000	
Less allowance for doubtful accounts	2,000	38,000
Notes receivable		32,000
Merchandise inventory		41,000
Prepaid expenses		2,000
Total current assets		**$182,000**

Fixed assets

Delivery equipment	$110,000	
Less accumulated depreciation	20,000	$ 90,000
Furniture and store equipment	62,000	
Less accumulated depreciation	15,000	47,000
Total fixed assets		137,000

Intangible assets

Patents	$ 6,000	
Goodwill	15,000	
Total intangible assets		21,000
TOTAL ASSETS		**$340,000**

LIABILITIES AND STOCKHOLDERS' EQUITY

Current liabilities

Accounts payable	$ 35,000	
Notes payable	25,675	
Salaries payable	4,000	
Taxes payable	5,325	
Total current liabilities		$ 70,000

Long-term liabilities

Mortgage payable on store equipment	$ 40,000	
Total long-term liabilities		$ 40,000
TOTAL LIABILITIES		$110,00

Stockholders' equity

Common stock	$150,000	
Retained earnings	80,000	
TOTAL OWNERS' EQUITY		$230,000
TOTAL LIABILITIES AND OWNERS' EQUITY		**$340,000**

FIGURE 15.2

Business Balance Sheet

A balance sheet summarizes a firm's accounts at the end of an accounting period, showing the various dollar amounts that enter into the accounting equation. Note that assets ($340,000) equal liabilities plus owners' equity ($340,000).

fixed assets assets that will be held or used for a period longer than one year

depreciation the process of apportioning the cost of a fixed asset over the period during which it will be used

Sometimes inventory is cute!

As part of their regular inventory process, employees at the Hanover, Germany zoo must count, weigh, and measure more than 2000 animals and 200 different species. In this photo, a zoo employee checks the length of a small neotropical animal named "Diego." For retailers, wholesalers, and manufacturers, inventory procedures are important to ensure that there is enough inventory for customers who want to purchase their products.

intangible assets assets that do not exist physically but that have a value based on the rights or privileges they confer on a firm

first. Next are *marketable securities*—stocks, bonds, and other investments—that can be converted into cash in a matter of days.

Next are the firm's receivables. Its *accounts receivables*, which result from allowing customers to make credit purchases, generally are paid within thirty to sixty days. However, the firm expects that some of these debts will not be collected. Thus it has reduced its accounts receivables by a 5 percent *allowance for doubtful accounts*. The firm's *notes receivables* are receivables for which customers have signed promissory notes. They generally are repaid over a longer period of time than the firm's accounts receivables.

Northeast's *merchandise inventory* represents the value of goods on hand for sale to customers. Since Northeast Art Supply is a wholesale operation, the inventory listed in Figure 15.2 represents finished goods ready for sale to retailers. For a manufacturing firm, merchandise inventory also may represent raw materials that will become part of a finished product or work that has been partially completed but requires further processing.

Northeast's last current asset is *prepaid expenses*, which are assets that have been paid for in advance but have not yet been used. An example is insurance premiums. They are usually paid at the beginning of the policy year. The unused portion (say, for the last four months of the time period covered by the policy) is a prepaid expense. For Northeast Art, all current assets total $182,000.

Fixed Assets Fixed assets are assets that will be held or used for a period longer than one year. They generally include land, buildings, and equipment used in the continuing operation of the business. Although Northeast owns no land or buildings, it does own *delivery equipment* that originally cost $110,000. It also owns *furniture and store equipment* that originally cost $62,000.

Note that the values of both fixed assets are decreased by their *accumulated depreciation*. Depreciation is the process of apportioning the cost of a fixed asset over the period during which it will be used, that is, its useful life. The depreciation amount allotted to each year is an expense for that year, and the value of the asset must be reduced by the amount of depreciation expense. Although the actual method used to calculate the dollar amounts for depreciation expense reported on a firm's financial statements are beyond the scope of this text, you should know that there are a number of different methods that can be used. In the case of Northeast's delivery equipment, $20,000 of its value has been depreciated (or used up) since it was purchased. Its value at this time is thus $110,000 less $20,000, or $90,000. In a similar fashion, the original value of furniture and store equipment ($62,000) has been reduced by depreciation totaling $15,000. Furniture and store equipment now has a reported value of $47,000. For Northeast Art, all fixed assets total $137,000.

Intangible Assets Intangible assets are assets that do not exist physically but that have a value based on the rights or privileges they confer on a firm. They include patents, copyrights, trademarks, franchises, and goodwill. By their nature, intangible assets are of value to the firm for a number of years.

Northeast Art Supply lists two intangible assets. The first is a *patent* for a special oil paint that the company purchased from the inventor. The firm's accountants estimate that the patent has a current market value of $6,000. The second intangible asset, *goodwill,* is the value of a firm's reputation, location, earning capacity, and other intangibles that make the business a profitable concern. Goodwill normally is not listed on a balance sheet unless the firm has been purchased from previous owners. In such a case, the new owners actually have paid an additional amount over and above the fair market value of the firm's assets for goodwill. Goodwill exists because most businesses are worth more as going concerns than as a collection of assets. Northeast Art's accountants included a $15,000 amount for goodwill. The firm's intangible assets total $21,000. Now it is possible to total all three types of assets for Northeast Art. As calculated in Figure 15.2, total assets are $340,000.

Liabilities and Owners' Equity

The liabilities and the owners' equity accounts complete the balance sheet. The firm's liabilities are separated into two categories—current and long term.

Current Liabilities A firm's current liabilities are debts that will be repaid in one year or less. For Northeast Art Supply, current liabilities include

* *Accounts payable*—short-term obligations that result from a firm making credit purchases.
* *Notes payable*—obligations that have been secured with promissory notes. Only the obligations that must be paid within the year are listed under current liabilities.
* *Salaries payable*—payroll expense that has been incurred during the current accounting period but will be paid in the next accounting period.
* *Taxes payable*—tax obligations that have been incurred during the current accounting period but will be paid in the next accounting period.

As shown in Figure 15.2, current liabilities for Northeast Art Supply total $70,000.

Long-Term Liabilities Long-term liabilities are debts that need not be repaid for at least one year. Northeast lists only one long-term liability—a $40,000 *mortgage payable* for store equipment. Loans and other long-term obligations would be included here as well, if they existed. As you can see in Figure 15.2, Northeast's current and long-term liabilities total $110,000.

Owners' or Stockholders' Equity For a sole proprietorship or partnership, the owners' equity is shown as the difference between assets and liabilities. In a partnership, each partner's share of the ownership is reported separately in each owner's name. For a corporation, the owners' equity usually is referred to as *stockholders' equity.* The dollar amount reported on the balance sheet is the total value of stock plus retained earnings that have accumulated to date. Retained earnings are the portion of a business's profits not distributed to stockholders.

CONCEPT CHECK
How are current assets distinguished from fixed assets? Why are fixed assets depreciated on a balance sheet?

current liabilities debts that will be repaid in one year or less

long-term liabilities debts that need not be repaid for at least one year

retained earnings the portion of a business's profits not distributed to stockholders

The original investment by the owners of Northeast Art Supply was $150,000. In addition, $80,000 of Northeast's earnings have been reinvested in the business since it was founded. Thus owners' equity totals $230,000.

As the two grand totals in Figure 15.2 show, Northeast's assets and the sum of its liabilities and owners' equity are equal—at $340,000. The accounting equation (assets = liabilities + owners' equity) is still in balance.

TEST PREPPER 15.4

True or False?

___ 1. A balance sheet can be constructed for an individual or a company.

___ 2. Patents, copyrights, trademarks, franchises, and goodwill are all examples of intangible assets.

___ 3. For a sole proprietorship or partnership, the owners' equity is shown as the difference between assets and liabilities.

Multiple Choice

___ 4. Accounts receivables will be listed under

    a. current liabilities.
    b. fixed liabilities.
    c. current assets.
    d. fixed assets.
    e. owners' equity.

___ 5. Accounts payable would be listed under

    a. current assets.
    b. current liabilities.
    c. long-term liabilities.
    d. owners' equity.
    e. fixed assets.

ACE the Test
ACE & ACE+
Practice Test 15.4

The Income Statement

Learning Objective 5

Read and interpret an income statement.

income statement a summary of a firm's revenues and expenses during a specified accounting period

revenues the dollar amounts earned by a firm from selling goods, providing services, or performing business activities

gross sales the total dollar amount of all goods and services sold during the accounting period

Question: Where can you find the profit or loss amount for The Gap, Inc.?

Answer: The firm's income statement.

An **income statement** is a summary of a firm's revenues and expenses during a specified accounting period—one month, three months, six months, or a year. The income statement is sometimes called the *earnings statement* or the *statement of income and expenses*. Let's begin our discussion by constructing a personal income statement for Marty Campbell. **EXAMPLE** Having worked as a sales representative for an office supply firm for the past three years, Marty now earns $33,600 a year, or $2,800 a month. After deductions, his take-home pay is $1,900 a month. As illustrated in Figure 15.3, Marty's typical monthly expenses include payments for an automobile loan, credit-card purchases, apartment rent, utilities, food, clothing, and recreation and entertainment.

While the difference between income and expenses is referred to as *profit* or *loss* for a business, it is normally referred to as a *cash surplus* or *cash deficit* for an individual.

Fortunately for Marty, he has a surplus of $250 at the end of each month. He can use this surplus for savings, investing, or paying off debts.

Figure 15.4 shows the income statement for Northeast Art Supply. Generally, revenues *less* cost of goods sold *less* operating expenses equals net income.

Revenues

Revenues are the dollar amounts earned by a firm from selling goods, providing services, or performing business activities. Like most businesses, Northeast Art obtains its revenues solely from the sale of its products or services. The revenues section of its income statement begins with gross sales. Gross sales are the total dollar amount of all goods and services sold during the accounting period. From this amount are deducted the dollar amounts of

* *Sales returns*—merchandise returned to the firm by its customers

* *Sales allowances*—price reductions offered to customers who accept slightly damaged or soiled merchandise

* *Sales discounts*—price reductions offered to customers who pay their bills promptly

The remainder is the firm's net sales. Net sales are the actual dollar amounts received by the firm for the goods and services it has sold after adjustment for returns, allowances, and discounts. For Northeast Art, net sales are $451,000.

Cost of Goods Sold

The standard method of determining the cost of goods sold by a retailing or wholesaling firm can be summarized as follows:

Cost of goods sold = beginning inventory + net purchases − ending inventory

A manufacturer must include raw materials inventories, work in progress, and direct manufacturing costs in this computation.

According to Figure 15.4, Northeast began its accounting period on January 1 with a merchandise inventory that cost $40,000. During the next twelve months, the firm purchased merchandise valued at $346,000. After taking advantage of *purchase discounts*, however, it paid only $335,000 for this merchandise. Thus, during the year, Northeast had total *goods available for sale* valued at $40,000 plus $335,000, or $375,000.

Twelve months later, at the end of the accounting period on December 31, Northeast had sold all but $41,000 worth of the available goods. The cost of goods sold by Northeast therefore was $375,000 less ending inventory of $41,000, or $334,000. It is now possible to calculate gross profit. A firm's gross profit is its net sales *less* the cost of goods sold. For Northeast, gross profit was $117,000.

Marty Campbell
Personal Income Statement
For the month ended December 31, 20XX

INCOME (Take-home pay)		$1,900
LESS MONTHLY EXPENSES		
Automobile loan	$ 250	
Credit card payment	100	
Apartment rent	500	
Utilities	200	
Food	250	
Clothing	100	
Recreation & entertainment	250	
TOTAL MONTHLY EXPENSES		1,650
CASH SURPLUS (or profit)		$ 250

FIGURE 15.3

Personal Income Statement

By subtracting expenses from income, anyone can construct a personal income statement and determine if they have a surplus or deficit at the end of the month.

net sales the actual dollar amounts received by a firm for the goods and services it has sold after adjustment for returns, allowances, and discounts

cost of goods sold the dollar amount equal to beginning inventory *plus* net purchases *less* ending inventory

gross profit a firm's net sales *less* the cost of goods sold

FIGURE 15.4

Business Income Statement

An income statement summarizes a firm's revenues and expenses during a specified accounting period. For Northeast Art, net income after taxes is $30,175.

CONCEPT CHECK

How does a firm determine its net income after taxes?

NORTHEAST ART SUPPLY, INC.

Income Statement
For the Year Ended
December 31, 20XX

Revenues			
Gross sales		$465,000	
Less sales returns and allowances	$ 9,500		
Less sales discounts	4,500	14,000	
Net sales			$451,000
Cost of goods sold			
Beginning inventory, January 1, 20XX		$ 40,000	
Purchases	$346,000		
Less purchase discounts	11,000		
Net purchases		335,000	
Cost of goods available for sale		$375,000	
Less ending inventory December 31, 20XX		41,000	
Cost of goods sold			334,000
Gross profit			$117,000
Operating expenses			
Selling expenses			
Sales salaries	$ 22,000		
Advertising	4,000		
Sales promotion	2,500		
Depreciation—store equipment	3,000		
Depreciation—delivery equipment	4,000		
Miscellaneous selling expenses	1,500		
Total selling expenses		$ 37,000	
General expenses			
Office salaries	$ 28,500		
Rent	8,500		
Depreciation—office furniture	1,500		
Utilities expense	2,500		
Insurance expense	1,000		
Miscellaneous expense	500		
Total general expense		42,500	
Total operating expenses			$ 79,500
Net income from operations			$ 37,500
Less interest expense			2,000
NET INCOME BEFORE TAXES			$ 35,500
Less federal income taxes			5,325
NET INCOME AFTER TAXES			$ 30,175

Operating Expenses

A firm's operating expenses are all business costs other than the cost of goods sold. Total operating expenses generally are divided into two categories: selling expenses or general expenses.

Selling expenses are costs related to the firm's marketing activities. For Northeast Art, selling expenses total $37,000. *General expenses* are costs incurred in managing a business. For Northeast Art, general expenses total $42,500. Now it is possible to

operating expenses all business costs other than the cost of goods sold

total both selling and general expenses. As Figure 15.4 shows, total operating expenses for the accounting period are $79,500.

Net Income

When revenues exceed expenses, the difference is called **net income**. When expenses exceed revenues, the difference is called **net loss**. As Figure 15.4 shows, Northeast Art's *net income from operations* is computed as gross profit ($117,000) *less* total operating expenses ($79,500). For Northeast Art, net income from operations is $37,500. From this amount, *interest expense* of $2,000 is deducted to obtain a *net income before taxes* of $35,500. The interest expense is deducted in this section of the income statement because it is not an operating expense. Rather, it is an expense that results from financing the business.

Northeast's *federal income taxes* are $5,325. Although these taxes may or may not be payable immediately, they are definitely an expense that must be deducted from income. This leaves Northeast Art with a *net income after taxes* of $30,175. This amount may be used to pay a dividend to stockholders, it may be retained or reinvested in the firm, it may be used to reduce the firm's debts, or all three.

Sometimes a firm must spend money to make money.

The cost of this advertisement for eebee's Adventures—a series of DVDs to help infants learn—is reported on the firm's income statement as a marketing expense. Marketing expenses—along with all other expenses are deducted from sales revenue to determine if a firm earns a profit during a specific accounting period.

TEST PREPPER 15.5

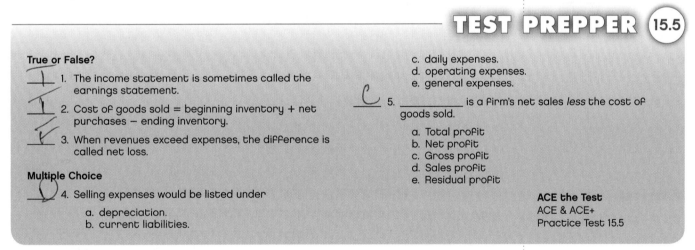

True or False?

T 1. The income statement is sometimes called the earnings statement.

T 2. Cost of goods sold = beginning inventory + net purchases − ending inventory.

F 3. When revenues exceed expenses, the difference is called net loss.

Multiple Choice

D 4. Selling expenses would be listed under

    a. depreciation.
    b. current liabilities.
    c. daily expenses.
    d. operating expenses.
    e. general expenses.

C 5. _____ is a firm's net sales *less* the cost of goods sold.

    a. Total profit
    b. Net profit
    c. Gross profit
    d. Sales profit
    e. Residual profit

ACE the Test
ACE & ACE+
Practice Test 15.5

The Statement of Cash Flows

Learning Objective 6

Describe business activities that affect a firm's cash flow.

net income occurs when revenues exceed expenses

net loss occurs when expenses exceed revenues

Cash is the lifeblood of any business. In 1987, the SEC and the Financial Accounting Standards Board required all publicly traded companies to include a statement of

FIGURE 15.5

Statement of Cash Flows

A statement of cash flows summarizes how a firm's operating, investing, and financing activities affect its cash during a specified period—one month, three months, six months, or a year. For Northeast Art, the amount of cash at the end of the year reported on the statement of cash flows is $59,000—the same amount reported for the cash account on the firm's balance sheet.

NORTHEAST ART SUPPLY, INC.

Statement of Cash Flows
For the Year Ended
December 31, 20XX

Cash flows from operating activities

Cash received from customers	$ 451,000	
Cash paid to suppliers and employees	(385,500)	
Interest paid	(2,000)	
Income taxes paid	(5,325)	
Net cash provided by operating activities		$ 58,175

Cash flows from investing activities

Purchase of equipment	$(2,000)	
Purchase of investments	(10,000)	
Sale of investments	10,000	
Net cash provided by investing activities		$(2,000)

Cash flows from financing activities

Payment of short-term debt	$(9,000)	
Payment of long-term debt	(17,000)	
Payment of dividends	(15,000)	
Net cash provided by financing activities		$(41,000)
NET INCREASE (DECREASE) IN CASH		$ 15,175
Cash at beginning of year		43,825
CASH AT END OF YEAR		$ 59,000

statement of cash flows
a statement that illustrates how the operating, investing, and financing activities of a company affect cash during an accounting period

cash flows along with their balance sheet and income statement in their annual report. The **statement of cash flows** illustrates how the operating, investing, and financing activities of a company affect cash during an accounting period. A statement of cash flows for Northeast Art Supply is illustrated in Figure 15.5. It provides information concerning the company's cash receipts and cash payments and is organized around three different activities: operations, investing, and financing.

* *Cash flows from operating activities.* This is the first section of a statement of cash flows. It addresses the firm's primary revenue source—providing goods and services. The amounts paid to suppliers, employees, interest, taxes, and other expenses are deducted from the amount received from customers. Finally, the interest and dividends received by the firm are added to determine the total. After all adjustments are made, the total represents a true picture of cash flows from operating activities.

* *Cash flows from investing activities.* The second section of the statement is concerned with cash flow from investments. This includes the purchase and sale of land, equipment, and other assets and investments.

※ *Cash flows from financing activities.* The third and final section deals with the cash flow from all financing activities. It reports changes in debt obligation and owners' equity accounts. This includes loans and repayments, the sale and repurchase of the company's own stock, and cash dividends.

The totals of all three activities are added to the beginning cash balance to determine the ending cash balance. For Northeast Art Supply, the ending cash balance is $59,000. Note that this is the same dollar amount reported for the cash account on the firm's balance sheet. Together the cash flow statement, balance sheet, and income statement illustrate the results of past business decisions and reflect the firm's ability to pay debts and dividends and to finance new growth.

Evaluating Financial Statements

Learning Objective 7
Summarize how managers evaluate the financial health of a business.

All three financial statements—the balance sheet, the income statement, and the statement of cash flows—can provide answers to a variety of questions about

* A firm's ability to do business and stay in business
* Its profitability
* Its value as an investment
* Its ability to repay its debts
* Its present financial statements compared with those prepared for past accounting periods

Using Annual Reports to Compare Data for Different Accounting Periods

In addition to providing printed annual reports to stockholders and other interested parties, it is possible to view a firm's annual report by accessing the company's website. Typically, an annual report contains a great deal of information about the company, its operations, current financial statements, and its past and current financial health. The following five suggestions can help you to get to the "bottom line" of a corporation's annual report:

1. Look at the firm's income statement to determine whether the company is profitable or not.
2. Read the letters from the chairman of the board and chief executive officer (CEO) that describe the corporation's operations, prospects for the future, new products or services, financial strengths, *and* any potential problems.

What's so big about GE?

To answer that question, look at General Electric's "BIG" annual report. For investors, an annual report provides a great deal of information about the company, its operations, and its current financial statements. General Electric's annual report is yet another tool that can be used to showcase how the company continues to earn profits, as well as the respect of customers, employees, and investors.

3. Compare the corporation's current income statement and balance sheet with previous financial statements. Look at trends for sales, expenses, profits or losses, assets, liabilities, and owners' equity.

4. Examine the footnotes closely, and look for red flags that may be in the fine print. Often the footnotes contain (and sometimes hide) important information about the company and its finances.

5. Learn how to calculate financial ratios, and determine how they may predict a change in the firm's financial condition. Some of the most important financial ratios are discussed in the last part of this section.

Comparing Data with Other Firms' Data

Many firms also compare their financial results with those of competing firms and with industry averages. Comparisons are possible as long as accountants follow generally accepted accounting principles.

Comparisons among firms give managers a general idea of a firm's relative effectiveness and its standing within the industry. Competitors' financial statements can be obtained from their annual reports—if they are public corporations. **EXAMPLE** Industry averages are published by reporting services such as D&B (formerly Dun & Bradstreet) and Standard & Poor's, as well as by some industry trade associations.

Financial Ratios

Still another type of analysis of a firm's financial health involves computation of financial ratios. A **financial ratio** is a number that shows the relationship between two elements of a firm's financial statements. Among the most useful ratios are *profitability ratios, short-term financial ratios, activity ratios,* and the *debt-to-owners'-equity ratio.* Like the individual elements in financial statements, these ratios can be compared with the firm's past ratios, with those of competitors, and with industry averages. The information required to form these ratios is found in a firm's balance sheet and income statement (in our examples for Northeast Art Supply, Figures 15.2 and 15.4).

CONCEPT CHECK

Do the balance sheet, income statement, and statement of cash flows contain all of the information you might want as a potential lender or stockholder? What other information would you like to examine?

financial ratio a number that shows the relationship between two elements of a firm's financial statements

FIGURE 15.6

Comparisons of Present and Past Financial Statements for Microsoft Corporation

Most corporations include in their annual reports comparisons of the important elements of their financial statements for recent years.

Source: Adapted from the Microsoft Corporation 2006 and 2005 Annual Reports, **www.microsoft.com,** November 14, 2006. December 3, 2005.

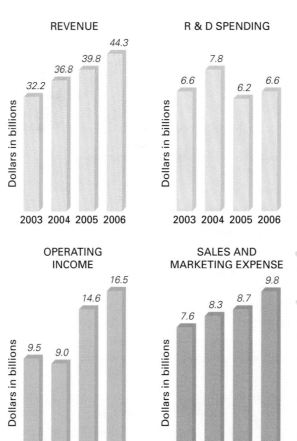

Profitability Ratios

A firm's net income after taxes indicates whether the firm is profitable. It does not, however, indicate how effectively the firm's resources are being used. For this latter purpose, three ratios can be computed.

Return on Sales *Return on sales*, sometimes called *profit margin*, is a financial ratio calculated by dividing net income after taxes by net sales. For Northeast Art Supply,

$$\text{Return on sales} = \frac{\text{net income after taxes}}{\text{net sales}} = \frac{\$30,175}{\$451,000}$$

$$= 0.067, \text{ or } 6.7 \text{ percent}$$

The return on sales indicates how effectively the firm is transforming sales into profits. A higher return on sales is better than a low one. Today, the average return on sales for all business firms is between 4 and 5 percent. With a return on sales of 6.7 percent, Northeast Art Supply is above average. A low return on sales can be increased by reducing expenses, increasing sales, or both.

Return on Owners' Equity *Return on owners' equity* is a financial ratio calculated by dividing net income after taxes by owners' equity. For Northeast Art Supply,

$$\text{Return on owners' equity} = \frac{\text{net income after taxes}}{\text{owners' equity}} = \frac{\$30,175}{\$230,000}$$

$$= 0.13, \text{ or } 13 \text{ percent}$$

Return on owners' equity indicates how much income is generated by each dollar of equity. Northeast is providing income of 13 cents per dollar invested in the business. The average for all businesses is between 12 and 15 cents. A higher return on owners' equity is better than a low one, and the only practical ways to increase return on owners' equity is to reduce expenses, increase sales, or both.

Earnings per Share From the point of view of stockholders, *earnings per share* is one of the best indicators of a corporation's success. It is calculated by dividing net income after taxes by the number of shares of common stock outstanding. If we assume that Northeast Art Supply has issued 25,000 shares of stock, then its earnings per share are

$$\text{Earnings per share} = \frac{\text{net income after taxes}}{\text{common stock shares outstanding}} = \frac{\$30,175}{25,000}$$

$$= \$1.21 \text{ per share}$$

There is no meaningful average for this ratio mainly because the number of outstanding shares of a firm's stock is subject to change as a result of stock splits and stock dividends. Also, some corporations choose to issue more stock than others. As a general rule, however, an increase in earnings per share is a healthy sign for any corporation.

Short-Term Financial Ratios

Two short-term financial ratios permit managers (and lenders) to evaluate the ability of a firm to pay its current liabilities. Before we discuss these ratios, we should examine one other easily determined measure: working capital.

Working Capital *Working capital* is the difference between current assets and current liabilities. For Northeast Art Supply,

Current assets	$182,000
Less current liabilities	$ 70,000
Equals working capital	$112,000

Working capital indicates how much would remain if a firm paid off all current liabilities with cash and other current assets. The "proper" amount of working capital depends on the type of firm, its past experience, and its particular industry. A firm with too little working capital may have to borrow money to finance its operations.

Current Ratio A firm's *current ratio* is computed by dividing current assets by current liabilities. For Northeast Art Supply,

$$\text{Current ratio} = \frac{\text{current assets}}{\text{current liabilities}} = \frac{\$182,000}{\$70,000} = 2.6$$

This means that Northeast Art Supply has $2.60 of current assets for every $1 of current liabilities. The average current ratio for all industries is 2.0, but it varies greatly from industry to industry. A high current ratio indicates that a firm can pay its current liabilities. A low current ratio can be improved by repaying current liabilities, by reducing dividend payments to increase the firm's cash balance, or by obtaining additional cash from investors.

Acid-Test Ratio This ratio, sometimes called the *quick ratio*, is a measure of the firm's ability to pay current liabilities *quickly*—with its cash, marketable securities, and receivables. The *acid-test ratio* is calculated by adding cash, marketable securities, and receivables and dividing the total by current liabilities. The value of inventory and other current assets is "removed" from current assets because these assets are not converted into cash as easily as cash, marketable securities, and receivables. For Northeast Art Supply,

$$\text{Acid-test ratio} = \frac{\text{cash + marketable securities + receivables}}{\text{current liabilities}} = \frac{\$139,000}{\$70,000} = 1.99$$

For all businesses, the desired acid-test ratio is 1.0. Northeast Art Supply is above average with a ratio of 1.99, and the firm should be well able to pay its current liabilities. To increase a low acid-test ratio, a firm would have to repay current liabilities, reduce dividend payments to increase the firm's cash balance, or obtain additional cash from investors.

Activity Ratios

Two activity ratios permit managers to measure how many times each year a company collects its accounts receivables or sells its inventory.

Accounts Receivable Turnover A firm's *accounts receivable turnover* is the number of times the firm collects its accounts receivable in one year. If the data are available, this ratio should be calculated using a firm's net credit sales. Since data for Northeast Art Supply's credit sales are unavailable, this ratio can be calculated by dividing net sales by accounts receivable. For Northeast Art Supply,

$$\text{Accounts receivable turnover} = \frac{\text{net sales}}{\text{accounts receivable}} = \frac{\$451,000}{\$38,000}$$
$$= 11.9 \text{ times per year}$$

Northeast Art Supply collects its accounts receivables 11.9 times each year, or about every thirty days. If a firm's credit terms require customers to pay in twenty-five days, a collection period of thirty days is considered acceptable. There is no meaningful average for this measure mainly because credit terms differ among companies. A high accounts receivable turnover is better than a low one. As a general rule, a low accounts receivable turnover ratio can be improved by pressing for payment of past-due accounts and by tightening requirements for prospective credit customers.

Inventory Turnover A firm's *inventory turnover* is the number of times the firm sells its merchandise inventory in one year. It is approximated by dividing the cost of goods sold in one year by the average value of the inventory.

The average value of the inventory can be found by adding the beginning inventory value and the ending inventory value (given on the income statement) and dividing the sum by 2. For Northeast Art Supply, average inventory is $40,500. Thus

$$\text{Inventory turnover} = \frac{\text{cost of goods sold}}{\text{average inventory}} = \frac{\$334,000}{\$40,500}$$
$$= 8.2 \text{ times per year}$$

Northeast Art Supply sells its merchandise inventory 8.2 times each year, or about once every forty-five days. The average inventory turnover for all firms is about 9 times per year, but turnover rates vary widely from industry to industry. For example, supermarkets may have turnover rates of 20 or higher, whereas turnover rates for furniture stores are generally well below the national average. The quickest way to improve inventory turnover is to order merchandise in smaller quantities at more frequent intervals.

Debt-to-Owners'-Equity Ratio

Our final category of financial ratios indicates the degree to which a firm's operations are financed through borrowing. Although other ratios can be calculated, the debt-to-owners'-equity ratio is used often to determine whether a firm has too much debt. The debt-to-owners'-equity ratio is calculated by dividing total liabilities by owners' equity. For Northeast Art Supply,

$$\text{Debt-to-owners' equity ratio} = \frac{\text{total liabilities}}{\text{owners' equity}} = \frac{\$110,000}{\$230,000}$$
$$= 0.48, \text{ or } 48 \text{ percent}$$

A debt-to-owners'-equity ratio of 48 percent means that creditors have provided about 48 cents of financing for every dollar provided by the owners. The higher this ratio, the riskier the situation is for lenders. A high debt-to-owners'-equity ratio may make borrowing additional money from lenders difficult. It can be reduced by paying off debts or by increasing the owners' investment in the firm.

Northeast's Financial Ratios: A Summary

Table 15.2 compares the financial ratios of Northeast Art Supply with the average financial ratios for all businesses. It also lists the formulas we used to calculate Northeast's ratios. Northeast seems to be in good financial shape. Its return on sales, current ratio, and acid-test ratio are all above average. Its other ratios are

RATIO	FORMULA	NORTHEAST RATIO	AVERAGE BUSINESS RATIO	DIRECTION FOR IMPROVEMENT
Profitability Ratios				
Return on sales	net income after taxes / net sales	6.7%	4–5%	Higher
Return on owners' equity	net income after taxes / owners' equity	13%	12–15%	Higher
Earnings per share	net income after taxes / common stock shares outstanding	$1.21 per share	—	Higher
Short-Term Financial Ratios				
Working capital	current assets − current liabilities	$112,000	—	Higher
Current ratio	current assets / current liabilities	2.6	2.0	Higher
Acid-test ratio	cash + marketable securities + receivables / current liabilities	1.99	1.0	Higher
Activity Ratios				
Accounts receivable turnover	net sales / accounts receivable	11.9	—	Higher
Inventory turnover	cost of goods sold / average inventory	8.2	9	Higher
Debt-to-owners' ~~equity ratio~~ *leverage*	total liabilities / owners' equity	48 percent	—	Lower

---

TABLE 15.2

Financial Ratios of Northeast Art Supply Compared with Average Ratios for All Businesses

about average, although its inventory turnover and debt-to-equity ratio could be improved.

This chapter ends our discussion of accounting information. In Chapter 16 we see why firms need financing, how they obtain it, and how they ensure that funds are used efficiently, in keeping with their organizational objectives.

TEST PREPPER

True or False?

 1. Cash flows from operating activities is the first section of a statement of cash flows.

2. Working capital is the difference between current assets and long-term liabilities.

3. A debt-to-owners'-equity ratio of 35 percent means that lenders have provided about 35 cents of financing for every dollar provided by the owners.

Multiple Choice

 4. Return-on-sales, return-on-equity, and earnings-per-share ratios can tell us

a. the future stock price of a company.
b. the overall financial health of a company.
c. employee effectiveness.
d. the net income potential.
e. how effectively a firm's resources are being used.

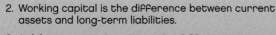 5. The inventory turnover of a furniture store compared with a supermarket would be

a. higher.
b. lower.
c. the same.
d. higher if the store is in a high-traffic area.
e. dependent on the state of the economy.

ACE the Test
ACE & ACE+
Practice Test 15.6, 15.7

Prepare for Class
CL News Feeds
CL News Now

→ **RETURN TO INSIDE BUSINESS**

Laws such as the Sarbanes-Oxley Act require top executives to certify that the data in the company's financial reports are accurate and complete. Even though an annual report must contain specific financial data, it can still be fascinating as well as factual. A growing number of corporations are posting eye-catching, interactive annual reports on the web for anyone to click on and read.

In fact, NewAlliance Bancshares of New Haven, Connecticut, has noticed so much interest in its online annual report that the company now produces fewer printed copies. Printed reports aren't going away anytime soon, but "the time for the wired, living annual report has arrived," says public relations expert Leslie Gaines-Ross. You can see a variety of online annual reports on sites such as **annualreports.com.**

Questions

1. How much weight should lenders and stockholders give to management's discussion of the financial data in an annual report? Explain your answer.
2. Some companies say that employees or customers are their most important asset. Do you think that a company should mention employees or customers as intangible assets in its annual report? Why?

LEARNING OBJECTIVES REVIEW

1 Explain why accurate accounting information and audited financial statements are important.

- Accounting is the process of systematically collecting, analyzing, and reporting financial information.
- A firm's accountants and its accounting system often translate goals, objectives, and plans into dollars and cents to help determine if a decision or plan of action makes "financial sense."
- A large number of accounting scandals have caused people to doubt not only the financial information reported by a corporation but also the accounting industry.
- The purpose of an audit is to make sure that a firm's financial statements have been prepared in accordance with generally accepted accounting principles (GAAPs).
- To help ensure that corporate financial information is accurate and in response to the many accounting scandals that surfaced in the last part of the 1990s and the first part of the twenty-first century, the Sarbanes-Oxley Act was signed into law.

2 Identify the people who use accounting information and possible careers in the accounting industry.

- To be successful in the accounting industry, employees must be responsible, honest, and ethical; have a strong background in financial management; know how to use a computer and software to process data into accounting information; and be able communicate with people who need accounting information.
- Primarily, management uses accounting information, but it is also demanded by lenders, suppliers, stockholders, potential investors, and government agencies.
- While many people think that all accountants do the same tasks, there are special areas of expertise, including managerial, financial, cost, tax, government, and not-for-profit accounting.
- A private accountant is employed by a specific organization to operate its accounting system.
- A public accountant performs these functions for various individuals or firms on a fee basis. Most accounting firms include on their staffs at least

one certified public accountant (CPA). In addition to CPAs, there are also certified management accountants (CMAs).

3 Discuss the accounting process.

- The accounting process is based on the accounting equation: Assets = liabilities + owners' equity.
- The accounting process involves five steps:
  - Source documents are analyzed.
  - Each transaction is recorded in a journal.
  - Each journal entry is posted in the appropriate general ledger accounts.
  - At the end of each accounting period, a trial balance is prepared to make sure that the accounting equation is in balance.
  - Financial statements are prepared from the trial balance and the books are closed for the accounting period.
- A firm's financial statements are included in its annual report. An annual report is a report distributed to stockholders and other interested parties that describes a firm's operating activities and its financial condition.

4 Read and interpret a balance sheet.

- A balance sheet is a summary of a firm's assets, liabilities, and owners' equity accounts at the end of an accounting period.
- This statement must demonstrate that the accounting equation is in balance.
- On the balance sheet, assets are categorized as current, fixed, or intangible.
- Liabilities can be divided into current and long-term liabilities.
- For a sole proprietorship or partnership, owners' equity is shown as the difference between assets and liabilities.
- For a corporation, the owners' equity section reports the values of stock and retained earnings.

5 Read and interpret an income statement.

- An income statement is a summary of a firm's revenues and expenses during a specified accounting period.

- On the income statement, the company's gross profit is computed by subtracting the cost of goods sold from net sales.
- Operating expenses and interest expense then are deducted to compute net income before taxes. Finally, income taxes are deducted to obtain the firm's net income after taxes.

6 Describe business activities that affect a firm's cash flow.

- Since 1987, the Securities and Exchange Commission (SEC) and the Financial Accounting Standards Board (FASB) have required all publicly traded companies to include a statement of cash flows in their annual reports.
- The cash-flow statement illustrates how the operating, investing, and financing activities of a company affect cash during an accounting period.
- Together the cash-flow statement, balance sheet, and income statement illustrate the results of past decisions and the business's ability to pay debts and dividends and to finance new growth.

7 Summarize how managers evaluate the financial health of a business.

- A firm's financial statements and its accounting information become more meaningful when compared with corresponding information for previous years, for competitors, and for the industry in which the firm operates.
- Such comparisons permit managers and other interested people to pick out trends in growth, borrowing, income, and other business variables and to determine whether the firm is on the way to accomplishing its long-term goals.
- A number of financial ratios can be computed from the information in a firm's financial statements.
- Like the information on the firm's financial statements, these ratios can and should be compared with those of past accounting periods, those of competitors, and those representing the average of the industry as a whole.

Improve Your Grade
Audio Chapter Summary & Quiz

VIDEO CASE

The Ethics of "Making the Numbers"

Will sales and profits meet the expectations of investors and Wall Street analysts? Managers at public corporations must answer this vitally important question quarter after quarter, year after year. In an ideal world—one in which the economy never contracts, expenses never go up, and customers never buy competing products—the corporation's share price would soar, and investors would cheer as every financial report showed ever-higher sales revenues, profit margins, and earnings.

In the real world, however, many uncontrollable and unpredictable factors can affect a corporation's performance. Customers may buy fewer units or postpone purchases, competitors may introduce superior products, energy costs and other expenses may rise, interest rates may climb, and buying power may plummet. Faced with the prospect of releasing financial results that fall short of Wall Street's expectations, managers may feel intense pressure to "make the numbers" using a variety of accounting techniques.

For example, some executives at WorldCom made earnings look better by booking billions of dollars in ordinary expenses as capital investments. The company was forced into bankruptcy a few weeks after the accounting scam was exposed. As another example, top managers at the drug retailer Rite Aid posted transactions improperly to inflate corporate earnings. Ultimately, Rite Aid had to lower its earnings figures by $1.6 billion, and investors fled, driving the share price down.

Under the Sarbanes-Oxley Act, the CEO and CFO now must certify the corporation's financial reports. This has led hundreds of companies to restate their earnings in recent years, a sign that stricter controls on accounting practices are having the intended effect. "I don't mean to sugarcoat the figure on restatements," says Steve Odland, CEO of Office Depot, "but I think it is positive—it shows a healthy system." Yet not all earnings restatements are due to accounting irregularities. "The general impression of the public is that accounting rules are black and white," Odland adds. "They are often anything but that, and in many instances the changes in earnings came after new interpretations by the chief accountant of the SEC."

Because accounting rules are open to interpretation, managers sometimes find themselves facing ethical dilemmas when a corporation feels pressure to live up to Wall Street's expectations. Consider the hypothetical situation at Commodore Appliances, a fictional company that sells to Home Depot, Lowe's, and other major retail chains. Margaret, the vice president of sales, has told Rob, a district manager, that the company's sales are down 10 percent in the current quarter. She points out that sales in Rob's district are down 20 percent and states that higher-level managers want him to improve this month's figures using "book and hold," which means recording future sales transactions in the current period.

Rob hesitates, saying that the company is gaining market share and that he needs more time to get sales momentum going. He thinks "book and hold" is not good business practice, even if it is legal. Margaret hints that Rob will lose his job if his sales figures don't look better and stresses that he will need the book-and-hold approach for one month only. Rob realizes that if he doesn't go along, he won't be working at Commodore for very much longer.

Meeting with Kevin, one of Commodore's auditors, Rob learns that book and hold meets generally accepted accounting principles. Kevin emphasizes that customers must be willing to take title to the goods before they're delivered or billed. Any book-and-hold sales must be real, backed by documentation such as e-mails to and from buyers, and the transactions must be completed in the near future.

Rob is at a crossroads: His sales figures must be higher if Commodore is to achieve its performance targets, yet he doesn't know exactly when (or if) he actually would complete any book-and-hold sales he might report this month. He doesn't want to mislead anyone, but he also doesn't want to lose his job or put other people's jobs in jeopardy by refusing to do what he is being asked to do. Rob is confident that he can improve his district's sales over the long term. On the other hand, Commodore's executives can't wait—they are pressuring Rob to make the sales figures look better right now. What should he do?[11]

For more information about the Sarbanes-Oxley Act, go to **www.aicpa.org.** This is the website for the American Institute of Certified Public Accountants and is a good source of information about the act.

Questions

1. What are the ethical and legal implications of using accounting practices such as the book-and-hold technique to inflate earnings?

2. Why would Commodore's auditor insist that Rob document any sales booked under the book-and-hold technique?

3. If you were in Rob's situation, would you agree to use the book-and-hold technique this month? Justify your decision.

4. Imagine that Commodore has taken out a multimillion-dollar loan that must be repaid next year. How might the lender react if it learned that Commodore was using the book-and-hold method to make revenues look higher than they really are?

BUILDING SKILLS FOR CAREER SUCCESS

1. Exploring the Internet

To those unacquainted with current activities and practices in larger accounting firms, there is often some surprise at just how varied the accounting work involved actually is. Although setting up and maintaining accounting software for clients are standard, accounting firms also can provide a wide range of specialized services. For example, research into mergers or acquisitions of other firms, investment advice, and solutions to financial problems are now common strategies for revenue growth within accounting firms. Most websites for large accounting firms also post information about current employment opportunities.

Assignment

1. Visit the website of a major accounting firm such as Deloitte Touche Tohmatsu (**www .deloitte.com**), KPMG (**www.kpmg.com**), PricewaterhouseCoopers (**www.pwc.com**), or Ernst & Young (**www.ey.com**). Describe in general terms how the website is used to communicate with clients and prospective clients. Visit the text website for updates to this exercise.

2. What are some of the content items presented on the site? What do these tell you about the firm and its clients?

3. Search the site for career information. Often the firm will post descriptions of employment opportunities along with educational and experience requirements. Describe what you find.

2. Building Team Skills

This has been a bad year for Miami-based Park Avenue Furniture. The firm increased sales revenues to $1,400,000, but total expenses ballooned to $1,750,000. Although management realized that some of the firm's expenses were out of control, including cost of goods sold ($700,000), salaries ($450,000), and advertising costs ($140,000), it could not contain expenses. As a result, the furniture retailer lost $350,000. To make matters worse, the retailer applied for a $350,000 loan at Fidelity National Bank and was turned down. The bank officer, Mike Nettles, said that the firm already had too much debt. At that time, liabilities totaled $420,000; owners' equity was $600,000.

Assignment

1. In groups of three or four, analyze the financial condition of Park Avenue Furniture.

2. Discuss why you think the bank officer turned down Park Avenue's loan request.

3. Prepare a detailed plan of action to improve the financial health of Park Avenue Furniture over the next twelve months.

3. Researching Different Careers

As pointed out in this chapter, job opportunities for accountants and managers in the accounting area are expected to grow faster than average between now and the year 2014. Employment opportunities range from entry-level positions for clerical workers and technicians to professional positions that require a college degree in accounting, management consulting, or computer technology. Typical job titles in the accounting field include bookkeeper, corporate accountant, public accountant, auditor, managerial accountant, and controller.

Assignment

1. Answer the following questions based on information obtained from interviews with people employed in accounting, from research in the library or by using the Internet, or from information gained from your college's career center.

    a. What types of activities would a person employed in one of the accounting positions listed above perform on a daily basis?

    b. Would you choose this career? Why or why not?

2. Summarize your findings in a report.

Prepare for Class
Exploring the Internet

CHAPTER 16

Mastering Financial Management

Your Guide to Success in Business

Why this chapter matters

The old saying goes, "Money makes the world go around." For individuals and business firms, this is true. It's hard to live *or* operate a business without money. In this chapter we discuss how financial management is used to obtain money and insure that it is used effectively.

LEARNING OBJECTIVES

1. Explain the need for financial management in business.

2. Summarize the process of planning for financial management.

3. Identify the services provided by banks and financial institutions for their business customers.

4. Describe the advantages and disadvantages of different methods of short-term debt financing.

5. Evaluate the advantages and disadvantages of equity financing.

6. Evaluate the advantages and disadvantages of long-term debt financing.

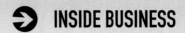

Mighty Microfinance Goes Multinational

Muhammad Yunus won the 2006 Nobel Peace Prize for pioneering a revolutionary financing concept: microfinance, lending entrepreneurs a little *(micro)* money *(finance)* to start or expand a small business. Traditionally, banks have been reluctant to lend money to people who have no inventory, no credit history, no equipment, and little (if anything) of value to back up their repayment promises.

In contrast, microfinance helps even poor entrepreneurs over that high hurdle. What's really revolutionary about microfinance is that it offers would-be business owners the opportunity to borrow in the first place, on the assumption that they'll ultimately become self-supporting. Borrowers who use microfinance to fuel a business are expected to repay every loan, with interest, no matter how small—and well over 95 percent do.

Over the years, Yunus's Grameen Bank, based in Bangladesh, has loaned more than $5 billion to seven million borrowers who could pledge nothing but their personal promise to repay the money. In addition to Grameen Bank, 7,000 microfinance institutions worldwide now lend small amounts to small business borrowers. These include nonprofit organizations such as the Gates Foundation (created by Microsoft's founder) and the Omidyar Network (created by eBay's founder). Increasingly, commercial banks such as BancoSol in Bolivia and even the New York–based banking giant Citigroup are getting involved.

In all, more than 100 million people each year borrow an average of $50 to $150 to start or grow a wide variety of small businesses. Most of these entrepreneurs are women with business ideas such as making tortillas to sell on market day or buying a cell phone and charging villagers to use it. Even a tiny loan can make a big difference. In Africa, a woman who was reselling fish bought from a local distributor borrowed money for a bus trip to the Nile River, where she could buy directly from fishermen and pay far less for her merchandise. "A $10 bus ticket separated her from vastly expanding her profit," says Jessica Flannery, cofounder of the web-based nonprofit Kiva.org, which arranged the loan.[1]

DID YOU KNOW?

Through microfinance, more than 100 million people each year borrow an average of $50 to $150 to start or grow their small businesses.

KEY TERMS

financial management (510)
short-term financing (511)
cash flow (511)
speculative production (511)
long-term financing (512)
risk-return ratio (512)
chief financial officer (CFO) (513)
financial plan (514)
budget (515)
cash budget (515)
capital budget (515)

equity capital (517)
debt capital (517)
certificate of deposit (CD) (518)
check (518)
line of credit (519)
revolving credit agreement (519)
collateral (519)
debit card (520)
electronic funds transfer (EFT) system (520)
letter of credit (521)

banker's acceptance (521)
unsecured financing (522)
trade credit (522)
promissory note (523)
prime interest rate (523)
commercial paper (524)
factor (525)
initial public offering (IPO) (526)
investment banking firm (527)
convertible preferred stock (528)
retained earnings (528)

private placement (529)
financial leverage (530)
term-loan agreement (531)
corporate bond (531)
maturity date (531)
registered bond (532)
bond indenture (532)
serial bonds (532)
sinking fund (532)
trustee (532)

ACE the Test
Crossword Puzzle
Flashcards

In Chapter 1, we defined a *business* as the organized effort of individuals to produce, and sell for a profit, the products and services that satisfy society's needs. Now, after reflecting on this definition, imagine that you are a would-be entrepreneur. You have a good idea for a successful business and with hard work, a little luck, *and* some financing you could turn your dream into a reality. That's the situation that many would be entrepreneurs around the world face when attempting to start a business. For some, the microfinance loan programs described in the Inside Business feature for this chapter provide the financing—even small dollar amounts—that can be used to start their businesses. And while other entrepreneurs may use more traditional methods to raise the money they need, the fact is that all businesses need money to open the doors and to stay in business.

In this chapter we focus on

- ＊ How firms meet the two financial needs of all business organizations:
  - ＊ The need for money to start a business and keep it going.
  - ＊ The need to manage that money effectively.
- ＊ How firms develop financial plans and evaluate financial performance.
- ＊ The services provided by banks and other financial institutions for their business customers.
- ＊ Various sources for short- and long-term financing.

What Is Financial Management?

Learning Objective ❶

Explain the need for financial management in business.

financial management all the activities concerned with obtaining money and using it effectively

Financial management consists of all the activities concerned with obtaining money and using it effectively. Within a business organization, the financial manager not only must determine the best way (or ways) to raise money, but he or she also must ensure that projected uses are in keeping with the organization's goals.

The Need for Financing

Money is needed both to start a business and to keep it going. The original investment of the owners, along with money they may have borrowed, should be enough to open the doors. After that, it would seem that sales revenues could be used to pay the firm's expenses and to provide a profit as well.

This is exactly what happens in a successful firm—over the long run. However, income and expenses may vary from month to month or from year to year. Temporary financing may be needed when expenses are high or sales are low. Then, too, situations such as the opportunity to purchase a new facility or expand an existing plant may require more money than is currently available within a firm. In either case, the firm must look for outside sources of financing.

Short-Term Financing Short-term financing is money that will be used for one year or less. As illustrated in Table 16.1, there are many short-term financing needs, but two deserve special attention.

Cash-Flow Management First, certain business practices may affect a firm's cash flow and create a need for short-term financing. Cash flow is the movement of money into and out of an organization. The ideal is to have sufficient money coming into the firm in any period to cover the firm's expenses during that period. The ideal, however, is not always achieved. **EXAMPLE** California-based Callaway Golf offers credit to retailers and wholesalers that carry the firm's golf clubs and balls. Credit purchases made by Callaway's retailers generally are not paid until thirty to sixty days (or more) after the transaction. Callaway therefore may need short-term financing to pay its bills until its customers have paid theirs.

Inventory Management A second major need for short-term financing is inventory. For most manufacturers, wholesalers, and retailers, inventory requires considerable investment. Moreover, most goods are manufactured four to nine months before they are actually sold to the ultimate customer. This type of manufacturing is often referred to as *speculative production*. Speculative production refers to the time lag between the actual production of goods and when the goods are sold. **EXAMPLE** Consider what happens when a firm such as Black & Decker begins to manufacture electric tools and small appliances for sale during the Christmas season. Manufacturing begins in February, March, and April, and Black & Decker negotiates short-term financing to buy materials and supplies, to pay wages and rent, and to cover inventory costs until its products eventually are sold to wholesalers and retailers later in the year. Take a look at Figure 16.1. Although Black & Decker manufactures and sells

Inventory management: A complex problem.

For retailers like Best Buy, managing inventory can be a problem, especially before Christmas and other peak selling periods. Although retailers don't want to get stuck with unsold inventory, they must have the right mix and amount of inventory to meet consumer demand. Despite the problems associated with inventory, it's a good feeling to see customers at the cash register purchasing the products they need.

short-term financing money that will be used for one year or less

cash flow the movement of money into and out of an organization

speculative production the time lag between the actual production of goods and when the goods are sold

CORPORATE CASH NEEDS	
SHORT-TERM FINANCING NEEDS	**LONG-TERM FINANCING NEEDS**
Cash-flow problems	Business start-up costs
Current inventory needs	Mergers and acquisitions
Speculative production	New product development
Monthly expenses	Long-term marketing activities
Short-term promotional needs	Replacement of equipment
Unexpected emergencies	Expansion of facilities

TABLE 16.1

Comparison of Short- and Long-Term Financing

Whether a business seeks short- or long-term financing depends on what the money will be used for.

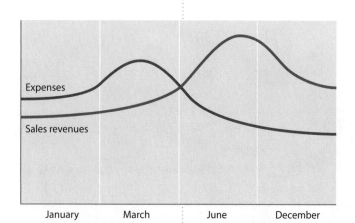

January   March   June   December

long-term financing money that will be used for longer than one year

risk-return ratio a ratio based on the principle that a high-risk decision should generate higher financial returns for a business and more conservative decisions often generate lesser returns

finished products all during the year, expenses peak during the first part of the year. During this same period, sales revenues are low. Once the firm's finished products are shipped to retailers and wholesalers and payment is received (usually within thirty to sixty days), sales revenues are used to repay short-term financing.

Retailers that range in size from Wal-Mart to the neighborhood drugstore also need short-term financing to build up their inventories before peak selling periods.

Long-Term Financing Long-term financing is money that will be used for longer than one year. Long-term financing obviously is needed to start a new business. As Table 16.1 shows, it is also needed for business mergers and acquisitions, new product development, long-term marketing activities, replacement of equipment, and expansion of facilities.

The amounts of long-term financing needed by large firms can seem almost unreal. **EXAMPLE** Merck invested $3.8 billion in research and development (R&D) to create new or improved prescription drugs in 2005—the last year that complete dollar amounts are available at the time of this publication.[2]

Functions of Effective Management

To some extent, financial management can be viewed as a two-sided problem. On one side, how a firm uses its funds dictates the type or types of financing needed by a business. On the other side, what activities a business can undertake are determined by the types of financing available. Financial managers must ensure that funds are

* Available when needed
* Obtained at the lowest possible cost
* Used as efficiently as possible
* Allocated on the basis of the risk-return ratio
* Available for repayment of debt

Financial managers must consider the risk-return ratio when making decisions. The **risk-return ratio** is based on the principle that a high-risk decision should generate higher financial returns for a business. On the other hand, more conservative decisions (with less risk) often generate lesser returns. While financial managers want higher returns, they often must strive for a balance between risk and return.

Finally, financial managers must ensure that funds are available for the repayment of debts in accordance with lenders' financing terms. Prompt repayment is essential to protect the firm's credit rating and its ability to obtain financing in the future.

Many firms have failed because their managers did not pay enough attention to finances. In fact, poor financial management was one of the major reasons why over 31,500 businesses filed for bankruptcy for the twelve-month period ending in June 2006—the most recent twelve-month period for which complete statistics are available.[3] In addition, many fairly successful firms could be highly successful if they managed their finances more carefully. However, many people often take finances for granted. Their first focus may be on production or marketing. As long as there is sufficient financing today, they don't worry about how well it is used or whether it will be there tomorrow. Proper financial management can ensure that

* Financing priorities are established in line with organizational goals and objectives.

* Spending is planned and controlled.

* Bills are paid promptly to protect the firm's credit rating.

* Excess cash is invested in certificates of deposit (CDs), government securities, or conservative, marketable securities.

These functions define effective management as applied to a particular resource—money. And like all effective management, financial management begins with people who must set goals and plan for the future.

Careers in Finance

When you hear the word *finance*, you may think of highly paid executives who determine what a corporation can afford to do and what it can't. At the executive level, most large business firms have a chief financial officer for financial management. A **chief financial officer (CFO)** is a high-level corporate executive who manages a firm's finances and reports directly to the company's chief executive officer or president. Some firms prefer to use the titles vice president of financial management, treasurer, or controller instead of the CFO title for executive-level positions in the finance area.

While some executives in finance do make $300,000 a year or more, many entry-level and lower-level positions that pay quite a bit less are available. Banks, insurance companies, and investment firms obviously have a need for workers who can manage and analyze financial data. So do businesses involved in manufacturing, services, and marketing. Colleges and universities, not-for-profit organizations, and government entities at all levels also need finance workers.

People in finance must have certain traits and skills. In addition to honesty, managers and employees in the finance area must

1. Have a strong background in accounting or mathematics.

2. Know how to use a computer to analyze data.

3. Be an expert at both written and oral communication.

SPOTLIGHT

Without financial management, businesses often fail.

The number of business bankruptcies over an extended period of time.

2004	35,739
2005	39,201
Today	31,562

Source: *Statistical Abstract of the United States, 2006,* Table 749, p. 519, and The Federal Judiciary, website: **www.uscourts.gov;** accessed June 3, 2006.

chief financial officer (CFO) a high-level corporate executive who manages a firm's finances and reports directly to the company's chief executive officer or president

A career in finance can mean handling a lot of money.

Anna Escobedo Cabral is the Treasurer of the United States, one of the top positions in the U.S. government. Cabral has held a number of leadership positions, which include serving as director of the Smithsonian Institution's Center for Latino Initiatives and as deputy staff director for the United States Senate Judiciary Committee.

Typical job titles in finance include bank officer, consumer credit officer, financial analyst, financial planner, loan officer, insurance analyst, and investment account executive. Depending on qualifications, work experience, and education, starting salaries generally begin at $25,000 to $35,000 a year, but it is not uncommon for college graduates to earn $40,000 a year or more.

TEST PREPPER 16.1

True or False?

___F___ 1. The financial manager's job is to raise money. This may or may not be in accordance with the company's goals.

___T___ 2. One of the long-term financing needs could be for new product development.

___T___ 3. People choosing finance as a career must have a strong background in accounting or mathematics.

Multiple Choice

___C___ 4. Short term financing is money that is needed

   a. for the next two years.
   b. for the next three years and beyond.
   c. for one year or less.
   d. for the next two months.
   e. for the next six months.

___B___ 5. While financial managers want higher returns, they must

   a. often have cash reserves.
   b. strive for a balance between risk and return.
   c. make decisions strictly in accordance with the wishes of shareholders.
   d. make sure that they take risky decisions regardless of the return.
   e. make sure that the return far outweighs the risk.

ACE the Test
ACE & ACE+
Practice Test 16.1

Planning—The Basis of Sound Financial Management

Learning Objective ②

Summarize the process of planning for financial management.

financial plan a plan for obtaining and using the money needed to implement an organization's goals

In Chapter 7 we defined a *plan* as an outline of the actions by which an organization intends to accomplish its goals. A **financial plan,** then, is a plan for obtaining and using the money needed to implement an organization's goals.

Steps in Developing the Financial Plan

The three steps involved in financial planning are as follows:

1. Financial planning (like all planning) begins with establishing a set of valid goals and objectives.

2. Financial managers next must determine how much money is needed to accomplish each goal and objective.

3. Finally, financial managers must identify available sources of financing and decide which to use. The three steps involved in financial planning are illustrated in Figure 16.2.

> **CONCEPT CHECK**
>
> What is the function of a cash budget? A capital budget?

Establishing Organizational Goals and Objectives

As pointed out in Chapter 7, a *goal* is an end state that an organization expects to achieve over a one- to ten-year period. *Objectives* are specific statements detailing what the organization intends to accomplish within a certain period of time. If goals and objectives are not specific and measurable, they cannot be translated into dollar costs, and financial planning cannot proceed. Goals and objectives also must be realistic. Otherwise, they may be impossible to finance or achieve. For large corporations, goals and objectives also can be expensive. **EXAMPLE** Bank of America paid $3.3 billion to purchase U.S. Trust from Charles Schwab.[4]

Budgeting for Financial Needs Once planners know what the firm's goals and objectives are for a specific period—say, the next calendar year—they can budget the costs the firm will incur and the sales revenues it will receive. Specifically, a budget is a financial statement that projects income and/or expenditures over a specified future period.

Usually the budgeting process begins with the construction of budgets for sales and various types of expenses. (A typical sales budget—for Stars and Stripes Clothing, a California-based retailer—is shown in Figure 16.3.) Financial managers can easily combine each department's budget for sales and expenses into a company-wide cash budget. A cash budget estimates cash receipts and cash expenditures over a specified period. Notice in the cash budget for Stars and Stripes Clothing, shown in Figure 16.4, that cash sales and collections are listed at the top for each calendar quarter. Payments for purchases and routine expenses are listed in the middle section. Using this information, it is possible to calculate the anticipated cash gain or loss at the end of each quarter.

To develop a plan for long-term financing needs, managers often construct a capital budget. A capital budget estimates a firm's expenditures for major assets, including new product development, expansion of facilities, replacement of obsolete equipment, and mergers and acquisitions. **EXAMPLE** Bank of America constructed a capital budget to determine the best way to finance its $3.3 billion purchase of U.S. Trust from Charles Schwab.[5]

Identifying Sources of Funds The four primary sources of funds, listed in Figure 16.2, are sales revenue, equity capital, debt capital, and proceeds from the sale of assets. Future *sales revenue* generally provides the greatest part of a firm's financing. Figure 16.4 shows that for Stars and Stripes Clothing, sales for the year are expected to cover all expenses and to provide a cash gain of $106,000, or about 16 percent of sales. However, Stars and Stripes has a problem in the first quarter, when sales are expected to fall short of expenses by $7,000. In fact, one of the primary reasons for financial planning is to provide management with adequate lead time to solve this type of cash-flow problem.

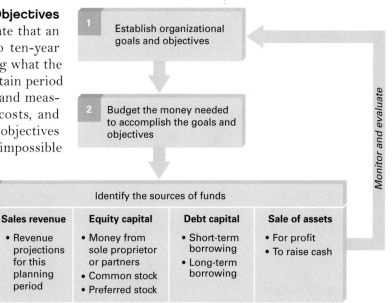

FIGURE 16.2

The Three Steps of Financial Planning

After a financial plan has been developed, it must be monitored continually to ensure that it actually fulfills the firm's goals and objectives.

budget a financial statement that projects income and/or expenditures over a specified future period

cash budget a financial statement that projects cash receipts and cash expenditures over a specified period

capital budget a financial statement that estimates a firm's expenditures for major assets and its long-term financing needs

STARS AND STRIPES CLOTHING
Sales Budget   For January 1, 2008 to December 31, 2008

Department	First Quarter	Second Quarter	Third Quarter	Fourth Quarter	Totals
Infants'	$ 50,000	$ 55,000	$ 60,000	$ 70,000	$235,000
Children's	45,000	45,000	40,000	40,000	170,000
Women's	35,000	40,000	35,000	50,000	160,000
Men's	20,000	20,000	15,000	25,000	80,000
Totals	$150,000	$160,000	$150,000	$185,000	$645,000

FIGURE 16.3

Sales Budget for Stars and Stripes Clothing

Usually the budgeting process begins with the construction of departmental budgets for sales.

A second type of funding is **equity capital**. For a sole proprietorship or partnership, equity capital is provided by the owner or owners of the business. For a corporation, equity capital is money obtained from the sale of shares of ownership in the business. Equity capital is used almost exclusively for long-term financing. Thus it would not be considered for short-term financing needs, such as Stars and Stripes Clothing's first-quarter $7,000 shortfall.

A third type of funding is **debt capital**, which is borrowed money. Debt capital may be borrowed for either short- or long-term use—and a short-term loan seems made

STARS AND STRIPES CLOTHING
Cash Budget   For January 1, 2008 to December 31, 2008

	First Quarter	Second Quarter	Third Quarter	Fourth Quarter	Totals
Cash sales and collections	$150,000	$160,000	$150,000	$185,000	$645,000
Less payments					
Purchases	$110,000	$ 80,000	$ 90,000	$ 60,000	$340,000
Wages/salaries	25,000	20,000	25,000	30,000	100,000
Rent	10,000	10,000	12,000	12,000	44,000
Other expenses	4,000	4,000	5,000	6,000	19,000
Taxes	8,000	8,000	10,000	10,000	36,000
Total payments	$157,000	$122,000	$142,000	$118,000	$539,000
Cash gain or (loss)	$ (7,000)	$ 38,000	$ 8,000	$ 67,000	$106,000

FIGURE 16.4

Cash Budget for Stars and Stripes Clothing

A company-wide cash budget projects sales, collections, purchases, and expenses over a specified period to anticipate cash surpluses and deficits.

to order for Stars and Stripes Clothing's shortfall problem. The firm probably would borrow the needed $7,000 (or perhaps a bit more) at some point during the first quarter and repay it from second-quarter sales revenue.

Proceeds from the *sale of assets* are the fourth type of funding. Selling assets is a drastic step. However, it may be a reasonable last resort when neither equity capital nor debt capital can be found. Assets also may be sold when they are no longer needed or do not "fit" with the company's core business. **EXAMPLE** To concentrate on its core business and to raise financing, General Motors sold its 8.7 percent stake in Japan's Fuji Heavy Industries, the maker of Subaru cars, to Toyota Motor Corporation for $315 million. General Motors also plans to sell its remaining 11.4 percent in Fuji on the open market in an effort to raise an additional $425 million.[6]

Monitoring and Evaluating Financial Performance

It is important to ensure that financial plans are being implemented properly and to catch potential problems before they become major ones. To prevent problems, financial managers should establish a means of monitoring financial performance. Interim budgets (weekly, monthly, or quarterly) may be prepared for comparison purposes. These comparisons point up areas that require additional or revised planning—or at least areas calling for a more careful investigation.

It takes more than a cute advertising gimmick.

Although most people enjoyed seeing the **Pets .com** sock puppet, they didn't buy the firm's products. **Pets.com,** a dot com start-up backed by Amazon, spent millions of dollars on television and other media advertising, but failed to generate enough sales revenue to avoid the cash crisis that eventually led to the company's failure.

TEST PREPPER 16.2

True or False?

___T___ 1. Financial planning begins with establishing a set of valid goals and objectives.

___T___ 2. Sale of assets may be a reasonable last resort when neither equity capital nor debt capital can be found.

___T___ 3. Interim budgets (weekly, monthly, or quarterly) may be prepared for comparison purposes to monitor financial performance.

Multiple Choice

___A___ 4. If goals and objectives are not _____, they cannot be translated into dollar costs, and financial planning cannot proceed.

a. specific and measurable
b. broadly defined
c. developed company-wide
d. historically defined
e. based on market trend

___E___ 5. Which one of the following is *not* one of the four primary sources of funds?

a. Sales revenue
b. Equity capital
c. Debt capital
d. Proceeds from the sale of assets
e. Retained sales

ACE the Test
ACE & ACE+
Practice Test 16.2

Financial Services Provided by Banks and Other Financial Institutions

Learning Objective 3

Identify the services provided by banks and financial institutions for their business customers.

For a business owner, it helps to know your banker. Banking services can be divided into three broad categories: traditional services, electronic banking services, and international services.

equity capital money received from the owners or from the sale of shares of ownership in a business

debt capital borrowed money obtained through loans of various types

BUSINESS AROUND THE WORLD

South of the Border, Banking in Aisle One

Buy a toaster, borrow some pesos. A growing number of financial institutions are expanding by offering banking services in stores across Mexico. The market is low- and middle-income people who haven't traditionally used banking services but would like to build their savings or borrow modest amounts to buy appliances or make home improvements. Banco Azteca, for example, maintains branches in hundreds of stores operated by its parent company, Grupo Elektra. Shoppers can open a savings account with the equivalent of $2 and apply for personal loans to buy merchandise as well.

Banamex, a bank owned by Citigroup, contracts with shopkeepers in rural areas to take deposits and loan payments. Now Wal-Mart has applied for permission to open bank branches in its Mexican stores. This is a sure sign that providing financial services to low- and middle-income consumers has significant profit potential while providing a needed service for customers.

Sources: Based on information in "Mexican Banking: Underwear and Overdrafts," *The Economist,* November 25, 2006, p. 76; "Grupo Elektra Gain," *MMR,* November 13, 2006, p. 13; Scott Johnson, "Money on the Move," *Newsweek International,* January 20, 2003, p. 30; "Case Study: A Successful Distribution Alliance, Grupo Elektra and Western Union," *LatinFinance,* April–May 2006, p. 56.

Prepare for Class
Career Snapshot

Traditional Banking Services for Business Clients

Traditional services provided by banks and other financial institutions include savings and checking accounts, loans, processing credit- and debit-card transactions, and providing professional advice.

Savings and Checking Accounts Savings accounts provide a safe place to store money and a very conservative means of investing. The usual *passbook savings account* earns between 0.50 and 2 percent in banks and savings and loan associations (S&Ls) and slightly more in credit unions. A business with excess cash that is willing to leave money on deposit with a bank for a set period of time can earn a higher rate of interest. To do so, the business firm buys a certificate of deposit. A **certificate of deposit (CD)** is a document stating that the bank will pay the depositor a guaranteed interest rate on money left on deposit for a specified period of time.

Business firms (and individuals) also deposit money in checking accounts so that they can write checks to pay for purchases. A **check** is a written order for a bank or other financial institution to pay a stated dollar amount to the business or person indicated on the face of the check. For businesses, monthly charges are based on the average daily balance in the checking account and/or the number of checks written.

Business Loans Banks, S&Ls, credit unions, and other financial institutions provide short- and long-term loans to businesses. *Short-term business loans* must be repaid

**certificate of deposit
(CD)** a document stating
that the bank will pay the
depositor a guaranteed
interest rate on money
left on deposit for a
specified period of time

check a written order for
a bank or other financial
institution to pay a stated
dollar amount to the business or person indicated
on the face of the check

within one year or less. Typical uses for the money obtained through short-term loans include solving cash-flow problems, purchasing inventory, financing promotional needs, and meeting unexpected emergencies. To help ensure that short-term money will be available when needed, many firms establish a line of credit. A **line of credit** is a loan that is approved before the money is actually needed. Because all the necessary paperwork is already completed and the loan is preapproved, the business can obtain the money later without delay, as soon as it is required. Even with a line of credit, a firm may not be able to borrow money if the bank does not have sufficient funds available. For this reason, some firms prefer a **revolving credit agreement**, which is a guaranteed line of credit. Under this type of agreement, the bank guarantees that the money will be available when the borrower needs it. In return for the guarantee, the bank charges a commitment fee ranging from 0.25 to 1.0 percent of the *unused* portion of the revolving credit agreement. The usual interest is charged for the portion that *is* borrowed.

Long-term business loans are repaid over a period of years. The average length of a long-term business loan is generally three to seven years but sometimes as long as fifteen to twenty years. Long-term loans are used most often to finance the expansion of buildings and retail facilities, mergers and acquisitions, replacement of equipment, or product development. Most lenders require some type of collateral for long-term loans. **Collateral** is real estate or property (e.g., stocks, bonds, equipment, or any other asset of value) pledged as security for a loan.

Repayment terms and interest rates for both short- and long-term loans are arranged between the lender and the borrower. For businesses, repayment terms may include monthly, quarterly, semiannual, or annual payments.

Why Has the Use of Credit Transactions Increased?

Approximately 176 million Americans use credit cards to pay for everything from tickets on American Airlines to Zebco fishing gear.[7] Why have credit cards become so popular? For a merchant, the answer is obvious. By depositing charge slips in a bank or other financial institution, the merchant can convert credit-card sales into cash. In return for processing the merchant's credit-card transactions, the bank charges a fee that generally ranges between 1.5 and 5 percent. Typically, small, independent businesses pay more than larger stores or chain stores. Let's assume that you use a Visa credit card to purchase a microwave oven for $300 from Richardson Appliance, a small retailer in Richardson, Texas. At the end of the day, the retailer deposits your charge slip, along with other charge slips, checks, and currency collected during the day, at its bank. If the bank charges Richardson Appliance 5 percent to process each credit-card transaction, the bank deducts a processing fee of $15 ($300 × 0.05 = $15) for your credit-card transaction and immediately deposits the remainder ($285) in Richardson Appliance's account. The number of credit-card transactions, the total dollar amount of credit sales, and how well the merchant can negotiate the fees the bank charges determine actual fees.

line of credit a loan that is approved before the money is actually needed

revolving credit agreement a guaranteed line of credit

collateral real estate or property pledged as security for a loan

debit card a card that electronically subtracts the amount of a customer's purchase from her or his bank account at the moment the purchase is made

electronic funds transfer (EFT) system a means of performing financial transactions through a computer terminal or telephone hookup

Do not confuse debit cards with credit cards. Although they may look alike, there are important differences. A debit card electronically subtracts the amount of a customer's purchase from her or his bank account at the moment the purchase is made. (By contrast, when you use your credit card, the credit-card company extends short-term financing, and you do not make payment until you receive your next statement.) Debit cards are used most commonly to obtain cash at automatic teller machines (ATMs) and to purchase products and services from retailers.

Electronic Banking Services

An electronic funds transfer (EFT) system is a means of performing financial transactions through a computer terminal or telephone hookup. The following three EFT applications are changing how banks help firms do business:

1. *Automated clearinghouses (ACHs).* Designed to reduce the number of paper checks, automated clearinghouses process checks, recurring bill payments, Social Security benefits, and employee salaries. **EXAMPLE** Large companies use ACHs to transfer wages and salaries directly into their employees' bank accounts, thus eliminating the need to make out individual paychecks.

2. *Point-of-sale (POS) terminals.* A POS terminal is a computerized cash register located in a retail store and connected to a bank's computer. **EXAMPLE** At the cash register, you pull your bank credit or debit card through a magnetic card reader. A central processing center notifies a computer at your bank that you want to make a purchase. The bank's computer immediately adds the amount to your account for a credit-card transaction. In a similar process, the bank's computer deducts the amount of the purchase from your bank account if you use a debit card. Finally, the amount of your purchase is added to the store's account. The store then is notified that the transaction is complete, and the cash register prints out your receipt.

3. *Electronic check conversion (ECC).* Electronic check conversion is a process used to convert information from a paper check into an electronic payment for merchandise, services, or bills. **EXAMPLE** When you give your completed check to a store cashier, the check is processed through an electronic system that captures your banking information and the dollar amount of the check. Once the check is processed, you are asked to sign a receipt, and you get a voided (canceled) check back for your records. Finally, the funds to pay for your transaction are transferred into the business firm's account. ECC also can be used for checks you mail to pay for a purchase or to pay on an account.

Bankers and business owners generally are pleased with EFT systems. EFTs are fast, and they eliminate the costly processing of checks. However, many customers are reluctant to use online banking or EFT systems. Some simply do not like "the technology," whereas others fear that the computer will garble their accounts. Early on, in 1978, Congress responded to such fears by passing the Electronic Funds Transfer Act, which protects the customer in case the bank makes an error or the customer's credit or debit card is stolen.

International Banking Services

For international businesses, banking services are extremely important. Depending on the needs of an international firm, a bank can help by providing a letter of credit or a banker's acceptance.

A **letter of credit** is a legal document issued by a bank or other financial institution guaranteeing to pay a seller a stated amount for a specified period of time—usually thirty to sixty days. (With a letter of credit, certain conditions, such as delivery of the merchandise, may be specified before payment is made.)

A **banker's acceptance** is a written order for a bank to pay a third party a stated amount of money on a specific date. (With a banker's acceptance, no conditions are specified. It is simply an order to pay without any strings attached.)

Both a letter of credit and a banker's acceptance are popular methods of paying for import and export transactions. **EXAMPLE** Imagine that you are a business owner in the United States who wants to purchase some leather products from a small business in Florence, Italy. You offer to pay for the merchandise with your company's check drawn on an American bank, but the Italian business owner is worried about payment. To solve the problem, your bank can issue either a letter of credit or a banker's acceptance to guarantee that payment will be made. In addition to a letter of credit and a banker's acceptance, banks also can use EFT technology to speed international banking transactions.

One other international banking service should be noted. Banks and other financial institutions provide for currency exchange. If you place an order for Japanese merchandise valued at $50,000, how do you pay for the order? Do you use U.S. dollars or Japanese yen? To solve this problem, you can use a bank's currency-exchange service. To make payment, you can use either currency, and if necessary, the bank will exchange one currency for the other to complete your transaction.

letter of credit a legal document issued by a bank or other financial institution guaranteeing to pay a seller a stated amount for a specified period of time

banker's acceptance a written order for a bank to pay a third party a stated amount of money on a specific date

TEST PREPPER (16.3)

ACE the Test
ACE & ACE+
Practice Test 16.3

True or False?

___ 1. Savings accounts provide a safe place to store money and a very conservative means of investing.

___ 2. A debit card and a credit card essentially have very little to no differences at all.

___ 3. When a letter of credit is used in international trade, no conditions are specified before payment is made.

Multiple Choice

___ 4. A loan that is approved before the money is actually needed is called a(n)

a. revolving installment purchase.
b. credit card.
c. loan.
d. line of credit.
e. advance loan.

___ 5. A computerized cash register located in a retail store and connected to a bank's computer is known as a(n)

a. electronic terminal.
b. automated clearinghouse (ACH).
c. electronic check conversion (ECC).
d. ATM.
e. point-of-sale (POS) terminal.

Sources of Short-Term Debt Financing

Learning Objective 4

Describe the advantages and disadvantages of different methods of short-term debt financing.

CONCEPT CHECK
Why would a supplier offer both trade credit and cash discounts to its customers?

The decision to borrow money does not necessarily mean that a firm is in financial trouble. On the contrary, astute financial management often means regular, responsible borrowing of many different kinds to meet different needs. In this section we examine the sources of *short-term debt financing* available to businesses. In the next two sections we look at long-term financing options: equity capital and debt capital.

Sources of Unsecured Short-Term Financing

Short-term debt financing (money repaid in one year or less) is usually easier to obtain than long-term debt financing for three reasons:

1. For the lender, the shorter repayment period means less risk of nonpayment.
2. The dollar amounts of short-term loans usually are smaller than those of long-term loans.
3. A close working relationship normally exists between the short-term borrower and the lender.

Most lenders do not require collateral for short-term financing. When they do, it is usually because they are concerned about the size of a particular loan, the borrowing firm's poor credit rating, or the general prospects of repayment. **Unsecured financing** is financing that is not backed by collateral. A company seeking unsecured short-term financing has several options.

unsecured financing financing that is not backed by collateral

Trade Credit Manufacturers and wholesalers often provide financial aid to retailers by allowing them thirty to sixty days (or more) in which to pay for merchandise. This delayed payment, known as **trade credit**, is a type of short-term financing extended by a seller who does not require immediate payment after delivery of merchandise. It is the most popular form of short-term financing; in fact, 70 to 90 percent of all transactions between businesses involve some trade credit.

trade credit a type of short-term financing extended by a seller who does not require immediate payment after delivery of merchandise

EXAMPLE Let's assume that a Barnes & Noble bookstore receives a shipment of books from a publisher. Along with the merchandise, the publisher sends an invoice that states the terms of payment. Barnes & Noble now has two options for payment. First, the book retailer may pay the invoice promptly and take advantage of any cash discount the publisher offers. Cash-discount terms are specified on the invoice. For instance, "2/10, net 30" means that the customer—Barnes & Noble—may take a 2 percent discount if it pays the invoice within ten days of the invoice date. Let's assume that the dollar amount of the invoice is $140,000. In this case, the cash discount is $2,800 ($140,000 × 0.02 = $2,800).

A second option is to wait until the end of the credit period before making payment. If payment is made between eleven and thirty days after the date of the invoice, the customer must pay the entire amount. As long as payment is made before the end of the credit period, the customer maintains the ability to purchase additional merchandise using the trade-credit arrangement.

Promissory Notes Issued to Suppliers A **promissory note** is a written pledge by a borrower to pay a certain sum of money to a creditor at a specified future date. Suppliers uneasy about extending trade credit may be more inclined to offer credit to customers who sign promissory notes. Unlike trade credit, however, promissory notes usually require the borrower to pay interest. Although repayment periods may extend to one year, most short-term promissory notes are repaid in 60 to 180 days.

Advantages of Promissory Notes

1. A promissory note is a legally binding and enforceable document that has been signed by the individual or business borrowing the money.

2. Most promissory notes are negotiable instruments, and the supplier (or company extending credit) may be able to discount, or sell, the note to its own bank. If the note is discounted, the dollar amount the supplier would receive is slightly less than the maturity value because the bank charges a fee for the service. The supplier would recoup most of its money immediately, and the bank would collect the maturity value when the note matured.

Unsecured Bank Loans Banks and other financial institutions offer unsecured short-term loans to businesses at interest rates that vary with each borrower's credit rating. The **prime interest rate**, sometimes called the *reference rate*, is the lowest rate charged by a bank for a short-term loan. This lowest rate generally is reserved for large corporations with excellent credit ratings. Organizations with good to high credit ratings may pay the prime rate plus 2 percent. Firms with questionable credit ratings may have to pay the prime rate plus 4 percent. (The fact that a banker charges a higher interest rate for a higher-risk loan is a practical application of the risk–return ratio discussed earlier in this chapter.) Of course, if the banker believes that loan repayment may be a problem, the borrower's loan application may well be rejected.

Banks generally offer unsecured short-term loans through promissory notes, a line of credit, or a revolving credit agreement. A bank promissory note is similar to the promissory note issued by suppliers described in the preceding section. For both types of promissory notes, interest rates and repayment terms may be negotiated between the borrower and a bank or supplier. A bank that offers a promissory note or line of credit may require that a *compensating balance* be kept on deposit at the bank. This balance may be as much as 20 percent of the borrowed funds. **EXAMPLE** Assume that Bank of America requires a 20 percent compensating balance on a short-term promissory note or a line of credit. If you borrow $50,000, at least $10,000 ($50,000 × 0.20 = $10,000) of the loan amount must be kept on deposit at the bank.

When automakers don't sell cars, financial troubles build.

In this photo, a group of demonstrators attempts to convince Ford to increase its research efforts to develop automobiles that operate on alternative fuels. For the automaker, this protest couldn't have come at a worse time. Because of lower sales revenues and operating losses, Ford has less money for research and development projects.

promissory note a written pledge by a borrower to pay a certain sum of money to a creditor at a specified future date

prime interest rate the lowest rate charged by a bank for a short-term loan

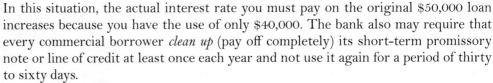

commercial paper a short-term promissory note issued by a large corporation

In this situation, the actual interest rate you must pay on the original $50,000 loan increases because you have the use of only $40,000. The bank also may require that every commercial borrower *clean up* (pay off completely) its short-term promissory note or line of credit at least once each year and not use it again for a period of thirty to sixty days.

Commercial Paper Commercial paper is a short-term promissory note issued by a large corporation. Commercial paper is secured only by the reputation of the issuing firm; no collateral is involved. It is usually issued in large denominations, ranging from $5,000 to $100,000. Corporations issuing commercial paper pay interest rates slightly below the interest rates charged by banks for short-term loans. Thus, issuing commercial paper is cheaper than getting short-term financing from a bank. The interest rate a corporation pays when it issues commercial paper is tied to its credit rating and its ability to repay the commercial paper. Large firms with excellent credit reputations can raise large sums of money quickly by issuing commercial paper. **EXAMPLE** GE Capital, for example, may issue commercial paper totaling millions of dollars. However, commercial paper is not without risks. If a corporation has severe financial problems, it may not be able to repay commercial paper. Enron Corporation, for instance, had issued commercial paper worth millions of dollars at the time of its bankruptcy.[8]

Sources of Secured Short-Term Financing

If a business cannot obtain enough capital through unsecured financing, it must put up collateral to obtain additional short-term financing. Almost any asset can serve as collateral. However, *inventories* and *accounts receivable* are the assets most commonly pledged for short-term financing. Even when it is willing to pledge collateral to back up a loan, a firm that is financially weak may have difficulty obtaining short-term financing.

Loans Secured by Inventory Normally, manufacturers, wholesalers, and retailers have large amounts of money invested in finished goods. In addition, manufacturers carry raw materials and work-in-process inventories. All three types of inventories may be pledged as collateral for short-term loans. However, lenders prefer the much more salable finished merchandise to raw materials or work-in-process inventories.

A lender may insist that inventory used as collateral be stored in a public warehouse. In such a case, the receipt issued by the warehouse is retained by the lender. Without this receipt, the public warehouse will not release the merchandise. The lender releases the warehouse receipt—and the merchandise—to the borrower when the borrowed money is repaid. In addition to paying the interest on the loan, the borrower must pay for storage in the public warehouse. As a result, this type of loan is more expensive than an unsecured short-term loan.

Loans Secured by Receivables As defined in Chapter 15, *accounts receivable* are amounts owed to a firm by its customers. They are created when trade credit is given to customers and usually are due within thirty to sixty days. A firm can pledge its accounts receivable as collateral to obtain short-term financing. A lender may advance 70 to 80 percent of the dollar amount of the receivables. First, however, it conducts a thorough investigation to determine the *quality* of the receivables. (The quality of the

receivables is the credit standing of the firm's customers, coupled with the customers' ability to repay their credit obligations.) If a favorable determination is made, the loan is approved. When the borrowing firm collects from a customer whose account has been pledged as collateral, it must turn the money over to the lender as partial repayment of the loan. An alternative approach is to notify the borrower's credit customers to make their payments directly to the lender.

Factoring Accounts Receivable

Accounts receivable may be used in one other way to help raise short-term financing: They can be sold to a factoring company (or factor). A **factor** is a firm that specializes in buying other firms' accounts receivable. The factor buys the accounts receivable for less than their face value, but it collects the full dollar amount when each account is due. The factor's profit thus is the difference between the face value of the accounts receivable and the amount the factor has paid for them. Generally, the amount of profit the factor receives is based on the risk the factor assumes. Risk, in this case, is the probability that the accounts receivable will not be repaid when they mature.

Even though the firm selling its accounts receivable gets less than face value, it does receive needed cash immediately. Moreover, it has shifted both the task of collecting and the risk of nonpayment to the factor, which now owns the accounts receivable. In many cases, the firm selling its accounts receivable must obtain approval from the factor *before* selling merchandise to a credit customer. Thus the firm receives instant feedback on whether the factor will purchase the credit customer's account. Generally, customers whose accounts receivable have been factored are given instructions to make their payments directly to the factor.

factor a firm that specializes in buying other firms' accounts receivable

Cost Comparisons

Table 16.2 compares the various types of short-term financing. As you can see, trade credit is the least expensive. Factoring of accounts receivable is typically the highest-cost method shown.

TABLE 16.2

Comparison of Short-Term Financing Methods

TYPE OF FINANCING	COST	REPAYMENT PERIOD	BUSINESSES THAT MAY USE IT	COMMENTS
Trade credit	Low, if any	30–60 days	All businesses	Usually no finance charge
Promissory note issued to suppliers	Moderate	1 year or less	All businesses	Usually unsecured but requires legal document
Unsecured bank loan	Moderate	1 year or less	All businesses	Promissory note, a line of credit, or revolving credit agreement generally required
Commercial paper	Moderate	1 year or less	Large corporations with high credit ratings	Available only to large firms
Secured loan	High	1 year or less	Firms with questionable credit ratings	Inventory or accounts receivable often used as collateral
Factoring	High	None	Firms that have large numbers of credit customers	Accounts receivable sold to a factor

For many purposes, short-term financing suits a firm's needs perfectly. At other times, however, long-term financing may be more appropriate. In this case, a business may try to raise equity capital or long-term debt capital.

TEST PREPPER 16.4

True or False?

___F___ 1. Most lenders require collateral for short-term financing.

___T___ 2. A bank that offers a promissory note or line of credit may require that a compensating balance be kept on deposit at the bank.

___T___ 3. The firm selling its accounts receivable shifts the risk of a customer not paying the amount owed to a factor.

Multiple Choice

___E___ 4. Short-term debt financing is usually easier to obtain than long-term debt financing. Which one of the following is one of the reasons why this is so?

    a. Short-term financing is repaid in two years or less.

b. Short-term financing has more risk associated with it.

c. Banks are eager to loan money in the short term.

d. There are a lot more financial institutions willing to lend for the short term than for the long term.

e. The dollar amounts of short-term loans usually are smaller than those of long-term loans.

___C___ 5. Which one of the following is *not* an example of unsecured loans?

    a. Line of credit

    b. Trade credit

    c. Revolving credit agreement

    d. Commercial paper

    e. Factoring accounts receivables

ACE the Test
ACE & ACE+
Practice Test 16.4

Sources of Equity Financing

Learning Objective ❺

Evaluate the advantages and disadvantages of equity financing.

Sources of long-term equity financing vary with the size and type of business. As mentioned earlier, a sole proprietorship or partnership acquires equity capital (sometimes referred to as *owner's equity*) when the owner or owners invest money in the business. For corporations, equity-financing options include the sale of stock and the use of profits not distributed to owners. All three types of businesses also can obtain venture capital.

Selling Stock

Some equity capital is used to start every business—sole proprietorship, partnership, or corporation. In the case of corporations, stockholders who buy shares in the company provide equity capital.

Initial Public Offerings An **initial public offering (IPO)** occurs when a corporation sells common stock to the general public for the first time. **EXAMPLE** One of the

initial public offering (IPO) when a corporation sells common stock to the general public for the first time

largest IPOs in recent history was for the search engine Google, which raised over $2.7 billion that be could used to fund expansion and other business activities.[9] Established companies that plan to raise capital by selling subsidiaries to the public also can use IPOs. For example, McDonald's sold a part of its stake in its Chipotle casual restaurant subsidiary. McDonald's will use the money it receives from the IPO to fund capital expenditures and expansion of its current business activities.[10]

A corporation selling stock often will use an **investment banking firm**—an organization that assists corporations in raising funds, usually by helping to sell new issues of stocks, bonds, or other financial securities. The investment banking firm generally charges a fee of 2 to 20 percent of the proceeds received by the corporation issuing the securities. The size of the commission depends on the financial health of the corporation issuing the new securities and the size of the new security issue.

Advantages of Selling Stock

1. The corporation does not have to repay money obtained from the sale of stock because the corporation is under no legal obligation to do so. If you purchase corporate stock and later decide to sell your stock, you may sell it to another investor—not the corporation.
2. The corporation is under no legal obligation to pay dividends to stockholders. A *dividend* is a distribution of earnings to the stockholders of a corporation. For any reason (if a company has a bad year, for example), the board of directors can vote to omit dividend payments. Earnings then are retained for use in funding business operations.

There are two types of stock: common and preferred. Each type has advantages and drawbacks as a means of long-term financing.

Common Stock   In Chapter 5, *common stock* was described as the most basic form of corporate ownership whose owners may vote on corporate matters but whose claims on profits and assets are subordinate to the claims of others. In return for the financing provided by selling common stock, management must make certain concessions to stockholders that may restrict or change corporate policies. By law, every corporation must hold an annual meeting, at which the holders of common stock may vote for the board of directors and approve or disapprove major corporate actions. Among such actions are

1. Amendments to the corporate charter or by-laws
2. Sale of certain assets
3. Mergers and acquisitions
4. New issues of preferred stock or bonds
5. Changes in the amount of common stock issued

You recognize their credit card, but did you know that they just sold stock for the first time?

That's right; MasterCard sold stock for the first time in 2006. Although the company has been issuing credit cards for years, its long-awaited initial public offering (IPO) created quite a stir on Wall Street and was one of the largest in the past two years.

investment banking firm an organization that assists corporations in raising funds, usually by helping to sell new issues of stocks, bonds, or other financial securities

convertible preferred stock preferred stock that an owner may exchange for a specified number of shares of common stock

retained earnings the portion of a corporation's profits not distributed to stockholders

ACE the Test
Hangman

Few investors will buy common stock unless they believe that their investment will increase in value. Basically, there are three ways to profit from stock investments:

* From dividend payments
* From an increase in the value of the stock
* Because of stock splits

Preferred Stock As noted in Chapter 5, the owners of *preferred stock* must receive their dividends before holders of common stock receive theirs. Moreover, the preferred-stock dividend amount is specified on the stock certificate. And the owners of preferred stock have first claim, after bond owners and general creditors, on corporate assets if the firm is dissolved or enters bankruptcy. For investors, these features make preferred stock a more conservative investment with an added degree of safety and a more predictable source of income when compared with common stock. Even so, as with common stock, the board of directors must approve dividends on preferred stock, and this type of financing does not represent a debt that must be legally repaid. In return for preferential treatment, preferred stockholders generally give up the right to vote at a corporation's annual meeting.

To make preferred stock more attractive to investors, some corporations include a conversion feature. **Convertible preferred stock** is preferred stock that an owner may exchange for a specified number of shares of common stock. **EXAMPLE** The Textron Corporation—a manufacturer of component parts for the automotive and aerospace industries—has issued convertible preferred stock. Each share of Textron preferred stock is convertible to 4.4 shares of the firm's common stock. This conversion feature provides the investor with the safety of preferred stock and the hope of greater speculative gain through conversion to common stock.

Retained Earnings

Most large corporations distribute only a portion of their after-tax earnings to stockholders. The portion of a corporation's profits not distributed to stockholders is called **retained earnings**. Because they are undistributed profits, retained earnings are considered a form of equity financing.

The amount of retained earnings in any year is determined by corporate management and approved by the board of directors. Most small and growing corporations pay no cash dividend—or a very small dividend—to their stockholders. All or most earnings are reinvested in the business for R&D, expansion, or the funding of major projects. Reinvestment tends to increase the value of the firm's stock while it provides essentially cost-free financing for the business. More mature corporations may distribute 40 to 60 percent of their after-tax profits as dividends. Utility companies and other corporations with very stable earnings often pay out as much as 80 to 90 percent of what they earn. For a large corporation, retained earnings can amount to a hefty bit of financing. **EXAMPLE** For example, in 2006, the total amount of retained earnings for General Electric was almost $108 billion.[11]

Venture Capital and Private Placements

To establish a new business or expand an existing one, an entrepreneur may try to obtain venture capital. In Chapter 6 we defined *venture capital* as money invested in small (and sometimes struggling) firms that have the potential to become very successful. Most venture capital firms do not invest in the typical small business—a neighborhood convenience store or a local dry cleaner—but in firms that have the potential to become extremely profitable. Generally, a venture capital firm consists of a pool of investors, a traditional partnership established by a wealthy family, or a joint venture formed by corporations with money to invest. In return for financing, these investors generally receive an equity position in the business and share in its profits.

Another method of raising capital is through a private placement. A **private placement** occurs when stock and other corporate securities are sold directly to insurance companies, pension funds, large institutional or wealthy investors. When compared with selling stocks and other corporate securities to the public, there are often fewer government regulations and the cost is generally less when the securities are sold through a private placement. Typically, terms between the buyer and seller are negotiated when a private placement is used to raise capital.

> **private placement** occurs when stock and other corporate securities are sold directly to insurance companies, pension funds, or large institutional or wealthy investors

ENTREPRENEURIAL CHALLENGE

Meeting the Venture Capitalists

If you're an entrepreneur with a promising business idea—or you're running a small business that needs financial fuel for future growth—how do you attract venture capital? Maha Ibrahim, a California-based venture capitalist, stresses that "there is no lack of money for highly promising entrepreneurs with good, well-formulated ideas, whether they're creating a startup from scratch or seeking later-stage financing for a growing venture with promise." You just have to know what to do (and what not to do) when you prepare to meet a venture capitalist.

Do:

- Create a detailed business plan with realistic costs and profits.
- Gather solid, recent data about your market and your competitors.
- Develop a compelling story about your business idea and your background.

- Identify venture capitalists interested in your type of business.

Don't:

- Have unrealistic expectations for investment and growth.
- Exaggerate your projected revenues and profits.
- Overlook venture capital possibilities outside your local area.

Sources: Based on information from Maha Ibrahim, "Preparing Your Pitch for Venture Capital, *Electronic Engineering Times,* November 27, 2006, p. 40; Robert Weisman, "Where's Web 2.0? Greater Boston Venture Capitalists Are Seeking the Second Wave of Internet Start-Ups Based on Web Content, Social Networking, Digital Media," *Boston Globe,* August 7, 2006, p. D1.

TEST PREPPER 16.5

True or False?

 1. Equity-financing options for corporations include the sale of stock only.

 2. One of the ways common stockholders can make money is by receiving dividends on their stock holdings.

 3. Private placement occurs when stock and other corporate securities are sold privately to some preferred stockholders.

Multiple Choice

_____ 4. An organization that assists corporations in raising funds usually by helping to sell new issues

of stocks, bonds, or other financial securities is called

  a. a commercial bank.
  b. a venture capitalist firm.
  c. an investment banking firm.
  d. a private placement firm.
  e. a credit union.

 5. Which one of the following is *not* a source of equity financing?

  a. IPO's
  b. Venture capital
  c. Preferred stock
  d. Trade credit
  e. Retained earnings

ACE the Test
ACE & ACE+
Practice Test 16.5

Sources of Long-Term Debt Financing

Learning Objective 6

Evaluate the advantages and disadvantages of long-term debt financing.

As we pointed out earlier in this chapter, businesses borrow money on a short-term basis for many valid reasons other than desperation. There are equally valid reasons for long-term borrowing. In addition to using borrowed money to meet the long-term needs listed in Table 16.1, successful businesses often use the financial leverage it creates to improve their financial performance. **Financial leverage** is the use of borrowed funds to increase the return on owners' equity. The principle of financial leverage works as long as a firm's earnings are larger than the interest paid for the borrowed money. The most obvious danger when using financial leverage is that the firm's earnings may be less than expected. If this situation occurs, the fixed interest charge actually works to reduce or eliminate the return on owners' equity. Of course, borrowed money eventually must be repaid. Finally, because lenders always have the option to turn down a loan request, many managers are reluctant to rely on borrowed money.

For a small business, long-term debt financing generally is limited to loans. Large corporations have the additional option of issuing corporate bonds.

financial leverage the use of borrowed funds to increase the return on owners' equity

Long-Term Loans

Many businesses finance their long-range activities such as those listed in Table 16.1 with loans from banks and other financial institutions. Manufacturers and suppliers of heavy machinery also may provide long-term debt financing by granting extended credit to their customers.

Term-Loan Agreements When the loan repayment period is longer than one year, the borrower must sign a term-loan agreement. A **term-loan agreement** is a promissory note that requires a borrower to repay a loan in monthly, quarterly, semiannual, or annual installments. Although repayment may be as long as fifteen to twenty years, long-term business loans normally are repaid in three to seven years.

The interest rate and repayment terms for term loans often are based on such factors as the reasons for borrowing, the borrowing firm's credit rating, and the value of collateral. Acceptable collateral includes real estate, machinery, and equipment. Lenders also may require that borrowers maintain a minimum amount of working capital.

The Basics of Getting a Loan Preparation is the key when applying for a business loan. To begin the process, you should get to know potential lenders before requesting debt financing. While there may be many potential lenders that can provide the money you need, the logical place to borrow money is where your business does its banking. This fact underscores the importance of maintaining adequate balances in the firm's bank accounts. Before applying for a loan, you also may want to check your firm's credit rating with a national credit bureau such as D&B (formerly known as Dun & Bradstreet).

Typically, you will be asked to fill out a loan application. In addition to the loan application, the lender also will want to see your current business plan. Be sure to explain what your business is, how much funding you require to accomplish your goals and objectives, and how the loan will be repaid. Most lenders insist that you submit current financial statements that have been prepared by a certified public accountant (CPA). Then compile a list of references that includes your suppliers, other lenders, or the professionals with whom you are associated. Once you submit your application, business plan, supporting financial documents, and list of references, a bank officer or a loan committee will examine the loan application and supporting documentation. You also may be asked to discuss your request with a loan officer. Hopefully, your loan will be approved. If not, try to determine why your loan request was rejected.

Corporate Bonds

In addition to loans, large corporations may choose to issue bonds in denominations of $1,000 to $50,000. Although the usual face value for corporate bonds is $1,000, the total face value of all the bonds in an issue usually amounts to millions of dollars. In fact, one of the reasons why corporations sell bonds is that they can borrow a lot of money from a lot of different bondholders and raise larger amounts of money than could be borrowed from one lender. A **corporate bond** is a corporation's written pledge that it will repay a specified amount of money with interest. The **maturity date** is the date on which the corporation is to repay the borrowed money.

Until a bond's maturity, a corporation pays interest to the bond owner at the stated rate. **EXAMPLE** Owners of a Honeywell International corporate bond receive 5.4 percent per year for each bond. Because interest for corporate bonds is usually paid semiannually, bond owners receive half the annual interest in a payment every six months.

term-loan agreement a promissory note that requires a borrower to repay a loan in monthly, quarterly, semiannual, or annual installments

corporate bond a corporation's written pledge that it will repay a specified amount of money with interest

maturity date the date on which a corporation is to repay borrowed money

registered bond a bond registered in the owner's name by the issuing company

bond indenture a legal document that details all the conditions relating to a bond issue

serial bonds bonds of a single issue that mature on different dates

sinking fund a sum of money to which deposits are made each year for the purpose of redeeming a bond issue

trustee an individual or an independent firm that acts as the bond owners' representative

Types of Bonds Today, most corporate bonds are registered bonds. A **registered bond**—is a bond registered in the owner's name by the issuing company. Until the maturity date, the registered owner receives periodic interest payments. On the maturity date, the owner returns a registered bond to the corporation and receives cash equaling the face value.

Corporate bonds generally are classified as debentures, mortgage bonds, or convertible bonds.

* *Debenture bonds* are backed only by the reputation of the issuing corporation.
* *Mortgage bonds* are secured by various assets of the issuing firm.
* *Convertible bonds* can be exchanged, at the owner's option, for a specified number of shares of the corporation's common stock.

Repayment Provisions for Corporate Bonds Maturity dates for bonds generally range from ten to thirty years after the date of issue. If the interest is not paid or the firm becomes insolvent, bond owners' claims on the assets of the corporation take precedence over the claims of both common and preferred stockholders. Some bonds are callable before the maturity date; that is, a corporation can buy back, or redeem, them. For these bonds, the corporation may pay the bond owner a call premium. The amount of the call premium is specified, along with other provisions, in the bond indenture. The **bond indenture** is a legal document that details all the conditions relating to a bond issue.

Before deciding if bonds are the best way to obtain corporate financing, managers must determine if the company can afford to pay the interest on the corporate bonds. It should be obvious that the larger the bond issue, the higher the dollar amount of interest will be. If the corporation defaults on (does not pay) either interest payments or repayment of the bond at maturity, owners of bonds can force the firm into bankruptcy.

A corporation may use one of three methods to ensure that it has sufficient funds available to redeem a bond issue. First, it can issue the bonds as **serial bonds**, which are bonds of a single issue that mature on different dates. **EXAMPLE** A company may use a twenty-five-year $50 million bond issue to finance its expansion. None of the bonds mature during the first fifteen years. Thereafter, 10 percent of the bonds mature each year until all the bonds are retired at the end of the twenty-fifth year. Second, the corporation can establish a sinking fund. A **sinking fund** is a sum of money to which deposits are made each year for the purpose of redeeming a bond issue. **EXAMPLE** When Pacific Gas & Electric Company sold a $200 million bond issue, the company agreed to contribute to a sinking fund twice a year until the bond's maturity in the year 2024. Third, a corporation can pay off an old bond issue by selling new bonds. Although this may appear to perpetuate the corporation's long-term debt, a number of utility companies and railroads use this repayment method.

A corporation that issues bonds also must appoint a **trustee**, an individual or an independent firm that acts as the bond owners' representative. A trustee's duties are handled most often by a commercial bank or other large financial institution. The corporation must report to the trustee periodically regarding its ability to make interest payments and eventually redeem the bonds. In turn, the trustee transmits this information to the bond owners, along with its own evaluation of the corporation's ability to pay.

Cost Comparisons

Table 16.3 compares some of the methods that can be used to obtain long-term equity *and* debt financing. Although the initial cost of issuing stock is high, selling common stock generally is the first choice for most financial managers. Once the stock is sold and upfront costs are paid, the *ongoing* costs of using stock to finance a business are low. The type of long-term financing that generally has the highest *ongoing* costs is a long-term loan (debt).

TYPE OF FINANCING	REPAYMENT	REPAYMENT PERIOD	COST/DIVIDENDS INTEREST	BUSINESSES THAT MAY USE IT
Equity				
Common stock	No	None	High initial flotation cost; low ongoing costs because dividends and repayment not required	All corporations that sell stock to investors
Preferred stock	No	None	Dividends not required but must be paid before common stockholders receive any dividends	Large corporations that have an established investor base of common stockholders
Debt				
Long-term loan	Yes	Usually 3–7 years	Interest rates between 7 and 13 percent depending on economic conditions and the financial stability of the company requesting the loan	All firms that can meet the lender's repayment and collateral requirements
Corporate bond	Yes	Usually 10–30 years	Interest rates between 5 and 10 percent depending on economic conditions and the financial stability of the company issuing the bonds	Large corporations that investors trust

TABLE 16.3

Comparison of Long-Term Financing Methods

TEST PREPPER 16.6

True or False?

F 1. The principle of financial leverage works as long as a firm's interest payments are larger than the earnings of the firm.

T 2. Before deciding if bonds are the best way to obtain corporate financing, managers must determine if the company can afford to pay the interest on the corporate bonds.

T 3. Although the initial cost of issuing stock is high, selling common stock generally is the first choice for most financial managers.

Multiple Choice

D 4. The usual face value for a corporate bond is
  a. $50,000.
  b. $25,000.
  c. $5,000.
  d. $1,000.
  e. $500.

E 5. Debenture bonds are backed by the issuing firm's
  a. collateral.
  b. revenues.
  c. credit rating.
  d. sales.
  e. reputation.

ACE the Test
ACE & ACE+
Practice Test 16.6

⊃ RETURN TO INSIDE BUSINESS

Often budding entrepreneurs in developing countries are located many miles from the nearest bank branch or lack the official identification documents that banks usually require. As microfinance becomes more commonplace, institutions are finding ways around these barriers. Some banks and financial institutions send representatives to villages every week to meet borrowers and collect payments. Others are taking a more high-tech approach. In India, Citigroup is installing ATMs that use customers' fingerprints as identification.

Microfinance is also opening business doors for American entrepreneurs who need money for equipment or marketing. However, these loans can run to $10,000 or higher because "the cost of starting and running a business in the United States is very much more than in developing countries," observes a microfinance authority.

Questions

1. Why would a financial institution choose *not* to engage in microfinance?
2. If you were a banker deciding whether to approve a microfinance loan, what would you ask the business borrower before you make your decision?

LEARNING OBJECTIVES REVIEW

 Explain the need for financial management in business.

- Financial management consists of all activities concerned with obtaining money and using it effectively.

- Short-term financing is money that will be used for one year or less.

- Short-term financing may be used for cash-flow problems, current inventory needs, speculative production, monthly expenses, short-term promotional needs, and unexpected emergencies.

- Long-term financing is money that will be used for more than one year.

- Long-term financing may be required for a business start-up, for a merger or acquisition, for new product development, for long-term marketing activities, for replacement of equipment, or for expansion of facilities.

- Financial management can be viewed as a two-sided problem. On one side, the uses of funds often dictate the type or types of financing needed by a business. On the other side, the activities a business can undertake are determined by the types of financing available.

- Financial managers also must consider the risk-return ratio when making decisions.

 Summarize the process of planning for financial management.

- A financial plan begins with an organization's goals and objectives, which are "translated" into departmental budgets that detail expected income and expenses.

- These budgets, when combined into an overall cash budget, determine what funding will be needed and where it may be obtained.

- Departmental and cash budgets emphasize short-term financing needs; a capital budget can be used to estimate a firm's expenditures for major assets and its long-term financing needs.

- Four principal sources of financing are sales revenues, equity capital, debt capital, and proceeds from the sale of assets.
- The financial manager is also responsible for monitoring and evaluating the firm's financial activities.

3 Identify the services provided by banks and financial institutions for their business customers.

- The most important and attractive banking services for businesses are savings and checking accounts, loans, processing of credit-card and debit-card transactions, and professional advice.
- Increased use of electronic banking services (automated clearinghouses, point-of-sale terminals, and electronic check conversion) is also changing how banks help firms do business.
- A bank can provide letters of credit and banker's acceptances for firms in the global marketplace that will reduce the risk of nonpayment for sellers.
- Banks and financial institutions also can provide currency exchange to reduce payment problems for import or export transactions.

4 Describe the advantages and disadvantages of different methods of short-term debt financing.

- Most short-term financing is unsecured; that is, no collateral is required.
- Sources of unsecured short-term financing include trade credit, promissory notes issued to suppliers, unsecured bank loans, and commercial paper.
- Sources of secured short-term financing include loans secured by inventory and accounts receivable.
- A firm also may sell its receivables to factors.
- Trade credit is the least expensive source of short-term financing.
- The cost of financing through other sources generally depends on the source and on the credit rating of the firm that requires the financing. Factoring generally is the most expensive approach.

5 Evaluate the advantages and disadvantages of equity financing.

- A sole proprietorship or partnership acquires equity when the owner or owners invest money in the business.
- A corporation can raise equity capital by selling either common or preferred stock.
- Common stock is voting stock; holders of common stock elect the corporation's directors and must approve major corporate actions.
- Holders of preferred stock must be paid dividends before holders of common stock are paid any dividends.
- Another source of equity funding is retained earnings, which is the portion of a business's profits not distributed to stockholders.
- Venture capital—money invested in small (and sometimes struggling) firms that have the potential to become very successful—is yet another source of equity funding.
- Generally, venture capital is provided by investors, partnerships established by wealthy families, or a joint venture formed by corporations with money to invest. In return, they receive an equity position in the firm and share in the profits of the business.
- Finally, a private placement can be used to sell stocks and other corporate securities.

6 Evaluate the advantages and disadvantages of long-term debt financing.

- For a small business, debt financing generally is limited to loans, whereas large corporations have the additional option of selling corporate bonds.
- Financial leverage is the use of borrowed funds to increase the return on owners' equity.
- Rate of interest for long-term loans usually depends on the financial status of the borrower, the reason for borrowing, the borrowing firm's credit rating, and the kind of collateral pledged to back up the loan.
- Acceptable collateral includes real estate, machinery, and equipment.

- Long-term business loans normally are repaid in three to seven years but can be as long as fifteen to twenty years.

- Term loan agreements usually require a business to repay borrowed money in monthly, quarterly, semiannual, or annual installments.

- Money realized from the sale of corporate bonds must be repaid when the bonds mature. In addition, the corporation must pay interest—usually every six months—on the borrowed money from the time the bonds are sold until maturity.

- Maturity dates for bonds generally range from ten to thirty years after the date of issue.

- Three types of bonds—debentures, mortgage bonds, and convertible bonds—are sold to raise debt capital.

- When comparing the cost of equity and debt long-term financing, the ongoing costs of using stock (equity) to finance a business are low.

- The type of long-term financing that generally has the highest ongoing costs is a long-term loan (debt).

Improve Your Grade
Audio Chapter Summary & Quiz

VIDEO CASE

Gilford Securities' Financial Matchmaking: Easier than Dating

Companies need money for operations and growth, and investors need good investments. This is where Gilford Securities comes in. Since 1979, Gilford has served as an investment matchmaker, helping small and midsized companies to raise money through IPOs and private debt placements. In addition to investment banking expertise, it has a full-service brokerage unit to buy and sell securities for individual and institutional investors. And to enhance its match-making capabilities, Gilford maintains a staff of expert research analysts who study undervalued securities to identify good investment opportunities for the investors who use its brokerage services.

In a twenty-four-month period, matchmaker Gilford helped fifteen companies obtain capital. Its initial and secondary public offerings range in size from $5 million to more than $25 million; its private placements range from $5 million to $20 million. Not long ago, Gilford was one of several firms co-managing an IPO that raised $28 million for RAM Energy Resources.

Although such numbers generally are too small to capture the attention of giant Wall Street investment banking firms, they are the right size for Gilford. Its specialists know that preparing for an IPO can be traumatic for a growing company and its management team. This is why they work closely with companies during every step in the process, from compiling and filing the necessary financial information to scheduling the offering, setting the initial share price, and arranging for the stock to begin and continue trading. After a transaction, Gilford tracks the performance of the stock and issues regular research reports for current and prospective investors.

The first contact some companies have with Gilford is through its research analysts. For example, the CEO of Pennsylvania Enterprises was impressed after a Gilford analyst researched his company and wrote a report demonstrating a thorough understanding of the company and the industry. Pennsylvania Enterprises became an enthusiastic customer, and soon its growth led to a merger with Southern Union, a major energy company.

Casey Alexander, a senior vice president, explains that thoroughly researching companies is essential if Gilford is to unearth potential investment opportunities for its brokerage customers. One clue he uses is whether managers and directors are buying their own company's stock and the level of their purchases. If insiders are buying heavily, he looks for the catalyst prompting these investments so that he can alert Gilford's brokerage customers to the opportunity. Does the company have a new product, a new process, or a new patent? What special circumstances might induce insiders to make sizable investments that clearly are not guaranteed to pay off? Alexander and his team keep looking until they find answers.

By analyzing companies that few other firms research and recognizing stocks that seem poised to increase in value, Gilford helps its brokerage customers wring the most from their investment dollars. Sometimes the firm arranges for large investors to meet with the management of companies whose stock its analysts are recommending for purchase. However, not every recommendation is a "buy." When they uncover competitive challenges or other emerging problems that can affect a corporation, Gilford's analysts will issue reports explaining their reasoning and suggesting that customers consider selling the stock.

Having an investment banking group to advise companies and a research team to advise customers on the brokerage side of the business is a delicate balancing act these days. Yet, because of the company's high ethical standards and professionalism, top brokers join because they'll have the freedom to do what's right for their customers. Over time, this customer orientation has helped Gilford build a loyal customer base and expand nation-wide despite intense competition. Today the firm has 150 employees spread across offices in New York City and other locations.[12]

For more information about this company, go to www.gilfordsecurities.com.

Questions

1. Imagine that you're an analyst researching a toy manufacturer that relies on speculative production to prepare for the year-end holiday sales period. What questions would you ask the company before determining whether to recommend its stock to investors?
2. In addition to significant insider buying, what other clues might Casey Alexander use in identifying companies that could be profitable investments for Gilford's brokerage customers?
3. Why do you think going public can be traumatic for a company's management team? How does Gilford make the process easier for a firm selling a new securities issue?
4. If you were the owner of a growing business in need of capital, what questions would you ask when choosing an investment bank to take your company public?

BUILDING SKILLS FOR CAREER SUCCESS

1. Exploring the Internet

Finding capital for new business start-ups is never an easy task. Besides a good business plan, those seeking investor funds must be convincing and clear about how their business activities will provide sufficient revenue to pay back investors who help to get them going in the first place. To find out what others have done, it is useful to read histories of successful start-ups as well as failures in journals that specialize in this area. Visit the text website for updates to this exercise.

Assignment

1. Examine articles that profile at least three successes or failures in the following sources and highlight the main points that led to either result.

   American Venture magazine (**www.americanventuremagazine.com**)

   Business 2.0 (**www.business2.com**)

   Red Herring (**www.redherring.com**)

   Fast Company (**www.fastcompany.com**)

2. What are the shared similarities?

3. What advice would you give to a start-up venture after reading these stories?

2. Building Team Skills

Suppose that for the past three years you have been repairing lawn mowers in your garage. Your business has grown steadily, and recently, you hired two part-time workers. Your garage is no longer adequate for your business; it is also in violation of the city code, and you have been fined twice for noncompliance. You have decided that it is time to find another location for your shop and that it also would be a good time to expand your business. If the business continues to grow in the new location, you plan to hire a full-time employee to repair small appliances. You are concerned, however, about how you will get the money to move your shop and get it established in a new location.

Assignment

1. With all class members participating, use brainstorming to identify the following:

   a. The funds you will need to accomplish your business goals

   b. The sources of short-term financing available to you

   c. Problems that might prevent you from getting a short-term loan

   d. How you will repay the money if you get a loan

2. Have a classmate write the ideas on the board.

3. Discuss how you can overcome any problems that might hamper your current chances of getting a loan and how your business can improve its chances of securing short-term loans in the future.

4. Summarize what you learned from participating in this exercise.

3. Researching Different Careers

Financial managers are responsible for determining the best way to raise funds, for ensuring that the funds are used to accomplish their firm's goals and objectives, and for developing and implementing their firm's financial plan. Their decisions have a direct impact on the firm's level of success. When managers do not pay enough attention to finances, a firm is likely to fail.

Assignment

1. Investigate the job of financial manager by searching the library or Internet and/or by interviewing a financial manager.

2. Find answers to the following questions:

   a. What skills do financial managers need?

   b. How much education is required?

   c. What is the starting salary? Top salary?

   d. What will the job of financial manager be like in the future?

   e. What opportunities are available?

   f. What types of firms are most likely to hire financial managers? What is the employment potential?

3. Prepare a report on your findings.

Prepare for Class
Exploring the Internet

RUNNING A BUSINESS PART 6
Finagle A Bagel Counts on Accounting and Finance

Like the hole in a bagel, any hole in Finagle A Bagel's accounting and financial management systems means less dough for the company. Copresidents Alan Litchman and Laura Trust could not profitably build the business without quick access to details such as how much money the stores take in, how much money is spent on ingredients, how much money is needed for rent, and so on.

Tracking Sales, Cash, and Profits
Regina Jerome is Finagle A Bagel's director of information systems. She and her assistant are responsible for running the computerized accounting system as well as for the point-of-sale system that stores use to ring up all customer orders. "Every transaction in every store is recorded and can be retrieved by minute, by day, by store, by cashier, and by terminal," notes Jerome. The copresidents use all this financial data to reconcile daily store sales with daily bank deposits.

As a result, copresident Litchman knows by 7:30 each morning how much money was deposited on the previous day and the total amount the company has to cover payroll, food purchases, and other expenses. He also knows if a store's reported sales match its bank deposit. If not, a senior manager immediately looks into the discrepancy, which usually turns out to be some kind of error. Once in a while, however, the discrepancy is a sign of store-level theft that requires

further investigation and—when warranted—legal action.

Although Finagle A Bagel makes about 8 cents in profit from every sales dollar, Litchman is aiming to make a profit of 10 cents per dollar. He needs timely reports showing retailing and wholesaling revenues, the cost of goods sold, and operating expenses to calculate the company's pretax profit and measure progress toward this profit goal. Food and labor costs constitute more than two-thirds of Finagle A Bagel's costs—so the faster managers can see these numbers, the faster they can act if expenses are higher than expected.

Bagels, Banking, and Borrowing
Like many other entrepreneurs, when Laura Trust and Alan Litchman decided to buy a business, they raised some money from friends and family. Unlike many entrepreneurs, however, they were so adamant about retaining full control of Finagle A Bagel that they never considered venture capital financing or going public. Instead, Litchman says, "We made the decision to get banks to finance this company, which is a difficult thing."

Banks prefer to make loans secured by assets such as inventory or accounts receivable. However, Finagle A Bagel has no inventory aside from each day's raw ingredients and fresh-baked bagels, which cannot be repossessed and resold if the company is unable to repay a

loan. Nor does it have significant accounts receivable because most of its revenues come from cash transactions in the seventeen stores. The company has commercial ovens and other equipment, but, says copresident Litchman, banks do not consider such assets sufficient collateral for a secured loan. And not every bank is willing to offer an unsecured line of credit to a small, fast-growing company like Finagle A Bagel.

Fortunately, the copresidents bought Finagle A Bagel after the previous owner (who stayed on for a time after the purchase) had built the business into a highly successful chain. To a bank, a company with a proven record of success and a detailed, practical business plan for continued growth looks less risky as a borrower than a newly established company without customers, assets, or cash flow. Thus Finagle A Bagel was able to negotiate an unsecured line of credit of nearly $4 million. As long as Trust and Litchman could show that the company was healthy and achieving certain financial ratios, they were allowed to draw on the credit line to open new stores or for other business purposes.

Initially, the copresidents only paid the interest on borrowed money so that they would have more money available for growth. Within a few years, however, they began repaying the principal as well as the interest. This meant less money to fuel growth, but it also lightened the company's debt load.

Juggling Three Banks and Two Checking Accounts

Even though Finagle A Bagel operates numerous stores plus a wholesale division, it deals with three banks and needs only two corporate checking accounts. Here's how the system works: For safety reasons, management does not want general managers or their assistants traveling too far to deposit each day's receipts. So the company deals with three New England banks that have local branches located near the stores. For each store, Finagle A Bagel opens an account in the closest branch of one of these three banks. After the day's deposits are made, money is transferred using an electronic funds transfer system to the company's main checking account.

Every morning, Litchman looks at the current balance in the main checking account and examines the report showing the previous day's sales and deposits. That tells him how much money he has to cover the bills to be paid that day. Given the slim profit margin in the food-service business—only pennies per sales dollar—Finagle A Bagel uses most of its cash to pay for food and labor.

Clearly, cash flow is critical for a small, fast-growing business. Especially on slower sales days, Litchman observes, "You may be one check away from being cash-negative." If its main checking account balance is too low to cover checks that are presented for payment that day, the company may have to draw on its line of credit. Once this happens, the company must pay interest on any money it borrows, even for just a day.

Finagle A Bagel uses its second checking account only for payroll. This is a zero-balance account containing no money because its sole function is to clear payroll checks. Having two checking accounts allows the company to separate its payroll payments from its payments for supplies, rent, and other business expenses, a convenience for tax and accounting purposes. It also helps the copresidents maintain tight financial control: No check can be issued without either Litchman's or Trust's signature.

The Future of Finagle A Bagel

The future of Finagle A Bagel could take a very different turn. "The opportunity to be bought by, just for an example, a McDonald's or a Wendy's or one of the larger operators becomes more plausible as you start to prove to people that you can survive as a multiunit chain with twenty or more stores," says Trust. Because big companies are always on the lookout for innovative food-service concepts, Finagle A Bagel's owners might receive an acquisition offer that's too good to pass up.

A few years ago the company was named Greater Boston's Small Business of the Year, and *Boston* magazine put it on the "Best of Boston" list for two consecutive years. The company also has been named to the list of Top 100 Women-Led Businesses in Massachusetts. As important and gratifying as such honors may be for a small business, money always must be—literally—the bottom line for Finagle A Bagel. "You have to make money," Trust emphasizes. "If you don't make money, you're not in business."

Questions

1. Finagle A Bagel tracks cash, sales revenues, and expenses on a daily basis. How does this type of accounting system encourage effective decision making and discourage store-level theft?

2. As a small business, which of the financial ratios might Finagle A Bagel want to track especially closely? Why?

3. If the copresidents of Finagle A Bagel had approached venture capitalists for funding, they probably would have been able to open more new stores in less time. Instead, they opted to use bank financing that has to be repaid. Do you agree with their decision? Why?

4. Given their growth plans, why would the copresidents repay principal and interest on borrowed money rather than pay interest only? Which repayment plan would Finagle A Bagel's bank prefer?

Sources: Based on information from Clara Silverstein, "Look Around Finagle A Bagel," *Boston Globe*, April 19, 2006, p. E2; Sasha Pfeiffer, "Bagel Tribute to the Sox Becomes a Daily Sellout," *Boston Globe*, April 12, 2006, n.p.; Matt Viser, "Small, But Thinking Big," *Boston Globe*, October 27, 2005, **www.boston.com**; "Finagle A Bagel to Move HQ to Newton," *Boston Business Journal*, January 13, 2005, **www.bizjournals.com/boston**; Donna Hood Crecca, "Higher Calling," *Chain Leader*, December 2002, p. 14; "State Fare: Finagle A Bagel, Boston," *Restaurants and Institutions*, October 1, 2002, **www.rimag.com/1902/sr.htm**; "Finagle Sees a Return to More Normal Business Mode," *Foodservice East*, Fall 2002, pp. 1, 17; "Sloan Grads Bet Their Money on Bagels," *Providence Business News*, October 25, 1999, p. 14; interview with Laura B. Trust and Alan Litchman, February 25, 2003; **www.finagleabagel.com**.

Notes

CHAPTER 1

1. Based on information in "Gatorade Sports Drink Revamps Site for European Focus," *New Media Age*, May 31, 2007, p. 3; "PepsiCo's Profit Rises 61% on International Sales," *New York Times*, February 9, 2007, p. C6; Chris Reidy, "Pepsi to Help Ocean Spray Get on More Store Shelves," *Boston Globe*, July 14, 2006, p. E1; Stephanie Thompson, "Pepsi Dons Disguise in Attempt to Seduce the Whole Foods Devotees," *Advertising Age*, November 6, 2006, p. 3; Christina Cheddar Berk, "PepsiCo's CEO Sees No Need to Change Current Strategy," *Wall Street Journal*, October 24, 2006, p. B4; Betsy McKay and Janet Adamy, "Food Companies Vow to Tighten Limits on Kids' Ads, *Wall Street Journal*, November 15, 2006, p. B3; "PepsiCo to Buy Naked Juice," *Los Angeles Times*, November 22, 2006, p. C2.
2. Ibid.
3. The Dudley Products, Inc., website at **www.dudleyq.com;** accessed August 7, 2007.
4. The Horatio Alger website at **www.horatioalger.com;** accessed August 7, 2007.
5. Alan Goldstein, "Most Dot.Coms Doomed to Fail, Cuban Tells Entrepreneurs," *Dallas Morning News*, April 7, 2000, p. 1D.
6. Idy Fernandez, "Julie Stav," *Hispanic*, June–July 2005, p. 24.
7. The Wal-Mart website at **www.walmart.com;** accessed September 11, 2006.
8. U.S. Census Bureau, *Statistical Abstract of the United States*, 2007, 126th ed. (Washington: U.S. Government Printing Office, 2007), p. 429.
9. The CBS News website at **www.cbsnews.com;** accessed September 30, 2005.
10. The Bureau of Economic Analysis website at **www.bea.gov;** accessed September 11, 2006.
11. The Bureau of Economic Analysis website at **www.bea.gov;** accessed September 12, 2006.
12. U.S. Census Bureau, *Statistical Abstract of the United States*, 2006, 125th ed. (Washington: U.S. Government Printing Office, 2006), p. 317.
13. The Bureau of Labor Statistics website at **www.bls.gov;** accessed August 7, 2007.
14. Bill Weir, "Made in China: Your Job," ABC News website at **www.abcnews.com;** accessed September 21, 2005.
15. Based on information from Andrew Martin, "In Live Bacteria, Food Makers See A New Bonanza," *New York Times*, January 22, 2007, pp. A1+; Andrew Martin, "Stonyfield Farm Yogurt President Oversees Natural Fast-Food Restaurant Chain," *Chicago Tribune*, June 15, 2005, **www.chicagotribune.com;** Jim Johnson, "Yogurt Maker Gets Handle on Recycling Partnership," *Waste News*, January 3, 2005, p. 5; "French Conglomerate Groupe Danone SA Has Increased Its Stake in the Stonyfield Farm," *Food Management*, February 2004, p. 84; David Goodman, "Culture Change," *Mother Jones*, January–February 2003, pp. 52–78; **www.stonyfield.com.**

CHAPTER 2

1. Sources: Based on information from Michael Arndt, "3M's Seven Pillars of Innovation," *BusinessWeek*, May 10, 2006, **www.Businessweek.com;** Toni Randolph, "3M Names New CEO," Minnesota Public Radio, December 7, 2005, **http://news.minnesota.publicradio.org/features/2005/12/07_ap_3mboss;** "EPA Cites 3M, Motorola, Pfizer Facilities, Others, for Environmental Progress Beyond Current Regulatory Requirements," U.S. Environmental Protection Agency news release, April 8, 2005, **www.epa.gov;** "Businesses Turn Energy Savings into a Profit for the Environment," U.S. Environmental Protection Agency news release, March 21, 2006, **www.epa.gov;** "3M Ergonomic Optical Mouse," *Extreme Tech*, November 9, 2006, **www.ExtremeTech.com; www.3m.com.**
2. Charles Haddad and Amy Barrett, "A Whistle-Blower Rocks an Industry," *BusinessWeek*, June 24, 2002, pp. 126–130.
3. Albert B. Crenshaw, "Tax Shelter Leaders Get Jail Time, Must Pay Restitution," *Washington Post*, April 23, 2005, p. E2.
4. *Frontlines* (Washington: U.S. Agency for International Development), September 2005, p. 16.
5. Anthony Bianco, William Symonds, and Nanette Byrnes, "The Rise and Fall of Dennis Kozlowski," *BusinessWeek*, December 23, 2002, pp. 64–77
6. James Underwood, "Should You Watch Them on the Web," CIO, **www.cio.com/archive/051500_face.html;** accessed May 15, 2000.
7. Paula Dwyer et al., "Year of the Whistleblower," *BusinessWeek*, December 16, 2002, pp. 107–110.
8. **www.whistleblowers.org/;** accessed September 21, 2005.
9. Dell Sustainability Report, Dell Fiscal Year 2006 in Review, pp. 68–69, **www.dell.com;** accessed September 29, 2006.
10. **www.ibm.com/ibm/responsibility/world/communities/;** accessed September 23, 2006.
11. **www.ge.com/en/citizenship/community/vol/index.htm;** accessed September 24, 2006.
12. **http://merck.com/cr/company_profile/philanthropy_at_Merck/home_print.html;** accessed September 26, 2006.
13. **http://solutions.3m.com/wps/portal/3m/en;** accessed September 27, 2006.
14. **http://att.sbc.com/gen/corporate-citizenship?pid=7736;** accessed September 28, 2006.
15. *The Lamp* (ExxonMobil), vol. 88, no. 1 (2006), p. 31, **www.exxonmobil.com;** accessed September 28, 2006.
16. U.S. Government Accountability Office, *Agricultural Conservation: USDA Should Improve Its Process for Allocating Funds to States for the Environmental Quality Insentive Program (EQIP)*, GAO-06-969 (Washington: U.S. Government Printing Office, September 2006), p. 5.
17. Based on information from "New Belgium Expands Production," *Beverage Industry*, June 2006, p. 14; "New Belgium Brewing Wins Ethics Award," *Denver Business Journal*, January 2, 2003, **Denver.bizjournals.com/Denver/stories/2002/12/30/daily21.html;** Richard Brandes, "Beer Growth Brands," *Beverage Dynamics*, September–October 2002, pp. 37ff; **www.newbelgium.com; www.followyourfolly.com.**

CHAPTER 3

1. Sources: Based on information from Alex Markels, "Turning the Tide at P&G," *U.S. News & World Report*, October 30, 2006, pp. 69–71; Ellen Byron, "And Now a Word From . . . P&G's Global Marketing Chief," *Wall Street Journal*, July 10, 2006, p. R7; Geoffrey A. Fowler, "For P&G in China, It's Wash, Rinse, Don't Repeat," *Wall Street Journal*, April 7, 2006, p. B3; James T. Areddy, "Spent Force: As Families Splurge, Chinese Savings Start to Take a Hit," *Wall Street Journal*, May 2, 2006, p. A1; "A Post-Modern Proctoid, Face Value," *The Economist*, April 16, 2006, p. 68; Mark Schoeff, "P&G Places a Premium on International Experience," *Workforce Management*, April 10, 2006, p. 28; **www.pg.com.**

2. U.S. Department of Commerce, International Trade Administration, and the U.S. Census Bureau, **www.census.gov/foreign-trade/Press-Release/ current-press-release/exh1.pdf;** accessed May 18, 2007.

3. *Business Review*, Federal Reserve Bank of Philadelphia, Second Quarter 2005, p. 70.

4. "The Global Economic Outlook and Risks from Global Imbalances," remarks by Rodrigo de Rato, managing director of International Monetary Fund, September 30, 2005.

5. Michael Chriszt and Elena Whisler, "China's Economic Emergence," *Econ South*, Federal Reserve Bank of Atlanta, Second Quarter 2005, pp. 4–7.

6. **www.whitehouse.gov/news/releases/2005/08/print/20050803-1.html;** accessed September 21, 2005.

7. William M. Pride and O.C. Ferrell, *Marketing*, 12th ed. (Boston: Houghton Mifflin, 2003), p. 128.

8. *Ibid.*, 127.

9. Based on information from "IDG: Ten Years in China," *Asia Africa Intelligence Wire*, September 23, 2005, n.p.; "IDG Develops Partnerships in Vietnam to Expand Its Activities," *Tradeshow Week*, July 18, 2005, p. 5; Sean Callahan, "Publishers Explore Vast Chinese Market," B to B, December 9, 2002, p. 3; "'Let Many Gardens Bloom': IDG's Pat Kenealy Sees the Future Everywhere," *Min's B to B*, April 11, 2005, n.p.; **www.idg.com.**

CHAPTER 4

1. Based on information in Terry Pristin, "Out of the Kitchen and into the Shopping Mall," *New York Times*, October 25, 2006, p. C9; Julie Naughton, "Carol's Daughter Gives Birth to New Store," *WWD*, September 16, 2005, p. 20; "Will Smith, Jay-Z Back Beauty Line," *CNN Money*, May 18, 2005, **www.money.cnn.com/2005/05/18/news/newsmakers/cossmetics;** Erika Kinetz, "DanceAfrica Spills onto Brooklyn Streets in a Bazaar of Goods for Near and Far," *New York Times*, May 27, 2005, pp. E1, E17; Julie Naughton, "Carol's Daughter Poised for Growth," *WWD*, August 5, 2005, p. 6.

2. Ibid.

3. "The Web at Your Service," *BusinessWeek Online*, **www.businessweek.com,** accessed March 18, 2002.

4. Bradley Mitchell, "What Is (Wireless/Computer) Networking," About.com website, **www.about.com;** accessed August 11, 2007.

5. Bradley Mitchell, "LAN—Local Area Network," About.com website, **www .about.com;** accessed August 11, 2007.

6. Charlene Li and Shar VanBoskirk, "U.S. Online Marketing Forecast: 2005 to 2010," Forrester Research, Inc., website, **www.forrester.com/Research/ Document/Excerpt/0,7211,36546,00.html;** accessed May 2, 2005.

7. "Worldwide Internet Users Will Top 1 Billion in 2005. USA Remains #1 with 185M Internet Users," *Computer Industry Almanac* website, **www.c-i-a.com/ pr0904.htm;** accessed September 3, 2004.

8. Nielsen//NetRatings, "Two Out of Every Five Americans Have Broadband Access at Home," Nielsen//NetRatings website, **www.nielsen-netratings .com/pr/pr_050928.pdf;** accessed September 28, 2005.

9. Source: Based on information in Suzanne Marta, "Travelocity Adds Destination Activity Information," *Dallas Morning News*, January 15, 2007, n.p.; Dennis Schaal, "Satisfaction 'Guaranteed' by Travelocity," *Travel Weekly*, May 2, 2005, pp. 1+; Suzanne Marta, "Travelocity Trying to Expand Services beyond Lower Prices," *Dallas Morning News*, March 1, 2005, **dallasnews.com;** Avery Johnson, "Booking a $51 Flight to Fiji Online," Flyertalk website, **www.flyertalk.com,** accessed April 26, 2005; **www.travelocity.com.**

CHAPTER 5

1. Based on information from Vito J. Racanelli, "A Good Name Above All," *Barron's*, September 11, 2006, pp. 1+; Stephanie Saul, "Johnson & Johnson Buys Pfizer Unit for $16.6 Billion," *New York Times*, June 27, 2006, p. C2; **jnj.com.**

2. The Ivy Group website at **www.ivygroupllc.com;** accessed October 1, 2006.

3. The Yahoo! Small Business website at **http://smallbusiness.yahoo.com/;** accessed October 22, 2006.

4. The Hispanic PR Wire website at **www.hispanicprwire.com;** accessed August 21, 2007.

5. The Internal Revenue Service website at **www.irs.gov;** accessed August 21, 2007.

6. The Company Corporation website at **www.corporate.com;** accessed August 21, 2007.

7. The Sony Ericsson Mobile Communications website at **www.sonyericsson .com;** accessed October 19, 2006.

8. The Wal-Mart website at **www.walmart.com;** accessed October 19, 2006.

9. The Oracle website at **www.oracle.com;** accessed October 18, 2006.

10. The Internet Security Systems website at **www.iss.net;** accessed October 18, 2006.

11. The Procter & Gamble website at **www.pg.com;** accessed October 18, 2006.

12. Based on information from Keith Reed, "Bowing Out at Jordan's," *Boston Globe*, December 22, 2006, p. C1; David Gianatasio, "Rooms to Grow," *Adweek*, January 14, 2003, p. 3; Jon Chesto, "Buffet Helps Jordan's Flip Switch," *Boston Herald*, August 22, 2002, p.37; "At the Movies with Buffet," *Financial Express*, October 28, 2002; Barry Tatelman, "You Can't Take That Away from Us," *Operations Management* (n.d.), **www.furninfo.com/ operations/jordans0402.html; www.jordansfurniture.com.**

CHAPTER 6

1. Based on information from Sheena Harrison, "Kate Richard, 28," *Crain's Detroit Business*, April 17, 2006, p. 28; Cyndia Zwahlen, "Women's Support Group Gets Creative," *Los Angeles Times*, May 17, 2006, p. C7; Joanna L. Ossinger, "Women Entrepreneurs Have an Increasing Number of Places to Reach Out for Funding," *Wall Street Journal*, September 25, 2006, p. R11; Amy Ann Stoessel, "On the Job," *Crain's Cleveland Business*, October 9, 2006, p. 25.

2. U.S. Small Business Administration, **www.sba.gov/size/summary-whatis .html;** accessed August 22, 2007.

3. U.S. Small Business Administration, Office of Advocacy, **www.sba.gov/ advo;** accessed August 27, 2007.

4. *Ibid.*

5. **www.richmondfed.org/community_affairs/;** accessed October 20, 2005.

6. Thomas A. Garrett, "Entrepreneurs Thrive in America," *Bridges*, Federal Reserve Bank of St. Louis, Spring 2005, p. 2

7. *2004 The Small Economy*, A Report to the President, U.S. Small Business Administration, Washington, D.C., 2004, p. 2.

8. Kim Girard and Sean Donahue, "Crash and Learn: A Field Manual for e-Business Survival," *Business2.0*, **www.business2.com/content/magazine/ indepth/2000/06/28/13700,** accessed June 11, 2000.

9. U.S. Small Business Administration, **http://app1.sba.gov/faqs/faqindex .cfm?areaID=24;** accessed August 25, 2007.

10. *Ibid.*

11. U.S. Small Business Administration, Office of Advocacy News Release, August 2007, **www.sba.gov/advo;** accessed August 28, 2007.

12. U.S. Small Business Administration, **http://www.sba.gov/idc/groups/ public/documents/sb;** accessed August 23, 2007, and **http://www .score.org/explore_score.html,** accessed August 23, 2007.

13. Special Advertising Supplement, *New York Times*, April 25, 2005, p. ZN4.

14. U.S. Small Business Administration, **www.score.org/media_fact_sheet .html;** accessed August 28, 2007.

15. U.S. Small Business Administration, Office of Advocacy, Frequently Asked Questions, August 2007, p. 2., **www.sba.gov/advo/;** accessed August 28, 2007.

16. Cindy Elmore, "Satisfaction Guarateed," *Marketwise*, Federal Reserve Bank of Richmond, Issue III, 2004, p. 21.

17. U.S. Small Business Administration News Releases, September 12, 2005 and November 8, 2005., **www.sba.gov/news/;** accessed October 26, 2006.

18. U.S. Small Business Administration, "SBA FY 2005 Performance and Accountability Report," p. 11, **www.sba.gov;** accessed October 29, 2006.

19. U.S. Small Business Administration, **www.sba.gov/INV/stat/table1.doc;** accessed October 28, 2006.

20. William M. Pride and O. C. Ferrell, *Marketing*, 12th ed. (Boston: Houghton Mifflin, 2003), p. 414.

21. Cindy Elmore, "Putting the Power into the Hands of Small Business Owners," *Marketwise*, Federal Reserve Bank of Richmond, Issue II, 2005, p. 13.

22. U.S. Small Business Administration, **www.sba.gov/managing/marketing/ intlsales.html;** accessed October 4, 2005.

23. Based on information from Ed Christian, "Mike Dreese, CEO, Newbury Comics," Billboard, December 23, 2006, p. 22; Ed Christman, "Newbury Comics Cuts Staff," Billboard, September 10, 2005, p. 8; Wendy Wilson, "Newbury Comics," Video Business, December 20, 2004, p. 18; Ed Christman. "We Have All Had to Grow Up a Little," Billboard, September 27, 2003, pp. N3ff; **www.newburycomics.com;** Accessed January 3, 2007.

CHAPTER 7

1. Based on information from Adrienne Carter, "Lighting a Fire Under Campbell," *BusinessWeek*, December 4, 2006, pp. 96–101; Carol Hymowitz, "Business Is Personal, So Managers Need to Harness Emotions," *Wall Street Journal*, November 13, 2006, pp. B1+; Saj-nicole Joni, "The Power of Purpose," *Forbes.com*, December 4, 2006, **www.forbes.com; www. campbell.com;** "Canned and Packaged Foods—Soup," *Progressive Grocer*, November 15, 2006, pp. 34+.

2. Geoff Armstrong, "People Strategies Are Key to Future Success," *Personnel Today*, January 7, 2003, p. 2.

3. Stephanie Mehta and Fred Vogelstein, "AOL: The Relaunch," *Fortune*, November 14, 2005, pp. 78–84.

4. **www.google.com/corporate/.**

5. Curtis Sittenfeld, "Get Well Soon!" *Fast Company*, April 2005, p. 32.

6. Herold Hamprecht, "Chrysler Group Has Big Plans for Europe," *Automotive News Europe* 10(8), April 18, 2005.

7. Lucas Conley, "Climbing Back Up the Mountain," *Fast Company*, April 2005, p. 84.

8. Scott Morrison, "From Tactics to Strategy," *Financial Times*, January 24, 2003, p. 8.

9. **www.monster.com.**

10. Henry Mintzberg, "The Manager's Job: Folklore and Fact," *Harvard Business Review*, July–August 1975, pp. 49–61.

11. Chana R. Schoenberger, "The Greenhouse Effect," **www.forbes.com/ global/2003/0203/030_print.html;** accessed February 3, 2003.

12. Robert Kreitner, *Management*, 9th ed. (Boston: Houghton Mifflin, 2004), p. 505.

13. Ricky W. Griffin, *Fundamentals of Management*, 3d ed. (Boston: Houghton Mifflin, 2003), p. 96.

14. "IBM Announces PC Division's 2005 Plan," *SinoCast China Business Daily News*, London, January 24, 2005, p. 1.

15. Paul R. La Monica, "After Carly, Is HP a Bargain?" *Money*, April 2005, p. 108.

16. Paul Loftus, "Viewpoint: Tackling Talent Management," IndustryWeek, January 10, 2007, **www.industryweek.com;** "Kimberly-Clark Hires Accenture to Provide Broad Range of Human Resources Services," Accenture news release, January 29, 2007, **www.accenture.com;** Loretta Chao, "Sabbaticals Can Offer Dividends for Employers," Wall Street Journal, July17, 2006, p. B.

CHAPTER 8

1. Based on information from Patrick J. Kiger, "Power of the Individual: Small Groups Big Ideas," *Workforce Management*, February 27, 2006, pp. 1+; Chris Taylor, "What's In a Name?" *Sales and Marketing Management*, January–February 2006, pp. 31+.

2. "Mercedes-Benz USA Selects Workstream," *Business Editors; Automotive Writers*, March 2005.

3. Bill Saporito, "Can Wal-Mart Get Any Bigger? (Yes, a lot Bigger . . . Here's How)," *Time*, January 13, 2003, p. 38.

4. Robert Kreitner, *Foundations of Management: Basics and Best Practices* (Boston: Houghton Mifflin, 2005), pp. 186–187.

5. Paul Kaihla, "Raytheon on Target," *Business 2.0*, **www.business2.com/ articles/mag/0,1640,46335,00.html;** accessed February 4, 2003.

6. Stephanie Thompson, "'God Is in the Details': Campbell Soup Chief Energizes Marketing; Fingerman Pushes Innovation Agenda to Stimulate Sleepy Sales," *Advertising Age*, January 27, 2003, p. 3.

7. Kreitner, *Foundations of Management*, p. 192.

8. Marriott International Fact Sheet, *Hoovers Online*, September 5, 2007, http://www.hoovers.com/marriott/—ID__56078—/free-co-factsheet .xhtml

9. Rob Goffee and Gareth Jones, "The Character of a Corporation: How Your Company's Culture Can Make or Break Your Business," *Jones Harper Business*, p. 182.

10. Paul Sloan, "Dells Man on Deck," *Business 2.0*, February 2003.

11. "Mergers' Missing Link: Cultural Integration," *PR Newswire*, January 23, 2003.

12. Kreitner, *Foundations of Management*, p. 49.

13. Source: Based on information from Mara Der Hovanesian, "Green Mountain Could Really Percolate," *BusinessWeek*, January 8, 2007, p. 84; Tony Baer, "Brewing a New Kind of Connection," *Manufacturing Business Technology*, January 2005, pp. 40–42; Mark Pendergrast, "Green Mountain Coffee Roasters: Doing Well by Doing Good," *Tea & Coffee Trade Journal*, April 20, 2004, pp 100+; Ellyn Spragins, "The Three-Peat," *Fortune Small Business*, July–August 2003, n.p.; **www.greenmountaincoffee.com.**

CHAPTER 9

1. Based on information from Jena McGregor, "Six Sigma Still Pays Off at Motorola," *BusinessWeek*, December 4, 2006, p. 50; Amol Sharma, "Testing, Testing," *Wall Street Journal*, October 23, 2006, p. R7; Kate Norton, "Nokia and Motorola on Earnings Seesaw?" *BusinessWeek Online*, October 19, 2006, **www.businessweek.com.**

2. The Bureau of Labor Statistics website at **www.bls.gov;** accessed August 31, 2007.

3. Robert Kreitner, *Management*, 10th ed. (Boston: Houghton Mifflin, 2007), pp. 577–578.

4. The 3M website at **www.3m.com**; accessed November 3, 2006.

5. Berry Plastics website at **www.berryplastics.com**; accessed November 8, 2006.

6. The National Institute for Standards and Technology (NIST) website at **www.nist.gov**; accessed September 1, 2007.

7. Robert Schroeder, "Productivity Growth Bodes Well for U.S.: Bernanke," Market Watch website at **www.marketwatch**; accessed June 9, 2006.

8. "International Factory Productivity Gains in 2005," The Bureau of Labor Statistics website at **www.bls.gov**; accessed November 3, 2006.

9. David Shook, "A Tool-and-Die Maker for Genesmiths," *BusinessWeek Online*, **www.businessweek.com**; accessed October 15, 2002.

10. The Dell website at **www.dell.com**; accessed November 10 2006.

11. Source: Based on information from Andrew Martin, "In Live Bacteria, Food Makers See a New Bonanza," *New York Times*, January 22, 2007, p. A1+; Clara Silverstein, "Look Around Finagle A Bagel," *Boston Globe*, April 19, 2006, p. E2; Stephen Hochman, "Flexibility—Finding the Right Fit," *Supply Chain Management Review*, July–August 2005, p. 10; www .finaglebagel.com, **www.stonyfield.com; www.bakersbestcatering.com; www.newbalance.com.**

CHAPTER 10

1. Based on information in Daniel Roth, "Trading Places," *Fortune Magazine*, January 20, 2006, pp. 120+; Bill Leonard, "Taking Care of Their Own: Under Chairman Bill Greehey, Valero Energy Demonstrates How a Commitment to Compassion and Community Service Can Lead to Success," *HR Magazine*, June 2006, pp. 112+; Ed Frauenheim, "2006 Winner Innovation Valero Energy," *Workforce Management*, March 13, 2006, p. 23; **www.Valero.com.**

2. Ivy Schmerken, "The Hiring Game," *Wall Street & Technology*, Spring 2005, pp. 28+.

3. Joseph Mann, "Fort Lauderdale, Florida-Based AutoNation Reports Earnings Increase," *South Florida Sun-Sentinel*, February 7, 2003.

4. Bureau of Labor Statistics website at **www.dol.gov**; accessed October 17, 2005.

5. "ManTech to Provide C4ISR Training Support," *Aerospace Daily & Defense Report*, January 6, 2005, p. 5.

6. **http://careers.bankofamerica.com/overview/overview.asp** accessed January 17, 2003.

7. Linnea Anderson, "Monster Worldwide, Inc.," Hoovers.com, **http://premium .hoovers.com/subscribe/co/factsheet.xhtml?ID=crjrkfhfckrkhc.**

8. Nanette Byrnes, "Start Search," *BusinessWeek*, October 10, 2005, pp. 74–76.

9. Harry Wessel, "Jobs Column," *The Orlando Sentinel*, January 15, 2003.

10. U.S. Department of Labor, Bureau of Labor Statistics, News Release, June 18, 2002, **www.dol.gov.**

11. "Employees, HR Out of Sync," *Employee Benefit News*, January 1, 2003, p. 5.

12. Douglas Harbrecht, "When Active Duty Calls IBM'ers," *BusinessWeek Online*, **www.businessweek.com:/print/careers/content/feb2003/ca/ 20030210_9434_ca030.html**, accessed February 10, 2003.

13. Robert Levering, Milton Moskowitz, Ann Harrington, and Christopher Tkaczyk, "100 Best Companies to Work For," *Fortune*, January 20, 2003, p. 127.

14. Based on information from Megan Tench, "N.E. Aquarium Regains Its Accreditation," Boston Globe, September 26, 2006, **www.boston.com**; Geoff Edgers, "With Eye on Growth, Aquarium Names New Chief," Boston Globe, June 15, 2005, **www.boston.com**; Stephanie Vosk, "It's February, But on Summer Jobs, Hope Springs Eternal," Boston Globe, February 20, 2005, p. 3; Jeffrey Krasner,

"New England Aquarium Plunges into Financial Turmoil," Boston Globe, December 13, 2002, **www.boston.com; www.neaq.org.**

CHAPTER 11

1. Based on information from Betsy Morris, "Genentech: The Best Place to Work Now," *CNNMoney.com*, January 20, 2006, n.p; Ed Frauenheim, "On the Clock, But Off on Their Own," *Workforce Management*, April 24, 2006, p. 40; Andrew Pollack, "Genentech Caps Cost of Cancer Drug for Some Patients," *New York Times*, October 12, 2006, p. C2; **www.gene.com.**

2. Sheree R. Curry, "Retention Getters," *Incentive*, April 2005, pp. 14+.

3. Christopher Bowe and Andrew Hill, "This Month's Strike at General Electric Highlights the Growing Tensions Between Management and Workers over Healthcare and Retirement Benefits," *Financial Times*, January 30, 2003, p. 11.

4. "Isle of Capri Casinos, Inc., Creates Real-Life Employee 'Survivor' Event," *PR Newswire*, January 20, 2003.

5. Douglas McGregor, *The Human Side of the Enterprise* (New York: McGraw-Hill, 1960).

6. William Ouchi, *Theory Z* (Reading, MA: Addison-Wesley, 1981).

7. Ricky W. Griffin, *Fundamentals of Management*, 3d ed. (Boston: Houghton Mifflin, 2006), p. 334.

8. Rochelle Garner, "Company Growth and Rankings," *Computer Reseller*, January 31, 2005.

9. Alison Overholt, "Power up the People: Economy Stuck in the Doldrums? Morale Stuck There Too? Here Are a Few Things That You Can Do to Jazz Things up in 2003," *Fast Company*, January 2003, p. 50.

10. "Is Job Stress Taking Its Toll in Your Facility," *Safety Management*, February 2003, p. 3.

11. Alan Deutschman, "Making Change," *Fast Company*, May 2005, pp. 52+.

12. Leah Carlson, "Benefits that Meet Mom's Needs," *Employee Benefits News*, December 1, 2005, n.p.

13. Nanette Byrnes, "Star Search," *BusinessWeek*, October 10, 2005, p. 78.

14. Leigh Strope, "More Workers Have Option of Growing Flex-Time Trend," Associated Press, January 6, 2003.

15. **www.starbucks.com/aboutus/jobcenter.asp**

16. Alison Maitland, "Two for the Price of One." *Financial Times Limited*, January 24, 2001, p. 17.

17. *World News This Morning*, Transcript, ABC News, January 10, 2003.

18. "Telework Succeeds for U.S. Agencies," *Work & Family Newsbrief*, January 2003, p. 7.

19. "Boston College Report Presents Challenges and Advantages of Telework," *Work & Family Newsbrief*, January 2003, p. 8.

20. Arif Mohamed, "Bosses Split Over Productivity of Teleworkers," *Computer Weekly*, March 29, 2005, p. 55.

21. Matthew Boyle and Ellen Florian Kratz, "The Wegmans Way," *Fortune*, January 24, 2005, p. 62.

22. "A Short History of ESOP," **www.nceo.org**, January 2006.

23. Bruce Upbin, "Work and Buy and Hold," *Forbes*, January 20, 2003, p. 56.

24. Daniel Kadlec, "Meet the No-Star Team," *Time*, December 19, 2005, p.58.

25. Barry L. Reece and Rhonda Brandt, *Effective Human Relations: Personal and Organizational Applications* (Boston: Houghton Mifflin, 2005), pp. 280–285.

26. "Jones Walker Law Firm Taps Harvard for New Orleans Rebuild Advice," *New Orleans CityBusiness*, News Section, January 3, 2006, n.p.

27. "Case Study: Using the Right Incentive Can Improve Cooperation Among Departments," *Report on Customer Relationship Management*, September 2003, p. 5.

28. Bill Fischer and Andy Boynton, "Virtuoso Teams" *Harvard Business Review,* July–August 2005, pp. 116–123.

29. Milton Moskowitz and Robert Levering, "10 Great Companies to Work For," *Fortune International,* January 20, 2003, p. 26.

30. "Trusted Computer Solutions Names Top Military IT Expert to Advisory Board," *PR Newswire,* October 12, 2004.

31. Based on information from Patricia Harris and David Lyon, "On Weekends, the Pizza Stays on the Premises," Boston Globe, April 9, 2006, p. M.15; Pioneering American Flatbread, video by Houghton Mifflin; Andrew Nemethy, "Waitsfield: American Flatbread," See Vermont, February 21, 2001, **seevermont.nybor.com/dining/story/20722.html; www.americanflatbread.com.**

CHAPTER 12

1. Based on information from Janet Adamy, "A Little Wasabi Ginger with That Burger?" *Wall Street Journal,* December 28, 2006, p. D1; Melanie Warner, "Family-Style Restaurants Deliver Food to Cars at Curbside, For Meals That Nobody at Home Had to Cook," *New York Times,* June 6, 2006, pp. C1+; Joseph T. Hallinan, "For Dining Chains, Lucrative Drinks Could Make for Very Happy Hours," *Wall Street Journal,* October 12, 2006, p. B1; Monica Rogers, "Speedy Delivery: Kurt Hankins Shortens the Development Cycle at Applebee's to Quickly Deliver Bolder, More Upscale Fare," *Chain Leader,* July 2006, pp. 27+; Steve McClellan, "Applebee's Puts VOD on Marketing Menu," *Brandweek,* February 6, 2006, p. 6.

2. *Marketing News,* September 15, 2004, p. 1.

3. Jagdish N. Sheth and Rajendras Sisodia, "More than Ever Before, Marketing Is under Fire to Account for What It Spends," *Marketing Management,* Fall 1995, pp. 13–14.

4. Coca-Cola 2004 Annual Report, **www2.coca-cola.com/investors/annualandotherreports/2004/pdf/Coca-Cola_10-K_Item_01.pdf;** accessed January 6, 2006.

5. Lynette Ryals and Adrian Payne, "Customer Relationship Management in Financial Services: Towards Information-Enabled Relationship Marketing," *Journal of Strategic Marketing,* March 2001, p. 3.

6. Werner J. Reinartz and V. Kumark, "On the Profitability of Long-Life Customers in a Noncontractual Setting: An Empirical Investigation and Implications for Marketing," *Journal of Marketing,* October 2000, pp. 17–35.

7. Roland T. Rust, Katherine N. Lemon, and Valarie A. Zeithaml, "Return on Marketing: Using Customer Equity to Focus Marketing Strategy," *Journal of Marketing* 68 (January 2004), pp. 109–127.

8. Rajkumar Venkatesan and V. Kumar, "A Customer Lifetime Value Framework for Customer Selection and Resource Allocation Strategy," *Journal of Marketing* 68 (October 2004), pp. 106–125.

9. Gina Chon, "Toyota's Marketers Get Respect—Now They Want Love," *Wall Street Journal,* January 11, 2006, p. B1.

10. Megan E. Mulligan, "Wireless for the Well Off," *Forbes.com,* **http://forbes.com/2003/01/21/cz_mm_0121tentech_print.html;** accessed January 21, 2003.

11. Michael J. Weiss, "To Be About to Be," *American Demographics,* September 2003, pp. 29–36.

12. Cliff Edwards, "Inside Intel," *BusinessWeek,* January 9, 2006, p. 46.

13. Kenneth Hein, "Disney Puts Pooh, Power Rangers, Princess under Wing with $500M," *Brandweek,* January 27, 2003, p. 6.

14. Mark Jewell, "Dunkin' Donuts Eyes Turn Westward: Chain Evolves from No Frills," *The Coloradoan,* January 17, 2005, p. E1.

15. William M. Pride and O. C. Ferrell, *Marketing: Concepts and Strategies* (Boston: Houghton Mifflin, 2006), p. 233.

16. Chad Kaydo, "A Position of Power," *Sales and Marketing Management,* June 2000, p. 106.

17. Based on information from "New Balance 'Heroes' Celebrate Centenary," *Marketing Week,* August 31, 2006, p. 6; Stephen Hochman, "Flexibility—Finding the Right Fit," *Supply Chain Management Review,* July–August 2005, p. 10; Naomi Aoki, "New Balance's Latest Ads Celebrate the (Older) Amateur," *Boston Globe,* February 28, 2005, n.p.; Barbara Schneider-Levy, "Woman's Touch: Comfort," *Footwear News,* May 30, 2005, p. 38; Daren Fonda, "Sole Survivor," *Time,* November 8, 2004, p. 48; Thomas J. Ryan, "The Price Is Right," *Footwear Business,* February 2004, n.p.; interviews with Jim Sciabarrasi, Christine Epplett, and Paul Heffernan of New Balance, Houghton Mifflin video, 2003.

18. Kay Parker, "Old-Line Goes Online", *Business 2.0,* **http://www.business2.com/content/magazine/marketing/2000/06/01/1270,** June 1, 2000.

CHAPTER 13

1. Based on information in Seth Porges, "The Top Design Houses: Saving the World, One Laptop at a Time," *PC Magazine,* December 5, 2006, pp. 130–131; John Markoff, "For $150, Third-World Laptop Stirs a Big Debate," *New York Times,* November 30, 2006, pp. 1, C6; David Kirkpatrick, "This PC Wants to Save the World," *Fortune,* November 30, 2006, p. 82; Bruce Einhorn, "In Search of a PC for the People," *BusinessWeek,* June 12, 2006, pp. 40+; Robert A. Guth, "Microsoft Launches Effort to Cut PC Costs in Developing Nations," *Wall Street Journal,* May 22, 2006, p. B6.

2. Peter Lewis, "Play That Funky Music, White Toy," *Fortune,* February 7, 2005, pp. 38–39.

3. William Hall, "Logitech Proves No Mouse Among Men," *Financial Times,* January 6, 2003, p. 15.

4. Procter & Gamble, **www.pg.com;** accessed April 27, 2006; Chennai, *Businessline,* February 6, 2005, p. 1; **www.pg.com/common/sitemap.jhtml.**

5. **www.gefn.com/search/index;** accessed January 24, 2003.

6. Kate MacArthur, "Drink Your Fruits, Veggies: Water's the New Fitness Fad," *Advertising Age,* January 3, 2005, p. 4.

7. Joseph B. White and Norihiko Shirouzu, "Ford Gambles in Rolling Out New F-150," *Wall Street Journal,* January 6, 2003, p. A15.

8. Mike Beirne, "Hershey Gets Sweet with Sugarfree," *Brandweek,* January 20, 2003, p. 4.

9. Peter D. Bennett (ed.), *Dictionary of Marketing Terms* (Chicago: American Marketing Association and NTC Publishing Group, 1995), p. 27.

10. "Market Profile," **www.plma.com;** accessed January 23, 2006.

11. Deborah Ball and Sarah Ellison. "Two Shampoos Lather Up for Duel," *Wall Street Journal,* January 28, 2003, p. B7.

12. "World's Most Valuable Brands," Interbrand, **www.interbrand.com,** accessed July 2005.

13. Emily Lambert, "The Buck Stops Here," *Forbes.com,* **www.forbes.com/forbes/2003/0106/052.html;** accessed January 6, 2003.

14. Alex Taylor III, "Porsche's Risky Recipe," *Fortune,* **www.fortune.com/fortune/print/0,15935,418670,00.html;** accessed February 3, 2003.

15. **www.netzero.com;** accessed September 13, 2007

16. **www.verizon.com;** accessed April 27, 2006.

17. Based on information from "Fuel Costs Hurt Profit at JetBlue," New York Times, July 22, 2005, n.p.; Jeremy W. Peters, "Rougher Times Amid Higher Costs at JetBlue," New York Times, November 11, 2004, pp. C1; Chuck Salter, "And Now the Hard Part," Fast Company, May 2004, pp. 66; Amy Goldwasser, "Something Stylish, Something Blue," Business 2.0, February 2002, pp. 94–95; "Blue Skies: Is JetBlue the Next Great Airline—Or Just a Little Too Good to Be True?" Time, July 30, 2001, pp. 24; Darren

Shannon, "Three of a Kind," Travel Agent, July 23, 2001, pp. 60; Ann Keeton and Stephen Wisnefski, "JetBlue, Following Disruptions, Unveils Customer Bill of Rights," Wall Street Journal, February 21, 2007, p. A4; **www.jetblue.com.**

CHAPTER 14

1. Based on information in Jane Bennett Clark, "Great Things from Big Boxes," *Kiplinger's Personal Finance Magazine*, January 2007, p. 102; Matthew Boyle, "Why Costco Is So Damn Addictive," *Fortune*, October 30, 2006, pp. 126+; Doug Desjardins, "Costco Edges Closer to the Top with Record Earnings," *DSN Retailing Today*, June 12, 2006, p. 40.
2. "Industry Report 2005," *Convenience Store News*, April 18, 2005.
3. Sandra O'Loughlin and Barry Janoff, "Retailers Seek New Ways to Sell Wares," *Brandweek*, January 6, 2003, p. 12.
4. Michael Barbaro, "Readings," *Washington Post*, January 23, 2005, p. F3; David Moin, "Category Killers' Concerns: Overgrowth and Extinction," *WWD*, January 6, 2005, p. 17.
5. **www.dsa.org;** accessed July 12, 2007.
6. **www.donotcall.gov/FAQ;** accessed January 27, 2006.
7. John Eggerton, "DirecTV Settles $10 Million in Complaints," *Broadcasting & Cable*, December 19, 2005, pp. 4, 30.
8. **www.netflix.com;** accessed July 13, 2007.
9. Robert McMillan, "Got 796 Quarters Handy? Get Yourself an iPod," *PC World*, January 2006, p. 54.
10. Sandra O'Loughlin, "Out with the Old: Malls versus Centers," *Brandweek*, May 9, 2005, p. 30.
11. Robert Coen, "Insider's Report," December 2005, **www.universalmccann.com.**
12. "The Impact of Direct-to-Consumer Drug Advertising on Seniors' Health," States News Service, October 10, 2005.
13. Paul Sloan, "The Sales Force that Rocks," *Business 2.0*, July 1, 2005, **cnnmoney.com.**
14. Terence Shimp, *Advertising, Promotion, and Supplemental Aspects of Integrated Marketing Communications* (Mason, OH: Southwestern, 2006), p. 527.
15. Natalie Schwartz, "Clipping Path," *Promo's 12th Annual SourceBook 2005*. p. 15.
16. "Berry & Homer Wraps Bus Leading Lance Armstrong and Tour of Hope Team on Cross-Country Trek," *Business Wire*.
17. Based on information from "100 Best Companies to Work for," Fortune, January 22, 2007, **http://money.cnn.com/magazines/fortune/bestcompanies/2007;** David Biederman, "Breaking New Ground (Recreational Equipment, Inc.)," The Journal of Commerce, November 6, 2006, pp, 24; Denise Power, "REI Woos Customers with Delivery Options," WWD, May 18, 2005, pp. 6B; "REI Climbs Data Mountain to Gain Single View of Customers," Chain Store Age, October 2005, p. S7; Ken Clark, "REI Scales New Heights," Chain Store Age, July 2004, pp. 26A; "REI Climbs to New Heights Online," Chain Store Age, October 2003, pp. 72; **www.rei.com;** Mike Gorrell, "New REI Store Opens in Salt Lake City Area," Salt Lake Tribune, March 28, 2003, **www.sltrib.com.**

CHAPTER 15

1. "Annual Reports Could Use Some Life," *PR Week (US)*, October 9, 2006, p. 10; "Sears' Lampert Shows Value of Annual Report as Comms Tool," *PR Week (US)*, April 10, 2006, p. 9; Charles Keenan, "If It's Spring, It Must Be Annual Report Season," *Community Banker*, May 2006, pp. 64+.

2. Arthur Andersen, The Wikipedia web site at **www.wikipedia.org;** accessed September 28, 2007.
3. American Institute of Certified Public Accountants (AICPA) website at **www.aicpa.org;** accessed November 14, 2006.
4. Nanette Byrnes and William Symonds, "Is the Avalanche Headed for Pricewaterhouse?" *BusinessWeek*, October 14, 2002, pp. 45–46.
5. Steve Rosenbush, "The Message in Ebbers' Sentence," *BusinessWeek Online*, **www.businessweek.com,** July 14, 2005.
6. "Ex-Tyco CEO Dennis Kozlowski Found Guilty," MSNBC, **www.msnbc.msn.com,** June 17, 2005.
7. Wendhy Grossman-Houston, "The Enron Case Drags On," Time, **www.time.com,** October 24, 2006.
8. "System Failure," *Fortune*, June 24, 2002, p. 64.
9. Bureau of Labor Statistics website at **www.bls.gov;** accessed September 28, 2007.
10. American Institute of Certified Public Accountants (AICPA) website at **www.aicpa.org;** accessed September 28, 2007.
11. Sources: Based on information from Jane Sasseen, "White-Collar Crime: Who Does Time?" *BusinessWeek*, February 6, 2006, **www.businessweek.com;** Stephen Labaton, "Four Years Later, Enron's Shadow Lingers as Change Comes Slowly," *New York Times*, January 5, 2006, p. C1; *Making the Numbers at Commodore Appliance* (Houghton Mifflin video).

CHAPTER 16

1. Based on information in Jay Greene, "Taking Tiny Loans to the Next Level," *BusinessWeek*, November 27, 2006, pp. 76+; Jay Greene, "A Big Stage for Small Loans," *BusinessWeek*, November 27, 2006, p. 82; Connie Bruck, "Millions for Millions," *New Yorker*, October 30, 2006, pp. 62+; Sonia Narang, "Sixth Annual Year of Ideas: Web-Based Microfinancing," *New York Times Magazine*, December 10, 2006, p. 84; Joseph P. Fried, "From a Small Loan, a Jewelry Business Grows," *New York Times*, November 12, 2006, sec. 10, p. 1; "Face Value: Macro Credit," *The Economist*, October 21, 2006, p. 78.
2. The Merck & Company website at **www.merck.com;** accessed November 27, 2006.
3. The U.S. Courts website at **www.uscourts.gov/bankruptcycourts.html;** accessed November 28, 2006.
4. Rachel Beck, "All Business: Buyout Binge Boosts Stocks," AP Newswire, Tuesday, November 28, 2006.
5. *Ibid.*
6. Ian Rowley, "Fuji Heavy Trades GM for Toyota," *BusinessWeek Online*, **www.businessweek.com,** October 6, 2005.
7. U.S. Census Bureau, *Statistical Abstract of the United States*, 2006, 125th ed. (Washington: U.S. Government Printing Office, 2006), p. 766.
8. "Amicus Briefs in Enron Bankruptcy Litigation," BondMarkets.com website at **www.bondmarkets.com,** March 18, 2004.
9. Paul R. LaMonica "Google Sets $2.7 Billion IPO," CNN/Money website at **http://money.cnn.com,** November 30, 2006.
10. Scott Reeves "Chipotle's IPO: Mild to Medium," Forbes website at **http://forbes.com;** accessed October 2, 2007.
11. General Electric website at **www.ge.com;** accessed October 2, 2007.
12. Based on information from "RAM Energy Prices Offering at $4 a Share," Associated Press, February 8, 2007, **www.forbes.com/feeds/ap/2007/02/08/ap3408567.html;** the Gilford Securities website at **www.gilfordsecurities.com;** accessed July 1, 2007; and "Newsreel," *Pipeline & Gas Journal*, August 1999, p. 2.

Credits

PHOTO CREDITS

Chapter 1 p. 2: © Image Source/CORBIS; p. 7: © 2007 Monster, Inc. All Rights Reserved; p. 11: Courtesy Best Buy; p. 12: © CORBIS; p. 13: AP Photo/ *The Journal Record*, Jennifer Pitts; p. 14: AP Photo/ *Alaska Journal of Commerce*, Claire Chandler; p. 20: AP Photo/Xinhua, Chen Fei; p. 23: © Peter Morgan/Reuters/CORBIS; p. 30: © Underwood & Underwood/CORBIS; p. 32: PRNewsFoto; p. 34: PRNewswire/ Pepsi-Cola Company.

Chapter 2 p. 38: PRNewsFoto/Habitat for Humanity of Greater Los Angeles; p. 40: PRNewswire/Quest Communications International, Inc; p. 47: Copyright © Time, Inc. All Rights Reserved; p. 50: PRNewswire/Bechtel National Inc; p. 51: PRNewswire/Whirlpool Corporation; p. 51: "WORLD COMMUNITY GRID," the name and logo, are trademarks of International Business Machines Corporation in the U.S., other countries, or both, and are used under license. Used with permission; p. 52: Logo designed by John Beske Communications; p. 68: www.reduce.org; p. 63: U.S. Equal Employment Opportunity Commission, www.eeoc.gov; p. 71: Courtesy www.energystar.gov.

Chapter 3 p. 76: AP Photo/Eugene Hoshiko; p. 79: Feature Photo Service/Japan Airlines; p. 83: Feature Photo Service/Washington AgriNews Service; p. 84: PRNewswire/Gilden Tree; p. 88: Courtesy Ten Thousand Villages; photograph Carol Lefkov; p. 92: AP Photo/ Denis Sarkic; p. 95: AP Photo/M. Lakshman; p. 97: AP Photo/Eugene Hoshiko; p. 102: Feature Photo Service/Procter & Gamble.

Chapter 4 p. 108: PRNewswire/Verizon Wireless Communications; p. 112:Courtesy Ford Motor Company; p. 115: AP Photo/Luis M. Alvarez; p. 118: Courtesy United Devices; p. 119: PRNewswire/Sealy Inc.; p. 125: AP Photo/Don Ryan; p. 129: AP Photo/Richard Vogel; p. 130: PRNewswire; p. 131: NYTimes.com © 2007 The New York Times Company; p. 132: AP Photo/Richard Drew; p. 138: Courtesy Carol's Daughter.

Chapter 5 p. 144: AP Photo/Tony Avelar; p. 148: AP Photo/Pat Vasquez-Cunningham; p. 150: PRNewswire/Black Enterprise; p. 156: PRNewswire/Schwan's Consumer Brands; p. 157: PRNewswire/Gap; p. 159: AP Photo/Paul Sakuma; p. 161: PRNewswire/Smith & Company Architects; p. 165: PRNewswire/Busch Entertainment Corp; p. 167, Business Around the World: AP Photo/Eugene Hasiko; p. 167: AP Photo/Shizuo Kambayashi; p. 172: Feature Photo Service/McNeil Specialty Products Co.

Chapter 6 p. 178: AP Photo/*Akron Beacon Journal*, Mike Cardew; p. 184: Feature Photo Service/Microsoft Corp; p. 184: AP/Wide World; p. 185: Courtesy City Lights Electrical Company, Inc; p. 186: Art Direction: Laura Jaworski, Web Development/Coding: Anthony T. Damasco III; p. 195: Courtesy Little Scoops; p. 196: AP Photo/ Mark Saltz; p. 198: PRNewswire/Putt-Putt Golf Courses of America; p. 199: Courtesy Dream Dinners; p. 201: © 2007 Susan Holtz; p. 204: Courtesy Ladies Who Launch/Greg Hinsdale.

Chapter 7 p. 210: © Image Source/CORBIS; p. 213: PRNewswire/ Giant Eagle Inc; p. 214: AP Photo/Ted S. Warren; p. 217: PRNewswire/ careerbuilder.com; p. 218: AP Photo/Marcio Jose Sanchez; p. 220: PRNewswire/Marriott International Inc; p. 221: AP Photo/Nati Harnik; p. 226: © Getty Images; p. 231: PRNewswire/ Campbell's Center for Nutrition.

Chapter 8 p. 236: © Annie Griffiths Belt/CORBIS; p. 242: AP Photo/ Kathy Willens; p. 244: © Jack Hollingsworth/CORBIS; p. 251: Feature Photo Service/McDonald's; p. 252: PRNewswire/Newsweek; p. 255: Copyright 2007, Linden Research, Inc. All Rights Reserved; p. 256: AP Photo/Mark Lennihan; p. 259: © 2007 Midway Home Entertainment, Inc. All rights reserved; p. 260: Courtesy W.L. Gore & Associates.

Chapter 9 p. 266: PRNewsFoto/Honda Manufacturing of Alabama; p. 269:PRNewswire/Microsoft Corp; p. 272: © 2007 Caterpillar All Rights Reserved. Used with permission; p. 273: © 2007 Starbucks Corporation. All rights reserved; p. 275: AP Photo/Chiaki Tsukumo; p. 277: PRNewswire/Newsweek; p. 282: Feature Photo Service/Novartis Turf & Ornamental Products; p. 284: AP Photo/Alexandria Boulat/ VII; p. 285: © 2005-2007 iSixSigma LLC. All rights reserved; p. 288: © 2007 Dell Inc. All Rights Reserved; p. 290: PRNewswire/Cingular Wireless.

Chapter 10 p. 296: AP Photo/Elaine Thompson; p. 307: PRNewswire/ NAACP Diversity Job Fair; p. 308: AP Photo/Elizabeth Dalziel; p. 314: Courtesy Ernst & Young; p. 316: PRNewswire/Clay Lacy Aviation; p. 317: © CORBIS; p. 322: Occupational Safety and Health Administration; p. 323: © Bob Rowan; Progressive Image/CORBIS; p. 324: PRNewswire/Valero Energy Corporation.

Answer Key

1.1
1. False   2. True   3. e   4. b   5. c

1.2
1. False   2. True   3. d   4. c   5. a

1.3
1. True   2. False   3. d   4. c   5. e

1.4
1. True   2. False   3. False   4. True
5. a

1.5
1. True   2. True   3. True   4. c
5. b

1.6
1. True   2. False   3. True   4. d   5. b

1.7
1. True   2. True   3. b   4. a   5. d

2.1, 2.2
1. T   2. F   3. b   4. c   5. c

2.3
1. T   2. T   3. T   4. c   5. b

2.4
1. T   2. T   3. F   4. d   5. c

2.5
1. T   2. F   3. e   4. b   5. b

2.6
1. F   2. T   3. T   4. a   5. c

2.7
1. T   2. T   3. c   4. e   5. b

2.8
1. F   2. F   3. F   4. a   5. b

2.9
1. F   2. F   3. c   4. a   5. a

2.10
1. F   2. T   3. d   4. c

3.1
1. F   2. d   3. c   4. b   5. d

3.2
1. T   2. T   3. a   4. c   5. e

3.3
1. T   2. F   3. T   4. c   5. d

3.4
1. T   2. F   3. T   4. F   5. F
6. d   7. a

3.5, 3.6
1. F   2. T   3. F   4. e   5. a
6. c   7. c   8. d

4.1
1. F   2. T   3. d   4. a   5. a

4.2
1. F   2. F   3. T   4. b   5. c

4.3
1. T   2. F   3. e   4. a   5. e

4.4
1. e   2. c   3. a   4. c   5. e

4.5
1. F   2. T   3. F   4. c   5. d

4.6
1. T   2. T   3. T   4. a   5. c

4.7
1. T   2. F   3. a   4. b   5. d

4.8
1. T   2. T   3. F   4. d   5. b

5.1
1. F   2. T   3. d   4. a   5. e

5.2
1. F   2. T   3. F   4. e   5. d

5.3
1. F   2. T   3. T   4. d   5. b

5.4
1. T   2. T   3. d   4. a   5. d

5.5
1. T   2. T   3. T   4. c   5. d

5.6
1. F   2. T   3. F   4. e   5. c

5.7
1. T   2. b   3. b   4. d   5. a

5.8
1. T   2. T   3. F   4. c   5. d

6.1
1. F   2. T   3. T   4. d   5. d

6.2
1. T   2. T   3. F   4. T   5. c

6.3, 6.4
1. F   2. T   3. e   4. b   5. e

6.5
1. T   2. T   3. F   4. T   5. c

6.6, 6.7
1. F   2. T   3. d   4. e   5. a

7.1, 7.2
1. T   2. F   3. T   4. b   5. a

7.3
1. T   2. T   3. T   4. b   5. b

7.4, 7.5
1. T   2. F   3. T   4. b   5. a

7.6
1. T   2. T   3. T   4. e   5. b

7.7, 7.8
1. T   2. T   3. F   4. a   5. d

8.1, 8.2
1. T   2. F   3. F   4. c   5. d

8.4, 8.5
1. F   2. F   3. T   4. e   5. a

8.3
1. T   2. F   3. T   4. a   5. b

8.6, 8.7
1. F   2. T   3. F   4. b   5. e

8.8
1. T   2. F   3. T   4. c   5. b

9.1
1. T   2. F   3. T   4. b   5. e

9.2
1. T   2. F   3. T   4. b   5. c

9.3
1. T   2. T   3. d   4. b   5. b

9.4
1. T   2. F   3. F   4. e   5. b

9.5
1. F   2. T   3. F   4. e   5. c

9.6
1. T   2. F   3. T   4. d   5. b

10.1
1. a   2. b   3. b   4. a   5. e

10.2
1. F   2. T   3. F   4. e   5. b

10.3
1. T   2. T   3. a   4. d   5. d

10.4, 10.5
1. F   2. T   3. T   4. F   5. b
6. c   7. e

10.6
1. T   2. T   3. b   4. c   5. a

10.7
1. F   2. F   3. F   4. a   5. a

10.8
1. T   2. a   3. b   4.b   5.a

11.1, 11.2
1. F   2. F   3. T   4. e   5. d

11.3
1. T   2. T   3. T   4. a   5. c

11.4
1. T   2. F   3. T   4. b   5. c

11.5
1. T   2. T   3. F   4. c   5. a

12.1, 12.2
1. T   2. T   3. b   4. b   5. b

12.3, 12.4
1. F   2. T   3. T   4. d   5. a

12.5
1. T   2. T   3. T   4. a

12.6, 12.7
1. T   2. T   3. F   4. a

12.8, 12.9
1. T   2. F   3. T   4. b   5. a

12.10
1. F   2. F   3. T   4. a

13.1
1. F   2. T   3. T   4. c   5. c

13.2
1. T   2. F   3. T   4. b   5. a

13.3, 13.4
1. T   2. T   3. T   4. a   5. b

13.5
1. T   2. F   3. F   4. b   5. d

13.6
1. F   2. F   3. T   4. b   5. c

13.7
1. T   2. F   3. T   4. d   5. a

13.8, 13.9
1. F   2. T   3. F   4. b   5. a

13.10
1. F   2. T   3. F   4. e   5. c

13.11
1. T   2. T   3. F   4. a   5. a

14.1
1. T   2. T   3. d   4. b

14.2
1. T   2. F   3. b   4. a

14.3
1. T   2. T   3. T   4. d

14.4
1. T   2. F   3. T   4. T   5. c

14.5
1. F   2. T   3. d   4. b   5. a

14.6, 14.7
1. F   2. T   3. F

14.8
1. T   2. T   3. b   4. c   5. a   6. a

14.9
1. T   2. T   3. c   4. d

14.10
1. T   2. T   3. b   4. b

14.11
1. T   2. T   3. F   4. d   5. d

15.1
1. T   2. F   3. T   4. b   5.a

15.2
1. F   2. F   3. T   4. a   5. e

15.3
1. F   2. T   3. F   4. b   5. e

15.4
1. T   2. T   3. T   4. c   5. b

15.5
1. T   2. T   3. F   4. d   5. c

15.6,7
1. T   2. F   3. T   4. e   5. b

16.1
1. F   2. T   3. T   4. c   5. b

16.2
1. T   2. T   3. T   4. a   5. e

16.3
1. T   2. F   3. F   4. d   5. e

16.4
1. F   2. T   3. T   4. e   5. e

16.5
1. F   2. T   3. F   4. c   5. d

16.6
1. F   2. T   3. T   4. d   5. e

Name Index

Subject Index